HARD DRIVE
TO THE
KLONDIKE

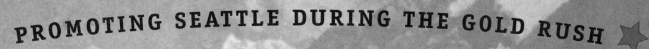

PROMOTING SEATTLE DURING THE GOLD RUSH

HARD DRIVE
TO THE
KLONDIKE

LISA MIGHETTO and MARCIA MONTGOMERY

Northwest Interpretive Association
in association with
University of Washington Press
SEATTLE AND LONDON

Library of Congress Cataloging-in-Publication Data

Mighetto, Lisa, 1955-
    Hard drive to the Klondike : promoting Seattle during the
    Gold Rush / Lisa Mighetto and Marcia Montgomery.
    p. cm.
Includes bibliographical references and index.
    ISBN 0-295-98227-6
1. Seattle (Wash.)--History. 2. Frontier and pioneer life--Washington
(State)--Seattle. 3. Historic sites--Washington (State)--Seattle.
4. Klondike River Valley (Yukon)--Gold discoveries. 5. Klondike Gold
Rush National Historical Park (Alaska and Wash.)--History. I.
Montgomery, Marcia Babcock. II. Title.

F899.S457 M54 2002
979.7'772--dc21
2002024561

Published in partnership by:

 University of Washington Press
1326 Fifth Avenue, Suite 555
Seattle, WA 98101-2604

 Northwest Interpretive Association
909 First Avenue, Suite 630
Seattle, WA 98104-3627
206-220-4140
nwpubliclands.com

Book Design: Mark MacKay, Northwest Interpretive Association

Contents

Foreword

When the steamer *Portland* sailed into Seattle in July 1897, laden with more than a ton of gold from the Canadian Far North, hundreds of townspeople gathered eagerly at the dock to greet the 68 ragtag "argonauts" who hit paydirt and changed their lives. What the crowds may have only dimly perceived, however, was that the life of the city, too, would change almost immediately, in ways both profound and lasting. For while the gold fields lay far to the north, Seattle became the jumping-off point to riches, and the frontier town was suddenly transformed into the metropolis of the Northwest.

As *Hard Drive to the Klondike: Promoting Seattle During the Gold Rush* so effectively recounts, the remarkable story of the Klondike Gold Rush is far more than the story of hardy adventurers striking it rich. It is also the story of a city galvanized to recast itself in the eyes of the world. It is the story of a regional economy revitalized seemingly overnight as it housed, outfitted, entertained and transported thousands of fortune seekers. It is the story of a dramatic surge in population that would forever change the flavor and fabric of city life. The Klondike Gold Rush was at once the last frontier fantasy of the 19th century and the birth of modern Seattle.

When a decade later Seattle paused to reflect on its good fortune at the Alaska-Yukon-Pacific Exposition of 1909, the city was hardly recognizable from ten years before. After years of gold fever, the civic landscape included a booming downtown of tall buildings, an impressive system of parks and boulevards, and an atmosphere charged with the "Seattle Spirit," that powerful blend of entrepreneurial energy, civic boosterism, and fortuitous happenstance. Indeed, *Hard Drive to the Klondike* makes clear that the most enduring fortune of the Gold Rush era was not the riches gained by individual prospectors (although names like Nordstrom figure among them) nor even by the merchants who mined the prospectors (like the Bon Marche), but rather by Seattle itself, which aggressively invited gold-seekers to its doors with the promise that it was the portal to prosperity.

Seattle's promotional zeal was unbounded, and its civic marketing efforts rarely equaled in American history. So vigorous was Seattle's claim to its gateway status that even the seasoned ports of Vancouver, Portland and San Francisco took a back seat in the last great gold rush in American history. *Hard Drive to the Klondike* explores the amazing history behind that effort. It looks at the promoters and con men, the businesses that grew to serve and facilitate the "rush," and the economic, demographic, and physical changes — some planned; some unexpected — that characterized Seattle's boom period.

Now, a century later, *Hard Drive to the Klondike* places these stories within the larger context of what came before and what followed. Richly illustrated with photographs, drawings, maps, advertisements and more, *Hard Drive to the Klondike* is the complete story of Seattle during the gold rush, exploring that rare moment in time when, enthralled by tales of distant riches, a city saw its own best chance, and took it.

Leonard Garfield
Executive Director
Museum of History & Industry

Acknowledgments

The National Park Service contracted with Historical Research Associates, Inc. to prepare this study in 1997-1998, to commemorate the centennial of the Klondike Gold Rush. The authors would like to thank the following individuals who reviewed this work for the National Park Service: Edwin C. Bearss, Marc Blackburn, Betsy Duncan-Clark, Gretchen Luxenberg, and Frank Norris. Terrence Cole of the Department of History at the University of Alaska, Fairbanks reviewed the manuscript as well, and he provided illustrations and research materials. Richard Engeman, formerly of the Special Collections Division at the University of Washington; Lorraine McConaghy of the Museum of History and Industry, Seattle; and Robert Weaver of Hart-Crowser, Inc., Seattle also provided research materials and valuable suggestions.

Additional repositories consulted included the following: Alaska and Polar Regions Archives, Rasmuson Library, University of Alaska, Fairbanks; Bellingham Public Library; British Library, London; Klondike Gold Rush National Historical Park Library, Seattle; Jefferson County Historical Society Museum, Port Townsend; Oregon History Center, Portland; Seattle City Archives; Seattle Department of Construction and Land Use; Seattle Department of Neighborhoods, Office of Urban Conservation; Seattle Public Library; Tacoma Public Library; Vancouver City Archives, British Columbia; Washington State Archives, Puget Sound Regional Branch; and the Washington State Historical Society, Tacoma. We are grateful to their staffs for their time and attention.

Lisa Mighetto
Marcia Montgomery
Seattle, 2002

The Legacy of the Klondike Gold Rush

It was through the gold rush that Seattle learned the marketing flair it now applies to selling computer software or persuading people to pay $2 ... for a cup of coffee.

— *The Economist, 1997*

Seattle, according to an article in The Economist, "is remarkable for its golden touch." The metropolitan area serves as a base for Bill Gates, America's richest man, along with several thousand Microsoft millionaires. The city supports numerous companies recognized as "standard-setters in their businesses," including Boeing, Nordstrom, and Starbucks. Seattle became the largest city in the Pacific Northwest almost a century ago — and for nearly that long historians and other analysts have examined the reasons for this growth. The Economist has offered an intriguing, if somewhat ahistorical, interpretation: what sets Seattle apart from other successful cities is a series of characteristics resulting from the Klondike Gold Rush of 1897-1898.[1]

During these years, thousands of prospectors headed for the Far North, passing through San Francisco, Portland, Tacoma, Seattle, Victoria, and Vancouver, British Columbia. Of the approximately 100,000 miners who started for the gold fields, 70,000 used Seattle as their point of departure.[2] For the most part, however, it was not the stampeders who struck it rich. As was the case with other gold rushes in the western United States, it was the merchants who profited from the Klondike Gold Rush — and Seattle provides an excellent example of how this event encouraged population growth and the development of businesses that outfitted and transported the miners. During the late 1890s, "Klondike" became a "magic word," and Seattle merchants used it to sell a variety of goods and services.[3]

Above: This proposed design for a city seal illustrated the spirit of determination that characterized Seattle in 1897.

The Klondike Gold Rush fueled a longstanding commercial spirit in Seattle that has continued through the present. John Nordstrom and George Bartell, for example, started companies during this era, providing clothing and supplies — and both remain thriving businesses today. As The Economist observed, the Klondike Gold Rush helped Seattle develop the "marketing flair" now applied to selling computer software and coffee. Few public relations campaigns in American history could match the advertising blitz organized by the Seattle Chamber of Commerce during the stampede to the Yukon and Alaska. As a result of that marketing effort, Seattle became linked to Alaska and the Far North in the public mind. Moreover, according to The Economist, the energetic, risk-taking entrepreneurship that developed in the city during the late nineteenth century remains a "recipe for business achievement."[4]

Of course, this interpretation is very much a product of the 1990s. It is difficult to imagine The Economist printing such an idea 25 years earlier, with Boeing laying off thousands of employees and Seattle's economy plunging into recession. The late 1990s, however, exhibited a resurgence of the commercial success, along with the vitality and energy, which characterized the gold-rush era of the late 1890s and the early twentieth century. As an article in Pacific Northwest observed, during the 1990s Seattle transformed from a "modest place" to "musical mecca, center of the coffee universe, hip tourist destination, hacker heaven, and superliveable place."[5] Because 1997-1998 marked the centennial of the Klondike Gold Rush, this seemed an especially appropriate time to examine its legacy.

As noted, the Seattle area owes a good measure of its current good fortune to the presence of Microsoft. As chairman of this company, Bill Gates has seen a connection between the gold rush and the development of the software industry. "The Internet," he wrote in 1997, "is another case where people who are selling pans to the prospectors often will do better than the prospectors themselves. Analysts, the people who assemble trade shows, consultants, and others providing internet-related services may have a more sure-fire way of benefiting than the poor prospectors out there wielding picks and axes...."[6] No one in America has demonstrated this point better than Gates. He personifies a quality called "hard drive," which is manifested in the philosophy "work hard, make better products, and win."[7] Persistence and assertiveness are essential components of Microsoft's ethos.[8]

Interestingly, 100 years earlier a miner by the name of Swiftwater Bill Gates (no relation to the current chairman of Microsoft) supposedly leaned from the window of a Seattle hotel, showering gold nuggets from the Klondike on the passersby below.[9] The new "gold rush" of the 1990s has once again brought recognition and prosperity to Seattle.

Not all historians, however, see the connection between the gold rush and the current economy. Neither do historians agree as to the importance of the gold rush to Seattle's development. Some view it as a pivotal event affecting the course of the city's history. Others argue that the arrival of the transcontinental railroad proved to be far more significant in encouraging population growth and the expansion of local industries that had already gained a foothold in the area. Few historians, however, would deny the importance of the late nineteenth century in the development of Seattle. At the very least, the Klondike Gold Rush coincided with major events, including the arrival of the railroad, and it exemplified continuing trends in the city's history. If not the primary cause of the city's growth and prosperity, the Klondike Gold Rush nonetheless serves as a colorful reflection of the era and its themes, including the celebrated "Seattle spirit."

This book examines these issues, beginning in the early 1850s with the founding of Seattle, and ending in 1909 with the Alaska-Yukon-Pacific Exposition commemorating the Klondike Gold Rush and the growth of the city. Chapter One describes early Seattle and the gold strike in the Klondike, while the following three chapters analyze how the city became the gateway to the Yukon, how the stampede to the Far North stimulated local businesses, and how the city's infrastructure and boundaries changed during the era of the gold rush. Chapter Five looks at how historians have interpreted the Klondike Gold Rush throughout the twentieth century. The final chapter brings the Klondike story up to the present, describing the establishment of the Pioneer Square Historic District and the Klondike Gold Rush National Historical Park. It also describes the buildings and structures associated with the gold rush that remain standing, emphasizing those that have not yet been recognized or listed in the National Register. These historic resources serve as reminders of the period that, in the words of one observer, "put Seattle on the map."[10]

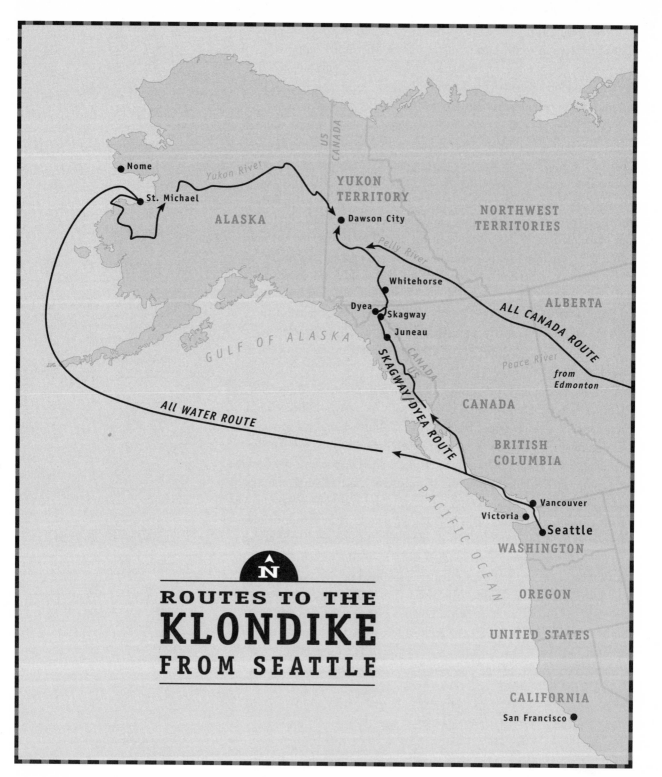

Nome

St. Michael

Yukon River

ALASKA

YUKON
TERRITORY

Dawson City

NORTHWEST
TERRITORIES

US
CANADA

Pelly River

ALL CANADA ROUTE

ALBERTA

Whitehorse

Dyea

Skagway

Juneau

GULF OF ALASKA

Peace River

from
Edmonton

CANADA
US

CANADA

ALL WATER ROUTE

SKAGWAY/DYEA ROUTE

BRITISH
COLUMBIA

PACIFIC OCEAN

Vancouver

Victoria

Seattle

WASHINGTON

OREGON

UNITED STATES

CALIFORNIA

San Francisco

^N

ROUTES TO THE
KLONDIKE
FROM SEATTLE

By and By: The Early History of Seattle

In a sense, Seattle itself arrived on the steamer Portland.
—Ross Anderson, The Seattle Times, 1997

Founding The City

Seattle has a long history of profiting from gold rushes. Beginning with the stampede to California in the mid-nineteenth century and continuing through the Klondike craze of 1897-1898, Seattle business interests were quick to spot economic opportunity. The California Gold Rush rapidly expanded the development of San Francisco in the early 1850s, opening a market for the lumber that grew in abundance in the Puget Sound region. Seattle's first business was a sawmill located at the foot of what is now Yesler Way. "You have the timber up there that we want and must have," one California miner advised an early Seattle resident. "By selling us lumber … you'll soon be rich."[1] The city's founders swiftly recognized the potential value of the area's natural resources. They named their initial settlement in what is now West Seattle "New York-Alki," reflecting their ambition that "by-and-by" it would enjoy a prosperity rivaling that of the large cities on the eastern seaboard.[2]

The Denny party, which included 24 people led by former Illinois resident Arthur Denny, first settled on Alki Point in 1851. They arrived aboard the schooner *Exact* on a dreary November day. As many historians have recounted, some of the party's women responded to the wet, unfamiliar landscape by weeping.[3] This site proved to be unsuitable, prompting Denny, Carson Boren, and William Bell to explore the sheltered shoreline of Elliott Bay to the east. Here, in February of 1852, they chose a new location for their town, calling the site "Duwamps," after the nearby Duwamish River. That summer, they changed the name to Seattle, after the Indian leader Sealth.[4]

The new settlement consisted of an eight-acre island bordered by a saltwater lagoon to the east, and tideflats to the south. The settlers' initial claims ran from the foot of what is now Denny Way south to the island, near the intersection of First Avenue and King Street. The island's high point was located between Jackson and King streets on First Avenue. Throughout the nineteenth century, Seattle residents filled the surrounding tidelands, which today stand approximately 12 feet above the high-water level.[5]

Shortly after the members of the Denny party had staked their claims, Dr. David Swinson (known as "Doc") Maynard arrived. Perhaps the most colorful of Seattle's pioneers, he headed west from Ohio in 1850, hoping to escape a bad marriage and to strike it rich in the California gold fields.[6] "The first entry in his travel diary," observed historian Murray

This illustrated map was adapted from a sketch and map made by Lieutenant Thomas S. Phelps of the U.S. Sloop-of-War *Decatur* during the Indian War of 1855. This map includes street names and identifies important landmarks such as Yesler's Mill and the Elliot Hotel. An attentive reader will note that the schematic illustration at the bottom begins with the Methodist church and concludes with Madame Damnable's residence.

Hard Drive to the Klondike

Morgan, "expressed the intention of many another man who eventually settled in Seattle: 'Left here for California.'"[7] A personable, gregarious, and "hard-drinking" man, Maynard was also a "buyer and a seller." In 1852, he settled in Seattle, where he opened the first store. He established a 58-block tract that included part of the island and the lagoon, and joined other settlers in donating land to Henry Yesler for the creation of a sawmill.[8] Maynard served as a physician, justice of the peace, and the town's first booster.[9] As historian Roger Sale explained, he "was willing to do anything to make Seattle grow."[10]

Yesler's business became the hub of Seattle's economy, and the new town's labor force expanded. Workers skidded enormous trees down Mill Street — or "Skid Road" (now Yesler Way), to be cut into lumber. In 1854, Yesler constructed a wharf, and he began depositing sawdust from his mill into the bay and saltwater lagoon, thus increasing the land base along the waterfront. He also built a cookhouse, which became Seattle's first restaurant, along with a hall that became the town's meeting place.[11] By 1860, Seattle's population had reached approximately 150 residents. The commercial district on First Avenue South ran four blocks, from Yesler's mill to King Street. The city, incorporated in 1865, began to address the transportation problems created by the wet climate, which turned dirt streets into impassable bogs. Road crews planked Third Avenue with wood, marking the eastern border of the town.[12]

In 1869, when Seattle received its first charter, Yesler became mayor. Like Maynard, he hailed from Ohio. In contrast to Maynard, however, he remained "dour and tight-fisted," eventually selling his sawmill to pursue a more lucrative career in real estate. In Sales' estimation, had Seattle been settled mostly by people like Yesler, it would have evolved into little more than a company town rather than the largest city on Puget Sound.[13]

From the outset, Seattle's character differed from that of other early communities on Puget Sound, such as Port Gamble. According to numerous historians, Arthur Denny embodied the nature of this difference. A man with "an innate business sense," he had left his home in Illinois to take advantage

In 1854, Yesler constructed a wharf, and he began depositing sawdust from his mill into the bay and saltwater lagoon, thus increasing the land base along the waterfront.

Seattle, early in 1865, from Main Street and First Avenue South, looking north.

of the opportunities that the West presented — and he realized the economic connection between Seattle and San Francisco very quickly. During the early 1850s, ships arrived from California loaded with merchandise to be sold on commission in Seattle. Denny found a way to keep the profits by building a store on the corner of First Avenue and Washington Street, and purchasing stock directly in San Francisco. His entrepreneurial activities helped "reduce San Francisco's hold on Seattle."[14]

Throughout the remainder of his life, Denny engaged in a variety of businesses, ranging from banking to producing building materials. He also surveyed and platted much of the downtown area, donating land for establishing a university. Perhaps the best example of Denny's foresight was his interest in the railroad and his efforts to expand Seattle's transportation system, described below. Taken individually, these activities were not unique in burgeoning western communities. What set Denny apart was the extent of his "energy and vision." When he saw a need in the community, he stepped in to fill it, sometimes turning a handsome profit in the process. Even so, he was motivated by more than money, "feeling the growth of his own property to be a part of the growth of Seattle." Denny's activities led to "a decreasing dependence on the outside world for Seattle's essential livelihood," paving the way for future development.[15] He thus represented the vitality and the entrepreneurism that would characterize Seattle later in the century — qualities that would place the city in an advantageous position during the Klondike Gold Rush era.

Early Local Industries

The Donation Land Claim Act of 1850 encouraged settlement of the Pacific Northwest. This early homestead measure offered each white male adult 320 acres of land if single, and if he married by December 1, 1851, his wife was entitled to an additional 320 acres in her own right. To take advantage of this measure, settlers were required only to reside on the land and cultivate it for four years.[16]

Seattle further benefited from its proximity to farmlands in the Duwamish Valley. While the town's lumber industry developed during the 1850s, farmers staked claims along the river and prairies as far south as Auburn. Here they raised livestock and a variety of crops, including wheat, oats, peas, and potatoes, which they traded with Seattle settlers.[17]

Probably no development proved more influential to the early growth of Seattle than the arrival of the railroad. Arthur Denny realized the importance of connecting the town by rail line from the outset of his settlement on Puget Sound. His dream was delayed, however, by conflicts with Indians during the 1850s, and by the opening of Kansas and Nebraska for homesteading, which diverted potential settlers. During the 1860s, the Civil War further slowed railroad development in the West. Denny's hopes were rekindled in 1870, when the Northern Pacific Railroad began building a road west from Minnesota and a branch line from the Columbia River to Puget Sound. To help finance construction, the federal government gave the Northern Pacific the rights to millions of acres of land.[18]

Seattle and Tacoma competed for the position as terminus for this transcontinental railroad. In 1873, Seattle residents urged the Northern Pacific to build its terminal in their town, extending offers of $250,000 in cash and 3,000 acres of undeveloped land — much of which was located along the waterfront. The railroad company, however, decided to make Tacoma its terminus, owing to the greater opportunities for land speculation that the "City of Destiny" to the south presented. As *The Oregonian*, a Portland newspaper, explained, Tacoma became a company town, "largely the creation of the Northern Pacific" for "the benefit of some of its managers who compose the Tacoma Land Company."[19] Disappointed Seattle residents, including Denny, formed the Seattle & Walla Walla Railroad, resolving to build their own connection over Snoqualmie Pass. On May Day of 1874, they organized a picnic and started laying track. Historians came to view this "bold and amusing" incident as reflecting a distinctive "spirit" in Seattle, characterized by optimism and determination.[20]

The effort to build a rail line from Seattle across the Cascade Mountains soon languished, due to lack of funds. Similarly, the Northern Pacific had collapsed in 1873, when Jay Cooke, its financier, went bankrupt.[21] Meanwhile, the discovery of coal deposits south and east of Seattle further encouraged city residents to develop local rail lines. By the 1870s, Seattle had nearly exhausted its supply of timber — and the coal located in Renton, on the southern shore of Lake Washington, presented the opportunity for an additional export. In 1876, James Colman purchased Yesler's wharf, taking over construction of the Seattle & Walla Walla Railroad. He extended the rail line to Renton and Newcastle, and Seattle

Probably no development proved more influential to the early growth of Seattle than the arrival of the railroad. Arthur Denny realized the importance of connecting the town by rail line from the outset of his settlement on Puget Sound.

began sending coal to markets in Portland and San Francisco. Trains carried coal across the tideflats, to docks on Elliott Bay. The rail connections, along with deposits discovered in Issaquah and Black Diamond, helped make coal a significant export, second only to lumber. So significant was the development of coal that Seattle came to be called "the Liverpool of the North."[22]

During the 1880s, Seattle enjoyed its "first great spurt of growth."[23] Residents established a chamber of commerce to promote business interests in 1882, and five years later the Northern Pacific Railroad completed its transcontinental line to Tacoma, thus linking Puget Sound to the markets of the eastern United States. The railroad also helped make Seattle accessible to migrants, who traveled north from Tacoma on a branch line.[24] As the mayor of Seattle, Henry Yesler viewed these railroad connections with considerable enthusiasm. He predicted in 1886 that "in the near future more than one transcontinental railroad will be humbly asking for our trade and support." So bright were Seattle's prospects that Yesler downplayed its competition with Tacoma. Once the transcontinental railroad reaches Seattle, he suggested, "it will be a matter of wonder that any other city upon Puget Sound ever dreamed of being our rival, far less our superior."[25] By 1888, a tunnel through Stampede Pass, which cut through the Cascade Mountains, had allowed for direct rail service from eastern points to Seattle.

During the 1880s, the city's population expanded from 3,500 to more than 43,000.[26] Rapid growth had its drawbacks, at least from an aesthetic perspective. Ernest Ingersoll, a writer who visited Seattle at this time, characterized it as "scattered" and disorganized. "The town has grown too fast to look well or healthy," he informed readers of *Harper's New Monthly Magazine*. "Everybody has been in [such] great haste to get there and get a roof over his head that he has not minded much how it looked or pulled many stumps out of his door-yard."[27]

Seattle's commercial district remained centered around the waterfront, which, by the late 1880s, had featured a patchwork of piers and frame buildings extending over the bay.[28] While developing its rail connections, the city relied heavily on maritime traffic — some of which focused on the Far North, due to an increasing commercial interest in the region's fur seals and fisheries. Although the Alaska Commercial Company was based in San Francisco, by the 1880s, Seattle also had become a center of water trade between Puget Sound and the Far North.[29] The construction of

So bright were Seattle's prospects that Yesler downplayed its competition with Tacoma. Once the transcontinental railroad reaches Seattle, he suggested, "it will be a matter of wonder that any other city upon Puget Sound ever dreamed of being our rival, far less our superior."

Hard Drive to the Klondike

"larger and better wharves" and improved shipping facilities hastened this transition.[30]

The Pacific Coast Steamship Company provided the first direct, regular service from Seattle to Alaska in 1886. During the mid-1890s, the Alaska Steamship Company formed in Seattle, and the Japan Steamship Company placed its western American terminus at the city, contracting with the railroad for exchange of freight and delivery. This development represented an "immense advance in the commerce of the city."[31] When the Japanese steamship *Miiki Maru* sailed into Elliott Bay with a cargo of silk and tea in 1896, the Seattle city council declared a holiday.[32] In the years before the Klondike Gold Rush, then, Seattle established a trade link with Alaska and the Far North as well as with the Far East.

A variety of shipping company offices were located along First Avenue South, which also supported such businesses as meat packing, food processing, furniture manufacturing, and breweries. These industries served Seattle residents as well as the outlying logging, farming, and mining communities.[33] City laborers found lodging in hotels, tenements, and boarding houses located off Main Street.[34]

During this era, Seattle included a Chinese community, located initially in the area around First Avenue South and Occidental Avenue. Chinese immigrants came to the Northwest in the 1870s, to work on the region's rail lines and in its mines. For the next two decades, they also labored on regrading projects and in laundries, canneries, and stores. By the 1880s, the Chinese community had moved to Washington Street, between Second and Third avenues, where residents often lived above stores and retail businesses. Anti-Chinese sentiment, encouraged by white laborers, erupted in riots during the mid-1880s, prompting declaration of martial law. Before troops arrived, many Chinese workers were evicted from the city. Those remaining in Seattle continued to live along Washington Street, where they were joined by an influx of Japanese workers.[35]

Most of the town's infrastructure — including streets, wharves, businesses, and residences — was made of wood. In 1889, however, Seattle had the opportunity to rebuild itself. On June 6 of that year, a devastating fire swept through downtown, beginning in a store on the corner of First Avenue and Madison Street eventually destroying more than 30 blocks. Although destructive, this blaze resulted in new development, as Seattle passed an ordinance requiring that buildings downtown be constructed of brick and stone.[36]

Observers — and investors — noted that the fire sparked the "Seattle spirit" of optimism and determination. Seattle resident Judge Thomas Burke, for example, described the post-fire mood of the town as one of "vigor and energy." The flames "had scarcely been extinguished before the rebuilding of the City and the re-establishment of business in the various lines had been begun," he stated in July of 1889. "Banks have now on deposit more than they ever had before."[37] Early historians similarly praised the pluck and resolve of Seattle citizens for their swift response to the disaster. "Fate lit a torch," explained Welford Beaton in 1914, "which called to arms the enterprise and spirit of the people," who began the task of rebuilding "while the ashes were still warm."[38] Citizens in Seattle had further cause for optimism in July of 1889, when territorial delegates met in Olympia to draft a state constitution and by-laws. On November 11 of that year, Washington was admitted to the Union as the 42nd state.[39]

After the fire, the center of business activity in Seattle gradually expanded from Yesler's wharf to the north, east, and southeast. Neighborhoods emerged along the electric streetcar lines, established in 1884, that ran north and east from downtown.[40] Many residents lived in the core of the city, in the five blocks on either side of Yesler Way, between First and Third Avenues. According to Sale, downtown Seattle featured "furniture and cabinet makers, machine shops, groceries, laundries, dressmakers, meat and fish merchants, and in a great many

This photograph of Seattle's waterfront is dated circa 1885. It shows the Seattle harbor north of Main Street. Denny Hill appears at the left.

Hard Drive to the Klondike

instances the owners and employees of these businesses lived there or nearby." In short, "light industry and office work were next to each other, and both were next to all kinds of residences."[41] The presence of these various industries, along with the transportation infrastructure, helped business interests in Seattle take advantage of the opportunities presented at the onset of the Klondike Gold Rush.

The 1890s

The rebuilding of Seattle and the continued expansion of the town's infrastructure encouraged some residents to meet the 1890s with high expectations — and the decade began favorably in Seattle. In 1890, *The Overland Monthly*, a national publication, characterized the industrial growth in Puget Sound as "very remarkable."[42] By that year, the population of Seattle had reached 40,000. According to *The Seattle Post-Intelligencer*, newcomers were attracted to the town's "independent enterprise and go-aheadiveness."[43] The decade began in Seattle with a "building boom" prompted not only by the fire but also by the arrival of James J. Hill's Great Northern Railway. Judge Burke persuaded Hill to select the town as the terminus for his transcontinental line, which reached Puget Sound in 1893. Historians would later view this event as monumental in significance for its contribution to the growth of the city's economy and infrastructure.

Early Population Growth in Seattle

1860	c. 150
1865	c. 350
1870	1,107
1875	1,512
1880	3,533
1885	9,786

Source: Clarence B. Bagley, *History of Seattle from the Earliest Settlement to the Present Time*, Vol. 2 (Chicago: S. J. Publishing Co. 1916), p. 698.

In 1887 Seattle's waterfront was a vibrant and busy neighborhood. Prior to the fire Frye's Opera House, the domed building in the center, was located here. The Seattle fire began in the white building on the extreme left of the photograph.

The 1890s, however, proved to be anything but gay. In 1893, unchecked speculation on Wall Street and overexpansion of railroads created the worst economic downturn that the nation had yet experienced. Europe, South Africa, and South America also felt the effects of what came to be known as the Panic of 1893. Frightened foreign investors sold their American bonds, draining gold from the U.S. Treasury. The prosperity in Seattle stimulated by the Great Northern Railway "collapsed with an abruptness that ruined thousands."[44] Edith Feero Larson, who lived in Tacoma during the Panic of 1893, later recalled that "the Northwest should have boomed with the completion of the railroads.... It did for a few months, then money began to disappear and no one had any work. For a while our papa cut firewood for the railway for a dollar a day — a fourteen-hour day. 'It keeps us eating,' he said."[45] So dismal was the economic depression during the 1890s that one local historian has portrayed it as "the decade of misery."[46]

Economic hard times strengthened interest in the People's or Populist party throughout the Pacific Northwest. Populism appealed to voters who regarded the "Gilded Age" of the late nineteenth century with disenchantment. While the industrialization of the country after the Civil War had brought vast fortunes to a few individuals, the gap between the wealthy and the poor had widened considerably. The misery of the depression gave rise to unrest. In 1894 unemployed workers from the Pacific Northwest — known as Coxey's Army — marched east toward Capitol Hill, intending to demand jobs. The U.S. Army overtook these desperate men in Wyoming, after they had commandeered a train. That year, the Pullman strike also marked the first nationwide walkout by railroad workers. Corruption in government added to the dissatisfaction that fueled Populist sentiment — and by the early 1890s unprecedented unemployment increased calls for reforms. These included government ownership of railroad, telegraph, and telephone lines as well as federal anti-trust legislation to curtail corporate power.[47]

One of the most prominent platforms of the Populist party became the free and unlimited coinage of silver by the federal treasury. The hope was that this inflationary measure would stimulate the national economy, while bolstering the flagging silver mining industry in the West. Opposition to the Free Silver Movement generally came from eastern-based bankers and financiers who favored the traditional hard money, or gold standard. Many voters in Washington state, however, embraced the

Populist party — especially after the Panic of 1893.[48] By 1896, *The Seattle Daily Times* had become a voice of the Populist party, advocating free coinage of silver. The newspaper's masthead supported laborers against "the silk-stockinged gentlemen" who favored the gold standard.[49]

In the presidential election of 1896, Washington and Idaho supported William Jennings Bryan, the Populist and Democratic candidate and an advocate of free silver. "You shall not press down upon the brow of labor this crown of thorns," he warned the opposition at the Democratic convention. "You shall not crucify mankind upon a cross of gold!" His words revealed that free silver had become "almost as much a religious as a financial issue." Even so, Republican "Gold Bugs" triumphed over what they regarded as the "silver lunacy," with their candidate, William McKinley, winning the presidency.[50] The advocacy of Free Silver as a means to alleviate the depression in the 1890s directed national attention to the discovery and mining of precious metals throughout the West and Far North, helping to set the stage for the Klondike Gold Rush.[51]

The anxious tone of the early 1890s was further reflected in Frederick Jackson Turner's Frontier Thesis. Delivered in 1893 before a Chicago meeting of the American Historical Association, this bold interpretation of American history suggested the national identity had been shaped by the so-called "frontier experience." As Turner explained, "The existence of an area of free land, its continuous recession, and the advance of American settlement westward, explain American development." According to him, the expansion into western lands had transformed immigrants into self-reliant, independent, inventive Americans. The frontier, moreover, represented the opportunity for fresh starts. Turner's thesis touched a nerve in the 1890s, as the forces that he claimed had shaped the American character seemed to be fast disappearing. Three years earlier, the U.S. Census had declared the frontier to be "closed," ending an era in American history. As the Superintendent of the Census explained in 1890, "at present the unsettled area has been so broken into by isolated bodies of settlement that there can hardly be said to be a frontier line."[52]

Scholars have debated Turner's thesis since it appeared in the 1890s. The New Western Historians in the 1980s and 1990s, for example, criticized its ethnocentric assumptions, pointing out that the "free land" Turner described was hardly a "frontier" to the Indian and Latino peoples already living there.[53] Even so, during the 1890s, Turner's thesis signaled a concern that the West no longer represented a land of promise or a safety valve for the laborers of the East. Although the number of Americans aware of it would have been limited in 1893, Turner's thesis exemplified "a growing perception that the frontier era was over."[54]

This concern was not limited to the perceived availability of western lands. The dispirited tone of the 1890s appeared in a variety of forums, including popular journals, which summarized the "mood of the age" as one of "pessimism."[55] As *The Seattle Daily Times* explained in 1897, "the great majority of the American people ... have suffered so much loss of property and the ordinary comforts of life, during the last four years." So "burdensome" had the economic hard times become "that endurance for another year seemed almost impossible."[56] For many Americans, the Klondike Gold Rush provided a welcome distraction. Although its precise impact on the depression is difficult to determine, the stampede became a focus for hope and expectation during the late 1890s — even for those who did not leave for the Far North.

As the historian Roderick Nash pointed out, for many Americans the Yukon promised more than economic gain. The timing of the Klondike stampede, he explained in *Wilderness and the American Mind*, was particularly significant:

> When the forty-niners rushed to California's gold fields in the mid-nineteenth century, the United States was still a developing nation with a wild West. The miners did not seem picturesque and romantic so much as uncouth and a bit embarrassing to a society trying to mature. But with the frontier officially dead (according to the 1890 census), the time was ripe for a myth that accorded cowboys and hunters and miners legendary proportions. Americans of the early twentieth century were prepared to romanticize the "ninety-eighters" and paint their rush to the gold of the north in glowing colors.

The image of the Far North as a wild, savage place proved appealing. The wide circulation of Jack London's novel, *The Call of the Wild* (1903), exemplified the popularity of this romanticized view of the gold rush.[57]

Gold Fever Strikes

Few events in the history of Seattle have produced more excitement than the stampede to the Yukon. Gold discoveries at Circle City and Cook Inlet in Alaska sparked a small rush in Seattle in 1896, but the fervor did not equal that generated by the Klondike strike. The discovery of gold in

Gold discoveries at Circle City and Cook Inlet in Alaska sparked a small rush in Seattle in 1896, but the fervor did not equal that generated by the Klondike strike.

1896 on Rabbit Creek, a tributary of the Klondike River, heralded a momentous era for the city. In July of 1897, the ships *Excelsior* and *Portland* docked in San Francisco and Seattle respectively, carrying three tons of gold between them from the Far North. The media lost no time in spreading the news, sparking the "Klondike Fever" that gripped much of the nation and Seattle for the next two years. *The Seattle Post-Intelligencer* produced one of the most memorable accounts of the *Portland's* arrival. The paper chartered a tug so that one of its correspondents could meet this vessel as it sailed, laden with gold nuggets, into Puget Sound. "GOLD! GOLD! GOLD! GOLD!," the headline of July 17, 1897 read. "Sixty-Eight Rich Men on the Steamer Portland. STACKS OF YELLOW METAL!"[58] This would prove to be one of the most enduring images in Seattle's history, contributing to the city's identity. As one reporter observed 100 years later, "in a sense, Seattle itself arrived on the steamer Portland."[59]

The Seattle Daily Times conveyed the sense of excitement and exhilaration that swept the town. "All that anyone hears at present is 'Klondyke,'" it reported on July 23, 1897. "It is impossible to escape it. It is talked in the morning; it is discussed at lunch; it demands attention at the dinner table; it is all one hears during the interval of his after-dinner smoke; and at night one dreams about mountains of yellow metal with nuggets as big as fire plugs."[60] Similarly, the celebrated nature writer John Muir, hired by the *San Francisco Examiner* to describe the Far North, observed, "The Klondyke! The Klondyke! Which is the best way into the yellow Klondyke? Is all the cry nowadays." [61]

Confusion about the term "Klondike" added to the mystery of the gold fields. The press typeset the words "Klondike," "Klondyke," and "Clondyke," sometimes seemingly at random, although the *Post-Intelligencer* favored "Clondyke," while the *Times* preferred using a "K." In August of 1897, the U.S. government and the Associated Press chose "Klondike" as the official spelling.[62]

Whatever the spelling, it soon became clear what the word conveyed to readers. The national journal *Leslie's Weekly*, for example, reported that it "stands for millions of gold, and is a synonym for the advancement, after unspeakable suffering, of hundreds of miners from poverty to affluence in a brief period of a few months."[63] Four years of depression had increased the appeal of the gold fields. One ounce of gold was worth $16 in 1897 — a year when typical wages totaled approximately $14 for 78 hours of

Fortunes from the Klondike

Anderson	$10,000
G.W. Anderson	25,000
Clarence Barry	45,000
James Clemons	50,000
James Coslow	15,000
George Gray	10,000
Frank Keller	10,000
Jack Moffit	12,000
Frank Phiscator	70,000
James Pickett	20,000
Simms	10,000
William Sloan	10,000
William Stanley	10,000
Charles Warden	10,000
Wilkerson	10,000

Source: Miners on board the *Portland*, along with their fortunes from the Klondike gold fields, reported in the *San Francisco Chronicle*, July 17, 1897

Much of Tacoma's fire department resigned to leave for the Yukon, while several Seattle policemen also quit. Some stores had to close because their clerks left abruptly for the Far North.

work. Moreover, the Far North offered opportunity for adventure and exploration during an era that had witnessed the close of the "frontier."[64]

News of the Klondike strike quickly spread to the Midwest and East Coast, where stories of instant wealth were circulated with a vigor that matched the media coverage in the West — at least initially. Two days after the *Portland* docked in Seattle, New York City was "touched" with gold fever. "Klondyke Arouses the East," announced *The Seattle Daily Times* on July 20, 1897. "Effete Civilization … Affected by the Reports." New York City had contributed a large number of Forty-niners to the California Gold Rush, and observers expected it would again be well represented among the eastern argonauts headed for the Far North.[65] *The New York Times* reported the Klondike strike as monumentally significant. This publication quoted Clarence King, a celebrated geologist, as asserting, "The rush to the Klondike is one of the greatest in the history of the country."[66]

The Post-Intelligencer proved even more enthusiastic, describing the Klondike stampede as "one of the greatest migrations in the history of the world."[67] Both the *Times* and the *Post-Intelligencer* sent correspondents to the gold fields. Reporter S.P. Weston took a dozen carrier pigeons to send messages to the Associated Press and the *Post-Intelligencer*.[68] These Seattle papers also produced special Klondike editions, providing information on outfitting and prospecting.[69] *Harper's Weekly*, a national publication, sent special correspondent Tappan Adney to the Yukon to keep its readership informed, while *The Illustrated London News* sent Julius Price.[70]

The impact of this kind of media attention was immediate. Hundreds of spectators had crowded the waterfront in Seattle to greet the *Portland*. On July 18, 1897 — just one day after that vessel arrived, the steamer *Al-Ki* departed for the Yukon, filled to capacity with miners and 350 tons of supplies.[71] As a *Times* headline explained on July 19, "Men With the Gold Fever" were "Hustling to Go."[72]

So strong was the lure of the Klondike that cities along Puget Sound had difficulty retaining employees. Much of Tacoma's fire department resigned to leave for the Yukon, while several Seattle policemen also quit. Some stores had to close because their clerks left abruptly for the Far North. The Rainier Produce Company lost its manager when news of the gold strike hit Seattle.[73] The labor shortage similarly affected the Seattle District of the U.S. Army Corps of Engineers, which had difficulty retaining workers to complete its fortification projects in the Puget Sound

Hard Drive to the Klondike

region. "Due to the Klondike excitement," explained one contractor, it is "impossible to secure steady and reliable men in anything like adequate numbers."[74] Even Seattle's mayor, W.D. Wood, succumbed to gold fever, as did Col. K.C. Washburn, a King County and state legislator. "Seattle is Klondike Crazy," one *San Francisco Chronicle* headline explained on July 17, 1897. "Men of All Professions [Are] Preparing for the Gold Fields."[75]

Within a week, the Seattle city council raised the salaries of police officers, and the *Post-Intelligencer* issued a warning to job hunters that there was no labor shortage in the city, to prevent a rush for the abandoned positions.[76] The discovery of gold in the Yukon was even credited with lowering the crime rate in the Puget Sound area, "since the men who would ordinarily commit offenses against the laws of the city or state now have something else to think about."[77] These were crimes such as burglary, for the gold rush encouraged the development of vice-related offenses.

When the gold craze hit the nation, few Americans were familiar with the geography of the Far North. Many assumed that the Klondike was located in Alaska, instead of in the Yukon, in Canadian territory. Klondike guidebooks — some of which were hastily produced in a matter of days — further obscured the issue. *The Chicago Record's Book for Gold Seekers*, for example, used the terms "Klondike" and "Alaska Gold Fields" interchangeably. Blinded by visions of treasure, many prospective miners were ignorant of what a trip to the Far North would entail.[78] Upon hearing the news of the Klondike strike, a group of enterprising New Yorkers made plans to walk to the gold fields from the East Coast.[79] Similarly, one New York woman inquired upon arriving in Seattle, "Can I walk to the Klondike or is it too far?"[80]

Others planned to reach the Yukon by balloon. Charles Kuenzel, a resident of Hoboken, New Jersey, organized an airship expedition. "We may get lost away up in the air somewhere," he conceded. "The Western and Klondike country is strange to me, and I may make some mistakes in steering. There are no charts for

Some people planned to walk to the Klondike and others opted for the train. A group of inventive travelers planned to reach the gold fields by air.

TO THE KLONDYKE BY BALLOON.
Four Daring Aeronauts to Sail to the Gold Fields in the World's Fair Monster Airship.

Above left: This illustration from *Leslie's Weekly* depicts Klondike miners arriving in Seattle in 1897. Feature stories like this one fueled stories about the gold rush across the United States and the world.

Above right: This guide book was written by William Ogilvie, the foremost Canadian expert on the gold fields. Some stampeders were unfortunate and purchased guide books written by authors with questionable Klondike expertise.

the air. But I'll land all right."[81] Similarly, a group of enthusiastic Canadians planned to launch a "line of airships" to the Klondike.[82]

Although these whimsical, optimistic schemes can appear charming today, the stampede to the Klondike brought tragedy to many — even to those who remained home. By 1898, the Seattle police had received hundreds of inquiries about missing persons. One distraught woman from Olympia reported that her husband had left for Seattle and was not heard from again. She feared he had fallen ill, or had become a victim of "the wicked part of the city." As *The Times* described the situation, "Children left behind and forgotten want to come to their fathers and mothers; old fathers in the East inquire for sons; wives in destitute circumstances for husbands; old, gray haired mothers write tear stained letters pitifully begging the Chief of Police to hunt up their wayward boys."[83]

The gold rush, according to the *Post-Intelligencer*, had resulted in a "Nest of Missing People."[84] Clearly some gold seekers did not want to be found. Even so, many died attempting to reach the Klondike — and their identities were not always known. On a February evening in 1898, for example, the steamer *Clara Nevada* exploded and burned while en route between Skagway and Seattle. More than 70 of its passengers were lost, and aside from the crew it was not clear who was on board.[85] A month after the disaster, the ship's carpenter notified *The Seattle Daily Times* that although the newspaper reported his death, he remained "alive and hardy and well."[86]

The Klondike Gold Rush attracted approximately 100,000 miners, 70,000 of whom passed through Seattle, nearly doubling the population of the city. So extensive was this migration that the *Post-Intelligencer* ran a regular column titled "The Passing Throng."[87] Although the majority were white men, African-Americans traveled to the gold fields as well. Many women went, too, sometimes bringing their families. The Klondike Gold Rush was a multi-national event, attracting argonauts of various ages and ethnicity.[88]

For the most part, however, it was not the prospectors who profited from the stampede to the Klondike. Instead, it was the merchants who struck pay dirt, as the gold rush encouraged the development of businesses that outfitted and transported the miners. As noted, Seattle already had the transportation network, infrastructure, and local industries needed to benefit from the migration to the Far North. Seattle also benefitted from the farmlands, coal deposits, and forests in the surrounding area. All that was needed was publicity promoting the city — a theme that is analyzed throughout the following chapter.

This issue of the *Seattle Post-Intelligencer*, published in July of 1897, is devoted to Klondike Gold Rush. During the gold rush, newspapers helped link Seattle, Alaska, and the Klondike in the public mind.

CHAPTER TWO

Selling Seattle

*There is probably no city in the Union today so much talked about as Seattle
and there is certainly none toward which more faces are at present turned.
From every nook and corner of America and from even the uttermost parts of
the earth, a ceaseless, restless throng is moving — moving toward the land of
the midnight sun and precious gold, and moving through its natural gateway
— the far-famed City of Seattle.*

— *The Seattle Daily Times, 1898*

*"We are taking advantage of the Klondike excitement to let the world know
about Seattle."*

— *Erastus Brainerd, 1897*

Erastus Brainerd and the Seattle Chamber of Commerce

Seattle's reputation as the gateway to Alaska and the Far North is widespread. Alaska Airlines remains based in this city, providing a modern
example of the transportation connections that were established in the
late nineteenth century. As historian Murray Morgan observed, Seattle
residents "tend to look on Alaska as their very own....Seattle stores display sub-arctic clothing, though Puget Sound winters are usually mild;
Seattle curio shops feature totem poles, though no Puget Sound Indian
ever carved one."[1] This perception is in part a legacy of the Klondike
Gold Rush, which linked Seattle and the Far North in the public mind. It
resulted from an extensive advertising campaign designed and launched
by the Seattle Chamber of Commerce in 1897.

From the outset of the gold rush, Seattle newspapers promoted their
city as the obvious point of outfitting and departure for the Yukon. "If
there ever was competition between Seattle and other cities on the Pacific

Coast relative to Alaska business," *The Seattle Post-Intelligencer* boasted on July 25, 1897, "it has entirely disappeared….Seattle controls the trade with Alaska. There is no other way to state the fact — the control is complete and absolute." As the *Post-Intelligencer* concluded, the rush to the Klondike was "centered in Seattle."[2] Despite such bold assertions, however, it took the Seattle Chamber of Commerce months of effort in public relations to make this "fact" a reality. Comprised of only seven key members, it proved to be a very vocal force in promoting Seattle.

Cooper and Levy — a major outfitter in the city — moved Seattle boosters to action. One of the owners notified the Chamber of Commerce that railroad companies were not routing many of the early Klondike stampeders through Seattle. Initially, only the Great Northern Railway took Yukon-bound passengers to this city, while the Southern Pacific routed passengers to San Francisco, the Northern Pacific advertised Portland, and the Canadian Pacific promoted Vancouver, British Columbia. The Chamber of Commerce thus established the Bureau of Information on August 30, 1897, to devise a plan for promoting Seattle as the Klondike outfitting and departure center. It also charged the Bureau of Information with counteracting the efforts of other cities in this direction. Even more significant, members appointed Erastus Brainerd as secretary and executive officer.[3] Were it not for this move, Seattle might not have figured as prominently as it did in the Klondike trade.

Brainerd proved to be the most influential of Seattle's boosters during the Klondike Gold Rush. What was most remarkable about his advertising campaign was that it was waged during an era before the practice of swaying public opinion had become commonplace. His social status and his professional contacts helped his publicity efforts. Born in the Connecticut River Valley in 1855, Brainerd attended Phillips Exeter Academy, and graduated from Harvard at the tender age of 19. After serving as curator of engravings at the Boston Museum of Arts, he traveled to Europe, where he promoted a tour for W. Irving Bishop, a "lecturing showman." While in Europe, Brainerd displayed his gregarious personality and his propensity for joining, becoming a Knight of the Order of St. John of Jerusalem, a Knight of the Red Cross of Rome, a Knight Templar, and a Mason.[4]

Returning to the United States, Brainerd turned to journalism, landing a job as a news editor of the Atlanta Constitution. In 1882, he married Jefferson Davis' granddaughter, which endeared him to Southern readers. One reporter described Brainerd at this time as "an accomplished gentleman, a desirable citizen, and an engaging friend." Moving to Philadelphia,

Brainerd proved to be the most influential of Seattle's boosters during the Klondike Gold Rush. What was most remarkable about his advertising campaign was that it was waged during an era before the practice of swaying public opinion had become commonplace.

Routes to the Klondike

Seattle or Vancouver to Skagway

Steamships sailed 800 miles through the Inside Passage to Skagway. This trip took approximately three days. From Skagway, gold seekers crossed the White Pass or Chilkoot Trails to reach the headwaters of the Yukon River, and from there they continued to Dawson City – a distance of 500 miles. Most prospectors took this route.

All-Water Route

Steamships sailed to the Bering Sea and the delta of the Yukon River. From St. Michael, gold seekers took a riverboat upstream to Dawson City – a distance of 1,700 miles. This was the longest and most expensive route to the gold fields.

All-Canada Route

Gold seekers reached Edmonton on the Canadian Pacific Railroad. From there, they traveled overland to the Athabasca River, where they caught a steamboat to the Mackenzie River. After traveling on the river, stampeders still needed to surmount a mountain range to the west before reaching Dawson City. This was an extremely difficult route, due to the muskeg and willow thickets that covered the trail.

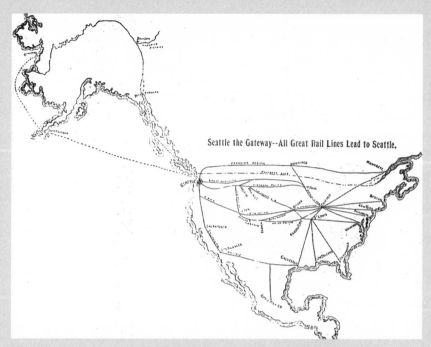

This map, which appeared in The Seattle Post Intelligencer in October of 1897, depicted "all great rail lines" leading to Seattle. San Francisco, Vancouver, and other rival cities — which also offered rail connections — did not appear.

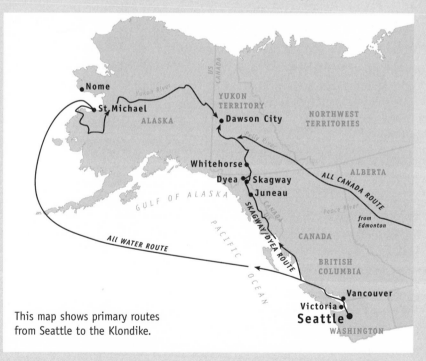

This map shows primary routes from Seattle to the Klondike.

Brainerd again joined a variety of organizations, including the Union League, Penn Club, and the Authors and Press clubs of New York.[5]

In 1890, Brainerd suffered from several attacks of influenza. His desire for employment opportunities as well as his ill health prompted him to relocate to Seattle, where he became the editor of *The Press-Times*. Brainerd joined the Rainier Club and organized a local Harvard Club, becoming known as "a social swell and an authority on terrapin [edible turtles]." His activities included fishing trips with the eminent Judge Thomas Burke. By 1897, when Brainerd became secretary of the Bureau of Information, he had developed valuable social — and editorial — connections in the Puget Sound area and throughout the nation. As one biographer summarized, Brainerd was a "man of the world, confident and self assertive." He was also an "unusually facile writer" — a characteristic that would serve Seattle well in the publicity campaign.[6]

The Advertising Campaign

Brainerd's strategy was to promote the city as the only place to outfit for the Klondike. He devised a plan to finance the Bureau of Information by taxing Seattle merchants who stood to profit from the expected influx of population and increased trade.[7] Businesses that paid dues received lists of prospective customers. Brainerd devoted some of this money to advertising in newspapers and popular journals. He purchased a three-quarter-page ad in William Randolph Hearst's *New York Journal* for $800, along with quarter-page advertisements in *Munsey*, *McClure's*, *Cosmopolitan*, *Harper's Weekly*, *Scribner's*, and *Review of Reviews*.[8] One of these advertisements pointed out that as the "Queen City of the Northwest," Seattle served as the manufacturing, railroad, mining, and agricultural center of Washington state. "Look at your map!" the ad urged readers. "Seattle is a commercial city, and is to the Pacific Northwest as New York is to the Atlantic coast."[9]

Brainerd also encouraged the *Post-Intelligencer* to issue a special Klondike edition on October 13, 1897, which began with the headline, "Seattle Opens the Gate to the Klondike Gold Fields." Seattle, the lead article assured readers, "is not a mushroom, milk-

Bureau of Information, Seattle Chamber of Commerce, 1897

Erastus Brainerd, Secretary
Edward F. Sweeney, president of Seattle Brewing and Malt Company
J.W. Goodwin, J. W. Goodwin & Company
Emil Lobe, Golden Rule Bazaar
Samual Rosenberg, Kline and Rosenberg, clothiers
A. B. Stewart, Stewart and Holmes, wholesale druggists
F. S. Sylvester, president of Seattle Trading Company, grocers

Source: Answers to Queries, *Seattle Post-Intelligencer*, October 13, 1897, p.6.

and-water town with only crude frontier ways." Instead, "it is a city of from 65,000 to 70,000 population, with big brick and stone business blocks and mercantile establishments that would be a credit to Chicago, New York, or Boston." The issue featured a map of transcontinental railroad lines leading to Seattle, "the Gateway."[10] The special Klondike edition offered advice to prospectors on what to bring to the gold fields, how to obtain an outfit, and which route to select. It provided much of the same information as the guidebooks produced throughout the nation during the late nineteenth century, while promoting Seattle.

For a week preceding the publication of the special Klondike edition, Brainerd placed advertisements announcing the upcoming issue and urging readers to send copies to friends and relatives in the East. The *Post-Intelligencer* printed 212,000 copies, making it the largest newspaper run that had been produced west of Chicago. Brainerd sent more than 70,000 to postmasters across the nation, requesting that they distribute them. Various newspaper editors received 20,000 copies, while 10,000 copies went to librarians, mayors, and members of town councils. The Great Northern Railway and Northern Pacific received 10,000 and 5,000 copies respectively.[11]

In addition, Brainerd wrote feature stories on Seattle's virtues, which he distributed to publications throughout the nation. "The 'Seattle Spirit' has accomplished wonders," he assured readers of *The Argus* in 1897. "My impression is that wonders are yet to come." He claimed that observers in the East were convinced "Seattle is a remarkable place" and "something remarkable is sure to occur here." Relentlessly upbeat in tone, Brainerd's writing, like most booster literature, was given to hyperbole: "everybody in the East says Seattle is an extraordinary place."[12]

A subscription to a clippings service helped Brainerd keep track of his efforts as well as those of competing cities. Always vigilant, when he encountered a negative or misinformed article, he wrote to the editors, demanding a retraction.[13] Often Brainerd's letters employed a deceptively innocent tone, as though the publicity for his city had erupted spontaneously, and was not the result of his calculated efforts. "Seattle is not advertising the Klondike," he argued in one letter-to-the-editor. "The Klondike is advertising Seattle, and we are taking advantage of the Klondike excitement to let the world know about Seattle."[14]

Also effective was Brainerd's correspondence campaign, which employed tactics similar to those of modern political lobbyists. He sent a

For a week preceding the publication of the special Klondike edition, Brainerd placed advertisements announcing the upcoming issue and urging readers to send copies to friends and relatives in the East.

This advertisement is an example of Brainerd's promotional genius. A close read of the copy describes Seattle as "*the* point of departure for the Klondike," other cities on the west coast offering services to miners are not mentioned.

confidential letter to employers, organizational leaders, ministers, and teachers, encouraging them to ask the large numbers of people with whom they came in contact to write letters about Seattle to out-of-town friends and newspapers. The more spontaneous these letters could appear, the greater their impact. Brainerd thus generated what looked like a groundswell of unsolicited support. The Bureau of Information offered to furnish the details about Seattle as well as the postage to those who agreed to write letters.[15] "It is very important," Brainerd explained, "that Seattle should be first to catch the eye of the reading public and of the intending Klondiker."[16]

Another masterful public relations effort was the production of circulars that promoted Seattle as the gateway to the Klondike. Brainerd designed and wrote one of these to look like an official government publication — and he convinced Will D. Jenkins, Washington's Secretary of State, to sign it. The circular reassured gold seekers of the safety of the trip to the Yukon, "making it sound like no more than an invigorating outing." The publication also cautioned that no person should embark on the journey with less than $500.[17] A number of European countries — including France, Belgium, Italy, and Switzerland — found the circular so appealing that they reprinted it and had it distributed. Encouraged by this success, Brainerd sent pictures and information about Seattle and the Klondike as Christmas presents to the heads of European nations. When

Kaiser Wilhelm II of Germany refused the gift, fearing it was a bomb, Brainerd used his distrust to gain further publicity.[18]

The Bureau of Information sent additional circulars to every governor and mayor in the United States. These included a series of questions about prospective gold seekers and where they planned to be outfitted. Ostensibly, the purpose of the information acquired was to help Seattle businesses prepare for the stampede of prospectors. The circulars served to advertise Seattle, however, and most recipients turned them over to local newspapers, which printed them. Also, Brainerd provided the information he received from the circulars to Seattle's merchants.[19]

Brainerd's questions elicited some humorous responses. An official of the city of Plymouth, Connecticut, for instance, informed the Bureau of Information that "the 'fever' has had but one victim here as far as we can learn. The young man having married since....has recovered. Think there

In 1898 Erastus Brainerd, pictured here in the Yukon, headed north to search for gold. He did not strike it rich and returned to Seattle the following year.

Hard Drive to the Klondike

is no danger from this point."[20] Similarly, a Detroit official indicated that he could not answer Brainerd's questions, reporting as follows: "How many women there are who intend to go; where people would secure their outfits if they did go; when they expect to go, I respectfully submit is a matter probably known only to Providence himself, and I doubt that if you could communicate with Providence that he would give you reliable data."[21] Omaha responded with some boosterism of its own: "'Klondike fever' has not reached us nor is it likely to do so. This species of disease is apt to strike Cities where business is stagnated and people have lost their faith in the return of prosperity. In Omaha however prosperity is no longer a prophecy but a grand reality."[22]

One of the most celebrated of Brainerd's publicity schemes was a traveling exhibit of $6,000 of Klondike gold. Although it cost the Bureau of Information only $275, the Great Northern Express Company carried this display all over the nation, providing exposure to thousands of spectators and prospective stampeders.[23]

In March of 1898, the Bureau of Information's charter expired. At that time, the Chamber of Commerce's finance committee reported that $9,546.50 had been collected for the advertising campaign — and Brainerd had "made the most of every penny."[24] As a result of his efforts, Seattle received five times the advertising exposure as other cities on the West Coast.[25] In early 1898, *The Seattle Daily Times* reported that Seattle had become the recognized center of Klondike trade. "There is probably no city in the Union today so much talked about as Seattle," the article informed readers, "and there is certainly none toward which more faces are at present turned. From every nook and corner of America and from even the uttermost parts of the earth, a ceaseless, restless throng is moving — moving toward the land of the midnight sun and precious gold, and moving through its natural gateway — the far-famed City of Seattle."[26]

For six months, Brainerd had promoted Seattle at a furious pace. By March of 1898, the work had become "wearing."[27] The next month, he took a new job for the Chamber of Commerce: lobbying in Washington, D.C. for an assay office in Seattle, which would convert the prospectors' gold into cash. An assay office in Seattle would provide returning miners with money that they could spend in the city, allowing merchants to prosper from their business not only on their way to the Klondike but also on their return. While Seattle boosters had advocated this measure from the outset of the gold rush, delegations from San Francisco to

In early 1898, The Seattle Daily Times reported that Seattle had become the recognized center of Klondike trade. "There is probably no city in the Union today so much talked about as Seattle," the article informed readers, "and there is certainly none toward which more faces are at present turned."

Philadelphia opposed the idea, fearing a loss of business in their assay offices. Even so, Brainerd's efforts were successful — and in June of 1898 Congress passed a bill establishing an assay office in Seattle.[28] The government selected a building owned by Thomas Prosch, a prominent city resident. Located at 613 Ninth Avenue, it was a two-story concrete structure featuring a spectacular view of Puget Sound and the busy harbor.[29]

The assay office opened in mid-July of 1898 to a long line of miners recently returned from the Klondike. They received money for their "glittering piles," which employees melted into bars and shipped to Philadelphia to be coined.[30] "It was a sight not quickly to be forgotten," noted one observer. "The looks of anxiety depicted upon the faces of those in waiting, the furrows caused by the rough touch of the north wind, and the general unkempt appearance of the miners, told the bystander that these were men who had escaped none of the hardships incident to life in the wilds of the [Far North]."[31] The first day it opened, the assay office took in $1 million in gold, and for the next six months the average receipts totaled one million dollars per month — far exceeding expectations.[32] By 1902, the assay office had cleared $174 million in gold.[33]

After helping Seattle obtain the assay office in 1898, Brainerd himself headed for the Klondike, perhaps succumbing to his own "gold-rush propaganda." Like many prospectors, Brainerd did not strike it rich in the Far North. He returned to Seattle the following year, becoming involved in numerous professional ventures. He served as "an irrepressible editor" of *The Seattle Post-Intelligencer*, for instance, from 1904 to 1911. During the early twentieth century, he argued for harbor improvements, public health measures, and civic beautification. He also became vice chairman of the Republican City Committee of Seattle. Given the extent of Brainerd's contributions, his final years seem especially tragic. By 1920, he had become mentally ill — and the next year he entered Western State Hospital at Steilacoom. He died there on Christmas Day of 1922.[34]

Strangely, Brainerd's obituary in *The Seattle Post-Intelligencer* mentions very little about the Klondike — and nothing about his role in promoting Seattle.[35] This omission could suggest that the gold rush represented a minor event in Brainerd's expansive career — yet later biographers would note that if Brainerd is remembered at all it is for publicizing the link between Seattle and the Far North.[36] It would be difficult to credit Brainerd with single-handedly securing Seattle's place as the outfitting center, since the city's press and business leaders seized the opportunity to advertise weeks before he assumed responsibility for the publicity campaign. Still, Brainerd's efforts to promote the city proved to be enthusiastic and inventive — even for a booster.

Competition Among Cities

Although it is difficult to evaluate Brainerd's precise impact on the Klondike Gold Rush or on the growth of Seattle, it is certain that the objective of his advertising campaign was reached: Seattle indeed became the gateway to the Klondike. As noted, of the approximately 100,000 prospectors who set out for the Far North, 70,000 selected this city as the place for outfitting and transportation. To some extent, this development was dictated by location. San Francisco and Portland did not enjoy the relative proximity to the gold fields that cities on Puget Sound offered. Meanwhile, smaller cities such as Everett, Bellingham, and Port Townsend did not sustain a population base sufficient to support large-scale businesses that could easily outfit tens of thousands of miners.

Still, the question of why Tacoma did not benefit more from the Klondike trade remains an interesting one, as does the question of why an American city should profit more than Victoria and Vancouver from a gold strike located on Canadian soil. The efforts of Erastus Brainerd help explain how Seattle emerged the victor in the battle for gold-rush business. No other city mounted an advertising campaign that could rival his. Part booster and part huckster, Brainerd was "an optimist and an enthusiast" who had the vision necessary to sell Seattle to the public.[37]

At the outset of the Klondike Gold Rush, it was not clear that Seattle would emerge as the point of departure. Like Seattle, other cities also advertised their merits. It was a measure of Brainerd's success that as the competition for the Yukon trade progressed, other towns agreed on only one thing — that Seattle was not the place for outfitting and transportation.[38]

San Francisco

Initially, San Francisco seemed to be a formidable rival. The vessel *Excelsior* had landed there heavy with Klondike gold three days before the *Portland* docked in Seattle in July of 1897. The *Excelsior's* berths sold quickly a week later, as the steamer prepared to return to the Far North.[39] The oldest and most populated of the cities vying for the Klondike trade,

The efforts of Erastus Brainerd help explain how Seattle emerged the victor in the battle for gold-rush business. No other city mounted an advertising campaign that could rival his.

San Francisco promoted its vast experience outfitting Forty-niners during the California Gold Rush.[40]

Moreover, this city featured significant rail and shipping connections — and it enjoyed a longstanding link to the industries of the Far North. Before the Klondike Gold Rush, San Francisco served as the gateway city for the Yukon.[41] The Alaska Commercial Company, associated with fur sealing and other activities, was based in San Francisco — and it was this firm that operated the *Excelsior*. As the Alaskan Trade Committee pointed out, San Francisco was "many times larger" than other cities on the West Coast — and its size kept prices competitive.[42] At the time of the Klondike craze, San Francisco had more than 300,000 residents.[43]

Tacoma promoted itself as "the starting point for all steamers for Alaska." To avoid promoting their competition the word "Seattle" was avoided in their promotional material.

Yet San Francisco's advertising campaign was no match for that of Seattle. To be sure, its newspapers publicized the gold strike and the Bay Area's role. As noted, the *Examiner* hired John Muir to provide observations on the stampede. This naturalist, however, was hardly a booster,

KLONDIKE

INFORMATION FREE.

Authentic and reliable information regarding the New Gold Fields of Alaska, ways and means and cost of reaching them, when and how to go; together with maps of the country and directions for traveling and outfitting will be furnished free by addressing the undersigned committee of citizens of Tacoma, Wash,, head of navigation on Puget Sound and the most economical outfitting point for the Klondike.

All Transportation Companies' Steamers start from Tacoma.

COMMITTEE:

ED. S. HAMILTON, Chairman.
Of McCabe & Hamilton Stevedoring Co.

FREDERIC MOTTET, Treasurer.
Manager and Owner Hunt & Mottet Co.

GEORGE BROWNE, Secretary.
President Tacoma Smelting and Refining Co.

F. W. MERRICK,
Clothier.

GEORGE H. STONE,
Of Sanford, Stone & Fisher Co.

C. P. FERRY,
Capitalist.

Address TACOMA CITIZEN'S KLONDIKE COMMITTEE, 942 Pacific Avenue, Tacoma, Wash.

viewing the gold rush as "a wild and discouraging mess."[44]

San Francisco also established an Alaska-Klondike Bureau of Information. Staffed with "competent, courteous and painstaking men," the Bureau maintained up-to-date reports on the Yukon, along with an "educational exhibit." It advised prospective miners to travel through San Francisco "because you save time, money and annoyance." Among the more compelling arguments in favor of this city included the number of businesses, which kept prices low and goods in stock, and the ample hotel accommodations. Interestingly, the Bureau also highlighted recreational opportunities, promising that those who traveled to San Francisco would encounter scenery superior to that of northern routes. San Francisco itself, moreover, was "worth seeing."[45]

According to the *The Seattle Daily Times*, San Francisco merchants organized an advertising campaign in 1897 that emphasized the California city's advantages over Seattle. "The stocks of San Francisco merchants are practically inexhaustible," they claimed, "as against the similar stores of Seattle, which on several occasions….were totally depleted in several lines. Being forced to telegraph to San Francisco for goods, prices were boosted out of sight in Seattle." Not surprisingly, such disparaging claims provoked Seattle promoters, who complained that the California city was "scheming" to take the Yukon trade. [46]

The Seattle Daily Times assured its readers in 1897 that most of San Francisco's Klondike business was local.[47] Located much farther south of the Yukon than the other competing cities, San Francisco encouraged argonauts to take the all-water route. Seattle boosters counteracted this approach by claiming that the trip up the Inside Passage from Puget Sound was safer.[48]

The route over Chilkoot Pass to the interior, developed during the 1880s, gave Seattle an advantage over San Francisco.[49] Even so, rail line connections made San Francisco accessible and attractive to prospectors outside California. These included Wyatt Earp, who departed from Yuma, Arizona. "It was hot as Hades," his wife recalled, "and we were fondly remembering cool San Francisco."[50]

For all the early interest in San Francisco, the city did not seriously threaten Seattle's position as the gateway to the Klondike. As Seattle author and historian Archie Satterfield has explained, "somehow the chemistry wasn't right" in San Francisco.[51] The California city did not experience the level of excitement that gripped towns farther north —

Population Growth in Competing Cities

City	Population Increase 1890-1900			
	1890	1900	Number	%
San Francisco	298,997	342,782	43,785	15
Portland	46,385	90,426	44,041	95
Tacoma	36,006	37,714	1,708	5
Seattle	42,837	80,671	37,834	88
Vancouver	13,709	27,010	13,301	97
Victoria	16,841	20,919	4,078	24

Source: Alexander Norbert MacDonald, "Seattle, Vancouver, and the Klondike," *The Canadian Historical Review* (September 1968), p. 246

and attempts to advertise itself as the point of departure were lukewarm. John Bonner, writing from San Francisco to the national journal *Leslie's Weekly*, offered a similar explanation in December of 1897. "San Francisco has only just begun to wake up," he pointed out, while Seattle "was the first in the field" to take advantage of the opportunities that the gold rush presented. He characterized Seattle residents as "energetic" and "enterprising" people of the "git-up-and-git kind," who flooded eastern cities with advertising. The people of San Francisco, on the other hand, were "torpid," inclined to "jaw-smithing when they should be acting."[52] In summary, Seattle proved far more aggressive than San Francisco in pursuing the Klondike trade.

Portland

Portland had numerous advantages in the battle for the Klondike trade: a strong, stable financial foundation and extensive rail connections and port facilities. With approximately 60,000 residents, Portland also boasted a higher population than Seattle — a distinction it retained even after the gold rush. In September of 1897, Portland's business leaders organized an advertising campaign that resembled Brainerd's plan. It included providing maps, pamphlets, and circulars to railroads and prominent eastern publications. W.A. Mears, one of the primary forces behind this campaign, assured fellow businessmen that success in this venture would require extraordinary contributions. "You will have yourself to thank," he warned them, "if you see Seattle go ahead with a bound and distance this city in wealth and population."[53]

The Seattle Chamber of Commerce did not take this threat lightly. As Brainerd explained, "Portland will not do this by halves." Clearly he viewed the city as a rival, asking "Is it likely that Portland with its great aggregated corporate and individual wealth will fail to spend money like water when it thinks that a failure [to do so] will help Seattle?"[54] A large advertisement for Portland appeared in the *New York Journal* in December of 1897, prompting Brainerd to respond with an advertisement of his own.[55]

The Klondike Gold Rush indeed brought profit to Portland's merchants. From 1896 to 1898, more than 300 new businesses incorporated in Oregon — and 136 of them were mining-related enterprises. Henry Wemme exemplified a Portland businessman who capitalized on the Klondike stampede by establishing "an immense business in selling tents."[56]

For all this success, however, the Webfoot City, as newspapers called it, did not succeed in wresting much of the business from Seattle. Portland was farther from the gold fields than the Puget Sound cities, and it did not have the frequent shipping service to the Far North that Seattle offered. As a number of historians have pointed out, Portland was established earlier than Seattle, and the older city retained a conservative, complacent character that contrasted with the energy of Seattle promoters. Jonas A. Jonasson, for example, explained in a comparison of Portland in Seattle that "Seattle's favored location on Puget Sound and the vigor of the famous 'Seattle Spirit' that saw its opportunity and took advantage of it was an unbeatable combination."[57]

Tacoma

Tacoma and Seattle had a longstanding rivalry. As the "City of Destiny," Tacoma had won the coveted position as terminus for the Northern Pacific — the first transcontinental railroad to arrive in Washington. Like

Tacoma promoted itself as the terminus for the Great Northern Railroad. This map, published in the *Tacoma Daily News*, is a direct copy of a map used in the *Seattle Post-Intelligencer's* Klondike issue. Notice that no competing cities appear on this version of the map.

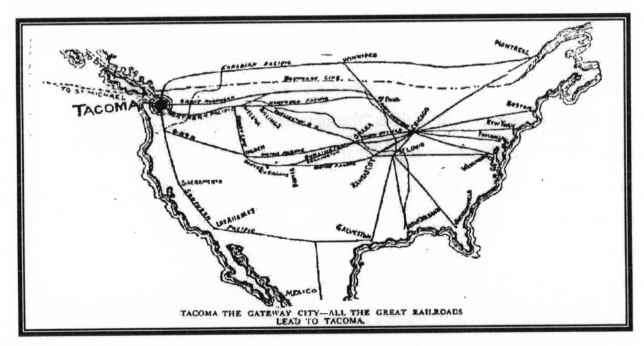

TACOMA THE GATEWAY CITY—ALL THE GREAT RAILROADS LEAD TO TACOMA.

Seattle, Tacoma boasted port as well as rail facilities, and it was relatively the same distance from this location to the Klondike. According to historian Murray Morgan, what distinguished Tacoma from Seattle in the race for Klondike trade was its slow pace and lack of vigor. "Before Tacoma awoke to the full possibilities of the rush north," he explained, "Seattle was synonymous with Alaska." Significantly, Charles Mellen, president of the Northern Pacific, arranged for company steamships to leave from commercial docks in Seattle, even though he had to pay rent for those facilities. Ironically, at the outset of the gold rush, the only ship that sailed regularly from Tacoma to the Far North was named *The City of Seattle*.[58]

Early accounts by the Tacoma press indicated a lack of recognition of the significance of the gold rush. Two days after the *Portland* arrived in Seattle, *The Tacoma Daily News* reported that the city "has not gone wild over the Klondike." As the article advised, "It is not well for people to lose their heads over distant gold fields, only to be reached after extreme hardship.... Careful people who are making a living will stay where they are."[59] Initially, Tacoma business responded to the gold rush with "lethargy."[60] While such caution appears prudent in retrospect, it did not help increase Tacoma's share of the Klondike trade.

Similarly, on July 29, *The Tacoma Daily News* sneered at Seattle's aggressive approach, suggesting that the city "should not make a spectacle of herself." Moreover, the article found "the Seattle spirit" to be "unlovely." While others praised Seattle's "energy and enterprise," Tacoma saw only "hoggishness and snarling."[61] The Tacoma press further pointed out that other Puget Sound cities shared its sentiments. In late July of 1897, *The Skagit News-Herald*, for example, urged Seattle promoters to "remember this is not yet the harvest time," advising them to proceed more slowly.[62] Tacoma, then, was not alone in failing to recognize the importance of speed in pursuing the Klondike trade.

A few weeks after the gold rush began, Tacoma businessmen began to realize what they were missing. They suggested advertising in eastern newspapers and establishing a bureau of information. "The principal thing for Tacoma to do just now is to advertise," one promoter advised in August of 1897. "Pick up any of the eastern newspapers today and you will find just how much this town is losing by not keeping to the front as a starting and outfitting point for miners bound for Alaska."[63] Another observer in Tacoma noted that "there is the greatest difference in the

While others praised Seattle's "energy and enterprise," Tacoma saw only "hoggishness and snarling." The Tacoma press further pointed out that other Puget Sound cities shared its sentiments.

world between Tacoma and Seattle in this Klondike excitement.... Over there they are all up in arms about it."[64]

The Tacoma City government, however, was not in a position to respond, as it was "bitterly divided" over a mayoral election that had come down to two votes. Because the ballot boxes had been stolen from the city clerk's office, a recount was not possible. As a result, Tacoma was encumbered by two mayors and two civil service commissions. Moreover, the Chamber of Commerce, established in 1884, split three ways when attempting to select a publicity director for a Klondike advertising campaign.[65]

A longstanding rivalry between Tacoma and Seattle intensified during the Klondike Gold Rush. This advertisement promotes Tacoma and Pierce County as destinations as profitable as the Klondike Gold Fields.

Accordingly, in late September of 1897, *The Seattle Daily Times* featured an article titled "Tacoma Has Given Up," suggesting that Seattle promoters did not view Tacoma as a serious threat. It quoted Brainerd as follows: "It is best for the Coast cities to set forth their merits as outfitting points in their own way, and let the intending Klondiker make his own choice. In that case Seattle will stand the best chance to keep and to enlarge the trade she now controls."[66]

By late 1897, Tacoma's Chamber of Commerce had produced a circular titled *Tacoma: Gateway to the Klondike.* This publication promoted Tacoma as "the starting point of all steamers for Alaska." Perhaps attempting to avoid inadvertent advertising for rival cities, its authors refused to use the word "Seattle," referring to W.D. Wood as mayor "of one of the Puget Sound cities."[67] The Chamber of Commerce and Board of Trade also printed a booklet titled *Tacoma Souvenir,* which announced that the city "is not the result of an accident," since the Northern Pacific Railroad selected it as the terminus after "exhaustive examinations of the entire northwest."[68]

Like boosters in Seattle, Tacoma promoters distributed advertisements to railroads. These billed Tacoma as "the most economical outfitting point for the Klondike."[69] Despite these efforts, however, the Tacoma press revealed that the city remained in a weak position.

Attempting to deflect attention from Seattle and the Yukon, *The Tacoma Daily News* emphasized that there were other "Klondikes" in Washington, where prospectors could strike it rich. This newspaper published a map as part of a special Klondike edition December of 1897 that prominently featured Tacoma as the gateway to the Yukon. Displaying the rail connections that led to the city, it was a direct copy of the map featuring Seattle that the *Post-Intelligencer* had published in its special Klondike edition two months earlier (see map on page 42). Even the organization of *The Tacoma Daily News* article resembled the earlier Seattle piece.[70]

In summary, Tacoma's efforts to gain the Klondike trade lagged behind that of Seattle every step of the way. When the gold rush ended, according to Morgan, "the race for dominance on Puget Sound was over. Tacoma was the second city. Its struggle in the next years was not for triumph but for survival." During the decade 1890-1900, Seattle's population nearly doubled, reaching 80,676. Tacoma's population increased only 4.7 percent, reaching a total of 37,714.[71] It is interesting to speculate how this outcome might have differed had Erastus Brainerd been named head of the publicity campaign of Tacoma. Even so, it is doubtful that Tacoma, characterized as a "company town" dominated by the railroad, could have surpassed Seattle in the rush for the Klondike trade.[72] Brainerd's enthusiasm and his advertising schemes might not have proven effective without the vision and support of Seattle's business community, which, as noted, immediately seized the opportunity to promote the city.

Additional American Cities

A number of smaller cities on the West Coast attempted to secure some of the Klondike trade. Juneau, for instance, billed itself as "the metropolis of Alaska" and "the gateway to the interior gold fields." Its merchants argued that miners outfitting in their town would reduce or eliminate the cost of transporting freight to the Yukon, and they warned that outfits purchased in Seattle were stowed at the bottom of the ship's hold, where horses and mules stood over them for the duration of the trip to the Far North.[73] Juneau business interests also distributed circulars advertising Juneau on trains that ran between Seattle and Tacoma.[74]

Port Townsend similarly promoted itself as "the principal city on the west side of Puget Sound" and the port entry for the Puget Sound customs district. At the outset of the gold rush, some Port Townsend merchants recognized the need for "prompt interest and vigorous action." Seattle, they noted, had benefited from this approach.[75] "The Seattle papers," one observer pointed out in July of 1897, "are full of advertisements of business houses, giving lists of articles that should be purchased by intending Klondyke gold seekers… It has been generally believed by them that Seattle was the only place where such goods can be procured."[76]

Port Townsend merchants, along with the Board of Trade, thus launched a relatively modest publicity campaign touting the advantages of their town. Advertisements described Port Townsend as "the principal city on the west side of Puget Sound" and the port entry for the Puget Sound customs district. Steamers bound for the Far North stopped at Port Townsend — and its businesses offered goods from San Francisco "at the lowest possible rates." Promoters promised that miners who purchased their outfits at Port Townsend would enjoy the advantage of having their goods loaded last on the ship — since this was the last port stop — making them the first to be unloaded at the port of discharge in the Far North. The Board of Trade further suggested "that all Eastern parties who come through direct to Port Townsend will be so well pleased that they will all write to their friends to come here as the starting point for the great gold fields of the North."[77]

Without the rail connections that Seattle and Tacoma enjoyed, however, Port Townsend was not positioned to become the "starting point" to the Klondike. Moreover, with a population of only 3,600 residents in 1897, the town did not support the number of businesses that larger cities offered.[78] Although the gold rush renewed the determination of town residents to secure a rail link to Portland, it did not play a major role in the development of the community.

Similarly, Everett and Bellingham, for all their railroad and water connections, boasted fewer than 10,000 residents apiece — and as historian Alexander Norbert MacDonald has indicated, "their smallness ruled them out as significant competitors."[79] They could not pursue the Klondike trade with the zeal, vigor, and resources that Seattle merchants brought to the enterprise. Newspapers in the Bellingham area, in fact, reported that the Klondike Gold Rush was not what it was "cracked up to be," and advertised placer mines in Whatcom County as rivaling those in the Yukon.[80]

Vancouver and Victoria

Vancouver and Victoria enjoyed an advantage in the scramble for Klondike profits: location. Not only were these cities closer to the gold fields than most West Coast communities but they were Canadian as well. If American stampeders purchased and bonded their outfits in

Canada, they were not required to pay an import duty — and merchants in Vancouver and Victoria made the most of this point in attempting to lure prospectors their way. Business interests in the cities mobilized quickly to mount a publicity campaign that included distributing leaflets and printing articles and advertisements in Vancouver's *News-Advertiser* and Victoria's *The Daily Colonist*. These promotions emphasized that the gold fields were located in Canada, and that the British Columbia cities were accessible by rail and steamer.[81] Interestingly, this effort sparked very little friction between the two cities, whose merchants felt the need to cooperate against their American rivals.[82]

Tappan Adney, correspondent for *Harper's Weekly*, observed a flurry of business activity. "Victoria sells mittens and hats and coats only for Klondike," he wrote. "Flour and bacon, tea and coffee, are sold only for Klondike. Shoes and saddles and boats, shovels and sacks — everything for Klondike." He reported that some "wide-awake" merchants from Victoria and Vancouver purchased an outfit in Seattle to compare American and Canadian prices.[83]

Despite the responsiveness of Canadian businesses, however, the gold rush had caught the nation unprepared to address confusing trade regulations. For approximately eight months, newspapers in Vancouver, Victoria, and American cities exchanged heated arguments about Canadian customs. Encouraged by U.S. railway officials, Brainerd lobbied Congress to pressure Canada for resolution of the tariff issue.[84] In September of 1897, the Vancouver Board of Trade advertised that all goods purchased in that city "will be certified by the Customs Officers there, and be admitted free of duty, thus saving time, trouble and money to the miner." Seattle newspapers, on the other hand, suggested that no Canadian customs would be collected on goods purchased on American soil. At the outset of the gold rush, duties were seldom collected in the Yukon, since Canada had not yet posted customs officials there. In the fall of 1897, however, Canada established a customs post at Lake Tagish, and by January 1 of the following year, regular duties were established.[85]

Advertisements promoting Vancouver and Victoria informed readers that they were closer to the Klondike gold fields, a detail often overlooked in competing publications and promotions.

For the Yukon ...

... VANCOUVER

is the Nearest Port;
the Best Outfitting Place; and
the Starting Point for all
the Best Routes to the

KLONDIKE

See that your Ticket reads
"via Vancouver"

and that your Baggage is checked
"to Vancouver"

In addition to the lack of import duties, Vancouver and Victoria offered accessibility to prospectors. The Canadian Pacific Railway had completed its transcontinental line to British Columbia in 1885 — and the railroad advertised its services to gold seekers. Vancouver, however, lacked Seattle's trade connections with the Far North. At the outset of the gold rush the Pacific Coast Steamship Company and the North American Transportation and Trading Company, both of which maintained trading posts in the Yukon, were based in Seattle. Vancouver, according to MacDonald, enjoyed no such facilities, and "had to start virtually from scratch in its attempt to capture some of the trade."[86] As noted, the foothold that Seattle had gained in Alaska and the Far North before the gold rush helped the city eclipse the efforts of rivals, including Vancouver.

~~~~~THE~~~~~

KLONDYKE GOLD FIELDS

ARE IN CANADA.

Goods purchased elsewhere than in Canada are subject to Customs Duty on entering the Yukon. Strong force of Customs Officers and Mounted Police stationed at the Passes Customs Certificates on purchases in Canada will prevent any delay from Canadian or United States officials.

VICTORIA, BRITISH COLUMBIA,

Is the best place to Fit Out and Sail from. All Steamboats going North start from or call at Victoria.

G. A. KIRK,
President B. C. Board of Trade.

Vancouver and Victoria merchants worked together against rival American cities. They emphasized that the gold fields were located in Canada, and explained that purchases made in Canada were exempt from import duty.

Moreover, as was the case with other competing cities, Victoria and Vancouver could not match the pace and extent of Seattle's advertising campaign. In 1897, one Canadian publication urged stampeders to exercise caution, noting "there is plenty of time….the gold won't run away. It has been there for several million years already, and will no doubt wait a month or two longer."[87] It is difficult to imagine Brainerd issuing such a statement, which contradicts the spirit of the term "gold rush." Similarly, the *Vancouver News-Advertiser* cautioned that "only one out of every hundred who risks the venture [to the Klondike] can expect to realize any big results from their hazardous undertaking."[88] In addition to contributing to newspapers, Brainerd published articles in a variety of magazines. Canadian journals, on the other hand, carried few, if any, articles on the gold rush in the fall of 1897.[89] As one historian explained, Canadians were sober, moderate people, not given to the sense of urgency that characterized the American response to the gold strike in the Klondike. Canadians valued "safety and security, order and harmony," whereas "for the Americans who rushed north in 1897 and 1898, [the Klondike] was a last frontier; for them there were no more wilderness worlds to conquer or even to know."[90]

Perhaps it was the British influence that resulted in this conservative, restrained tone. *The Illustrated London News* portrayed an unappealing side of the gold rush that Seattle newspapers avoided, if not ignored. "Thousands of men are quitting their safe abodes and proved industries or trades," observed one article in 1897, "and making their way, at any cost, with certain loss of what they leave behind." In addition to this dismal assessment of the risks involved in gold seeking, *The Illustrated London News* described the Yukon as "that remotest and naturally most uninviting north-western corner of the vast British American dominion."[91] Similarly, *Punch*, a British journal, published a striking cartoon in 1897 that depicted dying miners clawing their way toward a gold nugget, which was guarded by the Angel of Death.[92] Such images were not designed to send gold seekers racing toward Canadian cities for outfitting. In contrast, when Seattle publications depicted the hardships of the Yukon, the narrative typically ended with advice about obtaining sufficient supplies and warm clothing, which could be purchased in Seattle.[93]

Even guidebooks published in Canada touted Seattle — not Victoria or Vancouver — as the best place to begin the journey to the gold fields, while *The Seattle Post-Intelligencer* pronounced the All-Canadian route "worthless."[94] In fact, most American promoters, including Brainerd, downplayed the point that the gold fields were located in Canada — a tactic that irritated promoters in Victoria and Vancouver.[95] In the end, the Klondike Gold Rush turned out to be primarily an American phenomenon, with as many as 65 percent of the prospectors coming from the United States.[96] Although many miners were immigrants who had recently naturalized, the fact that they started out from the United States might have made them more likely to outfit from an American city.[97]

In summary, although cities such as San Francisco, Portland, Tacoma, Victoria, and Vancouver succeeded in gaining some of the Klondike trade, they were not able to take the majority of it from Seattle, which became the "Queen City" of the Pacific Northwest and the "emporium" of the Far North.[98] None could boast a promoter as effective as Brainerd. Although *The Seattle Daily Times* expressed concern in 1897 about Seattle's "busy" competitors, fearing "they stop at nothing," it was Seattle's boosters who "stopped at nothing."[99] *The Trade Register*, a publication produced weekly in Seattle, derided Tacoma in 1897 as "our crotchety, jealous and notoriously unreliable little rival." According to this source, the eastern press "now recognizes Seattle's importance as the leading commercial center and headquarters for the Yukon trade." As *The*

"Thousands of men are quitting their safe abodes and proved industries or trades," observed one article in 1897, "and making their way, at any cost, with certain loss of what they leave behind."

This striking illustration depicted dying miners clawing their way toward a gold nugget, guarded by the Angel of Death. A watchful bear and a pair of wolves (pictured right) added to the sense of doom. This cartoon appeared in *Punch* on August 28, 1897.

Trade Register further explained, "Seattle is all life and bustle, while Tacoma is as dead as a post."[100]

In addition to its superior efforts at promotion, Seattle had established trade connections to the Far North, as well as railroad and shipping facilities, before the Klondike stampede. Seattle also supported numerous local industries that could activate quickly for the outfitting business. "The gold excitement did not start the wheels going," *The Trade Register* explained in 1897, "it only gave them a big whirl."[101] The following chapter explores how this "big whirl" affected Seattle businesses.

If you want the very best Klondike outfit that money can buy, and want it put up on short notice, we can serve you well and faithfully.

COOPER & LEVY

CHAPTER THREE

Reaping the Profits of the Klondike Trade

"This town of thirty to forty thousand was all Klondike"
— *Robert B. Medill, Klondike Diary:*
True Account of the Gold Rush of 1897-1898

"The stores are ablaze with Klondike goods; men pass by robed in queer garments; … teams of trained dogs, trotting about with sleds; men with packs upon their backs, and a thousand and one things which are of use in the Klondike trade."

— *The Seattle Daily Times, 1897*

An "All-Klondike" Town

Descriptions of Seattle from 1897 and 1898 share a common theme: a sense of energy and purpose had gripped the city. After years of depression, the stampede to the Klondike invigorated the economy, rekindling the Seattle spirit. As was the case with many gold rushes throughout the West, it was generally not the miners who struck it rich. The business district — centered around what is now Pioneer Square — flourished, as thousands of gold seekers bound for the Yukon poured into the city, and a variety of merchants stepped forward to meet their needs.

One observer, returning to Seattle after a seven-month absence in the late 1890s, marveled that the sluggish, stagnant town he left bustled with new prosperity. "Up First Avenue and down Second Avenue is one train of fanciful, kaleidoscopic pictures from real life," he wrote. "The stores are ablaze with Klondike goods; men pass by robed in queer garments; … teams of trained dogs, trotting about with sleds; men with packs upon their backs, and a thousand and one things which are of use for the Klondike trade."[1] Martha Louise Black, a prospector headed for the

Yukon, had a similar reaction to Seattle's streets. "Everywhere were piles of outfits," she recalled. These included camp supplies, sleds, carts, and harnesses, together with dogs, horses, cattle, and oxen.[2] The increased commercial activity affected the mood of the city. As one miner summarized, "We found no discouragement in Seattle. This town of thirty to forty thousand was all Klondike."[3]

So profitable was the Klondike trade that during the late 1890s Seattle became the financial center of the Pacific Northwest.[4] By 1900 Seattle's bank clearances — the amount of money that changed hands in the daily course of the city's commercial life — had soared more than 400 percent, surpassing those of Portland and Los Angeles. At the turn of the century, only San Francisco enjoyed a greater volume of business among West Coast cities. Seattle bankers attributed this prosperity to the gold rush.[5] The city's merchants, too, remained well aware of the source of their profits. Wa Chong & Company, for example, reported in 1898 that "times are very good….Klondike gold has helped things very much."[6]

The amount and variety of goods in a typical Klondike grubstake boosted numerous businesses in Seattle. During the winter of 1898, the Northwest Mounted Police required that each miner bring enough provisions to last a year, which could weigh between 1,500 and 2,000 pounds. The "one-ton rule" helped ensure that prospectors would arrive at least somewhat prepared to withstand the difficult environment of the Far North. It also benefited the merchants, who sold the miners this vast quantity of supplies, along with a myriad of services. Approximately 70,000 stampeders passed through Seattle during the Klondike Gold Rush — each one a potential customer. Some gold seekers invested as much as $1,000 for supplies and transportation. During the winter of 1898, the Northwest Mounted Police required that each miner bring enough provisions to last a year, which could weigh between 1,500 and 2,000 pounds.[7]

Not all were men.[8] Although the Seattle Chamber of Commerce discouraged women from traveling to the Yukon, it established a Women's Department, which distributed advice on purchasing an outfit. Moreover, some entire families set out for the Klondike, providing additional opportunities for sales. Articles commonly purchased included groceries, clothing, bedding, sleds, hardware, medicine chests, tents, and harnesses and packsaddles.[9]

Some of the materials marketed to gold seekers were manufactured in the city. The Seattle Woolen Mill, for example, produced blankets and robes "for the Arctic Regions."[10] Another firm made a "special miner's shoe," turning out several dozen pairs per day.[11] Seattle also featured food

So profitable was the Klondike trade that during the late 1890s Seattle became the financial center of the Pacific Northwest.

Klondike Insect-Proof Mask

A newly patented device which is
an absolute protection against
all insects.

Made of Galvanized Steel wire and Cape
of Linen scrim.

Cannot break or tear.

Sold by all Outfitters on Pacific Coast.

Alaska Novelty Mfg. Co., Tacoma

Outfitters offered a variety of items to stampeders. Crystallized eggs, frost extractors, and insect-proof masks were just a few of the items available.

processing plants, breweries, and foundries that supplied gold seekers.[12] Even so, Seattle merchants obtained many products — including dry goods and clothing — from suppliers in New York and Chicago, who shipped their goods west. Sometimes wholesalers in Seattle re-packaged these products under new, Klondike-related brand names. Lilly, Bogardus, and Company, Inc., a Seattle grain and feed dealer, sold products purchased from the Chicago stockyards as "Alaska Dog Feed."[13] By purchasing goods from the East and Midwest, Seattle merchants forged important commercial connections that allowed large stocks to move quickly and efficiently, at reduced costs.[14]

In addition to collecting fees from various merchants to finance its advertising campaign, the Chamber of Commerce gathered testimonials from miners to help Seattle businesses. "I never ate better bacon," one prospector vouched for The Seattle Trading Company. "The flour and beans could not be beat." Moreover, he and his partner did not lose any provisions, indicating that "the packing was first-class." Erastus Brainerd published these testimonials, many of which mentioned specific businesses, in Seattle newspapers.[15]

From the summer of 1897 throughout 1898, the Seattle press was filled with large, illustrated advertisements directed at stampeders. Merchants used the word "Klondike" to sell everything from arctic underwear to insect-proof masks. Crystallized eggs and evaporated foods were heavily advertised. Advertisements promoted an array of ingenious gadgets, including Klondike frost extractors (boilers) and air-tight camp stoves. The smaller "want ads" during this period further demonstrated the range of businesses that used the gold rush to sell their products and services. Vashon College, for example, offered Yukon-bound parents a place to leave their sons and daughters, "while their home is broken up."[16] The connection between the Yukon and what was being sold often appeared tenuous. One business advertised, "Going to the Klondyke? Have your watch repaired."[17] Even clairvoyants used the Klondike craze to sell their services. Flo Marvin, for instance, had predicted the gold strike — and she frequently advertised her "occult powers," which included locating mines.[18]

Such an array of advertised products made it difficult for gold seekers to distinguish the essential from the useless and cumbersome. Miners had to decide whether to buy an air-tight camp stove, for example, or whether one of Palmer's Portable Houses would prove to be a better investment than a tent.[19] Purchasing agents were available to assist gold seekers in selecting and buying an outfit, but this approach had its drawbacks. Some unscrupulous purchasing agents — called "cappers" — took money from naive miners and bought inexpensive, inadequate food and equipment, pocketing large profits.[20] In any case, some observers reveled in the city's unbridled consumerism during the gold rush. "I like Seattle," William Ballou noted in 1898, "all its different fakirs trying to sell you a gold washer, a K. stove, or a dog team with one lame dog which would get well by tomorrow."[21]

Outfitters

Seattle offered numerous companies that could outfit miners — sometimes in a single stop. Some of the city's retailers captured Klondike trade by marketing complete outfits that included food, equipment, and clothing. The Columbia Grocery Company, Seattle Trading Company, and Fischer Brothers, for example, offered this service. While gold seekers in other cities had to locate and visit a variety of stores, Seattle businesses developed a reputation for providing outfits quickly and efficiently. The Seattle Trading Company, established in 1893, printed special forms listing supplies, and miners could check the items they wished to purchase.[22]

Cooper and Levy was among the largest and most heavily advertised of the city's outfitters. Isaac Cooper and his wife's brother, Louis Levy, formed a partnership in 1892, providing retail and mail-order groceries, hardware, and woodenware. Their business was located in Seattle's commercial center, at the southeast corner of First Avenue and Yesler (photo, above). During the gold rush, large stacks of goods outside this store became a common sight — and it remains an enduring image of Seattle street scenes from the period. In 1903, Cooper and Levy sold their business to the Bon Marche.[23]

Schwabacher Brothers and Company was another prominent merchandising business. Established in Seattle in 1869, it was also one of the city's oldest. In 1888, Schwabacher Hardware Company incorporated as a separate business. Schwabacher Brothers and Company sold groceries, clothing, and building materials. The store was located in Seattle's commercial district, and the company also maintained a wharf. These facilities, along with the Schwabachers' longstanding presence in Seattle, placed the company in an advantageous position when the gold rush began. Schwabacher's wharf received considerable publicity in July of 1897, when the *Portland*, laden with Klondike gold, docked there and set off the rush to the Yukon.[24]

Some Seattle companies that prospered during the stampede continue to serve customers today. These include the Bon Marche, which frequent-

Cooper and Levy was among the largest and most heavily advertised of the city's outfitters. Isaac Cooper and his wife's brother, Louis Levy, formed a partnership in 1892, providing retail and mail-order groceries, hardware, and woodenware.

The Bon Marche ran a mail order business and also advertised arctic clothing, in Seattle newspapers in 1897 and 1898. Blankets, shoes, bedding, and items were offered for sale.

ly advertised arctic clothing as well as a mail order business, in Seattle newspapers in 1897 and 1898. Its wares included blankets, shoes, bedding, and general furnishings. Edward Nordhoff, a German immigrant, founded this company, naming it after the famous store in Paris. "Le Bon Marche" translates into "The Good Bargain." During the gold rush, the Bon Marche operated at Second Avenue and Pike Street.[25]

Additional outfitting stores that remained in business a century after the gold rush era included the Clinton C. Filson Company, which operated the Pioneer Alaska Clothing and Blanket Manufacturer, and continues to provide outdoor wear.[26] Similarly, the Bartell Drug Company continues to maintain a chain of stores throughout Puget Sound.

Nordstrom Department Store remains one of the best-known businesses still in operation. John W. Nordstrom, a Swedish immigrant, arrived in the Klondike gold fields in 1897. He struggled there for two years, supporting himself by taking odd jobs. When Nordstrom finally hit pay dirt, another miner challenged his claim, and he sold it. In 1899, he arrived in Seattle with $13,000, which "looked like a lot of money" to him. Two years later Nordstrom invested $4,000 of his newfound wealth in a shoe store, which he opened with his partner, Carl F. Wallin. Located at Fourth Avenue and Pike Street, the business prospered for nearly 30 years — and Nordstrom and Wallin bought another store on Second Avenue. By the late 1920s, the partnership had soured, and Nordstrom bought Wallin's shares. Nordstrom's sons bought the shoe store during the 1930s, expanding it into a retail business with multiple locations.[27] Although Nordstrom's was not founded during the stampede of 1897-1898, it benefited from the vigorous economy that the Klondike Gold Rush encouraged in Seattle. Subsequent gold strikes in Alaska at the turn of the century continued the momentum, bringing additional customers to Seattle outfitters as well as other businesses, described below.

Transportation

Seattle's transportation facilities proved crucial to its success in securing Klondike trade. As noted, at the outset of the gold rush the city already had rail and marine connections in place. Miners could take a train to the city, where they could then obtain passage on a steamship to the Far North.

Railroads

Rail links were especially significant. Seattle served as the terminus for the Great Northern Railway, completed in 1893. By the early 1890s, the city had also developed an extensive local railroad network. The Columbia and Puget Sound Railroad (originally the Seattle and Walla Walla), linked the city with the coal fields at Newcastle, Renton, Franklin, and Black Diamond. The Seattle Lake Shore and Eastern transported produce from the east side of Lake Washington to the city, while its northern branch connected Seattle with Snohomish, Skagit, and Whatcom counties. Moreover, Seattle could be reached through spur lines via the Canadian Pacific in Vancouver, British Columbia, and the Union Pacific in Portland, Oregon. In addition to carrying passengers, railroads shipped lumber, coal, fish, and agricultural products from Seattle.[28]

While bringing stampeders to the city, these rail connections also delivered goods to merchants who supplied the miners. Rail shipments in Washington state increased dramatically — as much as 50 percent per year — during the late nineteenth century. Seattle became the "central point" of rail traffic, in part due to the "Alaskan trade."[29]

Shipping

By the time of the Klondike Gold Rush, Seattle also functioned as the central point for water traffic of freight and passengers to Alaska. Before the 1890s, San Francisco controlled trade with the Far North. During that decade, however, Seattle merchants gained a strong foothold. In 1892, the Pacific Coast Steamship Company of San Francisco shifted its center of operations from Portland to Seattle, which was closer and could offer an ample supply of coal.[30] As noted, the Alaska Steamship Company formed in Seattle in the mid-1890s — and the North American Transportation and Trading Company also operated there.[31]

The Klondike stampede boosted Seattle's shipping to the Far North considerably. According to a newspaper report, Seattle's fleet tripled in size between 1897 and 1898, in part due to the "Alaskan business."[32] So pressing was the demand for steamships in the late 1890s that some vessels of marginal quality were placed in service. Seattle's shipping "never was so entirely engaged," explained one reporter in 1897. "Not a single vessel seaworthy and capable of use" was overlooked.[33]

During the late nineteenth century, shippers filled these vessels to capacity. The Alaska Steamship Company, for instance, operated vessels that carried as many as 700 passengers apiece. In general, each ship ran between Seattle and the Far North one and one-half times per month.[34] To prospector Martha Louise Black, it seemed that steamships left Seattle for Alaska "almost every hour."[35] The historian Clarence B. Bagley noted that all this activity resulted in a "scene of confusion" on the Seattle waterfront that "has never been equaled by any other American port."

The One Ton Rule

During the winter of 1898, the Northwest Mounted Police required that each miner bring enough provisions to last a year, which could weigh between 1,500 and 2,000 pounds. Schwabacher's wharf received considerable publicity in July of 1897, when the Portland, laden with Klondike gold, docked there and set off the rush to the Yukon. William B. Haskell list the items in his outfit as follows:

Total Weight 2,327

Clothing

3	Suits Underwear, extra heavy
2	Extra heavy double breasted Flannel Over shirts
1	Extra heavy Mackinaw Overshirt
4	Parils All-Wool Mittens
1	Pair Leather Suspenders
6	Pairs long German knit Socks
1	Extra Heavy Packing Bag
2	Pairs German knit and shrunk stockings, leather heels
2	Pairs Leopard Seal Waterproof Mittens
2	Pair Overalls
1	Fur cap
1	Pair Mackinaw Pants
1	Extra heavy all-wool double Sweater
1	Suit Oil Clothing and Hat
1	Pair Hip Boots
2	Pair Rubber Shoes
2	Pairs Blanets
1	Wool Scarf
1	Mackinaw Coat, extra heavy
1	Waterproof, Blanket-Lined Coat
1	Canvas Sleeping Bag
1	Doz,. Bandana Handkerchiefs

Source: William B. Haskell, *Two Years in the Klondike and Alaskan Gold-Field, 1896-1898* (Fairbanks, University of Alaska Press, 1998).

Provisions

Flour	800 lbs.
Corn Meal	50 lbs.
Rolled Oat	80 lbs.
Pilot Bread	50 lbs.
Baking Powder	20 lbs.
Yeast Cakes	6 lbs.
Baking Soda	6 lbs.
Rice	100 lbs.
Beans	200 lbs.
Split Peas	50 lbs.
Evaporated Potatoes	50 lbs.
Bacon	300 lbs.
Bried Beef	60 lbs.
Dried Salt Pork	50 lbs.
Roast Coffee	50 lbs.
Tea	25 lbs.
Condensed Milk	50 lbs.
Butter, hermetically sealed	40 lbs.
Salt	40 lbs.
Ground Pepper	3 lbs.
Ground Mustard	3 lbs.
Evaporated Onions	20 lbs.
Beef Extract	3 lbs.
Evaporated Apples	50 lbs.
Evaporated Peaches	50 lbs.
Evaporated Apricots	50 lbs.
Ginger	2 lbs.
Jamaica Ginger	3 lbs.
Evaporated Vinegar	12 lbs.
Matches	25 lbs.
Candles, 2 boxes containing 240 candles	80 lbs.

Equipment

1	Handsaw
2	Handled Axes
1	Gold Scale
2	Butcher knives
1	Measuring Tape
2	Cartridge Belts
1	Whetstone
6	Towels
2	Grub Bags
15	lbs. Pitch
2	Scissors
	Fish Lines and Hooks
2	Hatchets
2	Draw Knives
2	Compasses
2	Hunting Knives
1	Brace and 4 Bits
1	Caulking
2	Prospector's Picks
2	Pairs Snow Glasses
1	Camp Kettle
4	Galvanized Pails
20	lbs. Oakum
	Pack Straps
2	Shovels
1	Jack Plane
1	Chalk Line
2	Pocket Knives
2	Money Belts
2	Gold Pans
2	Picks and Handles
2	Coffee Pots
2	Frying Pans
2	Large Spoons
	Knives and Forks
	Table and Teaspoons
1	Whip Saw
30	lbs. Nails (assorted sizes)
1	Set Awls and Tools
3	Chisels, assorted

2	Gold Dust Bags (buckskin)
1	Medicine Case
150	feet 5/8 inch Rope
1	Stove (Yukon)
4	Granite Buckets
	Granite Plates
	Granite Cups

Cooper and Levy was among the largest and most heavily advertised of Seattle's outfitters.

Miners used many different methods to move their supplies from one place to another. This photograph was taken at Crater Lake on Chilkoot Trail circa 1898.

The docks were piled high with outfits, and crowds of impatient miners "anxiously sought for some floating carrier to take them to the land of gold."[36]

Shipping continued to expand in Seattle during the subsequent gold rush to Nome in 1899-1900. By that time, according to Bagley, the city's fleet had become a "great armada." He detected an interesting trend: at the end of the nineteenth century, only 10 percent of the ships sailing from Seattle to Alaska were owned and operated by people based in Seattle. In 1905, however, more than 90 percent of the vessels sailing from Seattle to Alaska were controlled by Seattle residents and businesses based in the city.[37]

The docks were piled high with outfits, and crowds of impatient miners "anxiously sought for some floating carrier to take them to the land of gold."

Shipbuilding

The increase in shipping stimulated the boatbuilding industry during this era. At the end of the nineteenth century, many shipbuilders in Seattle tripled their output as well as their number of employees.[38] Prior to this point, most ships constructed in the city included small fishing vessels or boats for local trade. During the decade 1880 to 1890, Seattle shipbuilders produced approximately 75 vessels, the average weight of each totaling 33 tons. In 1898, Seattle shipyards built 57 steamers, 17 steam barges and scows, and 13 tugs.[39] Wood Brothers of West Seattle constructed and launched the first steamer built "wholly for Yukon trade."

Hard Drive to the Klondike

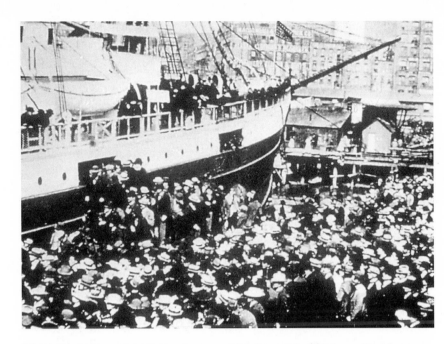

This vessel measured 75 feet long and 20 feet wide.[40] Moran Brothers Shipbuilding Company produced many of the vessels constructed during the gold rush era. In early August of 1897, the North American Transportation and Trading Company ordered a fleet of 15 ships from this business. "A stroll through the extensive works of Moran Bros. discloses a veritable [sic] hive of industry," observed one reporter. "About 400 men are employed and separate forces are at work day and night." The "immediate cause" of this activity was the Alaska trade.[41] Gold strikes in western Alaska at the turn of the nineteenth century — which required ocean-going vessels that could sail the Bering Sea — further stimulated the shipbuilding industry in Seattle.[42]

Animals for the Yukon

In addition to encouraging the development of rail and marine transportation in Seattle, the Klondike Gold Rush also fostered businesses that assisted miners in getting around once they arrived in the Yukon. The stampede increased the market for dogs, horses, goats, and oxen — all of which moved people and supplies to the gold fields.

Dogs became the most heavily publicized animals for sale. The use of these animals in the Far North dated back centuries. By the turn of the century, Tappan Adney, a correspondent for Harper's Weekly, had observed an "extraordinary demand" for dogs to carry sleds and saddlebags. Yukon miners had "raked and scraped" the Canadian Northwest in search of dogs, resulting in a shortage.[43] A single dog could draw 200 pounds on a sled, and six of these animals could carry a year's worth of supplies for a miner.[44]

Adney described a variety of breeds, including Eskimo, husky, malamute, and siwash. So similar were these dogs in physical appearance that he had difficulty distinguishing them. He did, however, detect differences in characteristics among the various animals. The Eskimo dog, for instance, featured a "wolf-like muzzle," but lacked the "wild wolf's hard, sinister expression." The malamute, on the other hand, was a dog "without moral sense," often approaching "the lowest depths of turpitude."[45] The Klondike trade in canines was not limited to these large animals; Seattle dealers also sold "little dogs not much larger than pugs."[46]

The scarcity of dogs made sale of these animals a lucrative business. Miners, according to Adney, were "willing to pay almost any price," and dogs brought "fabulous" sums in the Yukon during the winter of 1897-1898. The best dogs sold for $300-400 apiece. By the summer of 1898, approximately 5,000 dogs had arrived at Dawson City, indicating the size of the market.[47] Teams of dogs waiting for transport remained a common sight throughout the commercial district in Seattle during the gold rush.[48]

Businesses such as the Seattle-Yukon Dog Company imported "all kinds of canines" from as far away as Chicago and St. Paul. In addition to transporting the animals, the company trained them in preparation for their service in the Yukon. "Dog drivers" placed the animals two at a time

During the gold rush it was common to see teams of dogs in Seattle waiting to be transported to the Klondike. It has been reported that stampeders were willing to pay up to $500 dollars for a dog of the best quality.

in a harness attached to a sled, compelling them to pull it for half an hour. "At first it is hard work," noted one observer, "but nearly all of the dogs soon understand what is wanted and pull the sled without trouble."[49] As Adney pointed out, however, not all dogs that reached the Yukon were trained.[50]

The vast number of dogs brought into Seattle for the Klondike trade created problems for merchants as well as for the animals. Some dog yards held as many as 400 animals at once — all waiting to be shipped to the Yukon. One November morning in 1897, 200 canines, held together in a single yard, engaged in "one big dog fight." The noise was "deafening," prompting The Seattle Daily Times to dispatch a reporter to investigate the event. He described the animals as "snarling, biting, fighting canines who were doing their best to annihilate each other." Not surprisingly, nearly every dog was wounded in the brawl.[51]

The Klondike stampede also created a demand for horses. A Yukon horse market operated on Second Avenue and Yesler — and the commercial district also offered horses "at every corner" for $10 to $25. By early October of 1897, within three months of the onset of the gold rush, 5,000 horses had been shipped to the Far North from Seattle. Encouraged by the volume of sales, one Seattle firm ordered 4,000 burros from the Southwest. Merchants selling tack and horseshoes also benefited from the trade. Many of these animals died, however, killed by exposure, lack of food, and overwork. Their carcasses littered the trails to the gold fields, serving as a grim reminder of the consequences of hasty marketing and ignorance of northern conditions.[52] Even so, the trade in horses, burros, and dogs remained active, prompting the Seattle newspapers to carry a special section devoted to this topic in the want ads.

Gold seekers not inclined to buy dogs, horses, or burros had another choice: goats. While merchants advertised dogs as faithful, hard-working animals, businesses trading in goats pointed out that their animals were less expensive to purchase and maintain — and they could furnish milk, butter, food, and clothing.[53] Goats, they argued, also proved to be sure-footed on steep, icy inclines, and they could "gather their feed on the trail."[54] Miners also purchased oxen in Seattle, which they shipped to the gold fields.[55]

Wheels on Ice

One of the most colorful, whimsical means of getting around the Yukon was by bicycle — and Seattle merchants advertised them during the stampede.[56] The gold rush coincided with the worldwide bicycle craze of the 1890s, when riding "wheels" became a fashionable pastime. One New

Bicycles were a popular method of transportation in the Klondike. They were less expensive and easier to maintain than dogs.

York Company considered producing a "Klondike Bicycle," which representatives claimed could carry gold seekers across Chilkoot Pass to Dawson City. For all the impracticality of that particular idea, numerous miners brought bikes to Alaska — and they were available for purchase in Seattle. Spelger & Hurlbut, dealers operating on Second Avenue, sold bicycles that they obtained from the Western Wheel Works factory in Chicago. By 1900, one Seattle newspaper had reported that "scarcely a steamer leaves for the North that does not carry bicycles."[57]

This mode of transportation offered several advantages: cyclists could follow the tracks in the snow left by dogsleds with relative ease; they could travel faster than dog teams and horses; and "iron steeds" were less expensive and easier to maintain than animals. Cycling in the Far North was not without hazards, which included snowblindness and eyestrain from attempting to follow a narrow track through the ice, and frequent breakdowns due to frozen bearings and stiff tires.[58]

"A Hot Town" and "A Very Wicked City"

By day, Seattle bustled with activities associated with outfitting and transportation. By night, according to one newspaper headline, it became "A Hot Town" that catered to the needs of a largely transient population.[59]

Hard Drive to the Klondike

The influx of people during the Klondike stampede included dock workers, ship crews, and various merchants, as well as miners — most of whom were passing through. They increased the demand for accommodations, food and drink, entertainment, and other services. "The town is overrun with strangers," marveled one observer, "the hotels are crowded; the restaurants are jammed;" and "a number of theaters are running full blast."[60] The large number of people pouring into the city created a need for hotels, rooming houses, and other service industries.[61] As a result, downtown Seattle was a lively place — "a great carnival of the senses" — at all hours.[62]

The hotel business thrived in Seattle during the gold rush. Accommodations at the high end included the Hotel Seattle (originally the Occidental) at First Avenue and Yesler, the Butler Hotel at Second Avenue and James, and the Grand Pacific and Northern hotels on First Avenue. These were elegant buildings that offered a variety of amenities, including suites and dining rooms.[63] Less expensive rooming houses were also available throughout the commercial district. These featured small units arranged along a narrow corridor, providing very little privacy.[64]

The supply of rooms, however, could not always meet the demand. "More Klondykers than ever were in town last night," noted one newspaper article from August of 1897. "For the first time since the fire men were walking the streets in the lower part of the city unable to get a bed, although they had money in plenty. The parlors in many of the hotels were filled with cots."[65]

In addition to searching for accommodations, a "great number" of people spent their evenings "out doing the town." Much of their activity centered around the Tenderloin — an area bordered by Yesler Way, Jackson Street, Railroad Avenue, and Fifth Avenue. Here, gold seekers could enjoy "all kinds" of activities, not all of which were legal.[66] So lively was this district that in the fall of 1897 Seattle's City Council increased the size of the police force by approximately 40 percent. The town grew 500 percent "in rogues and rascals," one newspaper article explained.[67] Robberies and assaults became especially common crimes in this area. By November of 1897, Seattle had become "the greatest petty larceny town on the Coast."[68] As one reporter summarized, it is "a very wicked city just now."[69]

The excitement in the Tenderloin was encouraged by the sales of alcohol and the openings of numerous saloons. New drinking establishments in 1897 included the Torino and People's Café on Second Avenue South, and the Dawson Saloon on Washington Street. Typically, these businesses served beer, whiskey, and even champagne. They attracted "the

By November of 1897, Seattle had become "the greatest petty larceny town on the Coast." As one reporter summarized, it is "a very wicked city just now."

The Hotel Seattle, originally the Occidental, offered a variety of amenities including suites and dining rooms.

Klondikers going and coming, for the majority of them get drunk at both stages of the game."[70] One visitor claimed that Seattle boasted one saloon for every 50 citizens, and he published these observations in The New York Times. Accordingly, the Tenderloin acquired a reputation like that of the Barbary Coast in San Francisco.[71]

Seattle newspapers were filled with stories illustrating the consequences of widespread drinking. In August of 1897, one gold seeker reported to city police that he had been robbed of $300 while "doing" Washington Street during the evening. The police could locate no suspects. Just as they were about to give up the search, the man sheepishly informed the authorities that he had apparently deposited the missing $300 at his hotel while intoxicated — an act of good sense that he could not remember.[72]

Captain Bensely Collenette of Boston was not so fortunate. He had come to Seattle to lead a party of miners to the Yukon. Upon arriving in the city, he "went on a glorious drunk," spending "his money like wind." On Washington Street, he was robbed of $185. Even so, Collenette was later observed "riding around the city in the finest hack in town," and he left for the Yukon on the steamer Cleveland.[73]

Along with the problems that alcohol presented, the police contended with morphine and opium "fiends" in the Tenderloin. Many drug stores sold these substances, often remaining open at night for that purpose. Newspapers credited morphine and opium with murder, robbery, and leading women to a "life of shame."[74]

During the late nineteenth century, Seattle featured a variety of brothels, including the Klondike House. Located on the corner of Main Street and Second Avenue South, this establishment functioned as the "stopping place for the worst of Seattle's fallen women," and it gained the reputation of being one of the "worst dives in the city."[75] Newspaper reports of the Tenderloin focused on prostitutes — known as "soiled doves." Prostitution had existed in the city long before the late 1890s, but the gold rush increased its visibility. Women also worked as comediennes, singers, dancers, and actors in the district's theaters — and they dealt cards in the gambling houses that sprang up during the gold rush.[76]

Gambling was a lucrative business that caught gold seekers before and after their trip to the Klondike. By the turn of the century, the Standard Gambling House, for example, had averaged more than $120,000 per year.[77] In addition to card games, customers could try their luck with the "Klondike dice game."[78]

At the turn of the century, a banner across the top of the Grand Pacific Hotel advertised the Seattle Woolen Mill's office and salesroom, located at the building's street-level.

In summary, vice became a prominent industry in Seattle during the stampede — one that attracted as much immediate attention as outfitting and transporting miners. Newspapers focused on this topic from 1897 through 1910 — in part because sensational and scandalous stories increased sales. The Seattle Daily Times condemned Mayor J. Thomas Humes for his failure to suppress gambling and other "social evils" in Seattle, likening his supporters to an army of "besotted drunks." In 1902, voters approved a reform measure that controlled vice through saloon license fees of $1,000 and evening and Sunday closings.[79]

The excesses of the Tenderloin during the Klondike stampede link the gold seekers to other figures in western history. During the early nineteenth century, mountain men and trappers emerged once a year from the remote, far-flung areas where they hunted beaver. They met at a rendezvous — a caravan that purchased their beaver pelts and sold them supplies. After transacting their business, many trappers drank and gambled away their annual earnings, turning the rendezvous into a "scene of roaring debauchery." The caravan's owners, on the other hand, profited handsomely from this arrangement, often enjoying returns that reached 2,000 percent.[80] For the most part, those who made fortunes from the fur trade, like those who reaped profits from the gold rush, were not the people directly involved in extracting the resource; they were the ones that sold the goods and services.

Population and Economic Growth During the Gold-Rush Era

It was during the late 1890s that Seattle eclipsed other Puget Sound communities as the state's most populous city. By 1890, Tacoma's population had reached 36,006 — which was fairly close to Seattle's 42,837 residents. During the decade of the 1890s, however, Tacoma gained only 1,708 residents, while Seattle's population rose by 37,834, to a total of 80,671.[81]

Most of this growth — approximately two-thirds — occurred between 1897 and 1900, when the city increased from 56,842 to 80,671.[82] This

Growth of Selected American Cities

City	Population		% Increase
	1880	1910	
Washington, D. C.	177,624	331,069	86
Los Angeles	11,183	319,069	2,700
Minneapolis	46,887	301,408	504
Jersey city	120,722	267,799	122
Kansas City	55,785	248,381	345
Seattle	3,533	237,194	6,600
Indianapolis	75,056	233,650	210
Providence	104,857	224,326	116
Louisville	123,785	223,928	81
Rochester	89,366	218,149	145
St. Paul	41,473	214,744	417

Source: Alexander Norbert McDonald, "Seattle's Economic Development, 1880-1910," Ph.D. Dissertation, University of Washington, 1959

development suggests the influence of the Klondike Gold Rush. By 1910, Seattle had developed into a city of 237,194 residents. Seattle's growth exceeded that of many other comparable cities in other regions of the country during this period.

For all this dramatic growth, the ethnic composition of Seattle's population did not change appreciably during the late nineteenth and early twentieth centuries. In 1880, native-born whites comprised approximately 69 percent of the population, while in 1910 they accounted for 70 percent. The percentage of foreign-born whites also remained stable, at around 26-27 percent. Between 1890 and 1910, African-Americans made up one percent of the city's population, while Asians comprised around 3 percent.[83]

Most native-born residents in Seattle came from somewhere else — particularly the Midwest and East Coast. In 1910 only 16 percent of the city's residents were from Washington. Seattle's foreign-born population

Composition of Seattle's Population, 1880-1890

	1880		1890		1900		1910	
	Number	%	Number	%	Number	%	Number	%
Native-born White	2,450	69	28,906	67.5	58,159	72.1	166,918	70.4
Foreign-born White	950	27	13,150	30.7	18,656	23.1	60,835	25.6
African-American	25	1	286	0.7	406	0.5	2,296	1.0
Asian and Other	108	3	495	1.2	3,450	4.3	7,145	3.0
Total Population	**3,533**		**42,837**		**80,671**		**237,194**	

Source: Alexander Norbert McDonald, "Seattle's Economic Development, 1880-1910," Ph.D. Dissertation, University of Washington, 1959

Population Composition of Selected American Cities

	Percentage Distribution			
	Native-born White	Foreign-born White	African-American	Asian and Others
Washington, D. C.	64.0	7.4	28.5	0.1
Los Angeles	76.7	19.0	2.4	2.0
Minneapolis	70.6	28.5	0.9	0.1
Jersey city	68.7	29.0	2.2	0.1
Kansas City	80.3	10.2	9.5	0.1
Seattle	70.4	25.6	1.0	3.0
Indianapolis	82.2	8.5	9.3	0.1
Providence	63.4	34.0	2.4	0.2
Louisville	74.1	7.8	18.1	0.1
Rochester	72.5	27.0	0.4	0.1
St. Paul	72.2	26.3	1.5	0.1

Source: Alexander Norbert McDonald, "Seattle's Economic Development, 1880-1910," Ph.D. Dissertation, University of Washington, 1959

Occupation of Seattle Work Force

	1880	1890	1900		1910	
		number	number	%	number	%
Agriculture		350	625	1.4	2,025	1.6
Fishing		250	478	1.1	1,097	0.9
Logging		350	664	1.5	1,338	1.1
Mining		1,900	3,595	8.1	1,915	1.6
Manufacture	138	2,750	5,190	11.6	14,014	11.5
Hand Trades		2,850	5,383	12.0	25,625	20.9
Trade and Transportation		6,900	13,102	29.2	47,635	38.8
Domestic and Persoanl Service		6,800	12,802	28.5	19,874	16.3
Professional		1,600	3,029	6.7	8,762	7.2
Total Employment		23,750	44,868		122,285	
Total Population	**3,533**	**42,837**	**80,671**		**237,194**	

Source: Alexander Norbert McDonald, "Seattle's Economic Development, 1880-1910," Ph.D. Dissertation, University of Washington, 1959

was comprised of migrants from Canada, Sweden, Norway, Great Britain, and Germany in 1880. Immigration from Japan, Italy, and Russia had become more common by 1910.[84]

Rapid population growth could be viewed as an indication of economic prosperity. Seattle's population figures reveal that the late 1890s and early twentieth century — the era of the Klondike stampede — was a period of vigorous expansion.[85] Even so, an examination of population figures for other western cities during the 1890s demonstrates comparable growth. Although Portland and Vancouver, British Columbia, did not attract the Klondike trade to the extent that Seattle enjoyed, they both expanded at a faster rate than Seattle, perhaps due to momentum gained early in the decade, before the gold strike. This trend suggests that the continuing movement west of the population of the two nations proved to be a significant influence on growth. [86]

By 1910, Seattle's position as the state's commercial center was assured. The region's rail and water transportation network also concentrated in the city. Foreign trade grew during the early twentieth century as well, shifting from British Columbia to Asia. On the surface, Seattle's manufacturing base seemed sound, as the city produced an array of products ranging from shoes to beer to bicycles. Yet, according to historian Alexander Norbert MacDonald, Seattle continued to rely mostly on extractive industries, including lumbering, fishing, and agriculture. Although the gold rush helped ensure Seattle's position as a commercial center for the region, it did not provide a broad, diversified manufacturing base that could rival the industrial cities of the eastern seaboard.[87]

The Alaska-Yukon-Pacific Exposition

In May of 1898, The New York Times announced that the Klondike excitement was "fizzling out."[88] Although this assertion proved to be premature, it signaled that the frenetic pace of the stampede was slowing down and that the media's interest was waning. The outbreak of the Spanish American War in April provided a new arena for the nation's

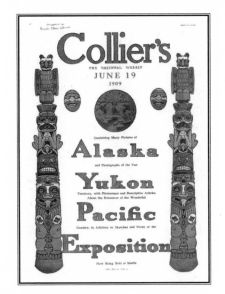

The Great Northern Railway advertised special fares to the Alaska-Yukon-Pacific Exposition while national magazines such as *Collier's* also promoted it.

reporters, and that topic pushed the Klondike out of the headlines.[89] By late 1898, the rush to the Klondike had subsided considerably. The following year new gold discoveries in Nome deflected attention from the Yukon to western Alaska, and Seattle continued to function as an outfitting center.[90] In April and May of 1900, approximately 8,000 gold seekers passed through Seattle on their way to Nome.[91] During the early twentieth century, miners continued to travel through Seattle on their way to subsequent gold rushes to Fairbanks, Kantishna, Iditarod, Ruby, Chisana, and Livengood.[92]

The trade to the Far North never regained the excitement of the Klondike Gold Rush. Seattle, however, retained its dominant connection to this region — and it continued to supply Alaska with lumber, coal, food, clothing, and other goods. By 1900, Alaska's population had reached 63,592 residents, many of whom remained "heavily dependent" on Seattle for trade.[93] This link between Seattle and the Far North endured throughout the twentieth century.

To celebrate its ties to the Far North and to commemorate the Klondike Gold Rush, Seattle hosted the Alaska-Yukon-Pacific Exposition in 1909. This world's fair represented a "coming-of-age party" for the city, signaling the end of its pioneer era. In 1905, Portland similarly hosted the Lewis and Clark Exposition to commemorate the centennial of the 1805 expedition to the Pacific. Its fair attracted three million visitors — a point Seattle boosters noted with interest. Four years later, Seattle's exposition drew nearly four million people, focusing national attention on the city and the region.[94]

Organizers wanted to hold the event in 1907, to honor the 10-year anniversary of the Klondike Gold Rush. Jamestown, Virginia, however, also planned to celebration its 300-year anniversary with a fair in 1907. In any case, the Panic of 1907, a nationwide depression that slowed the economy in Seattle, would have reduced the scale of festivities and the visitation — so it was a fortuitous turn of events that delayed the exposition until June of 1909.[95] On that date, President William H. Taft at the national capitol pressed the gold nugget Alaska key, setting the fair's operations in motion. Railroad magnate James J. Hill greeted 80,000 spectators in the commencement celebration, which included a parade in downtown Seattle.[96]

The Olmsted Brothers served as landscape architects of the fair, while John Galen Howard became its principal architect. Held on the grounds of the University of Washington campus, the exposition featured pools, fountains, gardens, and statuary that opened on a vista of Mount Rainier. A variety of ornate buildings designed in the French Renaissance style housed exhibits from all over the world.[97]

The exposition included an amusement park with carnival rides and other entertainment. It was called the "Paystreak" — a term for the richest deposit of gold in a placer claim and an allusion to the importance of gold mining to Seattle. The Paystreak featured an attraction called "Gold Camps of Alaska" as well as an Eskimo village. Additional references to the Far North at the exposition included a large gold nugget, on display from the Yukon. Especially visible was the Alaska monument, a column measuring 80 feet high. Covered in pieces of gold from Alaska and the Yukon, it stood in front of the U.S. Government Building, reminding visitors of the ties between Seattle and the Far North.[98]

While reflecting on the past, the exposition also looked to the future — and organizers hoped to boost interest in Seattle and the Northwest. "This summer's show is essentially a bid to settlers," noted one reporter, "and an advertisement for Eastern capital to come West and help develop the natural resources which offer wealth on every hand." The exposition featured numerous promotional booths from cities such as Tacoma and Yakima. Washington and other western states financed construction of buildings that featured their products and resources. The exposition also celebrated the Pacific Rim, promoting increased trade with Asia. Japan, China, Hawaii, and the Philippines provided exhibits, and a Japanese battleship docked in Seattle's port in honor of the fair.[99]

Seattle merchants and residents hoped that the economy would boom as a result of the Alaska-Yukon Exposition. Irene and Zacharias Woodson,

The Alaska-Yukon-Pacific Exhibition included an amusement park called the "Paystreak" a term for the richest deposit of gold in placer mining. The Paystreak featured an attraction called "Gold Camps of Alaska."

for example, expected the demand for housing to expand in the summer of 1909. This African-American couple operated a cigar store and rooming houses in downtown Seattle, using the profits to purchase new properties. The Woodson Apartments, constructed in 1908 at 1820 24th Avenue, represented these hopes.[100]

The exposition ended in October of 1909, marking the end of an era. Although most of the infrastructure was removed, several buildings remained, including Cunningham and Architecture halls. Today, they stand on the University of Washington campus as testaments to a significant point in Seattle's history.

Another legacy of the Alaska-Yukon-Pacific Exposition was that it strengthened the link between Seattle and the Far North in the public mind. Seattle had developed a significant connection to Alaska before the Klondike Gold Rush, and promoters such as Erastus Brainerd had used the stampede as an occasion to publicize that tie in the late 1890s. The exposition similarly advertised it in 1909. As historian Clarence B. Bagley summarized, the fair successfully met the city's objectives: it demonstrated "the enormous value of Alaska to the United States and the greatness of its entry port, Seattle. The city's guests left the fair with the knowledge that Alaska was a golden possession and Seattle a growing metropolis."[101]

These "official" postcards document the Alaska-Yukon-Pacific Exhibition. The postcard on the top advertises "Lily's Seeds," which were used on the AYP lawns and shows the Court of Honor with Mount Rainier in the distance. The postcard on the bottom shows the Manufacturers and Oriental Foreign Exhibit Buildings.

It is difficult to measure the precise impact of the fair and the worldwide exposure it provided to Seattle. As noted, by 1910, the city's population had jumped to 237,194 residents. According to MacDonald, however, the dramatic growth in the city's economy occurred before 1910. After that point, the city "settled down to the moderate growth of the region," abandoning the "independent, enthusiastic" mood of the previous era.[102] Seattle's foreign trade had grown rapidly during the first decade of the twentieth century, but for all the hopes of exposition promoters, there was no immediate increase in trade with Asia after the fair.[103] Not until the late twentieth century would Seattle again experience the vibrance and energy exhibited during the gold-rush era.

Outfits for the Klondike

Some companies offered one-stop shopping by providing complete outfits. Cooper and Levy, one of the most heavily advertised outfitters, warned gold seekers that "you are going to a country where grub is more valuable than gold." This company also ran advertisements showing hapless miners who outfitted with "greenhorns," which left them stranded in the Far North with inadequate provisions.

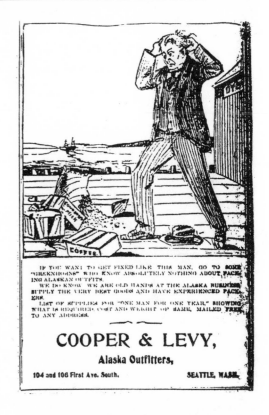

IF YOU WANT TO GET FIXED LIKE THIS MAN, GO TO SOME "GREENHORNS" WHO KNOW ABSOLUTELY NOTHING ABOUT PACKING ALASKAN OUTFITS.

WE DO KNOW WE ARE OLD HANDS AT THE ALASKA BUSINESS SUPPLY THE VERY BEST GOODS AND HAVE EXPERIENCED PACKERS.

LIST OF SUPPLIES FOR "ONE MAN FOR ONE YEAR," SHOWING WHAT IS REQUIRED, COST AND WEIGHT OF SAME, MAILED FREE TO ANY ADDRESS.

COOPER & LEVY,
Alaska Outfitters,

104 and 106 First Ave. South.   SEATTLE, WASH.

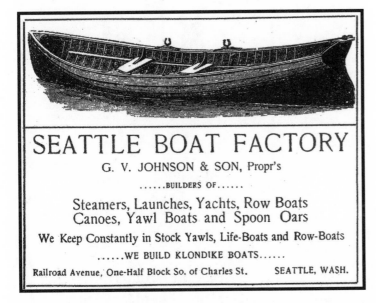

SEATTLE BOAT FACTORY

G. V. JOHNSON & SON, Propr's

......BUILDERS OF......

Steamers, Launches, Yachts, Row Boats
Canoes, Yawl Boats and Spoon Oars

We Keep Constantly in Stock Yawls, Life-Boats and Row-Boats

......WE BUILD KLONDIKE BOATS......

Railroad Avenue, One-Half Block So. of Charles St.   SEATTLE, WASH.

Sources for these advertisements include the following: *The Seattle Daily Times, The Seattle Post-Intelligencer, The Tacoma Daily News, The Morning Leader* (Port Townsend), and *Vancouver News-Advertiser,* 1897-1898.

Clondyke Outfits
of the BEST QUALITY can be bought from

The Seattle Clothing Co.

719 Second Av.   Hinckley Block.

Clothing for the Klondike

As one advertisement indicated, "The Skagway winds blow hard and cold and reach the bones thro' blankets, woolens and mackinaws." Clothing was an important purchase for Klondike stampeders.

The Skagway Winds

Blow hard and cold and reach the bones thro' blankets, woolens and mackinaws.

BUCKSKIN STOPS 'EM

So say those who have returned. We have the buckskin suits for big lunged men and plucky women.

SOFT, WARM AND IMPERVIOUS

STEWART & HOLMES DRUG CO.   703 First Ave.

xxvii   ADVERTISEMENTS.

Shorey's Patent Blizzard Resister Suits

Made under Patent No. 1062 are the Most Comfortable Garments Sold.

Shorey's Miners' Suit

Made in all Shades of Mackinaw, Warmly Lined, With or Without Capot. Also in Khaki Duck.

These Goods can be Purchased at

Vancouver - - B. C.
Victoria   "
Kamloops   "
Ashcroft   "
Nanaimo   "
Glenora   "

Shorey's Arctic Suit

Made in all Shades of Heavy Mackinaw. With or Without Capot.

These Goods can be Purchased at

Edmonton, N.W.T.
Calgary   "
Prince Albert   "
Winnipeg   Man.
and all Eastern Towns.

SHOREY'S KLONDYKE SHIRT

..See that Shorey's Guarantee Card is in the Pocket of Every Garment..

YOU WILL NEED A PAIR OF THESE

When You go to the

KLONDIKE

Alaska Footwear

SEATTLE is the only place to outfit and get just what you will need. We carry a complete stock of **Alaska Footwear** of every description, including Miners' Boots, Shoes and Rubber Goods, Moccasins, Leggings, German Sox, Felt Boots with Overs, etc.

San Francisco Shoe Co.

722 First Ave., Cor. Columbia

The Only Manufacturers in the City of—

BLANKET CLOTHING FOR THE KLONDYKE

SEATTLE WOOLEN MANUFACTURING CO.
1119 FIRST AVENUE.

Klondike Equipment and Services

Among the goods advertised were asbestos-lined Yukon stoves, Winchester rifles, banking, transportation by sea to the gold fields, and frost extractors.

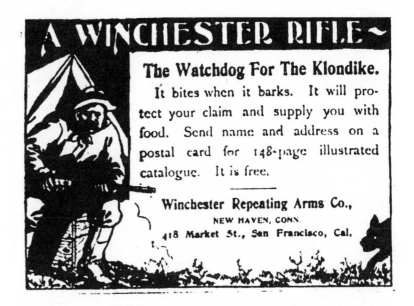

A WINCHESTER RIFLE~

The Watchdog For The Klondike.

It bites when it barks. It will protect your claim and supply you with food. Send name and address on a postal card for 148-page illustrated catalogue. It is free.

Winchester Repeating Arms Co.,
NEW HAVEN, CONN.
418 Market St., San Francisco, Cal.

Yukon Gold Fields, Alaska.

Clondyke!

THE NORTH AMERICAN TRANS-
PORTATION & TRADING
COMPANY'S

Steamer Cleveland

Leaves Seattle Aug. 5,

Connecting at St. Michael's with elegant river steamers direct for the mines. For rates and further information apply at the company's office, 615 First avenue, Seattle.

WASHINGTON NATIONAL BANK, OF SEATTLE

U. S. GOVERNMENT DEPOSITARY

BUYS GOLD DUST or makes advances against shipments to Mint.
RECEIVES CONSIGNMENTS OF DUST or bullion and makes immediate returns.
ISSUES LETTERS OF CREDIT good at Juneau, St. Michaels, Circle City, Fort Cudahy and Dawson.
INVITES CORRESPONDENCE with miners and business men in Alaska.

✦KLONDYKE✦

We have a few of our celebrated asbestos-lined

YUKON STOVES

which we are disposing of at reduced prices.
....COMPLETE OUTFITS....

Z. C. MILES CO.

A. L. PIPER, Receiver

Clondyke Frost Extractor.

Patent applied for in U. S. and Canada.

For Thawing Frozen Placer Dirt.

Steamed up and on exhibition on West street, rear of Z. C. Miles Co's. on and after Monday Aug 2, 1897. Simple at Hardy-Hall Arms Co's.

Light, cheap and highly efficient. Standard sizes—1, 2 and 3 horse power; weights 100, 140 and 165 pounds complete. Larger sizes to order. Easily taken to pieces in convenient sizes and shapes for packing. For further particulars call on or address

Barron Bros. & Co., 619 First Av.

ANDERSON'S MAP OF ALASKA
AND A PORTION OF
The Northwest Territory

Just issued. Best, most complete and latest map published, showing the famous **KLONDYKE GOLD FIELDS** and the routes thereto. Size 24x30 inches. Price 75c, in covers $1. Postage free. Published and for sale by

THE O. P. ANDERSON MAP AND BLUE PRINT CO.

SEATTLE, WASH.

Outfitted for the Klondike: A Special Advertising Section

65

Pharmaceuticals for the Klondike

Medicine cases and drugs were widely advertised during the gold rush. "You will be tired and sore," one advertisement for liniments noted. Another advertisement used humor: "Klondycitis is very prevalent disease which cannot be cured by medical science."

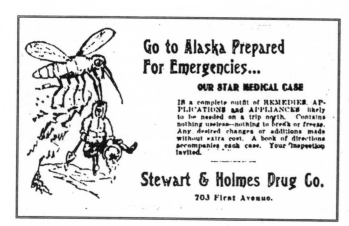

Go to Alaska Prepared For Emergencies...

OUR STAR MEDICAL CASE

Is a complete outfit of REMEDIES, APPLICATIONS and APPLIANCES likely to be needed on a trip north. Contains nothing useless—nothing to break or freeze. Any desired changes or additions made without extra cost. A book of directions accompanies each case. Your inspection invited.

Stewart & Holmes Drug Co.

703 First Avenue.

Food for the Klondike.

"Your life may depend upon your getting the very best groceries," one advertisement warned gold seekers. Evaporated food was heavily advertised, and LaMont's frequently ran advertisements for crystallized eggs, prompting challenges from Halls, a competitor.

KLONDYCITIS

Is a very prevalent disease which cannot be cured by medical science. We have unusual advantages which enable us to make the ailment one of pleasure. Come and see us before going North.

Lee's Pharmacy

Cor. Second Avenue and Columbia Street.

WE THROW DOWN THE GAUNTLET

HALL'S PULVERIZED EGGS

PARALYZE COMPETITION

Half the Price of the Self-Inflated and Sensationally Advertised High-Priced Prepared Eggs Offered on this Market.

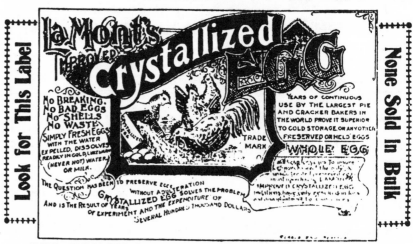

Advertising in Canada

Canadian companies advertised "no duty for Klondike goods purchased in British Columbia." The Klondike stampede created geographical confusion. This advertisement for a Canadian company was more appropriate for an African outfit than an outfit for the Klondike.

Advertising in Tacoma

The longstanding rivalry between Tacoma and Seattle intensified during the Klondike Gold Rush. These advertisements from Tacoma touted the "City of Destiny" as the "best place on Puget Sound." One Tacoma company offered investments in mining "better than Klondike."

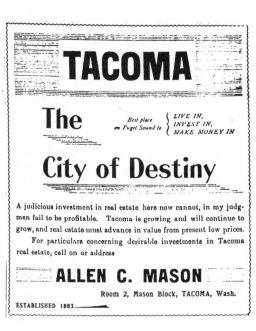

CHAPTER FOUR

Building the City

"Seattle is the result of a patriotic, unselfish, urban spirit which has been willing to sacrifice in order to gain a desired end — the upbuilding of a great city….Seattle has well-paved streets, a thorough and satisfactory street car system, large and handsome business blocks, and residence districts adorned by palatial homes and green and velvety lawns."

—Daniel L. Pratt, "Seattle, The Queen City," The Pacific Monthly, 1905

Seattle changed more during the gold-rush era than in any other period in its history. The rapid economic and population growth of the late nineteenth and early twentieth centuries spurred the development of the city's infrastructure, transforming it from a town to a metropolis. As one historian observed, if Rip Van Winkle had appeared in 1883 after a 30-year absence, he would have easily recognized what he saw: a town dependent on the lumber industry and water transportation. Similarly, if he awakened in the 1940s after a 30-year absence, he would find the city bigger but not fundamentally changed. However, if he fell asleep in 1880 and returned in 1910, he would not have known where he was. Although natural landmarks such as Mount Rainier and Puget Sound remained in their familiar positions, "Seattle had undergone more profound changes during these thirty years than in any other thirty year period."[1] An examination of the city's infrastructure reveals the extent of these changes.

Buildings

During the gold-rush era, building along the waterfront increased dramatically. Schwabacher's rebuilt and extended its wharf. The Northern Pacific Railway extended its Yesler dock, and the Great Northern Railway added a new facility that included docks, warehouses, and a wheat elevator.[2]

The changes within the commercial district were especially visible. As noted, brick and masonry buildings replaced wooden structures after the fire in 1889. Building in the downtown area became denser, and the size and scale of structures increased. The Alaska Building, the city's first steel-frame skyscraper, appeared in 1904. Located at Second and Cherry, this 14-story structure symbolized the significance of the gold rush to Seattle. The porthole windows along the top floor looked out over the waterfront, providing a view of the shipbuilding, shipping, and rail industries that the gold rush encouraged. For many years a gold nugget embedded in the front door of this building reminded visitors of the stampede and the city's connection to the Far North. Construction of the Arctic Building at Third and Cherry in 1914 similarly represented Seattle's connection to Alaska. This stately structure was noteworthy for its Italianate terra-cotta façade, tusked walrus heads, and rococo-gilt Dome Room.[3]

Street and Transportation Improvements

The influx of people during the late nineteenth century increased the need to provide access to the city's commercial district, requiring street improvements within the downtown area. During the 1880s, many streets had been covered with wood planking. This material had its drawbacks: it did not last long and engineers feared it was unsanitary. By the early 1890s, gravel was used to pave some Seattle roads, but hauling the quantities required proved expensive and difficult. By that time, brick had become another favored material.[4]

In 1898, engineers at Smart and Company leveled First Avenue from Pine Street to Denny Way, using the earth to fill Western and Railroad avenues, located along the waterfront.[5] That year, the city also laid new planking and paving from First Avenue to Fourth Avenue, between Yesler Way and Pine Street. One article in The Seattle Daily Times cited 1898 as a record-breaking year for improvements, noting that contractors "flourished as they have not done before."[6]

Streetcars also facilitated movement in the downtown area. The first street railway appeared in 1884, offering nickel-a-fare service. Operated by the Seattle Street Railway Company, it used horses to pull the cars. Five years later an electric streetcar began operating in Seattle — and even the fire did not interrupt its service. During the 1880s, Seattle's downtown area also featured a cable railway, which ran along Yesler Way and First and Second avenues. By the early 1890s, passengers could travel to Lake Union along Westlake Avenue and to points farther north.[7] Promoters praised these developments, noting how they had transformed the city during the gold-rush era. An article in The Pacific Monthly, pub-

The Alaska Building, the city's first steel-frame skyscraper, appeared in 1904. Located at Second and Cherry, this 14-story structure symbolized the significance of the gold rush to Seattle.

lished in 1905, informed readers that "Seattle has well-paved streets, a thorough and satisfactory street car system, large and handsome business blocks, and residence districts adorned by palatial homes and green and velvety lawns."[8]

Electric rail lines also connected Seattle to communities to the north and south of the city. An interurban train ran between Seattle and Tacoma, and the completion in 1910 of a line from Seattle to Everett further opened opportunities for growth, encouraging development in new communities such as Alderwood Manor.[9]

City Parks

Another development in early twentieth-century Seattle was the creation of the city's park system. As early as 1884, the Denny Family had donated a five-acre tract located at the foot of what is now Battery Street. Although first used as a cemetery, this parcel became Denny Park, a "verdant oasis" that featured the headquarters building of the board of park commissioners. The park commissioners also developed Volunteer Park, at the north end of Capitol Hill, and Woodland Park, east of Green Lake. Located outside the city limits, these reserves became accessible by streetcar lines. Additional acquisitions included Washington Park — which is now the Arboretum — Ravenna Park, and Leschi Park.[10]

The Alaskan window appears on the first floor of the Morrison Hotel, located at 501 Third Avenue. This building, constructed in 1908, was the original home of the Arctic Club, comprised of the city's leaders and entrepreneurs.

That year, the Arctic Club merged with the Alaska Club, a commercial organization of Alaskans in Seattle. For years, the Alaska Club had maintained a reading room featuring Alaska newspapers and mineral exhibits, and its leaders promoted the Alaska-Yukon-Pacific Exposition. In 1916, the Arctic Club moved to the Arctic Building.

Hard Drive to the Klondike

Seattle's connection with the Far North is reflected in a variety of structures, including the Alaska Building located at Second and Cherry, and the Arctic Building, located at Third and Cherry.

Prominent architect Elmer Fisher designed the Pioneer Building, pictured here. Constructed in 1889-1890, this building reflected the optimism of the developing city after the fire. This Victorian structure is embellished with Romanesque Revival features, including rusticated stone columns extending above the building's central entrance. This striking building was located in the heart of the city's commercial center during the Klondike Gold Rush.

Established in 1890, the Merchants Cafe located at Yesler and Marion, advertises itself as Seattle's oldest restaurant. It operated during the Klondike Gold Rush.

Regrading

From the 1880s through 1910, the city limits grew dramatically, extending northward past Green Lake and southward to West Roxbury and Juniper streets. The commercial district expanded eastward away from the waterfront, as the shoreline became increasingly devoted to shipping and manufacturing. It also moved northward, toward Denny Hill. During the early twentieth century, Seattle's hills blocked further expansion of the city. In some places, the grades on streets over the hills measured 20 per cent, making transportation, as well as construction, difficult.[11]

City engineers addressed this problem with extensive regrading projects, radically altering the topography of the city. As historian Clarence B. Bagley pointed out, during the early twentieth century the business section of Seattle became "one vast reclamation project." As he defined it, this area extended from Denny Way and the foot of Queen Anne Hill on the north to the Duwamish River toward the south.[12] Two of the most noteworthy reclamation projects included the Denny and Jackson Street regrades.

Reginald H. Thomson supervised much of this work. He was a civic-minded visionary — a leader reminiscent of Arthur Denny. Born in Indiana, Thomson arrived in Seattle in 1881 at the age of 26. He dreamed of building a large city on Puget Sound, and investigated a number of possibilities, including Bellingham, Everett, and Tacoma, before settling on Seattle. He became City Engineer in 1892, quickly developing a reputation for dedication. "Thompson is a man who loves work," noted one observer, who further characterized him as "the greatest influence in Seattle."[13] Within two years he garnered support for the project to level Denny Hill, which presented a considerable barrier to northward expansion of the city.[14]

This leveling — called the Denny Regrade — proceeded in two stages: 1902-1910 and 1929-1930. By 1905, engineers had removed the west side of the hill, leaving the Washington Hotel precariously perched 100 feet above Second Avenue. Engineers used sluicing techniques similar to those used in gold mining, drawing water from Lake Union by large electric pumps through woodstave pipes. The water sprayed from hoses that featured a pressure of approximately 125 pounds at the nozzle, washing clay and rocks down into flumes and a central tunnel. Heralded as a monumental engineering feat, the Denny Regrade created more than 30 blocks of level land for new construction.[15]

Between 1900 and 1914, Thomson also transformed the southern end of the city. Called the Jackson Street Regrade, this project resurfaced and cut down approximately fifty blocks between Main Street on the north

The Arctic Building was constructed in 1914. Twenty-seven walruses rim the third-floor exterior.

and Judkins Street on the south, and Twelfth Avenue on the east and Fourth Avenue on the west. The Jackson Street Regrade resulted in the removal of approximately five million cubic yards of earth at a cost of $471,547.10. A smaller regrade at Dearborn Street also removed more than one million cubic yards of earth, leveling areas for new construction. These projects improved access to the waterfront, Rainier Valley, and Lake Washington. According to Bagley, the regrade projects were among Thomson's most notable achievements — and they dramatically changed the look of the city.[16]

Engineers used much of the earth removed from the regrades to fill the tideflats, a process that changed the appearance of the waterfront. The filled tideflats encouraged further development of rail yards and terminals — and this expansion forced the relocation of ethnic groups, including Japanese and Chinese, that had resided and worked around Washington and King streets. The growth of an industrial complex in this area pushed them east of Fifth Avenue, where they formed a new community, now

Engineers used sluicing methods drawn from placer mining to level the hills of Seattle. Pictured here is the Denny Regrade, early twentieth century.

called the International District.[17]

As a result of the regrades, the city was level enough by 1910 to accommodate automobiles, which greatly increased the volume and speed of land transportation. Most land traffic in the Puget Sound area flowed through Seattle, further securing its status as the metropolis of the region.[18]

Sewage, Water, and Electricity

As City Engineer, Thomson's chief concerns were sewage, water, and electricity. He was alarmed by the longstanding practice of individuals and businesses dumping waste into Lake Washington, which had no natural outlet. He suggested that sewage be discharged at West Point, at the edge of Fort Lawton on Magnolia Bluff, since the deep and constant current there could carry waste into Puget Sound. After lengthy negotiations with the U.S. Army, Thomson won approval to run sewer lines out to West Point.[19]

Providing for the expanding city was a major issue in the late nineteenth and early twentieth centuries. Before Thomson became City Engineer, Seattle had relied on a number of early water systems, included the operations of the Spring Hill Water Company. This firm secured its supply of water from the west slope of First Hill, storing it in wooden tanks in the south end of the city. In 1886, the company also constructed a pumping station at Lake Washington and a reservoir at Beacon Hill. Four years later, the city purchased the Spring Hill Water Company's system. By that time, city officials had already looked to the Cedar River, which flowed out of the Cascade Mountains, as the ultimate source of water supply. One of his first tasks as City Engineer was to design a plan for its development. A citywide fight over public versus private construction and management delayed the project until the late 1890s.[20]

In 1899, the city contracted with the Pacific Bridge Company to construct the headworks, dam, and pipeline. It also hired Smith, Wakefield & David to build the reservoirs in Lincoln and Volunteer parks. In 1901, the system went into commission, delivering 22 million gallons of water per day. By the end of the decade, however, city officials realized that this amount was not sufficient for the needs of the growing metropolis, and a second pipeline was constructed in 1909. By 1916, the expanded system had delivered 66 million gallons per day.[21]

Thomson also tackled the issue of electricity. In the early twentieth century, Seattle Electric — a predecessor company of Puget Sound Energy — enjoyed a near monopoly on electric power as well as public transportation. Thomson, however, wanted the city to build a hydroelec-

As City Engineer, Thomson's chief concerns were sewage, water, and electricity. He was alarmed by the longstanding practice of individuals and businesses dumping waste into Lake Washington, which had no natural outlet.

tric plant at Cedar River, and he garnered support among city officials and residents. In 1902, voters decided in favor of the city power plant.[22]

Harbor and Waterway Improvements

During the early twentieth century, construction of the Panama Canal encouraged cities along the West Coast to plan for increased maritime traffic. Seattle promoters, including local newspapers and the Chamber of Commerce, advocated setting up a municipal corporation to own, expand, and manage Seattle's harbor. This enthusiasm inspired Virgil Bogue, a civil engineer, to draw up the city's first comprehensive plan for harbor improvement in 1910. Bogue had enjoyed an impressive career, designing Prospect Park in Brooklyn with Frederick Law Olmsted. He also constructed a trans-Andean railroad in Peru, and had identified Stampede Pass in the Cascade Mountains for the passage of the railroad.[23]

Bogue's plan for Seattle's harbor included two large marinas on the central waterfront, one for ferries and Alaska steamers and the other for Seattle's "mosquito fleet" (a fleet of small ships). He further envisioned 1,500-foot coal docks and the addition of piers and slips at Lake Union, which would be transformed into an industrial waterway. His plan also included a 3,000-foot waterway between Shilshole and Salmon Bays in Ballard — a project for which Erastus Brainerd had lobbied in 1902. Bogue's most ambitious idea was to develop seven 1,400-foot piers at Harbor Island, which could increase Seattle's annual marine commerce by seven times. "Seattle's harbor is Seattle's opportunity," he wrote. "With cheap power in abundance, and an inexhaustible supply of coal at her very gates and the vast resources of its hinterland, all that remains to be done by Seattle, the gateway to Alaska and the Orient, is to adopt a comprehensive scheme for its development."[24]

In 1910, Congress authorized construction of the Lake Washington Canal connecting Lake Washington and Lake Union to Puget Sound. The following year, voters in King County created the Port of Seattle and passed Bogue's plan.[25] These improvements to navigation and harbor facilities helped Seattle become a major port, ensuring the city's continued connections to the Far North and Asia.

In general, the expansion of Seattle's infrastructure during the early twentieth century accommodated the population growth spurred by the Klondike stampede and subsequent gold rushes in Alaska. As historian Murray Morgan explained, "without Brainerd, Seattle might not have tripled its population in a decade; ... without Thomson, it could not have handled the newcomers."[26]

Interpreting the Klondike Gold Rush

"The Seattle gold rush of 1897-98 was more than just an interesting story. It was the major turning point in the city's history."

— David V. and Judith A. Clarridge, A Ton of Gold:
The Seattle Gold Rush, 1897-98, 1972

"The boost Seattle received from the Gold Rush was not a major contributor to its essential economic development."

— Roger Sale, Seattle, Past to Present, 1976

Historians and other commentators wasted no time taking on the task of interpreting the Klondike Gold Rush. Early in the twentieth century they began examining the stampede's influence on the development of Seattle and the region, starting a process that has continued for nearly 100 years. Although popular and scholarly accounts have varied greatly throughout this period, a general trend emerged: many early histories downplayed the gold rush's role in economic and population growth, while later interpretations increasingly presented the stampede as a major influence in the city's history. Throughout the twentieth century, most historians have agreed that the gold-rush era brought monumental changes to the city; it would be very difficult to argue otherwise. The following chapter focuses on how the stampede as a single event has been interpreted.

Early Interpretations

During the early twentieth century, popular, promotional publications continued to tout the Klondike Gold Rush as a pivotal event. An article in *The Pacific Monthly* in 1905, for example, retained the spirit of the advertising campaign that the Seattle Chamber of Commerce had waged during the late 1890s. "Seattle is an achievement, not a mere growth," boasted the author. "Seattle is the result of a patriotic, unselfish, urban spirit which has been willing to sacrifice in order to gain a desired end — the upbuilding of a great city." To his mind, the "turning point in Seattle's career came in the summer of 1897," when Seattle became "a busy, prosperous port" focused on outfitting thousands of gold seekers.[1] In 1909, four years after this article appeared, the Alaska-Yukon-Pacific Exposition celebrated the gold rush as part of Seattle's connection to the Far North.

Edmond Meany was one of the first historians to tackle the significance of the gold rush. In 1910, he noted that the stampede brought immediate improvements in Seattle's economy. In assessing its long-term impact, however, he broadened the picture beyond the events of 1897 and 1898, concluding that "the industrial and economic life of Washington was profoundly affected by the series of events known as the golden era of Alaska."[2]

Welford Beaton, another early historian, presented the stampede in a different light. In *The City That Made Itself*, published in 1914, he claimed that the "greatest single factor in the upbuilding of Seattle was not the Klondike rush." To his mind, "it was the coming of the Great Northern Railway" that marked the turning point for the city, "for without the railway service which that company provided Seattle would not have been able to avail itself to the upmost of the possibilities the gold presented."[3]

Beaton was not the only observer to emphasize the importance of the railroad. In 1909, the Seattle Chamber of Commerce produced a pamphlet promoting the Alaska-Yukon-Pacific Exposition. Looking back, the publication credited the city's rail connections for its economic growth during the late nineteenth century. The pamphlet did not mention the stampede. Although this was a piece of boosterism and not a thoughtful reflection on the past, it is revealing that the very promoters who had once focused so intensely on the gold rush had all but forgotten the event a decade later.[4]

Similarly, Clarence B. Bagley's portrayal of the gold rush is interesting mostly for what he did not say. One of the best known early-Seattle historians, Bagley also served as secretary of the City's Board of Public Works. He produced detailed, year-by-year accounts of various events in his three-volume, *History of Seattle From the Earliest Settlement to the Present Time*, published in 1916. Although this work mentions the Klondike stampede and the frenzied activity on the city's waterfront, Bagley's brief description is buried in a chapter on Alaska shipping interests. He did not indicate that the gold rush was responsible for the city's

"Seattle is the result of a patriotic, unselfish, urban spirit which has been willing to sacrifice in order to gain a desired end — the upbuilding of a great city."

Opposite: Detail of map showing development of Seattle's waterfront in 1891, two years after the fire.

Hard Drive to the Klondike

"P.-I."
Clondyke Extra.

READY THIS MORNING.

Contains a summary of all the latest news, maps, interviews, etc., relating to the great Alaskan Gold Fields. Procure your copies at Business Office of the Post-Intelligencer. Price 5 cents. Special rates given on large orders. Every reader of the Post-Intelligencer should send this Special Clondyke Edition to his Eastern friends and those making inquiries about the new Eldorado.

8 PAGES—ALL CLONDYKE.

For historians studying the gold rush the most readily available primary documents incude newspaper articles, advertisements, and promotional materials.

prosperity in the late 1890s. Nor did he present the stampede itself as an event of long-term significance. Bagley presented Alaska trade and commerce as the important influence during the era — and presumably to him the Klondike stampede represented one small part of that larger topic.[5] Also revealing is the absence of Erastus Brainerd in Bagley's discussions of individuals important to the city's development.

Six years after Bagley's work appeared, Jeannette Paddock Nichols offered a similarly low-key interpretation. In 1922, she published an article devoted to advertising and the Klondike Gold Rush in *The Western Historical Quarterly*. Her strongest statement read as follows: "It cannot be gainsayed that the Bureau of Information of the Seattle Chamber of Commerce gave momentum to the growth of both the Klondike and Seattle."[6] The idea that promotions of Seattle "gave momentum" to the city's growth is very different from the notion that advertising proved to be essential to the city's growth.

In summary, the first historians to examine the Klondike Gold Rush had the difficult task of assessing the long-term impact of events that occurred only 10 or 20 years previously. Perhaps the early commentators needed sufficient time to place the stampede in a larger context, witnessing more of its aftermath. On the other hand, historians who lived during the gold-rush era, experiencing it firsthand, were perhaps in a good position to evaluate different types of evidence. In 1998, the most readily available primary documents specifically pertaining to the gold rush include newspaper articles, guidebooks, and promotional materials — sources that by their very nature emphasize the importance and success of the event. As Nichols pointed out, the Klondike Gold Rush is a study in the effectiveness of advertising. It is possible that promotional sources wielded less influence on early historians, who were well aware of their intent — and perhaps this point accounts for the reserved manner in which some of them presented the stampede.

Also, some of the early histories mentioned here generally focused on politics, economics, and prominent community leaders, in accordance with the standards of the time. Typically, they remained subdued in tone, avoiding a more lively, spirited presentation appropriate for a popular, general audience. It is difficult to imagine Bagley adopting a style that would later characterize the work of Murray Morgan or William C. Speidel — whatever the topic.

Mid-Twentieth Century Interpretations

Various anniversaries of the gold rush prompted popular examinations of what it meant to Seattle. At the 40-year mark, for example, an article by Irving Sayford in *Travel* reflected on how the stampede increased the city's prosperity. Written in an enthusiastic, hyperbolic tone that would have won Brainerd's approval, the article portrayed the Klondike Gold Rush as "the greatest treasure hunt in the annals of the western world." Sayford portrayed the importance of the gold strike in the Yukon as follows:

> [Seattle], founded on the Northern fisheries industry and its commerce, overnight shot up through municipal adolescence and became a gangling, boisterous, delighted, bawdy and infelonious landlord to transients twice the number of its permanent inhabitants. It was faced with the job of feeding the hordes, bedding them, entertaining them, while they were outfitting themselves in the town and shouting for ships to take them away from there to the Northland to hunt gold!

With a heavy dose of exclamation points, Sayford's article conveyed the excitement of the stampede, depicting it as a romantic, colorful event that profoundly affected the city. "No municipality ever changed more suddenly than Seattle," he concluded. Moreover, in his estimation, it was the Klondike Gold Rush that "put Seattle on the map."[7]

Two years later, Archie Binns's history of the Port of Seattle echoed these sentiments. His book, *Northwest Gateway*, published in 1941, celebrated Seattle as the "Gateway to Gold" during the Klondike stampede. Unlike Bagley, he devoted an entire chapter to the topic. "The city roared, and the waterfront roared," he wrote. With embellished prose reminiscent of nineteenth-century accounts, Binns informed readers that "in dull streets all over the United States, and farther away, men heard the blaring of the master calliope and the roll of golden chariots. The great parade was happening at last and it was forming in Seattle."[8] In addition to leaving the impression that the gold rush was a noisy event, Binns' book portrayed it as being significant to the city's development.

The 50-year anniversary further rekindled interest in the gold rush. At that time, *The Seattle Times Magazine* carried a series of articles describing how "the city went mad" during the gold rush. Although the author

With embellished prose reminiscent of nine-teenth-century accounts, Binns informed readers that "in dull streets all over the United States, and farther away, men heard the blaring of the master calliope and the roll of golden chariots. The great parade was happening at last and it was forming in Seattle."

Seattle and Tacoma competed against one another to attract stampeders heading to the gold fields. This advertisement for the *Tacoma Daily and Weekly News* appeals to families and friends at home hoping for news about distant relatives and friends.

acknowledged the hardships of mining, for the most part the stampede was portrayed as a great adventure that began in Seattle.[9]

Like Binns, Murray Morgan devoted an entire chapter to the stampede in his well-known history of Seattle, *Skid Road*. First published in 1951, this book credited Brainerd with "making Seattle the main port of the Klondike and Nome gold rushes." Morgan, alert to interesting and colorful details, conveyed the story in a manner that appealed to a wide audience — and his book underwent numerous printings. In an exaggerated style, he portrayed the economic benefits that the stampede brought to Seattle: "Every business prospered. Real-estate values boomed. Papers increased their circulation. Anyone who owned or could lease a ship, no matter how old, no matter how unseaworthy, could find passengers." Significantly, Morgan's chapter on the gold rush ends with Seattle's transformation to a metropolis. "The city's dominance of the region was secure," he concluded.[10]

Even scholarly examinations assumed a tone of enthusiasm that was missing from works produced 20 and 30 years earlier. In 1944, Calvin F. Schmid, a professor of sociology at the University of Washington, described the Klondike gold strike (which he placed in Alaska) as "momentous."[11] Alexander Norbert MacDonald's lengthy dissertation on Seattle's economic development, completed in 1959, also included the stampede as an event important to the prosperity of the city. "The impact of the gold rush in the Klondike was quickly apparent in Seattle," he wrote. "Everything boomed." MacDonald cited Seattle newspaper articles to support this expansive statement.[12]

Yet nineteenth-century newspapers also included information to the contrary. Buried in reports on Seattle businesses, for example, were peevish statements from merchants who did not realize the profits that they had been led to expect during the gold rush. By 1898, one business that lost $5,000 had become "sore on Seattle."[13] Although this kind of information appeared only occasionally in newspapers bent on promoting the city, it provided a broader perspective, indicating that "everything" did not "boom." Many mid twentieth-century interpretations avoided this point, choosing to emphasize the more successful, glamorous stories of the gold rush. In any case, in an article in 1968, MacDonald approached the topic more cautiously, writing "it seems reasonable to conclude that the rush of the 1890s helped establish Seattle as the dominant city on Puget Sound."[14]

Modern Interpretations

During the last 30 years, historians have continued to emphasize the economic growth that the gold rush sparked. Many contrasted the success of Seattle businesses with the relative failure of most miners. Some commentators took an additional step, analyzing what it was about Seattle that positioned the city to take advantage of the opportunities that the stampede presented.

Earl Pomeroy offered one of the most intriguing interpretations, drawing on longstanding descriptions of the "Seattle spirit." In *The Pacific Slope*, published in the mid-1960s, Pomeroy presented the gold rush as Seattle's "most colorful experience" — one that set it apart from other western cities. He argued that Seattle lacked the complacency of Portland, which remained economically secure in its "reliable traffic with the farmers of the Columbia Basin." Seattle businesses were "free in their imaginations to seek after new visions of fortune overseas," which motivated them to "improve themselves by developing and advertising their city." To achieve economic prosperity, Seattle merchants had to cultivate ambition and acumen. When gold arrived in Seattle in 1897, the city perfected these qualities, cultivating a "speculative excitement" that "remained for a long time," fueling a continuing interest in the Far North and Asia. In Pomeroy's estimation, the success of the gold rush represented "a triumph for generations of frontier optimists who had dreamed of a thriving city rising out of the wilderness to traffic in silk and gold as well as in salmon and lumber."[15]

In their classic book, *Empire of the Columbia*, Dorothy O. Johansen and Charles M. Gates offered a similar analysis. Published in 1967, this work claimed that partly through its "energetic promotion" during the gold rush, "Seattle helped establish itself as the fastest growing city in the Northwest."[16] As noted, MacDonald demonstrated that Portland actually

In Pomeroy's estimation, the success of the gold rush represented "a triumph for generations of frontier optimists who had dreamed of a thriving city rising out of the wilderness to traffic in silk and gold as well as in salmon and lumber."

What's in a name? The various spellings of the stampeder's destination included "Clondyke," "Klondyke," and "Klondike."

grew at a faster rate during that period.

William C. Speidel put a different spin on this interpretation. A popular historian who reached thousands of readers through his books, Speidel also launched the well visited tours of underground Seattle. These tours continue to feature what remained of the city's infrastructure before the fire of 1889 had raised the level of construction, and they include numerous stories of the gold-rush era. While historians like Morgan and Pomeroy presented the drive and pluck of Seattle promoters in a positive light, Speidel adopted the cynical view that the city's leaders were simply consumed by one longstanding pursuit: the desire for monetary gain.

His book, *Sons of the Profits*, published in 1967, applied this thesis to most of the major events in Seattle's history. In keeping with his theme, Speidel titled his chapter on the gold rush "This Little Piggy Stayed Home." Like other observers, Speidel noted that the merchants in Seattle benefited far more from the stampede than did most prospectors who traveled to the Yukon. "By the time the big strike came along in 1897," he wrote, "we had the business of mining the miners honed to a fine edge…. We got the miners coming and going."[17]

Despite Speidel's relentlessly flip tone, he did place the gold rush in the larger context of Seattle's longstanding cultivation of the Alaskan trade and the development of shipping and rail connections. In essence, Speidel's interpretation was not radically different from that of Binns or Morgan. It was his style of expression and his desire to shock readers that distinguished his writing.

For all the discussion of the economic impact of the gold rush on Seattle, popular historians also continued to focus on the flamboyant details of the stampede. As a journalist and former editor of the *Post-Intelligencer*, Nard Jones depicted the gold rush as a raucous event that rocked "Seattle to its foundations." According to his book, Seattle, published in 1972, "virtually all of Seattle crowded the waterfront" to greet the Portland in July of 1897. Jones regaled his readers with stories of Diamond-tooth Lil, a leading madame who sported a large gem embedded in her front tooth, along with descriptions of brothels featuring "plush red velvet interiors hung with oil paintings of provocative nudes."[18] Such vivid images made for more interesting reading than did discussions of the number of grocers and shoe makers that prospered during the gold rush. In part, the colorful aspects of the stampede seemed to attract attention from historians because they provided appealing anecdotes. As historian Pierre Berton noted, "the Klondike odyssey has been subject in the past to some fantastic misstatements, errors, half-truths, garblings, over-romanticizations, and out-and-out fabrications."[19]

Hard Drive to the Klondike

Yet most modern historians continued to present the Klondike Gold Rush as a pivotal event essential to the city's development. David and Judith Clarridge, for example, claimed in 1972 that the stampede was "more than just an interesting story." To them, "It was the major turning point in the city's history."[20]

Not everyone agreed with this view. Roger Sale, an English professor at the University of Washington turned historian, conceded in 1976 that the gold rush "was exciting and of course it did help." Even so, he concluded that "the boost Seattle received from the gold rush was not a major contributor to its essential economic development." According to his reasoning, "if it had been the crucial event it often has been taken to be, we would expect a falling off in Seattle when the gold ran out, as it quickly did." Nor did Sale place much stock in the value of Seattle advertising. In his analysis, Bellingham, Port Townsend, and Tacoma "could have had five Brainerds and would have gained little from them." Seattle already possessed the transportation facilities and the manufacturing goods to supply the gold seekers.[21]

This interpretation is noteworthy mostly because it presented a novel perspective in the modern era. Sale himself acknowledged that historians have "often" depicted the gold rush to be a "crucial event"; his book in fact refuted half a century of commentators. In any case, Sale's narrative skirted the point that the gold rush might have stimulated business that could be sustained after "the gold ran out."

His assessment of Tacoma also seems off the mark. As noted, Tacoma had transportation connections and access to manufactured goods that could rival those of Seattle — and it was comparable in size. While it is simplistic to credit Brainerd with single-handedly focusing national attention on Seattle, the point that advertising of the city increased dramatically during the Klondike Gold Rush — and that the publicity benefited city businesses — is difficult to deny. And historians have demonstrated that the gold rushes of the late nineteenth century proved essential to Seattle's continuing trade links to Alaska, which in turn represented an important component of the city's economy.[22] Moreover, the Klondike Gold Rush and the Alaska-Yukon-Pacific Exposition were specific events that strengthened the link between Seattle and the Far North in the public mind — a point supported by the sheer numbers of people that participated, as well as the pervasive nature of the advertising.

Furthermore, Sale's interpretation implies that the Klondike Gold Rush was an isolated event, when in fact placer production continued in the Far North into the early twentieth century. The Alaska trade was an ongoing process for Seattle, and it did not end abruptly in 1898. Sale was

All manner of goods were available for the stampeder outfitting his or her expedition – everything from sleds to gold dredging machinery. One question which may have been posed by a miner preparing his trip: How many sleds are required to transport that heavy machinery?

CORNELL BROS.,

MANUFACTURERS OF

Klondike Sleds

754 C ST., TACOMA.

OUR EASTERN HICKORY SLEDS ARE THE LIGHTEST AND STRONGEST ON THE MARKET.

Weight 32 pounds and guaranteed to carry 1500 lbs.
Take no other until you see them.
Handled by all the Leading Dealers in Tacoma

Price List:

Hickory Sleds,	-	-	$5.00
Fir "		-	3.50
Oak "		-	4.00

The volume of books and articles on the California Gold Rush of 1849 far exceeds that pertaining to the Klondike stampede. That the California rush occurred 50 years earlier — and it involved more people and a greater quantity of gold — might help explain this discrepancy in attention.

mistaken in assuming that there should be a spike in the city's growth in 1897-1898, followed by a collapse. Such an assumption misses the significance of the Klondike as the first in a series of northern gold rushes, followed by stampedes to Nome, Fairbanks, Kantishna, Iditarod, Ruby, Chisana, Livengood, and others.[24] Although Sale's estimation of the Klondike Gold Rush differed from those of many modern historians, it could help explain why scholars and academics have not devoted more effort to this topic. The volume of books and articles on the California Gold Rush of 1849 far exceeds that pertaining to the Klondike stampede. That the California rush occurred 50 years earlier — and it involved more people and a greater quantity of gold — might help explain this discrepancy in attention. Even so, major books on western history, including Ray Allen Billington's *Westward Expansion* and Richard White's *"It's Your Misfortune and None of My Own": A New History of the American West*, barely mentioned the Klondike or its importance to Seattle. White devoted half a line to the gold rush — which he placed in Alaska — in his 600-page book, published in 1991.[24] Yet as Paula Mitchell Marks pointed out in 1994, the Klondike fever exhibited numerous similarities to the California rush, including "the international scope of the response and the high level of interest exhibited by the American populace."[25]

Analyzing the significance of the stampede in Seattle's history prompts the question of what the city might be like today had the event not occurred. Would Seattle be the same place? As Sale pointed out, the city had already established transportation connections, trade with the Far

86   *Hard Drive to the Klondike*

Risdon Iron Works,

MANUFACTURERS OF

GOLD DREDGING MACHINERY

FOR YUKON AND KLONDIKE.

Our Mining River Dredge is just the thing for placer mining in Alaska. Shipped knocked down and, if desired, erected, in running order.

We also manufacture all kinds of Stern-wheel Boats, Mining and Milling Machinery, Engines and Boilers, Evans' Patent Hydraulic Elevators and Hydraulic Giants, Water Wheels and Sheet Iron Riveted Pipe.

Office and Works: Howard and Beale Sts., San Francisco, Cal.

North, and thriving businesses. Kathryn Taylor Morse noted a similar point in her dissertation on the Klondike stampede, completed in 1997. She observed that it was during the gold rush that Seattle became the gateway to the Far North, replacing San Francisco as the principal link between Alaska and the "outside" world. The Klondike Gold Rush assured Seattle's position as "the urban marketplace which funneled people and supplies to and from the north." In Morse's estimation, however, this point does not explain Seattle's development. "The gold certainly boomed the Alaska trade," she wrote, "but it was not, in and of itself, the only cause of Seattle's subsequent emergence as the Northwest's leading metropolis. The initial 1897-1900 boom was accompanied by, and then followed by, a prolonged economic expansion, beyond the Alaska trade, into world-wide markets in wheat, flour, fruit, forest products, salmon, and general merchandise. Those markets included Alaska, but the expansion was fueled as much by rail and steamer connections to the eastern United States, California, Europe, Hawaii, and South America."[26]

If it was not a pivotal event, however, the gold rush can at least be viewed as a striking and colorful manifestation of the larger forces that shaped the city. Although the railroad arrived in Seattle long before the stampede, the story of special "Klondike cars" that displayed gold nuggets reveal the general importance of railroads in late nineteenth-century America. Promotions by steamship companies similarly indicated Seattle's longstanding association with the Far North and its importance to the city's commerce. Similarly, the advertisements that pervaded local newspapers and national publications reveal the range of businesses operating in Seattle during the era.

The story of the gold rush also offers a glimpse of the city in a major period of transition, since the event occurred during the era that transformed it from a town to a metropolis. The event has become an important symbol of this development; as one reporter recently observed, "in a sense, Seattle itself arrived on the steamer *Portland*."[27] The gold rush also makes an interesting story. As historians throughout the century have demonstrated, the Klondike story has high drama (bringing hope to a nation reeling from a depression); spectacle (the image of gold seekers crowding the waterfront); tragedy (the wreck of the *Clara Nevada*, to name just one); and whimsy (marketing and design of Klondike opera glasses, bicycles, and other products of ingenuity and questionable utility).

The gold rush further provides an interesting look at the character of the city. As Pomeroy pointed out, Seattle exhibited distinctive qualities during the gold-rush era that pushed it ahead of other communities, expanding its economy and population. Similarly, an article in *The Economist* reported in 1997 that Seattle "is remarkable for its golden touch." The metropolitan area serves as a base for Bill Gates, America's richest man, along with several thousand Microsoft millionaires — and the city supports numerous companies recognized as "standard-setters in their businesses." According to this article, what sets Seattle apart from other successful cities is a series of traits, including energy and risk-taking entrepreneurship, that resulted from the Klondike Gold Rush of 1897-1898. Today, these qualities remain a "recipe for business achievement," fueling sales of everything from coffee to computer software.[28] Bill Gates, the personification of a quality called "hard drive," exemplifies the commercial spirit that was also evident during the stampede — and he has observed the parallels between the industry that he helped build and the business of outfitting gold seekers.[29]

As noted, this interpretation is a product of its time. The parallels between the late 1890s and the late 1990s are striking: both were periods of rapid growth, high energy, and national attention. What makes this analysis intriguing is that it explains the significance of the gold rush in terms that are relevant to Seattle today. As the city's history continues to evolve, historians will continue to reassess the legacy of the Klondike Gold Rush.

The story of the gold rush also offers a glimpse of the city in a major period of transition, since the event occurred during the era that transformed it from a town to a metropolis.

CHAPTER SIX

Historic Resources in the Modern Era

*Today we need not regret that the commercial center moved on, leaving the
area to stagnate. This lack of interest and investment insured that a remarkable stand of urbanistically compatible buildings from the end of the nineteenth century would remain. Streetscapes like that from Pioneer Square
south along First Avenue are rare in a modern metropolis forced to reuse the
same downtown area over and over.*

— Sally Woodbridge and Roger Montgomery,
A Guide to Architecture in Washington State, 1980

Pioneer Square: Seattle's First Commercial District

When the Klondike Gold Rush began in 1897, the area now called
"Pioneer Square" was a thriving commercial district. A variety of businesses served the stampeders, including outfitting, hardware, and grocery
stores. Today, most of Seattle's historic resources associated with the
Klondike Gold Rush are located within this commercial district, extending from Columbia Street south to King Street and from Third Avenue
west to Alaskan Way S. In 1970, this 52-acre area was listed in the
National Register of Historic Places (National Register). In 1978, the
boundaries of the district were expanded to 88 acres, and an additional
three acres along the district's southwest end were added in 1987.[1] After
Pioneer Square was listed in the National Register, the City of Seattle
established its own preservation district to facilitate management at the
local level.

Buildings within the Pioneer Square Historic District date from three
periods between the years 1889-1916. The first period, lasting from 1889
to 1899, represents the city's redevelopment after the fire. In the follow-

ing period, which lasted from 1900 to 1910, Pioneer Square experienced tremendous growth and underwent significant development projects including regrading and filling in the tide flats. Just prior to World War I, the district experienced a final surge of construction.[2] After the war, Seattle's retail district moved north of Pioneer Square along First and Second avenues.

Over the years, this shift resulted in the abandonment of Pioneer Square. Buildings in Pioneer Square that once hummed with commercial activity were left vacant or used for storage.

In 1966, an "urban renewal" project proposed by a local planning group known as the Central Association threatened the area. Under the Central Association's plan, buildings in Pioneer Square would have been replaced by modern parking garages.[3] However, as architectural historians Sally Woodbridge and Roger Montgomery explained, "streetscapes like that from Pioneer Square south along First Avenue are rare in a modern metropolis forced to reuse the same downtown area over and over."[4] Recognizing the importance of this intact historic district, preservationists, led by the non-profit Allied Arts of Seattle, worked to raise awareness of Pioneer Square's historic and architectural significance. As a result of these efforts, Pioneer Square became the city's first National Register district in 1970.[5] Historic designation revitalized Pioneer Square by attracting the attention of private developers interested in rehabilitating buildings; businesses seeking commercial space; and individuals interested in the area's stores and colorful history.

In 1976, as Pioneer Square regained its foothold as an important commercial center, Congress established the Klondike Gold Rush National Historical Park, which included a Seattle Unit, in the district. Today, the Park's interpretive exhibits and tours of Pioneer Square allow visitors to envision Seattle during the gold-rush years of the late 1890s.

Seattle's Gold-Rush Era Properties Located Outside the Pioneer Square Historic District

Although most buildings associated with the gold rush in Seattle are located within the Pioneer Square Historic District, some properties lie outside the district's boundaries. This study involved the identification of gold-rush era resources that are located outside the district and which date from after the Seattle fire in 1889 until the Alaska-Yukon-Pacific Exposition (AYP) in 1909. Seattle expanded rapidly during this period, in

In 1966, an "urban renewal" project proposed by a local planning group known as the Central Association threatened the area. Under the Central Association's plan, buildings in Pioneer Square would have been replaced by modern parking garages.

part due to the influx of miners and mining-related businesses. The study also includes properties associated with the AYP because it represents the culmination of Seattle's fascination with the Far North. The already familiar AYP properties located at the original fairgrounds on the University of Washington campus, however, have not been included in this study.

Historians conducting the research for the original project contacted historical preservation agencies and organizations to inquire about their knowledge of gold rush resources located outside the Pioneer Square Historic District. Those contacted include the Office of Archaeology and Historic Preservation, Seattle Office of Urban Conservation, Allied Arts, and Historic Seattle Preservation and Development Authority. The latter assisted in identifying the house of George Carmack, who filed the first claim for Klondike gold.

The researchers obtained the addresses of additional properties through research in Seattle City Directories. Using key words such as "Alaska, Klondike, Miner, and Yukon," they identified addresses of businesses located outside the Pioneer Square Historic District. A similar process was used to go through Klondike guidebooks, which advertised businesses associated with the gold rush. The National Park Service (NPS) developed a database that includes gold-rush images from historic newspaper articles, advertisements, and photographs. Historians can use this database to help identify addresses of gold rush businesses.

The project historians also used Seattle City Directories to determine the addresses of individuals who played an important role in the gold rush. They researched the residences of Seattle promoter Erastus Brainerd, Mayor William Wood, and miners Tom Lippy and George Carmack. Information relating to the architectural characteristics and history of the Wood and Carmack residences is included later in this chapter. It was determined that the Brainerd and Lippy homes had been demolished. During the early 1900s, Brainerd lived in downtown Seattle at 1116 Fifth Avenue and in 1909 he moved to Richmond Beach. The YMCA building replaced Brainerd's downtown address in 1913.[6] From 1900 until 1931, Thomas Lippy lived in a grand house located at 1019 James Street. Constructed by Seattle Pioneer James Scurry in 1890, the house was demolished in 1966.[7]

Further research was conducted on identified buildings by looking at their specific addresses in Sanborn Fire Insurance maps and obtaining King County Assessor's historic property cards for each building.

Historians obtained information about the historic use of some properties by accessing articles and advertisements listed in the NPS database of gold mining businesses. They obtained available records associated with the early history of buildings from the Seattle Department of Construction and Land Use. Researchers also consulted historic preservation records filed at the Seattle Office of Urban Conservation and Office of Archaeology and Historic Preservation. These records included National Register and City landmark nominations.

The nine gold-rush era buildings identified outside the Pioneer Square Historic District include the U.S. Assay Office (613 9th Avenue), the Colman Building (801-821 First Avenue), the Grand Pacific Hotel (1117 First Avenue), the Holyoke Building (1018 First Avenue), the Globe Building (1007 First Avenue), the Moore Theatre and Hotel (1932 Second Avenue), the George Carmack House (1522 East Jefferson Street), the William Wood House (816 35th Avenue) and the Woodson Apartments (1820 24th Street). Six of these buildings are listed in the National Register and as Seattle Landmarks. The unlisted Carmack and Wood houses appear eligible for the National Register. Although the Woodson Apartment building possesses an association with the AYP as an example of residential development that occurred prior to the event, physical alterations have compromised its integrity making it ineligible for the National Register. A catalog at the end of this section provides current and historic photographs, along with a summary of each property's architectural characteristics, past uses, and potential eligibility for the National Register.

While the Pioneer Square Historic District's gold rush resources are located within a cohesive group of properties built soon after Seattle's 1889 fire, most of the buildings identified outside the district were constructed later. Six of the properties outside Pioneer Square are associated with two phases of development: the northward expansion of downtown along First Avenue (1889-1909) and Seattle's preparation for the AYP (1907-1909). The development of a commercial district along First Avenue began as early as 1889 with the construction of the Holyoke Building at the southeast corner of First Avenue and Spring Street.[8] It was not until the turn of the century, however, that a considerable amount of development occurred in this area. Construction associated with the AYP was limited to the years just prior to the event. Three properties, notably the U.S. Assay Office and the houses of George Carmack and William

Wood, do not correspond to the above listed phases.

Historians determined that the Holyoke Building, the Grand Pacific Hotel, the Globe Building, and the Colman Building are associated with both the northward expansion of Seattle's retail district and the gold rush. During the 1970s, the Seattle Office of Urban Conservation recognized the historic significance of buildings along First Avenue and worked to establish a First Avenue Historic District stretching from Pioneer Square (Columbia Street) north to the Pike Place Market (Union Street). The Office of Urban Conservation determined after numerous public hearings and the demolition of an entire block of these buildings that the historic First Avenue properties should be nominated individually rather than as a district. Several of the historic First Avenue properties, including the Holyoke and the Colman buildings, had already been listed in the National Register. Consequently, in 1980, the Office of Urban Conservation prepared a National Register nomination for the following seven buildings, referring to them as the First Avenue Groups: the Globe Building (1001-1011 First Avenue), the Beebe Building (1013 First Avenue), the Cecil Hotel (1019-1023 First Avenue), the Coleman Building (94-96 Spring Street), the Grand Pacific Hotel (1115-1117 First Avenue), the Colonial Hotel (1119-1123 First Avenue), and the National Building (1006-1024 Western Avenue). The Coleman Building is the only property from this group that was not listed in the National Register.

According to the First Avenue Groups' National Register nomination, the Grand Pacific Hotel, the Globe Building, the Beebe Building, the Cecil Hotel, and the Colonial Hotel were constructed to house Seattle's large transient labor population, which had grown as a result of the Klondike Gold Rush.[9] Research indicated the Grand Pacific Hotel and the Globe Building also housed businesses associated with the gold rush. The Seattle Woolen Mill, which outfitted miners with clothing and blankets, was located in the street-level commercial space of the Grand Pacific Hotel from 1899 until 1914. From 1903 until 1912, the Globe Building housed the offices of the Alaska Gold Standard Mining Co., and from 1908 until 1909 the Treasurer's Office for the AYP was also located in the Globe Building.[10] Because HRA did not find additional information connecting the gold rush and the Beebe, Cecil, and Colonial hotels, these buildings were not included in the catalog.

According to the First Avenue Groups' National Register nomination, the Grand Pacific Hotel, the Globe Building, the Beebe Building, the Cecil Hotel, and the Colonial Hotel were constructed to house Seattle's large transient labor population, which had grown as a result of the Klondike Gold Rush.

The Holyoke Building, located at the southeast corner of Spring Street and First Avenue, is also part of the commercial district's northward expansion. In 1976, the Office of Urban Conservation nominated the Holyoke Building as a fine example of the Victorian Style. The nomination also noted that the Holyoke was the "first office building to be completed after Seattle's disastrous fire of 1889."[11] HRA determined that during the gold rush the Northwest Fixture Company, a supplier of lighting equipment for Klondike miners, occupied the Holyoke from 1894 until 1900.[12]

The Colman Building, located on the west side of First Avenue between Columbia and Marion streets, was constructed in 1889 as Seattle's commercial district spread northward. Architect Stephen Meany originally designed the Colman Building as a two-story Romanesque Revival building. In 1904, architect August Tidemand redesigned it into a six-story Chicago Style building.[13] It has been listed in the National Register as a fine example of the Chicago Style of architecture and for its association with James Colman an influential businessman in Seattle.[14] The Colman Building housed two businesses that catered to gold seekers. The grocer Louch, Augustine & Co. occupied the Colman Building from 1894 until 1907, and the Klondike clothing outfitter, Rochester Clothing Co. was located in the building from 1897 until 1899. HRA also determined that during the AYP years, the Colman Building housed the offices of the exposition's publisher and legal counsel.[15]

The Moore Theatre and Hotel and the Woodson Apartments were constructed in direct response to the AYP. Anticipating the event, land developer James A. Moore constructed his namesake Theatre and Hotel in downtown Seattle. When the theatre opened on December 28, 1907, its connection to the AYP was stressed by featuring a comic opera entitled *The Alaskan*.[16] The Moore is listed in the National Register because of its unique design, association with the AYP, and its role as a "leading cultural house in the city."[17] Expecting an increased need for housing due to the AYP, Irene and Zacharais Woodson constructed the Woodson Apartments in the Central District. Although the Woodson Apartment building possesses an important tie to the AYP, it is not eligible for the National Register because physical changes have compromised its integrity.

The U.S. Assay Office and the houses of miner George Carmack and Mayor William Wood are not associated with either the commercial district's northward expansion along First Avenue or the AYP. Among the

properties included in this study, the U.S. Assay Office is the most directly related to the gold rush. Although it was not originally constructed as
an assay office, public demand for a federal assayist required that this
entertainment hall be converted for government use as an assay office in
1897. According to this property's 1969 National Register nomination, it
continued to be used for this purpose until 1932.[18]

When George Carmack first returned from the Far North, he lived in
hotels in the Pioneer Square area. From 1905 until 1909, he lived in a
house at 3007 East Denny, which no longer remains standing.[19] The
house Carmack lived in from 1910 until his death in 1922 is still standing in Seattle's Central District. This property appears eligible for the
National Register for its association with Carmack, who filed the first
claim for Klondike gold.

As the mayor who left his post to try his hand at mining in the Yukon,
William Wood played a significant role in Seattle's gold rush history. Prior
to the gold rush Wood owned a large amount of land east of Greenlake,
which he was responsible for platting. According to Seattle City
Directories, from 1892 until 1900 he lived at the intersection of
Woodlawn and Greenlake. Because historical maps do not show that
Woodlawn and Greenlake intersect, HRA could not identify the location
of Wood's house during this period. Between 1900 and 1904, Wood lived
at two different addresses and from 1905 until 1915, he lived at 816 35th
Avenue.[20] The latter property appears to be eligible for the National
Register because of its association with him.

The following pages include the six National Register-listed and three
unlisted properties that HRA identified as associated with the Klondike
Gold Rush. For each building, we have included a description of the
property's design and its association with the Klondike Gold Rush.

A Visit to Pioneer Square in 1898

Imagine that you're a stampeder beginning to outfit your expedition to the Klondike Gold Fields. You've just arrived in Seattle after a long trip from Philadelphia. You've read all of the Klondike guide books and countless articles in *Leslie's Weekly*. Today you will wander the streets of Pioneer Square trying to get the most items for the least amount of money. Beware of the charlatans and remember that you must carry everything you purchase.

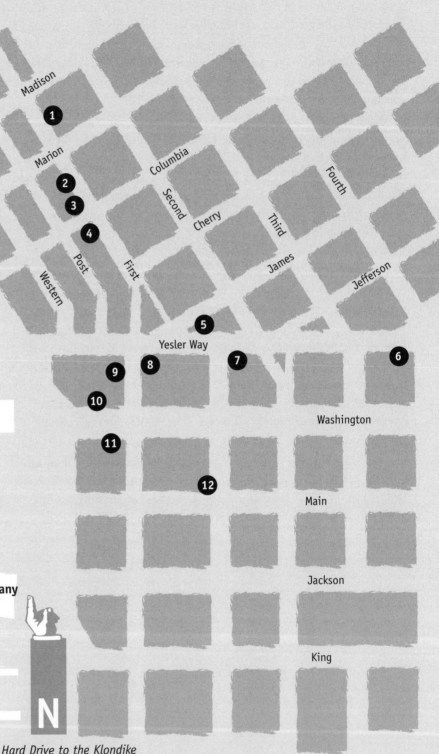

1. N. H. Thedinga Hardware
2. Seattle Klondike Company
3. Seattle Hardware Company
4. MacDougall Southwick Company
5. Argonaut Outfitting Company
6. Pacific Hardware Company
7. Seattle Wool Manufacturing Company
8. Cooper and Levy Company
9. Schwabacher Hardware Company
10. Seattle-Alaska General Supply
11. Benjamin Olswang Hardware
12. Carroll, Cosh, and Company

Hard Drive to the Klondike

U.S. Assay Office
613 Ninth Avenue
Seattle, WA

Built in 1886 by Thomas Prosch, a secretary of the Seattle Chamber of Commerce and owner of the *Post-Intelligencer*, the U.S. Assay office was originally used an entertainment hall and office building. The first floor was used as offices and the second floor was rented as a ballroom. This historical photograph is dated circa 1937.

Architectural Description

The two-story U.S. Assay Office is an "excellent example of a 19th century commercial cast-iron and masonry building, typified with larger, open street level bays and narrow vertical window openings on other facades and on the upper street-front level."[21] The front facade includes two traditional style storefronts consisting of large windows, kick plates, and transoms. The arched entrance to the second floor space is surrounded by columns and a pediment. Five centrally located arched windows on the second floor are flanked by narrow rectangular windows. The protruding central portion of the parapet wall is decorated with a wooden cornice and brackets.

The U.S. Assay Office has undergone several minor alterations, including a narrow addition featuring arched windows similar to the rest of the building added to the south side of the building. Many of the building's windows have been replaced or filled-in. Two first-floor windows on the north side of the building have been filled with brick. One south side window and all the second story windows on the rear (west) of the building have been replaced. A small wood sided addition has been added to the southwest corner of the building's second floor.

Historical Significance

The building that housed the U.S. Assay Office was erected in 1886 by Thomas Prosch, a secretary of the Seattle Chamber of Commerce and owner of the Post-Intelligencer, for use as an entertainment hall and office building. Originally, the first floor was used as offices and the second floor was rented as a ballroom. During the gold rush, the Seattle Chamber of Commerce recognized the city's need for a federal assay office. The Chamber of Commerce, represented by Erastus Brainerd, successfully lobbied for the establishment of an assay office. In May of 1898, the federal government rented Prosch's building and on July 15, 1898, the U.S. Assay Office opened. The Assay Office included a melting department. During the early years of the Klondike Gold Rush, deposits in the office reached approximately $20 million. In 1932, the U. S. Assay Office moved to a government-owned building.

In 1935, the Deutsches Haus (German House) purchased this property and renovated it for use as a social center. During World War II it was used as an entertainment center. After the war, the Deutsches Haus again occupied the structure.[22] The building is currently owned by the German Heritage Society.

The U.S. Assay Office is historically significant as a fine example of commercial cast-iron and masonry architecture, and because of its association with the Klondike Gold Rush, an event that contributed to the economic growth of Seattle. [23]

U.S. Assay Office's east facade, 2001

Hard Drive to the Klondike

The Colman Building was built by James Colman, an influential businessman, who reached in Seattle 1861. It was home for two companies serving stampeders — the grocer Louch, Augustine & Co. occupied the building from 1894 until 1907 and the Klondike clothier, Rochester Clothing Co. was located in the building from 1897 until 1899. This photograph shows the Colman Building prior to 1904.

Architectural Description

The six-story Chicago Style Colman Building occupies the east half of the block located on the west side of First Avenue between Columbia Street and Marion Street. In a Seattle Landmark nomination form, the Seattle Office of Urban Conservation described the Colman Building as follows:

The Colman Building is a six-story concrete and brick office building with stone and marble trim that epitomizes the Chicago Style and its influence upon Seattle architecture.... The exterior of the lower floors was faced with rusticated stone and the additional floors with red brick. A central bay which, at the First Avenue ground level houses the main entrance to the building, protrudes from the rest of the facade and is faced in the same stone as the lower floors. On either side of this central section, the building facade is divided into four equal sections consisting of five structural piers and four window spandrels each. The outermost corner sections extend outward slightly from the adjacent sections, providing a subtle undulation of the surface. A narrow banding just below the top floor and a modestly extended copper cornice crown the building.... The ground level retail shops were embellished by small multi-paned transoms and pediment and column entrances. The building is also distinguished by a metal and glass awning, which stretches along the entire east or front facade.[24]

Historical Significance

The original two-story Colman Building was erected by James Colman, an influential businessman who arrived in Seattle in 1861. Colman's entrepreneurial tendencies involved him in a variety of businesses, including owning woolen mills, land acquisition, and railroading. Colman was one of the major promoters of the railroad to the Renton Coal mines. He operated this railroad for one year until Henry Villard of the Northern Pacific Railroad took it over.[25]

In 1890, the two-story Colman Building was constructed on the site of the old Colman Block, a wooden building that burned in the fire of 1889. The Colman Block had been built on the remains of the ship Winward, which had wrecked near Whidbey Island. Intending to salvage the boat, James Colman bought it and towed it to his dock in Seattle. When the Colman Block was constructed the ship was surrounded by land and buried under the foundation of the Colman Block.[26]

Architect Stephen Meany originally designed the Colman Building as two-story Romanesque Revival structure. In 1904, the Danish architect August Tidemand remodeled it into Seattle's "earliest example of the Chicago Style of commercial architecture."[27] All that was retained of the original facade were the cast iron columns between the storefront bays on First Avenue. The Colman Building has been recognized as historically important for its architectural style and association with James Colman.[28]

The Colman Building housed two businesses that catered to gold seekers. The grocer Louch, Augustine & Co. occupied the Colman Building from 1894 until 1907 and the Klondike clothing outfitter, Rochester Clothing Co. was located in the building from 1897 until 1899. HRA also determined that from 1908 until 1909, the Colman Building housed the offices of the AYP's publisher and legal counsel.[29]

Colman Building, 2001.

Hard Drive to the Klondike

Grand Pacific Hotel
1117 First Avenue
Seattle, WA

The Grand Pacific Hotel was constructed in response to Seattle's growing number of transients, dock workers, lumber workers and ship's crews. From 1899 until 1914, the it housed the office and salesroom for the Seattle Woolen Mill, an important outfitter for the Klondike. This photograph was taken circa 1900.

Architectural Description

The Grand Pacific Hotel is part of a collection of turn-of-the-century commercial buildings north of Pioneer Square on First Avenue. In 1980, the Seattle Office of Urban Conservation prepared a National Register nomination for this cluster of buildings referred to as the First Avenue Groups. The Seattle Office of Urban Conservation described the Grand Pacific Hotel in the following way:

> The former Grand Pacific Hotel exemplifies the Richardsonian Romanesque Style in the composition and detailing of its primary or First Avenue elevation. Beginning at the ground floor, the elevation incorporates a bold central entrance arch flanked by clerestoried storefronts. The arch is constructed of lightly rusticated limestone blocks and voussoirs, as are the two stone block piers at the extreme ends of the store front zone.... Above the store front area and the archway, the First Avenue facade is dominated by a rhythmic two story arcade composed of nine square-based brick piers and eight round, cut stone arches which spring from elegant and compact stone capitals. Deeply recessed between these piers, the second and third story windows are separated by slightly recessed spandrels, faced in small, square, rusticated blocks. The fourth story of the First Avenue facade begins above a stone dentil course and consists of eight rectangular windows framed between short piers aligned with

those of the arcade below. A parapet wall rising above the fourth story is detailed with recessed panels and a corbelled cornice.[30]

The First Avenue Groups' nomination noted that the hotel's storefronts suffered from uncomplimentary signage and a boarded-up central building entrance. Although the original storefront windows have been replaced in recent years, the new windows are well suited for the building. The building's main arched entrance is currently in use.

Historical Significance

Although the architect for the Grand Pacific Hotel is undetermined, this building has been recognized as "one of Seattle's finest examples of Richardsonian Romanesque commercial architecture." It has also been identified as one of "the last major buildings in Seattle to be designed in this style."[31] Circa 1898, the Grand Pacific Hotel opened under the name "First Avenue Hotel." This hotel, along with others included in the First Avenue Groups, was constructed in part to cater to the needs of Seattle's growing transient laborer population. Growth resulting from the Klondike Gold Rush resulted in an "acute need for new structures to provide necessary retail outlets and hotels for the large number of transients, dock workers, lumber workers and ship's crews."[32] The Grand Pacific Hotel filled the growing need for both housing and commercial space.

From 1899 until 1914, the Grand Pacific Hotel also housed the office and salesroom for the Seattle Woolen Mill, an important outfitter for the Klondike. According to Seattle City Directories, this company moved its offices from a neighboring building at 1119 First Street. This earlier building was replaced by the Colonial Hotel in 1901.[33] During the gold rush, the Seattle Woolen Mill advertised "Llama underwear, heavy Mackinaw clothing and double woven blankets for the Arctic Regions" as well as, "Blanket Clothing for the Klondike."[34]

East elevation of the Grand Pacific Hotel, 2001.

Hard Drive to the Klondike

In 1890, lumberman Richard Holyoke constructed the Holyoke Building. It was one of the first office buildings to be completed after Seattle's 1889 fire. During the gold rush, the Holyoke Building housed the Northwest Fixture Co., which outfitted miners with electric motors and generators for mining and lighting. This photograph was taken circa 1900.

Architectural Description

The five-story Holyoke Building is essentially Victorian in style. The building's emphasis on verticality evidenced in the tall narrow windows and closely spaced repeating piers is characteristic of Victorian buildings. It was framed with post and beam construction and clad in red brick. A continuous band of concrete runs across the top of the building and is repeated on the upper-stories in the form of interrupted concrete bands above each of the windows. These details off-set the strong vertical emphasis by providing distinct horizontal lines.

Concrete detailing compliments the gray-colored rusticated stone block first-floor facade. The Holyoke Building's principal facade faces First Avenue. Because the building is set into the hillside formed by Seneca Street, the stonework along this secondary street-facing facade is cut-off by the incline. The Holyoke Building's commercial store-fronts, complete with recessed doorways, kick plates, and large store-front windows are still intact. Few alterations have been made to the original design of this building.

Historical Significance

In 1890, lumberman Richard Holyoke constructed the Holyoke Building. Architects Thomas Bird and George Dornbach had planned the construction of the Holyoke Building prior to Seattle's 1889 fire. After the fire had occurred, the Holyoke Building was one of the first office buildings to be completed.[35]

This building represents the northward expansion of Seattle's downtown spreading out from Pioneer Square. In the late 1890s, the Klondike Gold Rush caused increased development activity resulting in the construction of hotels and commercial properties near the Holyoke Building.[36] During the gold rush, the Holyoke Building housed the Northwest Fixture Co. This company outfitted miners with electric motors and generators for mining and lighting.[37] This business was located in the Holyoke Building from 1894 until 1900. In the following years, the Northwest Fixture Co. moved to 313 First Avenue, where it was located until 1902. According to Seattle City Directories, it no longer existed after 1902.[38]

Southwest corner of the Holyoke Building, 2001.

Hard Drive to the Klondike

Globe Building
1007 First Avenue
Seattle, WA

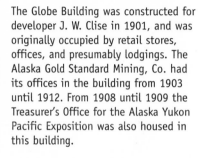

The Globe Building was constructed for developer J. W. Clise in 1901, and was originally occupied by retail stores, offices, and presumably lodgings. The Alaska Gold Standard Mining, Co. had its offices in the building from 1903 until 1912. From 1908 until 1909 the Treasurer's Office for the Alaska Yukon Pacific Exposition was also housed in this building.

Architectural Description

The Globe Building is part of a collection of turn-of-the-century commercial buildings located just north of Pioneer Square and referred to as the First Avenue Groups. In 1980, the Seattle Office of Urban Conservation prepared a National Register nomination for the First Avenue Groups which provided the following physical description of the Globe Building's street-facing elevations:

> The First Avenue façade is organized into three vertically ascending layers consisting of a continuous ground floor storefront zone, a two story body and an arcaded upper story. The storefront zone consists of large display windows and clerestories, many of which have been cosmetically altered with garish signage and other reversible accretions. Masonry walls above the storefronts are supported by a series of slender iron columns and horizontal girders encased within a terra cotta entablature. The walls are faced in tan-colored press brick and are penetrated by pairs of double hung windows at the second and third stories, and a nearly continuous arcade of round arched windows at the fourth story. Neo-classical detailing executed in ivory-colored terra cotta includes corner quoins, bracketed lintels above the second story windows, segmented flat arches above the third story windows and a terminating cornice detailed with an egg and

dart motif. An arched entrance canopy, four iron balconies and a small roofline pediment originally incorporated at the center of the First Avenue facade no longer remain.

The Madison Street facade incorporates similar fenestration and detailing. The wall plane of this facade is interrupted at the center where a slight recess occurs beneath an elliptical terra cotta arch. The recess appears to have originally opened into an internal light court, which has since been enclosed. The wall surface now contains unadorned double hung windows. Openings at the basement level of this facade relate to the Arlington Garage, which occupied the lower floors of the building several decades after the building's initial construction.

Historical Significance

The First Avenue Groups National Register nomination indicates that the Globe Building was "constructed for developer J. W. Clise in 1901, and was originally occupied by retail stores, offices, and presumably lodgings."[39] This nomination indicates that the Globe Building, along with the Grand Pacific Hotel, housed the influx of transient laborers that arrived with the gold rush.

Southeast facade of the Globe Building, 2001.

Among the offices housed in the Globe Building were two businesses associated with ties to the Far North that Seattle established during the Klondike Gold Rush. From 1903 until 1912, the offices of the Alaska Gold Standard Mining Co. were located in the Globe Building. Seattle's fascination with the Far North culminated in 1909 with the Alaska Yukon Pacific Exposition. From 1908 until 1909, the Treasurer's Office for this noteworthy event was housed in the Globe Building.[40] Today, this building houses the Alexis Hotel.

Moore Theatre, Seattle, Wash.

The Moore Theatre and Hotel was opened by James A. Moore in 1907 to accommodate anticipated crowds associated with the 1909 Alaska-Yukon-Pacific Exhibition. The theatre's first production was a comic opera entitled, The Alaskan. This view of the building is from a postcard circa 1909.

Architectural Description

The seven-story Moore Theatre and Hotel building is located at the corner of Second Avenue and Virginia Street. The primary facade faces Second Avenue with another street-facing facade along Virginia. It is constructed of reinforced concrete with white glazed brick cladding. Accents of tan-colored terra-cotta appear over the main arched entrances, on the window sills, and on a panel which bears the name "Moore Theatre." These details along with a decorative cornice and freeze are the building's principal exterior embellishments.

In 1937, the building was reported to have 11 stores and 146 hotel rooms.[41] The building's commercial spaces along Second Avenue are still in use, although the original store fronts have been replaced with aluminum-framed windows and black siding. The theatre's original marquee has been replaced with a larger modern version. The windows throughout the building have been replaced.

Historical Significance

This building was constructed by James A. Moore, an early Seattle real estate developer who was responsible for erecting over 200 homes on Capitol Hill and platting Latona and part of what is now the University District.[42] In 1907, he opened the Moore Theatre and Hotel to accommodate anticipated crowds associated with the 1909 AYP. The building's design "was immediately noted nation-wide, and its use made it the leading cultural house of the city."[43] Moore Theatre and Hotel Architect E. W. Houghton designed a lavish interior which included onyx and marble in the theatre lobby and foyer.

The theatre opened on December 28, 1907, eight months after the hotel. James A. Moore had been convinced to open a theatre by the manager of the Northwestern Theatrical Association, James Cort. Cort became the manager of the Moore Theatre and attracted well-known entertainers to the theatre. Cort's successor Celia Schultz outdid him by regularly bringing a fantastic array of singers, dancers, and instrumentalists to the theatre until 1949 when she resigned. Until the 1950s, the Moore Theatre played a leading role in the Seattle entertainment industry. It continues to hold musical concerts today. The National Register Nomination for this building notes the following:

> The Moore is significant not only for theatrical contributions, but also for its outstanding theatre architecture. From the expensive exterior construction, withstanding both climatic and earthquake stresses, to interior design features of exiting ramps, excellent sight lines, superior stage "life," and acoustics, the Moore is among the best examples of theatre architecture and engineering ahead of its time, to be found in the country.[44]

Northwest corner of the Moore Theatre and Hotel, 2001.

The Moore Theatre and Hotel building was closely associated with the AYP. As noted, it was constructed in part to cater to AYP visitors. When the theatre opened, its first production was a comic opera entitled, The Alaskan. Journalist Jane Lotter explained that during that time period "Seattle was still in the midst of a love affair with the North that had begun with the 1897 gold rush and *The Alaskan* was a guaranteed crowd pleaser." As expected, the opening performance was a hit with 2,500 people- including the governor, the mayor, James A. Moore and John Cort-attending the performance.

On August 16, 1897, George Washington Carmack discovered gold along Bonanza Creek, a tributary of the Klondike River. By 1910, Carmack moved to 1522 East Jefferson Street. According to *Seattle City Directories*, he lived at this address until he died in 1922. This photograph was taken circa 1937.

Architectural Description

The George Carmack (1910-1922) residence is located at the corner of East Jefferson and 16th Avenue. It is a two and a half-story Colonial Revival house with a rectangular plan and a side-gambrel roof. This wood frame building is clad with white-painted clapboards at the first floor and shingles above. Dense vegetation currently surrounds the property, making it difficult to view the house. The original porch, which stretches across the front of the house (facing East Jefferson), has been enclosed with corrugated plastic siding. On the second floor above the porch is a shed roof dormer with bay windows. At the first level on the 16th Avenue side of the house is a bay with three double-hung windows. Like most of the building's lights, these windows have multiple panes above and a single pane below. Another bay with two double-hung windows and a bracketed eve is located above the first-story bay. Over the years, this building has undergone few exterior alterations.

Historical Significance

George Washington Carmack, the "official discover of Klondike gold," lived in this house from 1910 until 1922. On August 16, 1897, Carmack discovered gold along Bonanza Creek, a tributary of the Klondike River. Carmack was married to a Tagish Indian woman named Kate. When he discovered the gold, he was accompanied by two Tagish men Skookum Jim Mason, and Dawson (Tagish) Charley. By filing a claim first,

Carmack became credited with finding the Klondike lode. After Carmack arrived in Seattle on July 17, 1897, the stampede to the Klondike began.[45]

When Carmack and his wife disposed of their holdings in the Klondike, they moved to Seattle where they took residence at the prestigious Hotel Seattle. Kate Carmack did not enjoy living in Seattle and returned to her northern home.[46] Carmack soon thereafter married a woman named Marguerite. Carmack eventually left the Hotel Seattle, but continued residing in the Pioneer Square area. From 1905 until 1909, he lived in a house at 3007 East Denny Way, which has since been removed. By 1910, Carmack moved to 1522 East Jefferson. According to Seattle City Directories, Carmack lived at this address until he died in 1922.[47] Marguerite Carmack continued living in the house until the 1940s. A considerable amount of development has occurred around this house, which is still used as a residential structure.

Southeast side of the Carmack House, 2001.

Hard Drive to the Klondike

In 1908, Zacharias and Irene Woodson built this apartment expecting an increased demand for housing due to the Alaska-Yukon-Pacific Exhibition. By 1903 Zacharias was the proprietor of a rooming house at 1216 Second Avenue. In 1909, the Woodsons were the proprietors of both the Woodson Apartments and a rooming house at 1530 Fifth Avenue. This photograph was taken circa 1937.

Architectural Description

The Woodson Apartments, known today as the Cascade View Apartments, have undergone numerous alterations over the years. This two-story rectangular building is located on the east side of 24th Avenue and stretches from the street to an alley east of the property. The building originally had a two-story porch that protruded from the center of the east facade to shelter the main entrance on the first floor and a similar space at the second level. The second-story porch had a low-pitched gable roof supported by classical columns. The same style columns also supported the porch at the first level. A cornice once extended across the principle facade and around the building's north and south corners.

Today, the architectural details that once characterized the Woodson Apartments have been removed. The two-story porch has been replaced with a simple metal awning over the main entrance. A metal railing borders the concrete stairway leading to the entrance. The cornice has been removed and the original double hung windows have been replaced with aluminum frame versions. The east side of the building is covered in a composite concrete and the rest of the building is clad in vinyl.

Historical Significance

In 1908, Zacharias and Irene Woodson built this apartment anticipating that the AYP would increase the demand for housing in Seattle.

According to Esther Mumford's Seattle's Black Victorians, the Woodsons came to Seattle in 1897 and operated rooming houses during the first three decades of the century.[48] Seattle City Directories list Zacharias as a "bootblack" in 1899. By 1903, however, Zacharias is listed as being the proprietor of a rooming house at 1216 Second Avenue In 1909, the Woodsons are listed as the proprietors of both the Woodson Apartments and a rooming house at 1530 Fifth Avenue.[49] This property represents the growth Seattle experienced due to the AYP.

Woodson Apartments (Cascade View Apartments), 2001.

Hard Drive to the Klondike

William Wood and his wife Emma lived in this house from 1905 until 1915. The year the gold rush began, Wood became the Mayor of Seattle. It is unknown if Wood commissioned the construction of this house; however, it is likely that he and his wife were the first people to live here. This photograph was taken circa 1937.

Architectural Description

This two-and-a-half story Classic Box house is located in Madrona, on the edge of a hill overlooking Lake Washington. The house is set back from 35th Avenue and is approached by an alley-like driveway that runs between two houses set closer to the street. The east facing principal facade overlooks Lake Washington.

The house has a hip roof with hip-roof dormers on the east and west elevations. The exposed rafter tails that once decorated the eaves have been removed. The clapboard walls of the second floor flare slightly before meeting a flat board that separates the first and second floors. The northeast corner of the house has an inset porch supported by classical columns. The railing surrounding the porch has turned balusters. Most of the house's original windows are one-over-one and double hung. On the north side of the house is a ribbon of three leaded glass windows. The principle facade has a one-story bay window on its north side. The north, south, and west sides of the house are unaltered. The south elevation is obscured by thick vegetation making it difficult to discern if alterations have occurred to this side of the house.

Historical Description

Seattle City Directories indicate that Seattle Mayor William Wood and his wife Emma lived in this house from 1905 until 1915. Wood had many interests which included working as a realtor, lawyer, and businessman. As a realtor in 1888, Wood owned a large amount of land on the east side of Greenlake, which he platted. Prior to becoming mayor in 1897, he acted as the president of W.D. Wood & Co. lawyers. His business interests included serving as president for both the Seattle-Yukon Transportation Co. and the Antimony Smelting & Refining Co.

The year the gold rush began, Wood became the Mayor of Seattle. Unable to resist the temptation of striking it rich, he, too, went to the Yukon for a short period. In the years following his return from the Far North, he lived in several different houses for short periods. It is unknown if Wood commissioned the construction of this house; however, it is likely that he and his wife were the first people to live here.[50]

William Wood House, 1998.

Hard Drive to the Klondike

Hard Drive to the Klondike:
Promoting Seattle During the Gold Rush

Introduction

1 "American Survey: The Heirs of the Klondike," *The Economist* (February 15-21, 1997), p. 25.

2 *The Trade Register, December Trade Summary, 1898,* p. 28; Pierre Berton, *The Klondike Fever: The Life and Death of the Last Great Gold Rush* (New York: Alfred A. Knopf, 1958). Neither source explains how the precise number of gold seekers was obtained.

3 William B. Haskell, *Two Years in the Klondike and Alaska Gold-Fields, 1896-1898* (Fairbanks: University of Alaska Press, 1998), p. 17.

4 "American Survey: The Heirs of the Klondike," p. 25.

5 Kimberly B. Marlowe, "Seattitude," Pacific Northwest, *The Seattle Times*, August 16, 1998, p. 8.

6 Bill Gates, "The Internet 'Gold Rush': Where's the Gold?," Microsoft Internet Column, URL http://www.microsoft.com./Bill Gates_L/column/1995essay/12-6-95.htm, p. 1.

7 James Wallace and Jim Erickson, *Hard Drive: Bill Gates and the Making of the Microsoft Empire* (New York: John Wiley & Sons, Inc. 1992), p. 125.

8 "American Survey: The Heirs of the Klondike," p. 25.

9 Murray Morgan, *Skid Road: An Informal Portrait of Seattle* (Seattle: University of Washington Press, 1982), p. 10.

10 Irving Sayford, "The Klondike Put Seattle on the Map," *Travel*, March 1939.

Chapter One

1 Murray Morgan, *Skid Road: An Informal Portrait of Seattle* (Seattle: University of Washington Press, 1982), p. 19.

2 Morgan, *Skid Road: An Informal Portrait of Seattle*, pp. 4 and 8; Gordon B. Dodds, The American Northwest: A History of Oregon and Washington (Arlington Heights, Illinois: The Forum Press, Inc., 1986), p. 99.

3 See, for example, Roger Sale, *Seattle, Past to Present* (Seattle: University of Washington Press, 1976), p. 7.

4 Sale, *Seattle, Past to Present*, p. 8.

5 William C. Speidel, *Sons of the Profits* (Seattle: Nettle Creek Publishing Company, 1967), pp. 214-215.

6 Sale, *Seattle, Past to Present*, p. 12.

7 Morgan, *Skid Road: An Informal Portrait of Seattle*, p. 12.

8 Sale, *Seattle, Past to Present*, p. 12.

9 Gerald B. Nelson, *Seattle: The Life and Times of an American City* (New York: Alfred A. Knopf, 1977), p. 7.

10 Sale, *Seattle, Past to Present*, p. 12.

11 James R. Warren, *The Day Seattle Burned* (published by the author, 1989), p. 1; Sale, *Seattle, Past to Present*, p. 12.

12 Clarence B. Bagley, *History of Seattle From the Earliest Settlement to the Present Time, vol. II* (Chicago: S.J. Clarke Publishing Company, 1916), p. 698.

13 Sale, *Seattle, Past to Present*, p. 12.

14 Sale, *Seattle, Past to Present*, p. 19; Nelson, *Seattle: The Life and Times of an American City*, p.12.

15 Sale, *Seattle, Past to Present*, pp. 19-22.

16 Carlos Schwantes, *The Pacific Northwest: An Interpretive History* (Lincoln: University of Nebraska Press, 1996), p. 121; Nard Jones, *Seattle: A Fresh Look at One of America's Most Exciting Cities* (Garden City, New York: Doubleday & Company, Inc., 1972), p. 37.

17 Clarence B. Bagley, *History of King County Washington, vol. 1*, (Chicago: S.J. Clarke Publishing Company, 1929), p. 104.

18 Sale, *Seattle, Past to Present*, pp. 32-33.

19 Quoted in Neil Clifford Kimmons, "The Historical Development of Seattle As a Metropolitan Area," Master's Thesis, University of Washington, 1942, p. 71.

20 See, for example, Dorothy O. Johansen and Charles M. Gates, *Empire of the Columbia: A History of The Pacific Northwest* (New York: Harper & Row, 1967), p. 312.

21 Sale, *Seattle, Past to Present*, pp. 32-33.

22 Bagley, *History of Seattle From the Earliest Settlement to the Present Time, vol. 1*, pp. 131-134.

23 Sale, *Seattle, Past to Present*, p. 50.

24 Warren, *The Day Seattle Burned*, p. 2.

25 Quoted in Kimmons, "The Historical Development of Seattle as a Metropolitan Area," p.6.

26 Bagley, *History of Seattle From the Earliest Settlement to the Present Time*, p. 698.

27 Carlos Schwantes, *The Pacific Northwest: An Interpretive History*, p. 239.

28 Sanborn Map, 1888.

29 Kimmons, "The Historical Development of Seattle as a Metropolitan Area," p. 53.

30 *Seattle Chamber of Commerce Report, 1898*, p. 28, Klondike Gold Rush National Historical Park Library, Seattle.

31 Richard C. Berner, *Seattle 1900-1920: From Boomtown, Urban Turbulence, to Restoration* (Seattle: Charles Press). p. 10; J. Willis Sayre, *The Early Waterfront of Seattle* (1937), p. 9; Thomas W. Prosch, *A Chronological History of Seattle From 1850 to 1897, vol. 2* (c. 1900), p. 482.

32   Murray Morgan, *Puget's Sound: A Narrative of Early Tacoma and the Southern Sound* (Seattle: University of Washington Press, 1979), p. 298;

Alexander Norbert MacDonald, "Seattle, Vancouver, and the Klondike," *The Canadian Historical Review* (September 1968), p. 237.

33 Sale, *Seattle, Past to Present*, p. 35.

34 Speidel, *Sons of the Profits,* pp. 214-215.

35 Edward and Elizabeth Burke, *Seattle's Other History: Our Asian-American Heritage* (Seattle: Profanity Hill Press, c. 1979); Johansen and Gates, *Empire of the Columbia: A History of the Pacific Northwest*, p. 349.

36 City of Seattle Ordinance, "Construction of Buildings in the Fire Limits," July 1, 1889, City of Seattle Archives; Warren, *The Day Seattle Burned.*

37 Judge Thomas Burke quoted in Nelson, *Seattle, The Life and Times of an American City*, p. 28.

38 Welford Beaton, *The City That Made Itself: A Literary and Pictorial Record of the Building of Seattle* (Seattle: Terminal Publishing Company, 1914), p. 10.

39 Warren, *The Day Seattle Burned*, p. 2.

40 Walt Crowley, *National Trust Guide, Seattle* (New York: John Wiley & Sons, Inc., 1998), p. 91.

41 Sale, *Past to Present*, pp. 53-56.

42 "The Boom in Western Washington," *The Overland Monthly 16* (September 1890), p. 225.

43 Victoria Hartwell Livingston, "Erastus Brainerd: The Bankruptcy of Brilliance," Master's Thesis, University of Washington, 1967, p. 12.

44 Murray Morgan, *One Man's Gold Rush: A Klondike Album* (Seattle: University of Washington Press, 1967), p. 14.

45 Melanie J. Mayer, *Klondike Women: True Tales of the 1897-1898 Gold Rush* (Ohio: Swallow Press, 1989), pp. 13-14.

46 Archie Satterfield, *Klondike Park: From Seattle to Dawson City* (Golden, Colorado: Fulcrum Publishing), p. 32.

47 Schwantes, *The Pacific Northwest: An Interpretive History*, pp. 262-267.

48 Schwantes, *The Pacific Northwest: An Interpretive History*, p. 265.

49 Sharon A. Boswell and Lorraine McConaghy, *Raise Hell and Sell Newspapers: Alden J. Blethen and The Seattle Times* (Pullman: Washington State University Press, 1996), pp. 96-97.

50 Thomas A. Bailey and David M. Kennedy, *The American Pageant, ninth edition* (Lexington, Massachusetts: D.C. Heath and Company, 1991), pp. 621-623.

51 Satterfield, *Klondike Park: From Seattle to Dawson City*, p. 32.

52 Frederick Jackson Turner, "Statement of the Frontier Thesis," in Ray Allen Billington, editor, *The Frontier Thesis: Valid Interpretation of American History?* (Huntington, New York: Robert E. Krieger Publishing Company, 1977), pp. 9-20. See also Bailey and Kennedy, *The American Pageant*, pp. 608-609.

53 See, for example, Patricia Limerick, *The Legacy of Conquest: The Unbroken Past of the American West* (New York: Norton, 1987).

54 Roderick Nash, *Wilderness and the American Mind, third edition* (New Haven: Yale University Press, 1982), p. 145.

55 See, for example, E.A. Ross, "Turning Towards Nirvana," Arena 4 (November 1891), pp. 739 and 742, and Herbert Ernest Cushman, "Professor August Weismann," *Outlook* (January 16, 1897), p. 253.

56 "Unfair Criticism," *The Seattle Daily Times*, August 16, 1897.

57 Roderick Nash, *Wilderness and the American Mind*, pp. 284-285.

58 "GOLD! GOLD! GOLD! GOLD!," *The Seattle Post-Intelligencer*, July 17, 1897, p. 1.

59 Ross Anderson, "Poor Man, Rich Man," *The Seattle Times Magazine*, July 13, 1997, p. 22.

60 "All in Now Excitement," *The Seattle Daily Times*, July 3 1897, p. 8.

61 Bruce Merrell, "'A Wild and Discouraging Mess': John Muir Reports on the Klondike Gold Rush," *Alaska History 7* (Fall 1992), p. 34.

62 Boswell and McConaghy, *Raise Hell and Sell Newspapers: Alden J. Blethen and The Seattle Times*, p. 107; Terrence Cole, "Klondike Visions: Dreams of

a Promised Land," *The Alaska Journal 16* (1986), p. 90; Announcement in *The Seattle Daily Times*, August 7, 1897.

63 *Leslie's Weekly*, August 12, 1897.

64 "Seattle: Launch Pad to Gold," *The Seattle Post-Intelligencer*, September 13, 1990, p. 5.

65 "Klondyke Arouses the East," *The Seattle Daily Times*, July 20, 1897, p. 1; "GOLD! Is Still Causing Excitement in New York," The Seattle Daily Times, July 23, 1897, p.1.

66 "Clarence King's Views," *The New York Times*, August 7, 1897.

67 *The Seattle Post-Intelligence*r, January 21, 1898.

68 "Bound for the Klondike," *The New York Times*, July 23, 1897, p. 1; Boswell and McConaghy, *Raise Hell and Sell Newspapers: Alden J. Blethen and The Seattle Times*, p. 109.

69 *The Seattle Post-Intelligencer*, July 29, 1897 and October 13, 1897; *The Seattle Times*, August 21, 1897.

70 Tappan Adney, *The Klondike Stampede* (New York: Harper & Brothers Publishers, 1900); Dianne Newell, "The Importance of Information and Misinformation in the Making of the Klondike Gold Rush," *Journal of Canadian Studies 21* (Winter 1986-1987), p. 103.

71 Satterfield, *Klondike Park: From Seattle to Dawson City*, p. 43.

72 "Where's Your Grubstake," *The Seattle Daily Times*, July 19, 1897.

73 Kathryn Taylor Morse, "The Nature of Gold: An Environmental History of the Alaska/Yukon Gold Rush," Ph.D. Dissertation, University of Washington, 1997, p. 374.

74 Letter, C.F. Swigert to Capt. Harry Taylor, June 30, 1898, Record Group 77, Office of the Chief of Engineers, Seattle District, Box 250, Folder Defenses #262 to #346, National Archives, Seattle; William F. Willingham, *Northwest Passages: A History of the Seattle District, U.S. Army Corps of Engineers, 1896-1920* (Seattle: U.S. Army Corps of Engineers, 1992), p. 104.

75 "Rush for the Land of the Golden Fleece," *San Francisco Chronicle*, July 17, 1897, p. 1. See also "Wood to Resign," *The Seattle Post-Intelligencer*, July 31, 1897, p. 1.

76 "Police Salaries Raised," *The Seattle Daily Times*, July 21, 1897; Mark R. Shipley, "The Impact of the Klondike Gold Rush on Seattle: A Research Report," in the Klondike Gold Rush National Historical Park Library, Seattle, n.p.

77 "A Queer Effect," *Tacoma Daily News*, August 3, 1897, n.p. , vertical file, Alaska Gold Rush, Tacoma Public Library.

78 Terrence Cole, "Klondike Visions: Dreams of a Promised Land," pp. 84-87.

79 "Will Not Go to Klondike," *The New York Times*, July 29, 1897, p. 2.

80 Barbara E. Kelcey, "What to Wear to the Klondike: Outfitting Women for the Gold Rush," *Material History Review 37* (Spring 1993), p. 22.

81 "By Air Ship to Klondike," *The New York Times*, August 30, 1897, p. 1. See also "To the Klondike By Balloon," *The New York Times*, April 4, 1898, p. 2.

82 "Canadians for Klondike," *New York Times*, September 26, 1897, p. 4.

83 *The Seattle Daily Times*, September 8, 1897.

84 "A Nest of Missing People," *The Seattle Post-Intelligencer*, February 15, 1898, p. 5.

85 "What Steamer is This?," *The Seattle Post-Intelligencer*, February 15, 1898, p. 1; Shipley, "The Impact of the Klondike Gold Rush on Seattle: A Research Report," n.p.

86 "Was On Clara Nevada," *The Seattle Daily Times*, March 17, 1898, p. 1.

87 See, for example, "The Passing Throng," *The Seattle Post-Intelligencer*, August 17, 1897; Shipley, "The Impact of the Klondike Gold Rush on Seattle: A Research Report," n.p.

88 See, for example, Melanie J. Mayer, *Klondike Women: True Tales of the 1897-1898 Gold Rush*,; Esther Hall Mumford, *Seattle's Black Victorians, 1852-1901* (Seattle: Ananse Press, c. 1980), p. 209; Paula Mitchell Marks: *Precious Dust: The American Gold Rush Era*, 1848-1900 (New York: William Morrow and Company, 1994), p. 48.

Chapter Two

1 Murray Morgan, *Skid Road: An Informal Portrait of Seattle* (Seattle: University of Washington Press, 1982), p. 5.

2 "Centered in Seattle," *The Seattle Post-Intelligencer*, July 25, 1897, p. 1; David V. Clarridge, *A Ton of Gold: The Seattle Gold Rush, 1897-1898* (Seattle, c. 1972), p. 15.

3 *The Trade Register, December Trade Summary, 1898*, p. 28. See also Archie Satterfield, "He Sold the Klondike," *The Seattle Times Magazine*, January 2, 1972, p. 10.

4 Victoria Hartwell Livingston, "Erastus Brainerd: The Bankruptcy of Brilliance," Master's Thesis, University of Washington, 1967, pp. 128 and 3.

5 Livingston, "Erastus Brainerd: The Bankruptcy of Brilliance," pp. 4-7.

6 Livingston, "Erastus Brainerd: The Bankruptcy of Brilliance," pp. 13 and 127.

7 Satterfield, "He Sold the Klondike," p. 10.

8 Livingston, "Erastus Brainerd: The Bankruptcy of Brilliance," p. 28-29.

9 "Seattle, 'The Queen City,'" Advertisement, Erastus Brainerd Scrapbooks, University of Washington, A1698.

10 "Seattle Opens the Gate to the Klondike Gold Fields," *The Seattle Post-Intelligencer*, October 13, 1897, p. 1.

11 Jeannette Paddock Nichols, "Advertising and the Klondike," *The Western Historical Quarterly 13* (January 1972), pp. 22-23; Mark R. Shipley, "The Impact of the Klondike Gold Rush on Seattle," Klondike Gold Rush National Historical Park Library, Seattle, n.p.

12 Erastus Brainerd, "Seattle's Outlook," *The Argus*, December 18, 1897, p. 1.

13 Satterfield, "He Sold the Klondike," p. 10.

14 "Is Advertising Seattle," *The Seattle Daily Times* [?], p. 8.

15 Satterfield, "He Sold the Klondike," p. 10.

16 Erastus Brainerd, General Letter to Organizations, November 20, 1897, Erastus Brainerd Scrapbooks, University of Washington, A1698.

17 Livingston, "Erastus Brainerd: The Bankruptcy of Brilliance," pp. 29-30.

18 Satterfield, "He Sold the Klondike," p. 10.

19 Erastus Brainerd, Circular, Seattle Chamber of Commerce, October 1, 1897, Erastus Brainerd Scrapbooks, University of Washington, A1698; Livingston, "Erastus Brainerd: The Bankruptcy of Brilliance," p. 29.

20 George L. Gordon, Letter to Bureau of Information, n.d., Erastus Brainerd Scrapbooks, University of Washington, A1698.

21 James Q. Robeson [illegible], Letter to Erastus Brainerd, October 18, 1897, Erastus Brainerd Scrapbooks, University of Washington, A1698.

22 Letter to Erastus Brainerd from Omaha, n.d., Erastus Brainerd Scrapbooks, University of Washington, A1698.

23 Livingston, "Erastus Brainerd: The Bankruptcy of Brilliance," p. 32.

24 Livingston, "Erastus Brainerd: The Bankruptcy of Brilliance," p. 32.

25 Satterfield, "He Sold the Klondike," p. 10.

26 "A Heavy Modern Exodus," *The Seattle Daily Times*, February 17, 1898, p. 5.

27 Shipley, "The Impact of the Klondike Gold Rush on Seattle," n.p. See also *The Trade Register, December Trade Summary, 1898*, p. 28.

28 Livingston, "Erastus Brainerd: The Bankruptcy of Brilliance," pp. 33-34.

29 Larry Rumley, "When Gold Poured Into Seattle From the North," *The Seattle Times*, May 1, 1966, pp. 14-15.

30 Rumley, "When Gold Poured Into Seattle From the North," pp. 14-15.

31 George Edward Adams, "Where the Klondike Gold is Valued," *The Cosmopolitan 28* (1900), p. 425.

32 Seattle Chamber of Commerce Report, 1898, n.p., Erastus Brainerd Scrapbooks, University of Washington, A1698; "The Assay Office," *The Seattle Daily Times*, December 22, 1900, p. 1.

33 Sharon A. Boswell and Lorraine McConaghy, *Raise Hell and Sell Newspapers: Alden J. Blethen and The Seattle Times* (Pullman: Washington

State University Press, 1996), p. 110.

34 Livingston, "Erastus Brainerd: The Bankruptcy of Brilliance," pp. 34, 48, and 125.

35 "Erastus Brainerd, Former Seattle Editor, is Dead," *The Seattle Post-Intelligencer*, December 26, 1922, p. 1.

36 Livingston, "Erastus Brainerd: The Bankruptcy of Brilliance," Foreword.

37 Livingston, "Erastus Brainerd: The Bankruptcy of Brilliance," p. 127.

38 William C. Speidel, *Sons of the Profits* (Seattle: Nettle Creek Publishing Company, 1967), p. 313.

39 "The Passenger Rush," *Seattle Daily Times*, July 23, 1897, p. 1.

40 John Bonner, "The Competition for the Klondike," *Leslie's Weekly* (December 30, 1897), p. 444.

41 Kathryn Taylor Morse, "The Nature of Gold: An Environmental History of the Alaska/Yukon Gold Rush," Ph.D. Dissertation, University of Washington, 1997, p. 327.

42 Alaskan Trade Committee Advertisement, Erastus Brainerd Scrapbooks, University of Washington A1698.

43 Alexander Norbert MacDonald, "Seattle's Economic Development, 1880-1910," Ph.D. Dissertation, University of Washington, 1959, p. 136.

44 Merrell, "'A Wild and Discouraging Mess': John Muir Reports on the Klondike Gold Rush," *Alaska History 7* (Fall 1990).

45 San Francisco Pamphlet, provided by Klondike Gold Rush National Historical Park Library, Seattle.

46 "San Francisco After It," *The Seattle Daily Times*, November 5, 1897, p. 5.

47 "San Francisco After It," p. 5.

48 Seattle Chamber of Commerce, Annual Report, 1897, p. 66, Erastus Brainerd Scrapbooks, University of Washington, A1698.

49 Terrence Cole, Personal Communication, September 22, 1998.

50 Glenn G. Boyer, editor, *I Married Wyatt Earp: The Recollections of Josephine Sarah Marcus Earp* (Tucson: University of Arizona Press, 1981), p. 159.

51 Archie Satterfield, *Klondike Park: From Seattle to Dawson City* (Golden, Colorado: Fulcrum Publishing), p. 43.

52 Bonner, "The Competition for the Klondike Trade," p. 444.

53 "Portland is After It," *The Seattle Times*, September 28, 1897.

54 "Portland is After It."

55 Shipley, "The Impact of the Klondike Gold Rush on Seattle," p. 12.

56 E. Kimbark MacColl, *The Shaping of a City: Business and Politics in Portland, Oregon, 1885-1915* (Portland, Oregon: The Georgian Press Company, 1976), pp. 215-217. See also E. Kimbark MacColl, *Merchants, Money and Power: The Portland Establishment*, 1843-1913 (Portland, Oregon: The Georgian Press, 1988), pp. 335-336.

57 Jonas A. Jonasson, "Portland and the Alaska Trade," *The Pacific Northwest Quarterly 30* (April 1939), p. 144. Se also Earl Pomeroy, *The Pacific Slope: A History of California, Oregon, Washington, Idaho, Utah, and Nevada* (New York: Alfred A. Knopf, 1965), pp. 138-139.

58 Murray Morgan, *Puget's Sound: A Narrative of Early Tacoma and the Southern Sound* (Seattle: University of Washington Press, 1979), p. 299.

59 "No Craze Here," *The Tacoma Daily News*, p. 2.

60 "Purchase in Tacoma," *The Tacoma Daily News*, July 28, 1897, n.p., vertical file, Alaska Gold Rush, Tacoma Public Library.

61 "A Perturbed Spirit," *The Tacoma Daily News*, July 29, 1897, p. 2.

62 Quoted in "The Seattle Spirit," *The Tacoma Daily News*, July 28, 1897.

63 "Tacomans Should Advertise," August, 1897 [title of article, newspaper, date, and page number illegible], vertical file, Alaska Gold Rush, Tacoma Public Library.

64 "Ho! For Alaska," n.d., n.p., vertical file, Alaska Gold Rush, Tacoma Public Library.

65 Morgan, *Puget's Sound: A Narrative of Early Tacoma and the Southern Sound*, pp. 299-300.

66 "Tacoma Has Given Up," *The Seattle Daily Times*, September 28, 1897, p. 3.

67 *Tacoma: The Gateway to the Klondike*, 1897, Washington State Historical Society, Tacoma.

68 Tacoma Souvenir, n.d., n.p., Washington State Historical Society, Tacoma.

69 Klondike Advertisement, Erastus Brainerd Scrapbooks, University of Washington, A1698.

70 "Tacoma: The Gateway to the Klondike," *The Tacoma Daily News*, December 14, 1897, p. 1.

71 Morgan, *Puget's Sound: A Narrative of Early Tacoma and the Southern Sound*, p. 301.

72 Personal Communication, Alfred Runte, May 23, 1998.

73 Juneau: The Great Outfitting Point, Erastus Brainerd Scrapbooks, University of Washington, A1698; Richard P. Emanual, "The Golden Gamble." *Alaska Geographic 24* (1997), p. 23.

74 Morse, "The Nature of Gold: An Environmental History of the Alaska/Yukon Gold Rush," p. 362.

75 "Vigorous Action," *The Morning Leader*, August 4, 1897, p. 1.

76 "Merchants Lose," *The Morning Leader*, July 23, 1897, p. 1.

77 "For Klondike and Northern Goldfields!," *The Morning Leader*, August 4, 1897, p. 4.

78 E.J. White, *Directory, Port Townsend and Hadlock* (Seattle: Metropolitan Printing & Binding Company, 1897), n.p., The Richard F. McCurdy Historical Research Library, Jefferson County Historical Society Museum, Port Townsend.

79 Alexander Norbert MacDonald, "Seattle's Economic Development, 1880-1910," Ph.D. Dissertation, University of Washington, 1959, p. 135.

80 See, for example, "Whatcom Placer Mines Rival the Klondike," *Bellingham Bay Reveille*, November 19, 1897, p. 9, and "C.I. Roth in Klondike," *Bellingham Bay Reveille*, December 3, 1897, p. 7.

81 See, for example, *Vancouver News-Advertiser*, September 8, 1897, p. 5; Nichols, "Advertising and the Klondike," p. 24.

82 Alexander Norbert MacDonald, "Seattle, Vancouver, and the Klondike," *The Canadian Historical Review* (September 1968), p. 236.

83 Tappan Adney, *The Klondike Stampede* (New York: Harper & Brothers, 1900), pp. 12-13.

84 Nichols, "Advertising and the Klondike," pp. 24-25.

85 MacDonald, "Seattle, Vancouver, and the Klondike," pp. 241-243.

86 MacDonald, "Seattle, Vancouver, and the Klondike," p. 238. See also Report of the Vancouver Board of Trade, 1896-1897, City of Vancouver Archives, p. 32.

87 MacDonald, "Seattle, Vancouver, and the Klondike," pp. 245-246.

88 "The Clondyke Excitement," *Vancouver News-Advertiser*, July 28, 1897, p. 5.

89 Dianne Newell, "The Importance of Information and Misinformation in the Making of the Klondike Gold Rush," *Journal of Canadian Studies 21* (Winter 1986-1987), p. 103.

90 Pierre Berton, *Klondike: The Last Great Gold Rush, 1896-1899*, revised edition (Toronto, Ontario: McClelland & Stewart, Inc. 1997), p. xiii-xviii.

91 *The Illustrated London News*, August 14, 1897, p. 2, British Library, London.

92 Terrence Cole, "Klondike Visions: Dreams of a Promised Land," p. 92.

93 See, for example, Erastus Brainerd's circular quoted in Victoria Hartwell Livingston, "Erastus Brainerd: The Bankruptcy of Brilliance," p. 30.

94 Joseph LaDue, *Klondyke Facts: Being a Complete Guide Book to the Great Gold Regions of the Yukon and Klondyke in the North West Territories* (Montreal: John Lovell and Son, c.1897), p. 21; "All Canadian Route Worthless," *The Seattle Post-Intelligencer*, March 16, 1898, p. 18.

95 See, for example, *Vancouver News-Advertiser*, July 28, 1897, p. 4.

96 MacDonald, "Seattle, Vancouver, and the Klondike," p. 245; Personal Communication with Terrence Cole, March 1, 1998. See also Paula Mitchell Marks, *Precious Dust: The American Gold Rush Era, 1848-1900* (New York: William Morrow Company, 1994), p. 125.

97 Charlene L. Porsild, "Culture, Class and Community: New Perspectives on the Klondike Gold Rush, 1896-1905," Ph.D. dissertation, Carleton University, Canada, 1994, pp. 48-52.

98 Morse, "The Nature of Gold: An Environmental History of the Alaska/Yukon Gold Rush," p. 328.

99 "Seattle's Enemies Busy," *The Seattle Daily Times*, September 24, 1897, p. 5.

100 *The Trade Register*, August 21, 1897, p. 22; *The Trade Register*, September 18, 1897, p. 24.

101 *The Trade Register*, August 21, 1897, p. 22.

Chapter Three

1 "The Seattle of Today," *The Seattle Daily Times* [date illegible], Klondike Gold Rush National Historical Park Library, Seattle.

2 Flo Whyard, editor, Martha Louise Black, *My Ninety Years* (Anchorage: Alaska Northwest Publishing Company, c. 1976), p. 21.

3 Robert B. Medill, *Klondike Diary: True Account of the Klondike Rush of 1897–1898* (Portland, Oregon: Beattie and Company, 1949), p. 3.

4 Neil Clifford Kimmons, "The Historical Development of Seattle as a Metropolitan Area," M.A. Thesis, University of Washington, 1942, p. 37.

5 "The Clearing House," *The Seattle Daily Times*, December 22, 1900, p. 13. See also Polk's Seattle City Directory, 1898, pp. 33-34.

6 "Seattle Business Men Continue Their Cheering Reports of the Improved Condition of Trade," *The Seattle Daily Times*, August 1898 [complete date illegible], Museum of History and Industry, Seattle.

7 Dorothy O. Johansen and Charles M. Gates, *Empire of the Columbia: A History of the Pacific Northwest*, second edition (New York: Harper & Row, 1967), pp. 370-371.

8 Melanie Mayer, *Klondike Women: True Tales of the 1897-1898 Gold Rush* (Ohio: Swallow Press, 1989).

9 "Answers to Queries," *The Seattle Post-Intelligencer*, October 13, 1897, p. 6.

10 Seattle Woolen Mill, Advertisement, Seattle Polk Directory, July 20, 1897, p. 5. Kathryn Taylor Morse, however, reported that Seattle Woolen Manufacturing had to dispatch a buyer to the East in 1897. See "The Nature of Gold: An Environmental History of the Alaska/Yukon Gold Rush," Ph.D. Dissertation, University of Washington, 1997, pp. 368-369.

11 "Answers to Queries," p. 6.

12 "Seattle's Trade Growth," *The Trade Register*, October 1, 1898, p. 24.

13 Morse, "The Nature of Gold: An Environmental History of the Alaska/Yukon Gold Rush," p. 369. See also Charles M. Gates, "Human Interest Notes on Seattle and the Alaskan Gold Rush," *The Pacific Northwest Quarterly* (April 1943), p. 209.

14 Morse, "The Nature of Gold: An Environmental History of the Alaska/Yukon Gold Rush," p. 368.

15 "Seattle Merits the Outfitting Trade," *The Seattle Daily Times*, November 13, 1897, p. 11.

16 Want Ads, *The Seattle Post-Intelligencer*, February 15, 1898.

17 Want Ads, *The Seattle Daily Times*, August 6, 1897, p. 6.

18 See, for example, Want Ads, *The Seattle Daily Times*, March 18, 1898.

19 Gates, "Human Interest Notes on Seattle and the Alaskan Gold Rush," p. 209.

20 "Condition of the Market," *The Trade Register*, April 23, 1898, p. 21.

21 Kathryn Taylor Morse, "The Nature of Gold: An Environmental History of the Alaska/Yukon Gold Rush," pp. 363 and 374.

22 Kathryn Taylor Morse, "The Nature of Gold: An Environmental History of the Alaska/Yukon Gold Rush," pp. 371-372; Richard Ralph Still, "Historical and Competitive Aspects of Grocery Wholesaling in Seattle, Washington," Ph.D. Dissertation, University of Washington, 1953, p. 35.

23 Description, "Cooper-Levy Family Papers," Manuscripts and Archives, University of Washington, n.d.

24 Description, "Schwabacher Brothers and Company," Manuscripts and Archives, University of Washington, n.d.

25 "What Merchants Say," *The Seattle Daily Times*, July 31, 1897, n.p., Museum of History and Industry. See also advertisements throughout The Seattle Daily Times, 1897-1898.

26 Richard P. Emanuel, "The Golden Gamble," *Alaska Geographic 24* (1997), p. 83.

27 Robert Spector and Patrick D. McCarthy, *The Nordstrom Way: The Inside Story of America's #1 Service Company* (New York: John Wiley & Sons, Inc., c. 1995), pp. 37-50; John W. Nordstrom, *The Immigrant in 1887* (Seattle: F. McCaffrey, Dogwood Press, 1950), pp. 44-50.

28 Alexander Norbert MacDonald, "Seattle's Economic Development, 1880-1910," Ph.D. Dissertation, University of Washington, 1959, pp. 89-101.

29 "Railroad Tonnage and Construction," *The Seattle Daily Times*, December 22, 1900, p. 16.

30 MacDonald, "Seattle's Economic Development, 1880-1910," pp. 129-132.

31 Clarence B. Bagley, *History of Seattle From the Earliest Settlement to the Present Time, vol. 2* (Chicago: S.J. Clarke Publishing Company, 1916), p. 534.

32 "Marvelous Increase of Business in Coastwise and Foreign Shipping," *The Seattle Daily Times*, December 1898 [precise date unknown], Museum of History and Industry, n.p.

33 "Our Commercial Supremacy," *The Seattle Daily Times*, December 18, 1897, p. 24.

34 "The Alaska Steamship Co.," *The Seattle Daily Times*, December 18, 1897, n.p., Museum of History and Industry.

35 *My Ninety Years*, p. 21.

36 Bagley, *History of Seattle From the Earliest Settlement to the Present Time, vol. 2*, p. 534.

37 Bagley, *History of Seattle From the Earliest Settlement to the Present Time, vol. 2*, p. 538.

38 Bagley, *History of Seattle From the Earliest Settlement to the Present Time, vol. 2*, p. 535.

39 MacDonald, "Seattle's Economic Development, 1880-1910," pp. 194-195.

40 Bagley, *History of Seattle From the Earliest Settlement to the Present Time, vol. 2*, p. 535.

41 "Boats for the Yukon," *The Seattle Daily Times*, August 5, 1897, p. 2. See also C.T. Conover, "Yukon Gold Rush Speeded Shipbuilding in Seattle," *The Seattle Times*, May 11, 1960, n.p.

42 Bagley, *History of Seattle From the Earliest Settlement to the Present Time, vol. 2*, pp. 536-537.

43 Tappan Adney, "The Sledge Dogs of the North," *Outing 38* (April 1901), p. 130.

44 "Dogs in Alaska," *The Seattle Daily Times*, July 31, 1897, n.p., Museum of History and Industry.

45 Adney, "The Sledge Dogs of the North," pp. 130 and 137.

46 "At the Yukon Dog Yard," *The Seattle Daily Times*, November 11, 1897, p. 8.

47 Adney, "The Sledge Dogs of the North," pp. 134 and 137.

48 "At the Yukon Dog Yard," p. 8.

49 "At the Yukon Dog Yard," p. 8. See also "Bureau of Information Doing a Successful Business in Advertising Seattle, *The Seattle Daily Times*, January 26, 1898, p. 5.

50 Adney, "The Sledge Dogs of the North," p. 131.

51 "At the Yukon Dog Yard," p. 8.

52 "Horse Mart Established," *The Seattle Daily Times*, July 23, 1897, p. 8; "Equine Market is Empty," *The Seattle Daily Times*, October 1, 1897, p. 5. See also Tappan Adney, *The Klondike Stampede* (New York: Harper & Brothers, 1900), p. 18, for a discussion of the poor condition of many of the horses shipped to the Yukon.

53 "Dogs or Goats, Which?," *The Seattle Daily Times*, n.d., n.p., Museum of History and Industry.

54 Want Ads, "For Sale – Large Goats," *The Seattle Daily Times*, February 13, 1898, p. 18.

55 Black, *My Ninety Years*, p. 21.

56 Mark R. Shipley, "The Impact of the Klondike Gold Rush on Seattle," Klondike Gold Rush National Historical Park Library, Seattle, n.p.

57 Spelger & Hurlbut, Advertisement, Seattle Polk Directory, July 6, 1897; Terrence Cole, editor, "Wheels on Ice: Bicycling in Alaska, 1898-1908," book insert, *The Alaska Journal 15* (Winter 1985), p. 6.

58 Terrence Cole, editor, "Wheels on Ice: Bicycling in Alaska, 1898-1908," pp. 6-7.

59 "Seattle 'A Hot Town,'" *The Seattle Daily Times*, October 7, 1897, p. 5.

60 "The Seattle of Today," n.p.

61 National Register of Historic Places Inventory – Nomination Form, First Avenue Groups, 1979, p. 4.

62 Sharon A. Boswell and Lorraine McConaghy, *Raise Hell and Sell Newspapers: Alden J. Blethen and The Seattle Times* (Pullman: Washington State University Press, 1996), p. 110.

63 Walt Crowley, *National Trust Guide Seattle: America's Guide for Architecture and History Travelers* (New York: John Wiley & Sons, Inc., 1998.

64 Sanborn Maps, 1893. See also Craig Holstine, Multiple Property Documentation Form, Single Room Occupancy Hotels in the Central Business District of Spokane, WA, 1900-1910, 1993 and Frances Amelia Sheridan, "Apartment House Development on Seattle's Queen Ann Hill Prior to World War II," Master's Thesis, University of Washington, 1994.

65 "Last Night Was Lively," *The Seattle Daily Times*, August 6, 1897, n.p., Museum of History and Industry.

66 "Last Night Was Lively," n.p.; "Seattle 'A Hot Town,'" p. 5.

67 "Police Protection," *The Seattle Daily Times*, September 1, 1897, n.p., Museum of History and Industry.

68 "A Seige of Petty Larceny," *The Seattle Daily Times*, November 6, 1897, n.p., Museum of History and Industry.

69 "Last Night Was Lively," n.p.

70 "Seattle 'A Hot Town,'" p. 5. See also Boswell and McConaghy, *Raise Hell and Sell Newspapers: Alden J. Blethen and The Seattle Times*, p. 110.

71 Nard Jones, *Seattle* (Garden City, New York: Doubleday & Company Inc., 1972), p. 151.

72 "Last Night Was Lively," n.p.

73 "Last Night Was Lively," p. 5.

74 "Seattle Has Its Fiends," *The Seattle Daily Times*, February 3, 1897, n.p., Museum of History and Industry; "Ran Away From the Mission," *The Seattle Daily Times*, September 6, 1897, n.p., Museum of History and Industry.

75 "He is a Human Devil," *The Seattle Daily Times*, October 7, 1897, n.p., Museum of History and Industry.

76 Murray Morgan, *Skid Road: An Informal Portrait of Seattle* (New York: Viking Press, 1960), pp. 59-61; Boswell and McConaghy, *Raise Hell and Sell Newspapers: Alden J. Blethen and The Seattle Times,* p. 110.

77 Boswell and McConaghy, *Raise Hell and Sell Newspapers: Alden J. Blethen and The Seattle Times*, p. 112.

78 "Gambling is Closed," *The Seattle Daily Times*, February 28, 1902, n.p., Museum of History and Industry.

79 Boswell and McConaghy, *Raise Hell and Sell Newspapers: Alden J. Blethen and The Seattle Times*, p. 112; "Gambling is Closed," n.p.

80 Ray Allen Billington, *Westward Expansion: A History of the American Frontier, fifth edition* (New York: MacMillian Publishing Company, Inc., 1982), p. 402.

81 MacDonald, "Seattle's Economic Development, 1880-1910," p. 145.

82 MacDonald, "Seattle's Economic Development, 1880-1910," p. 145.

83 MacDonald, "Seattle's Economic Development, 1880-1910," pp. 320-321.

84 MacDonald, "Seattle's Economic Development, 1880-1910," pp. 321-322.

85 MacDonald, "Seattle's Economic Development, 1880-1910," p. 67.

86 Alexander Norbert MacDonald, "Seattle, Vancouver, and the Klondike" *Canadian Historical Review 49* (1968), p. 246.

87 MacDonald, "Seattle's Economic Development, 1880-1910," pp. 163 and 327.

88 "Klondike Excitement Fizzling Out," *The New York Times*, May 1, 1898, p. 10.

89 J. Kingston Pierce, "Words of Gold: Reporters Bring the World News of the Klondike Stampede," 12 Columbia (Spring 1988), p. 11.

90 MacDonald, "Seattle's Economic Development, 1880-1910," p. 143.

91 Terrence Cole, "A History of the Nome Gold Rush: The Poor Man's Paradise," Ph.D. Dissertation, University of Washington, 1983, p. 116.

92 Terrence Cole, Personal Communication, September 22, 1998.

93 MacDonald, "Seattle's Economic Development, 1880-1910," p. 144.

94 Schwantes, *The Pacific Northwest: An Interpretive History*, pp. 306-309.

95 MacDonald, "Seattle's Economic Development, 1880-1910," p. 314.

96 Bagley, *History of Seattle From the Earliest Settlement to the Present Time*, vol. 2, pp. 526-527.

97 "The Seattle Exposition of 1909," *The Western Architect 14* (July 1909), pp. 3-6.

98 "What It All Means," *Collier's 43* (September 18, 1909), pp. 14-15.; "The Seattle Exposition of 1909," p. 6.

99 Schwantes, *The Pacific Northwest: An Interpretive History*, pp. 308-309.

100 Paul Dorpat, "Now & Then: Central Area Tour," *Pacific Magazine*, June 14, 1998, p. 3.

101 Clarence B. Bagley, *A History of Seattle From the Earliest Settlement to the Present, vol. 2*, p. 527.

102 MacDonald, "Seattle's Economic Development, 1880-1910," p. 337.

103 Rickerson, Lecture on the Alaska-Yukon-Pacific Exposition, Museum of History and Industry, March 10, 1998.

Chapter Four

1 Alexander Norbert MacDonald, "Seattle's Economic Development, 1880-1910," Ph.D. Dissertation, University of Washington, 1959, p. 318.

2 Kathryn Taylor Morse, "The Nature of Gold: An Environmental History of the Alaska/Yukon Gold Rush," Ph.D. Dissertation, University of Washington, 1997, pp. 378-379.

3 Walt Crowley, *National Trust Guide, Seattle: America's Guide for Architecture and History Travelers* (New York: John Wiley & Sons, Inc., 1998), pp. 49-51.

4 Myra L. Phelps, *Public Works in Seattle: A Narrative History, The Engineering Department, 1875-1975* (Seattle: Kingsport Press, 1978), pp. 18-19; 99-101.

5 Phelps, *Public Works in Seattle: A Narrative History, The Engineering Department, 1875-1975*, pp. 18-19; 99-101.

6 "New Streets and Sewers: 1898 Has Been a Record Breaker," *The Seattle Daily Times*, n.d., n.p., Museum of History and Industry.

7 Crowley, *National Trust Guide, Seattle*, pp. 91-92; Myra L. Phelps, Public Works in Seattle: A Narrative History, The Engineering Department, 1875-1975, p. 162-164; Janice L. Reiff, "Urbanization and the Social Structure: Seattle, Washington, 1852-1910," Ph.D. Dissertation, University of Washington, 1981, p. 66.

8 Daniel L. Pratt, "Seattle, The Queen City," *The Pacific Monthly 14* (August 1905), p. 122.

9 Warren W. Wing, *To Seattle by Trolley: The Story of the Seattle-Everett Interurban and the "Trolley That Went to Sea,"* (Edmonds, WA: Pacific Fast Mail, 1988), pp. 13-21.

10 Roger Sale, *Seattle, Past to Present* (Seattle: University of Washington Press, 1976), p. 82.

11 Murray Morgan, *Skid Road: An Informal Portrait of Seattle* (New York: Viking Press, 1960), p. 168.

12 Clarence B. Bagley, *History of Seattle From the Earliest Settlement to the Present Time, vol. 2* (S.J. Clarke Publishing Company, 1916), p. 354.

13 R.H. Thompson, *That Man Thompson* (Seattle: University of Washington Press, 1950), pp. 4-5.

14 Sale, *Seattle, Past to Present*, pp. 68-70; Bagley, *History of Seattle from the Earliest Settlement to the Present Time*, pp. 359-361.

15 V.V. Tarbill, "Mountain-Moving in Seattle," *Harvard Business Review* (July 1930), pp. 482-489; Sale, *Seattle, Past to Present*, pp. 75-76.

16 Bagley, *History of Seattle From the Earliest Settlement to the Present*, pp. 361-362.

17 Personal Communication with Robert Weaver, May 8, 1998.

18 Morgan, *Skid Road: An Informal Portrait of Seattle*, p. 168.

19 Sale, *Seattle, Past to Present*, p. 70.

20 Bagley, *History of Seattle From the Earliest Settlement to the Present Time, vol. 2.*, pp. 265-272.

21 Bagley, *History of Seattle From the Earliest Settlement to the Present Time, vol. 2.*, pp. 265-272.

22 Sale, *Seattle, Past to Present*, p. 72.

23 Padraic Burke, *A History of the Port of Seattle* (Port of Seattle, 1976), pp. 32-33.

24 Burke, *A History of the Port of Seattle*, pp. 33-34; Victoria Hartwell Livingston, "Erastus Brainerd: The Bankruptcy of Brilliance," Master's Thesis, University of Washington, 1967, pp. 40-45.

25 Bagley, *History of Seattle From the Earliest Settlement to the Present Time, vol 2.*, p. 363.

26 Morgan, *Skid Road: An Informal Portrait of Seattle*, p. 167.

1 Daniel L. Pratt, "Seattle, The Queen City," *The Pacific Monthly 14* (August 1905), p. 121.

2 Edmond Meany, *History of the State of Washington* (New York: MacMillan Company, 1910), p. 294.

3 Welford Beaton, *The City That Made Itself* (Seattle: Terminal Publishing Company, 1914), p. 11.

4 Seattle Chamber of Commerce, *Seattle and Western Washington: A Statement of Resources*, 1909, n.p., Special Collections Division, University of Washington.

5 Clarence B. Bagley, *History of Seattle From the Earliest Settlement to the Present Time*, (S.J. Clarke Publishing Company, 1916), pp. 530-534.

6 Jeannette Paddock Nichols, "Advertising and the Klondike," *Western Historical Quarterly 13* (January 1922), p. 26.

7 Irving Sayford, "The Klondike Put Seattle on the Map," *Travel* (March 1939), pp. 24-27; 48.

8 Archie Binns, *Northwest Gateway: The Story of the Port of Seattle* (Portland, Oregon: Binfords & Mort, 1941), pp. 271 and 273.

9 D.E. Griffith, "When Seattle Went Mad," July 20, 1947, pp. 1-7.

10 Murray Morgan, *Skid Road: An Informal Portrait of Seattle*, (New York: Viking Press, 1960), pp. 159-168.

11 Calvin F. Schmid, *Social Trends in Seattle* (Seattle: University of Washington Press, 1944), p. 2.

12 Alexander Norbert MacDonald, "Seattle's Economic Development, 1880-1910," Ph.D. Dissertation, University of Washington, 1959, p. 137.

13 "Seattle Business Men," *The Seattle Daily Times*, August 3, 1898, p. 9.

14 Alexander Norbert MacDonald, "Seattle, Vancouver, and the Klondike," *Canadian Historical Review 49* (1968), p. 246.

15 Earl Pomeroy, *The Pacific Slope: A History of California, Oregon, Washington, Idaho, Utah, and Nevada*, (New York: Alfred A. Knopf, 1965), pp. 146-148.

16 Dorothy O. Johansen and Charles M. Gates, *Empire of the Columbia: A History of the Pacific Northwest, second edition* (New York: Harper & Row, 1967), p. 371.

17 William C. Speidel, *Sons of the Profits* (Seattle: Nettle Creek Publishing Company, 1967), p. 307.

18 Nard Jones, *Seattle* (New York: Doubleday & Company, Inc., 1972), pp. 145-151.

19 Pierre Berton, *Klondike: The Last Great Gold Rush,* 1896-1899, p. 427.

20 David V. and Judith A. Clarridge, *A Ton of Gold: The Seattle Gold Rush, 1897-98* (Seattle, 1972), p. 24.

21 Roger Sale, *Seattle, Past to Present* (Seattle: University of Washington Press, 1976), pp. 52-53.

22 See, for example, Terrence Cole, "A History of the Nome Gold Rush: The Poor Man's Paradise," Ph.D. Dissertation, University of Washington, 1983.

23 Terrence Cole, Personal Communication, September 22, 1998.

24 Richard White, *It's Your Misfortune and None of My Own: A New History of the American West* (Norman: University of Oklahoma Press, 1991), p. 418.

25 Paula Mitchell Marks, *Precious Dust: The American Gold Rush Era, 1848-1900* (New York: William and Morrow Company, 1994), p. 125.

26 Kathryn Taylor Morse, "The Nature of Gold: An Environmental History of the Alaska/Yukon Gold Rush," Ph.D. Dissertation, University of Washington, 1997, pp. 327-330.

27 Ross Anderson, "Poor Man, Rich Man," *The Seattle Times Magazine,* July 13, 1997, p. 22.

28 "American Survey: The Heirs of the Klondike," *The Economist* (February 15-21, 1997), p. 25.

29 James Wallace and Jim Erickson, *Hard Drive: Bill Gates and the Making of the Microsoft Empire* (John Wiley & Sons, Inc., 1992), p. 125. See also the related discussion in the Introduction.

Chapter Six

1 Margaret Corley, Pioneer Square – Skid Road District National Register Nomination, Washington Office of Archaeology and Historic Preservation, Olympia, 1969; Elizabeth Walton Potter, Pioneer Square Historic District National Register Nomination, Washington Office of Archaeology and Historic Preservation, Olympia, 1976; Katherine Hills Krafft, Pioneer Square – Skid Road Historic District (Boundary Increase) National Register Nomination, Washington Office of Archaeology and Historic Preservation, Olympia, 1987.

2 Elizabeth W. Potter, Pioneer Square Historic District National Register Nomination, 1976.

3 Walt Crowley, *National Trust Guide, Seattle: America's Guide for Architecture and History Travelers*. New York: John Wiley & Sons, Inc., 1998, p. 35.

4 Sally Woodbridge and Roger Montgomery, *A Guide to Architecture in Washington*, Seattle: University of Washington Press, 1980, p.110.

5 Crowley, *National Trust Guide Seattle*, 1998, p.35.

6 *Seattle City Directories, 1897-1909*; Crowley, *National Trust Guide, Seattle*, p. 112.

7 City Directories, 1897-1909. "Wreckers Fell 1890 Mansion," *Seattle Post Intelligencer*, January 11, 1966, p.3.

8 Office of Urban Conservation, First Avenue Groups National Register Nomination, Washington Office of Archaeology and Historic Preservation, Olympia, 1980.

9 Office of Urban Conservation, First Avenue Groups National Register Nomination, 1980, p. 4; Paul Dorpat, *Seattle Now & Then, vol. 3*, (Seattle: Self Published, 1989), p.82.

10 *Seattle City Directories*, 1903-1912.

11 Nancy Susman, Holyoke Building National Register Nomination, Washington Office of Archaeology and Historic Preservation, Olympia, 1976, p. 2.

12 *Seattle City Directories, 1894-1900*, Northwest Fixture Co. Advertisement for Mining Equipment, *Seattle Post Intelligencer*, June 7, 1897, p.4.

13 Crowley, *National Trust Guide, Seattle*. p.46; Jeffery Karl Oschsner, Shaping

Seattle Architecture: A Historical Guide to the Architects. Seattle: University of Washington Press, 1994, p. 348.

14 Margaret Corley, Colman Building National Register Nomination, Washington Office of Archaeology and Historic Preservation, Olympia, 1969; Washington Office of Archaeology and Historic Preservation, Washington State Department of Community Trade and Economic Development, Historic Places in Washington: National Historic Landmarks, National Register of Historic Places, and Washington Heritage Register. Washington Office of Archaeology and Historic Preservation, Olympia, 1997, p.27; Dorpat, Seattle Now & Then, p. 79.

15 *Seattle City Directory, 1908*, p.149 and 1909, p.147.

16 Jane Lotter, "The Life and Hard Times of the Moore Theatre." *The Weekly.* April 29-May 5 1981. pp. 19

17 Margaret Corley, Moore Theatre and Hotel Building National Register Nomination, Washington Office of Archaeology and Historic Preservation, Olympia, 1973.

18 Margaret Corley, German Club National Register Nomination, Washington Office of Archaeology and Historic Preservation, Olympia, 1969.

19 *Seattle City Directories 1905-1909*; Sanborn Fire Insurance Maps 1905 and 1916.

20 *Seattle City Directories, 1892-1915.*

21 Roberta, Deering. Designation/Staff Recommendation to the Board – U.S. Assay Office, Seattle Office of Urban Conservation, 1983.

22 Roberta Deering, Landmark Nomination Form, U.S. Assay Office, Seattle Office of Urban Conservation, 1983.

23 Roberta Deering, Landmark Nomination Form, U.S. Assay Office, 1983; Margaret Corley, German Club National Register Nomination.

24 Office of Urban Conservation, Landmark Nomination Form, Colman Building. Seattle Office of Urban Conservation, n.d.

25 Margaret Corley, Colman Building National Register Nomination, Washington Office of Archaeology and Historic Preservation, 1969.

26 Office of Urban Conservation, Landmark Nomination Form, Colman

Building, n.d.; Corley, Colman Building National Register Nomination, 1969; Ochsner, Shaping Seattle Architecture, p. 348; Crowley, National Trust Guide, Seattle, p. 46-47.

27 Office of Urban Conservation, Landmark Nomination Form-Colman Building, n.d.

28 Earl Layman, Landmarks Preservation Board, Seattle Historic Building Data Sheet, Seattle Office of Urban Conservation, July 8, 1975.

29 *Seattle City Directory*, Polk's Seattle Directory Co., Publishers, Seattle, 1908, p. 149 and 1909, p.147.

30 Office of Urban Conservation, First Avenue Groups National Register Nomination, Washington Office of Archaeology and Historic Preservation, 1980.

31 Office of Urban Conservation, First Avenue Groups National Register Nomination Form, 1980.

32 Office of Urban Conservation, First Avenue Groups National Register Nomination Form, 1980.

33 *Seattle City Directories, 1898-1914.*

34 *Seattle City Directory, 1897*; "Seattle Woolen Manufacturing Co. Advertisement," *Seattle Post Intelligencer*. July 20, 1897, p.5.

35 Nancy Susman, National Register Nomination-Holyoke Building, Washington Office of Archaeology and Historic Preservation, 1976; Crowley, National Trust Guide, 1998, p.75.

36 Office of Urban Conservation, First Avenue Groups National Register Nomination, 1980.

37 Advertisement for the Northwest Fixture Company. *Seattle Post Intelligencer*. June 7, 1897, p.4.

38 *Seattle City Directories, 1894-1902.*

39 Office of Urban Conservation, First Avenue Groups National Register Nomination, 1980.

40 *Seattle City Directories, 1903-1912.*

41 King County Assessor's Records, History Card for 1932 Second Avenue, Puget Sound Regional Branch of the Washington State Archives, Bellevue, 1938.

42 Lotter, "The Life and Hard Times of the Moore Theatre," p. 19.

43 Margaret Corley, Moore Theatre and Hotel National Register Nomination Form, Washington Office of Archaeology and Historic Preservation, 1973.

44 Corley, Moore Theatre and Hotel National Register Nomination Form, 1973.

45 Richard Emanuel, "Outfitting the Rush: 'Ho! For the Klondike!'" in *Alaska Geographic*. (24) 1997, p. 12.

46 James R. Little, "Squaw Kate," *Alaska Life*, March 1943, vol. 3, p.18.

47 *Seattle City Directories, 1897-1922*; "Klondike Discoverer Is Called by Death," *Seattle Times*, June 6, 1922, p.9

48 Esther Hall Mumford, *Seattle's Black Victorians, 1852-1901*. Seattle: Ananse Press, 1980, pp.14 and 93.

49 *Seattle City Directories, 1897-1909*; Paul Dorpat, "Now & Then" *Parade Magazine, The Seattle Times*, June 14, 1998.

50 Seattle City Directories, 1892-1915; Folke Nyberg and Victor Steinbrueck, Green Lake: An Inventory of Buildings and Urban Design Resources, Historic Seattle Preservation and Development Authority, 1975.

51 Pioneer Square Planning Committee, Draft 1998 Pioneer Square Neighborhood Plan, 1998, p. 3.

Index

Photo and Art Credits

Cover - *Harper's Weekly*, August 1897 - courtesy Terrence Cole

Back cover - Dog Team in front of Times Building, Second Ave and Cherry Street - Klondike Gold Rush National Historical Park, National Park Service

Page xi - early proposed Seattle City Seal - Museum of History and Industry, Seattle

Page xiv - Routes to the Klondike - Mark MacKay

Page 2 - Illustrated map of Seattle, 1856 - Calvin F. Schmid, *Social Trends in Seattle, Seattle*: University of Washington Press, 1944

Page 3 - Early photo of Seattle, ca. 1865 - Clarence B. Bagley, *History of Seattle from the Earliest Settlement to the Present Time* Chicago: S. J. Clarke Publishing Company, 1916

Page 8 - Seattle waterfront north of Main Street, ca. 1885-88 - Klondike Gold Rush National Historical Park, National Park Service

Page 9 - Seattle waterfront from Madison Street to Columbia Street, ca. 1887 - Klondike Gold Rush National Historical Park, National Park Service

Page 15 - To the Klondyke by Balloon - courtesy Terrence Cole

Page 16 left - *Leslie's Weekly*, August 1897 - courtesy Terrence Cole

Page 16 right - *Klondike Official Guide*, 1898 - courtesy Terrence Cole

Page 17 - *The Seattle Post-Intelligencer*, July 1897 - courtesy Terrence Cole

Page 20 top map - *The Seattle Post-Intelligencer*, October 1897

Page 20 bottom map - Water Routes to the Klondike - Mark MacKay

Page 23 - Bureau of Information ad - Erastus Brainerd Scrapbook, University of Washington

Page 24 - Erastus Brainerd in the Yukon, 1898 - courtesy Special Collections Division, University of Washington

Page 28 - Tacoma Citizens Klondike Committee Klondike Information Free ad - Erastus Brainerd Scrapbook, University of Washington

Page 36 - For the Yukon, via Vancouver - courtesy Terrence Cole

Page 37 - Klondyke Gold Fields are in Canada - courtesy Terrence Cole

Page 39 - Angel of Death - *Punch* magazine, August 28, 1897 - courtesy Terrence Cole

Page 47 - Cooper and Levy outfitters storefront and Southern Hotel at First Avenue and Yesler, ca. 1897 - Klondike Gold Rush National Historical Park, National Park Service

Page 48 - Crater Lake, Chilkoot Trail ca. 1898 - Klondike Gold Rush National Historical Park, National Park Service

Page 105 - Globe Building, ca. 1900 - courtesy Special Collections Division, University of Washington

Page 106 - Globe Building 2001 - Ben Nechanicky

Page 107 - postcard of Moore Theatre and Hotel, ca. 1909 - courtesy Office of Urban Conservation, Seattle

Page 108 - Moore Theatre and Hotel, 2001 - Ben Nechanicky

Page 109 - Carmack House, 1937 - courtesy Washington State Archives, Puget Sound Regional Branch

Page 110 - Carmack House, 2001 - Ben Nechanicky

Page 111 - Woodson Apartments, ca. 1937 - courtesy Washington State Archives, Puget Sound Regional Branch

Page 112 - Woodson (Cascade View) Apartments, 2001 - Ben Nechanicky

Page 113 - William Wood House, ca.1937 - courtesy Washington State Archives, Puget Sound Regional Branch

Page 114 - William Wood House, 1998 - Historic Research Associates

*Sources for newspaper advertisements used throughout this publication not otherwise credited included the following: *The Seattle Daily Times, The Seattle Post-Intelligencer, The Tacoma Daily News, The Morning Leader* (Port Townsend), and the *Vancouver News-Advertiser,* ca. 1897-1898.

Hard Drive to the Klondike

北美 GRE®

范文精讲

作者 · **Mark Alan Stewart, J.D.**

中文作者 · 修 锐　张雷东

世界知识 出版社

图书在版编目（CIP）数据

北美 GRE 范文精讲 ／（美）斯图尔特（Stewart, M. A. J. D.），
修锐，张雷东著．—北京：世界知识出版社，2004.4
书名原文：GRE CAT Answers to the Real Essay Questions
ISBN 7 – 5012 – 2211 – 8

Ⅰ.北... Ⅱ.①斯...②修...③张... Ⅲ.英语 – 写作 – 研究
生 – 入学考试 – 美国 – 自学参考资料 Ⅳ.H315

中国版本图书馆 CIP 数据核字（2004）第 034969 号
图字：01 – 2004 – 2528

Mark Alan Stewart, J. D.
GRE CAT Answers to the Real Essay Questions（Second Edition）
© 2003 by Arco, a division of Thomson Learning
First published by Arco, a division of Thomson Learning.
All Rights Reserved
Authorized Adaptation Edition by Thomson Learning and NOS and WAP.
No part of this book may be reproduced in any form without the express
written permission of Thomson Learning and NOS and WAP.

责任编辑 ／ 刘 砻 张雅坤
封面设计 ／ 孙 轶
责任出版 ／ 尧 阳
责任校对 ／ 陆 露

出版发行 ／ 世界知识 出版社
地址电话 ／ 北京市东城区干面胡同 51 号 （010）65265933
E-mail：gcgjlz@public.bta.net.cn
邮政编码 ／ 100010
经 销 ／ 新华书店
排 版 ／ 世界知识出版社电脑科
印 刷 ／ 北京市京科印刷有限公司
开本印张 ／ 787×1092 1/16 25¼印张 835 千字
版 次 ／ 2004 年 5 月第一版 2005 年 2 月第二次印刷
定 价 ／ 42.00 元

新东方丛书策划委员会

总 策 划　包凡一

决策委员　包凡一　　胡　敏　　王　强
　　　　　徐小平　　周成刚

委　　员　（按姓氏笔画为序）

王文山　　王文成　　白　勇
江　博　　许　杨　　杜　伟
杜子华　　李传伟　　邱政政
汪海涛　　陈向东　　杨　继
周　雷　　俞敏洪　　钱永强
铁　岭　　徐小平　　蔡　箐

前　言

从 2002 年 10 月起，所有 GRE 考生参加 GRE 考试时，必须撰写两篇作文：

- 对一个是非问题（Issue）提出你自己的见解（45 分钟）
- 分析一个逻辑问题（Argument）（30 分钟）

机考系统会从官方的题库中随机抽取题目作为你的 GRE 写作考题。

好消息：

GRE 考题的制定方——美国教育考试服务中心（ETS）已经预先透露了 GRE 写作考题的完全题库。这样，只要你愿意付出努力，就可以对每一道题都有所准备。

更好的消息：

本书囊括了超过 200 道的 GRE 官方作文题库高分样文！（你在第二至第五章中可以找到它们。）而且，本书的第一章还介绍了在作文考题上获得高分的所有技巧。

怎样在线升级 GRE 作文题库

不要忘记查看作者对本书的在线补充和修订。有时候，考试的制定方（ETS）会将其官方题库中的题目次序加以变更，同时也会在题库中添加新的题目。更新题库请访问下列网址：

www. west. net/ ~ stewart/ grewa

或者访问作者的 GRE 主页，在这里你可以找到使用指南和针对整个 GRE 考试每部分的小测验以及书评、链接，甚至更多内容：

www. west. net/ ~ stewart/ gre

> **怎样将我们的文章与官方题库匹配**
>
> 有些时候，考试服务中心会将其官方题库中的题目次序加以变更，也会在题库中添加新的题目，同时删除旧题目。第二至第五章对每篇文章进行了预测，相当于对当前的题目进行了描述，而这种描述会帮助你将两者进行匹配。如果你在进行匹配的时候需要更多的帮助，请你根据我们的相关关键词，在官方题库电子版文件中进行搜索。（为了醒目，我们已经将关键词加粗。）而且，如果你需要升级官方题库，请点击以下网址的"升级"页面：www. west. net/ ~ stewart/ awa

当你学习本书中提供的范文时，需要记住三点：

1. 我写这些文章时没有定时限制。而且，为了使它们成为你们更好的学习范本，我还对它们进行了润色。所以，如果你写出的文章不像我的文章那样丰富流畅，别担心。对于在 30 分钟内写出的东西，要采取现实的态度。

2. 我在每篇文章的第一段中都扼要复述了题目，不过你要记住，读你文章的人不会指望、也不想要你在文章中复述题目。所以你的开头一段要尽量简洁。

3. 这些范文旨在为你提供真实的、系统的、流行的写作思路，但是决不是用于供你逐字抄袭的。我要预先警告你：GRE 的阅卷者会时刻警惕抄袭现象。

本书作者

目　录

第三章 Issue 范文精选

第四章　Argument 范文精讲

29. 34. 35. 36. 38. 39. 40. 41. 43. 46. 47. 48. 49. 52. 54. 57. 58. 60. 62.
66. 68. 69. 72. 77. 86. 89. 90. 98~101. 110. 112. 118. 120. 121. 128. 130.
132. 134. 138. 222. 228. 242.

第五章　Argument 范文精选

第一章　GRE 写作应试指导

自 2002 年 10 月起,GRE 考试新添了写作题:Issue(是非问题分析)作文和 Argument(逻辑问题分析)作文。如果您准备参加 GRE 考试,这本书能给您提供写出高分作文的所有技巧。在本章您会学到:

- 怎样组织和写作 Issue 高分作文
- 怎样组织和写作 Argument 高分作文
- 作文考试的计算机界面是怎样的
- 考试专用文字处理软件有何特点
- GRE 作文是怎样打分和评估的
- 怎样充分利用你有限的时间备考

在后四章中,我们给出了 200 多篇范文,全部和 GRE 考试官方题库中的问题相符。我们建议您登录互联网,下载 GRE 考试题库。ETS(美国教育考试服务中心)官方网站的题库可以免费下载。或许您不需要获取官方题库就能从这本书中获得很大的收获,但是您如果手头上有官方题库,您从本书中得到的收获会更多。获取考试题库,请参照本书附带的指示说明,并登录其网站(www.west.net/~stewart/grewa)。

一、GRE 写作概要

1.考试内容

GRE 作文考题由两个不同的部分组成:

- 针对某一是非问题给出你的个人见解(45 分钟)。考生需要有广泛的知识面。

- 对某一论点做出分析(30 分钟)。你必须对特定的论点进行评述。

2.作文题库

在计算机考试系统的题库中,储存的 Issue 题目和 Argument 题目分别超过了 200 道。在你考试的过程中,系统会为你随机抽取两道 Issue 题目,你要从中选择一道作为你的 Issue 作文题。但是,Argument 题目是不可选择的;系统会为你随机抽取一道题目作为你的 Argument 考题。

3.考试时间

总共 75 分钟(45 分钟写 Issue 作文,30 分钟写 Argument 作文)。

4.考场规则

① 两个写作任务之间没有休息时间。

② 考试系统不允许你用超过 45 分钟的时间来完成 Issue 考题。同样,也不允许你用超过30

分钟的时间来完成 Argument 考题。

③ 考试时，一旦开始第二个写作任务，你将无法返回到第一个任务。（但是如果你的第一个任务完成得较早，可以马上开始第二个任务，这由你自己决定。）

④ 考试时提供草稿纸和铅笔（同考多项选择题一样）。

⑤ 写文章时，你既可以使用考试系统内置的文字处理软件，也可以以手写的方式交卷。

注意：如果你希望以手写的方式提交作文考卷，你在指定考试座位的时候就得将答卷提交方式提出。

5.考查要点

内容　考生通过列举合理的推论性和支持性例子来提出恰到好处的、具有说服力的相关见解和论点的能力。

组织　考生以结构清楚紧凑的行文提出观点的能力。

语言　考生的英语语言支配能力，通过考生的词汇量、措辞（词汇的选择）以及俗语的应用得以体现。

结构　考生对标准书面英语的熟练程度，包括语法、句法（句型结构）以及词汇的应用。

注意：拼写和标点不是 GRE 作文的评分依据，除非考生犯了过多类似的错误，以致无法有效地表达考生的观点。（GRE 考试内置的文字处理软件没有拼写检查功能和语法检查功能。）

（编者注：在考场上你只能靠自己去避免这类低级错误，虽然 GRE 不像 TOEFL 考试那样重视拼写和语法问题，但是 ETS 所有的 6 分范文每篇中类似的低级错误都不超过三个。）

6.评分系统

两位打分员根据上述考查要点为每篇文章分别打分，从 0 分至 6 分（0,1,2,3,4,5, 或 6）,6 分是最高分；每篇作文的分数按照考生在四个考查重点上所获得的分数平均计算成绩（四舍五入精确到 0.5 分）。

注意：在本章中，我们会给出更加详细的打分和评估标准。

二、*Issue* 写作详解

Issue 作文考查考生针对某一是非问题有效、有理地提出自己见解的能力。你的任务是分析该是非问题，周全地考虑每个不同的观点，并给出自己对原观点的见解。在为你的 Issue 作文题打分的时候，GRE 评分者关注的是你的下列四种能力：

- 有效地识别并处理原论点的复杂性和各观点间的牵连关系
- 有效地组织、发展并表达你自己的见解
- 有效地支持自己的观点（通过列举原因和例证）
- 有效地支配标准书面英语的各项要素（语法、句型以及词语的运用）

注意：在 Issue 部分，从来没有"正确的"答案。也就是说，重要的是你怎样表达并支持你的见解，而不是你的见解是什么。

1.*Issue* 作文特征

Issue 考题由两部分组成：简洁的提示（对你的任务的描述），后面紧接的是 1~2 个主题句（观点陈述或论点的引语）。每篇 Issue 的提示差不多都一样，基本上是下面的语句：

Present your perspective on the following issue; use relevant reasons and/or examples to support your viewpoint. 针对下面的是非问题提出你的个人见解；运用相关原因和/或例证支持你的观点。

　　Issue 题涉及的范围很广泛，需要考生掌握大量而全面的知识，大学生或大学毕业生会经常接触到这些题材。下面是三个考题例子，你可以在 GRE 官方 Issue 题库中找到类似的题目。（注意：这些只是模拟题，并非 GRE 题库中题目。）

"In order to achieve greatness in a particular field—whether it be in the arts, sciences, or politics—any individual must challenge tradition as well as the conventional wisdom of the day." "为了在特定的领域塑造辉煌——不论是在艺术、科学抑或政治领域——任何人都必须勇于挑战当前的传统和常理。"

"The objective of science is largely opposed to that of art; while science seeks to discover truths, art seeks to obscure them." "科学的目的在很大程度上与艺术的目的背道而驰，科学所追求的是发现真理，而艺术的目标则是使之隐讳。"

"The only way to ensure that our natural environment will be protected and preserved is through government penalties and other regulatory measures. No society can rely on the voluntary efforts of its individuals and private businesses to achieve these objectives." "使我们的自然环境得以保护并保存的惟一途径，就是通过政府的强制力和其他法规性的措施。没有任何一个社会可以依赖个人和私有企业自发的努力来实现这一目标。"

2. Issue 作文要则

① **在你开始限时写作 Issue 作文前，考试系统会显示满满一屏幕的关于此项任务的详细说明。** 这些说明会指出上面讲过的四个综合评分标准，下面就是该说明的内容：

- 你的答题时间是 45 分钟。
- 选择你认为可以接受的那个题目进行写作。
- 题目会以对某一普遍问题的简单陈述这种形式出现。
- 你可以随心所欲地赞同、反对或者证明原论点。
- 你应该通过你的经历、观察和阅读等渠道提出原因和/或例证，支持你自己的观点。
- 在你开始写之前，最好花几分钟思考一下如何组织你的文章。
- 你应该预留出富裕的时间，检查自己写过的文章，做出必要的修改。

② **官方题库中的题目有很多共同的主题**。尽管每道官方 Issue 作文考题都有独特性，但是它们的基本主题有很多共同的背景。下面列出的主题能涵盖 Issue 题库中大部分题目（排列不分先后顺序）：

- 一致性和传统惯例 VS 个性和革新
- 实用性和用途 VS 创造性和个人致富
- 文化特性（习俗、礼节以及思想观念）的重要性
- 个人成功并取得进步的关键因素
- 社会进步的关键因素，以及我们怎样对其定义
- 我们如何获取知识，或者如何让我们的知识更加丰富，以及更加广泛的知识是怎样组成的

- 常规教育的目标和方法是怎样的
- 研究历史的价值何在
- 知识对社会和个人的冲击
- 社会上公认的英雄或伟大领袖的分类
- 艺术和科学的功用和分类(分别对于个人和社会来说)
- 在保证社会福利方面,政府、商界以及个人的恰当角色

　　总体来讲,Issue 作文题所探讨的范围涉及所有的知识领域——包括社会学、人类学、历史、教育、法律和政府、政治科学、经济学、哲学、生理和行为科学、美术以及表演艺术等等。

③ **对于任何 Issue 写作题目来讲,不存在"正确答案"一说。**在官方题库中,你既不会遇到无法反驳的题目,也不会找到完全错误的题目。题目编纂者如此出题的目的在于检验你赞成或反对某一立场的辩论能力,检验你证明或"推诿"自己观点的能力。

④ **对于每篇写作文章来说,不存在所谓限定的或"正确的"长度。**本考试系统惟一在长度方面施加的实质性限制就是 45 分钟的考试时间。那么,GRE 作文评分人员偏爱简短的还是较长的 Issue 文章呢? 其实,这完全取决于文章本身的质量。一篇简洁明了并且中肯扼要的文章的得分要远比漫无目的的长篇大论更高。但是话说回来,结构清晰、有大量独到见解并且附带足够论据的长文章,肯定会比缺乏实质性内容、过于简单的文章得分高。

　　我在 GRE Issue 写作方面的经验就是,你写一篇 400 字左右的简洁文章,就可以得到 6 分。在后面几页你看到的 Issue 范文都符合 ETS 相关标准,得到了 6 分。它是有意写得这样简短的——只有 400 字左右——只是为了要说明你不必为了追求高分而长篇大论。

　　本书第二章和第三章的范文较长;字数大约维持在 500 ~ 750 之间,而且大多数分为 5 或 6 段。ETS 公布的惟一一篇 6 分 Issue 范文大约 700 字,分为 7 段。但是,ETS 也承认,或许没有这篇文章更有说服力的其他作文也得到了 6 分。因此,要想得最高分 6 分,你的文章不必像我的范文或 ETS 的范文那样词句丰富或言辞精练。(编者注:实战中最合适的字数在 400 ~ 500 字之间。)

3. Issue 写作流程

　　为了在 Issue 写作题中得高分,你必须展现出前面提到的那四种能力。为了确保你能在 45 分钟内充分表现出这四种被考查的能力,请遵循下列七步走的方法:

① **动脑思考,同时动笔记录(2 ~ 3 分钟)。**努力提出几个赞同和反对原论点的理由,以及几个分别支持 Issue 各个方面的例子。记录下来你想到的任何想法,即使它似乎不着边际、看似陈腐、毫无理由或者不足以令人信服。当你写作的时候,它会帮你想到如何将较弱的想法转变成为较强的观点。也就是说,第一步的时候,请不要自我审查!

② **选择立场,组织你的想法(1 ~ 2 分钟)。**将你第一步记录下来的理由和例子标注为"正面"或"反面"。组织你的想法,分为 3 或 4 个主要段落,然后决定它们被提出的逻辑顺序,并据此为你的提纲编号。

③ **写简洁的开头段(3 ~ 4 分钟)。**在第一段中,你应该完成下列所有任务:

- 证明你对这道是非分析题目中的暗示或其复杂性已经有所了解。
- 让判卷者明白你对这篇 Issue 有着明确的观点。
- 为你将在文章主体部分提出的观点做出相应的铺垫。

　　　只用两三句话就能完成上述三个任务。先不要急于详细地罗列你的理由,也不要列举具体的例子。在你的文章主体部分再写这些内容。

注意:除非你是通过手写格式提交作文,否则你可以考虑等到写完 Issue 作文的其他部分以后再写文章的开头段。为什么? 当你撰写 Issue 文章论证段的时候,如果你的立场有所改变(有时会发生类似的情况),你就不必重写开头段了。

④ **根据你的回答撰写文章的论证段落(20～25 分钟)**。撰写文章时尽量贴近你的提纲,但有时也要灵活掌握。尽量选择最容易阐述清楚、看起来最深刻或最有说服力的观点作为开头。然后,在第六步中,如果你决定将这个要点安排在其他一个或多个要点之后,一定要注意合理用词,重视表达效果,以便使文章更具逻辑性和连贯性。在第四步中,你的主要任务就是狂敲键盘,以便把更多的思路搬上考卷。尽量运用简短的语言来表达提纲中的各个要点,最好每个要点不要超过三四句话。而且,假如时间太短,不足以逐一表达提纲中每一个要点的时候,你不必过于担心。判卷者明白,对于绝大多数考生来说,45 分钟的时间限制使大多数人都无法做到面面俱到。

⑤ **写一段总结性质的结尾(3～4 分钟)**。除非你的文章带有明显的结尾,否则判卷者会认为你没有在规定时间内完成写作题目。因此,一定要记住留出一定的时间来总结全文。最好用两三句话对文章的主旨进行概括。如果你想到了一个很特别的、见解深刻的要点,那么把它放到文章的最后一句话将会非常之好。

⑥ **根据情况对文章进行修改或润色,以确保文章的连贯性和平衡性(8～10 分钟)**。尽量留出足够的时间修改你的文章。下面就是你应该在第六步中完成的一些工作:

- 确保你在文章中针对原论点提出了多种形式的观点。极力坚持某一立场是可以的,但是你也应该知晓其他观点的优缺点。如果你的文章写得过于片面,你在这时就需要添加一段以弥补这个缺点。

- 重新整理你的各个段落,使文章在各个方面都更具逻辑性,更有说服力。确保每段的第一句话都能清楚明了地向判卷者传达本段的主要内容和思路。

- 检查你的各个段落,看看它们在长度上是否平衡。如果长度不平衡,或许是某一环节的讨论过于冗长,或许是罗列了重复的例子,而在论述其他要点时或许忘记提供足够的论证(理由和/或例子)。这时,就需要做出适当的增减,对文章进行修饰,已达到表达上的平衡。

- 检查你的开头段和总结段,确保它们能够前后呼应,并与题目相照应。

⑦ **校对一遍,检查低级错误(3～4 分钟)**。对"丑陋"的句子进行再加工,使它们表达得更流畅。检查措辞、用法、语法以及拼写等方面的错误。谨记:你的文章不需要完璧无瑕也可以得到 6 分。GRE 作文判卷者不会因为文章中偶尔出现的蹩脚句子或极少量的标点、拼写、语法或词语用法的错误而降低你的分数。不必追求将每个句子都写得像海明威或斯坦贝克的文字,否则你会背上沉重的包袱。把剩下的时间都用来修改最明显的低级错误即可。(这部分的时间安排并不固定,可根据各人情况进行灵活调整。)

4.Issue 作文范文

现在我们来看一篇范文,是关于第 112 页提到的第三个 Issue 题目的。在这篇文章中,我在某些起过渡作用的词汇和短语下面标注了下划线,帮助你看清我是怎样组织我的观点的——即第一步的"正面"和"反面"例子和理由——这样,它们可以自然而然地从一个要点过渡到下一个。(在真正考试的时候,你是无法使用下划线、斜体字或其他标记的。)

在你阅读下面的文章时,请牢记:

- 我所罗列的要点没有一个是不可反驳的,因为是非论断问题并不是"白与黑"的问题。它只是一个观点。这正是 Issue 作文的本质所在。

- 我的这篇文章无论在风格上还是在语言上都相对来说比较简单,而且足够简洁(400字),可以在45分钟之内完成。
- 我完成这篇文章的时候没有时间方面的压力,因此如果你的习作没有经过太多的润色,也不用过于担心。

针对下述论点的范文:

"The only way to ensure that our natural environment will be protected and preserved is through government penalties and other regulatory measures. No society can rely on the voluntary efforts of its individuals and private businesses to achieve these objectives."

While nearly everyone would agree in principle that certain efforts to preserve the natural environment are in humankind's best interests, exclusive reliance on volunteerism would be naive and imprudent, especially considering the stakes involved. For this reason, and because serious environmental problems are generally large in scale, I agree that government participation is needed to ensure environmental preservation.

Experience tells us that individuals and private corporations tend to act in their own short-term economic and political interest, not on behalf of the environment or the public at large. For example, current technology makes possible the complete elimination of polluting emissions from automobiles.

Nevertheless, neither automobile manufacturers nor consumers are willing or able to voluntarily make the short-term sacrifices necessary to accomplish this goal. Only the government holds the regulatory and enforcement power to impose the necessary standards and to ensure that we achieve such goals.

Admittedly, government penalties do not guarantee compliance with environmental regulations. Businesses often attempt to avoid compliance by concealing their activities, lobbying legislators to modify regulations, or moving operations to jurisdictions that allow their environmentally harmful activities. Others calculate the cost of polluting, in terms of punishment, then budget in advance for anticipated penalties and openly violate the law. However, this behavior only serves to underscore the need for government intervention, because left unfettered this type of behavior would only exacerbate environmental problems.

One must admit as well that government regulation, environmental or otherwise, is fraught with bureaucratic and enforcement problems. Regulatory systems inherently call for legislative committees, investigations, and enforcement agencies, all of which add to the tax burden on the citizens whom these regulations are designed to protect. Also, delays typically associated with bureaucratic regulation can thwart the purpose of the regulations, because environmental problems can quickly become grave indeed. However, given that the only alternative is to rely on volunteerism, government regulation seems necessary.

Finally, environmental issues inherently involve public health and are far too pandemic in nature for individuals to solve on their own. Many of the most egregious environmental violations traverse state and sometimes national borders. Individuals have neither the power nor the resources to address these widespread hazards.

In the final analysis, only the authority and scope of power that a government possesses can ensure the attainment of agreed-upon environmental goals. Because individuals are unable and businesses are by nature unwilling to assume this responsibility, government must do so.

5．Issue 写作的建议与禁忌

在下面这张简单的清单中，我列举了应考 Issue 作文题时的一些注意事项，帮助你更有效地组织和撰写 Issue 作文。为了加深对这些要点的理解，当你阅读第二章和第三章的范文时，请随时参考这张清单并做出相应的记号。

√ 要将原论点分成几个组成部分或非连续性的范围加以考虑。事实上，很多 Issue 的原论点都经过特殊设计，有意让考生这样操作。

√ 要给你自己的立场留有回旋的余地，这可以通过证明你自己的观点和承认其他观点来得以实现。这样，你的文章就不会显得空洞乏味，而你也会显得更加富有见地、更加博学！

√ 要解释清楚，你的每个例子是如何阐明你的观点的。任何人都可以列举出一长串的例子，并声明它们有效地说明了某一论点。但判卷者希望看到的是深刻的分析，而不是飞快的文字录入速度。

✗ 不要浪费时间去猜测判卷者会同意（或不同意）哪种观点。相反，一定要针对 Issue 本身提出自己独到的见解，总结出自己的立场，并予以很好的支持。

✗ 不要对 Issue 作文题目采取勉强的姿态；但也要避免过于武断或过于极端。处理 Issue 作文的时候，可以把它当做一次脑力练习，而不是当做分享你个人信仰体系的论坛。

✗ 不要过于详细地描述某个细节，但也不必照顾得面面俱到。结合你所剩的时间，尽量按照你的提纲涵盖更多的要点，不要过于"照顾"某一段落，而应保持各个段落之间的平衡。同时，如果你必须放弃草稿中的某些次级或不重要的写作要点，你也不必过于担忧。GRE 判卷者会理解你是受时间限制的。

✗ 不要显得过于夸张，尤其是当你要运用个人经历来支持你的论点时。相反，尽量将真实经历和学术知识加以广泛地结合，来论证你的观点。

✗ 不要将你的 Issue 作文当做一次关于琐事的争论。尽量运用判卷者可能知晓的人名和事件来支持你的立场，而不是仅仅罗列数据，援引晦涩的资料，或者引用鲜为人知的历史事件。

三、*Argument* 写作详解

Argument 写作题目用以检测考生评论性论证的技巧，以及考生的写作技巧。你的任务就是针对给出的论断进行评论，而评论的对象就是原文阐述的中肯程度（逻辑周到性）以及原作者为了支持论点而提出佐证的力度是否足够。在为你的 Argument 评分时，GRE 判卷者关注的是你的下列四种能力：

- 有效地辩明并分析论点的关键要素
- 有效地组织、发展并表达你的评论
- 有效地支持你的观点（通过列举理由和例子）
- 有效地支配标准书面英语的各项要素（语法、句型以及词语的运用）

1．Argument 作文特征

每道官方题库中的 Argument 考题都由两部分组成：一条简洁明了的指示（考生任务描述），后面紧接一段短文，提出了本题的考试论点。每篇 Argument 的提示差不多都一样：

Discuss how well reasoned you find the argument below. 讨论下面的论点的逻辑周全性。

Argument 题目的形式，通常是引用某篇小说中的某段文字。下面是两篇 GRE 风格的 Argument。谨记:这两篇例子在官方题库中没有出现,考试的时候你不会遇到它们。

The following appeared in an advertisement for United Motors trucks:

"Last year the local television-news program In Focus reported in its annual car-and-truck safety survey that over the course of the last ten years United Motors vehicles were involved in at least thirty percent fewer fatal accidents to drivers than vehicles built by any other single manufacturer. Now United is developing a one-of-a-kind computerized crash warning system for all its trucks. Clearly, anyone concerned with safety who is In the market for a new truck this year should buy a United Motors truck."

The following appeared in a memo from the manager of UpperCuts hair salon:

"According to a nationwide demographic study, more and more people today are moving from suburbs to downtown areas. In order to boost sagging profits at UpperCuts, we should take advantage of this trend by relocating the salon from its current location in Apton's suburban mall to downtown Apton, while retaining the salon's decidedly upscale ambiance. Besides, Hair-Dooz, our chief competitor at the mall, has just relocated downtown and is thriving at its new location. and the most prosperous hair salon in nearby Brainard is located in that city's downtown area. By emulating the locations of these two successful salons, UpperCuts is certain to attract more customers."

2. Argument 作文要则

① **在你开始限时写 Argument 作文之前,考试系统会显示满满一屏幕的详细说明。**这些说明不但指出四项综合评分标准,而且还会给你下列指示:

第一屏(总体指示和建议):

- 你的答题时间是 30 分钟。
- 你需要针对提出的论点评论它的逻辑周全性。
- 不可以对其他任何论点进行评论。
- 在你开始书写之前,最好花几分钟思考一下如何组织你的文章。
- 你需要完全展开你的观点并将它们串联起来,保持连贯性。
- 你应该留出富裕的时间,检查自己的文章,做必要的修改。

第二屏(对论点进行评论的具体指导):

- 这里没有要求你同意或反对论点中的任何一条陈述。
- 你应该对论点的推理过程提出自己的分析。
- 你应该考虑论点所隐含的某些可疑的假设。
- 你应该考虑为支持结论而提出的论据的范围。
- 你可以讨论哪些额外的论据可以有助于加强或反驳论点。
- 你可以讨论哪些额外的信息(如果可以找到的话)会帮助你对论点的结论进行评估。

② **你的分析必须紧贴 Argument 的逻辑特征和它的相关佐证。**不要混淆 Argument 写作与 Issue 写作。你的 Argument 作文不是用来表达你对 Argument 所涉及事件的个人观点的文章。例如,请考虑你刚刚读过的两个 Argument。一道涉及广告索赔的 Issue 考题或许需要你针对一个或多个商家的责任提出你自己的观点,以便为消费者提供完整而正确的产品信息。但是,这种观点在 Argument 考试中是与题目毫无关系的。需要你密切关注的是 Argument 本身内在的论证说服力(逻辑周全性)。

③ **Argument 的出题者有意在每篇 Argument 中添加了大量的瑕疵(谬论以及其他各种缺陷)，你必须有效地将它们指出才可以得到较高的分数。** 与 Issue 作文任务提示所不同的是，Argument 作文的提示并没有类似的陈述："没有所谓正确的答案。"为什么没有呢？在设计每道 Argument 作文题时，出题者故意在文章中添加了一定的逻辑错误(谬论以及其他各种缺陷)，让考生在自己的文章中加以辩明并进行阐述。这就是 Argument 作文的主要考查目的。如果你不能有效地辩明并阐述原文内在的逻辑陷阱，你将无法得到较高的分数。

一道典型的 Argument 文章通常会包含三到四个逻辑瑕疵。下面列出了七种 Argument 正式考试中最常见的逻辑问题：
- 两件事情之间的推论过于牵强
- 把因果关系混淆为简单的相互关系或时间顺序关系
- 误以为群组的特征就是每个组员的特征
- 误以为某种条件必然和/或足以引发相应的结果
- 以潜在的、不具代表性的统计结果作为论证依据
- 将不能反映真实情况的反馈或民意调查作为论证依据
- 误以为所有事情都会永远保持一成不变
后面你会读到关于这些瑕疵更为详尽的解释和说明。

④ **出题时，所有的 Argument 都不是均衡的。** 我已经撰写了大量的 Argument 作文，比一般人要多出很多。作为权威，我可以这样说：与其他文章相比，Argument 作文更加难以应付(编者注：对于语言不成问题的美国人来说，复杂的逻辑分析是最头疼的，而中国学生的难点反而在 Issue 部分)。当然，读过本书的第一章和第三章之后，你就不会有太大的问题了。然而，如果你仔细阅读官方题库中的 Argument 文章，你肯定会注意到，有些文章的逻辑瑕疵一眼就能发现，而另外一些文章中的错误论述却是与某些正确论证混杂在一起的，或者根本就隐藏在明显正确的论证背后，令它们更难提取、分离以及组织。而且，无法保证考试的时候你会遇到哪种题目。但是谁说过生活是公平的了？至少，你已经得到了本书的帮助。

⑤ **对于高分 Argument 文章来说，没有规定的或者所谓的"正确"长度。** 你的 Argument 文章长度仅仅受限于 30 分钟的考试时间以及可供讨论的逻辑错误的数量。据我在 Argument 写作方面的经验，对于 Argument 作文来说，400 字已经足够得到最高分了。(第四章和第五章中的几篇文章显得稍长，因为在每篇文章的第一段，我都对整篇 Argument 进行了摘要重述——供你参考。)

3. Argument 写作流程

如果想要在逻辑问题文章上拿到高分，你就至少需要展示出本章节列出的四种能力。为了确保你能够在规定的 30 分钟内表现出所有这四种能力，请按照如下的七步进行：

① **读题**：当你读题目的时候，分辨出它的结论和支持的论据(1 分钟)。当你第一次读题目的时候，要确保你看出了它的最终结论(你在题目的首句和末句都有可能发现结论)。把它速记在你的草稿纸上！在 Argument 题目中，结论可能是一个"主张"、"建议"或是"争论"。为什么说第一步非常重要呢？因为除非你非常清楚题目中的最终结论，否则无法评价作者的推理或是他用以支持其结论的论据是否有力。

② **灵机一动，然后开始动笔(2~3 分钟)。** 尝试着在题目中找到至少 3~4 个相对独立的错误。请把本章节列出的逻辑错误牢牢记住，它们可以助你一臂之力。假如你碰到了其他的逻辑问题，那么一定要把它们记下来。特别注意那些缺乏根据或者不合逻辑的假设，而题目结论又是基于这个假设得出的。不用担心你找出的有些错误是重复的，因为你可以在下一步

中把它们进行归类。

③ **组织你的文章(2～3分钟)**。以你在第二步中做的笔记为依据,把你的思路整理成段落(3段或4段,这取决于题目中存在的错误数量)。花1分钟时间考虑你找出的错误是否重复,或是有的错误是否可以再细分成两个不同的错误。在很多情况下,提出你评论观点的最佳顺序就是遵照逻辑错误在题目中出现的相应顺序。

④ **写简洁的开头段(1～2分钟)**。这段引言没有你的评论观点重要。以下是你在写开头段时应该做到的:

- 指出题目的最终结论。
- 简洁地描述题目推理的过程和相应的支持论据。
- 按照题目的推理过程和论据的顺序大概提一下主要错误。

请不要在开头段浪费时间去重复整个题目,因为考官肯定已经非常熟悉题目了,他们感兴趣的是你的想法而不是你的誊写技术。

注意:在第四章和第五章的文章中出现了更长的开头段落。我通过这些细节指出题目中的论据,供你参考,帮助分析 Argument。但是,在你的文章中不要出现这样的细节。

⑤ **组织你的论证段落(15～20分钟)**。除非你采取的是纸笔考试,否则就立刻跳过所有的说明。尽量紧扣你的提纲,但是要灵活。至于以哪一个逻辑错误开头,这就要看哪个是你最明白的,也最能表达清楚的。(你完全可以稍候再重新安排你的观点。)如同写 Issue 文章一样,在这一步的时候你只能玩命地打字,以便尽可能敲完你的所有观点。

⑥ **组织结尾段(3～4分钟)**。你应该在最后一段总结所有的逻辑错误。在这一段你可以通过如下问题来检查你的每一个重点:

- 这篇 Argument 如何能够更有说服力。
- 在评价题目结论的时候什么样的其他信息会有帮助。

不管你是否把所有的要素都包含在文中了,都要确保你的文章有一个清晰的结尾,否则判卷者会认为你没有按时写完文章。

⑦ **修改和检查你的文章(3～5分钟)**。检查书写、惯用法和语法中的错误。检查你的行文是否流畅,尤其是过渡部分。除非你选择的是纸笔考试,否则就重新排列你的段落,直到获得最好的逻辑顺序为止,同时重写一些生硬的句子以使它们更加自然。

4. Argument 作文范文

现在请看一篇 Argument 范文。我重点标出了一些起过渡作用的单词和短语,这些单词和短语将会在第四章和第五章的文章中反复出现。从中看到,我是如何模式化开头和结尾的,以及如何组织和表达我的各个分论点以获得它们之间最佳逻辑顺序的。(在真实考试的时候,你没有必要去做这些标记。)

当你读下面文章的时候,请牢记:

- 该文满足 ETS 6 分的全部标准。
- 该文简洁到足以在30分钟内构思和完成。(编者注:实战中中国考生不必追求这么多的字数,300～400字之间就可以了。)
- 我是在没有时间限制的情况下完成该文的,所以不必担心你在规定时间内写出的文章不像该文那样优美。

第8页 Argument 范文

Citing a general demographic trend and certain evidence about two other hair salons, the manager of UpperCuts (UC) concludes here that UC should relocate from suburban to downtown Apton in order to attract more customers and, in turn, improve its profitability. However, the manager's argument relies on a series of unproven assumptions and is therefore unconvincing as it stands.

To begin with, the argument assumes that Apton is demographic trend reflects the national trend. Yet, the mere fact that one hair salon has moved downtown hardly suffices to infer any such trend in Apton. Without better evidence of a demographic shift toward downtown Apton, it is just as likely that there is no such trend in Apton. For that matter, the trend might be in the opposite direction, in which event the manager's recommendation would amount to especially poor advice.

Even assuming that downtown Apton is attracting more residents, relocating downtown might not result in more customers for UC, especially if downtown residents are not interested in UC's upscale style and prices. Besides, Hair-Dooz might draw potential customers away from UC, just as it might have at the mall. Without ruling out these and other reasons why UC might not benefit from the demographic trend, the manager cannot convince me that UC would attract more customers, let alone increase its profits, by moving downtown.

Nor can the manager justify the recommended course of action on the basis of the Brainard salon's success. Or perhaps hair salons generally fare better in downtown Brainard than downtown Apton, due to demographic differences between the two areas. or perhaps the salon thrives only because it is long-established in downtown Brainard—an advantage that UC clearly would not have in its new location. In short, the manager cannot defend the recommended course of action on the basis of what might be a false analogy between two hair salons.

Finally, even assuming that the proposed relocation would attract more customers, an increase in the number of patrons would not necessarily improve UC's profitability. Should UC's expenses turn out higher downtown, they might very well offset increasing revenues, thereby frustrating UC's efforts to improve its profitability.

In sum, the argument relies on what might amount to two poor analogies between UC and two other salons, as well as a general demographic trend that may or may not apply to Apton. To strengthen the argument the manager should provide better evidence of a demographic shift in Apton toward the downtown area, and clear evidence that those demographics portend success there for an upscale hair salon. Even with this additional evidence, in order to properly evaluate the argument I would need to know why HairDooz relocated, what factors have contributed to the Brainard salon's success, what factors other than location might have contributed to UC's sagging profits at the mall, and what additional, offsetting expenses UC might incur at the new location.

5. Argument 写作的建议与禁忌

下面是你写 Argument 作文时需要注意的事项。为了加深对这些要点的理解,在阅读本书第四章和第五章的范文时要不时地回过头来参考这些要点。

√ 要仔细分析并找出 Argument 中至少三、四个论证或论据方面的错误。如果想拿到 5 分以上的分数,你就不能遗漏 Argument 中主要的逻辑错误,并且你必须至少挑出其中三、四个逻辑错误展开讨论。

√ 要用充分的理由和/或恰当的例子来支持你的观点。议论不要离题。不要在评论中掺杂自己的主观想法。

√ 要讨论一下使 Argument 的论点更有说服力还欠缺什么,以及如何才能使你更深入地评判它——如果时间充裕的话。这两点可以放在文章的最后一段进行陈述。

√ 要在你的文章中合乎逻辑地安排各个论点的顺序。要学会用过渡词或短语来衔接文章的各部分。注意：你的议论应该按照 Argument 中错误出现的先后顺序来进行。

✗ 不要仅仅重述或变相重述 Argument 的论点。得高分的诀窍是直截了当地说出对方的观点错在哪里。因此，你的开头段必须简短一些。（注：本书第四章和第五章范文的开头段较长，目的是为了概括 Argument 的内容——供你参考。）

✗ 不要在结尾段里提出 Argument 任何其他的错误。在结尾段里，你只能重申你的观点，或指出要使 Argument 更具说服力还需要什么，以及还有哪些信息会有助于你对它的评判。

四、GRE 写作中的建议和禁忌

根据 ETS 考试中心官员的说法，GRE 判卷者得到的指示是，侧重作文的内容和结构而不是语言质量。但这并不意味着你的语言质量不会影响判卷者，从而影响你的作文得分。我敢肯定影响一定是有的！要想得高分，你必须：

- 表述要清楚准确（注意措辞和表达形式的使用）
- 语法结构和用法准确无误（符合英语书面语言的要求）
- 具有说服力（有效地利用修辞手法）
- 句子长度和结构要有变化（以增加语言的趣味性和多样性；同时显示考生对英语写作娴熟高超的驾御水平）。

当然，这些说起来容易做起来难。虽然你只有几个星期或几个月的时间来提高你的写作水平，但这儿有一些具体的与语言相关的指导，你可以立刻就用在你的作文写作当中。

✗ **不要**使用俚语和俗语，用正式文体写作。否则，你将不但得不到高分，还会被判卷者打入不及格的行列。

✗ **不要**以嘲讽或幽默的方式论述你的观点。倒不是判卷者缺乏幽默感，而是幽默不适合用于这样的考试。

✗ **不要**过多使用拉丁语或其他外来语。偶尔使用拉丁语或缩略语，如 per se, i.e., e.g. 等是完全可以的。英语学术文章中常用的一些外来语，如 vis-à-vis, caveat 等也是可以接受的。但不要过多使用。（注：GRE 计算机考试不能识别变音符号，如 vis-à-vis 中 a 头上的"ˋ"这个符号。但也不用担心，判卷者清楚这些考试的局限性。）

✗ **不要**过于向判卷者炫耀你的词汇量。要尽量展示你有相当的词汇量（注意观察第 6 页范文中"imprudent"、"unfettered"和"pandemic"这三个词的使用），只是不要过头，而且要避免使用只有某一专门领域内的专家和学者才能理解的技术术语。

对引用的陈述或论述的来源要交代清楚。如果不能提供具体来源，也应在 Issue 中使用"speaker"、"statement"或在 Argument 中使用"author"、"argument"这样的字眼。

五、GRE 写作考试的计算机界面

正如下面所展示的，作文考试界面与多项选择部分的界面很相似。在屏幕上方可见：

- 当前写作考试所剩时间（分钟）
- 考试名称
- 考试题目、题号

屏幕下方是：

- 放弃考试键(用于停止或取消你的考试)
- 结束键(用于移动到第二个写作考题或考题的下面部分)
- 时间键(用于显示精确到秒的考试剩余时间)
- 帮助键(使用计算机和解答作文题的过程中寻求帮助时用)

为避免不小心而按下了放弃考试键或结束考试键,计算机在执行命令之前会让你对指令进行确认。

　　注:在下面的屏幕展示中,NEXT 这个指令呈灰色,这表明该指令没有被激活,即当前不能使用。

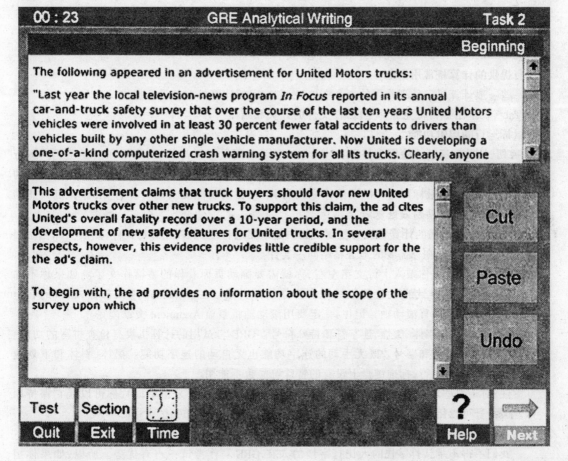

1.作文考试的计算机辅导

　　在计时考试前,考试系统会给你演示包括写作部分的整个考试过程(配合一系列屏幕演示)。包括：

- 如何使用鼠标
- 如何滚动窗口
- 如何使用屏幕下方的工具栏
- 如何使用计算机的内置字处理软件

　　在演示期间,你不能跳过任何内容而直接进入下一条内容。在你开始正式考试之前,计算机会考查你的操作能力。在考试之前你也可以先练习一下。

　　注:你也可选择手写作文考试。但在你报名考试时就要明确下来。

2.文字处理软件的特点和局限

① 导航和编辑——可供使用的键盘指令：

下面是考试时可用的计算机导航和编辑的键盘指令：

Backspace	删除光标左边的文字
Delete	删除光标右边的文字
Home	将光标移至一行文字的开首
End	将光标移至一行文字的末尾
Arrow Keys	将光标上下或左右移动
Enter	换行或在段落之间留出空白处
Page Up	将光标移至上一页(或上一屏幕)
Page Down	将光标移至下一页(或下一屏幕)

② 没有提供的计算机常用指令

有一些一般计算机字处理常用的指令在 GRE 考试用的计算机上却没有提供。

如 Tab（长空格键）：将光标移至段落/文件的开头和结尾

③ 由鼠标运行的编辑功能

* 剪切、粘贴和撤消　除键盘外，GRE 机考时还可以用鼠标运行剪切、粘贴和恢复功能。运行剪切时，用鼠标选中要剪切的文字，然后点击鼠标即可。粘贴的时候，将鼠标指向要粘贴的地方，然后点击鼠标即可。但用鼠标拖放的剪切、粘贴功能无法运行。另外，计算机只能储存近期的剪切、粘贴或恢复内容。

　　注：GRE 考试用的计算机没有复制功能。如果要进行复制，首先剪切文件，然后立即粘贴回原位，再移动光标，在你需要的地方粘贴同一文件。

* 垂直滚动轴　当你敲入十行文字左右，你就需要翻动页面看你的整篇作文了。如果你不知道怎样翻动页面，考前的计算机辅导将教你如何去做。在 Argument 考试部分，题目的右边也会出现一个垂直滚动轴。记住：一定要用滚动轴将整篇 Argument 文章读完。

* 关于检查拼写、字体、属性、连字符和特殊符号　GRE 考试用的计算机没有检查拼写的功能。也不能选择字体和字号。既无手动的连字功能也无自动的连字功能。黑体、斜体和下划线等属性都无法运行，标准键盘上没有的特殊符号也不能用。

　　注：对于那些本该采用斜体或下划线的部分（譬如书名或外来语单词），你可以让它保持原样。破折号可以用两条连字号表示，或在一个连字号的前后各加一个空格。

④ 提高 GRE 计算机字处理软件使用速度的窍门

　　　　我们不得不承认打字快的人比打字慢的人在 GRE 写作考试中占有优势。所以，如果你担心你的速度问题，可以尝试下面这些诀窍。（记住参加考试前一定要事先练习一下这些技巧）

* 在 Argument 作文部分使用专有名称的缩写。第一次采用缩写时一定要解释一下全称。例如，第 10 页范文中的 UpperCuts，我在首句表明 UpperCuts 可写做 UC，即：UpperCuts（UC），然后在文章以下的部分直接用 UC 来指 UpperCuts。

* 反复使用的短语可用剪切和粘贴的功能来录入。下面是 Argument 作文部分常用的三个表达方式：

"The argument depends on the assumption that..."

"Another problem with the author's recommendation is that..."

"Lacking evidence to support this assumption, the author cannot confidently conclude that..."

　　　　对于这样的字句你不需要一一地去敲。用剪切和粘贴就可以了。然后稍微做一些改动以避免雷同。

- 在 Issue 作文考试部分,如果你没有时间写开头段和结尾段(这两段都应该在你写完论证段后再写),就把你文章中总结性段落粘贴到文章的开头和结尾。然后把开头段稍做改动,使它读起来更像开场白而不是结束语。

六、*GRE* 写作评分、成绩通知和成绩评估

考试后不久,你的两篇作文将由考试中心的判卷者判阅。分数档次为 0 至 6,得分为两篇作文的综合得分。分数将通知你本人和你指定的学校。本章将介绍成绩通知和分数评定的过程。

1. *GRE* 考生两篇作文的分数是如何评定的

考试后一周内,你的两篇作文就会被评阅完毕。两篇作文将分别由两位判卷者评阅。在评阅过程中,判卷者之间不得交流评阅情况。评分采取综合给分的办法,即每个判卷者各自根据考生作文的整体质量在 0 分与 6 分的范围内打分(以 0.5 分为一个分数单位)。考生的最终得分为四个判卷者所给分数的平均值,4 舍 5 入精确到 0.5。

注:如果两位判卷者所给的分数相差 1 分以上,就由第三位经验丰富的判卷者复阅该考生作文,并决定最后得分。

同多项选择题一样,你的作文也会有一个百分制的得分,即从 0 至 99 的得分。例如,如果你的分数是 60 分,那就意味着你的分数高于参加考试的 60% 的考生(而低于参加考试的 40% 的考生)。因此,百分制的分数体现的是考生与所有 GRE 考生相比而得出的结果,并非你与写同样题目作文的考生相比较的结果。

2. *GRE* 作文的官方评分标准

GRE 作文的评分按照 GRE 官方网站www.gre.org 所发布的评分标准来进行。以下是最高分 6 分作文的基本要求(注意:即使其中偶尔有语法、用词、拼写和标点符号错误的作文也有可能得 6 分)。

① **Issue 作文最高分(6 分)要求**

- 作文用清晰的推理和具有说服力的例子来论述自己的观点。
- 文章思路清楚、扣题紧密、结构得当。
- 作文反映出考生在英语词汇、句型和习惯用语使用上的熟练、流利和老练。
- 作文反映出考生对英语书面语的娴熟掌握,包括语法、词汇应用、拼写和标点符号——但是在这几方面可以偶尔出现小错误。

② **Argument 作文最高分(6 分)要求**

- 作文逐一分析了 Argument 的特点,其分析有深度。
- 作文用有见识的推理和例证支持自己的辩驳观点。
- 作文思路表达清晰,条理性强。观点之间衔接得当。
- 作文反映出考生在英语词汇、句型和习惯用语使用上的熟练、流利和老练。
- 作文反映出考生对英语书面语的娴熟掌握,包括语法、词汇应用、拼写和标点符号——但是在这几方面可以偶尔出现小错误。

低于 6 分的作文,评分时所参照的因素同上。但给分标准会依照作文质量而递减。

你可以下载官方网站www.gre.org 上 GRE *Bulletin* 所发布的 ETS 0～6 分的评分标准。ETS

还在自己的网站上直接公布评分标准。

3.通知考生和学校分数

考试后的两周内,考试中心将寄给你包括作文成绩在内的成绩通知单。同时,考试中心还将给你所指定的学校寄出成绩通知单。从 2003 年 7 月开始,成绩通知单上还包括作文范文。

注:如果你选择的是手写作文,成绩通知单将在四周以后寄到。

4.学校如何利用 GRE 作文考试成绩

作文分数相对于其他入学要求(即 GRE 综合考试、GRE 单科考试、GPA、自我介绍、推荐信等)所占的比重之多寡,将由各个研究生院自行决定。招生部门也许会用作文成绩来筛选所有的申请者。或者,他们会用作文成绩来决定取舍两个实力相当的考生。建议你就相关政策询问具体学校的院系。

七、GRE 写作备考方略

面对如此多的 GRE 作文题目,你会感到要把这些题目都做一遍,就算不是一件不可能的任务,也是件很可怕的事。当然,阅读完本章后,你对 GRE 作文应该有相当的把握了。但本书第二章到第五章将讲些什么? 如何研究 Issue 作文的写作? 如何练习写作? 下面是本书就如何充分利用时间备考 GRE 作文考试的建议。

1.不要死记硬背本书范文

如果你背下本书所有的范文,然后在考试时复制其中两篇,你应该得高分,仅仅是看在你下的苦功的份上! 当然这是我的看法。可惜的是,考试中心的考官们不会发这种慈悲。在这儿提醒你一声:考官们也会有这本书,而且可能一眼就能看出你在抄袭。从本书的范文借用一些观点、推理和转换词是没有问题的。但是记住一定要用自己具体的例子,尤其是在 Issue 那篇作文里。两篇作文都要用自己的话来写。

2.练习、练习、再练习

也许你把这本书从头到尾读了 10 遍后,考试成绩仍然不佳。因为没有任何东西能替代有时间压力的模拟考试。尽量多地用考试中心提供的题目练习写作。同时请记住以下几点:

- 练习写作时一定要记时。这一点很重要。除非施加时间压力,否则你的练习都是没用的。
- 除非你决定选择提交手写作文试卷,否则你的练习都应该在计算机上进行。并且只练习那些考试时会用到的编辑指令。
- 评估自己的作文。如果同样的错误反复出现不能得到纠正,练习就没有意义了。所以,写完作文后应该参照权威机构的评分标准进行评估(如果能找到一位英语教授帮助评估就更好了)。然后看看自己的弱点在哪里,以后进行重点弥补。如果你的作文比本书第二章到第五章的范文逊色很多,不用着急。你只管集中精力进行改进和提高就行了。

3.阅读官方试题库并做笔记

通过本书提供的网址(www.west.net/~stewart/grewa)下载全部作文试题。挑选涉及各种题材的 10 ~ 15 个 Issue 作文题目以及同样数量的 Argument 题目。按照本章介绍的步骤逐一练习写作。注意在规定的时间内完成。动笔的同时还要动脑。

4.阅读本书范文并做笔记

准备 Issue 作文时,先确定你没信心的那些题目(参照本章的开头部分所列的清单)。然后阅读本书第二章和第三章的相应范文。阅读这些范文时要做到:

- 从文章的首尾段找出文章的主题。
- 对那些你认为最清楚、最有说服力或最有用的推论做笔记。
- 划出过渡词语和修辞部分(在你练习写作文时尽量用上这些你最欣赏的短语并形成你自己的写作风格)。

准备 Argument 作文时,只要有时间,就尽可能多地从本书第四章和第五章中选择一些范文。然后做以下两件事情:

- 搞清楚该文章所讨论的推论问题的类型并与你在本书第一章所学的相对照。
- 在衔接各论点的过渡词语上做上记号(在你练习写作文时把它们用在你的作文中)。

5.进一步挖掘 Issue 作文题材和例子

参考本章所列的题材清单。卷起袖子尽力搜寻题材。所有的渠道都不放过。

① 杂志

下面所列几种杂志常刊登关于常见话题的讨论:

U. S. News & World Report:刊登对当前热门事件的议论

The Economist:刊登世界政治和经济理论性文章

Reason:刊登意识形态和文化领域的文章

The New Yorker:刊登艺术、人文、社会和热门文化方面的文章

The Futurist:刊登有关文化和技术动向的文章

到当地图书馆去搜寻这些杂志,或者访问网站获取背景材料。你一定能找到大量可以用在 Issue 作文中的写作材料。

② 书籍

查阅有关重要人物、事件或人类重大活动的书籍。下面两本很有用的书可以起到抛砖引玉的作用:

A History of Knowledge: *Past*, *Present*, *and Future*, by Charles van Doren (Birch Lane Press, 1991)

The World's Greatest Ideas: *An Encyclopedia of Social Inventions*, by Nicholas Alberly (New Society Publications, 2001)

③ 学校的课堂笔记

把你在学校做的有关艺术、科学、历史、政治和社会学等科目的课堂笔记再翻出来。你会惊奇地发现,其中有很多东西你都能加以利用,作为准备 Issue 作文考试的材料。

④ 网络

利用网络寻找常用的 Issue 作文题材。

⑤ 电视与录像带

如果你喜欢看电视,那就把频道锁定在历史栏目。购买或租借《千年历史》。这个三小时的音像节目记录了从 1000～2000 年最有影响的人物,并将重点放在对几位艺术家、科学家、政治领袖和哲学家的专访上。你一定能从中找到好的题材。

6.坚持自己的观点

　　上面列举的策略可能很费时间。如果你考前有充裕的时间,倒也无关紧要。但是如果你没有这么多时间去阅读和搜寻题材,那怎么办呢? 别泄气。你用于 Issue 作文的那些例子和论据只是几项评分标准中的一项,而且绝对不是最重要的一项。你主要应该关注:

- 阐明一个观点或立场。而且该观点或立场能够解释原论点的复杂性和内在含义。同时兼顾可能存在的其他观点。
- 对该观点的表述要清楚,文章结构有序、均衡。

　　另外别忘了,考试时系统会提供给你两个 Issue 题目,你尽可选择你感觉写起来更得心应手的那一个。

第二章　Issue 范文精讲

Issue 写作要领

"它山之石,可以攻玉"。本书最大的资源之一就是大量的北美标准范文,同时辅以对 ETS 作文考试规律性的解密,以此来最大化地利用这些范文。以下寥寥数言是本书中文编著者日积月累得来的 Issue 作文实战要领,希望能够成为广大考生提高 Issue 写作分数的捷径!

一、题目分析

Issue 写作的第一步是对题目进行分析,从而使自己的思路具有条理性,立场更加鲜明。从审题的角度,根据题目的设计方式,我们可以把所有的题目分成两大类:细节类题目和抽象类题目。

1. 细节类题目

顾名思义,细节类题目有诸多的细节和限制。题目往往会给出话题的背景、例子或者出题者的观点,甚至会给出相互矛盾的观点!这种环环相扣的题目需要你做的第一步就是把这些关系理清,如果有一点照顾不到就有审题不清的嫌疑。怎么理清呢?简单地说就是:先抓大环,再抓小环!何为大环?就是题目的中心思想(整个的 244 道 Issue 题目其实就是八个大的主题!)。比如,Issue 31 题的中心思想就是未来(长远大计)和现实(当务之急)的取舍和矛盾。何为小环?就是题目涉及的特定范畴,例如长远大计中的保护濒危物种问题。

该题型在题库中占很大的比重,其应对方法非常明确,主要有两个:一个就是下面论证方法中详细解释的四种论证过程:比较型论证、因果型论证、问题解决型论证和结论型论证。根据这四种论证方法,就可以一步一步地展开论证的每一段了;第二个就是根据主题对题库进行分类,而每一个分题库内部的题目之间都可以互相借鉴和提供例子。

2. 抽象类题目

这类题目比较短,信息含量很少。题目的限定条件少不是好事,恰恰是命题作文的难点,因为题目没有限定范围,也就是说所有范围都有可能。类似的题目有"历史是今天的一面镜子"、"失败是成功之母"、"伟大来自于平凡"。这些更像是一本书或者一套书的名字。你能用几百字把这些话题说完整、说透彻、说深刻吗?不可能,想都别想!

既然说不清楚,我们是不是就束手就擒呢?其实抽象类题目的解决方法最简单!就是"伤其十指,不如断其一指",全说说不清楚,那就说清楚一部分!再直白地说,你只需分析几个特例,这些特例的对错就决定了你对题目观点是赞成还是反对。每个人一开始都会怀疑这样做的正确性:这不是 Argument 中逢见必打的"以偏概全"吗?那是在驳论文中,而在立论文中,考官关心的是你在分析这些特例的时候是否言之有理!无论是官方的范文(如,ETS 的第三篇范文六分文章),还是本书的范文都有许多这样的例子,但是切记它们都是:抽象类题目!

我们之所以要以偏概全地处理抽象类题目,是因为它很难写得完整。不过,运用四种论证方法也一样可以把它写成正反论证,只不过这样做对你的要求就高多了,没有上面的方法那么简易。Issue 的处理方法有很多种,要根据你自己的想法和掌握的资料得出你自己的结论。

二、立场

1.平衡观点

很多学员都存在一个疑问:平衡观点是不是就是中庸、骑墙、没有观点?答案当然是否定的。原因有两个:首先,平衡的正反论证不是没有观点,它自己本身就是一种更完整和更成熟的观点,只要你在开头段落的中心句明确表明你的这种立场;其次,GRE 的 Issue 题目无论从设计上还是难度上不同于其他的一些考试(TOEFL 或者雅思),其实它就是把你虚拟成一位拥有加工信息、处理信息、进行研究的学者或者决策者,考查你这方面的能力。它和 Argument 还不一样(后者不需要背景知识,同时仅限于题目本身的问题),有些 Issue 题目属于大是大非的问题(政治领导人是否应该向人民隐瞒信息?答案一定是完全否定么?),或者更复杂的问题,对这些问题进行单向或者倾向性的论述本身就有风险,甚至是错误的,如:The function of science is to reassure. / The purpose of art is to upset. / Herein lies the value of each one. 这种难度主要集中于题库中"最恶心"的三种话题:艺术、哲学和道德伦理。

2.有倾向的观点

即有保留的赞成或有保留的反对,也就是以赞成(反对)题目观点为主,附加少许的反对(赞成),体现在文章论证结构上就是绝大部分篇幅为一种倾向。这种立场一般用于漏洞比较小的题目,或者是你无法获得平衡论点的情况。

这种立场的使用频率最高,因为它把 Issue 的要求和中国同学想问题的习惯结合为一体。简单来说,可以用 GRE 的术语来概括这种立场的两种情况——大正小负和大负小正,这与 GRE 阅读文章十分相像。其实,除去语言因素外,我建议大家一定要把 GRE 的阅读和 Issue 联系起来,它们之间在结构和论证方面有着惊人的相似性,反之,掌握了 Issue 的基本知识对于提高你的阅读能力也是一大捷径!

3.一边倒的观点

即完全赞成或完全反对。在什么情况下会使用一边倒的观点呢?它似乎违反了我们一直强调的思维完整的原则。在很多题目中你的确不能持一边倒观点,但是有一种题目就可以——抽象类题目!当然有一些你很肯定的细节类题目也可以持一边倒观点,只不过比较少见。

另外,虽然可以用完全赞成或者完全反对的立场来写抽象类题目,但也不是绝对的,因为抽象类题目一样可以用我们四种论证类型中的某一种来进行正反论证,只不过难度要大一些,对你的思维能力、语言熟练度都有更高的要求!

三、开头方法

Issue 的开头方式比较灵活。本书每篇范文的开头都是一个模板,你需要明确的就是每种开头适用于什么题目。

1．让步语气＋表明立场

一种很常见的开头方式，其优点在于，你可以采用欲擒故纵的手法，先肯定原文的论点在某一领域成立，进而针对原论点的不足或不全面之处提出自己的立场，这样达到更加鲜明、更具针对性的效果。

2．提出问题＋表明立场

针对原文观点发问（推荐常用的四种疑问词：Do, Should, Whether, Why），然后结合自己的立场给出答案，形成一种自然的过渡，进而顺水推舟地表明立场。这是一种很"投机"的开头方式，一方面省去了挖空心思琢磨开头的时间（对原题稍作改动再加上一个疑问词不算是雷同！例如，本书第一篇范文。），另一方面，在切题的同时，又不会让考官觉得你懒惰到照抄题目的地步。

3．题目分析＋表明立场

这种行文的开头非常实际，平铺直叙中就可以把论点铺展开来，而且条理清晰，简单明了。其诀窍就在于：在后面的行文中一定要与开头的分析保持一致，产生呼应的效果。

4．表明立场＋概述理由

非常像全文提纲的一种开头方式，好处是非常清楚，就算你不看论证段也能知道下面是怎么展开的。提纲型开头较多用于一边倒观点的题目（换句话说，就是抽象类题目），原因很简单，因为一边倒观点的特点是立场明确，不像平衡型或倾向型立场，正反两方面在开头要胡搅蛮缠一番。

5．陈述题目观点＋原因＋驳斥题目观点

这种开头比较罕见，因为很容易在文章的展开过程中写成 Argument 文章，这是绝对不允许犯的错误！避免这种情况的诀窍就是在论证的前半部分一定要花相当的篇幅来支持题目观点的合理性，因为 Argument 与 Issue 的一个明显区别就在于，Argument 不会用一整段去支持题目中的任何一个观点。这种开头的好处也显而易见：首先，观点很理性，没有任何人称主语（I, we, they 等）的出现，具有相当的说服力；其次，文章结构和语言可以借鉴 Argument，准备的时候省时省力。

6．陈述题目观点＋表明立场

这种开头也很罕见，和 Argument 惊人地相似，很容易把文章写成 Argument，应对方法同上。请小心使用。

四、论证方法

Issue 文章的开头和结尾都是固定的，最大的难度在于论证。常用的四种论证类型为：比较型论证、因果型论证、问题解决型论证和结论型论证。这四种类型的名称就已经告诉了你论证应该怎么展开，互相之间是什么逻辑关系，这就是高于"语言模板"的"思维模板"。

1. 比较型论证

这种类型的论证过程中一般会出现明显的标志词 "more(less)...than..., not...but..., rather than..."来比较 A 和 B 两个方面，题目的设计会出现三种情况：A > B，A < B 或 A = B。这种文章很像 TOEFL 作文，将论证分成两大层次，把 A 和 B 这两者的优缺点都分析一番，最后得出综合结论。值得注意的是，TOEFL 文章可以二选一，而 Issue 文章则需要二者兼顾，可以是平衡的，也可以是有倾向的（因为如果不写支持方面就很容易写成 Argument，如果不写反对，就违反了论证文驳论部分好拿分的原则！）。

2. 因果型论证

Everything has cause and effect. 既然任何理论都有因有果，那么你在论证任何理论的时候就都可以使用因果型论证。凡是因果型题目必然写成两个层次：因果关系成立的情况和因果关系不成立的情况（cause→effect 和 cause≠effect），分别找例证进行阐述即可。

攻击因果关系的驳论部分有多种方法可以使用，反对 "A 推出 B" 最好用的方法有两个：(1) 拆桥法：攻击因果关系不成立，即 "A 推不出 B"；(2) 釜底抽薪法："原因 A 不成立"。

3. 问题解决型论证

这种论证类型的典型特点就是提出一个亟待解决的问题，再给出一个出题者的答案。出题者要求你不仅要考虑如何解决该问题，还得着手分析出题者给出的解决方法。论证展开的过程一般是：分析题目的解决方法 + 提出你的解决方法。

最常用于问题解决型的一种论证方法是他因法，即：题目：A 推出 B；反驳：C（D，E...）推出 B，所以 AB 之间不存在必然的因果关系。其实 Argument 中也到处可以看到他因法的使用。

4. 结论型论证

结论型论证公式为 why + if...then... + position。why 这个部分基本上是纯分析，其目的就是为驳论做准备，挖掘出题目观点成立的可能合理的原因（基础），然后攻击其原因（釜底抽薪），如果原因（基础）不成立了，出题者的结论（上层建筑）自然也就不成立了。结论型论证思维最缜密、最成熟，写 Issue 时有大量的机会可以使用这种方法。

此外，反证法也是 Issue 文章中常用的方法。如果你想反对题目观点，就先假设它是成立的，再由它推出一个谬误，最后它还是被证明为错误的。本书的范文中有大量反证法的例子。

最后还有一点是论证过程中不得不提到的：演绎分析。中国同学写文章习惯于以理论理，全是大话空话，大话西游可以，但是大话 Issue 就不具有说服力，所以在英文的论证中，演绎分析也就是举例子，是主要的论证方法。有同学怀疑整篇文章都用例证是不是太单调了，其实我们使用的例子已经不仅是一种论证方法了，而更多的是一种载体。分析空洞的理论不如分析有血有肉的事实来得更有说服力。因此，我们是在以例子作为媒介展现我们的各种论证方法。

Issue 31   Investing in research which may have **controversial** results

"Money spent on research is almost always a good investment, even when the results of that research are controversial."

花在研究上的资金基本上都是不错的投资,即使当研究的结果是有争议的时候。

I agree with the speaker's broad assertion that money spent on research is generally money well invested. However, the speaker unnecessarily extends this broad assertion to embrace research whose results are "controversial," while ignoring certain compelling reasons why some types of research might be unjustifiable. My points of contention with the speaker involve the fundamental objectives and nature of research, as discussed below.

I concede that the speaker is on the correct philosophical side of this issue. After all, research is the exploration of the unknown for true answers to our questions, and for lasting solutions to our enduring problems. Research is also the chief means by which we humans attempt to satisfy our insatiable appetite for knowledge, and our craving to understand ourselves and the world around us. **Yet**, in the very notion of research also lies my first point of contention with the speaker, who illogically presumes that we can know the results of research before we invest in it. **To the contrary**, if research is to be of any value it must explore uncharted and unpredictable territory. In fact, query whether research whose benefits are immediate and predictable can break any new ground, or whether it can be considered "research" at all.

While we must invest in research irrespective of whether the results might be controversial, **at the same time we should be circumspect about research whose objectives are too vague and whose potential benefits are too speculative. After all**, expensive research always carries significant opportunity costs—in terms of how the money might be spent toward addressing society's more immediate problems that do not require research. One apt illustration of this point involves the so-called "Star Wars" defense initiative, championed by the Reagan administration during the 1980s. In retrospect, this initiative was ill-conceived and largely a waste of taxpayer dollars; and few would dispute that the exorbitant amount of money devoted to the initiative could have gone a long way toward addressing pressing social problems of the day—by establishing after-school programs for delinquent latchkey kids, by enhancing AIDS awareness and education, and so forth. As it turns out, at the end of the Star Wars debacle we were left with rampant gang violence, an AIDS epidemic, and an unprecedented federal budget deficit.

The speaker's assertion is troubling in two other respects as well. First, no amount of research can completely solve the enduring problems of war, poverty, and violence, for the reason that they stem from certain aspects of human nature—such as aggression and greed. Although human genome research might eventually enable us to engineer away those undesirable aspects of our nature, in the meantime it is up to our economists, diplomats, social reformers, and jurists—not our research laboratories-to mitigate these problems. **Secondly**, for every new research breakthrough that helps reduce human suffering is another that serves primarily to add to that suffering. **For example**, while some might argue that physics researchers who harnessed the power of the atom have provided us with an alternative source of energy and invaluable "peace-keepers," this argument flies in the face of the hundreds of thousands of innocent people murdered and maimed by atomic blasts, and by nuclear meltdowns. **And**, in fulfilling the promise of "better living through chemistry" research has given us chemical weapons for human slaughter. **In short**, so-called "advances" that scientific research has brought about often amount to net losses for humanity.

In sum, the speaker's assertion that we should invest in research whose results are "controversial" begs the question, because we cannot know whether research will turn out controversial until we've invested in it. As for the speaker's broader assertion, **I agree that** money spent on research is generally a sound investment—because it is an investment in the advancement of human knowledge and in human imagination and spirit. **Nevertheless**, when we do research purely for its own sake—without aim or clear purpose—we risk squandering resources which could have been applied to relieve the immediate suffering of our dispirited, disadvantaged, and disenfranchised members of society. **In the final analysis**, given finite economic resources we are forced to strike a balance in how we allocate those resources among competing societal objectives.

投资可能产生有争议结果的研究项目

我同意演讲人的总体看法，即一般来说，把钱花在研究上是很明智的投资。然而，演讲人将这一总体看法所涵盖的范围不必要地扩大了。有令人信服的原因表明有些类型的研究是不合理的，而演讲者忽略了这些原因，从而将那些其结果有争议的研究也包括进自己的断言之中了。我与演讲人争辩的要点涉及研究的基本目标和本质，阐述如下：

我承认演讲人在这一问题上站在了正确的哲学立场上。毕竟，调查研究就是要探索未知从而为我们的问题找到正确的答案，以及为我们长久以来的问题找到永远的解决方法。研究也是我们人类试图去满足自己永无止境的求知欲望、渴望了解自身及我们周围的世界的一种重要的手段。但是，我要与演讲人所争论的第一个观点就是关于研究的确切定义。演讲人认为，在我们对研究投资之前我们就能够知道研究的结果，这是一种不合逻辑的假设。相反，如果一项研究要具有价值，那么它一定要去探索那些未知的、不可预见的领域。事实上，有着立竿见影、可以预见的效益的研究是否可能有所创新突破都是个问题，或者说它是否称得上是研究都是个问题。

虽然我们应该对研究进行投资，不必考虑它是否会产生有争议的结果，但同时，对于那些目标过于模糊，潜在收益过于不确定的研究我们也应该慎而行之。毕竟，这些用于研究的钱可以用来解决社会中更为迫在眉睫的问题，而这些问题可能并不需要进行什么研究，从这个角度来看，昂贵的研究机会成本是极高的。能证明这一点的一个很恰当的例子就是 19 世纪 80 年代里根政府支持的所谓的"星球大战"防御计划。现在看来，该计划失策，也大量浪费了纳税人的金钱。并且很少会有人反对以下这种说法，即把投资在这一计划上的大量金钱用于解决当时社会的一些紧迫问题将会更有用武之地，如用来为因家长无暇照管而犯过失的钥匙儿童建立课后照管项目，加强人们对艾滋病的认识和教育等等。正如后来事实所证明的一样，当"星球大战"计划最后失败的时候，它留给我们的是社会上黑帮暴力猖獗横行、艾滋病蔓延以及前所未有的联邦财政赤字。

演讲人的观点在另外两个方面也存在混淆。第一，再多的调查研究也不能完全解决战争、贫困和暴力这些长久以来的问题，因为他们是由人类本性的一些方面引起的，例如人类的侵略性和贪婪。尽管对人类基因的研究最终可能使我们除去人类本性中那些不良方面，但是同时这些问题的缓解有赖于我们的经济学家、外交官、社会改革家和法理学家，而不是研究实验室。第二，每一项用来帮助减轻人类痛苦的研究突破同时又主要是加深人类苦难的另一个因素。例如一些人可能会辩称，那些研究出如何利用原子能量的物理学家为人类提供了另一种可选择的能源，是宝贵的"和平卫士"，而完全无视那些成百上千的在原子弹爆炸和核泄漏事故中失去生命或受到伤害的无辜的人们。此外，当研究实现了"化学会给我们带来更美好的生活"这一承诺后，给我们带来的却是用于屠杀人类的化学武器。总之，科学研究所带来的所谓"进步"往往等同于人类的纯损失。

总之，演讲人关于我们应该对其结果有争议的研究进行投资的观点回避了问题，因为只有在我们对研究投资后，我们才能知道它是否会产生有争议的结果。至于演讲人的总体观点，我同意把钱花在研究上一般来说是很明智的投资。因为它是对推动人类知识前进的一种投资，也是对开发人类想像力和精神的一种投资。然而，当我们没有明确的目的或目标而单是为了研究而研究的时候，我们是在冒着浪费资源的危险。这些资源本可以用于减轻那些消沉沮丧的、贫穷而地位低下的、得不到平等权利的社会弱势群体所正在遭受的痛苦。归根结底，在经济资源有限的情况下，当我们在彼此冲突的社会目标中分配那些资源时，我们必须要做到分配的平衡合理。

论点 平衡观点　无条件的投资和合理研究在文中平分秋色。论点在开头和结尾中前后呼应，从结构到语言都十分接近，严格遵循平衡原则和"具体情况具体分析"。

开头方式 让步语气＋表明立场　I agree with...However, the speaker unnecessarily...unjustifiable.这是一个让步语气的变体，你在大多数的 GRE 细节题目中既要给出你自己独到的观点，又要针对出题者在题干中设定的范围，让步语气可以同时胜任这两项任务，对于复杂的细节题何不试试用让步语气的开头方式？

论证过程 结论型　论证部分的三个自然段分成两个层次。论证第一段前半部分，yet 之前，首先分析出题者持此观点可能的动机或者原因。值得一提的是 after all 这个短语，"毕竟，终究"在论证过程当中一般表示解释，属于一种比较弱的因果关系。从 yet 之后，作者从理论和例证两个层面驳斥出题者观点的谬误。简单地说，论证第一层次就是（why）为什么出题者会无条件赞成投资研究，第二层次就是（if）如果出题者观点成立的话，（then）那么就会出现哪些错误。

论证模式　论证中黑体部分是起承转合的关键语句，请仔细体会。

① I concede that the speaker is on the correct philosophical side of this issue. After all...

② While we must invest in research...at the same time we should be circumspect about research whose objectives are too vague and whose potential benefits are too speculative.

③ The speaker's assertion is troubling in two other respects as well.

Issue 190　The proper **use of public resources**

"As long as people in a society are hungry or out of work or lack the basic skills needed to survive, the use of public resources to support the arts is inappropriate—and, perhaps, even cruel—when one considers all the potential uses of such money."

只有社会上还有人正陷于饥饿、失业或者缺乏谋生的基本技能，那么运用公共资源去扶持艺术就是不恰当的——也许，甚至是残忍的——当你考虑到这些资金所有可能的用途时。

The speaker asserts that using public resources to support the arts is unjustifiable in a society where some people go without food, jobs, and basic survival skills. **It might be tempting to agree with the speaker on the basis that** art is not a fundamental human need, and that government is not entirely trustworthy when it comes to its motives and methods. **However,** the speaker overlooks certain economic and other societal benefits that accrue when government assumes an active role in supporting the arts.

The implicit rationale behind the speaker's statement seems to be that cultural enrichment pales in importance compared to food, clothing, and shelter. That the latter needs are more fundamental is indisputable; after all, what starving person would prefer a good painting to even a bad meal? **Accordingly, **I concede that** when it comes to the use of public resources it is entirely appropriate to assign a lower priority to the arts than to these other pressing social problems. **Yet**, to postpone public arts funding until we completely eliminate unemployment and hunger would be to postpone arts funding forever; any informed person who believes otherwise is envisioning a pure socialist state where the government provides for all of its citizens' needs—a vision which amounts to fantasy.

It might also be tempting to agree with the speaker on the basis that arts patronage is neither an appropriate nor a necessary function of government. **This argument has considerable merit, in three respects. First**, it seems ill-conceived to relegate decision and choices about arts funding to a handful of bureaucrats, who are likely to decide based on their own quirky notions about art, and whose decisions might be susceptible to influence-peddling. **Second**, private charity and philanthropy appear to be alive and well today. For example, year after year the Public Broadcasting System is able to survive, and even thrive, on donations from private foundations and individuals. **Third**, government funding requires tax dollars from our pockets—leaving us with less disposable dollars with which to support the arts directly and more efficiently than any bureaucracy ever could.

On the other hand are two compelling **arguments that public support for the arts is desirable**, whether or not unemployment and hunger have been eliminated. **One such argument is that** by allocating public resources to the arts we actually help to solve these social problems. Consider Canada's film industry, which is heavily subsidized by the Canadian government, and which provides countless jobs for film-industry workers as a result. The Canadian government also provides various incentives for American production companies to film and produce their movies in Canada. These incentives have sparked a boon for the Canadian economy, thereby stimulating job growth and wealth that can be applied toward education, job training, and social programs. The Canadian example is proof that public arts support can help solve the kinds of social problems with which the speaker is concerned.

A second argument against the speaker's position has to do with the function and ultimate objectives of art. Art serves to lift the human spirit and to put us more in touch with our feelings, foibles, and fate—in short, with our own humanity. With a heightened sensitivity to the human condition, we become more others-oriented, less self-centered, more giving of ourselves. **In other words**, we become a more charitable society—more willing to give to those less fortunate than ourselves in the ways with which the speaker is concerned. The speaker might argue, of course, that we do a disservice to others when we lend a helping hand—by enabling them to depend on us to survive. **However**, at the heart of this specious argument lies a certain coldness and lack of compassion that, in my view, any society should seek to discourage. **Besides**, the argument leads inexorably to certain political, philosophical, and moral issues that this brief essay cannot begin to address.

In the final analysis, the beneficiaries of public arts funding are not limited to the elitists who stroll through big-city museums and attend symphonies and gallery openings, as the speaker might have us believe. Public resources allocated to the arts create jobs for artists and others whose livelihood depends on a vibrant, rich culture—just the sort of culture that breeds charitable concern for the hungry, the helpless, and the hapless.

合理使用公共资源

演讲人认为，在一个有人挨饿、失业、没有基本生存技能的社会中，利用公共资源来支持艺术事业是不合理的。由于艺术不是人类的基本需要，而且说到其支持艺术事业的动机和方法这方面，政府并非完全值得信赖，因此，演讲人的观点或许容易得到人们的认同。但是，演讲人忽略了政府积极支持艺术事业时所得到的某些经济上的和其他社会上的效益。

演讲人所做的陈述的潜在理论基础似乎是，文化丰富的重要性与充饥、蔽体、容身之所的重要性相比就显得微不足道。后几种需求确是人类更为基础的需求，这一点是不争的事实。毕竟，饥饿的人难道会更想要一幅上佳的图画而不是一顿劣质的饭？因此，我承认当说到使用公共资源的时候，赋予其他急需解决的社会问题优先使用权，之后才轮到艺术，这样做是完全恰当的。但是，如果要等到我们完全消灭失业和饥饿之后才建立公共艺术基金就意味着这一基金将永远建立不起来。任何一个有知识的人，若认为情况并非如此的话，那么他就是在设想一个纯粹的社会主义国家，在这个国家中，政府满足所有的公民需求——这种设想等于是空想。

赞助艺术并不是一个政府当然和必然的职责，基于此，演讲人的观点也可能很容易得到认同。这一论点在三个方面有着相当大的价值。第一，把为艺术提供基金的决定权和选择权交到少数官僚的手中似乎是失策的。这些人可能会根据自己对艺术的奇思怪想来做决定，而他们的决定可能容易受到四处兜售的影响力的左右。第二，当今社会私人的慈善团体和慈善事业显得很有活力，运作良好。例如，在私人基金会和个人捐赠的帮助下，公众广播系统能够一年年地存活下来甚至成长壮大起来。第三，政府基金从我们的口袋里掏走了大量的税金，使我们可用来支持艺术事业的金钱减少了，而我们对艺术的支持原本可以比任何一个官僚所能做到的更加直接和更为有效。

另一方面，有两个很有说服力的观点，认为无论失业和饥饿的问题是否已经解决，对艺术事业的公众支持都是很需要的。其中的一个论点是通过把公共资源分配给艺术事业，实际上有助于我们解决这些社会问题。参考加拿大的电影工业，它得到了加拿大政府的大力补贴资助。其结果是，加拿大的电影工业为电影工作者提供了无数的就业机会。加拿大政府也为美国的电影制片商提供各种鼓励性措施，鼓励他们到加拿大拍摄和制作电影。这些鼓励措施为加拿大的经济增添了活力，从而刺激了就业增长和财富的积累，而这些增长和财富又可以应用于教育、职业培训和社会工程。加拿大的例子证明了，支持公共艺术事业有助于解决演讲人所关心的那些社会问题。

与演讲人观点相左的第二个论点与艺术事业的功能及其最终目的有关。艺术可用来提升人们的精神境界，使我们更贴近自己的感觉、弱点和命运，一句话，就是更贴近自己的本性。随着对人类生存状态敏感度的增加，我们那种以自我为中心的意识变得较为淡薄了，更加为他人着想了，更愿意奉献自我了。换句话说，我们正在变成一个更加仁爱的社会，更加愿意向那些在演讲人所关心的方面比我们不幸的人给予帮助。当然，演讲人也许会辩解说，当我们向那些人伸出援助之手的时候，实际上对他们造成了一种伤害，因为这使得他们要依赖我们来生存。但是，这一似是而非的论点的核心之处却体现出一种冷漠和同情心的缺乏，而在我看来，任何一个社会都应当努力加以消除。此外，这一论点必将导致一些政治、哲学和道德上的问题，这些问题并不是这篇短文所能开始解决的。

总而言之，公众艺术资金的受益者并不像演讲人要让我们相信的那样，只是那些漫步在各大城市博物馆中的、欣赏各种交响乐和参加画廊开幕典礼的精英人物。把公共资源分配到艺术事业上为艺术家们创造了就业的机会，也为那些以充满生机的、繁荣丰富的文化为生的人们提供了工作机会，也正是这种文化培育出了对那些饥饿者、无助者和不幸者怀有的仁爱之心。

论点　平衡观点　大部分篇幅看似都是在论述投资艺术的合理性，但是第二、三两段还是先做了让步，同意题目中的观点，这种套路在多篇文章中都被使用。

开头方式 陈述题目观点 + 原因 + 驳斥题目观点　　其特点有二：首先，这是一个与 Argument 非常相似的开头，从这一点来说，大家要慎用这种开头，因为 ETS 在其官方报告中明确声明，考生应该避免将 Issue 与 Argument 混淆，否则就失去了分开考核的意义；其次，整个开头没有出现"I"，没有直接的第一人称出现，具有十分客观的特点。

论证过程 结论型　　论证部分的四个自然段分成两个层次，第一段是典型的让步结构，先是支持题目观点的合理性，但是后面却没有提出作者标新立异的观点，而是在题目观点内部分析其不合理之处。与开头段相比，首先，论证第一段有更加具体的例子；其次，有更加具体的论证方法（反证法）。论证第二段也是在论述题目观点的合理性，为什么要花篇幅去分析题目的观点呢？因为大多数 Issue 的观点都是平衡的，你在进行正面论述的同时，就是在为后面的驳论做铺垫。后两段就是在驳斥题目观点的错误。

论证模式

① The implicit rationale behind the speaker's statement seems to be that...

② It might also be tempting to agree with the speaker on the basis that...

③ On the other hand are two compelling arguments that public support for the arts is desirable. One such argument is that...

④ A second argument against the speaker's position has to do with the function and ultimate objectives of art.

Issue 121　　Our responsibility to **save endangered species**

"**At various times in the geological past, many species have become extinct as a result of natural, rather than human, processes. Thus, there is no justification for society to make extraordinary efforts, especially at a great cost in money and jobs, to save endangered species.**"

在过去不同的地质时期，许多的物种因为自然作用而非人类行为而灭绝。因此，人类社会为了挽救濒危物种而付出的非常努力，尤其是以大量的资金和工作职位为代价的努力，是毫无道理的。

What are the limits of our duty to save endangered species from extinction? **The statement raises a variety of issues about** morality, conscience, self-preservation, and economics. **On balance, however, I fundamentally agree with the notion that** humans need not make "extraordinary" efforts—at the expense of money and jobs—to ensure the preservation of any endangered species.

As I see it, there are three fundamental arguments for imposing on ourselves at least some responsibility to preserve endangered species. The first has to do culpability. According to this argument, to the extent that endangerment is the result of anthropogenic events such as clear-cutting of forests or polluting of lakes and streams, we humans have a duty to take affirmative measures to protect the species whose survival we've placed in jeopardy.

The second argument has to do with capability. This argument disregards the extent to which we humans might have contributed to the endangerment of a species. Instead, the argument goes, if we are aware of the danger, know what steps are needed to prevent extinction, and can take those steps, then we are morally obligated to help prevent extinction. This argument would place a very high affirmative duty on humans to protect endangered species.

The third argument is an appeal to self-preservation. The animal kingdom is an intricate matrix of interdependent relationships, in which each species depends on many others for its survival. Severing certain relationships, such as that between a predator and its natural prey, can set into motion a series of extinctions that ultimately might endanger our own survival as a species. While this claim might sound far-fetched to some, environmental experts assure us that in the long run it is a very real possibility.

On the other hand are two compelling arguments against placing a duty on humans to protect endangered species. **The first** is essentially the Darwinian argument that extinction results from the inexorable process of so-called "natural selection" in which stronger species survive while weaker ones do not. Moreover, we humans are not exempt from the process. **Accordingly**, if we see fit to eradicate other species in order to facilitate our survival, then so be it. We are only behaving as animals must, Darwin would no doubt assert.

The second argument, and the one that I find most compelling, is an appeal to logic over emotion. It is a scientific fact that thousands of animal species become extinct every year. Many such extinctions are due to natural forces, while others are due to anthropogenic factors. In any event, it is far beyond our ability to save them all. By what standard, then, should we decide which species are worth saving and which ones are not? In my observation, we tend to favor animals with human-like physical characteristics and behaviors. This preference is understandable; after all, dolphins are far more endearing than bugs. But there is no logical justification for such a standard. Accordingly, what makes more sense is to decide based on our own economic self-interest. **In other words**, the more money and jobs it would cost to save a certain species, the lower priority we should place on doing so.

In sum, the issue of endangered-species protection is a complex one, requiring subjective judgments about moral duty and the comparative value of various life-forms. **Thus**, there are no easy or certain answers. Yet it is for this very reason I agree that economic self-interest should take precedence over vague notions about moral duty when it comes to saving endangered species. **In the final analysis**, at a point when it becomes critical for our own survival as a species to save certain others, **then** we humans will do so if we are fit—in accordance with Darwin's observed process of natural selection.

我们拯救濒临灭绝物种的职责

对于拯救濒临灭绝的物种，我们的责任有何限度呢？这一陈述引发了各种有关道德、良知、自我保护和经济学的问题。然而，总的来说，我基本上同意这一观点，即人类无须为保证濒临灭绝物种的生存做出"非常"的努力——即以金钱和职位为代价。

就我看来，有三条主要论据支持我们必须为保护濒临灭绝物种至少承担某种责任。第一个论据和负罪感有关。这一论据认为，正是伐光森林、污染江湖这些以人类为主角的事件造成了物种濒临灭绝的局面，在这种程度上来看，人类有责任采取积极的措施来保护那些濒临灭绝境地的物种，因为是我们危及了它们的生存。

第二条论据与能力有关。这一观点并不计较人类在何种程度上可能造成了一种物种濒危。相反，这一论据认为，如果我们已意识到这种危险，知道需要采取何种措施来防止物种灭绝，而且有能力将其付诸实施，那么我们在道义上就有责任来帮助阻止物种灭绝。这一观点要求人类在保护濒临灭绝物种方面负有非常积极的责任。

第三条论据是一种对人类自我保护的呼吁。动物王国的结构组成非常复杂，各物种间存在着相互依赖的关系。在这个结构矩阵中，每一个物种的存活都离不开其他物种的存在。当物种之间存在的某些关系（例如某种食肉动物与其天然猎物之间的关系）被破坏的时候，就会引发一系列的物种灭绝情况，而人类作为自然界中的一个物种，最终我们自身的生存也将受到威胁。尽管这种断言在有些人听来可能略觉牵强，但是环境学专家向我们保证长此以往这种情况极有可能发生。

另一方面，有两个令人信服的论据，反对人类应该为保护濒临灭绝动物承担责任的说法。第一个观点基本上承袭了达尔文的说法，认为物种灭绝是所谓"物竞天择"这一无情过程的结果，较强的物种在这一过程中生存下来而较弱的物种则被淘汰。而且，我们人类在这一过程中也难以幸免。因此，如果我们认为为了给我们人类自己的生存提供便利，根除其他一些物种是应当的，那么这么做就是应当的。达尔文肯定会说，我们只是在做动物必须做的事情罢了。

第二条论据，也是我认为最令人信服的一条论据，更多地诉诸于理性而非感情。每年都有成百上千的物种从地球上消失，这是一个科学的事实。这其中有很大一部分是由自然力量造成的，剩下的才是人为因素造成的。无论如何，要拯救所有的物种都是远远超出我们能力范围的。那么我们该用何种标准来决定哪些物种值得拯救，那些又不值得呢？依我看来，我们倾向于保护那些外表和行为与人相似的动物。这种偏好是可以理解的，毕竟，海豚要比臭虫可爱得多。但是这种标准没有理性的合理原因。所以，根据我们自身的经济利益来做出决定更为有理。换句话说，对某个物种的挽救需要花费的金钱和投入的人员越多，我们对其的考虑就应当越少。

总之，保护濒临灭绝物种是一个复杂的问题，需要对道义上的责任和不同生命形态的相对价值做主观判断。因此没有简单或者确定的答案。然而，正是基于上述原因，当谈到拯救濒临灭绝物种的时候，相比概念模糊的道德责任，我认为应该优先考虑自身的经济利益。总而言之，作为一个物种，当我们人类到了为自身的生存而不得不去拯救其他某些物种的危急关头时，如果我们应该去拯救它们的话，我们就会去这么做——这与达尔文所奉行的自然选择过程是一致的。

论点 平衡观点　本文的观点有一定的迷惑性，看似一边倒地赞成题目观点，其实是一方面承认必须为保护濒临灭绝物种承担一部分责任，另一方面又反对人类应该为保护濒临灭绝动物承担责任的说法。作者真正的立场还是"平衡观点"。

开头方式 提出问题＋表明立场　前面你曾经见过以一般疑问句方式开头的"投机"做法，这里是以设问的方式引出话题，作用和原理其实是一样的。

论证过程 因果型　论证部分的五个自然段泾渭分明，分成两个大的层次：前面三段支持必须为保护濒临灭绝物种承担一部分责任，给出了三个论据；后面两段反对人类应该为保护濒临灭绝动物承担责任的说法，给出了两个论据。其中大量使用例证法（达到五个之多），是一篇条理清晰、思路开阔、论证精彩的文章。

论证模式

① As I see it, there are three fundamental arguments for...The first...

② The second argument has to do with capability.

③ The third argument is an appeal to logic over emotion.

④ On the other hand are two compelling arguments against...

⑤ The second argument, and the one that I find most compelling, is an appeal to...

Issue 186　Is practicality our idol **in today's world**?

"Practicality is now our great idol, which all powers and talents must serve. Anything that is not obviously practical has little value in today's world."

实用性是我们现在崇拜的对象,一切的力量和才智都必须为其服务。任何并非显著实用的东西在当今世界几乎都是没有价值的。

In today's world is practicality our idol—one which all powers and talents must serve? While this claim has considerable merit with respect to most areas of human endeavor—including education, art, and politics—I take exception with the claim when it comes to the direction of scientific research today.

Practicality seems clearly to be the litmus test for education today. Grade-schoolers are learning computer skills right along with reading and writing. Our middle and high schools are increasingly cutting arts education, which ostensibly has less practical value than other course work. And, more and more college students are majoring in technical fields for the purpose of securing lucrative jobs immediately upon graduation. **Admittedly**, many college students still advance to graduate-level study; yet the most popular such degree today is the MBA; **after all**, business administration is fundamentally about practicality and pragmatism—that is, "getting the job done" and paying attention to the "bottom line."

Practicality also dictates what sort of art is produced today. Most new architecture today is driven by functionality, safety, and cost; very few architectural masterpieces find their way past the blueprint stage anymore. The content of today's feature films and music is driven entirely by demographic considerations—that is, by pandering to the interests of 18 – 35 year olds, who account for most ticket and CD sales. And, the publishing industry today is driven by immediate concern to deliver viable products to the marketplace. The glut of how-to books in our bookstores today is evidence that publishers are pandering to our practicality as well. It isn't that artists no longer create works of high artistic value and integrity. Independent record labels, filmmakers, and publishing houses abound today. It's just that the independents do not thrive, and they constitute a minuscule segment of the market. **In the main**, today's real-estate developers, entertainment moguls, and publishing executives are concerned with practicality and profit, and not with artistic value and integrity.

Practicality is also the overriding concern in contemporary politics. Most politicians seem driven today by their interest in being elected and reelected—that is, in short-term survival—rather than by any sense of mission, or even obligation to their constituency or country. Diplomatic and legal maneuverings and negotiations often appear intended to meet the practical needs of the parties involved—minimizing costs, preserving options, and so forth. Those who would defend the speaker might claim that it is idealists—not pragmatists—who sway the masses, incite revolutions, and make political ideology reality. Consider idealists such as the America's founders, or Mahatma Gandhi, or Martin Luther King. Had these idealists concerned themselves with short-term survival and immediate needs rather than with their notions of an ideal society, the United States and India might still be British colonies, and African Americans might still be relegated to the backs of buses. Although I concede this point, the plain fact is that such idealists are far fewer in number today.

On the other hand, the claim amounts to an overstatement when it comes to today's scientific endeavors. In medicine the most common procedures today are cosmetic; these procedures strike me as highly impractical, given the health risks and expense involved. **Admittedly**, today's digital revolution serves a host of practical concerns, such as communicating and accessing information more quickly and efficiently. Much of chemical research is also aimed at practicality—at providing convenience and enhancing our immediate comfort. **Yet**, in many other respects scientific research is not driven toward immediate practicality but rather toward broad, long-term objectives: public health, quality of life, and environmental protection.

In sum, practicality may be our idol today when it comes to education, the arts, and politics; but with respect to science I find the claim to be an unfair generalization. **Finally**, query whether the claim begs the question. **After all**, practicality amounts to far more than meeting immediate needs; it also embraces long-term planning and prevention aimed at ensuring our future quality of life, and our very survival as a species.

在当今的世界中，实用性是我们崇拜的对象吗？

在当今的世界中，实用性是不是我们所崇拜的对象，所有的能量和才能都要为其服务呢？这一主张在人类从事的大多数工作领域中是相当有价值的，包括教育、艺术和政治。但是当谈到当今的科学研究方向时，我却对这一主张持有异议。

实用性对今天的教育来说很像是一块试金石。小学生们在学习读写技能的同时也在学习计算机技能。我们的初中和高中正在不断地减少艺术类的课程，这些课程从表面上看不如其他课程的实用价值高。还有越来越多的大学生为了能够在毕业后立即找到一份好的工作而选择学习技术类的专业。无可否认，很多大学生毕业后仍然会继续深造，攻读研究生，但是今天最吃香的研究生学位却是工商管理学硕士。毕竟，工商管理从根本上来讲就是关于实用性和实用主义的，就是把"工作做成"，注意"底线"。

实用性也支配着今天何种艺术能被生产制造出来。如今，大多数新的建筑都受到了功能性、安全性和成本因素的影响，少有建筑杰作还能够通过图纸设计阶段了。人口统计上的考虑完全主宰着现今的故事片和音乐的内容，也就是说迎合 18 岁到 35 岁人群的兴趣，这一部分人是电影票和音乐 CD 的主要消费群体。而今天的出版业首先要考虑的就是要发行那些在市场上可能畅销的产品。我们的书架上充斥着各种教人实际操作方法的书籍，这一点也证明了出版商也正在努力迎合我们对实用性的要求。并不是说艺术家们不再创作具有极高艺术价值的完善作品。在今天仍有大量的独立唱片公司、电影制作人和出版社存在。只不过他们的发展并不繁荣，在市场中仅占有极其少的份额。从大体上看，今天的房地产开发商、娱乐业大亨和出版界巨头只关心产品的实用性和所能创造的利益，而不再关心它的艺术价值和是否完善。

实用性也是当今政治所考虑的首要问题。大多数的政客似乎都是受到能否当选和连任的利益驱使，即他们短期内的政治生命——并不是什么使命感，甚至也不是对他们的选民或国家的责任感。外交和法律上的策略和谈判看上去经常是为了满足相关各方的实际需要——花最少的钱、保留选择权等等。那些为演讲人观点辩护的人可能会声称，那些发动群众、煽动革命、要让政治意识形态成为现实的人是理想主义者，而不是实用主义者。那些美国的创立者们或是圣雄甘地或是马丁·路德·金都是这一类理想主义者。如果这些理想主义者只考虑自己短期的生存和眼前的需要，而不是追求他们对于理想社会的信念，那么美国和印度可能依旧是英国的殖民地，美国的黑人可能仍需要坐在公共汽车的后排位置。尽管我承认这一观点，但是实际的情况却是这样的理想主义者在如今已经少之又少了。

另一方面，当谈到今天的科研工作上时，这种说法就显得不合实际了。今天医学上最普通常见的一种手术就是整容手术，考虑到这一手术给健康带来的风险和所花费的大量金钱，我认为这一手术是极其不实用的。无可否认，今天的数字革命是为很多实用需求服务的，例如使通讯和信息获取变得更加的快捷高效。很多的化学研究也以实用性为目标——为我们提供便利，使我们感觉更加舒适。但是，在其他许多方面，科学研究并不是受立竿见影的实用性所驱使的，而是为了一些广阔的、长期的目标，如公共卫生、生活质量和环境保护。

　　总之，在教育、艺术、政治等领域，实用性可能是我们今天所崇尚的对象。但是我发现在科学领域这种说法并不是普遍适用的。最后，这种说法是否是回避问题时以假定为论据的狡辩还有待商榷。毕竟，实用性并不仅仅意味着满足眼前的需要。它同样也包括为保证我们未来的生活质量和我们作为一个物种的生存所做的长期规划和预防工作。

〔论点〕 **有保留的赞成**　作者一方面赞成题目的主张，即在人类从事的大多数工作领域中是正确的，另一方面用较小篇幅谈到对当今的科学研究的方向持有异议。

〔开头方式〕 **提出问题 + 回答 + 表明立场**

〔论证过程〕 **因果型**　题目的因果关系为：实用 = 价值。论证前三段为"实用 = 价值"成立的情况，分别举了三方面的例子——教育、艺术和政治；最后一段为"不实用也有价值"，举了长期科研为例子。

〔论证模式〕

① Practicality seems clearly to be the litmus test for...

② Practicality also dictates...

③ Practicality is also the overriding concern in...

④ On the other hand, the claim amounts to an overstatement when it comes to today's scientific endeavors.

Issue 4　Advancements in a **field of study** and outside experts

"**No field of study can advance significantly unless outsiders bring their knowledge and experience to that field of study.**"

在任何一个研究领域当中,除非有该领域之外的人引进他们的知识和经验,否则该领域就很难获得巨大的发展。

I strongly agree with the assertion that significant advances in knowledge require expertise from various fields. The world around us presents a seamless web of physical and anthropogenic forces, which interact in ways that can be understood only in the context of a variety of disciplines. Two examples that aptly illustrate this point involve the fields of cultural anthropology and astronomy.

Consider how a cultural anthropologist's knowledge about an ancient civilization is enhanced not only by the expertise of the archeologist—who unearths the evidence—but ultimately by the expertise of biochemists, geologists, linguists, and even astronomers. By analyzing the hair, nails, blood, and bones of mummified bodies, biochemists and forensic scientists can determine the life expectancy, general well-being, and common causes of death of the population. These experts can also ensure the proper preservation of evidence found at the archeological site. A geologist can help identify the source and age of the materials used for tools, weapons, and structures—thereby enabling the anthropologist, to extrapolate about the civilization's economy, trades and work habits, lifestyles, extent of travel and mobility, and so forth. Linguists are needed to interpret hieroglyphics and extrapolate from found fragments of writings. And an astronomer can help explain the layout of an ancient city as well as the design, structure and position of monuments, tombs, and temples—since ancients often looked to the stars for guidance in building cities and structures.

An even more striking example of how expertise in diverse fields is needed to advance knowledge **involves the area of astronomy and space exploration.** Significant advancements in our knowledge of the solar system and the universe require increasingly keen tools for observation and measurement. Telescope technology and the measurement of celestial distances, masses, volumes, and so forth, are the domain of astrophysicists. These advances also require increasingly sophisticated means of exploration. Manned and unmanned exploratory probes are designed by mechanical, electrical, and computer engineers. And to build and enable these technologies requires the acumen and savvy of business leaders, managers, and politicians. Even diplomats might play a role—insofar as major space projects require international cooperative efforts among the world's scientists and governments. And ultimately it is our philosophers whose expertise helps provide meaning to what we learn about our universe.

In sum, no area of intellectual inquiry operates in a vacuum. Because the sciences are inextricably related, to advance our knowledge in any one area we must understand the interplay among them all. **Moreover**, it is our non-scientists who make possible the science, and who bring meaning to what we learn from it.

一个研究领域的进步与其他领域的专家

我非常同意以下主张，即知识方面的重大进步需要各个领域的专门知识。我们周围的世界是一张天衣无缝的网，它由自然及人为力量组成，这些力量相互作用的方式只有在了解多个学科的情况下才能为人所理解。文化人类学和天文学领域的两个例子可以适当地阐明这一点。

想想一位文化人类学家对一种古代文明的了解是怎样既由挖掘证据的考古学家又最终由生化学家、地质学者、语言学家，甚至是天文学家的专门知识得以提高的吧。通过分析木乃伊尸体的头发、指甲、血液和骨骼，生化学家与法医专家可以确定发现的古人类的寿命、总体健康状况及通常死因。这些专家还可以确保对在考古地点发现的证据进行适当维护。地质学家能够识别用做工具、武器和建筑物的材料的来源与年代，因此可以使得人类学家推断出该人类文明的经济、贸易与工作习惯、生活方式、旅游和流动的范围等等。之所以需要语言学家是因为他们可以解释象形文字并能够从发现的只言片语中做出推断。由于古人经常通过看星星来指导他们修建城市与建筑物，所以天文学家可以有助于解释古城的布局、纪念碑、坟墓及庙宇的设计、结构和位置。

不同领域的专门知识对于促进知识的增长是如何必要，天文学和太空探索领域是一个更为显著的例子。我们对太阳系和宇宙的了解所取得的重大进步都越来越需要灵敏的观察工具和测量工具。望远镜技术与对太空的距离、质量、体积等等的测量都是天体物理学家的职责范围。这些进步还日益需要高级的探索手段。机械、电学和计算机工程师设计了载人或无人的探测器。而生产并且能够运用这些技术需要企业领导、管理人员和政界领导的才干和见识。甚至外交官也会起到作用——就主要的太空项目来说，都需要全世界的科学家和各国政府之间的国际合作才能完成。最终是哲学家的知识赋予了我们对宇宙的了解以意义。

总之，没有任何知识探索的领域是在真空中进行的。因为科学家之间的联系是必然的，我们必须理解他们之间所有的相互影响才能提高我们在任何一个领域的知识。而且，正是非科学家的专家使科学成为可能，并赋予其意义。

论点 **完全赞成**　大多数 Issue 题目都是采取平衡的立场，但是并不排除一边倒的情况。本文就是完全赞成题目观点。

开头方式 **表明立场 + 概述理由**　非常像全文提纲的一种开头方式，好处是非常清楚，就算你不看论证段也能知道下面是怎么展开的（是不是很没有悬念?）。这里的立场自然就是完全赞成或者完全反对，概述的理由自然就是后面给出的几个特例。

论证过程 **因果型**　题目中的"因"和"果"其实就是"引进外来知识＝巨大发展"，但由于该题同时也是一道抽象类题目（题目中只讲"在任何一个研究领域中"，也就是在所有领域中），所以本来应该写成一方面"引进外来知识＝巨大发展"，另一方面"引进外来知识≠巨大发展"，本文却只写了赞成的情况。论证只有两段，两个特例：人类学和天文学。

◆　*Tip*　我们之所以要用以偏概全处理抽象类题目，是因为它很难写完整；但是，"引进外来知识＝巨大发展"和"引进外来知识≠巨大发展"是不是可以看成是另外两个抽象类题目呢？你是不是可以在每个内部用特例来论证呢？再把两大部分合起来，还是一个完整的平衡观点！所以 Issue 的处理方法有很多种，根据你的想法和掌握的资料得出你自己的结论。

论证模式

　① Consider how a cultural anthropologist's knowledge about an ancient civilization...

　② An even more striking example...involves the area of astronomy and space exploration.

Issue 10　Government's duty to preserve **cultural traditions**

"**Governments must ensure that their major cities receive the financial support they need in order to thrive, because it is primarily in cities that a nation's cultural traditions are preserved and generated.**"

政府必须要确保主要城市繁荣发展所需的财政支持,因为一个国家的文化传统主要是在城市中得以保存和产生。

The speaker's claim is actually threefold: (1) ensuring the survival of large cities and, in turn, that of cultural traditions, is a proper function of government; (2) government support is needed for our large cities and cultural traditions to survive and thrive; and (3) cultural traditions are preserved and generated primarily in our large cities. **I strongly disagree with all three claims.**

　First of all, subsidizing cultural traditions is not a proper role of government. Admittedly, certain objectives, such as public health and safety, are so essential to the survival of large cities and of nations that government has a duty to ensure that they are met. **However**, these objectives should not extend tenuously to preserving cultural traditions. **Moreover**, government cannot possibly play an evenhanded role as cultural patron. Inadequate resources call for restrictions, priorities, and choices. It is unconscionable to relegate normative decisions as to which cities or cultural traditions are more deserving, valuable, or needy to a few legislators, whose notions about culture might be misguided or unrepresentative of those of the general populace. **Also**, legislators are all too likely to make choices in favor of the cultural agendas of their home towns and states, or of lobbyists with the most money and influence.

　Secondly, subsidizing cultural traditions is not a necessary role of government. A lack of private funding might justify an exception. **However**, culture—by which I chiefly mean the fine arts—has always depended primarily on the patronage of private individuals and businesses, and not on the government. The Medicis, a powerful banking family of Renaissance Italy, supported artists Michelangelo and Raphael. During the twentieth century the primary source of cultural support were private foundations established by industrial magnates Carnegie, Mellon, Rockefeller, and Getty. And tomorrow cultural support will come from our new technology and media moguls—including the likes of Ted Turner and Bill Gates. In short, philanthropy is alive and well today, and so government need not intervene to ensure that our cultural traditions are preserved and promoted.

Finally, and perhaps most importantly, the speaker unfairly suggests that large cities serve as the primary breeding ground and sanctuaries for a nation's cultural traditions. Today a nation's distinct cultural traditions—its folk art, crafts, traditional songs, customs and ceremonies—burgeon instead in small towns and rural regions. **Admittedly,** our cities do serve as our centers for "high art"; big cities are where we deposit, display, and boast the world's preeminent art, architecture, and music. **But** big-city culture has little to do anymore with one nation's distinct cultural traditions. **After all,** modern cities are essentially multicultural stew pots; accordingly, by assisting large cities a government is actually helping to create a global culture as well to subsidize the traditions of other nations' cultures.

In the final analysis, government cannot philosophically justify assisting large cities for the purpose of either promoting or preserving the nation's cultural traditions; nor is government assistance necessary toward these ends. Moreover, assisting large cities would have little bearing on our distinct cultural traditions, which abide elsewhere.

政府保护文化传统的职责

演讲人的观点实际上有三层含义：（1）确定保存大城市进而保护文化传统是政府的应有职责；（2）大城市与文化传统的保存和繁荣必须要有政府的支持；（3）文化传统主要是在大城市里产生并保存下来的。对这三层意思我都很不赞成。

首先，出资保护文化传统并不是政府的应有职责。诚然，某些目标计划，比如公共卫生与安全对大城市和国家的生存是必不可少的，政府的确有责任确保能够实现这些目标。但是，不应该空泛地把这些目标计划扩展到保护文化传统。而且，政府作为文化资助人不可能起到公正的作用，因为资源短缺要求对其使用进行限制、优先使用和有所选择。把关于哪些城市或文化传统更值得关注、更有价值、更需要保护的标准化决议提交给几个概念也许被误导、并不代表公众的立法者是很不合理的做法。而且，立法者都极其可能做出有利于自己城市和州的或者有利于那些有钱有势的说客的文化议程的选择。

其次，出资保护文化传统也不是政府的必要职责。缺乏私人资金也许可以算个例外。但是，文化，我主要指的是美术，总是主要依赖于私人和私人企业的赞助，而不是依靠政府。文艺复兴时意大利颇有权势的金融家族梅第奇，就曾经支持过艺术家米开朗基罗和拉菲尔。20世纪，主要的文化支持来源是由工业巨头卡耐基、梅隆、洛克菲勒和格蒂成立的私人基金会。未来的文化支持将来自新技术和媒体大亨，包括泰德·特纳与比尔·盖茨这些人物。简言之，慈善事业今天依然完好地存在，政府不需要进行干涉以保证我们的文化传统得以保护和发扬。

最终可能也是最重要的，讲话者提出大城市起着一个国家文化传统主要的生成场所及避难场所的作用，这很不公平。当今一个国家独特的民间艺术、工艺、传统歌曲、风俗以及仪式等文化传统反而是在小城镇和乡村地区快速发展的。无庸讳言，我们的城市的确起着"高雅文化"中心的作用；大城市是我们储存、展示、炫耀世界卓越的艺术、建筑以及音乐的地方。但是大城市的文化与我们国家独特的文化传统几乎不再有什么联系。毕竟，现代的城市从根本上来说是多文化的大熔炉，因此，通过帮助大城市政府实际上是帮助建立全球文化，也是在资助其他国家的文化传统。

最终，为了发扬或者保护国家的文化传统而帮助大城市，政府不能从哲学理念上证明这种做法是合理的，也不能证明这种政府帮助对于实现这些目标是必须的。而且，帮助大城市几乎对保护我们独特的文化传统没有什么影响，因为这些文化传统保留在其他地方。

论点 **完全反对**　该文是一个完全反对的典型例子，虽然题目并不是抽象类题目。注意：我们说过凡是抽象类题目都可以选择直线型立场，但并不等于只有抽象类题目才可以选用，有些你十分肯定的细节类题目也适用。

开头方式 **陈述题目观点＋表明立场**　本文的开头很罕见。作者将题目分解成三个逻辑片断，然后声明将各个击破。这种开头和 Argument 惊人地相似，如果依照这种思路，在后面展开过程中就很容易把文章写成 Argument，这是绝对不允许出现的错误！前面提过类似于 Argument 处理方法的文章，好处是可以把很多 Argument 的资源整合利用，这个开头对于有这种想法的读者会比较有价值，但是请小心使用。

论证过程 **釜底抽薪＋因果型**　论证的三个自然段是一种混合论证，本题的因果具有两个前提，为"因为政府应该保存和发展文化传统，而大城市保存和发展文化传统，所以政府应该发展大城市"。论证第一、二段采用的是釜底抽薪的论证方法，攻击第一个前提"政府应该保存和发展文化传统"；论证的最后一段则攻击第二个前提"大城市保存和发展文化传统"。

论证模式

① First of all, subsidizing cultural traditions is not a proper role of government.

② Secondly, subsidizing cultural traditions is not a necessary role of government.

③ Finally, and perhaps most importantly, the speaker unfairly suggests that ...

Issue 8　Should political leaders **withhold information from the public**?

"**It is often necessary, even desirable, for political leaders to withhold information from the public.**"

对于政治领导者来说，向人民大众隐瞒信息通常是必要的，甚至有益的。

I agree with the speaker that it is sometimes necessary, and even desirable, for political leaders to withhold information from the public. A contrary view would reveal a naiveté about the inherent nature of public politics, and about the sorts of compromises on the part of well-intentioned political leaders necessary in order to further the public's ultimate interests. **Nevertheless**, we must not allow our political leaders undue freedom to withhold information; otherwise, we risk sanctioning demagoguery and undermining the philosophical underpinnings of any democratic society.

One reason for my fundamental agreement with the speaker is that in order to gain the opportunity for effective public leadership, a would-be leader must first gain and maintain political power. In the game of politics, complete forthrightness is a sign of vulnerability and naiveté, neither of which earn a politician respect among his or her opponents, and which those opponents will use to every advantage to defeat the politician. In my observation, some measure of pandering to the electorate is necessary to gain and maintain political leadership. **For example**, were all politicians to fully disclose every personal foibles, character flaw, and detail concerning personal life, few honest politicians would ever by elected. While this view might seem cynical, personal scandals have in fact proven the undoing of many a political career; **thus**, I think this view is realistic.

　　Another reason why I essentially agree with the speaker is that fully disclosing to the public certain types of information would threaten public safety and perhaps even national security. **For example**, if the President were to disclose the government's strategies for thwarting specific plans of an international terrorist or a drug trafficker, those strategies would surely fail, and the public's health and safety would be compromised as a result. Withholding information might also be necessary to avoid public panic. While such cases are rare, they do occur occasionally. **For example**, during the first few hours of the new millennium the U.S. Pentagon's missile defense system experienced a Y2K-related malfunction. This fact was withheld from the public until later in the day, once the problem had been solved; and legitimately so, since immediate disclosure would have served no useful purpose and might even have resulted in mass hysteria.

　　Having recognized that withholding information from the public is often necessary to serve the interests of that public, legitimate political leadership **nevertheless** requires forthrightness with the citizenry as to the leader's motives and agenda. History informs us that would-be leaders who lack such forthrightness are the same ones who seize and maintain power either by brute force or by demagoguery—that is, by deceiving and manipulating the citizenry. Paragons such as Genghis Khan and Hitler, respectively, come immediately to mind. Any democratic society should of course abhor demagoguery, which operates against the democratic principle of government by the people. **Consider also** less egregious examples, such as President Nixon's withholding of information about his active role in the Watergate cover-up. His behavior demonstrated a concern for self-interest above the broader interests of the democratic system that granted his political authority in the first place.

　　In sum, the game of politics calls for a certain amount of disingenuousness and lack of forthrightness that we might otherwise characterize as dishonesty. And such behavior is a necessary means to the final objective of effective political leadership. **Nevertheless**, in any democracy a leader who relies chiefly on deception and secrecy to preserve that leadership, to advance a private agenda, or to conceal selfish motives, betrays the democracy—and ends up forfeiting the political game.

政界领导应该对公众封锁消息吗？

　　政界领导对公众封锁消息有时是必需的，甚至是适当的做法，我同意演讲者的这一观点。一个相反的观点暴露了对于公共政治固有本质和对于善意的政界领导一方为了促进公众的最终利益而需要采用的妥协方式的一种天真幼稚的行为。然而，我们一定不能允许政界领导拥有过度的自由来封锁消息，否则，我们就会难脱准许煽动群众行为以及削弱任何民主社会的哲学理论根基的嫌疑。

　　我从根本上同意演讲人的观点的一个原因是：为了得到有效的公众领导权的机会，一位想成为领导的人必须首先获得并且维持政治权力。在政治游戏中，完全的直率是软弱可欺、天真幼稚的标志，这两个缺点都不会在对手中赢得一个政治家应有的尊敬，那些政敌们反而会在每一个有利条件下利用这两个缺点来打败对手。据我的观察，某种迎合选民的方法对于赢得与维持政治领导权是必需的。比如，如果所有的政界领导都彻底暴露每一个私人弱点、性格缺陷以及有关个人生活的细节，那么几乎没有几个诚实正直的政界领导可以当选。尽管这种观点也许有些愤世嫉俗，但事实上个人的丑闻却证明确是许多官员政治生涯的祸根，所以，我认为此观点还是很现实的。

我基本上同意演讲人的观点的另一个原因是：完全彻底地对公众公开某些类别的信息可能会威胁到公众安全，甚至可能威胁到国家安全。比如，如果总统将要公开政府用于反对一个国际恐怖分子或者一个毒品走私贩的明确计划的策略，这些策略一定会失败，而导致的结果是公众的健康与安全将会受到威胁。封锁消息对于避免公众恐慌也是必需的。虽然这样的情形是罕见的，但是有时确实会发生。比如，在新千年最初的几个小时美国五角大楼导弹防御系统经受了与Y2K相关的故障。这一事实直到当天晚些时候问题被解决后才公诸于众。这样做是很合理的，因为立即公布该危险情况不会有任何用处，反而可能导致公众歇斯底里的恐慌。

意识到对公众封锁消息对于维护公众的利益通常是必需的，然而关于领导的做事动机和议事日程，正常的政治领导需要对全体公民坦诚直率。历史告诉我们，那些缺乏坦率的想成为领导的人与通过强力或者通过煽动行为来攫取并维护（也就是通过欺骗、操纵公民大众）他们权力的人同出一辙。我们头脑中会立刻分别想到像成吉思汗与希特勒这样的典范。当然任何民主社会都应该憎恨煽动群众的行为，因为这种煽动的操作违反了民治的政府的民主原则。再来考虑一下不是那么异乎寻常的例子吧。比如尼克松总统努力封锁关于他在水门事件中所起的积极作用的消息。他的行为显示了对于自我利益的关心超过对于民主制度更大利益的关心，而民主制度最初授予了他政治权力。

总之，政治游戏要求政治家有一定程度的、我们可能归结为虚伪欺骗的毫无诚意、缺乏坦率，而且这种行为对于有效政治领导的最终目标的实现是一种必要的方式。然而，在任何一种民主政治里，一个主要依赖欺骗与保密来维护领导权、来推进个人议事日程、或者来隐瞒自私动机的领导人，就是违背了民主的领导人，肯定会在政治游戏中以失败而告终。

论点 **平衡观点** 作者一方面认同政界领导对公众封锁消息有时是必需的，另一方面主张不能允许政界领导滥用自由来封锁消息。

开头方式 **陈述题目观点 + 表明立场**

论证过程 **结论型** 标准的"why + if...then..."展开模式。论证前两段分析题目观点背后的原因（动机），论证后一段陈述由此产生的不良后果以进行反驳。

论证模式

① One reason for my fundamental agreement with the speaker is that...

② Another reason why I essentially agree with the speaker is that...

③ Having recognized that...nevertheless...

Issue 113 Defining ourselves by identifying **with social groups**

"It is primarily through our identification with social groups that we define ourselves."
如果我们要定位自己最重要是要定位自己所处的社会团体。

I strongly agree that we define ourselves primarily through our identification with social groups, as the speaker asserts. Admittedly, at certain stages of life people often appear to define themselves in other terms. Yet, in my view, during these stages the fundamental need to define one's self through association with social groups is merely masked or suspended.

Any developmental psychologist would agree that socialization with other children plays a critical

role in any child's understanding and psychological development of self. At the day-care center or in the kindergarten class young children quickly learn that they want to play with the same toys at the same time or in the same way as some other children. They come to understand generally what they share in common with certain of their peers—in terms of appearance, behavior, likes and dislikes—and what they do not share in common with other peers or with older students and adults. **In other words**, these children begin to recognize that their identity inextricably involves their kinship with certain peers and alienation from other people.

As children progress to the social world of the playground and other after-school venues, their earlier recognition that they relate more closely to some people than to others evolves into a desire to form well-defined social groups, and to set these groups apart from others. Girls begin to congregate apart from boys; clubs and cliques are quickly formed—often with exclusive rituals, codes, and rules to further distinguish the group's members from other children. This apparent need to be a part of an exclusive group continues through high school, where students identify themselves in their yearbooks by the clubs to which they belonged. Even in college, students eagerly join clubs, fraternities, and sororities to establish their identity as members of social groups. **In my observation**, children are not taught by adults to behave in these ways; **thus**, this desire to identify oneself with an exclusive social group seems to spring from some innate psychological need to define one's self through one's personal associations.

However, as young adults take on the responsibilities of partnering, parenting, and working, they appear to define themselves less by their social affiliations and more by their marital status, parental status, and occupation. The last of these criteria seems particularly important for many adults today. When two adults meet for the first time, beyond initial pleasantries the initial question almost invariably is "What do you do for a living?" **Yet, in my opinion** this shift in focus from one's belonging to a social group to one's occupation is not a shift in how we prefer to define ourselves. **Rather**, it is born of economic necessity—we don't have the leisure time or financial independence to concern ourselves with purely social activities. I find quite telling the fact that when older people retire from the world of work an interest in identifying with social groups—whether they be bridge clubs, investment clubs, or country clubs—seem to reemerge. **In short**, humans seem possessed by an enduring need to be part of a distinct social group—a need that continues throughout life's journey.

In sum, I agree that people gain and maintain their sense of self primarily through their belonging to distinct social groups. Admittedly, there will always be loners who prefer not to belong, for whatever reasons; yet loners are the exception. **Also**, while many working adults might temporarily define themselves in terms of their work for practicality's sake, at bottom we humans are nothing if not social animals.

通过认同社会团体说明我们自己

我非常赞同主要应该通过认同社会团体来说明自己这个观点，正如讲话人所宣称的一样。诚然，在特定的人生阶段人们似乎经常用其他的方式来说明自己。然而，以我的观点看来，在这些阶段通过与社会团体的联系来说明自己的基本需要仅仅是被掩盖或者被搁置了。

任何一位成长心理学家都会承认，与其他孩子的社会交往在任何一个孩子对自我的理解与心理成长过程中都会起到关键作用。在日间托儿中心或者在幼儿园的班里，孩子很快就知道他们想和其他孩子一样在同一时间或者以同样的方式玩同样的玩具。他们逐渐开始了解他们和某些同龄人所共同拥有的东西，比如在外表、行为、喜好与厌恶方面；而且他们还了解到与同龄人或者年龄比他们大的学生以及成年人不同的地方。换言之，这些孩子开始意识到他们身份的确认都不可避免地涉及他们和某些同龄人的亲密关系以及和其他人的疏远关系。

随着孩子向操场以及其他课后地点等社交场所的发展，他们早期的关于与某些人的关系比与其他人的更紧密的认知发展成了一种组成定义明确的社会团体并想要把这些团体与其他团体分开的欲望。女孩子开始聚集在一起而与男孩子分开，俱乐部和小圈子迅速地形成了——通常有独有的仪式、章程和规则以便进一步区分本团体的成员与其他孩子。这种想要成为一个专有团体的明显需要一直持续到高中。高中阶段，学生通过他们所属的俱乐部所颁发的年鉴来认可身份。即使在大学阶段，学生也很渴望加入俱乐部、兄弟会、女学生联谊会来确立他们作为社团成员的身份。据我的观察，孩子不是经过大人教的才这样行为处事。于是，这种通过一个独有社会团体来认可自己的欲望好像来自某种内在的、通过一个人所拥有的个人联系说明自我的心理需要。

但是，随着成年的青年人承担起伴侣、父母以及工作的责任，他们似乎更少地通过社会联系来说明自己，而是更多地通过婚姻身份、父母身份以及职业来说明自己。在今天对许多成年人来说这些标准的最后一项也许尤其重要。当两个成年人初次见面时，除了最初的客套之外，第一个问题几乎毫无例外地是"你做什么工作？"然而，我认为这种从一个人属于一个社会团体到他属于一个职业的重心改变并不是我们喜欢说明自己的方式的改变。这种改变反而是一种经济需要的产物，因为我们没有悠闲的时间或经济上的独立让我们参加到纯粹的社会活动中去。当老年人从工作领域退休以后，一种认同社会团体的兴趣似乎又重新出现了，不管这样的团体是棋类俱乐部、投资俱乐部，或者是乡间俱乐部。简言之，人类似乎被一种成为一个独特无二的团体成员的永恒需要所支配，而且这种需要贯串人生整个旅程。

总的来说，我认为人们主要通过他们所属于某些与众不同的社会团体的方式来获得并且维持自我感。无庸讳言，不管出于什么原因，总是会有不喜欢从属于任何团体的不合群的人。然而，不合群的人只是例外。而且，虽然许多正在工作的成年人可能出于实用的缘故暂时按照所属职业来说明自己，归根结底，我们人类到底还是社会动物。

论点 有保留的赞成

开头方式 让步语气 + 表明立场 让步语气不仅可以用于平衡观点的开头，也一样可以用于倾向型题目的开头。事实上，大多数情况下，你是无法仅仅通过开头来判断一篇文章的立场的。

论证过程 问题解决型 本题关心的问题主要是我们应该如何定位自己。论证的三个自然段提出了两种答案，前两段是在人成年之前（幼儿期、小学、中学和大学），主要依靠所处的团体来定义自身；最后一段是成年的年轻人依靠独立的职业来定义自己，以及老年人靠团体定义自己。

◆ *Tip 他因法* 最常用于问题解决型的一种论证方法，即"题目：A 推出 B；反驳：C（D, E...）推出 B"，所以 AB 之间不存在必然的因果关系。

论证模式

① Any developmental psychologist would agree that socialization with other children...

② As children progress to the social world of the playground and other after-school venues...

③ However, as young adults take on the responsibilities of partnering, parenting, and working...

Issue 136　Is the **absence of choice** a rare circumstance?

"**The absence of choice is a circumstance that is very, very rare.**"

没有选择的情况少之又少。

I strongly agree with the contention that absence of choice is a rare circumstance, primarily because this contention accords with common sense and our everyday experience as human beings. **Besides, the reverse claim**—that we do not have free choice—serves to undermine the notions of moral accountability and human equality, which are critical to the survival of any democratic society.

Our collective life experience is that we make choices and decisions every day—on a continual basis. **Common sense dictates that** humans have free will, and therefore the true absence of choice is very rare. The only possible exceptions would involve extreme and rare circumstances such as solitary imprisonment or a severe mental or physical deficiency—any of which might potentially strip a person of his or her ability to make conscious choices. **Yet,** even under these circumstances, a person still retains choices about voluntary bodily functions and movement. **Thus,** the complete absence of choice would seem to be possible only in a comatose state or in death.

People often claim that life's circumstances leave them with "no choice." One might feel trapped in a job or a marriage. Under financial duress a person might claim that he or she has "no choice" but to declare bankruptcy, take a demeaning job, or even lie or steal to obtain money. **The fundamental problem with these sorts of claims is that** the claimants are only considering those choices that are not viable or attractive. That is, people in situations such as these have an infinite number of choices; it's just that many of the choices are unappealing, even self-defeating. For example, almost every person who claims to be trapped in a job is simply choosing to retain a certain measure of financial security. The choice to forego this security is always available, although it might carry unpleasant consequences.

Besides, the contention that we are almost invariably free to choose is far more appealing from a socio-political standpoint than the opposite claim. A complete lack of choice implies that every person's fate is determined, and that we all lack free will. According to the philosophical school of "strict determinism," every event, including human actions and choices, that occurs is physically necessary given the laws of nature and events that preceded that event or choice. **In other words,** the "choices" that seem part of the essence of our being are actually beyond our control. Recent advances in molecular biology and genetics lend some credence to the determinists' position that as physical beings our actions are determined by physical forces beyond our control. New research suggests that these physical forces include our own individual genetic makeup.

However, the logical result of strict determinism and of the new "scientific determinism" is that we are not morally accountable for our actions and choices, even those that harm other individuals or society. **Moreover,** throughout history monarchs and dictators have embraced determinism, at least ostensibly, to bolster their claim that certain individuals are preordained to assume positions of authority or to rise to the top levels of the socioeconomic infrastructure. **Finally,** the notion of scientific determinism opens the door for genetic engineering, which poses a potential threat to equality in socioeconomic opportunity, and could lead to the development of a so-called "master race." **Admittedly,** these disturbing implications neither prove nor disprove the determinists' claims. **Nevertheless,** assuming that neither free will nor determinism has been proven to be the correct position, the former is to be preferred by any humanist and in any democratic society.

In sum, despite the fact that we all experience occasional feelings of being trapped and having no choice, **the statement is fundamentally correct.** I would concede that science might eventually disprove the very notion of free will. **However**, until that time I'll trust my strong intuition that free will is an essential part of our being as humans and, accordingly, that humans are responsible for their own choices and actions.

没有选择余地的情况少见吗?

我完全同意没有选择余地的情况是少见的,主要因为这个论点与常识和我们人类日常经验相一致。此外,反面的说法——我们没有自由的选择——有损于道德责任和人类平等的观点,而这对任何民主社会的生存都是至关重要的。

我们集体生活的经验是我们每天都持续不断地做出选择和决定。常识告诉我们人有自由的意志,因此完全不能自主选择是很少见的。惟一可能的例外涉及孤独的监禁或生理或心理的不正常这些极端而少见的情况——其中任一种情况都可能剥蚀他或她做出理智选择的能力。但即使在这些环境之下,一个人仍然保有对自觉的身体功能和活动的选择。因此,完全不能自主选择只可能在昏睡或死亡的状态中发生。

人们经常说生活环境使他们"没有选择"。他会觉得陷入工作或婚姻之中。为财政所迫,一个人可能宣称他或她"没有选择"而只能宣布破产,干降级的工作,或者甚至撒谎乃至偷窃来赚钱。这些说法的根本问题在于说话的人认为这些选择是不可行或不诱人的。那就是说,在这些情况下人们可以有众多的选择,只不过许多选择是不诱人的,甚至是自相矛盾的。例如,那些说自己身陷工作之中的人只是在选择保有某种金融保障的办法。放弃这种保障的选择总是可行的,尽管可能会带来令人不悦的后果。

同时,我们总可以自主选择的论点从社会政治学的立场来看,比其悖论要更吸引人。完全缺乏决择意味着人命天定,我们都丧失自由意志。根据"严格决定论"这一哲学学派的观点,包括人类行为和选择在内的每一件发生的事,考虑到自然法则和先前发生的那件事或选择,都是物理上所必然的。换句话说,那些看起来是存在基础的一部分的"选择"却事实上超出了我们控制的范围。在分子生物学和基因学上的最新进展使决定论者的立场多了可信性,决定论者认为作为物理存在我们的行为是由不受我们控制的物理力量所决定。新的研究表明这些物理力量包括我们自己每个个体的基因组合。

然而,严格决定论和新"科学决定论"的逻辑结果就是我们对自己的行为和选择不负道德责任,甚至那些会伤害其他个人或社会的行为和选择。另外,纵观历史,君主和独裁者们都青睐决定论,至少表面上是,以支持他们的某些人的权利地位或跻身社会经济结构的上层都是天定的说法。最终,科学决定论的观点向基因工程敞开大门,这就对社会经济机会平等构成了潜在的威胁,并导致了所谓的"优秀种族"的发展。必须承认,这些烦人的联系既不能证明也不能反驳决定主义者们的观点。然而,假定自由意志和决定论都不能被证明是正确的立场,前者会成为任何人本主义者和民主社会的首选。

总而言之,尽管我们都曾偶然经历过受困和毫无选择的感觉,但是这个观点基本上是正确的。我承认科学可能将最终驳斥自由意志这一想法,管它呢,到时再说吧!我有一种强烈的直觉:自由意志是我们作为人类存在的基本组成部分,也因此,人类对其选择和行为承担责任,对此我深信不疑。

<u>论点</u> **完全赞成**　该题目是非常典型的抽象类题目,为一个哲学命题。越是抽象的题目越是要找

特例来从小处着手，不然是很难操作的。本文持完全赞成的立场，这样的论证已颇为艰难，更不要说写成平衡立场了。

开头方式 表明立场＋反证　非常规的开头方式，仅供参考。开头分成两个部分，前一部分表明立场，加以简单的解释；后一部分则采用了反证法，"如果没有选择自由的话，会多么地糟糕……"。

论证过程 结论型　由于是抽象类题目，作者在论证的四段中从几例个别的领域出发进行论述，寻找支持的证据：集体生活的经验、生活环境、社会政治学（很晦涩的领域，你最好不要选择这样的特例，纯粹是自找麻烦）。

论证模式

① Our collective life experience is that we make choices and decisions every day...

② People often claim that life's circumstances leave them with "no choice."...The fundamental problem with these sorts of claims is that...

③ Besides, the contention that we are almost invariably free to choose is far more appealing...

④ However, the logical result of...is that we are not morally accountable for our actions and choices,...

Issue 161　**Media scrutiny** of society's heroes

"**In this age of intensive media coverage, it is no longer possible for a society to regard any woman or man as a hero. The reputation of anyone who is subjected to media scrutiny will eventually be diminished.**"

在今天这个媒体铺天盖地的社会中，人们已经很难把任何人当做英雄了。任何人只要是沦为媒体的话题，那么他注定会名声扫地。

In general, I agree with the assertion that intense media scrutiny nearly always serves to diminish the reputation of society's would-be heroes, for the chief reason that it seems to be the nature of media to look for ways to demean public figures—whether heroic or not. **Moreover, while** in isolated cases our so-called heroes have vindicated themselves and restored their reputations diminished by the media, in my observation these are exceptional cases to the general rule that once slandered, the reputation of any public figure, hero or otherwise, is forever tarnished.

The chief reason why I generally agree with the statement has to do with the forces that motivate the media in the first place. The media generally consist of profit-seeking entities, whose chief objective is to maximize profits for their shareholders or other owners. **Moreover,** our corporate culture has sanctioned this objective by codifying it as a fiduciary obligation of any corporate executive. **For better or worse,** in our society media viewers, readers, and listeners find information about the misfortunes and misdeeds of others, especially heroic public figures, far more compelling than information about their virtues and accomplishments. **In short,** we love a good scandal. One need look no further than the newsstand, local television news broadcast, or talk show to find ample evidence that this is the case. **Thus,** in order to maximize profits the media are simply giving the public what they demand—scrutiny of heroic public figures that serves to diminish their reputation.

A second reason why I fundamentally agree with the statement is that, again for better or worse, intense media scrutiny raises a presumption, at least in the public's collective mind, that their hero is guilty of some sort of character flaw or misdeed. This presumption is understandable. **After all**, I think any demographic study would show that the vast majority of people relying on mainstream media for their information lack the sort of critical-thinking skills and objectivity to see beyond what the media feeds them, and to render a fair and fully informed judgment about a public figure—heroic or otherwise.

A third reason for my agreement with the statement has to do with the longer-term fallout from intense media scrutiny and the presumption discussed above. Once tarnished as a result of intense media scrutiny, a person's reputation is forever besmirched, regardless of the merits or motives of the scrutinizers. Those who disagree with this seemingly cynical viewpoint might cite cases in which public figures whose reputations had been tarnished were ultimately vindicated. For example, certain celebrities have successfully challenged rag sheets such as the National Enquirer in the courts, winning large damage awards for libel. **Yet, in my observation** these are exceptional cases; besides, a damage award is no indication that the public has expunged from its collective memory a perception that the fallen hero is guilty of the alleged character flaw or peccadillo.

In sum, the statement is fundamentally correct. As long as the media are motivated by profit, and as long as the public at large demands stories that serve to discredit, diminish, and destroy reputations, the media will continue to harm whichever unfortunate individuals become their cynosures. And the opportunity for vindication is little consolation in a society that seems to thrive, and even feed, on watching heroes being knocked off their pedestals.

社会英雄的媒体审视

总的来说，我同意这样的观点：严厉的媒体审视几乎总会降低社会潜在英雄的声望，其主要原因在于对于公众人物——无论是否英雄——媒体都会本能地贬低一下。而且，尽管在孤立的案例中我们所谓的英雄进行了自我辩护并维护他们被媒体侵蚀的形象，但据我观察，这些是普遍规律的例外，无论是否是英雄人物，任何公众形象一旦被人玷污，则永无出头之路。

我总体上同意上述观点的主要原因和最初促进媒体的动力有关。媒体基本上由那些以使股东或其他董事利益最大化为目的的创利实体构成。而且我们的公司文化已经把这种目的作为公司董事的一个受托义务天经地义地认可了。我们社会媒体的观察家、读者、听众都不管好歹地认为，别人尤其是英雄似的公众人物的不幸和罪行比他们美德和成就的消息更吸引人。简言之，我们喜欢真实的丑闻。人们只需驻足于报摊前、关注本地电视新闻或脱口秀节目就可获得充足的证据表明事实就是如此。因此，为了利益最大化，媒体就会满足大众需求——能够起到减少其声誉作用地对英雄式的公众人物进行审视。

其次，我之所以基本上赞同这一观点是因为严厉的媒体审视不论是好是坏提出一个假定：至少在民众集体心里，他们的英雄有某种性格缺陷或不轨行为。这种假设是可以理解的。毕竟，我以为任何人口统计调查都会表明依赖主流媒体获取信息的绝大多数人都没有那种批判思维技巧和客观性去看到媒体宣传背后的东西，并对公众人物——不管是否英雄——产生一个客观全面的评价。

再次，还有一个原因和严格媒体审视更长期的辐射尘及上面所讨论的假设有关。一个人一旦成为严格媒体审视的牺牲品，不管审视者的优点或者动机如何，他都是跳进黄河也洗不清了。不同意这个似乎是愤世嫉俗的观点的人可能会引证那些公众人物被毁谤名誉后又最终获得清白的例子。举例来说，某些名人在法庭上成功地挑战毁谤名誉的文章，像《国家调查者》（National Enquirer：发行量五百万的一份美国周刊——译者注），赢得了大量的诽谤赔偿。但是，据我观察，这些都是例外；此外，赔偿费不能把这个过气英雄的涉嫌个性缺点或过失从民众的集体记忆中抹杀。

　　总而言之，这个观点基本上是正确的。只要媒体受利润驱使，只要多数民众需要故事去贬低、毁谤名人，媒体就会继续把倒霉的家伙们当做他们伤害的目标。在一个渴望看到英雄被打倒的社会里，还有洗清名誉的机会就不过是小小的心理安慰了。

　　论点 **有保留的赞成**　在整篇文章中，只有开头和论证最后一段中有少量有保留的论述，你可能由此会把本文视为完全赞成的情况。请注意：文中只要有了例外情况的论述，就应该属于倾向型观点。这一点在你自己组织文章论点的时候一定要小心，防止中心句和文章展开不一致，导致文章逻辑混乱。

　　开头方式 表明立场 + 概述理由

　　论证过程 **结论型**　论证的三个自然段都在分析题目观点成立的原因（动机），论证最后一段提到了例外情况。

　　论证模式

　　① The chief reason why I generally agree with the statement has to do with...
　　② A second reason why I fundamentally agree with the statement is that...
　　③ A third reason for my agreement with the statement has to do with...

Issue 212　Do **worthy** ends justify **any means**?

"If a goal is worthy, then any means taken to attain it is justifiable."
只要值得，不择手段达到目的就是合理的。

　　The speaker asserts that if a goal is worthy then any means of attaining that goal is justifiable. **In my view this extreme position misses the point entirely.** Whether certain means are justifiable in reaching a goal must be determined on a case-by-case basis, by weighing the benefits of attaining the goal against the costs, or harm, that might accrue along the way. This applies equally to individual goals and to societal goals.

　　Consider the goal of completing a marathon running race. If I need to reduce my working hours to train for the race, thereby jeopardizing my job, or **if** I run a high risk of incurring a permanent injury by training enough to prepare adequately for the event, then perhaps my goal is not worth attaining. **Yet if** I am a physically challenged person with the goal of completing a highly-publicized marathon, risking financial hardship or long-term injury might be worthwhile, not only for my own personal satisfaction but also for the inspiration that attaining the goal would provide many others.

　　Or consider the goal of providing basic food and shelter for an innocent child. Anyone would agree that this goal is highly worthy—considered apart from the means used to achieve it. **But what if** those means involve stealing from others? Or **what if** they involve employing the child in a sweatshop at the expense of educating the child? Clearly, determining the worthiness of such goals requires that we confront moral dilemmas, which we each solve individually—based on our own conscience, value system, and notions of fairness and equity.

　　On a societal level we determine the worthiness of our goals in much the same way—by weighing competing interests. **For instance**, any thoughtful person would agree that reducing air and water pollution is a worthy societal goal; clean air and water reduce the burden on our health-care resources and improves the quality of life for everyone in society. **Yet** to attain this goal would we be justified in forcing entire industries out of business, thereby running the risk of economic paralysis and widespread unemployment? **Or consider** America's intervention in Iraq's invasion of Kuwait. Did our dual interest in a continuing flow of oil to the West and in deterring a potential threat against the security of the world justify our committing resources that could have been used instead for domestic social-welfare programs—or a myriad of other productive purposes? Both issues underscore the fact that the worthiness of a societal goal cannot be considered apart from the means and adverse consequences of attaining that goal.

In sum, the speaker begs the question. The worthiness of any goal, whether it be personal or societal, can be determined only by weighing the benefits of achieving the goal against its costs—to us as well as others.

有价值的目的就可以不择手段地去达到吗?

演讲人声称如果一个目的很有价值,那么采用任何方法来达到这个目的都是合理的。在我看来,这种极端的看法是彻底的理解错误。为了达到一个目的所采取的某种手段是否合理要就事论事,通过衡量达到目的后得到的好处,以及在追求这个目标的过程中可能要付出的代价或者所造成的损害,并将两者做一个比较,再做决定。这对于个人目标和社会目标都同样适用。

想一想跑完马拉松长跑比赛这一目标。如果我需要减少我工作的时间来为长跑比赛进行训练准备,从而对我的工作造成了损失,或者说如果我为了对这场比赛做充分的准备,保证足够的训练量,而冒着被伤病永久折磨的风险,那么也许我的这个目的就是不值得去追求达到的。但是,如果我是一个身体有缺陷的人,目标是跑完一场影响力非常大的马拉松比赛,那么冒着经济困难或者永久性伤病的风险可能就是值得的。这不仅是为了个人的满足感,也是为了在实现目标后能够激励许多其他的人。

或者,让我们来想一想这样一个目标,为一个天真无邪的孩子提供基本的食物和住处。如果不考虑为了实现这一目的所使用的方法,那么每一个人都会同意实现这个目标是很值得的。但是如果这些方法中包括从别人那里偷窃这种行为又会怎样呢?或者说如果方法中包括他们雇用这个孩子到一个活计苦累、工资微薄的工厂中去卖苦力受剥削,以牺牲这个孩子的教育为代价又会怎样呢?显而易见,决定这样目标的值不值得就需要我们面对道德上的两难境地,我们每个人,根据自己的良知、价值观以及对公平和平等的理解,都要独自解决。

在一个社会层面上,我们也以差不多同样的方法决定一个目标值不值得——即权衡利益得失。例如,任何有头脑的人都会同意减轻大气和水污染是一个很有价值的目标。清洁的空气和水可以减轻我们的卫生保健资源的压力,并提高社会中每一个人的生活质量。但是,为了实现这个目标,我们是否就有理由迫使整个工业停止运营,从而去冒经济瘫痪和大量失业的风险?或者让我们再想想这个例子,即美国对伊拉克入侵科威特所采取的干涉。在保证对西方的石油输入不间断和阻止世界安全的一个潜在威胁这种双重利益,但有这样的双重利益关系难道就意味着投入我们的资源就是合理的了吗?这些资源本可以用于国内社会福利事业或者数不胜数的其他各种生产目的。这两个问题都强调了一个事实,就是衡量一个社会目标是否有价值时,不能不考虑到为实现这个目标所采用的手段和实现这个目标所带来的负面结果。

总而言之,演讲人是以假定为论据进行讨论。无论是个人目标还是社会目标,任何一个目标值得与否只能通过权衡达成目标所能获得的利益和所要付出的代价孰重孰轻来决定——既要考虑到我们所要付出的代价，也要考虑到对他人的影响。

论点 **平衡观点** 典型的具体问题具体分析。作者从两个层面举出若干例子，一方面肯定"全力以赴"的合理性，另外一方面批评出题者片面地强调目的的价值，而忽视了手段的合理性和付出的代价。其实，题目的观点是非常极端的，类似于"any"这样的大话都是注定要成为驳论的靶子。

◆ *Tip 极端词汇* 如何从题目中寻找供你痛击的靶子？有很多的答案，其中有一个公认的小把戏，就是找题目中出现的极端词汇，你再打着"具体问题具体分析"的旗号将其折中。除了"any"以外，同类的词汇还有"always, never, no"等等。

开头方式 **陈述题目观点 + 表明立场** 上面提到过在问题解决型文章中经常使用这种开头方式：问题——不择手段达到目的是否合理，题目观点——目的有价值，作者立场——（不仅目的有价值）还要考虑手段和代价。

论证过程 **问题解决型** 论证部分的三个自然段分成两个层次：个人层面和社会层面。论证第一段和第二段从个人层面分析了两个例子：马拉松竞技和救助儿童；论证第三段从社会层面分析了两个例子：治理污染和中东问题。这四个例子都是具体情况具体分析，平衡观点。

论证模式

① Consider the goal of completing a marathon running race.

② Or consider the goal of providing basic food and shelter for an innocent child.

③ On a societal level we determine the worthiness of our goals in much the same way...

Issue 7　The growing significance of the **video camera**

"**The video camera provides such an accurate and convincing record of contemporary life that it has become a more important form of documentation than written records.**"

摄像机可以通过如此精确而有说服力的记录手段来再现当代生活，因此它已经代替书面记录成为了一种更重要的记录手段。

According to the speaker, the video recording is a more important means of documenting contemporary life than a written record because video recordings are more accurate and convincing. **Although I agree that** a video provides a more objective and accurate record of an event's spatial aspects, there is far more to document in life than what we see and hear. **Thus, the speaker overstates** the comparative significance of video as a documentary tool.

For the purpose of documenting temporal, spatial events and experiences, I agree that a video record is usually more accurate and more convincing than a written record. It is impossible for anyone, no matter how keen an observer and skilled a journalist, to recount in complete and objective detail such events as the winning touchdown at the Super Bowl, a Ballanchine ballet, the Tournament of Roses Parade, or the scene at the intersection of Florence and Normandy streets during the 1992 Los Angeles riots. **Yet** these are important events in contemporary life—the sort of events we might put in a time capsule for the purpose of capturing our life and times at the turn of this millennium.

The growing documentary role of video is not limited to seminal events like those described above. Video surveillance cameras are objective witnesses with perfect memories. Thus, they can play a vital evidentiary role in legal proceedings—such as those involving robbery, drug trafficking, police misconduct, motor vehicle violations, and even malpractice in a hospital operating room. **Indeed**, whenever moving images are central to an event the video camera is superior to the written word. A written description of a hurricane, tornado, or volcanic eruption cannot convey its immediate power and awesome nature like a video record. A diary entry cannot "replay" that wedding reception, dance recital, or surprise birthday party as accurately or objectively as a video record. **And** a real-estate brochure cannot inform about the lighting, spaciousness, or general ambiance of a featured property nearly as effectively as a video.

　　Nonetheless, for certain other purposes written records are advantageous to and more appropriate than video records. For example, certain legal matters are best left to written documentation: video is of no practical use in documenting the terms of a complex contractual agreement, an incorporation, or the establishment of a trust. And video is of little use when it comes to documenting a person's subjective state of mind, impressions, or reflections of an event or experience. **Indeed**, to the extent that personal interpretation adds dimension and richness to the record, written documentation is actually more important than video.

　　Finally, a video record is of no use in documenting statistical or other quantitative information. Returning to the not example mentioned earlier, imagine relying on a video to document the financial loss to store owners, the number of police and firefighters involved, and so forth. Complete and accurate video documentation of such information would require video cameras at every street corner and in every aisle of every store.

　　In sum, the speaker's claim overstates the importance of video records, at least to some extent. When it comes to capturing, storing, and recalling temporal, spatial events, video records are inherently more objective, accurate, and complete. **However**, what we view through a camera lens provides only one dimension of our life and times; written documentation will always be needed to quantify, demystify, and provide meaning to the world around us.

视频摄像机日益增长的重要性

　　因为摄像比书面记录更准确和使人信服，所以依照演讲人的观点，图像记录是比笔录更为重要的记录当代生活的方式。虽然我同意录像带可以提供事件在空间方面的更为客观和准确的记录，但是现实生活需要记录下来的远多于我们的所见所闻。因此，演讲人夸大了录像作为一个文件记录工具的相对重要性。

　　我同意，如果是要记录短期空间事件或经历，一份图像记录通常比一份书面记录更为准确和更使人信服。无论一位观察者多么敏锐或一位新闻记者多么熟练，任何人要想完全并客观地把类似超级保龄球赛中的制胜一击、一支巴兰钦编导的芭蕾舞、玫瑰巡回赛游行或是 1992 年洛杉矶暴动期间佛罗伦斯和诺曼第街道的十字路口的现场这样的事件的细节叙述下来，都是不可能的。然而这些事件都是我们当代生活中重要的一页——在新的千年之交为了捕捉我们的生活和时代，这类事件可能都将被载入史册。

　　摄像在记录中日益重要的地位不仅限于在像上面描述的重大事件中。视频监视照相机是有完美记忆的客观证人。因此，他们能在法律程序中扮演一个重要证据的角色，例如在涉及抢劫、贩毒、警察渎职、机动车违章甚至在医院手术室里不当治疗的案件中。的确，每当移动图像对描述一件事是十分重要时，摄像机就会甚于书面文字。飓风、龙卷风或火山爆发的书面描述就不能够像一个图像记录一样传递其即刻的爆发力和可怕的属性。一则日记不能够如一个图像记录那样客观公正地"重演"那次婚宴、歌舞会或惊喜的生日派对；同样一本不动产简介手册就不能像录像一样有效地说明一处美丽的房产的照明、宽敞或总体的气氛。

　　然而，在某些其他方面，书面记录就表现出它相对于视频记录的优势。举例来说，某些法律事务最好付诸文字：录像不能用于记录一份复杂的契约协议、一次合并或一个托拉斯的创建的条款。而且当要记录一个人的主观思想状态、感受或对一件事或经历的反应时，录像带就派不上用场了。的确，一定意义上人为解释使记录更为深刻而丰富，因此书面记录比录像带实际上更为重要。

　　最后，一份图像记录在处理统计信息或其他量化信息面前无可作为。回到上面那些反面的例子中，想像仰赖录像带来记录商店主的财产损失，参加的警察和消防队员的人数等等。如此全面而准确的图像文件需要在每个街道角落和在每间商店的每个走廊中都安放摄像机。

　　一言以蔽之，至少在某种程度上，演讲人的观点夸大了图像记录的重要性。当它用于抓拍、储存和再现即时的空间上的事件时，视频记录有其固有的更为客观、准确和全面的特性。然而，我们通过一个照相机透镜只能看到我们的生活和时代的一个方面，而在量化、阐明和提供我们周围世界的意义方面总是需要书面的文件。

论点　平衡观点　本文一方面赞同摄像技术可以在记录事件的空间方面更为客观和准确，但同时指出仅仅依靠图像和声音无法全面记录世界，书面记录也是不可替代的。

开头方式　陈述题目观点 + 表明立场　问题解决型文章中经常使用的开头方式：问题——如何记录我们的世界，题目观点——运用摄像技术，作者立场——（不仅运用摄像技术）还要使用书面记录手段。

论证过程　问题解决型　本文的思路十分清晰，论证部分的四个自然段平均分成两个层次：前两个自然段支持题目观点，赞同摄像技术可以提供更为客观和准确的记录；后两个自然段是驳论部分，说明书面记录也是不可替代的。

论证模式

① For the purpose of documenting temporal, spatial events and experiences, I agree that...

② The growing documentary role of video is not limited to seminal events like those described above.

③ Nonetheless, for certain other purposes written records are advantageous to and more appropriate than video records.

④ Finally, a video record is of no use in documenting statistical or other quantitative information.

Issue 114　Has technology failed to help **humanity** progress?

"Humanity has made little real progress over the past century or so. Technological innovations have taken place, but the overall condition of humanity is no better. War, violence, and poverty are still with us. Technology cannot change the condition of humanity."

　　人类在过去的一百年左右止步不前。技术在不断进步而人类的整体条件却没有改善。战争、暴力和贫困仍然困扰着我们。技术无法改变人类的处境。

　　Have technological innovations of the last century failed to bring about true progress for humanity, as the statement contends? **Although I agree that** technology cannot ultimately prevent us from harming one another, **the statement fails to** account for the significant positive impact that the modern-industrial and computer revolutions have had on the quality of life—at least in the developed world.

I agree with the statement insofar as there is no technological solution to the enduring problems of war, poverty, and violence, for the reason that they stem from certain aspects of human nature—such as aggression and greed. **Although** future advances in biochemistry might enable us to "engineer away" those undesirable aspects, **in the meantime** it is up to our economists, diplomats, social reformers, and jurists—not our scientists and engineers—to mitigate these problems.

Admittedly, many technological developments during the last century have helped reduce human suffering. Consider, for instance, technology that enables computers to map Earth's geographical features from outer space. This technology allows us to locate lands that can be cultivated for feeding malnourished people in third-world countries. **And, few would disagree that** humanity is the beneficiary of the myriad of twentieth-century innovations in medicine and medical technology—from prostheses and organ transplants to vaccines and lasers.

Yet, for every technological innovation helping to reduce human suffering is another that has served primarily to add to it. For example, while some might argue that nuclear weapons serve as invaluable "peace-keepers," this argument flies in the face of the hundreds of thousands of innocent people murdered and maimed by atomic blasts. **More recently**, the increasing use of chemical weapons for human slaughter points out that so-called "advances" in biochemistry can amount to net losses for humanity.

Notwithstanding technology's limitations in preventing war, poverty, and violence, **twentieth-century technological innovation has enhanced the overall standard of living and comfort level of developed nations.** The advent of steel production and assembly-line manufacturing created countless jobs, stimulated economic growth, and supplied a plethora of innovative conveniences. **More recently**, computers have helped free up our time by performing repetitive tasks; have aided in the design of safer and more attractive bridges, buildings, and vehicles; and have made possible universal access to information.

Of course, such progress has not come without costs. One harmful byproduct of industrial progress is environmental pollution and its threat to public health. Another is the alienation of assembly-line workers from their work. And, the Internet breeds information overload and steals our time and attention away from family, community, and coworkers. **Nevertheless**, on balance both the modern-industrial and computer revolutions have improved our standard of living and comfort level; and both constitute progress by any measure.

In sum, enduring problems such as war, poverty, and violence ultimately spring from human nature, which no technological innovation short of genetic engineering can alter. **Thus, the statement is correct in this respect. However**, if we define "progress" more narrowly—in terms of economic standard of living and comfort level—recent technological innovations have indeed brought about clear progress for humanity.

科技没有对人类的进步起到促进作用吗？

如这种说法争论的那样，上个世纪的科技革新对人类的进步没有起到促进作用吗？尽管我认同科技并不能最终阻止人与人之间的互相伤害，但这种说法并没能阐述现代工业和计算机革命对人们的生活——至少对在发达国家产生的积极而显著的影响。

还没找到可以解决长期困扰人类的战争、贫困以及暴力等问题的科技方案，在这个程度上，我认同这个观点，因为这些问题来源于人类本性的某些方面——例如侵略性和贪婪。尽管未来的生物化学或许能够使我们"除去"那些令人不快的阴暗面，但与此同时，如何缓解这些问题取决于我们的经济学家、外交家、社会改革运动者以及法理学家——而并不是科学家和工程师。

不可否认的是，上个世纪的许多科技发展已经缓解了人类的苦难。试想一下，比如使得计算机可以在外太空勾勒地球地貌特征的技术。这种技术使得我们可以找到适合耕种的土地来哺育第三世界国家中营养失衡的人民。同样，很少有人会否认人类已经从 20 世纪的众多医药和医学技术的革新中获益匪浅——从器官修复、器官移植到疫苗和激光的应用。

然而，每项有助于缓解人类苦痛的科技革新都有它的另一面——它在增加苦痛方面扮演了主要角色。举个例子来说：某些人认为核武器充当着无价的"和平维护者"，而完全无视在核爆炸中丧生或致残的成百上千的人。近来，越来越多地使用化学武器屠杀人类表明所谓的生物化学方面的进步导致了人类的纯粹丧失。

尽管科技在防止战争、贫困和暴行方面尚有其局限性，但 20 世纪的科技革新还是提高了发达国家人们的总体生活水平和舒适程度。钢制产品以及流水生产线的出现创造了大量的就业机会，从而刺激了经济的增长，并带来了过多的革新性便捷。特别是近来，计算机已经可以通过演算执行重复性的工作来帮助我们节省时间；帮助我们设计更安全、更美观的桥梁、建筑和车辆；并使得我们可以全面获取信息。

当然，这种进步并不是没有代价的。工业进步的不利环节之一就是带来了环境的污染，并威胁到公众的健康。另一个问题就是流水生产线工人们与他们的工作的疏离。同时，互联网导致信息的超负荷，并占用了我们更多的时间和注意力，使我们与家人、社区和同事变得更加疏远。尽管如此，总体而言，现代工业和计算机革命仍然提高了我们的生活水平和舒适程度；并且这两者从哪个方面讲都算是进步。

总而言之，长期困扰人类的战争、贫困和暴行等问题最终还是源于人类的本性，这是除了遗传工程之外的任何技术革新所无法改变的事实。因此，该说法在这个方面是正确无疑的。但是，如果我们根据经济的生活水平和舒适性更加狭义地对"进步"进行定义，近来的技术革新确实已经为人类带来了显著的进步。

论点 **平衡观点**　技术革新有没有对人类的进步带来促进作用？作者在这个论点上摆出了具体问题具体分析的态度——在肯定题目在某一方面是正确的同时，指出技术革新在某些领域（economic standard of living and comfort level）确实带来了显著的进步。

开头方式 **提出问题 + 让步语气 + 表明立场**　作者先以问句的形式开头，以"**as the statement contends...**"提出原文的观点，然后以让步语气（Although I agree...）提出自己的立场。这种开头形式不但可以归纳出原文的观点，还可以限定讨论的范围，同时给出自己的立场，可谓一箭三雕。

论证过程 **因果型论证**　这道题目比较啰嗦，第一句话和最后一句话没有什么本质区别，都是结论"人类没有因为技术进步而获得进步"，为什么呢？中间是原因"人类条件没有改善，很多问题困扰我们"，这道题按照因果型题目可以简化成"人类没改善→技术没用"。整个论证部分就是两个大层次：因果成立和不成立。值得注意的是，作者的论证部分比较乱，把这正反两方面掺杂在一块了，如果在考试的时候还是应该分得明确为上策。

论证模式

① I agree with the statement insofar as...

② Admittedly, many technological developments during the last century have helped reduce human suffering.

③ Yet, for every technological innovation helping to reduce human suffering is another that has served primarily to add to it.

④ Notwithstanding...twentieth-century technological innovation has enhanced the overall standard of living and comfort level of developed nations.

⑤ Of course, such progress has not come without cost...Nevertheless...

Issue 159　Will humans always be **superior to machines**?

"**The human mind will always be superior to machines because machines are only tools of human minds.**"

人类的智慧将总是高于机器,因为机器只是人类智慧的工具。

This statement actually consists of a series of three related claims: (1) machines are tools of human minds; (2) human minds will always be superior to machines; and (3) it is because machines are human tools that human minds will always be superior to machines. **While I concede the first claim, whether I agree with the other two claims depends partly on** how one defines "superiority," and partly on how willing one is to humble oneself to the unknown future scenarios.

The statement is clearly accurate insofar as machines are tools of human minds. After all, would any machine even exist unless a human being invented it? Of course not. **Moreover**, I would be hard-pressed to think of any machine that cannot be described as a tool. Even machines designed to entertain or amuse us—for example, toy robots, cars and video games, and novelty items—are in fact tools, which their inventors and promoters use for engaging in commerce and the business of entertainment and amusement. **And**, the claim that a machine can be an end in itself, without purpose or utilitarian function for humans whatsoever, is dubious at best, since I cannot conjure up even a single example of any such machine. **Thus**, when we develop any sort of machine we always have some sort of end in mind—a purpose for that machine.

As for the statement's second claim, in certain respects machines are superior. We have devised machines that perform number-crunching and other rote cerebral tasks with greater accuracy and speed than human minds ever could. **In fact**, it is because we can devise machines that are superior in these respects that we devise them—as our tools—to begin with. **However, if** one defines superiority not in terms of competence in performing rote tasks but rather in other ways, human minds are superior. Machines have no capacity for independent thought, for making judgments based on normative considerations, or for developing emotional responses to intellectual problems.

Up until now, the notion of human-made machines that develop the ability to think on their own, and to develop so-called "emotional intelligence," **has been pure fiction. Besides**, even in fiction we humans ultimately prevail over such machines—as in the cases of Frankenstein's monster and Hat, the computer in *2001: A Space Odyssey*. Yet it seems presumptuous to assert with confidence that humans will always maintain their superior status over their machines. Recent advances in biotechnology, particularly in the area of human genome research, suggest that within the twenty-first century we'll witness machines that can learn to think on their own, to repair and nurture themselves, to experience visceral sensations, and so forth. **In other words**, machines will soon exhibit the traits to which we humans attribute our own superiority.

In sum, because we devise machines in order that they may serve us, it is fair to characterize machines as "tools of human minds." **And insofar as** humans have the unique capacity for independent thought, subjective judgment, and emotional response, it also seems fair to claim superiority over our machines. **Besides**, should we ever become so clever a species as to devise machines that can truly think for themselves and look out for their own well-being, then query whether these machines of the future would be "machines" anymore.

人类会永远优于机器吗？

事实上，这种说法包括一系列三个互相关联的主张：（1）机器是人类智力的工具；（2）人类的智力总是优于机器；以及（3）正因为机器是人类智力的工具，人类的智力总是优于机器的。我仅能勉强认同第一个主张，而我能否认同另外两个主张部分取决于人们怎样对"优越"进行定义，部分取决于人们承认未知情况将优于自身的意愿程度。

在机器是人类智力的工具这个前提下，这种说法无疑是正确的。毕竟，如果人类没有发明机器，它们能够存在吗？当然不能。而且，我虽然穷尽所思，也不能想到哪种机器不能被称做工具。即使是那些设计出来服务和娱乐人类的机器——例如玩具机器人、汽车和视频游戏，以及新奇的玩意——事实上都是工具，它们的发明者或推广者用它们从事商业或娱乐业。无论如何，"某种机器自身就是目的，对于人类没有任何目的和任何功利主义功能"这种主张最多也只能算是令人怀疑的，因为我绞尽脑汁也无法列举出哪怕一个这类机器的例子。因而当我们研发任何一种机器的时候，我们自然而然的在脑海中为它设定了某种目的——这种机器的用途。

至于这种说法的第二个主张，在某些方面下，机器更优越。我们已经发明了可以执行特大数量的数字计算和其他死板的脑力劳动的机器，其精确性和工作速度是以往人类智力所无法企及的。事实上，首先正是因为在这些领域中机器更为优越我们才发明了它们——作为我们的工具。然而，如果人们以其他标准而不是以机器执行刻板任务的能力为标准来对优越性进行定义，那么人类的智力是优于机器的。机器无法进行独立的思考，无法进行正常的考虑而做出某种决定，也无法对理性的问题做出带有感情色彩的反应。

直到现在，衍生出自我思考的能力并带有"情感智能"的人造机器仍然属于凭空虚构。而且，即使在上述虚幻情节中，人类最终还是胜过了这种机器——例如弗兰肯斯坦的怪物和海特、《2001 年太空探险》（2001：A Space Odyssey）中的计算机。然而，如果要自信地坚持人类将永远保持对机器的优越性这一论断便显得有些专横了。近来在生物技术方面，尤其是在对人类基因组的研究领域所取得的进展表明，在 21 世纪，我们将亲眼目睹机器开始可以学习自我思考，可以自我修复和训练，可以体验发自内心的感情等等。换句话说，机器很快就会展示我们人类现有优越性的所有特征。

总而言之，正因为我们设计机器的目的在于让它们为我们服务，我们将机器定义为"人类智慧的工具"便显得顺理成章。而且只有人类才有能力进行独立思考、给出主观判断以及做出带有感情色彩的反应，因此在此限度内人类声称比机器更为优越似乎也显得合情合理。而且，万一我们成了如此聪明的物种，以致于我们可以设计真正为自身考虑并关心自身利益的机器的话，那个时候再问这些未来的机器还是不是"机器"也不迟。

论点 **平衡观点** 本文采取了部分肯定加部分否定的观点。开头就对论点做出了评判，将其分为三种情况，然后对于第一种状况予以肯定，随后针对第二和第三点提出自己的看法，达到了行文的目的，也让作者自己的论点更加精确与全面。

开头方式 题目分析 + 让步语气 + 表明立场　本文开头简要叙述题目的三个观点，然后紧接一个让步语气，随后对原文观点提出了质疑。这样既可以鲜明地提出论点，又可以为下文做出铺垫，具体问题具体分析，从而使论点更圆满。

论证过程 因果型

论证模式

① The statement is clearly accurate insofar as machines are tools of human minds... Moreover...

② As for the statement's second claim, in certain respects machines are superior... However, if...

③ Up until now, the notion of human-made machines that... has been pure fiction.

Issue 183　The impact of **acquiring more knowledge**

"As we acquire more knowledge, things do not become more comprehensible, but more complex and more mysterious."

当我们获得越来越多的知识，事情并没有变得更加透彻，相反是变得更复杂、更神秘。

Does knowledge render things more comprehensible, or more complex and mysterious? **In my view** the acquisition of knowledge brings about all three at the same time. This paradoxical result is aptly explained and illustrated by a number of advances in our scientific knowledge.

Consider, for example, the sonar system on which blind bats rely to navigate and especially to seek prey. Researchers have learned that this system is startlingly sophisticated. By emitting audible sounds, then processing the returning echoes, a bat can determine in a nanosecond not only how far away its moving prey is but also the prey's speed, direction, size and even specie! This knowledge acquired helps explain, of course, how bats navigate and survive. **Yet at the same time** this knowledge points out the incredible complexity of the auditory and brain functions of certain animals, even of mere humans, and creates a certain mystery and wonder about how such systems ever evolved organically.

Or consider our knowledge of the universe. Advances in telescope and space—exploration technology seem to corroborate the theory of a continually expanding universe that began at the very beginning of time with a "big bang". **On one level** this knowledge, assuming it qualifies as such, helps us comprehend our place in the universe and our ultimate destiny. **Yet on the other hand** it adds yet another chapter to the mystery about what existed before time and the universe.

Or consider the area of atomic physics. The naked human eye perceives very little, of course, of the complexity of matter. To our distant ancestors the physical world appeared simple—seemingly comprehensible by means of sight and touch. **Then** by way of scientific knowledge we learned that all matter is comprised of atoms, which are further comprised of protons, neutrons, and electrons. **Then** we discovered an even more basic unit of matter called the quark. **And now** a new so-called "string" theory posits the existence of an even more fundamental, and universal, unit of matter. **On the one hand**, these discoveries have rendered things more comprehensible, by explaining and reconciling empirical observations of how matter behaves. The string theory also reconciles the discrepancy between the quantum and wave theories of physics. **On the other hand**, each discovery has in turn revealed that matter is more complex than previously thought. In fact, the string theory, which is theoretically sound, calls for seven more dimensions—in addition to the three we already know about! I'm hard-pressed to imagine anything more complex or mysterious.

In sum, the statement overlooks a paradox about knowledge acquired, at least when it comes to understanding the physical world. When through knowledge a thing becomes more comprehensible and explainable we realize at the same time that it is more complex and mysterious than previously thought.

知识增多的影响

知识使事物变得更加明了还是更加复杂和神秘了呢？在我看来，知识的获取同时带来了这三种结果。科技知识中的众多发展适当地解释了这种自相矛盾的结论。

以看不见事物的蝙蝠赖以导航、尤其是捕食的声波定位系统为例。研究者已经知道了该系统极其复杂。通过发出声波和接收回应，蝙蝠在一纳秒间不仅能够判断出该猎物有多远，而且可以得知它的移动方向、速度、大小甚至物种。对这种知识的了解当然有助于解释蝙蝠如何导航和生存。但同时，该知识也指出了某些动物（甚至是人类）听觉和大脑功能的令人难以置信的复杂性，给该系统是如何有机进化演变而来的蒙上了一层神秘的面纱。

再考虑一下我们关于宇宙的知识。望远镜和空间探测技术的发展似乎印证了在时间之初由大爆炸形成的宇宙不断膨胀的理论。在某种程度上，该知识，假设它算得上是种知识，帮助我们了解了我们在宇宙中所处的位置以及最终的命运。但另一方面，何种物质存在于时间和宇宙之前又成了另外一个谜团。

原子物理领域也是例证之一。人裸眼仅能看到事务复杂性的极少方面。对我们的原始祖先来说，物质世界极其简单——看似仅凭视觉和触觉就能通晓一切。然后通过科学知识，我们得知所有的物质都是由原子组成的，而原子又是由中子、质子和电子组成。我们又进一步地发现了更基本的单位——夸克。如今，一种新的被成为"弦论"的理论指出一种更基本和普遍的物质单位的存在。一方面，这些发现通过解释和理顺对于物质运行之道的经验上的观察而使事物变得更加易于理解。弦论同时也调和了物理学中量子论和波动论之间的矛盾。而另一方面，任何一次发现都揭示出事物比以前想像的要复杂得多。事实上，理论上健全的弦论在我们已知的三维外又引发出了七个时空范围。我想不出比这更加复杂和更加神秘的东西了。

总之，该观点忽略了我们获得的知识的矛盾性，至少是在理解物质世界时是如此。在通过知识把一件事变得更加简单明了的同时，我们也意识到它该比以前想像的要复杂和神秘得多。

论点　平衡观点　作者的观点比较平衡，即 knowledge render (s) things more comprehensible（知识使事物更易于了解）和 more complex and mysterious（知识使事物更复杂、更神秘）。这两种情况贯穿全文，基本在每段都有所提及。即知识在使事物更易于了解的同时，也使事物变得更加复杂、更加神秘。在这方面，作者成功地达到了前后呼应的效果。

开头方式　提出问题 + 表明立场　作者首先以问句的形式开头，同时引出本文的论点。Does knowledge render things more comprehensible, or more complex and mysterious? 提问之后，将论点以答案的方式紧随其后给出，显得非常自然，与题目衔接得非常出色。

论证过程　结论型

论证模式

① Consider, for example, the sonar system on which blind bats rely to navigate and especially to seek prey.

② Or consider our knowledge of the universe.

③ Or consider the area of atomic physics.

Issue 196　Does technology threaten our **quality of life**?

　　"Technology creates more problems than it solves, and may threaten or damage the quality of life."

　　技术带来的问题比它解决的问题要多,并且可能会威胁或损害生活质量。

　　Whether technology enhances or diminishes our overall quality of life depends largely on the type of technology one is considering. While mechanical automation may have diminished our quality of life, **on balance**, digital automation is doing more to improve life than to undermine its quality.

　　First consider mechanical automation, particularly assembly-line manufacturing. With automation came a loss of pride in and alienation from one's work. In this sense, automation both diminished our quality of life and rendered us slaves to machines in our inability to reverse "progress." Admittedly, mechanical automation spawned entire industries, creating jobs, stimulating economic growth, and supplying a plethora of innovative conveniences. **Nevertheless**, the sociological and environmental price of progress may have outweighed its benefits.

　　Next consider digital technology. Admittedly, this newer form of technology has brought its own brand of alienation, and has adversely affected our quality of life in other ways as well. For example, computer automation, and especially the Internet, breeds information overload and steals our time and attention away from family, community, and coworkers. **In these respects**, digital technology tends to diminish our quality of life and create its own legion of human slaves.

　　On the other hand, by relegating repetitive tasks to computers, **digital technology has spawned great advances in medicine and physics**, helping us to better understand the world, to enhance our health, and to prolong our lives. Digital automation has also emancipated architects, artists, designers, and musicians, by expanding creative possibilities and by saving time. **Perhaps most important, however**, information technology makes possible universal access to information, thereby providing a democratizing influence on our culture.

　　In sum, while mechanical automation may have created a society of slaves to modern conveniences and unfulfilling work, digital automation holds more promise for improving our lives without enslaving us to the technology.

科技对我们的生活质量构成了威胁吗?

　　科技是否加强或削弱了我们的总体生活水平很大程度上取决于人们所考虑的科技的类型。机械自动化或许削弱了我们的生活质量,但总的来说,数字自动装置正在更大程度地提高我们的生活质量而不是去降低它。

　　首先来考虑机械自动化,特别是使用组装生产线的制造业。随自动化而出现的是人们不再将自己的工作引以为傲,同时导致了工人与工作的疏离。在这个意义上,自动化既降低了我们的生活质量,同时也使我们受制于机器,因为我们在扭转"发展"方面显得无能为力。不可否认,机械自动化促成了整个工业,创造了就业机会,刺激经济的增长,并带来了太多的革新性便捷。尽管如此,这种发展在社会学和环境方面付出的代价可能已经超过了它所带来的利益。

下一步我们来看数字技术。不可否认，这种新形式的技术带来了它自己新的疏离，在其他方面也不利地影响了我们的生活质量。例如计算机自动化，特别是互联网的出现导致了信息超负荷，并占用了我们更多的时间，吸引了我们更多的关注，使我们与家人、社区和同事变得更加疏远。在这些方面，数字技术有削减我们的生活质量并创造出了它的大量的人类奴隶的倾向。

另一方面，通过委派计算机重复性的任务，数字技术已经在医药和物理学方面做出了巨大贡献，帮助我们更好地理解这个世界，增强我们的健康，并延长我们的寿命。通过对拓展创作灵感和节省时间，数字自动化还解放了建筑师、艺术家、设计师和音乐家。但或许最为重要的是，数字技术使得全面的获得信息成为可能，并由此对我们的文化施加一种民主化的影响。

总而言之，机械自动化或许已经创造了一批现代化便捷和无成就感工作的奴隶，但数字自动化却更有可能提高我们的生活水平，而不需让我们受制于技术。

论点 平衡观点　作者在开头第一句话便开门见山地对原观点进行分析，Whether...or..., largely depend on...是其显著的标志。而我们的生活质量是否受到了威胁，作者也是从两方面加以阐述的，这种平衡将会贯穿全文。

开头方式 题目分析＋表明立场　本文开头第一句话就简洁明了地对论题进行了分析，即：我们的生活质量是否受到了来自科技方面的影响在很大程度上取决于科技的类型。进而，他根据科技的不同类型，阐述了对人们生活带来的不同后果，条理非常清楚。

论证过程 结论型

论证模式

① First consider mechanical automation...

② Next consider digital technology.

③ On the other hand... digital technology has spawned great advances in medicine and physics...

Issue 33　Is image more important than the **truth behind** it?

"**Creating an appealing image has become more important in contemporary society than is the reality or truth behind that image.**"

在当代社会,打造一个引人入胜的外表已经变得比外表下的现实或事实更加重要了。

Has creating an image become more important in our society than the reality or truth behind the image? **I agree that** image has become a more central concern, at least where short-term business or political success is at stake. **Nevertheless,** I think that in the longer term image ultimately yields to substance and fact.

The important role of image is particularly evident in the business world. Consider, for example, today's automobile industry. American cars are becoming essentially identical to competing Japanese cars in nearly every mechanical and structural respect, as well as in price. Thus, to compete effectively auto companies must now differentiate their products largely through image advertising, by conjuring up certain illusory benefits—such as machismo, status, sensibility, or fun. The increasing focus on image is also evident in the book-publishing business. Publishers are relying more and more on the power of their brands rather than the content of their books. Today mass-market books are supplanted within a year with products that are essentially the same—except with fresh faces, titles, and other promotional angles. I find quite telling the fact that today more and more book publishers are being acquired by large media companies. And the increasing importance of image is especially evident in the music industry, where originality, artistic interpretation, and technical proficiency have yielded almost entirely to sex appeal.

The growing significance of image is also evident in the political realm, particularly when it comes to presidential politics. **Admittedly**, by its very nature politicking has always emphasized rhetoric and appearances above substance and fact. **Yet**, since the invention of the camera presidential politicians have become increasingly concerned about their image. **For example**, Teddy Roosevelt was very careful never to be photographed wearing a tennis outfit, for fear that such photographs would serve to undermine his rough-rider image that won him his only term in office. With the advent of television, image became even more central in presidential politics. **After all**, it was television that elected J. EK. over Nixon. And our only two-term presidents in the television age were elected based largely on their image. Query whether Presidents Lincoln, Taft, or even ED. R. would be elected today if pitted against the handsome leading man Reagan, or the suave and politically correct Clinton. **After all**, Lincoln was homely Taft was obese, and ED. R. was crippled.

In the long term, however, the significance of image wanes considerably. The image of the Marlboro man ultimately gave way to the truth about the health hazards of cigarette smoking. Popular musical acts with nothing truly innovative to offer musically eventually disappear from the music scene. And anyone who frequents yard sales knows that today's best-selling books often become tomorrow's pulp. Even in politics, I think history has a knack for peeling away image to focus on real accomplishments. I think history will remember Teddy Roosevelt, for example, primarily for building the Panama Canal and for establishing our National Park System—and not for his rough-and-ready wardrobe.

In the final analysis, it seems that in every endeavor where success depends to some degree on persuasion, marketing, or salesmanship, image has indeed become the central concern of those who seek to persuade. And as our lives become busier, our attention spans briefer, and our choices among products and services greater, I expect this trend to continue unabated—for better or worse.

形象重于背后的真相吗?

在我们的社会中，创造形象已经重于形象背后的现实或实质了吗？我承认形象已经成了一个更主要的考虑，至少在事关短期贸易或政治活动成败的时候是这样。然而，从长远的角度讲，我还是认为形象最终是要屈服于本质和实际的。

在商贸领域，形象的重要作用十分明显。以现今的汽车业为例，几乎在机械、构造以及价格各个方面，美国的汽车都在变得与竞争对手日本汽车公司一样了。这样，为了有效地竞争，汽车公司现在必须通过形象广告来使其产品迥然有别于其他产品。这种形象广告像有魔力似地给汽车制造出虚幻的附加价值，如展示男子汉气概、地位、情感或幽默。在图书出版业，对形象越来越关注的趋势也十分明显。出版商越来越依靠其品牌的力量，而不是依靠图书的内容。如今，畅销书在一年内就会被另一批书所替代，这批书在实质上是相同的，不同的只是有了新的面孔、新的标题和其他的促销角度。说实话，我发现现今越来越多的图书出版商正在被大型的媒体公司所有。而且，形象日益重要的状况在音乐界表现得尤为明显，原创性、艺术演绎和技巧娴熟几乎已经全部都屈服于性的魅力。

在政治领域，形象日益重要的趋势也非常明显，尤其是涉及总统政治时。无可否认，在本质上，政治活动一直是对措辞和形象的注重多于本质和实际。然而，自从照相机问世，总统们已经越来越关注自己的形象。例如，特迪·罗斯福在穿着一身网球服的时候，就非常小心从不被拍照，因为他担心这样的照片会损坏他的骑士形象，骑士形象为他赢得了惟一的一次总统任期。随着电视的出现，在总统政治中形象变得更加重要。毕竟，是电视在约翰·F·肯尼迪和尼克松之间选择了前者，而且在电视机的时代里，任期只有两届的总统在很大程度上都是人们根据形象选出的。现在，如果同潇洒的领导人里根或文雅且政治上正确的克林顿竞争，不知道林肯、塔夫脱，甚至是富兰克林·罗斯福是否还会当选。毕竟，林肯相貌平平，塔夫脱身材肥胖，而罗斯福是一个跛子。

然而长远来看，形象的重要性要大幅地减弱。由于吸烟有害健康，万宝路品牌的形象最终被吸烟有害健康的真理所代替。流行音乐创作如果不能有真正的音乐创新，就会最终从乐坛消失。经常买卖家庭旧货的人都知道，今天的畅销书往往会成为明天的纸浆。甚至在政治领域，我认为历史有剔除形象、注重真实成绩的本领。例如，我认为历史将会记住特迪·罗斯福，主要是因为他建造了巴拿马运河、建立了我们的国家公园系统，而不是因为他简陋的衣柜。

综上分析，在依靠某种程度上的游说、营销、推销而获得成功的努力中，似乎形象已经真正的成为了这些去游说的人关注的中心。由于我们的生活越来越忙碌，我们集中注意力的时间更少了，我们在产品和服务间的选择却更多了。无论是好是坏，我都预料这种趋势将永不衰退。

论点 平衡观点 本文属于典型的"具体情况具体分析"的类型。一方面，在短期贸易或政治活动中，形象的作用有时候会甚于本质内容；另一方面，从长远的角度（历史）讲，形象最终是要屈服于本质和实际的。

开头方式 提出问题＋让步语气＋表明立场 该开头方式是我在最前面重点推荐过的，好处就不赘述了。首先，以提问的方式引出问题——在我们的社会中，创造形象是否已经重于形象背后的实质？其次，作者做出让步，同意题目中的观点——形象很重要；最后，作者提出自己的观点——（不仅形象很重要）本质内容也非常重要。

论证过程 比较型 题目中的"more...than..."已经明确告诉你，这道题最好当成比较型题目来处理。论证的三个自然段分成两个层次：一方面，作者举了若干的特例（商业和政治）来赞同形象的重要性；另一方面，作者又从相同的领域举出了反例，强调本质仍然非常重要。

◆ **Tip 推敲反例** 同学们在举例论证方面感到难度很大，因为他们认为自己找不到那么多贴切的例子。解决这个问题在于两点：第一，掌握四种论证过程，通过论证的逻辑过程推出例子（每一个明确分工的主题句都会引出若干例子），而不是凭空想像例子；第二，所有的文章观点都可以有正反两方面，你只要找到一方面的例子，就可以去推敲反面的情况。本文中畅销书和美国总统的例子就用了正反两面。

论证模式

① The important role of image is particularly evident in the business world.

② The growing significance of image is also evident in the political realm...

③ In the long term, however, the significance of image wanes considerably.

Issue 112　Should schools teach students to **explore their own emotions**?

"**Some educational systems emphasize the development of students' capacity for reasoning and logical thinking, but students would benefit more from an education that also taught them to explore their**

own emotions."

一些教育体系强调学生逻辑推理思维能力的发展,但是那些教学生们探究自身情绪的教育对学生们才更有好处。

The speaker asserts that educational systems should place less emphasis on reason and logical thinking and more emphasis on the exploration of emotions. **While I concede that** in certain fields students are well served by nurturing their emotions and feelings, **in most academic disciplines it is by cultivating intellect rather than emotions that** students master their discipline and, in turn, gain a capacity to contribute to the well-being of society.

I agree with the speaker insofar as undue emphasis on reason and logical thinking can have a chilling effect on the arts. After all, artistic ideas and inspiration spring not from logic but from emotions and feelings such as joy, sadness, hope, and love. And, the true measure of artistic accomplishment lies not in technical proficiency but rather in a work's impact on the emotions and spirit. **Nevertheless**, even in the arts, students must learn theories and techniques, which they then apply to their craft. And, creative writing requires the cognitive ability to understand how language is used and how to communicate ideas. Besides, creative ability is itself partly a function of intellect; that is, creative expression is a marriage of one's cognitive abilities and the expression of one's feelings and emotions.

Aside from its utility in the arts, however, the exploration of emotions has little place in educational systems. The physical sciences and mathematics are purely products of reason and logic. Even in the so-called "soft" sciences, emotion should play no part. Consider, for example, the study of history, political science, or public policy, each of which is largely the study of how the concepts of fairness, equity, and justice work themselves out. It is tempting to think that students can best understand and learn to apply these concepts by tapping feelings such as compassion, empathy, sympathy, and indignation. Yet fairness, equity, and justice have little to do with feelings, and everything to do with reason. **After all**, emotions are subjective things. **On the other hand**, reason is objective and therefore facilitates communication, consensus, and peaceful compromise.

Indeed, on a systemic scale undue emphasis on the exploration of our emotions can have deleterious societal consequences. Emotions invite irrationality in thought and action, the dangers of which are all too evident in contemporary America. For example, when it comes to the war on drugs, free speech and religion, abortion issues, and sexual choices, public policy today seems to simply mirror the voters' fears and prejudices. **Yet** common sense dictates that social ills are best solved by identifying cause-and-effect relationships—in other words, through critical thinking. The proliferation of shouting-match talk shows fueled by irrationality and emotion gone amuck is further evidence that our culture lends too much credence to our emotions and not enough to our minds. A culture that sanctions irrationality and unfettered venting of emotion is vulnerable to decline. **Indeed**, exploiting emotions while suppressing reason is how demagogues gain and hold power, and how humanity's most horrific atrocities have come to pass. **In contrast**, reason and better judgment are effective deterrents to incivility, despotism, and war.

In sum, emotions can serve as important catalysts for academic accomplishment in the arts. **Otherwise, however**, students, and ultimately society, are better off by learning to temper their emotions while nurturing judgment, tolerance, fairness, and understanding—all of which are products of reason and critical thinking.

学校应该教学生发掘他们自己的情感吗？

发言者认为教育系统应当把重点更多地放在对学生的情感发掘上，而较少强调逻辑和推理思维。我承认在一定的领域里，通过培养学生的情感和感觉而使他们大有裨益，但在多数的学术领域中，正是通过智力的提高而非感情的孕育而使他们成为学科能手，并反过来获得贡献社会的这样一种能力。

我同意该发言人对不当地强调推理和逻辑推理能力会给艺术带来可怕影响的观点。毕竟，艺术想法和灵感不是来自于逻辑而是迸发于诸如欢乐、悲伤、希望和爱情等情感和感觉。并且，艺术成就的真正分量在于该作品对情感和精神的冲击，而非技术的娴熟程度。但是，即使在艺术创作中，学生必须要学会应用他们作品中的理论和技艺。同时，创造性的写作需要一种运用语言和传达思想的认知能力。而且，创新能力本身也是智力功能的一部分，也就是说，创新的思想表达是该作者认知能力和情感表述的结合物。

然而，除了对艺术创作有益外，对情感的发掘在教育体系中无足轻重。物理学和数学纯是推理和逻辑的产物。即使在所谓的"软"科学中，情感也无立足之地。以历史学、政治学和公共政策学为例，每一门大都是对如何形成公正、平等和正义这些概念的学习和研究。我们很容易会认为学生通过挖掘自己的情感，像热情、同情、感知以及愤慨等，就会更好地理解和运用这些概念。但公正、平等和正义却与感情鲜有干系，而与推理却息息相关。毕竟，情感是主观的东西。另一方面，推理却是客观的，并因此使交流、共识和和平的让步更为容易。

系统地说来，对情感开发的过分强调的确会带来毁灭性的社会后果。情感容易导致思想和行动上的非理智，它带来的危险在当代美国是有目共睹的。例如，在禁毒、言论和宗教信仰自由、堕胎以及性选择上，今日的公共政策似乎仅折射出选民的恐惧与偏见。但根据常识，社会疾病只有通过认清因果关系才能得到最好的解决，换句话说，就是通过批判的思考。犹如大嗓门大赛的脱口秀的泛滥就是我们的文化过于信赖我们的情感而较少诉诸头脑的进一步证据，而这些脱口秀正是由失去理智和情感宣泄所支撑。一种认可非理智和情感无节制宣泄的文化很容易衰败。事实上，压制理性的同时利用情感就是蛊惑人心的政客获取和控制权力及世间最骇人听闻的暴行发生的方式。相反，理性和客观的判断可以有效地制止失礼、暴政和战争。

总之，在艺术创作中，情感是学术成就的重要的催化剂。然而，学生以及最终服务的社会只有通过学会限制他们的情感，同时培养判断、忍耐、公正和理解——所有这些都是理性和逻辑思维的产物——才能有更好地发展。

论点 **有保留的反对**　本文也属于典型的"具体情况具体分析"的类型。一方面，在艺术领域中，作者承认情感的重要性；另一方面，在其他大多数领域中，作者认为逻辑和客观才是至关重要的。虽然，本文观点也是从正反两个方面论述的，但是反对观点涉及的范围和篇幅都有明显的倾向，因此，它属于有保留的反对观点。

开头方式 **陈述题目观点＋表明立场**　问题解决型文章中经常使用的开头方式：问题——如何教育学生，题目观点——培养学生的情感和感觉，作者立场——（不仅把重点放在对学生的情感发掘上）还要提高智力。

论证过程 **问题解决型**　论证过程的三个自然段分成两个方面：一方面，作者承认题目的观点，在艺术领域中情感的确很重要，而且需要培养；另一方面，在论证过程的第二、三段，作者开始驳论，举了若干例子证明自然科学领域需要逻辑和推理而非感情，以及另外的例子说明过多的感性会导致的恶果。

论证模式

① I agree with the speaker insofar as undue emphasis on reason and logical thinking can have a chilling effect on. . . Nevertheless, . . .

② Aside from its utility in the arts, however, the exploration of emotions has little place in educational systems.

③ Indeed, on a systemic scale undue emphasis on the exploration of our emotions can have deleterious societal consequences.

Issue 127　Are facts "**stubborn things**," or can we alter them?

"**Facts are stubborn things. They cannot be altered by our wishes, our inclinations, or the dictates of our passions.**"

事实都是固执的。它不可能随着我们的愿望、喜好或者情绪的趋向而改变。

Can we alter facts according to our wishes or inclinations? **If** by "facts" the speaker means such phenomena as political, economic, social, or legal status quo, **then I concede that** we can alter facts. The reason for this is that such systems are abstract constructs of our inclinations, wishes, and passions to begin with. **Otherwise, I strongly agree with the speaker that** we cannot alter facts. When it comes to certain aspects of our personal lives, and to historical events and scientific truths, no measure of desire or even passion can change external reality.

　　On an individual level, we all engage in futile attempts to alter facts—by pretending that certain things are not the way they are because they are inconsistent with our wishes or personal interests. Psychologists refer to this psychological defensive mechanism, which seems to be part of human nature, as "denial." **Consider** curious pastimes such as mind-reading, psychic healing, rituals that purportedly impart immortality, and other such endeavors, which seems to transcend all cultures and periods of human history. **Understandably**, we would all like to have the ability to alter the physical world, including ourselves, as we see fit, or even to live forever by means of the sheer force of our will. **Yet**, not one iota of scientific evidence lends support to the claim that any human being has ever had any such ability.

　　Nor can we alter facts by virtue of our inclinations or passions when it comes to history. Admittedly, no person can truly know any particular past that the person did not experience firsthand. In this sense history is a construct, created for us by reporters, archivists, and historians. Historical facts are therefore susceptible to interpretation, characterization, and of course errors in commission and omission. **This is not to say, however, that** historical facts can be altered by our inventing versions that suit our inclinations or wishes. In short, a historical event is not rendered any less factual by either our ignorance or characterization of it.

　　Similarly, when it comes to science our wishes and desires ultimately yield to the stubbornness of facts—by which I mean empirical scientific evidence and the laws and principles of the physical world. **Admittedly**, in many cases it is difficult to distinguish between scientific "fact" and mere "theory." History is replete with examples of what were considered at one time to be facts, but later disproved as incorrect theories. **Yet** it is telling that many such obsolete theories were based on the subjective inclinations, desires, and wishes of theorists and of the societies in which the theorists lived. For example, the notions of an Earth-centered universe and of linear time and space were both influenced by religious notions—that is, by human wishes and passions. As our factual knowledge increased such theories ultimately give way.

In sum, I agree that facts are indeed "stubborn things." Understandably, all humans are guilty of ignoring, overlooking, and misunderstanding facts—at least to some extent. **After all**, human passion, desire, and individual bias and perspective are powerful influences when it comes to what we believe to be true and factual. **Moreover**, the statement carries deep epistemological implications regarding the nature of knowledge and truth, which I cannot begin to adequately address here. **Nevertheless**, on a less abstract level the speaker is correct that neither inclination, desire, nor passion, no matter how fervent, can alter that which is past or beyond our physical control.

事实是"顽固不化"吗？或我们能改变它们吗？

　　我们能够按自己的意愿或是喜好改变事实吗？如果该发言者口中的事实为诸如政治、经济、社会或法律现状这些现象的话，那么我承认我们能够改变事实。理由是这些体系首先就是我们喜好、意愿和热情的抽象组合。否则，我绝对赞同该发言人关于我们不能改变事实的观点。当涉及我们个人生活、历史事件和科学事实的某些方面时，再强烈的愿望甚至热情都不能改变外在的现实。

　　就个人而讲，我们试图改变事实的努力都是徒劳的——我们总是假装某些事情并非应是现在这种状况，因为它们与我们的意愿或是个人兴趣不符。心理学家将这种似乎是人类本性中一个组成部分的心理防卫机能称为"否认"。以一些奇特的消遣为例，像看透他人心思、精神治疗和据说可以得到永生的仪式以及其他诸如此类的努力，似乎都超越了所有文化和人类历史。我们都想有能力依自己的意愿改变物质世界，包括我们自己，甚至是仅依靠我们的意愿而获得永生，这可以理解。但是，没有任何的科学证据证明人类曾经拥有过任何这样的能力。

　　在历史方面，我们同样不能依自己的喜好或是热情来改变事实。我们必须承认，任何人在没有亲自经历的情况下，不可能真正知道过去特定的时期内所发生的事情。这样，历史就是记者、档案保管员和历史学家为我们构建的结构。因此，历史事实就有赖于人们的释义、勾勒，当然会产生遗漏和错误。但是这并不是说历史事实可以被符合我们意愿或喜好的杜撰所修改。总而言之，一个历史事件不会由于我们的无知或对其的描述而使其真实性受到损害。

　　同样，在科学方面，我们的愿望或意愿最终都要让步于事实的"顽固性"——这里的事实指的是由实践得出的科学证据以及物质世界的法规和原则。诚然，在许多情况下，人们很难区分科学"事实"和纯"理论"。历史充斥着这样的事例，一度被认为是事实的，后来被斥之为错误的理论。这些过时的理论许多都基于理论家以及他们所生活的社会的主观喜好、意愿和希望。例如，有关地心说以及线性时间和空间的理论都受到了宗教信仰的影响——也就是说受到了人的愿望和热情的影响。随着我们科学知识的增加，这些理论也寿终正寝了。

　　总之，我认为事实是"顽固的"。至少在一定的程度上，人们都会有意无意地忽略和曲解事实，这可以理解。毕竟，人类的热情、意愿及个人观点和视角在我们对事实的认定上具有很强的影响力。而且，就知识和真理的本性（篇幅有限，此处不能给出充足的叙述）而言，这种观点有着深刻的认识论上的含义。但是，具体点讲，发言人的关于无论个人喜好、意愿、热情如何强烈都不能改变超出我们物理控制能力之外的事情的观点是正确的。

论点　**有保留的赞成**　其实本文总的来说还是以赞成为主，但是就像基本上所有的 Issue 文章一

样，作者也没有把话说死：在一边倒地赞成我们无法按自己的意愿或是喜好改变事实的同时，还是做出了让步，承认存在很多例外情况（如政治、经济、社会或法律现实）。

开头方式 提出问题＋表明立场　常用的开头方式之一，用问句引出话题——人们是否能够通过意愿改变事实？作者观点则是"具体情况具体分析"。

论证过程 因果型　又要用到那句老话，"Everything has cause and effect"。本文的因果关系就是"事实不以人的意志而转移→事实都是固执的"，论证过程的三个自然段从三个角度（个人、历史和科学）分别进行纵向的正反论证（因果成立和因果不成立的情况）。

论证模式

① On an individual level, we all engage in futile attempts to alter facts...

② Nor can we alter facts by virtue of our inclinations or passions when it comes to history.

③ Similarly, when it comes to science...

Issue 184　Is it a mistake **to theorize** without data?

"It is a grave mistake to theorize before one has data."
在掌握足够资料之前建立理论会导致严重的错误。

Is it a "grave mistake" to theorize without data, as the speaker contends? **I agree insofar as to** theorize before collecting sufficient data is to risk tainting the process of collecting and interpreting further data. **However**, in a sense the speaker begs the question, by overlooking the fact that every theory requires some data to begin with. Moreover, the claim unfairly ignores equally grave consequences of waiting to theorize until we obtain too much data.

　　In one important respect I agree with the speaker's contention. A theory conjured up without the benefit of data amounts to little more that the theorist's hopes and desires—what he or she wants to be true and not be true. **Accordingly**, this theorist will tend to seek out evidence that supports the theory, and overlook or avoid evidence that refutes it. One telling historical example involves theories about the center of the Universe. **Understandably**, we ego-driven humans would prefer that the universe revolve around us. Early theories presumed so for this reason, and subsequent observations that ran contrary to this ego-driven theory were ignored, while the observers were scorned and even vilified.

　　By theorizing before collecting data the theorist also runs that risk of interpreting that data in a manner which makes it appear to lend more credence to the theory than it actually does. Consider the theory that the Earth is flat. **Any** person with a clear view of the horizon must agree in all honesty that the evidence does not support the theory. **Yet** prior to Newtonian physics the notion of a spherical Earth was so unsettling to people that they interpreted the arc-shaped horizon as evidence of a convex, yet nevertheless "flattish," Earth.

　　Despite the merits of the speaker's claim, I find it problematic in two crucial respects. First, common sense informs me that it is impossible to theorize in the first place without at least some data. How can theorizing without data be dangerous, as the speaker contends, if it is not even possible? While a theory based purely on fantasy might ultimately be born out by empirical observation, it is equally possible that it won't. Thus without prior data a theory is not worth our time or attention. **Secondly**, the speaker's claim overlooks the inverse problem: the danger of continuing to acquire data without venturing a theory based on that data. To postpone theorizing until all the data is in might be to postpone it forever. The danger lies in the reasons we theorize and test our theories: to solve society's problems and to make the world a better place to live. Unless we act timely based on our data we render ourselves impotent. For example, governments tend to respond to urgent social problems by establishing agencies to collect data and think-tanks to theorize about causes and solutions. These agencies and think-tanks serve no purpose unless they admit that they will never have all the data and that no theory is foolproof, and unless timely action is taken based on the best theory currently available—before the problem overwhelms us.

　　To sum up, I agree with the speaker insofar as a theory based on no data is not a theory but mere whimsy and fancy, and insofar as by theorizing first we tend to distort the extent to which data collected thereafter supports our own theory. **Nevertheless**, we put ourselves in equal peril by mistaking data for knowledge and progress, which require us not only to theorize but also to act upon our theories with some useful end in mind.

未掌握数据就得出理论是一个错误吗？

　　演讲者所说的，未掌握数据就得出理论是一个"大错误"吗？我只能认同在收集到足够的数据之前就得出理论会影响到收集和分析后来数据的程序。然而，从某种意义上讲，演讲者是在忽略每个理论都首先需要用一些数据来推断的前提下进行辩论的。而且，这种说法也不公平地忽视了在获得足够的数据之前等待得出理论的后果同样严重。

　　从一个重要的方面出发，我同意该演讲者的论点。一个没有数据支持而得出的理论，差不多就是理论家的希望和期望——他或她想要成为真实的或不想成为真实的东西。因此，理论家就会去寻找支持这个理论的证据，而忽略或避开否认它的证据。一个有力的历史例子是有关宇宙中心理论的。可以理解的是，我们以自我为中心的人类希望宇宙能够围绕着我们转。出于这个原因，早期的理论就假定为此，而随后的与这个自我中心理论相悖的观察结果就被忽视了，观察者也被蔑视，甚至被诋毁。

　　在收集数据前就做出结论，理论家还会冒这样一种风险：用一种使其看上去比事实上更可信的方式来解释数据。拿地球是平的这个理论来举例，任何一个能看清地平线的人都必须老老实实地承认这个证据不支持这个理论。然而，先于牛顿物理学说的地球球体论是如此的不得人心，以致于人们把球体论中的弧形地平线解释为一个凸面的证据，而地球还是"平的"。

　　尽管演讲者说的有一定道理，但我发现这个理论在两个关键方面有问题。首先，常理告诉我没有一点儿数据就得出理论是不可能的。正如演讲者所说，如果没有数据就得出理论连可能性都没有，那么又何谈危险性呢？一个完全以想像为依据的理论有可能最终通过实际观察得以产生，同样，也同样有可能被否掉。因此，早先没有数据依据的理论是不值得我们花费时间和精力的。其次，演讲者的观点忽略了一个反向问题：只是不断寻求数据而不依靠已有数据得出理论的做法是危险的。为了掌握所有数据而延迟得出理论有可能会导致永远延迟。危险就存在于我们得出理论和检验理论的原因：是为了解决社会问题，使世界成为人类生活的美好家园。除非我们根据数据及时地采取行动，否则就会使自己变得碌碌无为。例如，为了回应紧急的社会问题，政府通过建立机构来收集数据和建立智囊团来从理论上找出原因和解决的办法。这些机构和智囊团的工作没有任何目的性，除非他们承认自己永远不能掌握足够的数据，没有极简单明了的理论；除非他们能够在问题爆发之前根据目前所能获得的最好理论而及时地采取行动。

　　总之，我还是同意演讲者"没有数据验证的理论不能成为理论，只是异想天开和幻想"这种看法。我也同意演讲者的另一个观点，就是过早得出理论会歪曲我们收集多少数据来支持我们自己的理论的程度。然而，弄错知识和进展的数据会使我们同样困于险境，知识和进展不仅需要我们去得出理论，还需要我们根据头脑中的某种有用的目的实践这些理论。

论点 **平衡观点** 作者一方面认同在收集到足够的数据之前就得出理论会影响到理论的准确性，另一方面，作者认为题目忽视了一些重要的逻辑关系。

开头方式 **提出问题 + 回答 + 表明立场** 本文开头作者观点这一部分非常接近 Argument 的风格，这也是由本题的论证类型所决定的。

论证过程 **结论型** 本题是以判断句为标志的典型的结论型题目，同时它也是一道抽象类题目。遵循结论型论证（why + if... then...）。论证过程的三个自然段分成两个层次：前两段为第一层次，挖掘题目持此观点的原因——没有数据支持的理论没有真正意义（宇宙中心理论），以及会导致理论维护者带着偏见的自圆其说（地球是平面的理论）；论证过程的第三段为第二层次，这一个超长段落（if... then...），驳斥题目的绝对观点，举例说明有些情况不能只顾数据的完整（政府解决当务之急的问题）。

论证模式

① In one important respect I agree with the speaker's contention.

② By theorizing before collecting data the theorist also runs that risk of...

③ Despite the merits of the speaker's claim, I find it problematic in two crucial respects.

Issue 41　The role of **non-mainstream areas** of inquiry

"**Such non-mainstream areas of inquiry as astrology, fortune-telling, and psychic and paranormal pursuits play a vital role in society by satisfying human needs that are not addressed by mainstream science.**"

研究界的一些非主流领域，比如星象学、占卜术和意念及超自然探索，在社会中起到了很重要的作用，因为它们满足了人们无法从主流科学获得的需求。

This statement actually consists of two claims: (1) that non-mainstream areas of inquiry are vital in satisfying human needs, and (2) that these areas are therefore vital to society. I concede that astrology, fortune-telling, and psychic and paranormal pursuits respond to certain basic human needs. **However, in my view** the potential harm they can inflict on their participants and on society far outweighs their psychological benefits.

Admittedly, these non-mainstream areas of inquiry address certain human needs, which mainstream science and other areas of intellectual inquiry inherently cannot. One such need involves our common experience as humans that we freely make our own choices and decisions in life and therefore carry some responsibility for their consequences. Faced with infinite choices, we experience uncertainty, insecurity, and confusion; and we feel remorse, regret, and guilt when in retrospect our choices turn out be poor ones. **Understandably**, to prevent these bad feelings many people try to shift the burden of making difficult choices and decisions to some nebulous authority outside themselves—by relying on the stars or on a stack of tarot cards for guidance.

Two other such needs have to do with our awareness that we are mortal. This awareness brings a certain measure of pain that most people try to relieve by searching for evidence of an afterlife. Absent empirical proof that life extends beyond the grave, many people attempt to contact or otherwise connect with the so-called "other side" through paranormal and psychic pursuits. Another natural response to the prospect of being separated from our loved ones by death is to search for a deeper connection with others here on Earth and elsewhere, in the present as well as the past. This response manifests itself in people's enduring fascination with the paranormal search for extraterrestrial life, with so-called "past life" regression and "channeling," and the like.

While the sorts of pursuits that the speaker lists might be "vital" insofar as they help some people feel better about themselves and about their choices and circumstances, **query whether these pursuits are otherwise useful to any individual or society. In the first place**, because these pursuits are not rooted in reason, they are favorite pastimes of charlatans and others who seek to prey on dupes driven by the aforementioned psychological needs. And the dupes have no recourse. **After all**, it is impossible to assess the credibility of a tarot card that tells us how to proceed in life—simply because we cannot know where the paths not taken would have led. **Similarly**, we cannot evaluate claims about the afterlife because these claims inherently defy empirical proof—or disproof.

In the second place, without any sure way to evaluate the legitimacy of these avenues of inquiry, **participants become vulnerable to self-deception, false hopes, fantastic ideas, and even delusions.** In turn, so-called "insights" gained from these pursuits can too easily serve as convenient excuses for irrational and unreasonable actions that harm others. On a personal level, stubborn adherence to irrational beliefs in the face of reason and empirical evidence can lead to self-righteous arrogance, intolerance, anti-social behavior, and even hatred. **Moreover**, on a societal level these traits have led all too often to holy wars, and to such other atrocities as genocide and mass persecution.

In sum, I concede that the non-mainstream pursuits that the speaker lists are legitimate insofar as they afford many people psychological solace in life. **However**, when such pursuits serve as substitutes for reason and logic, and for honest intellectual inquiry, participants begin to distrust intellect as an impediment to enlightenment. In doing so, they risk making ill-conceived choices for themselves and unfair judgments about others—a risk that in my view outweighs the psychological rewards of those pursuits.

非主流探求的作用

该观点实际上包含两方面的意思：(1) 非主流的探询领域对满足人类的需要至关重要，(2) 因此，这些领域对社会也至关重要。我承认，占星术、占卜以及对超自然现象的研究迎合了人们一定的基本需要。但是，在我看来，它们对参与者以及社会的潜在危害远远超过了它们对人们心理需要的贡献。

诚然，这些人类探求中的非主流领域满足了人们一定的需要，而主流学科和智力探询的其他领域却生来无能为力。其中的一种需要牵涉到我们作为人类的共同经历，即在生活中我们自主做出选择和决定，并因此为它们的后果承担一定的责任。面对浩如烟海的选择，我们会遭遇不确定、不安全和迷惑；在回顾我们做出的差劲儿的选择时，我们会自责、懊悔和遗憾。可以理解，为了防止产生这样的不良感觉，许多人试图将做出困难选择和决定的负担转嫁给一些自身之外的不可名状的权威——通过星象或占卜纸牌来指点迷津。

另外的两个需要与我们意识到自己终究要入土有关。该意识带来了一定的痛苦，而多数人试图通过寻找来世的证据来减轻这种痛楚。由于没有实践证据证明生命可以在死后得以延续，许多人又尝试通过超自然的灵魂研究来接触或联络所谓的"来世"。死亡将会使自己与心爱的人分离，人们对此的自然反应是在地球上或其他的地方寻找一种与所爱的人在现在或是过去更紧密的联系。人们乐此不疲、近乎痴迷地对地外生命的超自然寻求和所谓的"往世"的回归和"转世"等等，就是该自然反应最好的见证。

演讲人列举的这些种研究在帮助一些人对自己、对自己所做出的选择和所处的环境感觉好一些这个方面或许是至关重要的，但除此之外，这些研究对任何个人或社会是否会有用是值得怀疑的。首先，因为这些研究并非根植于理性，仅是江湖郎中和那些以欺骗有着前面提到的心理需求的易受骗人群之徒所青睐的消遣而已。而这些被欺骗的人们毫无追索权。毕竟，我们不可能去评测一副指引生活方向的占卜牌的可信度——就是因为我们无从得知我们没有选择的那条路到底会通向何方。相同的是，我们不能够评价关于来世的看法，因为这些看法本质上是无法用实践证明是对是错的。

其次，因为没有确定的方法来评价这些探询途径的正当性，参与者就容易自欺欺人，产生虚假的希望和奇妙的想法，甚至是幻觉。反之，从这些探求中获得的所谓的"洞察力"很容易成为伤害他人的不理智和不合乎常理的行为的托词。就个人而言，在面对理智和实践证据时，固执地坚持荒谬的信仰会导致刚愎自用、心胸狭窄和反社会的行为，甚至是仇恨。而且，就社会而论，这些特性经常会导致圣战，以及其他诸如种族灭绝和大屠杀之类的暴行。

总而言之，我承认以上列举的非主流探求在生活中可以给许多人提供心理上的慰藉这个层面上是正当的。但是，当这些探求成为理性和逻辑以及真实的知识探求的替代品时，参与者就开始将理智视为精神启蒙的绊脚石而不再信任理智。因此，他们冒险做出错误的选择和对他人的不公正的判断——在我认为，其危害超出了这些探求对人们心理上的回报。

论点 **有保留的反对**　开头的中心句用的是大家见过很多次的让步语气句型"I concede that...However,...."，这暗示了作者在论证段要进行正反两方面的论证，最后由 outweigh 敲定了大负小正的结论。

◆ *Tip*　非常值得注意的一点是，考生们经常把 GRE 阅读中极端转折的让步语气概念照搬到 Issue 中，这两者之间是有很大区别的。如果你想判定这句话到底倾向前半部分还是后半部分，只看让步语气并不可靠，在很多情况下会把意思弄反，例如：It is true that...in most cases, however,...这句话大多数情况下是以前半句为准。这种情况在英文中非常普遍，看和用的时候请务必留心。

开头方式 **陈述题目观点 + 表明立场**　不特别推荐这种开头方式，看上去有些哗众取宠，如果对题目内涵分析不到位的话，很容易弄巧成拙。

论证过程 **结论型**　非常标准的"why + if...then..."结构，在讲课过程中，受 GRE 阅读和同学们反馈的启发，我把它简单地归纳成两个成语：欲擒故纵 + 釜底抽薪。驳论时不是只从正面去攻击它，而是先找理由支持它，再由该结论推出一些谬误，证明它最终是存在问题的，这样的思路最全面，最完整。

论证模式

① Admittedly, these non-mainstream areas of inquiry address certain human needs, ...

② Two other such needs have to do with our awareness that we are mortal.

③ While... query whether these pursuits are otherwise useful to any individual or society. In the first place...

④ In the second place...participants become vulnerable to self-deception, false hopes, fantastic ideas, and even delusions.

Issue 131 Do the arts reveal society's **hidden ideas and impulses**?

"**The arts (painting, music, literature, etc.) reveal the otherwise hidden ideas and impulses of a society.**"

艺术(绘画、音乐、文学等等)揭示了一个社会在其他方面隐藏着的理念和动力。

The speaker asserts that the arts reveal society's hidden ideas and impulses. While this assertion has merit, **I think it unfairly generalizes about art. Consider two particular art forms**: architecture and painting. In more important architecture one consistently sees a refection of society's ideas and urges. However, in more important paintings of the most recent century one sees instead the artists' personal and idiosyncratic visions of an aesthetic ideal.

Turning first to public architecture, one sees in ancient and Renaissance forms an impulse to transcend the human condition. Clearly, the most important architecture of these periods was built to honor deities and to propel humans into the afterlife. **Consider**, for example, the ancient pyramids and the great cathedrals of Europe, which rise upward toward the stars and heavens. **During** the Medieval period the most important architectural form was the castle, which reflected an overriding concern for military security and brute strength during a time of comparative anarchy. **During** the twentieth century it was first the steel-forged art deco forms and then the sky-scraping office building that dominated public architecture. These forms reflect modern, more mundane concerns for industrial and technological progress.

Turning next to important paintings and painters, it seems to me that the art of previous centuries reflected the attitudes and ideas of the prevailing culture to a far greater extent than today's art. The cynosures of the Medieval and Renaissance artists, for instance, were certain Christian themes—the Trinity, virgin birth of Christ, the Resurrection, and so forth—with which the society at large was also preoccupied. Later, during the eighteenth and nineteenth centuries, an emerging genteel class saw itself reflected in the bourgeois themes of impressionists such as Renoir and Monet.

But in the most recent century the picture has been much different. Consider three of the twentieth century's most influential painters: Picasso, Dali, and Pollock. Picasso's style underwent a series of radical changes throughout his career. Was the reason for Picasso's diverse "periods" a quick series of radical changes in society's ideas and impulses, or perhaps a reflection of society's hidden impulse for constant change? Or did Picasso's varied styles merely reflect the complex psychological profile of one eccentric artist? Dali is known for his surrealistic images; but do these images reveal some kind of existential angst on a societal level, or just the odd aesthetic vision of one man? Pollock's penchant was for dripping paint on the floor in order to create abstract images that would have the sort of visceral impact he was after. In fact, Pollock turned to this technique only after he tried but failed as a conventional painter, using brush and easel. So are Pollock's striking abstract murals a reflection of some mid-twentieth-century societal impulse, or merely the result of one struggling artist stumbling onto something he was good at? In all three cases, it seems that the art reflected the artist but not the society.

In sum, in the art of painting one can observe a shift from styles and themes reflecting broad societal impulses to a more recent concern for expressing personal impulses and creative urges. **In contrast**, the more public art form of architecture has always mirrored society's ideas and impulses, and probably always will—because architecture is so much more public than the are of painting.

艺术揭示了社会中隐藏的观念和冲动吗?

发言人断言,艺术揭示了社会中隐藏着的观念和冲动。尽管这种断言有其正确的一面,但我认为它对艺术的概括并不公平。试想两种特定的艺术形式:建筑和绘画。在更重要的建筑中,人们经常看到社会观念和迫切需求的折射。但是,在近一个世纪以来较为重要的绘画中,人们见到的却是艺术家个人的、更具特性的审美理念。

我们先看公共建筑,人们在古代和文艺复兴形式的建筑中看到的是超越人类环境的冲动。很显然,那些时期最重要的建筑的目的在于使神性更加荣耀,并促使人类步入来世。举个例子,参看一下朝向众星与天空修建的古代金字塔和欧洲大教堂。贯穿整个中世纪时期最重要的建筑形式就是城堡,它反映出在很长一段时期内,在相对混乱的割据的状况下,高于一切的对军事安全和控制实力的关注。进入 20 世纪以来,先是钢铁铸造的艺术装饰,然后是摩天而起的高级写字楼主导着公共建筑。这些形式反映出现代更加世俗的对工业和科技进步的关注。

我们再来看看重要的绘画和画家。我觉得,先前几个世纪的艺术所反映出来的主流文化的态度和理念似乎要远比当今艺术所反映的程度更深。例如,中世纪和文艺复兴时期艺术家的方向总是基督教主旨——圣灵、圣父、圣子的三位一体,耶稣基督的诞生,耶稣的复活,等等——这些在当时社会普遍占着主导的地位。后来,到了 18、19 世纪,新兴的上流社会在印象主义画家,例如雷诺阿和莫奈的资产阶级主题中看到了自己的影子。

但是最近一个世纪的绘画却大大不同了。我们可以看看 20 世纪最具影响力的三位画家:毕加索、达利和波洛克(Pollock)。在毕加索的绘画生涯中,他的风格经历了一系列的根本性的改变。导致毕加索拥有不同的“时期”的原因是因为社会观念和冲动的一系列的根本性的变更,还是或许它是社会的每一次变更中所隐藏的冲动的反映?抑或毕加索自己迥异的风格仅仅反映出一个行为古怪的艺术家自身的复杂的心理特征?达利以他超现实主义的画像闻名于世,但是这些画像是画家对社会存在的担忧的揭示,还是仅仅表达了个人怪癖的审美观?波拉克的趣味在于以滴墨的形式在地板上绘画以达到创作抽象画的目的,这些抽象的作品具有他一贯追求的触目惊心的效果。事实上,波洛克是在尝试用画笔和画板以常规方法进行创作失败的情况下才转而采用这种绘画方式的。因此,波拉克的惊世抽象壁画是 20 世纪中期一些社会冲动的折射吗?抑或仅仅是一位不屈不挠的艺术家误打误撞上了自己擅长之事的结果?在上述三个案例中,艺术仿佛仅仅反映艺术家而不是整个社会的状况。

总而言之,在绘画方面,人们可以看到风格和主旨这样一种变更:反映广阔社会冲动转变成为近来对明确的个人冲动和创造性的迫切要求的关注。相反,更加公众化的建筑艺术形式通常都折射出社会的理念和冲动,而且可能会一如既往地对此进行反映——因为相对于绘画作品,建筑更加公众化。

論点 **平衡观点**　对于艺术是在什么时候和什么地点由什么人创作,以及其对社会的反映和影响,作者做了一分为二的论述:这种断言有其正确的一面,但它对艺术的概括并不公平。

开头方式 **表明立场＋概述理由**　这个开头很不标准,因为第一句话其实是在重复题目的观点,后面的部分才是标准的表明立场＋概述理由。

論证过程 **比较型**　其实这个题目大可不必写成这种讨论艺术的比较型论证,因为中国考生最头疼的 Issue 题目有三种题材:哲学、伦理道德和艺术(包括文学、音乐和绘画等)。其中的难中之难就是有效的例子,其实大家看了以上的这么多范文就会发现,这种学术类文章是以例子作为载体来展示我们的逻辑论证方法和综合能力的。但是想讲清楚雷诺阿（Renoir）和莫奈（Monet），或者是毕加索、达利（Dali）、波洛克（Pollock）并不容易。

◆ *Tip* 这道题目可以当成是问题解决型，即揭示社会隐藏观点和动力的不只有艺术形式，还有其他的方面。这样不就可以紧扣题目而避开讨厌的艺术问题了么？

　论证模式

　　① Turning first to public architecture...

　　② Turning next to important paintings and painters...

　　③ But in the most recent century the picture has been much different. Consider...

Issue 138　Are mistakes necessary for **discovery or progress**?

"**Only through mistakes can there be discovery or progress.**"
失败是成功之母。

The speaker contends that discovery and progress are made only through mistakes. **I strongly agree with this contention, for two reasons.** First, it accords with our personal experiences. Secondly, history informs us that on a societal level trial-and-error provides the very foundation for discovery and true progress, in all realms of human endeavor.

To begin with, the contention accords with our everyday experience as humans from early childhood through adulthood. As infants we learn how to walk by falling down again and again. As adolescents we discover our social niche, and develop self confidence and assertiveness, only by way of the sorts of awkward social encounters that are part-and-parcel of adolescence. Through failed relationships not only do we discover who we are and are not compatible with, we also discover ourselves in the process. And, most of us find the career path that suits us only through trying jobs that don't.

This same principle also applies on a societal level. Consider, for example, how we progress in our scientific knowledge. Our scientific method is essentially a call for progress through trial-and-error. Any new theory must be tested by empirical observation, and must withstand rigorous scientific scrutiny. **Moreover**, the history of theoretical science is essentially a history of trial-and-error. One modern example involves two contrary theories of physics: wave theory and quantum theory. During the last quarter-century scientists have been struggling to disprove one or the other—or to reconcile them. As it turns out, a new so-called "string" theory shows that the quantum and wave theories are mistakes in the sense that each one is inadequate to explain the behavior of all matter; yet both so-called "mistakes" were necessary for physics to advance, or progress, to this newer theory.

The value of trial-and-error is not limited to the sciences. In government and politics, progress usually comes about through dissension and challenge—that is, when people point out the mistakes of those in power. In fact, without our challenging the mistaken notions of established institutions, political oppression and tyranny would go unchecked. Similarly, in the fields of civil and criminal law, jurists and legislators who uphold and defend legal precedent must face continual opposition from those who question the fairness and relevance of current laws. This ongoing challenge is critical to the vitality and relevance of our system of laws.

In sum, the speaker correctly asserts that it is through mistakes that discovery and true progress are made. Indeed, our personal growth as individuals, as well as advances in science, government, and law, depends on making mistakes.

错误对新事物的发现或发展来说是必需的吗？

发言者认为，新的发现和发展都是通过某些错误来得以实现的。对此，我非常赞同，有两点原因。第一，这符合我们个人的经历。第二，通过历史我们可以看出，在社会的层面上，在人类所有努力的领域，通过不断实验改正错误为新的发现和真正的进步奠定了基础。

首先，论点符合我们人类从孩童时期并贯穿整个成人阶段的日常经历。当我们还是婴儿的时候，我们正是通过一次又一次的跌倒而学会如何走路的。当我们步入青少年的时候，正是青春期非常重要的组成部分——各种各样的社会挫折——使我们发现自己的社会小环境，并充分建立自己的自信。通过各种人际关系的挫折，我们不仅可以发现我们与哪些人合得来、合不来，还可以在这个过程中发现我们自己。而且，我们中的大多数人都是在不断尝试不适合自己的职业的过程中找到自己的事业之路的。

相同的法则在社会的层面上同样适用。试想，例如，我们是如何在我们的科学知识方面取得进步的。我们的科学方法从本质上来说就是通过不断的尝试和失败而取得的进步。任何新的理论都必须通过实验性的观察加以检测，而且必须经受起严格的科学审查。而且，理论科学的历史从本质上来说就是不断实验和失败的历史。一个现代的例子就是物理学上的两个相对的理论：波动说和量子论。在上个世纪最后 25 年的期间内，科学家们一直在试图推翻这个或另一个理论——或是调和它们。而结果呢？一项新的所谓"弦性"理论表明，不论波动说还是量子论，在某种意义上都是错误的，这两种理论都不足以阐明所有物质的状态；但是，对于物理学的发展或进步或是这个新理论而言，这两个所谓的"错误"都是必不可少的。

不断尝试和失败的价值并不仅限于科学领域。在政府和政治方面，所取得的进步通常都经历了意见的分歧和质疑——也就是在人们指出当权者的错误的时候。事实上，如果我们不对已经建立起来的机构的错误意图提出质疑，政治压迫和暴政就会肆无忌惮。同样，在民法和刑法方面，支持并为法规上的先例辩护的法理学家和立法者，就必须面对来自那些质疑现行法律的公正性和适当性的人们的频繁挑战。对于我们法律体系的生命力和适当性来说，这种持续不断的质疑是至关重要的。

总而言之，发言人正确地断言，新的发现和真正的进步正是通过不断的错误而促成的。确实，我们个人的成长，以及科学、政府以及法律法规的进步，都依赖于出错。

论点 **完全赞成**　该题目虽然是抽象类题目，但是写成完全赞成的类型有很大风险，因为题目中的第一个词"only"就属于极端词汇，说"只有失败是成功之母"似乎有些过于武断了。如果让你来写这个题目，你会选择什么样的观点呢？

开头方式 **表明立场 + 概述理由**　典型的提纲型开头。

论证过程 **结论型**　作者遵从把抽象类题目简单化的原则，论证部分分成三个层面：整个成人阶段的日常经历、社会的层面和政府、政治方面，在这些层面中，作者都找到了支持的论据，因此得出了支持的结论。

论证模式

① To begin with, the contention accords with our everyday experience as humans from early childhood through adulthood.

② This same principle also applies on a societal level.

③ The value of trial-and-error is not limited to the sciences.

Issue 174　Should laws be **rigid or** flexible?

"**Laws should not be rigid or fixed. Instead, they should be flexible enough to take account of various circumstances, times, and places.**"

法律不应该是僵化或固定的,而应该足够灵活以照顾到不同的环境、时期和地点。

Some measure of consistency and stability in the law is critical for any society to function. Otherwise, **I strongly agree with the speaker's assertion that** laws should be flexible enough to adapt to different circumstances, times and places. The law of marital property aptly illustrates this point.

On the one hand, a certain measure of consistency, stability, and predictability in our laws is required in order for us to understand our legal obligations and rights as we go about our day-to-day business as a society. For example, in order for private industry to thrive, businesses must be afforded the security of knowing their legal rights and obligations vis-à-vis employees, federal regulatory agencies, and tax authorities-as well as their contractual rights and duties vis-à-vis customers and suppliers. Undue uncertainty in any one of these areas would surely have a chilling effect on business. **Moreover**, some measure of consistency in the legal environment from place to place promotes business expansion as well as interstate and international commerce, all of which are worthwhile endeavors in an increasingly mobile society.

On the other hand, rigid laws can result in unfairness if applied inflexibly in all places at all times. The framers of the U.S. Constitution recognized the need both for a flexible legal system and for flexible laws—by affording each state legal jurisdiction over all but interstate matters. The framers understood that social and economic problems, as well as standards of equity and fairness, can legitimately change over time and vary from region to region—even from town to town. And our nation's founders would be pleased to see their flexible system that promotes equity and fairness as it operates today.

Consider, for example, marital property rights, which vary considerably from state to state, and which have evolved considerably over time as inflexible, and unfair, systems have given way to more flexible, fairer ones. In earlier times husbands owned all property acquired during marriage as well as property brought into the marriage—by either spouse. Understandably, this rigid and unfair system ultimately gave way to separate-property systems, which acknowledged property rights of both spouses. More recently certain progressive states have adopted even more flexible, and fairer, "community property" systems, under which each spouse owns half of all property acquired during the marriage, while each spouse retains a separate-property interest in his or her other property. Yet even these more egalitarian community-property systems can operate unfairly whenever spouses contribute unequally; accordingly, some community-property states are now modifying their systems for even greater flexibility and fairness.

Thus, the evolution of state marital-property laws aptly illustrates the virtue of a legal system that allows laws to evolve to keep pace with changing mores, attitudes, and our collective sense of equity. This same example also underscores the point that inflexible laws tend to operate unfairly, and properly give way to more flexible ones—as our nation's founders intended.

<u>法律应该更严格还是应该更灵活?</u>
　　某些程度的法律的连贯性和稳定性对于任何社会的正常运转都是至关重要的。除此之外,

我极力赞同发言人关于法律应该更具灵活性以适应不同的情况、时间和地点的论断。婚姻财产法非常适宜地证明了这一点。

　　一方面，我们的法律必须具备一定程度的连贯性、稳定性和可预言性，以便让我们更能理解我们在日常事物和社会中的法定义务和权利。比如，为了使私营工业更加繁荣，必须给予商行获知其相对于雇员、联邦管制机构和税务当局的法定权利和义务以及他们相对于顾客和供应商的契约性的权利和义务的保障。在上述范围内的任何一个不恰当的非稳定因素一定会对业务带来不良影响。而且，不同地域之间某种程度上的较为连贯的法律有利于促进商业的发展，也同样能够有利于州际间乃至国际的商业，而这些在流动性越来越强的社会中是值得付出努力的。

　　另一方面，如果在所有的地方和所有的场合都不能灵活运用严格的法律，将会导致不公正。美国宪法的撰拟者认识到了灵活的法律制度和灵活的法律法规的需求——给予各个州全方位的法律权限，仅跨州事件除外。宪法的撰拟者明白，和公平与公正的标准一样，社会的和经济的问题可以合理地随时间改变，也可以根据地点的变化——甚至不同的城镇而改变。而我们国家的创始人也会欣喜地看到他们灵活的制度促进了公平与公正，正如它现在运行的一样。

　　例如，在各个州之间存在极大差异的婚姻财产权利。由于最初它们并不灵活而且不公平，随着时间发生了巨大的演化，它们逐渐被更加灵活、更加公平的法规体系所取代。在早期，丈夫拥有婚姻期间获得的全部财产，也同样拥有双方婚前全部财产。可以理解，这种严格而且不公平的制度最终被承认夫妻双方的财产权利的单独财产体系所取代。特别是最近，一些更加进步的州已经采用更加灵活、更加公平的"共有财产"体制。在这个体制下，丈夫和妻子在分别保留自己的财产的同时，平均拥有婚姻期间获得的全部财产。然而，当夫妻双方的贡献不均等时，即使这种更加灵活的共有财产制度也不能确保完全的公平性。因此，一些采用共有财产体制的州府现在正在修改它们的体制，以便具备更大的灵活性和公平性。

　　这样，不断健全的每个州的婚姻财产法，恰如其分地说明了这样的法律体系的优越性：允许法律自行发展以便适应不断变化的习俗、态度以及我们对公正的共同认识。同样的例子也强调了这样一个观点：不具备灵活性的法律容易导致不公，而且会被灵活的法规合理地取代——正如我们国家的创建者所希望的那样。

论点 **有保留的赞成**　作者没有全盘赞成题目的主张，即法律应该灵活，而是先做出让步，承认法律稳定的好处。

开头方式 **表明立场＋概述理由**　该文章开头的主体就是它的中心句，作者惟一使用的有分量的理由就是婚姻财产法这个例子。这篇文章写得并不工整，与前面讲过的文章不在一个档次上。

论证过程 **比较型**

论证模式

　① On the one hand, a certain measure of consistency, stability, and predictability in our laws is required in order for us to...

　② On the other hand, rigid laws can result in unfairness if applied inflexibly in all places at all times.

　③ Consider, for example, marital property rights...

Issue 176　The value and **function of science** and art

　　"The function of science is to reassure; the purpose of art is to upset. Therein lies the value of

each."

科学的作用是安心；艺术的目的是颠覆。只有这样他们才各得其所。

The speaker maintains that the function of art is to "upset" while the function of science is to "reassure," and that it is in these functions that the value of each lies. **In my view, the speaker unfairly generalizes about** the function and value of art, while completely missing the point about the function and value of science.

Consider first the intent and effect of art. In many cases artists set about to reassure, not to upset. Consider the frescos of Fra Angelico and others monks and nuns of the late medieval period, who sought primarily through their representations of the Madonna and Child to reassure and be reassured about the messages of Christian redemption and salvation. **Or consider** the paintings of impressionist and realist painters of the late nineteenth century. Despite the sharp contrast in the techniques employed by these two schools, in both genres we find soothing, genteel, pastoral themes and images—certainly nothing to upset the viewer.

In other cases, artists set about to upset. For example, the painters and sculptors of the Renaissance period, like the artists who preceded them, approached their art as a form of worship. Yet Renaissance art focuses on other Christian images and themes—especially those involving the crucifixion and apocalyptic notions of judgment and damnation—which are clearly "upsetting" and disconcerting, and clearly not reassuring. Or consider the works of two important twentieth-century artists; few would argue that the surrealistic images by Salvador Dali or the jarring, splashy murals by abstract painter Jackson Pollock serve to "upset," or at the very least disquiet, the viewer on a visceral level.

When it comes to the function and value of science, in my view the speaker's assertion is simply wrongheaded. The final objective of science, in my view, is to discover truths about our world, our universe, and ourselves. Sometimes these discoveries serve to reassure, and other times they serve to upset. For example, many would consider reassuring the various laws and principles of physics which provide unifying explanations for what we observe in the physical world. These principles provide a reassuring sense of order, even simplicity, to an otherwise mysterious and perplexing world.

On the other hand, many scientific discoveries have clearly "upset" conventional notions about the physical world and the universe. The notions of a sun-centered universe, that humans evolved from lower primate forms, and that time is relative to space and motion are all disquieting notions to anyone whose belief system depends on contrary assumptions. And more recently, researchers have discovered that many behavioral traits are functions of individual neurological brain structure, determined at birth. This notion has "upset" many professionals in fields such as behavioral psychology, criminology, mental health, and law, whose work is predicated on the notion that undesirable human behavior can be changed—through various means of reform and behavior modification.

In sum, the speaker over-generalizes when it comes to the function and value of art and science—both of which serve in some cases to reassure and in other cases to upset. In any event, the speaker misstates the true function and value of science, which is to discover truths, whether reassuring or upsetting.

科学和艺术的价值和功能

发言者主张艺术的功能在于"颠覆"而科学的功能在于"安心"，而它们各自的价值都存在于它们的这些功能之中。我认为，发言者对艺术的功能和价值的概括并不公平，而他又完全错误地解释了科学的功能和价值。

　　首先我们来看艺术的目的和作用。在很多情况下，艺术家的目的在于"安心"而不是"颠覆"。例如，中世纪晚期安吉里柯教士以及其他许多男女教士所作的壁画，他们最初通过圣母和圣子的画像保证并被保证基督教救赎和拯救的信息。或者我们来看 19 世纪晚期的印象派作家和现实主义画家的油画。暂且不论这两个派别所采用的差别迥然的绘画技巧，我们在每个流派中都可以发现令人宽慰的、上流社会的田园牧歌式的主题和画面——显然，没有任何"颠覆"视者的东西。

　　在其他情况下，艺术家有意地进行"颠覆"。例如，文艺复兴时期的画家和雕刻家，像在他们之前的艺术家一样，将他们的艺术作为一种膜拜的形式。然而，文艺复兴时期的艺术更着重于其他带有基督教色彩的画面和主题——尤其是那些涉及磨难和关于审判和诅咒的启示性意图的画面和主题——它们很明显地带有"颠覆"的意味，令人非常不安，显然并非"安心"。或者我们来看看 20 世纪两位重要艺术家的作品：几乎没有人会认为萨尔瓦多·达利的超现实主义绘画或抽象派画家杰克逊·波洛克略显杂乱的泼墨壁画带有"颠覆"的色彩，甚至连最低限度的令人不安的因素都没有。

　　我们再来看看科学的功能和价值，我认为发言人的断言是根本性的判断错误。科学的最根本的目标，我认为，在于发掘我们这个世界、我们的宇宙以及我们自身的真理。有时这些发现会带来"安心"的效果，但另外一些时候它们会有"颠覆"的作用。例如，很多人会考虑到对物理学的各种法则和原理的确定，可以对我们在物理世界所观测到的现象做出统一的解释。这些原理为其他神秘而且复杂的世界提供了一种令人安心的条理感，甚至是简易感。

　　另一方面，很多科学发现都明显"颠覆"了有关物理世界和宇宙的常规概念。对于任何信仰系统以相反的假设为基础的人来说，宇宙的日心说理论、人类由低级灵长目动物进化而来的理论以及时间与空间和运动相对的理论都是扰乱人心的概念。而在近期，研究人员发现，很多动作特征是个人大脑神经结构的功能，是与生俱来的。这个理论令很多行为主义心理学、犯罪学、精神健康以及法律等等领域内的专家感到"不安"——他们的工作是以这样的理论为基础的：人类的不良行为是可以通过各种感化和行为校正手段加以改变的。

　　总而言之，当涉及艺术和科学的功能和价值的时候，发言者给出了不恰当的总结——这两者在某些情况下使人安心，而在另外一些情况下，则有颠覆的作用。在很多情况下，发言者错误地对科学的真正功能和价值做出论断，其真正的功能和价值在于发现真理，无论是令人安心的真理还是颠覆的真理。

论点　有保留的反对　作者对于题目给艺术下的定义不置可否，而对于题目给科学下的定义只做出了小小的让步，主要以驳论为主。

开头方式　陈述题目观点 + 表明立场　请注意作者在开头时对原题所做的改动。

论证过程　比较型　作者把面铺得比较大，对于艺术和科学都在文内进行了正反分析，这其实也是由题目的设计所决定的，因为这道题目比较特殊的地方，就是它的题目设计的结构很松散，讲了两个方面的问题。

论证模式

① Consider first the intent and effect of art. In many cases artists set about to reassure, not to upset.

② In other cases, artists set about to upset.

③ When it comes to...in my view the speaker's assertion is simply wrongheaded.

④ On the other hand, many scientific discoveries have clearly "upset" conventional notions about the physical world and the universe.

Issue 221   The chief benefit of **the study of history**

"**The chief benefit of the study of history is to break down the illusion that people in one period of time are significantly different from people who lived at any other time in history.**"

研究历史最大的好处就是打破了这种假象:生活在不同时代的人们之间在很大程度上是不同的。

I concede that basic human nature has not changed over recorded history, and that coming to appreciate this fact by studying history can be beneficial in how we live as a society. **However, I disagree with the statement in two respects.** First, in other ways there are marked differences between people of different time periods, and learning about those differences can be just as beneficial. Second, studying history carries other equally important benefits as well.

I agree with the statement insofar as through the earnest study of human history we learn that basic human nature—our desires and motives, as well as our fears and foibles—has remained constant over recorded time. And through this realization we can benefit as a society in dealing more effectively with our enduring social problems. History teaches us, for example, that it is a mistake to attempt to legislate morality, because humans by nature resist having their moral choices forced upon them. History also teaches us that our major social ills are here to stay, because they spring from human nature. For instance, crime and violence have troubled almost every society; all manner of reform, prevention, and punishment have been tried with only partial success. Today, the trend appears to be away from reform toward a "tough-on-crime" approach, to no avail.

However beneficial it might be to appreciate the unchanging nature of humankind, **it is equally beneficial to understand and appreciate significant differences between peoples of different time periods**—in terms of cultural mores, customs, values, and ideals. For example, the ways in which societies have treated women, ethnic minorities, animals, and the environment have continually evolved over the course of human history. Society's attitudes toward artistic expression, literature, and scientific and intellectual inquiry are also in a continual state of evolution. And, perhaps the most significant sort of cultural evolution involves spiritual beliefs, which have always spun themselves out, albeit uneasily, through clashes between established traditions and more enlightened viewpoints. A heightened awareness of all these aspects of cultural evolution help us formulate informed, reflective, and enlightened values and ideals for ourselves; and our society clearly benefits as a result.

Another problem with the statement is that it undervalues other, equally important benefits of studying history. Learning about the courage and tenacity of history's great explorers, leaders, and other achievers inspires us to similar accomplishments, or at least to face own fears as we travel through life. Learning about the mistakes of past societies helps us avoid repeating them. For instance, the world is slowly coming to learn by studying history that political states whose authority stems from suppression of individual freedoms invariably fall of their own oppressive weight. And, learning about one's cultural heritage, or roots, fosters a healthy sense of self and cultivates an interest in preserving art, literature, and other cultural artifacts—all of which serve to enrich society.

To sum up, history informs us that basic human nature has not changed, and this history lesson can help us understand and be more tolerant of one another, as well as develop compassionate responses to the problems and failings of others. **Yet**, history has other lessons to offer us as well. It helps us formulate informed values and ideals for ourselves, inspires us to great achievements, points out mistakes to avoid, and helps us appreciate our cultural heritage.

研究历史的主要益处

我勉强认同在整个有记录的历史中，人类最基本的本性并没有改变，通过研究历史而认识到这个事实，对我们如何作为一个社会而生活是有利的。但是，在两个方面我不能认同文章的论点。第一，在很多方面，不同时期的人类存在着显著的区别，而认识到这些区别是同样有好处的。第二，对历史的研究还可以带来其他同等重要的益处。

通过认真地研究人类的历史，我们可以认识到人类的基本本性——我们的欲望和动机，以及我们的恐惧和弱点——自从有记录以来就一直保留至今，在这个范围内，我同意文章的观点。而且，通过这种认识，作为社会整体，我们在有效处理我们长期以来的社会问题上会获益匪浅。例如，历史教导我们，尝试在道德上进行立法是错误的，人类的本性抵制强加给他们道德上的选择。历史还教导我们，我们主要的社会弊病会存在下去，因为它们源自人类的本性。例如，犯罪行为和暴行几乎困扰着每一个社会，各种各样的革新、预防措施和惩罚措施都尝试过了，但只是取得了部分的成功。现在的趋势是"严厉打击犯罪"方法逐渐取代感化措施，但收效甚微。

对没有改变的人类本性的了解无论看上去是多么有益，了解人类在不同时期在文化道德观念、习俗、价值和理想方面的显著区别也是有着同样好处的。例如，在整个人类历史过程中，各个社会对妇女、少数民族、动物以及环境等问题的处理方式都在不断地发展完善。而社会对艺术表达、文学以及科学的、学术研究的态度也一直在不断地发展。而且，或许是最为显著的文化演变的类型涉及精神信仰，尽管并不容易，但它们经常在已经确立起来的传统和更具启迪性的观点的碰撞中自我发展。对文化演变所有这些方面的高度理解可以帮助我们为自己总结出有事实根据的、深思熟虑的、具有启迪性的价值观和理想，最终我们的社会很明显会从中得益。

文章的另一个问题在于，它低估了研究历史所带来的其他同等重要的好处。通过学习历史上伟大的探索者、领袖和其他成功者的勇气和坚韧，可以激发我们取得类似的成就，或者至少会鼓励我们在人生的旅途上直面自己的恐惧。学习以往各个社会的错误，可以帮助我们避免重蹈覆辙。例如，通过对历史的研究，全世界正在慢慢明白，那些将权力建立在对个人自由的镇压之上的国家，都会因为压迫深重而不可避免地步入灭亡。而且，研究人们的文化遗产或者文化根源，可以对自己认识得更加清楚，而且也会培养出对保留艺术、文学和其他文化遗产的兴趣——所有这些都有助于社会的充实。

总而言之，历史告诉我们，人类的基本本性并没有改变，这个历史教训可以帮助我们增强人与人之间的相互了解，对彼此更加宽容，同样对他人的困难和失败更富同情心。然而，历史还可以教导我们其他的东西。它可以帮助我们为自己总结正确的价值观和理想，激励我们取得更大的成就，指出我们的错误，让我们设法避免，并有助于我们欣赏我们的文化遗产。

论点 **有保留的反对**　作者用的是最常规的方法，让步赞成，再倾向于反对。

开头方式 **表明立场＋概述理由**　开头的最后部分把作者驳论的两个方面提前暴露出来，这对于一篇论证比较复杂的文章来说无疑是很明智的。

论证过程 结论型

论证模式

① I agree with the statement insofar as through...

② However beneficial it might be to appreciate...it is equally beneficial to understand and appreciate significant differences between peoples of different time periods...

③ Another problem with the statement is that it undervalues other, equally important benefits of studying history.

Issue 1   Do we learn the most from people whose **views we share**?

"**We learn more from people whose views we share in common than from those whose ideas contradict ours.**"

比起那些和我们意见相左的人，我们能从志同道合者那里学到更多的东西。

Do we learn more from people whose views we share in common than from those whose ideas contradict ours? **The speaker claims so**, for the reason that disagreement can cause stress and inhabit learning. **I concede that** undue discord can impede learning. **Otherwise, in my view** we learn far from discourse and debate with those whose ideas we oppose than from people whose ideas are in accord with our own.

Admittedly, under some circumstances disagreement with others can be counterproductive to learning. For supporting examples, one need look no further than a television set. On today's typical television or radio talk show, disagreement usually manifests itself in meaningless rhetorical bouts and shouting matches, during which opponents vie to have their own message heard, but have little interest either in finding any common ground with or in acknowledging the merits of the opponent's viewpoint. **Understandably,** neither the combatants nor the viewers learn anything meaningful. **In fact,** these battles only serve to reinforce the predispositions and biases of all concerned. The end result is that learning is impeded.

Disagreement can also inhibit learning when two opponents disagree on fundamental assumptions needed for meaningful discourse and debate. For example, a student of paleontology learns little about the evolution of an animal species under current study by debating with an individual whose religious belief system precludes the possibility of evolution to begin with. And, economics and finance students learn little about the dynamics of a laissez-faire system by debating with a socialist whose view is that a centralized power should control all economic activity.

Aside from the foregoing two provisos, however, I fundamentally disagree with the speaker's claim. Assuming common ground between two rational and reasonable opponents willing to debate on intellectual merits, both opponents stand to gain much from that debate. Indeed it is primarily through such debate that human knowledge advances, whether at the personal, community, or global level.

At the personal level, by listening to their parents' rationale for their seemingly oppressive rules and policies, teenagers can learn how certain behaviors naturally carry certain undesirable consequences. At the same time, by listening to their teenagers concerns about autonomy and about peer pressures parents can learn the valuable lesson that effective parenting and control are two different things. **At the community level,** through dispassionate dialogue an environmental activist can come to understand the legitimate economic concerns of those whose jobs depend on the continued profitable operation of a factory. Conversely, the latter might stand to learn much about the potential public-health price to be paid by ensuring job growth and a low unemployment rate. Finally, **at the global level**, two nations with opposing political or economic interests can reach mutually beneficial agreements by striving to understand the other's legitimate concerns for its national security, its political sovereignty, the stability of its economy and currency, and so forth.

　　In sum, unless two opponents in a debate are each willing to play on the same field and by the same rules, I concede that disagreement can impede learning. **Otherwise**, reasoned discourse and debate between people with opposing viewpoints is the very foundation upon which human knowledge advances. **Accordingly**, on balance the speaker is fundamentally correct.

我们从那些和我们意见一致的人那儿学到的东西最多吗？

　　比起那些和我们意见相左的人，我们能从志同道合者那里学到更多的东西吗？发言人是这样认为的，理由是分歧会形成压力并阻碍学习。我承认不恰当的争议会妨碍学习。除此之外，在我看来，我们从与那些不同意见者的言谈辩论中，比从和我们观点一致者那里可以学到更多的东西。

　　必须承认，在一些场合下，同别人争论是会降低学习效率的。例如，人们只需看一下电视就能找到有力的证据。在今天的电视或收音机里典型的脱口秀节目中，意见分歧常常表现为毫无意义的唇枪舌剑和吵架比赛，其中的各方都抢着宣传各自的观点，而对发现共识和承认对方观点的有理之处都不感兴趣。（从而）可以理解的是，无论是辩手还是观众都学不到任何有价值的东西。事实上，这些（口水）仗只能用于强化所有相关人员的偏见和癖好，其最终的结果是学习受到了抑制。

　　有意义的言谈辩论需要一些基本的假设，当双方在这些基本假定上存在争议时，意见不同也会阻碍认知。例如，一个古生物学学生和一个宗教信仰体系中首先就排除进化可能的人辩论，那么从中他对目前正在研究的某个动物物种进化状况几乎学习不到什么；或是经济学和金融学的学生，同一个主张中央集权控制所有经济行为的社会学家辩论，那么他们几乎学不到关于放任经济驱动系统论。

　　然而，除了上述两种情况，我基本上不赞同发言人的观点。如果愿意论辩的、有理性讲道理的双方，都是为了学术成果，那么他们都会从辩论中获益匪浅。事实上，人类知识主要就是通过这样的论辩而前进的，不论是在个人、社会或是全球的层面上。

　　在个人层面上，十来岁的孩子们可以通过听从其父母表面上强制性规定和方法，学到特定行为自然会产生某种不好的结果。同时，通过听取孩子们有关独立和同伴压力的忧虑，家长们可以学到宝贵的一课：有效的教子方式与控制是决然不同的两码事。在社会的层面上，一个环保积极分子在经过一番冷静对话之后，会逐渐理解那些靠工厂不断的营利经营为生者的合理经济考虑。反过来，后者可能会更多地了解到，确保工作增加和低失业率有可能会是以公共健康为代价。最后，在全球的层面上，两个有着相互冲突政治或经济利益的国家，通过努力了解对方的国家安全、政治主权、经济和货币的稳定等合理的诉求，是可以达成互利的协议的。

　　综上所述，我认为争议会妨碍学习，除非辩论双方都乐于在同一范围内遵守相同的游戏规则。要不然，合理的讨论和持不同观点的双方之间的辩论，正是人类知识进步的基础。因此，总的来看他说的是基本正确的。

|论点| **平衡观点**　赞成和反对在文中平分秋色，论点在开头和结尾中前后呼应，总之就是"具体

情况具体分析"。

开头方式 提出问题＋回答＋表明立场　问句是一种很"投机"的开头方式，一方面省去了挖空心思琢磨开头的时间，另一方面，在切题的同时，又不会让考官觉得你懒惰到照抄题目的地步。

论证过程 比较型　论证部分的四个自然段分成两个层次，前两段认同题目观点，每一段都是一种令题目观点成立的情况并举出具体例子。后两段驳斥题目观点，前一段承上启下引出反对题目的观点：分歧有助于交流和学习；后一段接着上一段展开，分别举出这三个层面中的例子。

论证模式

① Admittedly, under some circumstances disagreement with others can be counterproductive to learning.

② Disagreement can also inhibit learning when two opponents disagree on fundamental assumptions needed for meaningful discourse and debate.

③ Aside from the foregoing two provisos, however, I fundamentally disagree with the speaker's claim.

③ At the personal level,... At the community level,...at the global level...

Issue 17　Our duty to disobey unjust laws

"**There are two types of laws: just and unjust. Every individual in a society has a responsibility to obey just laws and, even more importantly, to disobey and resist unjust laws.**"

有两种法律：公正的和不公正的。每个社会成员都有责任遵守公正的法律，但是更重要的是，更应该不遵守和反抗不公正的法律。

According to this statement, each person has a duty to not only obey just laws but also disobey unjust ones. **In my view this statement is too extreme**, in two respects. **First**, it wrongly categorizes any law as either just or unjust; **and secondly**, it recommends an ineffective and potentially harmful means of legal reform.

First, whether a law is just or unjust is rarely a straightforward issue. The fairness of any law depends on one's personal value system. This is especially true when it comes to personal freedoms. Consider, for example, the controversial issue of abortion. Individuals with particular religious beliefs tend to view laws allowing mothers an abortion choice as unjust, while individuals with other value systems might view such laws as just.

The fairness of a law also depends on one's personal interest, or stake, in the legal issue at hand. After all, in a democratic society the chief function of laws is to strike a balance among competing interests. Consider, for example, a law that regulates the toxic effluents a certain factory can emit into a nearby river. Such laws are designed chiefly to protect public health. But complying with the regulation might be costly for the company; the factory might be forced to lay off employees or shut down altogether, or increase the price of its products to compensate for the cost of compliance. At stake are the respective interests of the company's owners, employees, and customers, as well as the opposing interests of the region's residents whose health and safety are impacted. **In short**, the fairness of the law is subjective, depending largely on how one's personal interests are affected by it.

The second fundamental problem with the statement is that disobeying unjust laws often has the opposite affect of what was intended or hoped for. Most anyone would argue, for instance, that our federal system of income taxation is unfair in one respect or another. Yet the end result of widespread disobedience, in this case tax evasion, is to perpetuate the system. Free-riders only compel the government to maintain tax rates at high levels in order to ensure adequate revenue for the various programs in its budget.

Yet another fundamental problem with the statement is that by justifying a violation of one sort of law we find ourselves on a slippery slope toward sanctioning all types of illegal behavior, including egregious criminal conduct. Returning to the abortion example mentioned above, a person strongly opposed to the freedom-of-choice position might maintain that the illegal blocking of access to an abortion clinic amounts to justifiable disobedience. **However**, it is a precariously short leap from this sort of civil disobedience to physical confrontations with clinic workers, then to the infliction of property damage, then to the bombing of the clinic and potential murder.

In sum, because the inherent function of our laws is to balance competing interests, reasonable people with different priorities will always disagree about the fairness of specific laws. Accordingly, radical action such as resistance or disobedience is rarely justified merely by one's subjective viewpoint or personal interests. And in any event, disobedience is never justifiable when the legal rights or safety of innocent people are jeopardized as a result.

反对不公正的法律是我们的责任

按照这一观点，每一个人都既有遵守合理法律的义务，又有反对不公正法律的责任。我认为，这就太绝对了，分两方面来说。一、法律不能以要么公正要么不公正来划分；二、这个观点推荐的是一种低效并具有潜在危害的法律改革方式。

首先，一部法律是否公正很少一眼就可以看出的。任何法律的合理性都取决于个人的价值体系。有关个人自由的问题尤为如此。例如，就人工流产这一有争议的问题，特定宗教信仰的个人倾向于把允许母亲堕胎看成是不合理，而其他价值体系的人又可能认为这种法律是合理的。

一部法律的公正合理与否还取决于人们的个人利益或在眼前的司法问题中的利害关系。毕竟，在一个民主社会中，法律的主要功用就是协调相互竞争利益之间的平衡。举例言之，一部关于某一工厂向附近河流排放污水的管制法，主要是为保护公共健康而订立的。但遵守管制对公司来说就可能意味着巨大的损失，工厂可能会被迫减员或整个停产，或者增加产品价格来弥补守法的损失。事关公司老板、雇员及顾客各方的利益，以及健康和安全受到冲击的地区居民的相对的利益。简言之，法律公正性是主观的，主要取决于个人的利益受影响的程度。

该观点的第二个基本问题在于反对不公正法律经常会产生事与愿违的作用。例如，大多数人会认为联邦个人所得税系统在这个方面或那个方面是不合理的。但广泛违法——在这个例子里就是逃税——的结果却是使这一系统永存。目无法纪者只能迫使政府保持高税率来确保各种预算计划的充足资金来源。

然而该观点还有一个基本问题，就是通过使违背某类法律的合理化会使我们滑向支持所有违法行为，包括惊人的犯罪行为的深渊。回到上面谈及的堕胎问题，一个持强烈反对自由选择立场的人可能主张非法地封锁堕胎渠道是合理的违背。但是，从这种民事违背，到对医护人员身体侵害，到财产蒙受损失，再到诊所爆炸和可能的谋杀，这之间仅仅是危险的一步之遥。

总而言之，正因为我们法律的内在功用在于平衡彼此竞争的利益，有着不同优先考虑的理性的人总会质疑特定法律的合理性。因此，像反抗或违背等激进行为很少会仅仅由人的主观看法来变得合理。在任何情况下，当无辜者的合法权利或安全最终受到侵害时，违背就永远不会是合理的。

论点 完全反对　作者从两个层次驳斥题目的观点：一、法律不能以公正不公正来划分；二、题目所推崇的是一种低效并具有潜在危害的法律改革方式。这种写法非常类似于 Argument 的找错误，尤其是第一个层次，完全在被题目牵着鼻子走。ETS 曾经明确表示过，如果考生把 Issue 写成了 Argument 题目，也就是挑题目的逻辑错误的话，那么就属于不符合考试要求，毕竟它们考查的方向是不一样的。而第二个层次，又提到了题目中从未提过的"法律改革"，可以说是论证得比较牵强。你可以试试用安全的方法进行正反论证。

开头方式 表明立场 + 概述理由

论证模式

① First, whether a law is just or unjust is rarely a straightforward issue.

② The fairness of a law also depends on one's personal interest...

③ The second fundamental problem with the statement is that...

④ Yet another fundamental problem with the statement is that...

Issue 46　Preparing **young people for leadership**

"**While some leaders in government, sports, industry, and other areas attribute their success to a well-developed sense of competition, a society can better prepare its young people for leadership by instilling in them a sense of cooperation.**"

政界、体育界、工业界和其他领域中的一些领导者将他们的成功归因于一种高度的竞争意识，而一个社会通过向年轻人灌输一种合作的意识却可以更好地为他们成为领导做准备。

Which is a better way to prepare young people for leadership: developing in them a spirit of competitiveness or one of cooperation? **The speaker favors the latter approach**, even though some leaders attribute their success to their keenly developed competitive spirit. **I tend to agree with the speaker, for reasons having to do with** our increasingly global society, and with the true keys to effective leadership.

The chief reason why we should stress cooperation in nurturing young people today is that, as tomorrow's leaders, they will face pressing societal problems that simply cannot be solved apart from cooperative international efforts. For example, all nations will need to cooperate in an effort to disarm themselves of weapons of mass destruction; to reduce harmful emissions that destroy ozone and warm the Earth to dangerous levels; to reduce consumption of the Earth's finite natural resources; and to cure and prevent diseases before they become global epidemics. Otherwise, we all risk self-destruction. In short, global peace, economic stability, and survival of the species provide powerful reasons for developing educational paradigms that stress cooperation over competition.

A second compelling reason for instilling in young people a sense of cooperation over competition is that effective leadership depends less on the latter than the former. A leader should show that he or she values the input of subordinates—for example, by involving them in decisions about matters in which they have a direct stake. Otherwise, subordinates might grow to resent their leader and become unwilling to devote themselves wholeheartedly to the leader's mission. In extreme cases they might even sabotage that mission, or even take their useful ideas to competitors. And after all, without other people worth leading a person cannot be a leader—let alone an effective one.

A third reason why instilling a sense of cooperation is to be preferred over instilling a sense of competition is that the latter serves to narrow a leader's focus on thwarting the efforts of competitors. With such tunnel vision it is difficult to develop other, more creative means of attaining organizational objectives. Moreover, such means often involve synergistic solutions that call for alliances, partnerships, and other cooperative efforts with would-be competitors.

Those who would oppose the speaker might point out that a thriving economy depends on a freely competitive business environment, which ensures that consumers obtain high-quality goods and services at low prices. Thus, key leadership positions, especially in business, inherently call for a certain tenacity and competitive spirit. And, a competitive spirit seems especially critical in today's hyper-competitive technology-driven economy, where any leader failing to keep pace with ever-changing business and technological paradigms soon falls by the wayside. However, a leader's effectiveness as a competitor is not necessarily inconsistent with his or her ability to cooperate with subordinates or with competitors, as noted above.

In sum, if we were to take the speaker's advice too far we would risk becoming a world without leaders, who are bred of a competitive spirit. We would also risk the key benefits of a free-market economy. Nevertheless, on balance I agree that it is more important to instill in young people a sense of cooperation than one of competition. The speaker's preference properly reflects the growing role of cooperative alliances and efforts in solving the world's most pressing problems. After all, in a world in which our very survival as a species depends on cooperation, the spirit of even healthy competition, no matter how healthy, is of little value to any of us.

培养年轻人的领导才能

怎样才能更好地培养年轻人的领导才能：发展他们的竞争精神抑或合作精神？演讲者倾向于后者，即使一些领袖们将他们的成就归功于敏锐的竞争精神。我同意他，理由与我们日益全球化的社会和有效领导的真正关键因素有关。

今天我们培育青年人之所以要强调合作是因为，作为明天的领袖，他们将面临紧迫的社会问题。这些问题如果缺少国际合作的努力是不能得到解决的。比如，所有的国家都需要共同合作去消除他们的大规模杀伤性武器；减少破坏臭氧层的气体排放以防止地球气温上升到危险的程度；减少消耗地球的有限自然资源；以及治疗和预防某些疾病使其不至于成为全球流行病。否则，我们要冒自我毁灭之险。简言之，全球和平、经济稳定、物种生存等为发展强调合作多过竞争的教育范例提供了强有力的理由。

另一个为青年灌输合作多过竞争意识的理由在于，有效的领导力依赖后者少于依赖前者。一个领导人应该表现出重视下属的参与——比如，令他们加入到与之直接相关的事务决策中来。否则，下属可能会逐渐对上级产生厌恶感，变得不愿意对领导人的目标全心投入。极端的例子可能是破坏那个目标，或把他们有用的想法提供给竞争者。毕竟，没有可领导的人是不能被称为领导的——更别提有效的领导了。

第三个强调合作胜于竞争的理由是，后者会窄化领导挫败竞争对手种种努力的关注。以这种短浅的目光很难开发出更有创造力实现组织目标的手段。而且，这些手段总牵涉到需要与潜在的竞争者联盟、参与或其他合作的努力的协同解决方案。

那些反对演讲者的人可能会指出，一个繁荣的经济体依赖于自由竞争的商业环境，那将确保消费者以低廉的价格获得高质的商品和服务。因此，重要的领导位置，尤其在商业中，天然地就需要某种特定的坚韧和竞争精神。还有，竞争的精神在今天高度竞争的技术驱动型社会，显得格外重要。在这样的社会中任何跟不上朝夕瞬变的商业与技术范式的领袖很快都会跌倒在路边。但是，作为竞争者领袖的效率与以上所述他或她和下属或竞争者合作的能力并不是矛盾的。

　　总而言之，如果把演讲者的看法理解得过于绝对，我们可能会令这个世界不再有领袖——那是些有着竞争精神的人。我们也将失去自由市场经济的一些关键好处。但不论如何，总体上我同意给青年灌输多于竞争意识的合作意识。演讲者的偏好恰当地反映了合作的联盟和努力在解决世界最为紧迫问题中日益重要的作用。毕竟，在这个世界上，作为一个物种我们的生存依赖于合作。健康的竞争精神，不论它有多健康，对我们来说都价值甚少。

论点 有保留的赞成

开头方式 提出问题 + 回答 + 表明立场

论证过程 比较型

论证模式

① The chief reason why we should stress cooperation in nurturing young people today is that...

② A second compelling reason for instilling in young people a sense of cooperation over competition is that...

③ A third reason why instilling a sense of cooperation is to be preferred over instilling a sense of competition is that...

④ Those who would oppose the speaker might point out that...

Issue 144　The value of art vs. that of **art critic**

"It is the artist, not the critic, ＊ who gives society something of lasting value."

＊ a person who evaluates works of art, such as novels, films, music, paintings, etc.

是艺术家而不是评论家带给了社会一些具有持久价值的东西。

＊评论家指的是评价例如小说、电影、绘画等这些艺术作品的人。

This statement asserts that art, not the art critic, provides something of lasting value to society. **I strongly agree with the statement.** Although the critic can help us understand and appreciate art, more often than not, critique is either counterproductive to achieving the objective of art or altogether irrelevant to that objective.

To support the statement the speaker might point out the three ostensible functions of the art critic. First, critics can help us understand and interpret art; a critic who is familiar with a particular artist and his or her works might have certain insights about those works that the layperson would not. **Secondly**, a critic's evaluation of an art work serves as a filter, which helps us determine which art is worth our time and attention. For example, a new novel by a best-selling author might nevertheless be an uninspired effort, and if the critic can call our attention to this fact we gain time to seek out more worthwhile literature to read. **Thirdly**, a critic can provide feedback for artists; and constructive criticism, if taken to heart, can result in better work.

However, reflecting on these three functions makes clear that the art critic actually offers very little to society. The first function is better accomplished by docents and teachers, who are more able to enhance a layperson's appreciation and understanding of art by providing an objective, educated interpretation of it. **Besides**, true appreciation of art occurs at the moment we encounter art; it is the emotional, even visceral impact that art has on our senses, spirits, and souls that is the real value of art. A critic can actually provide a disservice by distracting us from that experience.

The critic's second function—that of evaluator who filters out bad art from the worthwhile—**is one that we must be very wary of.** History supports this caution. In the role of judge, critics have failed us repeatedly. Consider, for example, Voltaire's rejection of Shakespeare as barbaric because he did not conform to neo-classical principles of unity. Or, consider the complete dismissal of Beethoven's music by the esteemed critics of his time. The art critic's judgment is limited by the narrow confines of old and established parameters for evaluation. Moreover, critical judgment is often misguided by the ego; thus, its value is questionable in any event.

I turn finally to the critic's third function: to provide useful feedback to artists. The value of this function is especially suspect. Any artist, or anyone who has studied art, would agree that true art is the product of the artist's authentic passion, a manifestation of the artist's unique creative impulse, and a creation of the artist's spirit. If art were shaped by the concern for integrating feedback from all criticism, it would become a viable craft, but at the same time would cease to be art.

In sum, none of the ostensible functions of the critic are of much value at all, let alone of lasting value, to society. **On the other hand**, the artist, through works of art, provides an invaluable and unique mirror of the culture of the time during which the work was produced—a mirror for the artist's contemporaries and for future generations to gaze into for insight and appreciation of history. The art critic in a subordinate role, more often than not, does a disservice to society by obscuring this mirror.

艺术的价值 vs. 艺术批评的价值

对于艺术而非艺术批评为社会提供了持续的价值这一论断，我非常同意。虽然批评能帮助我们理解和欣赏艺术，但通常批评对于艺术的目标起反作用或者与那个目标毫不相关。

为了支持这样的论断，演讲者可能举出了三个艺术批评的表面功能。首先，批评能帮助我们理解和解释艺术；一个熟悉某位艺术家及他或她作品的批评者或许对于这些作品有着某种门外汉没有的洞察力。其次，批评家对一件艺术作品的评价就类似一个筛子，帮助我们决定哪种艺术值得我们的时间和注意。比如，一个畅销书作者的新小说或许是没有创见的作品，如果批评家能提请我们的注意，那么我们就能把时间花在阅读更有意义的文学作品上。再次，批评可以为艺术家们提供反馈，建设性的批评如果被真心采纳，就会产生更好的作品。

然而，反思这三个功能却使人明白，艺术批评实际上对社会贡献甚少。第一个功能代课教师和教师们完成得更好，通过提供一个对艺术客观的有水平的解释，他们更有能力提高门外汉对该艺术的欣赏和理解水平。另外，真正理解艺术的时刻发生在我们与它接触的那一刹，艺术对我们的感官、精神、灵魂的感性的甚至是本能的冲击，才是艺术的真正价值。艺术批评会使我们从那种体验上分心，事实上在起反作用。

批评的第二个功能——把坏艺术视为无价值而加以滤去的评价者的功能——是我们必须非常谨慎的功能。历史支持着这种谨慎。艺术批评的判断作用不断地使我们失望。比如，伏尔泰拒斥莎士比亚为野蛮，因为后者没有遵从新古典的一体性原则。再考虑贝多芬的音乐在他那个时代被自负的评论所完全排斥的事实吧。艺术批评的判断为既有的、老旧的评价标准所限。更有甚者，批评时常为自负所误导。因此在任何情况中，它的价值都值得怀疑。

我最后谈谈批评的第三个功能：为艺术家提供有益的反馈。这一功能的价值尤其值得质疑。任何艺术家或者艺术学习者都会同意这样的一个观点，真正的艺术是艺术家真实激情的产品，是他独有创造冲动的体现，也是他精神的凝结。如果艺术被要整合所有批评者的反馈这种顾虑所塑造的话，那它只会是件合格的工艺品，同时不再是艺术了。

　　总而言之，对于社会，那些表面的功能没有一个拥有足够的，更别说是持续的价值了。另一方面，艺术家通过艺术品，提供了一面无价和独特的镜子，其中折射出作品产生时代的文化——以便艺术家的同代和后代从这面镜子中获得对历史的洞察和欣赏。艺术批评是个从属的角色，经常通过模糊那面镜子而危害社会。

论点 有保留的赞成　作者虽然在开头"强烈"地同意，但是他在论述过程中还是很小心地用了正反论证，即使他的倾向性非常"明显"。

开头方式 陈述题目观点 + 表明立场

论证过程 结论型

论证模式

① To support the statement the speaker might point out the three ostensible functions of the art critic.

② However, reflecting on these three functions makes clear that the art critic actually offers very little to society.

③ The critic's second function—is one that we must be very wary of.

④ I turn finally to the critic's third function:...

Issue 201　Should educators provide students with **a set of ideas** or with job preparation?

"The purpose of education should be to provide students with a value system, a standard, a set of ideas—not to prepare them for a specific job."

教育的目的应该是给予学生一个价值体系，一个标准，一整套理念——而不是为一个具体工作培养他们。

Should educators teach values or focus instead on preparing students for jobs? **In my view the two are not mutually exclusive.** It is by helping students develop their own principles for living, as well as by instilling in them certain fundamental values, that educators best prepare young people for the world of work.

One reason for my viewpoint is that rote learning of facts, figures, and technical skills does not help us determine which goals are worthwhile and whether the means of attaining those goals are ethically or morally acceptable. In other words, strong values and ethical standards are needed to determine how we can best put our rote knowledge to use in the working world. Thus, by helping students develop a thoughtful, principled value system educators actually help prepare students for jobs.

Another reason for my viewpoint lies in the fact that technology-driven industries account for an ever-increasing portion of our jobs. As advances in technology continue to accelerate, specific knowledge and skills needed for jobs will change more and more quickly. Thus it would be a waste of our education system to focus on specific knowledge and job skills that might soon become obsolete—at the expense of teaching values. It seems more appropriate today for employers to provide the training our workforce needs to perform their jobs, freeing up our educators to help students develop guiding principles for their careers.

Besides helping students develop their own thoughtful value systems, **educators should instill in students certain basic values** upon which any democratic society depends; otherwise, our freedom to choose our own jobs and careers might not survive in the long term. These values include principles of fairness and equity upon which our system of laws is based, as well as the values of tolerance and respect when it comes to the viewpoints of others. It seems to me that these basic values can best by instilled at an early age in a classroom setting, where young students can work out their value systems as they interact with their peers. Moreover, as students grow into working adults, practicing the basic values of fairness and respect they learned as students serves them well in their jobs. At the workplace these values manifest themselves in a worker's ability to cooperate, compromise, understand various viewpoints, and appreciate the rights and duties of coworkers, supervisors, and subordinates. This ability cannot help but serve any worker's career goals, as well as enhancing overall workplace productivity.

Admittedly, values and behavioral standards specific to certain religions are best left to parents and churches. After all, by advocating the values and teachings of any particular religion public educators undermine our basic freedom of religion. However, by exposing students to various religious beliefs, educators promote the values of respect and tolerance when it comes to the viewpoints of others. Besides, in my observation certain fundamental values—such as compassion, virtue, and humility—are common to all major religions. By appreciating certain fundamental values that we should all hold in common, students are more likely to grow into adults who can work together at the workplace toward mutually agreed-upon goals.

In sum, only when educators help students develop their own principles for living, and when they instill certain fundamental values, do young people grow into successful working adults. Although there will always be a need to train people for specific jobs, in our technological society where knowledge advances so rapidly, employers and job training programs are better equipped to provide this function—leaving formal educators to equip students with a moral compass and ballast to prevent them from being tossed about aimlessly in a turbulent vocational sea.

教育者该为学生提供一套理念还是职业准备?

教育者们是该教给学生价值观还是关注怎样为职业做准备? 在我看来, 这二者并不互相排斥。正是通过帮助学生发展他们自己的生活原则并灌输一定的基本价值观, 教育者们才能为年轻人在今后的工作世界做最佳准备。

我的这个观点的一个理由是, 熟知事实、数据与技巧并不能帮我们决定什么样的目标是值得的, 以及这些目标的手段是否为伦理道德所接受。换句话说, 我们需要强烈的价值观和伦理标准去决定如何最好地将所熟知的知识应用于这个世界。因此, 通过帮助学生发展出一套周详的、有原则的价值系统, 教育者们实际上是帮助他们为职业做准备。

另外一个理由在于这样的事实, 技术驱动的产业占据着越来越多的就业份额。因为技术发展的脚步正持续加快, 职业所需求的具体知识和技能将越来越快地发生改变。因此, 如果教育系统以牺牲教育价值观为代价, 将重点集中在提供或许很快就会过时的专业知识和技能, 就会是一种浪费。今天, 对雇主们而言为雇员提供我们的劳力所需要的技能培训, 而使教育者们得以解脱去帮助学生们发展他们职业的指导性原则似乎更为合适。

除了帮助学生发展自己的周详的价值系统外，教育者们还应向他们灌输某些任何民主社会赖以依存的基本价值观。否则，我们选择工作和职业的自由长远来看不会存在下去。这些价值观包括我们的法律系统作为基础的公平和平等，还有对他人观点的宽容和尊重。在我看来这些基本的价值在教室里可以最好地被灌输给年纪尚小的人，在那里年少的学生们可以在与同龄人的交往中实践这些价值。而且，随着学生们长大成为从业的成人，实践学生时期所学会的公平和尊重他人的基本价值在工作中将对他们大有裨益。在工作场所，这些价值表现为工人的合作、妥协、理解不同的观点的能力和欣赏同事、上级以及下级的权利和义务的能力。这种能力不仅有助于实现工作者本人的职业目标，也能提高经营体的整体生产率。

诚然，涉及某一宗教的具体价值观和行为标准最好留给父母或者教堂来教育。毕竟，公共的教育者们通过提倡任何一种特定宗教的价值观和教义将有损于我们基本的宗教自由原则。然而，通过将不同的宗教信仰展示给学生，教育者们实际上帮助提升了他们尊重和宽容不同观点的能力。另外，经我观察，一些基本的价值观——如悲悯、美德和谦虚——是所有主要宗教共有的。通过了解这些我们应该共有的基本价值观，学生们更可能成长为能够为取得共识的目标而一起工作的成年人。

总而言之，只有当教育者帮助学生发展自己的生活原则，并提供给他们一些基本价值观的时候，年轻人才能成长为成功的工作者。虽然，总有一种教给人们适应具体工作的技能的需要，但在我们这样一个技术日新月异的社会，雇主和职业训练教程能更好地提供这一功能。正统的教育者应为学生提供一种道德指南针和压舱物，以防止他们在汹涌的职业之海中迷失方向。

|论点| **平衡观点**　比较特殊的一篇文章，没有一半赞成一半反对，而是两者结合起来共同发挥作用，这很像是问题解决型的论点（各种方法结合起来才是最合理、最完整的解决办法）。

|开头方式| **提出问题＋表明立场**

|论证过程| **比较型**　本文没有特别成套路的论证过程，只是在按部就班地说明理由，每一段中都融合两个方面：原则和技能。

|论证模式|

① One reason for my viewpoint is that...

② Another reason for my viewpoint lies in the fact that...

③ Besides...educators should instill in students certain basic values...

④ Admittedly, values and behavioral standards specific to certain religions are best left to parents and churches.

Issue 228　Praising **positive** actions and ignoring negative ones

"**The best way to teach—whether as an educator, employer, or parent—is to praise positive actions and ignore negative ones.**"

无论是作为教育者、雇主或者是父母,教育最好的方法都是赞扬良好的行为而无视不良行为。

The speaker suggests that the most effective way to teach others is to praise positive actions while ignoring negative ones. In my view, this statement is too extreme. **It overlooks circumstances** under which praise might be inappropriate, as well as ignoring the beneficial value of constructive criticism, and sometimes even punishment.

The recommendation that parents, teachers, and employers praise positive actions is generally good advice. For young children positive reinforcement is critical in the development of healthy self-esteem and self-confidence. For students appropriate positive feedback serves as a motivating force, which spurs them on to greater academic achievement. For employees, appropriately administered praise enhances productivity and employee loyalty, and makes for a more congenial and pleasant work environment overall.

While recommending praise for positive actions is fundamentally sound advice, this advice should carry with it certain caveats. First, some employees and older students might find excessive praise to be patronizing or paternalistic. **Secondly,** some individuals need and respond more appropriately to praise than others; those administering the praise should be sensitive to the individual's need for positive reinforcement in the first place. **Thirdly,** praise should be administered fairly and evenhandedly. By issuing more praise to one student than to others, a teacher might cause one recipient to be labeled by classmates as teacher's pet, even if the praise is well deserved or badly needed. If the result is to alienate other students, then the praise might not be justified. Similarly, at the workplace a supervisor must be careful to issue praise fairly and evenhandedly, or risk accusations of undue favoritism, or even discrimination.

As for ignoring negative actions, I agree that minor peccadilloes can, and in many cases should, be overlooked. Mistakes and other negative actions are often part of the natural learning process. Young children are naturally curious, and parents should not scold their children for every broken plate or precocious act. Otherwise, children do not develop a healthy sense of wonder and curiosity, and will not learn what they must in order to make their own way in the world. Teachers should avoid rebuking or punishing students for faulty reasoning, incorrect responses to questions, and so forth. Otherwise, students might stop trying to learn altogether. And employees who know they are being monitored closely for any sign of errant behavior are likely to be less productive, more resentful of their supervisors, and less loyal to their employers.

At the same time, some measure of constructive criticism and critique, and sometimes even punishment, is appropriate. Parents must not turn a blind eye to their child's behavior if it jeopardizes the child's physical safety or the safety of others. Teachers should not ignore behavior that unduly disrupts the learning process; and of course teachers should correct and critique students' class work, homework and tests as needed to help the students learn from their mistakes and avoid repeating them. Finally, employers must not permit employee behavior that amounts to harassment or that otherwise undermines the overall productivity at the workplace. Acquiescence in these sorts of behaviors only serves to sanction them.

To sum up, the speaker's dual recommendation is too extreme. Both praise and criticism serve useful purposes in promoting a child's development, a student's education, and an employee's loyalty and productivity. Yet both must be appropriately and evenhandedly administered; otherwise, they might serve instead to defeat these purposes.

赞赏良好的而忽略不良行为

演讲者认为最有效的教育他人的办法就是对良好的行为给予赞赏而忽略不良行为。在我看来，这样的陈述过于极端。它忽略了赞赏有时可能并不恰当的情况，也忽视了富有建设性的批评，甚至惩戒的有益的价值。

推荐父母、老师、雇主们对于积极行为给予表扬在总体上说来是一个不错的建议。对孩子们来说，正面的强化对于他们自尊和自信的养成是至关重要的。对于学生们而言，恰当的积极反馈是一种激励的动力，将刺激他们在学术上取得更大成就。对雇员们而言，恰当地施予的赞赏将提高生产率和员工的忠实度，并有助于产生一个总体上更统一、更宜人的工作环境。

赞赏良好行为的建议基本上很好，但是这个建议也存在一些需要警戒的地方。首先，一些员工和年纪较大的学生或许认为过多的赞赏是屈尊俯就的和家长式作风的做法。其次，一些个人比他人需要和回应更恰如其分的赞扬，因此赞扬的施与者们必须首先对个人对积极强化的需求要敏锐。再次，赞扬应当被公正平等地给与。如果对一个学生给予比他人更多的褒扬，即使是应得的和急需的，也可能导致这位被表扬学生被同学贴上"老师宠物"的标签。如果结局是疏离其他的学生，那么这种赞赏可能就是不合理的。同样，在工作场所，一个主管也必须小心地、公正平等地给予赞赏，否则将有被指责为不当地偏护甚至是歧视的风险。

至于忽略不良行为，我同意对一些小错误可以，在许多时候甚至是应该被略过的。错误和其他的不良行为常常是自然学习过程中的一部分。孩子们总是天性好奇，父母们不应当为每个破碎的碟子或者是不成熟行为责备他们。否则孩子们将不能养成健康的惊异和好奇感，也不能学到那些对他们在世界上独自立足所必要的东西。教师们应当避免因为错误地推理和不正确地回答问题等等而责备或惩罚学生。不然，学生们也许会彻底放弃学习。了解到自身受到严密监视以防止任何过失行为的员工，可能生产率会降低，对于上级产生更深的厌恶感，对雇主的忠诚度更低。

与此同时，一定程度的建设性批评甚至惩戒却是恰当的。如果孩子的行为有可能伤害到自身安全或者他人的安全，父母千万不能视而不见。教师们对不当打断教学进程的行为也不能置之不理。当然他们还要批改学生的课堂作业和课后作业及测试题，需要这种批改来帮助他们从错误中学习并避免再犯。最后，如果员工的行为构成了骚扰或者损害了工作场所的整体生产率，雇主不应纵容，否则便是对他们自身的惩罚。

总的说来，演讲者的双重推荐过于极端。赞扬和批评对于促进孩子们的发展、学生的教育、员工的忠诚和生产率都能发挥有用的作用。但这两种手段都必须恰当、平等地实施，否则将阻碍最后目的的达到。

论点 有保留的反对

开头方式 陈述题目观点 + 表明立场

论证过程 结论型

论证模式

① The recommendation that parents, teachers, and employers praise positive actions is generally good advice.

② While recommending praise for positive actions is fundamentally sound advice, this advice should carry with it certain caveats.

③ As for ignoring negative actions, I agree that minor peccadilloes can, and in many cases should, be overlooked.

④ At the same time, some measure of constructive criticism and critique, and sometimes even punishment, is appropriate.

Issue 239　Should all so-called facts **be mistrusted**?

"**Much of the information that people assume is 'factual' actually turns out to be inaccurate. Thus, any piece of information referred to as a 'fact' should be mistrusted since it may well be proven false in the future.**"

大多数人们认为是事实的信息实际上最终都是不准确的。因此,任何一条据称是事实的信息都应该被质疑,因为它在将来很可能会被证明为是错误的。

The speaker contends that so-called "facts" often turn out to be false, and therefore that we should distrust whatever we are told is factual. **Although** the speaker overlooks certain circumstances in which undue skepticism might be counterproductive, and even harmful, **on balance I agree that** we should not passively accept whatever is passed off as fact; otherwise, human knowledge would never advance.

I turn first to so-called "scientific facts," by which I mean current prevailing notions about the nature of the physical universe that have withstood the test of rigorous scientific and logical scrutiny. The very notion of scientific progress is predicated on such scrutiny. Indeed the history of science is in large measure a history of challenges to so-called "scientific facts"—challenges which have paved the way for scientific progress. For example, in challenging the notion that the earth was in a fixed position at the center of the universe, Copernicus paved the way for the corroborating observations of Galileo a century later, and ultimately for Newton's principles of gravity upon which all modern science depends. The staggering cumulative impact of Copernicus' rejection of what he had been told was true provides strong support for the speaker's advice when it comes to scientific facts.

Another example of the value of distrusting what we are told is scientific fact involves the debate over whether human behavioral traits are a function of internal physical forces ("nature") or of learning and environment ("nurture"). Throughout human history the prevailing view has shifted many times. The ancients assumed that our behavior was governed by the whims of the gods; in medieval times it became accepted fact that human behavior is dictated by bodily humours, or fluids; this "fact" later yielded to the notion that we are primarily products of our upbringing and environment. Now researchers are discovering that many behavioral traits are largely a function of the unique neurological structure of each individual's brain. Thus only by distrusting facts about human behavior can we advance in our scientific knowledge and, in turn, learn to deal more effectively with human behavioral issues in such fields as education, juvenile delinquency, criminal reform, and mental illness.

The value of skepticism about so-called "facts" is not limited to the physical sciences. When it comes to the social sciences we should always be skeptical about what is presented to us as historical fact. Textbooks can paint distorted pictures of historical events, and of their causes and consequences. After all, history in the making is always viewed firsthand through the eyes of subjective witnesses, then recorded by fallible journalists with their own cultural biases and agendas, then interpreted by historians with limited, and often tainted, information. And when it comes to factual assumptions underlying theories in the social sciences, we should be even more distrusting and skeptical, because such assumptions inherently defy deductive proof, or disproof. Skepticism should extend to the law as well. While law students, lawyers, legislators, and jurists must learn to appreciate traditional legal doctrines and principles, at the same time they must continually question their correctness—in terms of their fairness and continuing relevance.

Admittedly, in some cases undue skepticism can be counterproductive, and even harmful. For instance, we must accept current notions about the constancy of gravity and other basic laws of physics; otherwise, we would live in continual fear that the world around us would literally come crashing down on us. Undue skepticism can also be psychologically unhealthy when distrust borders on paranoia. Finally, common sense informs me that young people should first develop a foundation of experiential knowledge before they are encouraged to think critically about what they are told is fact.

To sum up, a certain measure of distrust of so-called "facts" is the very stuff of which human knowledge and progress are fashioned, whether in the physical sciences, the social sciences, or the law. Therefore, with few exceptions I strongly agree that we should strive to look at facts through skeptical eyes.

是不是全部所谓的事实都该被怀疑?

演讲者主张所谓的"事实"经常最后被证明是错误的,因此我们应该怀疑任何被告知是事实的东西。虽然演讲者忽略了在某些情形下不正当的怀疑可能起到反作用,甚至有害,但总体上我同意我们不该被动地接受一切冒充的事实,否则人类的知识将无从进步。

我首先说说所谓的"科学事实",我指的是当下正流行的、已经经过了严格的科学和逻辑检验的有关宇宙本质的一些概念。科学进步的概念本身正是基于这些检验。的确,科学史在很大程度上是一部挑战所谓"科学事实"的历史,正是这些挑战为科学的发展扫平了道路。举个例子,通过挑战地球居于宇宙中心的一个固定位置的说法,哥白尼为伽利略一个世纪后的观察和牛顿提出全部现代科学所依据的地心引力说扫清了障碍。在科学事实方面,哥白尼拒绝接受被告知的事情是真的这个事实的惊人的、累计影响为演讲者的观点提供了有力的支持。

怀疑被告知是科学事实的价值的另一个例子,涉及关于人类性格是内在物理力量(天性)的功能还是后天学习和环境(培养)的功能的辩论。通观人类历史,主流观点几易其变。在古代,人们认为我们的行为是由神的兴致所统辖的;到了中世纪被广为接受的事实是人类的行为是由体液决定的,这样的"事实"不久又被我们主要是抚养和环境的产物的论断所取代。现在研究者发现许多行为特征在很大程度上是个体大脑的独特神经系统的一个功能。因此只有通过质疑关于人类行为的事实,我们才能推进科学知识的发展,反过来也学到了更有效地应对在诸如教育、青少年犯罪、刑罚改革以及精神疾病等领域内的人类行为问题。

怀疑所谓"事实"的价值并不局限于物理科学。当涉及社会科学,我们也应当总是对被呈现于眼前的历史事实保持怀疑。教科书会扭曲历史事实的图像及其原因和结果。毕竟,形成中的历史总是先由主观的目击者的眼睛所见,然后由难免受自身文化偏见和日程影响而犯错的记者记录下来,再由历史学家根据有限的、经常被篡改的信息加以解释。当涉及作为社会科学理论基础的事实上的假定时,我们更应该持怀疑态度,因为这样的假定就其本质而言无法进行推断性的证明或反证。怀疑主义也应被拓展到法律领域。法律系的学生、律师、立法者以及法官必须学习领会传统的法律条文和原则,同时他们也必须持续地质问它们的正确性——在它们的公正性和持续的适用性方面的正确性。

诚然,在某些情景中不适当的怀疑主义可能会起反作用,甚至是有害的。比如,我们必须接受目前的关于引力永恒和其他的物理基本法则,否则我们将会陷入对于周遭世界简直就要把我们压扁的持久恐慌中。当不信任的边界扩展到偏执的程度时,不适当的怀疑主义在心理上可能也是不健康的。最后,常识提醒我们,年轻人必须首先发展出一个经验知识根基,然后才能鼓励他们批判性地思考被告知的何为事实。

总而言之，对于所谓"事实"一定程度上的怀疑是人类知识和进步形成的题中之意，不论是物理科学、社会科学还是法律方面。因此，除了罕见的例外，我强烈认同我们必须用怀疑的眼光去看待事实。

论点 有保留的赞成

开头方式 陈述题目观点 + 表明立场

论证过程 比较型

论证模式

① I turn first to so-called "scientific facts,"...

② Another example of the value of distrusting what we are told is scientific fact involves the debate over...

③ The value of skepticism about so-called "facts" is not limited to the physical sciences.

④ Admittedly, in some cases undue skepticism can be counterproductive, and even harmful.

Issue 49　**Imaginative works** vs. factual accounts

"**Imaginative works such as novels, plays, films, fairy tales, and legends present a more accurate and meaningful picture of human experience than do factual accounts. Because the creators of fiction shape and focus reality rather than report on it literally, their creations have a more lasting significance.**"

想像作品，比如小说、戏剧、电影、童话和传奇要比真实的叙事作品更能精确而有意义地展现人类的经历。因为虚构作品的作者们塑造和关注现实而不是一板一眼地报道现实，所以他们的创作具有更加深远的意义。

Do imaginative works hold more lasting significance than factual accounts, for the reasons the speaker cites? **To some extent the speaker overstates fiction's comparative significance. On balance, however, I tend to agree with the speaker.** By recounting various dimensions of the human experience, a fictional work can add meaning to and appreciation of the times in which the work is set. Even where a fictional work amounts to pure fantasy, with no historical context, it can still hold more lasting significance than a factual account. Examples from literature and film serve to illustrate these points.

I concede that most fictional works rely on historical settings for plot, thematic, and character development. By informing us about underlying political, economic, and social conditions, factual accounts provide a frame of reference needed to understand and appreciate imaginative works. Fact is the basis for fiction, and fiction is no substitute for fact. **I would also concede that** factual accounts are more "accurate" than fictional ones—insofar as they are more objective. **But** this does not mean that factual accounts provide a "more meaningful picture of the human experience." To the contrary, only imaginative works can bring a historical period alive—by way of creative tools such as imagery and point of view. And, only imaginative works can provide meaning to historical events—through the use of devices such as symbolism and metaphor.

Several examples from literature serve to illustrate this point. Twain's novels afford us a sense of how nineteenth-century Missouri would have appeared through the eyes of 10-year old boys. Melville's "Billy Budd" gives the reader certain insights into what travel on the high seas might have been like in earlier centuries, through the eyes of a crewman. And the epic poems "Beowulf" and "Sir Gawain and the Green Knight" provide glimpses of the relationships between warriors and their kings in medieval times. Bare facts about these historical eras are easily forgettable, whereas creative stories and portrayals such as the ones mentioned above can be quite memorable indeed. In other words, what truly lasts are our impressions of what life must have been like in certain places, at certain times, and under certain conditions. Only imaginative works can provide such lasting impressions.

Examples of important films underscore the point that creative accounts of the human experience hold more lasting significance than bare factual accounts. Consider four of our most memorable and influential films: *Citizen Kane*, *Schindler's List*, *The Wizard of Oz*, *and Star Wars*. Did Welles' fictional portrayal of publisher William Randolph Hearst or Spielberg's fictional portrayal of a Jewish sympathizer during the holocaust provide a more "meaningful picture of human experience" than a history textbook? Did these accounts help give "shape and focus" to reality more so than newsreels alone could? If so, will these works hold more "lasting significance" than bare factual accounts of the same persons and events? I think anyone who has seen these films would answer all three questions affirmatively. Or consider *The Wizard of Oz and Star Wars*. Both films, and the novels from which they were adapted, are pure fantasy. Yet both teem with symbolism and metaphor relating to life's journey, the human spirit, and our hopes, dreams, and ambitions—in short, the human experience. Therein lies the reason for their lasting significance.

In sum, without prior factual accounts fictional works set in historical periods lose much of their meaning. Yet only through the exercise of artistic license can we convey human experience in all its dimensions, and thereby fully understand and appreciate life in other times and places. And it is human experience, and not bare facts and figures, that endures in our minds and souls.

想像作品 VS. 事实记述

　　想像作品是否因演讲者所持之理由要比事实记述拥有更为持久的影响力呢？在某种程度上演讲者夸大了小说的相对意义。但总体上我倾向于认同演讲者。通过重新考量各个方面的人类经验，一部虚构的作品能为作品产生的背景时代增加意义和加深对该时代的理解。即使一部虚构作品纯粹是幻想，而完全没有历史的背景，它仍然能比事实的记述拥有持久的意义。文学和电影的例子形象地说明了这些观点。

　　我承认大多数虚构作品在情节、主题和角色的发展方面有赖于历史背景。通过提醒我们基本的政治、经济和社会情况，事实的记述提供了一套理解和欣赏想像作品所必需的参考框架。事实是虚构的基础，虚构不能替代事实。我同样也承认事实的记述要比虚构更为"准确"——就其更为客观而言。但是这并不意味着事实的记述提供了一种"更为有意义的人类生活经历的图景"。相反，只有想像作品才能使一段历史时期生动——通过创造性的工具，诸如形象化的描述和视角。也只有想像作品能为历史事件提供意义——通过象征和隐喻等手段的运用。

　　许多文学作品的例子可用来证明这一观点。吐温的小说使我们通过一个 10 岁大的男孩的眼睛感知到了 19 世纪的密苏里会是什么样子。麦尔维尔的《巴特尔比》让读者通过船夫的眼睛看到了早几个世纪的远洋旅行。史诗《贝奥伍甫》和《高文爵士和绿衣骑士》使我们得以窥探中世纪骑士和他们的封君的关系。有关这些历史时代的明摆着的事实使人容易遗忘，而如上的富有创造性的故事和描写则确实令人难以忘怀。换句话说，真正持久的是我们对在某地某时和某种条件下的生活必然情形的印象。只有想像作品可以提供这样的持久印象。

许多重要电影的例子也强调了，创造性地记述人类经历历要比仅仅是事实记录拥有更持久的影响力。看看四部我们最为记忆深刻的电影吧：《公民凯恩》、《辛德勒的名单》、《绿野仙踪》、《星球大战》。是不是威尔士对威廉·鲁登道夫·希尔斯特的虚构描写和斯皮尔博格对大屠杀期间的一个犹太同情者的虚构描画比一本历史教科书提供了一幅更为"有意义的人类经历的图景"？这些记述是不是比单独的新闻报道更能赋予现实以"形态和专注"？如果是的话，这些作品是不是比赤裸的对事实和个人的记述要具有更为"持久的影响力"呢？我认为任何看过这些电影的人都能对这三个问题给出肯定的答案。或者看看《绿野仙踪》和《星球大战》，这两部电影以及它们改编所依据的小说纯属幻想。然而两者都充满了与生命旅程，人类精神，我们的希望、理想和雄心——简言之，人类历程——紧密相关的象征和隐喻。它们如此长盛不衰的原因就在于此。

总而言之，如果没有先前的事实记述，设定在历史时期的虚构作品便失去了意义。然而只有通过艺术加工我们才能从多方面传递人类经验，从而彻底理解和欣赏其他时空的生活。长存于我们的头脑与灵魂中的是人类经验，而不仅仅是事实和数据。

| 论点 | 有保留的赞成 |

| 开头方式 | 提出问题 + 表明立场 |

| 论证过程 | 比较型 |

| 论证模式 |

① I concede that most fictional works rely on historical settings for plot, thematic, and character development.

② Several examples from literature serve to illustrate this point.

③ Examples of important films underscore the point that...

Issue 99　**Pragmatic** vs. idealistic behavior

"In any realm of life—whether academic, social, business, or political—the only way to succeed is to take a practical, rather than an idealistic, point of view. Pragmatic behavior guarantees survival, whereas idealistic views tend to be superceded by simpler, more immediate options."

在任何生活领域中——无论学术、社会、商业还是政治——获得成功的惟一道路就是采取现实的而不是理想化的观点。实用的行为确保了生存，反之理想化的观点正在趋于被更简化的和更直接的选择所取代。

I agree with the speaker insofar as that a practical, pragmatic approach toward our endeavors can help us survive in the short term. **However**, idealism is just as crucial—if not more so—for long-term success in any endeavor, whether it be in academics, business, or political and social reform.

When it comes to academics, students who we would consider pragmatic tend not to pursue an education for its own sake. Instead, they tend to cut whatever corners are needed to optimize their grade average and survive the current academic term. **But**, is this approach the only way to succeed academically? Certainly not. Students who earnestly pursue intellectual paths that truly interest them are more likely to come away with a meaningful and lasting education. In fact, a sense of mission about one's area of fascination is strong motivation to participate actively in class and to study earnestly, both of which contribute to better grades in that area. Thus, although the idealist-student might sacrifice a high overall grade average, the depth of knowledge, academic discipline, and sense of purpose the student gains will serve that student well later in life.

In considering the business world it might be more tempting to agree with the speaker; after all, isn't business fundamentally about pragmatism—that is, "getting the job done" and paying attention to the "bottom line"? Emphatically, no. Admittedly, the everyday machinations of business are very much about meeting mundane short-term goals: deadlines for production, sales quotas, profit margins, and so forth. Yet underpinning these activities is the vision of the company's chief executive-a vision that might extend far beyond mere profit maximization to the ways in which the firm can make a lasting and meaningful contribution to the community, to the broader economy, and to the society as a whole. Without a dream or vision—that is, without strong idealist leadership—a firm can easily be cast about in the sea of commerce without clear direction, threatening not only the firm's bottom line but also its very survival.

Finally, when it comes to the political arena, again at first blush it might appear that pragmatism is the best, if not the only, way to succeed. Most politicians seem driven by their interest in being elected and reelected—that is, in surviving—rather than by any sense of mission, or even obligation to their constituency or country. Diplomatic and legal maneuverings and negotiations often appear intended to meet the practical needs of the parties involved—minimizing costs, preserving options, and so forth. But, it is idealists—not pragmatists—who sway the masses, incite revolutions, and make political ideology reality. Consider idealists such as America's founders, Mahatma Gandhi, or Martin Luther King. Had these idealists concerned themselves with short-term survival and immediate needs rather than with their notions of an ideal society, the United States and India might still be British colonies, and African Americans might still be relegated to the backs of buses.

In short, the statement fails to recognize that idealism—keeping one's eye on an ultimate prize—is the surest path to long-term success in any endeavor. Meeting one's immediate needs, while arguably necessary for short-term survival, accomplishes little without a sense of mission, a vision, or a dream for the long term.

务实行为 vs. 理想行为

　　在实际、务实的努力方法能使我们取得短期的成绩这点上，我同意演讲者的观点。然而，对于任何长期的成就，无论是学术的、商业还是政治与社会变革，理想主义却同样至关重要——如果不是更为重要的话。

　　涉及学术，我们视为务实的学生不会为了获得教育本身而接受教育。相反，他们会尽量投机取巧地取得最好的成绩水平，挨过眼下的学期。但这是学术成功的惟一路径吗？当然不。认真地在智力的道路上追求他们兴趣所在的学生会获得更为有意义和连贯的教育。实际上，对于某个迷人领域的一种使命感为他在课堂上主动参与和勤勉学习提供强烈的动力，而主动参与和勤勉学习都有助于在该领域中取得更好的成绩。因此，虽然理想主义学生也许会牺牲一点整体的成绩，但他们获得的知识的深度、学术的规范以及目的感在他们今后的生活中让他们获益匪浅。

　　考虑到商界，人们可能更倾向于同意演讲者。毕竟，难道做生意基本上不就是务实——"干完活儿"和注重"盈亏"吗？绝不是。诚然，日常的商业机制大多是为了实现短期的目标：生产期限、销售定额、利润空间等等。但首席执行官的设想是加强这些活动，他的设想远超过利润最大化，而推至公司为社区、为更宏观的经济乃至整个社会提供持续和有意贡献的种种方式。如果没有这样的一个设想或梦想，即没有强烈理想主义的领导——一个公司将在商海中迷失方向，威胁到的不仅仅是公司的盈亏，更危及生存。

最后，在政治领域务实主义猛一看似乎也是最好（如果不是惟一的）的成功方法。许多政客仅仅为当选与连任——生存——的利益所驱使，而不是出于对宪法和国家的任何使命感和义务。外交和法律的操作与谈判总是倾向于实现有关各方的实际需要——成本最小化、保留多种选择等等。但正是理想主义者——而非务实主义者——指挥着民众、煽动着革命，使政治的意识形态变为现实。看看理想主义者诸如美国建国者们、甘地或者马丁·路德·金吧。如果这些人仅仅考虑到短期的生存和直接的需要而不是他们心中的理想社会，那么美利坚和印度可能都仍然还是英国的殖民地呢，而非裔美国人或许还坐在公共汽车的后面。

简言之，那样的论断没有认识到理想主义——始终关注终极的奖赏——是任何一种努力长远成功的最可靠之路。实现一个人的直接需要，或许对短期生存必要，却因为使命感、视角、理想的缺失而成就甚少。

论点 有保留的反对

开头方式 表明立场 + 概述理由　作者在开头明确给出了支持自己观点的三个层次上的理由：学术方面的、商业方面的还有政治与社会变革方面的。

论证过程 比较型　作者在三个层次内部逐一进行正反论证，得出的结论当然都是统一的。

论证模式

① When it comes to academics, ...

② In considering the business world ...

③ Finally, when it comes to the political arena ...

Issue 164　**Imagination** vs. experience

"**Sometimes imagination is a more valuable asset than experience. People who lack experience are free to imagine what is possible and thus can approach a task without constraints of established habits and attitudes.**"

有时候想像力是比经验更有价值的财富。缺少经验的人得以自由地想像任何可能性,并且由此可以达成一个目标而不受既定习惯和态度的限制。

The speaker asserts that imagination is "sometimes" more valuable than experience because individuals who lack experience can more freely imagine possibilities for approaching tasks than those entrenched in established habits and attitudes. **I fundamentally agree; however**, as the speaker implies, it is important not to overstate the comparative value of imagination. Examples from the arts and the sciences aptly illustrate both the speaker's point and my caveat.

One need only observe young children as they go about their daily lives to appreciate the role that pure imagination can play as an aid to accomplishing tasks. Young children, by virtue of their lack of experience, can provide insights and valuable approaches to adult problems. Recall the movie *Big*, in which a young boy magically transformed into an adult found himself in a high-power job as a marketing executive. His inexperience in the adult world of business allowed his youthful imagination free reign to contribute creative—and successful—ideas that none of his adult colleagues, set in their ways of thinking about how businesses go about maximizing profits, ever would have considered. Admittedly, *Big* was a fictional account; yet, I think it accurately portrays the extent to which adults lack the kind of imagination that only inexperience can bring to solving many adult problems.

The speaker's contention also finds ample empirical support in certain forms of artistic accomplishment and scientific invention. History is replete with evidence that our most gifted musical composers are young, relatively inexperienced, individuals. Notables ranging from Mozart to McCartney come immediately to mind. Similarly, the wide-eyed wonder of inexperience seems to spur scientific innovation. Consider the science fiction writer Jules Verne, who through pure imagination devised highly specific methods and means for transporting humans to outer space. What makes his imaginings so remarkable is that the actual methods and means for space flight, which engineers settled on through the experience of extensive research and trial-and-error, turned out to be essentially the same ones Verne had imagined nearly a century earlier!

Of course, there are many notable exceptions to the rule that imagination unfettered by experience breeds remarkable insights and accomplishments. Duke Ellington, perhaps jazz music's most prolific composer, continued to create new compositions until late in life. Thomas Edition, who registered far more patents with the U.S. patent office than any other person, continued to invent until a very old age. Yet, these are exceptions to the general pattern. Moreover, the later accomplishments of individuals such as these tend to build on earlier ones, and therefore are not as truly inspired as the earlier ones, which sprung from imagination less fettered by life experience. 束缚 unfetter

On the other hand, it is important not to take this assertion about artistic and scientific accomplishment too far. Students of the arts, for instance, must learn theories and techniques, which they then apply to their craft—whether music performance, dance, or acting. And, creative writing requires the cognitive ability to understand how language is used and how to communicate ideas. Besides, creative ability is itself partly a function of intellect; that is, creative expression is a marriage of one's cognitive abilities and the expression of one's feelings and emotions. In literature, for example, a rich life experience from which to draw ideas is just as crucial to great achievement as imagination. For example, many critics laud Mark Twain's autobiography, which he wrote on his death bed, as his most inspired work. And, while the direction and goals of scientific research rely on the imaginations of key individuals, most scientific discoveries and inventions come about not by sudden epiphanies of youthful star-gazers but rather by years and years of trial-and-error in corporate research laboratories.

In sum, imagination can serve as an important catalyst for artistic creativity and scientific invention. **Yet,** experience can also play a key role; in fact, in literature and in science it can play just as key a role as the sort of imagination that inexperience breeds.

想像 *VS*. 经验

　　演讲者认为想像"有时"比经验更有价值，原因在于那些缺少经验的个人能比被习惯和态度所束缚的个人在完成任务时能够更自由地想像各种可能性。我基本上同意这种观点。然而，正如演讲者所暗示的，不要过分夸大想像的相对价值是很重要的。艺术和科学领域的例子能形象地证明演讲者的论点和我的提示。

　　要了解纯粹的想像帮助人们完成任务时起到的作用，那只需要看看孩子们的日常生活。孩子们由于缺少经验，在大人的问题方面往往能提供有见地和有价值的方案。想想《大》那部电影中神奇地将自己变为市场主管这样高位的那个孩子。他在大人的商业世界中的缺少经验，使想像力能产生出具有创造性的——并且是成功的——的点子。这些点子在他那些被利润最大化的思维方式所局限的大人同事看来，是绝对无法想像的。诚然，《大》是一部虚构作品，但我认为它准确地刻画出，在许多问题的解决中大人缺少那种只有无经验才能导致的想像。

演讲者同样也在某些艺术成就和科学发明中找到了足够的经验上的支持。我们许多杰出的作曲家都是年少的、相对而言缺乏经验的人，这样的例子在历史中不胜枚举。我们马上就会想到从莫扎特到麦卡尼这些名人。同样，由于没有经验而产生的令人吃惊的奇妙之事也能刺激科技的创新。想想朱尔斯·凡尔纳的科幻小说，他通过纯想像设计了许多将人类运送到外层空间的具体方式与手段。他的想像惊人之处就在于，科学家们通过广泛的经验研究和反复实验所发明的实际解决方法，与一个世纪前凡尔纳的想像基本相同！

当然，在不被经验束缚的想像能滋生出惊人的洞察和成就这点上，也有些值得注意的例外。爵士乐中可能最多产的作曲家杜克·艾林顿，即使在晚年他也能创造出新的作品。托马斯·爱迪生，他比任何人注册的专利都多，直到非常大的年纪仍然继续发明。但这是对总体的一些例外。人们后来的这些成就大多建筑在早期成就的基础上，因此不如那些不受生活经验束缚的想像富有灵感。

在另一方面，不要把关于这些艺术和科学成就的论断绝对化是很重要的。比如，学习艺术的学生必须学习理论和技艺，然后应用到他们的作品中去，不论是音乐、舞蹈或者表演。创作性的写作需要对语言是如何运用以及如何交流思想有所感知。同时，创造能力本身是智力功能的一部分，因此创造性的表达是个人感知能力与他的感觉和情感表达能力的共同产物。比如在文学方面，从中汲取思想的丰富生活经验与想像对于取得伟大成就是同等重要的。举个例子，许多评论家推崇马克·吐温的自传为他最有灵感的作品，而那是他在病床上写就的。当科学研究的方向和目标依赖于关键人物的想像的同时，许多科学发现和发明不是由年轻梦想家们的顿悟产生，而是在共同实验室中经多年的反复实验得来的。

总而言之，想像是艺术创造和科学发明的重要催化剂。但经验也能发挥重要的作用。事实上在文学和科学方面，经验和因缺少经验所滋生的想像能发挥同样重要的作用。

论点 有保留的赞成

开头方式 陈述题目观点 + 表明立场

论证过程 比较型

论证模式

① One need only observe young children as they go about their daily lives...

② Of course, there are many notable exceptions to the rule that imagination unfettered by experience breeds remarkable insights and accomplishments.

③ Of course, there are many notable exceptions to the rule that imagination unfettered by experience breeds remarkable insights and accomplishments.

④ On the other hand, it is important not to take this assertion about...too far.

Issue 210 Are people free to **choose a career**?

"**Most people choose a career on the basis of such pragmatic considerations as the needs of the economy, the relative ease of finding a job, and the salary they can expect to make. Hardly anyone is free to choose a career based on his or her natural talents or interest in a particular kind of work.**"

大多数人选择职业是基于一些实用考虑,诸如经济需求、较易谋职和称心的报酬之类。很少有人能够根据自己的天赋或者在某方面的兴趣来随心地择业。

The speaker believes that economic and other pragmatic concerns are what drive people's career decisions, and that very few people are free to choose their careers based on their talents and interests. **I tend to disagree**; although practical considerations often play a significant role in occupational trends, ultimately the driving forces behind people's career decisions are individual interest and ability.

At first glance the balance of empirical evidence would seem to lend considerable credence to the speaker's claim. The most popular fields of study for students today are the computer sciences—fields characterized by a relative glut of job opportunities. Graduates with degrees in liberal arts often abandon their chosen fields because they cannot find employment, and reenter school in search of more "practical" careers. Even people who have already achieved success in their chosen field are often forced to abandon them due to pragmatic concerns. For example, many talented and creative people from the entertainment industry find themselves looking for other, less satisfying, kinds of work when they turn 40 years of age because industry executives prefer younger artists who are "tuned in" to the younger demographic group that purchases entertainment products.

However, upon further reflection it becomes clear that **the relationship between career-seekers and the supply of careers is an interdependent one**, and therefore it is unfair to generalize about which one drives the other. Consider, for example, the two mainstream fields of computer science and law. In the computer industry it might appear that supply clearly drives job interest—and understandably so, given the highly lucrative financial rewards. But, would our legions of talented programmers, engineers, scientists, and technicians really pursue their careers without a genuine fascination, a passion, or at least an interest in those areas? I think not.

Conversely, consider the field of law, in which it would appear that **demand drives the job market, rather than vice versa**. The number of applications to law schools soared during the civil rights movement of the 1960s, and again in the 1980s during the run of the popular television series *L. A. Law*. More recently, the number of students pursuing paralegal and criminal-justice careers spiked during and immediately after the O.J. Simpson trial. Query, though, whether these aspiring lawyers and paralegals would have been sufficiently motivated had the supply of jobs and the financial rewards not already been waiting for them upon graduation.

Another compelling argument against the speaker's claim has to do with the myriad of ways in which people earn their living. Admittedly, the job market is largely clustered around certain mainstream industries and types of work. Nevertheless, if one peers beyond these mainstream occupational areas it becomes evident that many, many people do honor their true interests and talents—in spite of where most job openings lie and regardless of their financial rewards. Creative people seem to have a knack for creating their own unique vocational niche—whether it be in the visual or the performing arts; many animal lovers create work which allows them to express that love. Caregivers and nurturers manage to, find work teaching, socializing, counseling, and healing others. And people bitten by the travel bug generally have little trouble finding satisfying careers in the travel industry.

In sum, the speaker's threshold claim that it is strictly the pragmatic concerns of job availability and financial compensation that drive people's career decisions oversimplifies both why and how people make career choices. **Besides**, the speaker's final claim that people are not free to choose their work violates my intuition. **In the final analysis**, people are ultimately free to choose their work; it's just that they often choose to betray their true talents and interests for the sake of practical, economic considerations.

人们可以自由地选择职业吗？

　　说话者相信人们做出职业决定的驱动力是经济和其他实际的考虑，并且很少有人自由地根据他们的才能和兴趣选择职业。我倾向于不同意。虽然实际的考虑经常在择业趋势中扮演重要角色，但是最终躲藏在人们职业决定背后的驱动力是个人的兴趣和能力。

　　一眼看来，经验上的证据的对比似乎可以使说者的主张有了相当大的可信度。对于学生来说，今天最受欢迎的专业领域是计算机科学——一个被描绘成相对拥有许多工作机会的领域。文科学位的毕业生因为找不到工作通常放弃他们选择的领域，重新进入学校寻求更加"实用"的职业。甚至那些已经在所从事的领域中取得成功的人通常出于实际的考虑也会放弃自己的职业。比如，许多在娱乐业有才华和创造力的人当到了 40 岁的年龄时，发现他们不得不寻找其他的令人较不满意的工作，因为业内的经理们更欣赏比较年轻的艺术家，这些年轻人能够和那些购买娱乐产品的年轻的统计群体"和谐相处"。

　　尽管如此，通过进一步反思就会清楚地看到择业者和职业的供给之间是一种相互依赖的关系，所以草率地概括谁决定谁并不公正。拿计算机科学和法律两个主流领域举例。在计算机行业也许似乎是供给明显地决定工作利益——在经济回报丰厚的情况下，这也是可以理解的。但是，是不是我们大批有才华的程序师、工程师、科学家和技术员真的对他们所从事领域中的职业没有真实的迷恋、激情或者说兴趣呢？我认为并不是这样。

　　反过来，我们看到在法律领域中好像是需求决定工作市场，而不是反之亦然。在 20 世纪 60 年代的民权运动中申请到法律学校的人数剧增，并且在 20 世纪 80 年代随着广受欢迎的电视系列剧"法律代理人的法律"的热播再次激增。更近以来，从事律师专职助手和犯罪审判职业的学生数量，在 O.J 辛普森审判的过程中和接下来日子里达到顶峰。但是，我怀疑，如果他们一毕业没有充分的工作机会和经济回报在等着他们的话，这些积极的律师和律师助手是否还有这么大的动力。

　　另一个与演讲者主张相悖的令人信服的论据和人们谋生的无数途径有关。诚然，求职市场大量地聚集在某种主流工业和一定类型的工作周围。然而，如果超越这些主流职业领域去看的话，很明显，有许多许多人的确珍视他们的真实兴趣和才能——尽管大多数工作机会都存在于主流职业领域，也不顾及他们的经济报酬。有创造性的人似乎有一套创造他们独特职业地位的诀窍——不管是在视觉艺术还是表演艺术方面。许多喜爱动物的人创造了可以让他们表达那种喜爱的工作。照护者和育人者成功地找到了教育、社交、建议、治疗他人的工作。并且那些有旅游癖的人通常在旅游行业中几乎不会找不到满意工作。

　　综上所述，说话者开始宣称的，对工作可获得性和经济回报的实际考虑全然驱使着人们做有关职业选择的决定，这过分简单化了人们为什么和怎么样选择职业。另外，说话者最终宣称的人们没有自由选择他们的工作与我的直觉相左。归根结底，人们从根本上可以自由选择他们的工作，只是出于实际、经济的考虑，他们才经常选择违背他们真实的才能和兴趣。

论点　有保留的反对

开头方式　陈述题目观点 + 表明立场

论证过程 结论型

论证模式

① At first glance the balance of empirical evidence would seem to lend considerable credence to the speaker's claim.

② However...the relationship between career-seekers and the supply of careers is an interdependent one,...

③ Conversel...demand drives the job market, rather than vice versa.

④ Another compelling argument against the speaker's claim has to do with the myriad of ways in which people earn their living.

Issue 26　Historic buildings—preservation vs. practicality

"**Most people would agree that buildings represent a valuable record of any society's past, but controversy arises when old buildings stand on ground that modern planners feel could be better used for modern purposes. In such situations, modern development should be given precedence over the preservation of historic buildings so that contemporary needs can be served.**"

大多数人都会同意建筑物是任何一个社会有价值的历史的代表,但是当现代规划者们觉得这些以前的建筑物所占据的土地可以被更有价值地用于现代目的时,就产生了争议。在这种情形下,现代发展应该比保留历史建筑物更受重视以便于满足眼下的需求。

The speaker asserts that wherever a practical, utilitarian need for new buildings arises this need should take precedence over our conflicting interest in preserving historic buildings as a record of our past. **In my view, however,** which interest should take precedence should be determined on a case-by-case basis—and should account not only for practical and historic considerations but also aesthetic ones.

In determining whether to raze an older building, planners should of course consider the community's current and anticipated utilitarian needs. For example, if an additional hospital is needed to adequately serve the health-care needs of a fast-growing community, this compelling interest might very well outweigh any interest in preserving a historic building that sits on the proposed site. Or if additional parking is needed to ensure the economic survival of a city's downtown district, this interest might take precedence over the historic value of an old structure that stands in the way of a parking structure. **On the other hand,** if the need is mainly for more office space, in some cases an architecturally appropriate add-on or annex to an older building might serve just as well as razing the old building to make way for a new one. Of course, an expensive retrofit might not be worthwhile if no amount of retrofitting would meet the need.

Competing with a community's utilitarian needs is an interest preserving the historical record. Again, the weight of this interest should be determined on a case-by-case basis. Perhaps an older building uniquely represents a bygone era, or once played a central role in the city's history as a municipal structure. Or perhaps the building once served as the home of a founding family or other significant historical figure, or as the location of an important historical event. Any of these scenarios might justify saving the building at the expense of the practical needs of the community. On the other hand, if several older buildings represent the same historical era just as effectively, or if the building's history

Compelling.

is an unremarkable one, then the historic value of the building might pale in comparison to the value of a new structure that meets a compelling practical need.

Also competing with a community's utilitarian needs is the aesthetic and architectural value of the building itself—apart from historical events with which it might be associated. A building might be one of only a few that represents a certain architectural style. Or it might be especially beautiful, perhaps as a result of the craftsmanship and materials employed in its construction—which might be cost-prohibitive to replicate today. Even retrofitting the building to accommodate current needs might undermine its aesthetic as well as historic value, by altering its appearance and architectural integrity. Of course it is difficult to quantify aesthetic value and weigh it against utilitarian considerations. Yet planners should strive to account for aesthetic value nonetheless.

In sum, whether to raze an older building in order to construct a new one should never be determined indiscriminately. Instead, planners should make such decisions on a case-by-case basis, weighing the community's practical needs against the building's historic and aesthetic value.

历史性建筑——保存 vs. 实用

说话者宣称，对新建筑的实际、功利的需求应该在与保存过去见证的历史性建筑的利益冲突中居于优先地位。尽管如此，我的观点是哪种利益应该占优先地位应该就事论事地决定——并且不仅要出于实际的和历史性的考虑，而且还要有美学的考虑。

在决定是否摧毁一个古老的建筑时，规划者当然应该考虑到社区当前和预期的实际需求。比如，如果还需要一个医院才能充分地满足一个快速发展社区的保健需求，那么这个必要性就会比任何力图在规划的位置上保护历史性建筑的价值要重要得多。或者是需要一个额外的停车场来维持一个城市市区的经济生存需要，那么这种利益可能就优先于那些妨碍停车场位的古老建筑的历史价值。另一方面，如果主要是为了扩大更多的办公室空间，有些情况下，在一个建筑上适当地添加或连接一个旧建筑可能和拆掉古老的建筑为新建筑腾地方的效果一样好。当然，如果这些改造怎么也满足不了需求的话，一次昂贵的改造也许就是不值得的。

与一个社区的功利性需求相竞争的是一种保存历史记录的利益。同样，这种利益的重要性还是应该就事论事地决定。也许一幢比较古老的建筑独一无二地代表了一个过去的年代，或在一个城市的历史中作为一个市政结构曾一度扮演过一个中心角色。或者也许这幢建筑曾经是某个领域奠定人或是其他显赫历史人物的住宅，或者曾是一个重要的历史事件的发生地。任何这些情况中可能都可以使牺牲社区的实际需要而保留这幢建筑变得合情合理。另一方面，如果几个古老建筑等效地代表了相同的历史时代，或者说如果这幢建筑的历史并不突出，那么它的历史价值比起一幢能够满足一种迫切的实际需求的新建筑就微不足道了。

与社区实际需求相竞争的除了可能与之有关联的历史事件以外，还有建筑本身的审美价值和建筑上的价值。一幢建筑可能是少数代表某种建筑风格的建筑中的一个。或是一栋建筑也许因其建筑工艺和使用材料而特别地美丽，今天复制它的费用高得惊人。甚至为了提供当前的需求而通过改变它的外观和建筑上的整体性来进行翻新，都会破坏它的美学和历史价值。当然，想要量化其美学价值并与功利的考虑衡量孰重孰轻是很困难的。但虽然如此，规划者也应该努力说明其美学价值。

总之，是否应该为建一幢新建筑而拆掉一幢比较旧的建筑从来就不应该一刀切地下定论。相反，规划者应该在社区的实际需要与建筑的历史和美学价值间衡量，就事论事地做决定。

论点 **平衡观点**　作者持的是典型的"具体问题具体分析"的态度：应该在个案的基础上决定。

开头方式 陈述题目观点 + 表明立场

论证过程 比较型

论证模式

　① In determining whether to raze an older building, planners should of course consider the community's current and anticipated utilitarian needs.

　② Competing with a community's utilitarian needs is an interest preserving the historical record.

　③ Also competing with a community's utilitarian needs is the aesthetic and architectural value of the building itself...

Issue 36　Can only history determine an individual's **greatness**?

"**The greatness of individuals can be decided only by those who live after them, not by their contemporaries.**"

一个人是否伟大只能是由后人评定，而非他同时代的人。

Can a person's greatness be recognized only in retrospect, by those who live after the person, **as the speaker maintains**? In my view the speaker unfairly generalizes. In some areas, especially the arts, greatness is often recognizable in its nascent stages. However, in other areas, particularly the physical sciences, greatness must be tested over time before it can be confirmed. In still other areas, such as business, the incubation period for greatness varies from case to case.

We do not require a rear-view mirror to recognize artistic greatness—whether in music, visual arts, or literature. The reason for this is simple: art can be judged at face value. There's nothing to be later proved or disproved, affirmed or discredited, or even improved upon or refined by further knowledge or newer technology. History is replete with examples of artistic greatness immediately recognized, then later confirmed. Through his patronage, the Pope recognized Michelangelo's artistic greatness, while the monarchs of Europe immediately recognized Mozart's greatness by granting him their most generous commissions. Mark Twain became a best-selling author and household name even during his lifetime. And the leaders of the modernist school of architecture marveled even as Frank Lloyd Wright was elevating their notions about architecture to new aesthetic heights.

By contrast, in the sciences it is difficult to identify greatness without the benefit of historical perspective. Any scientific theory might be disproved tomorrow, thereby demoting the theorist's contribution to the status of historical footnote. Or the theory might withstand centuries of rigorous scientific scrutiny. In any event, a theory may or may not serve as a springboard for later advances in theoretical science. A current example involves the ultimate significance of two opposing theories of physics: wave theory and quantum theory. Some theorists now claim that a new so-called "string" theory reconciles the two opposing theories—at least mathematically. Yet "strings" have yet to be confirmed empirically. Only time will tell whether the string theory indeed provides the unifying laws that all matter in the universe obeys. In short, the significance of contributions made by theoretical scientists cannot be judged by their contemporaries—only by scientists who follow them.

In the realm of business, in some cases great achievement is recognizable immediately, while in other cases it is not. Consider on the one hand Henry Ford's assembly-line approach to manufacturing affordable cars for the masses. Even Ford could not have predicted the impact his innovations would have on the American economy and on the modern world. On the other hand, by any measure, Microsoft's Bill Gates has made an even greater contribution than Ford; after all, Gates is largely responsible for lifting American technology out of the doldrums during the 1970s to restore America to the status of economic powerhouse and technological leader of the world. And this contribution is readily recognizable now—as it is happening. Of course, the DOS and Windows operating systems, and even Gates' monopoly, might eventually become historical relics. Yet his greatness is already secured.

In sum, the speaker overlooks many great individuals, particularly in the arts and in business, whose achievements were broadly recognized as great even during their own time. **Nevertheless**, other great achievements, especially scientific ones, cannot be confirmed as such without the benefit of historical perspective.

只有历史才能决定一个人的伟大吗？

正如说话者主张的那样，一个人的伟大只有通过那些活在他身后的人的回顾才能得到确认吗？我认为他的概括有失公允。在某些领域中，特别是艺术领域，在起初阶段其伟大就经常得到认可。然而，在其他领域，特别是自然科学，其伟大必须通过长时间的检验才能被证实。还有其他领域，例如商业，伟大与否的潜伏期则根据情况的不同而不同。

要识别艺术的伟大我们并不需要一个后视镜——无论是在音乐、视觉艺术还是文学方面。理由很简单：艺术可以从其表面价值进行判定。没有什么需要后来证明或反证、确认或怀疑或者甚至是通过更进一步的知识或新的技术来改进或完善的。在历史中，伟大的艺术立即被认可，后来被证实，这样的例子有很多。通过赞助，罗马教皇识出了米开朗基罗艺术的伟大，而欧洲的帝王立刻看出了莫扎特的伟大，并给予他最慷慨的资助。马克·吐温甚至一生都是一个畅销作家和家喻户晓的人物。甚至在弗兰克·劳埃德·莱特把建筑学的现代主义学派的领袖们有关建筑学的观念提高到新的美学高度的时候，就已经使得他们惊叹不已了。

相反地，在科学领域，没有历史观察的帮助很难鉴别科学的伟大。任何科学的理论也许会在明天被证伪，从而降低了该理论家对于历史注脚的贡献地位。除非这个理论能经受几个世纪严厉的科学审查。无论如何，在理论科学中，一个理论可能会成为后来理论进展的跳板，也可能不能。一个当前的例子涉及物理学中最为重要的两种相反的理论——波动理论和量子理论。一些理论家现在宣称一个新的所谓"超弦"理论能协调这两种相反的理论，至少在数学上是如此。但是"超弦"理论还得被经验所证实。只有时间才能说明超弦理论是否的确提供了所有的宇宙物质都服从的统一法则。简而言之，理论科学家做出的贡献的重要性不能够被他们同时代的人判定，只有那些后来的科学家才能做到这一点。

在商业的王国里，在某些情况下卓越的成就会被马上认可，而在其他情况下却不是。一方面看看亨利·福特所采用的装配线方法，为大众制造负担得起的汽车。甚至福特自己也不能预测出他的革新给美国经济和现代世界带来的影响。另一方面，不管怎么比较，微软的比尔·盖茨已经做出了比福特更大的贡献。毕竟，是盖茨把美国的技术从 20 世纪 70 年代的萎靡不振中拉了出来，使美国恢复到世界经济动力和技术领袖的地位。并且这个贡献现在容易得到公认——正如它现在发生的那样。当然，DOS 和 Windows 操作系统，甚至盖茨的垄断最终可能会成为历史的遗迹。但是他的伟大已经确定无疑。

总的说来，说话者忽略了许多伟大的个人，特别是在艺术和商业领域里的重要人物，即使在他们自己生活的时代，他们的成就就广泛地被认可为伟大的了。然而，其他伟大的成就，尤其是科学成就，在没有历史观察的帮助是不能像这样被证实的。

论点 平衡观点　很完整的一个平衡观点：一方面赞成，一方面认为有失公允，持具体个案具体分析的态度。

开头方式 提出问题 + 表明立场

论证过程 比较型

论证模式

① We do not require a rear-view mirror to recognize artistic greatness—whether in music, visual arts, or literature.

② By contrast, in the sciences it is difficult to identify greatness without the benefit of historical perspective.

③ In the realm of business, in some cases great achievement is recognizable immediately...

Issue 103　Is history **relevant to our daily lives**?

"The study of history has value only to the extent that it is relevant to our daily lives."
对历史的研究只有与我们的日常生活相关时才有价值。

The speaker alleges that studying history is valuable only insofar as it is relevant to our daily lives. **I find this allegation to be specious.** It wrongly suggests that history is not otherwise instructive and that its relevance to our everyday lives is limited. To the contrary, studying history provides inspiration, innumerable lessons for living, and useful value-clarification and perspective—all of which help us decide how to live our lives.

To begin with, **learning about great human achievements of the past provides inspiration.** For example, a student inspired by the courage and tenacity of history's great explorers might decide as a result to pursue a career in archeology, oceanography, or astronomy. This decision can, in turn, profoundly affect that student's everyday life-in school and beyond. Even for students not inclined to pursue these sorts of careers, studying historical examples of courage in the face of adversity can provide motivation to face their own personal fears in life. In short, learning about grand accomplishments of the past can help us get through the everyday business of living, whatever that business might be, by emboldening us and lifting our spirits.

In addition, mistakes of the past can teach us as a society how to avoid repeating those mistakes. For example, history can teach us the inappropriateness of addressing certain social issues, particularly moral ones, on a societal level. Attempts to legislate morality invariably fail, as aptly illustrated by the Prohibition experiment in the U.S. during the 1930s. Hopefully, as a society we can apply this lesson by adopting a more enlightened legislative approach toward such issues as free speech, criminalization of drug use, criminal justice, and equal rights under the law.

Studying human history can also help us understand and appreciate the mores, values, and ideals of past cultures. A heightened awareness of cultural evolution, in turn, helps us formulate informed and reflective values and ideals for ourselves. Based on these values and ideals, students can determine their authentic life path as well as how they should allot their time and interact with others on a day-to-day basis.

Finally, it might be tempting to imply from the speaker's allegation that **studying history has little relevance even for the mundane chores** that occupy so much of our time each day, and therefore is of little value. However, from history we learn not to take everyday activities and things for granted. By understanding the history of money and banking we can transform an otherwise routine trip to the bank into an enlightened experience, or a visit to the grocery store into an homage to the many inventors, scientists, engineers, and entrepreneurs of the past who have made such convenience possible today. And, we can fully appreciate our freedom to go about our daily lives largely as we choose only by understanding our political heritage. In short, appreciating history can serve to elevate our everyday chores to richer, more interesting, and more enjoyable experiences.

In sum, the speaker fails to recognize that in all our activities and decisions—from our grandest to our most rote—history can inspire, inform, guide, and nurture. In the final analysis, to study history is to gain the capacity to be more human—and I would be hard-pressed to imagine a worthier end.

历史和我们的日常生活相关吗？

说话者宣称仅在和我们日常生活相关的范围内研究历史才是有价值的。我认为这个断言似是而非。它错误地暗示，历史在其他方面就不是有益的以及它和我们每天生活的联系是有限的。正相反，学习历史能够提供灵感、无数的生活经验和有用的澄清价值的方法和洞察力，所有这些都有助于我们决定怎样度过我们的人生。

首先，学习过去伟人的成就赋予我们灵感。比如，一个学生因受到历史上伟大探险家勇气和坚忍的鼓舞，结果可能决定在考古学、海洋学、天文学领域开创事业。这个决定，反过来会深刻地影响那个学生在学校和其他地方每天的生活。甚至对于那些无意于从事这类工作的学生而言，学习一些以勇气面对不幸的历史事实，也能够给他们提供在生活中战胜恐惧的动力。简而言之，学习关于昔日的重大成就可以通过鼓起我们的勇气并且提升我们的精神面貌来帮助我们解决每天的生活琐事，无论事情可能是什么。

除此以外，昔日的错误能够教给我们社会如何避免重复那些错误。举例来说，历史能告诉我们在社会层面上处理某种社会问题的不当之处，特别是伦理问题。尝试制定有关道德的立法总是以失败而告终，在 20 世纪 30 年代期间美国禁酒令试验正好阐明了这一点。希望我们社会能够吸取这一教训，采取一个更开明的立法途径处理这样的问题：言论自由、吸毒定罪、刑事审判和法律下的平等权利。

学习人类的历史也能够帮助我们理解和鉴赏过去文化的习俗、价值和理想。更高的对文化发展的意识反过来会帮助我们自己形成明达的和周详的价值观和理想。基于这些价值观和理想，学生能够决定他们的真实生活路径，以及他们每天应该如何分配时间和如何与他人交往。最后，从说话者的论断中可能很容易得出这样的暗示，学习历史对于占据我们每天大多数时间的世俗琐事，几乎没什么关系，因此没什么价值。然而，从历史中我们得知不要把每天的活动和事物想得理所当然。通过理解货币和银行的历史，我们能够把一种本来是例行的去一趟银行转变成一种文明的经历，或者是把一次到食杂店购物转变为一种向过去的许多发明家、科学家、工程师和企业家的致敬，是这些人创造了今天如此便利的生活。并且，只是通过理解我们的政治遗产才能完全了解我们绝大多数情况下按我们自愿的方式处理日常事务的自由。简而言之，了解历史能使我们每天的家务杂事变成更丰富、更有趣而且更令人愉快的体验。

总的说来，说话者没有认识到历史在我们所有的活动和决议中——从最宏大的到最死板的——都能起到启示、告知、引导和教育的作用。总而言之，学习历史是为了获得更加人性化的能力——我很难想像一个比这更有价值的目标了。

论点 有保留的反对

开头方式 陈述题目观点 + 表明立场 + 概述理由

论证过程 比较型

论证模式

① To begin with, learning about great human achievements of the past provides inspiration.

② In addition, mistakes of the past can teach us as a society how to avoid repeating those mistakes.

③ Studying human history can also help us understand and appreciate the mores, values, and ideals of past cultures.

④ Finally... studying history has little relevance even for the mundane chores...

Issue 120　　Studying the past to help us live in **the present**

"So much is new and complex today that looking back for an understanding of the past provides little guidance for living in the present."

现代社会是如此地崭新和复杂以至于对过去的回首了解对当代生活已经没有什么指导了。

The speaker claims that since so much in today's world is new and complex the past provides little guidance for living in the present. I agree with this assertion insofar as history offers few foolproof panaceas for living today. However, I disagree with the speaker's claim that today's world is so unique that the past is irrelevant. One good example that supports my dual position is the way society has dealt with its pressing social problems over time.

Admittedly, history has helped us learn the appropriateness of addressing certain social issues, particularly moral ones, on a societal level. Attempts to legislate morality invariably fail, as illustrated by Prohibition in the 1930s and, more recently, failed federal legislation to regulate access to adult material via the Internet. We are slowly learning this lesson, as the recent trend toward legalization of marijuana for medicinal purposes and the recognition of equal rights for same-sex partners both demonstrate.

However, the only firm lesson from history about social ills is that they are here to stay. Crime and violence, for example, have troubled almost every society. All manner of reform, prevention, and punishment have been tried. Today, the trend appears to be away from reform toward a "tough-on-crime" approach. Is this because history makes clear that punishment is the most effective means of eliminating crime? No; rather, the trend merely reflects our current mores, attitudes, and political climate.

Another example involves how we deal with the mentally-ill segment of the population. History reveals that neither quarantine, treatment, nor accommodation solves the problem, only that each approach comes with its own trade-offs. Also undermining the assertion that history helps us to solve social problems is the fact that, despite the civil-rights efforts of Martin Luther King and his progenies, the cultural gap today between African Americans and white Americans seems to be widening. It seems that racial prejudice is a timeless phenomenon.

To sum up, in terms of how to live together as a society I agree that studying the past is of some value; for example, it helps us appreciate the futility of legislating morality. However, history's primary sociological lesson seems to be that today's social problems are as old as society itself, and that there are no panaceas or prescriptions for solving these problems—only alternate ways of coping with them.

学习过去有助于我们生活在现在

演讲者认为既然今天的世界有如此多的新鲜和复杂的事物，过去的东西能为我们现在的生活提供的指导少之又少。如果说历史为我们今天的生活几乎提供不了简单易行的万能药，那我同意这种观点。然而，对于演讲者认为今天的世界是如此独特与过去毫无关联的说法，我不能苟同。一个不错的例子有助于说明我的双重立场：今天的社会处理紧迫的遗留问题的方式。

诚然，历史有助于使我们明白在社会层面处理某些社会问题，特别是道德方面的恰当性。对道德进行立法的尝试总是归于失败，就像20世纪30年代的禁酒令和未果的近期联邦立法对通过互联网浏览色情内容的管制。我们吸取教训的速度太慢，最近对大麻医用以及认可同性关系平等权利的立法化潮流都证明了这点。

但是，从历史中我们学到的有关社会痼疾的惟一牢固的教训是，它们会存在下去。就像犯罪和暴力，它们几乎困扰着每个社会。任何形式的感化、预防和惩戒都使用过。今天，社会的趋势似乎不再是感化而是采用"严打犯罪"的方式。是不是因为历史告诉了我们惩罚是最有效的消除犯罪的方法呢？不。而是这种趋势只是反映了我们当下的惯例、态度和政治气候。

另一个例子与我们对患有精神疾病的人的处置有关。历史告诉我们隔离、治疗和迁就都无助于问题的解决，每种方式都有它的代价。同样不利于历史帮助我们解决社会问题这一论断的事实是，尽管马丁·路德·金和他的后裔在民权运动中的努力，今天非裔美国人和美国白人的文化差异却似乎越来越深。种族歧视似乎是个永恒的现象。

总而言之，在关于如何作为一个社会共同生活这个方面，我同意学习历史有所裨益。比如，它帮助我们领会道德立法的无用。然而，历史的主要社会学上的教训在于今天的社会问题看来与社会本身一样古老。解决它们似乎没有什么万能药方——只有更换处理的手段而已。

论点 平衡观点

开头方式 陈述题目观点 + 表明立场

论证过程 比较型 论证部分的三个自然段分析了社会处理紧迫遗留问题的三例个案：对道德立法的尝试、犯罪和罪犯这样的社会痼疾和对精神疾病人员的隔离处置。

论证模式

① Admittedly, history has helped us learn the appropriateness of addressing certain social issues...

② However, the only firm lesson from history about social ills is that they are here to stay.

③ Another example involves how we deal with the mentally-ill segment of the population.

Issue 173 To what extent is **originality** truly original?

"Originality does not mean thinking something that was never thought before; it means putting old ideas together in new ways."

创新并不意味着一定要想到一些人们从未想过的东西;它意味着用新方法来重组老观点。

Does "originality" mean putting together old ideas in new ways, as the speaker contends, rather than conjuring up truly new ideas? **Although I agree that** in various realms of human endeavor, such as linguistics, law, and even the arts, so-called "new" or "original" ideas rarely are. **However**, when it comes to the physical sciences originality more often entails chartering completely new intellectual territory.

The notion that so-called "originality" is actually variation or synthesis of existing ideas finds its greatest support in linguistics and in law. Regarding the former, in spite of the many words in the modern English language that are unique to Western culture, modern English is derived from, and builds upon, a variety of linguistic traditions—and ultimately from the ancient Greek and Latin languages. Were we to insist on rejecting tradition in favor of purely modern language we would have essentially nothing to say. The same holds true for all other modern languages. As for law, consider the legal system in the United States, which is deeply rooted in traditional English common-law principles of equity and justice. The system in the U.S. requires that new, so-called "modern" laws be consistent with—and indeed build upon—those traditional principles.

Even in the arts—where one might think that true originality must surely reside—so-called "new" ideas almost always embrace, apply, or synthesize what came earlier. For example, most "modern" visual designs, forms, and elements are based on certain well-established aesthetic ideals—such as symmetry, balance, and harmony. Admittedly, modern art works often eschew these principles in favor of true originality. Yet, in my view the appeal of such works lies primarily in their novelty and brashness. Once the ephemeral novelty or shock dissipates, these works quickly lose their appeal because they violate firmly established artistic ideals. An even better example from the arts is modern rock-and-roll music, which upon first listening might seem to bear no resemblance to classical music traditions. Yet, both genres rely on the same 12-note scale, the same notions of what harmonies are pleasing to the ear, the same forms, the same rhythmic meters, and even many of the same melodies.

When it comes to the natural sciences, however, some new ideas are truly original while others put established ideas together in new ways. **One striking example of** truly original scientific advances involves what we know about the age and evolution of the Earth. In earlier centuries the official Church of England called for a literal interpretation of the Bible, according to which the Earth's age is determined to be about 6,000 years. If Western thinkers had simply put these established ideas together in new ways the fields of structural and historical geology might never have advanced further. A more recent example involves Einstein's theory of relativity. Einstein theorized, and scientists have since proven empirically, that the pace of time, and possibly the direction of time as well, is relative to the observer's motion through space. This truth ran so contrary to our subjective, linear experience, and to previous notions about time and space, that I think Einstein's theory can properly be characterized as truly original.

However, in other instances great advances in science are made by putting together current theories or other ideas in new ways. For example, only by building on certain well-established laws of physics were engineers able to develop silicon-based semiconductor technology. And, only by struggling to reconcile the quantum and relativity theories have physicists now posited a new so-called "string" theory, which puts together the two preexisting theories in a completely new way.

　　To sum up, for the most part originality does not reject existing ideas but rather embraces, applies, or synthesizes what came before. In fact, in our modern languages, our new laws, and even our new art, existing ideas are reflected, not shunned. But, when it comes to science, whether the speaker's claim is true must be determined on a case-by-case basis, with each new theory or innovation.

在何种程度上原创性是真正的原创？

　　原创性是如演讲者所说的那样将旧的思想用新的方式整合，还是思考出真正的新想法？虽然我同意在人类行为的许多领域，比如语言、法律，甚至是艺术，所谓的"新"和"原创"的想法极为罕见。但当涉及物理科学，原创性往往意味着开拓出全新的智力领域。

　　所谓"原创性"事实上是既有想法的变异或是综合这个概念，在语言和法律领域最能找到支持。关于前者，尽管许多英语词汇是西方文化所独有的，但现代英语是建筑在多种语言传统融合的基础上——最终是来自古希腊语和拉丁语。如果我们坚持将传统抛弃取而代之以全新的语言，那我们将无话可说。这点同样适用于其他现代语言。至于法律，以美国法律系统为例，它深深地植根于传统英语国家的平等与正义的普通法准则。美国法系要求那些新的，所谓"现代"的法律与这些传统原则相匹配——其实是以其为根基。

　　甚至在艺术中——人们可能认为那是真正原创性的必然所在——所谓的"新"思想也几乎总是会包容、应用和综合以前的东西。比如，最为"现代"的视觉设计、形式与成分也是基于某些早已确立的审美理想——如对称、平衡和和谐。诚然，现代艺术作品常避开这些原则以利于真实的创新。但在我看来，这些作品的吸引人之处主要在于它们的新颖和活跃。一旦这种转瞬即逝的新意渐渐消去，作品便因为它们对既有审美理想的违背而立刻失去了吸引力。艺术中的一个更好的例子是现代的摇滚乐，乍听起来似乎与古典音乐毫不相干。但两种类型的音乐都依靠同样的 12 个音符、相同的悦耳概念、同样的形式、同样的韵律节奏甚至许多都是同样的旋律。

　　但是当谈到自然科学时，有些想法是真正原创的而其他的就是重新整合旧的想法。一个最有力的真正原创科学进步的例子是关于我们对地球年龄和演进的认识。在早先的世纪里，英国的官方教会要求对《圣经》进行字面上的翻译，根据《圣经》地球的年龄被定为是 6000 年。如果西方的思想家只是简单地重新整合这些既有的观点，那么结构地理学和历史地理学领域可能永远也不会得到发展。另一个近一点儿的例子涉及爱因斯坦的相对论。爱因斯坦提出这个理论，从此许多科学家通过经验证明了，时间的步调或许还有它的方向对于观察者在空间中的移动是相对的。这样的真理与我们的主观、线性经验以及以前对时空的概念反差如此之大，我认为爱因斯坦的理论可谓真正的原创。

　　但是，在其他的一些例子中科学的重大进展是用新的方法重新整合既有的理论和其他的想法。比如，只有在遵从许多既有物理法则的基础上，工程师们才能发明出以硅为原料的半导体技术。只有通过尝试去调和量子理论和相对论，物理学家现在才能提出所谓的"弦"理论，后者是以一种全新的方式将既有的两种理论整合了。

　　总而言之，在大多数情况下原创性不会拒斥而是包容、应用和综合以往的东西。实际上，在我们的现代语言、新的法律甚至新艺术中，既有的思想也被反映出来，不是被回避。但是，当涉及科学的时候，演讲者观点的真实性则必须视每个新理论或创新的具体情况而定。

论点　有保留的赞成

开头方式	提出问题 + 表明立场
论证过程	比较型
论证模式	

① The notion that so-called "originality" is actually variation or synthesis of existing ideas finds its greatest support in linguistics and in law.

② Even in the arts...

③ When it comes to the natural sciences...

④ However, in other instances...

Issue 207　Rituals and ceremonies and cultural identity

"**Rituals and ceremonies help define a culture. Without them, societies or groups of people have a diminished sense of who they are.**"

仪式和礼仪有助于定义一个文化。如果没有这些，社会或者团体就会逐渐地迷失自我。

The speaker asserts that rituals and ceremonies are needed for any culture or group of people to retain a strong sense of identity. I agree that one purpose of ritual and ceremony is to preserve cultural identity, at least in modern times. However, this is not their sole purpose; nor are ritual and ceremony the only means of preserving cultural identity.

I agree with the speaker insofar as one purpose of ritual and ceremony in today's world is to preserve cultural identity. Native American tribes, for example, cling tenaciously to their traditional ceremonies and rituals, which typically tell a story about tribal heritage. The reason for maintaining these rituals and customs lies largely in the tribes' 500-year struggle against assimilation, even extinction, at the hands of European intruders. An outward display of traditional customs and distinct heritage is needed to put the world on notice that each tribe is a distinct and autonomous people, with its own heritage, values, and ideas. Otherwise, the tribe risks total assimilation and loss of identity.

The lack of meaningful ritual and ceremony in homogenous mainstream America underscores this point. Other than a few gratuitous ceremonies such as weddings and funerals, we maintain no common rituals to set us apart from other cultures. The reason for this is that as a whole America has little cultural identity of its own anymore. Instead, it has become a patchwork quilt of many subcultures, such as Native Americans, Hasidic Jews, Amish, and urban African Americans—each of which resort to some outward demonstration of its distinctiveness in order to establish and maintain a unique cultural identity.

Nevertheless, preserving cultural identify cannot be the only purpose of ritual and ceremony. Otherwise, how would one explain why isolated cultures that don't need to distinguish themselves to preserve their identity nevertheless engage in their own distinct rituals and ceremonies? In fact, the initial purpose of ritual and ceremony is rooted not in cultural identity but rather superstition and spiritual belief. The original purpose of a ritual might have been to frighten away evil spirits, to bring about weather conditions favorable to bountiful harvests, or to entreat the gods for a successful hunt or for victory in battle. Even today some primitive cultures engage in rituals primarily for such reasons.

Nor are ritual and ceremony the only means of preserving cultural identity. For example, our Amish culture demonstrates its distinctiveness through dress and lifestyle. Hasidic Jews set themselves apart by their dress, vocational choices, and dietary habits. And African Americans distinguish themselves today by their manner of speech and gesture. Of course, these subcultures have their own distinct ways of cerebrating events such as weddings, coming of age, and so forth. Yet ritual and ceremony are not the primary means by which these subcultures maintain their identity.

In sum, to prevent total cultural assimilation into our modern-day homogenous soup, a subculture with a unique and proud heritage must maintain an outward display of that heritage—by way of ritual and ceremony. **Nevertheless**, ritual and ceremony serve a spiritual function as well—one that has little to do with preventing cultural assimilation. Moreover, rituals and ceremonies are not the only means of preserving cultural identity.

仪式和礼仪与文化认同性

演讲者认为仪式与礼仪对于任何要保持强烈的身份感的文化或人群来说都是必要的。我同意至少在现代，仪式与礼仪的一个目的是保持文化身份。但这不是它们的惟一的目的，而保持文化身份仪式和礼仪也不是惟一的方式。

仪式与礼仪在今日世界的一个目标是保持文化认同，对于这点我表示同意。比方说，美洲的原始部落顽强地保持着那些反映它们部落遗产的仪式和礼仪。原因在于他们与欧洲人侵者长达500年的反同化、反灭绝斗争。需要外在地展示传统习俗与显著遗产以使世界认识到，每个部落都是独特自主的民族，有其自己的遗产、价值观和思想。否则，这些部落就有被完全同化和丧失身份的危险。

美国同质的主流文化中缺少有意义的仪式和礼仪这个事实加强了这种观点。除了婚礼和葬礼等无关紧要的仪式外，我们少有区别于其他文化的共同的仪式。原因在于美国人整体上缺少其自己的文化身份。相反，美国文化是由一些亚文化所拼凑而成的，诸如美洲原著民、哈西德派的犹太人、阿门宗派、城市的非裔美国人——每一类人为了建立和保持一种独特的文化身份都诉诸于外在地展示其与众不同之处。

尽管如此，保持文化身份并不是仪式和礼仪的惟一目的。否则我们怎么解释一些孤立的并不需要与他人区分以保持身份的文化，仍旧从事他们显著的仪式和礼仪？事实上，仪式和礼仪的最初目的并不植根于文化身份，而与迷信和精神信仰密切相关。仪式的最初目的也许是为了震慑邪恶，为了带来利于丰收的好气候或者是为了一次成功的狩猎和战役的胜利而祈神。即使今天一些原始文化还主要是出于这些目的而从事仪式。

仪式和礼仪也不是保持文化身份的惟一手段。比如，我们的阿门宗派文化通过穿着和生活方式来显示它的不同。哈西德犹太人通过穿着、职业的选择和饮食习惯与其他人相区别。而今天的非裔美国人则通过他们讲话的方式和手势来区别于其他人。当然，这些亚文化也有他们自己庆祝婚礼、成年等事件的独特方式。但是仪式和礼仪并不是这些亚文化用来保持身份的主要手段。

总而言之，为了防止被我们今日的同质文化完全同化，有着独特而骄傲传统的亚文化必须有保持外在地展示自己的那种传统——通过仪式和礼仪。尽管如此，仪式和礼仪也有精神方面的功用——而这与防止文化同化无关。而且，仪式和礼仪也不是保持文化认同的惟一手段。

论点 有保留的赞成

开头方式 陈述题目观点＋表明立场

论证过程 问题解决型

论证模式

① I agree with the speaker insofar as one purpose of ritual and ceremony in today's world is to preserve cultural identity.

② The lack of meaningful ritual and ceremony in homogenous mainstream America underscores this point.

③ Nevertheless, preserving cultural identify cannot be the only purpose of ritual and ceremony.

④ Nor are ritual and ceremony the only means of preserving cultural identity. For example, ...

Issue 226　Are we facing increasingly **complex and challenging** problems?

"People are mistaken when they assume that the problems they confront are more complex and challenging than the problems faced by their predecessors. This illusion is eventually dispelled with increased knowledge and experience."

人们总是错误地认为自己面临的问题要比前人来得更复杂和更具有挑战性。随着知识和经验的不断增加这种假象最终会被消除。

Is any sense that the problems we face are more complex and challenging than those which our predecessors faced merely an illusion—one that can be dispelled by way of knowledge and experience? The speaker believes so, although I disagree. In my view, the speaker unfairly generalizes about the nature of contemporary problems, some of which have no analog from earlier times and which in some respects are more complex and challenging than any problems earlier societies ever confronted. Nevertheless, I agree that many of the other problems we humans face are by their nature enduring ones that have changed little in complexity and difficulty over the span of human history; and I agree that through experience and enlightened reflection on human history we grow to realize this fact.

I turn first to my chief point of contention with the statement. The speaker overlooks certain societal problems unique to today's world, which are complex and challenging in ways unlike any problems that earlier societies ever faced. Consider three examples. The first involves the growing scarcity of the world's natural resources. An ever-increasing human population, together with over-consumption on the part of developed nations and with global dependencies on finite natural resources, have created uniquely contemporary environmental problems that are global in impact and therefore pose political and economic challenges previously unrivaled in complexity.

A second uniquely contemporary problem has to do with the fact that the nations of the world are growing increasingly interdependent—politically, militarily, and economically. Interdependency makes for problems that are far more complex than analogous problems for individual nations during times when they were more insular, more self-sustaining, and more autonomous.

A third uniquely contemporary problem is an outgrowth of the inexorable advancement of scientific knowledge, and one that society voluntarily takes up as a challenge. Through scientific advancements we've already solved innumerable health problems, harnessed various forms of physical energy, and so forth. The problems left to address are the ones that are most complex and challenging—for example, slowing the aging process, replacing human limbs and organs, and colonizing other worlds in the event ours becomes inhabitable. In short, as we solve each successive scientific puzzle we move on to more challenging and complex ones.

I turn next to my points of agreement with the statement. Humans face certain universal and time-less problems, which are neither more nor less complex and challenging for any generation than for preceding ones. These sorts of problems are the ones that spring from the failings and foibles that are part-and-parcel of human nature. Our problems involving interpersonal relationships with people of the opposite sex stem from basic differences between the two sexes. The social problems of prejudice and discrimination know no chronological bounds because it is our nature to fear and mistrust people who are different from us. War and crime stem from the male aggressive instinct and innate desire for power. We've never been able to solve social problems such as homelessness and hunger because we are driven by self-interest.

I agree with the statement also in that certain kinds of intellectual struggles—to determine the meaning of life, whether God exists, and so forth—are timeless ones whose complexities and mystery know no chronological bounds whatsoever. The fact that we rely on ancient teachings to try to solve these problems underscores the fact that these problems have not grown any more complex over the course of human history.

And, with respect to all the timeless problems mentioned above I agree that knowledge and experience help us to understand that these problems are not more complex today than before. In the final analysis, by studying history, human psychology, theology, and philosophy we come to realize that, aside from certain uniquely contemporary problems, we face the same fundamental problems as our predecessors because we face the same human condition as our predecessors whenever we look in the mirror.

我们是否面临日益增加的复杂和挑战性的问题？

觉得我们面对的问题比前人要更复杂和具有挑战性只是幻觉——一种能被知识和经验所驱散的幻觉吗？演讲者这么认为，但我不同意。在我看来，演讲者为当代问题的本质做的概括并不公正，当代问题中的一些的确为以前所没有，并在一些方面比我们以前社会面临的问题更复杂，更具挑战性。尽管如此，我同意这样的一种观点，我们人类面临的其他问题中有许多由于它们本质上是持久的，所以其复杂性和难度在人类历史的漫长时期中鲜有变化。我也同意，通过经验和反省人类历史我们正在逐渐意识到这一事实。

我首先说说我与该论断相左的主要观点。演讲者忽视了某些为今天的世界所独有的社会问题，它们因不同于以往社会所面临的社会问题而显得复杂而具有挑战性。我举三个例子。第一个与世界自然资源越来越少有关。持续增长的人口，加上发达国家的过度消耗，以及全球对于有限自然资源的依赖，造成了当代独有的环境问题，它具有全球性的影响，因此成为空前复杂的政治与经济挑战。

第二个当代独有的问题与这样的一个事实有关，世界上的国家正日益在政治、军事和经济上互相依赖。这种互相依存造成的问题要比国家在更加与世隔绝、更加自力更生和更自行其是的时代所产生的问题复杂得多。

第三个当代独有的问题是科学知识的爆炸性发展，社会情愿地以之为挑战。通过科技发展，我们已经解决了无数的健康问题，驾驭了各种形式的能源等等。剩下要解决的问题大多是最为复杂和具有挑战性的——比如，减慢老龄化进程，更换人类的肢体和器官，征服其他地方以备我们的世界不再适于居住。简言之，随着我们接二连三地解决科学难题，我们又会遭遇更具挑战性和更为复杂的难题。

我下面说说我肯定该论断的观点。人类的确碰到一些普遍而永恒的问题。这些问题在任何一代人看来都比前人面临的同样复杂和具有挑战性。这类问题与作为人类本性中必不可少部分的缺陷密切相关。我们处理异性之间关系的问题根源于男女两性的基本差异。偏见与歧视这些社会问题并没有时间范围，因为恐惧和不信任与我们不同的人是我们的天性。战争和犯罪起源于男性攻击的本能和对权力的内在渴望。我们永远也不能解决诸如流浪和饥饿等社会问题，因为我们总是为自身利益所驱动。

在这方面我也肯定该论断，即某种学术斗争——确定生命的意义，神是否存在等等——是永恒的，其复杂性与神秘性也没有任何时间范围。我们依靠古代经验来解决这些问题，这一事实强调了这些问题在人类历史进程中并没有变得更为复杂。

从以上我所谈到的永恒问题中，我认为知识与经验帮助我们理解到，这些难题在今天并不比以前更复杂。总之，通过学习历史、人类心理学、神学和哲学我们逐渐意识到，除了一些当代独有的问题外，我们与前人面临的基本问题相同，因为不论什么时候我们审视自己，我们都面对着与前人同样的人类条件。

论点 平衡观点

开头方式 提出问题 + 回答 + 表明立场

论证过程 比较型

论证模式

① I turn first to my chief point of contention with the statement.

② A second uniquely contemporary problem has to do with the fact that...

③ A third uniquely contemporary problem is...

④ I turn next to my points of agreement with the statement.

第三章　Issue 范文精选

Issue 5　The merits of a **national curriculum** for schools

in so far as 在…范围内

The speaker would prefer a national curriculum for all children up until college instead of allowing schools in different regions the freedom to decide on their own curricula. I agree insofar as some common core curriculum would serve useful purposes for any nation. At the same time, however, individual states and communities should have some freedom to augment any such curriculum as they see fit; otherwise, a nation's educational system might defeat its own purposes in the long term.

A national core curriculum would be beneficial to a nation in a number of respects. First of all, by providing all children with fundamental skills and knowledge, a common core curriculum would help ensure that our children grow up to become reasonably informed, productive members of society. In addition, a common core curriculum would provide a predictable foundation upon which college administrators and faculty could more easily build curricula and select course materials for freshmen that are neither below nor above their level of educational experience. Finally, a core curriculum would ensure that all school-children are taught core values upon which any democratic society depends to thrive, and even survive—values such as tolerance of others with different viewpoints, and respect for others.

However, a common curriculum that is also an exclusive one would pose certain problems, which might outweigh the benefits, noted above. First of all, on what basis would certain course work be included or excluded, and who would be the final decision-maker? In all likelihood these decisions would be in the hands of federal legislators and regulators, who are likely to have their own quirky notions of what should and should not be taught to children—notions that may or may not reflect those of most communities, schools, or parents. Besides, government officials are notoriously susceptible to influence-peddling by lobbyists who do not have the best interests of society's children in mind.

Secondly, an official, federally sanctioned curriculum would facilitate the dissemination of propaganda and other dogma—which because of its biased and one-sided nature undermines the very purpose of true education: to enlighten. I can easily foresee the banning of certain text books, programs, and Web sites that provide information and perspectives that the government might wish to suppress—as some sort of threat to its authority and power. Although this scenario might seem far-fetched, these sorts of concerns are being raised already at the state level.

Thirdly, the inflexible nature of a uniform national curriculum would preclude the inclusion of programs, courses, and materials that are primarily of regional or local significance. For example, California requires children at certain grade levels to learn about the history of particular ethnic groups who make up the state's diverse population. A national curriculum might not allow for this feature, and California's youngsters would be worse off as a result of their ignorance about the traditions, values, and cultural contributions of all the people whose citizenship they share.

Finally, it seems to me that imposing a uniform national curriculum would serve to undermine the authority of parents over their own children, to even a greater extent than uniform state laws currently do. Admittedly, laws requiring parents to ensure that their children receive an education that meets certain minimum standards are well justified, for the reasons mentioned earlier. However, when such standards are imposed by the state rather than at the community level parents are left with far less power to participate meaningfully in the decision-making process. This problem would only be exacerbated were these decisions left exclusively to federal regulators.

In the final analysis, homogenization of elementary and secondary education would amount to a double-edged sword. While it would serve as an insurance policy against a future populated with illiterates and ignoramuses, at the same time it might serve to obliterate cultural diversity and tradition. The optimal federal approach, in my view, is a balanced one that imposes a basic curriculum yet leaves the rest up to each state—or better yet, to each community.

Issue 11   The benefits of a **global university**

I agree that it would serve the interests of all nations to establish a global university for the purpose of solving the world's most persistent social problems. Nevertheless, such a university poses certain risks that all participating nations must be careful to minimize—or risk defeating the university's purpose.

One compelling argument in favor of a global university has to do with the fact that its faculty and students would bring diverse cultural and educational perspectives to the problems they seek to solve. It seems to me that nations can only benefit from a global university where students learn ways in which other nations address certain social problems—successfully or not. It might be tempting to think that an overly diversified academic community would impede communication among students and faculty. However, in my view any such concerns are unwarranted, especially considering the growing awareness of other peoples and cultures that the mass media, and especially the Internet, have created. Moreover, many basic principles used to solve enduring social problems know no national boundaries; thus, a useful insight or discovery can come from a researcher or student from any nation.

Another compelling argument for a global university involves the increasingly global nature of certain problems. Consider, for instance, the depletion of atmospheric ozone, which has warmed the Earth to the point that it threatens the very survival of the human species. Also, we are now learning that clear-cutting the world's rainforests can set into motion a chain of animal extinction that threatens the delicate balance upon which all animals—including humans—depend. Also consider that a financial crisis—or a political crisis or natural disaster—in one country can spell trouble for foreign companies, many of which are now multinational in that they rely on the labor forces, equipment, and raw materials of other nations. Environmental, economic, and political problems such as these all carry grave social consequences—increased crime, unemployment, insurrection, hunger, and so forth. Solving these problems requires global cooperation—which a global university can facilitate.

Notwithstanding the foregoing reasons why a global university would help solve many of our most pressing social problems, the establishment of such a university poses certain problems of its own that must be addressed in order that the university can achieve its objectives. First, participant nations would need to overcome a myriad of administrative and political impediments. All nations would need to agree on which problems demand the university's attention and resources, which areas of academic research are worthwhile, as well as agreeing on policies and procedures for making, enforcing, and a- mending these decisions. Query whether a functional global university is politically feasible, given that sovereign nations naturally wish to advance their own agendas.

A second problem inherent in establishing a global university involves the risk that certain intel- lectual and research avenues would become officially sanctioned while others of equal or greater po- tential value would be discouraged, or perhaps even proscribed. A telling example of the inherent dan- ger of setting and enforcing official research priorities involves the Soviet government's attempts dur- ing the 1920s to not only control the direction and the goals of its scientists' research but also to dis- tort the outcome of that research—ostensibly for the greatest good of the greatest number of people. Not surprisingly, during this time period no significant scientific advances occurred under the auspices of the Soviet government. The Soviet lesson provides an important caveat to administrators of a global university: Significant progress in solving pressing social problems requires an open mind to all sound ideas, approaches, and theories—irrespective of the ideologies of their proponents.

A final problem with a global university is that the world's preeminent intellectual talent might be drawn to the sorts of problems to which the university is charged with solving, while parochial social problem go unsolved. While this is not reason enough not to establish a global university, it neverthe- less is a concern that university administrators and participant nations must be aware of in allocating resources and intellectual talent.

To sum up, given the increasingly global nature of the world's social problems, and the escalat- ing costs of addressing these problems, a global university makes good sense. And, since all nations would have a common interest in seeing this endeavor succeed, my intuition is that participating na- tions would be able to overcome whatever procedural and political obstacles that might stand in the way of success. As long as each nation is careful not to neglect its own unique social problems, and as long as the university's administrators are careful to remain open-minded about the legitimacy and potential value of various avenues of intellectual inquiry and research, a global university might go a long way toward solving many of the world's pressing social problems.

Issue 13　Government's duty to preserve **lesser-known languages**

The speaker asserts that governments of countries where lesser-known languages are spoken should intervene to prevent these languages from becoming extinct. I agree insofar as a country's in- digenous and distinct languages should not be abandoned and forgotten altogether. At some point, however, I think cultural identity should yield to the more practical considerations of day-to-day life in a global society.

On the one hand, the indigenous language of any geographical region is part-and-parcel of the cultural heritage of the region's natives. In my observation, we humans have a basic psychological need for individual identity, which we define by way of our membership in distinct cultural groups. A culture defines itself in various ways—by its unique traditions, rituals, mores, attitudes, and beliefs, but especially language. Therefore, when a people's language becomes extinct the result is a dimin- ished sense of pride, dignity, and self-worth.

One need look no further than continental Europe to observe how people cling tenaciously to their distinct languages, despite the fact that there is no practical need for them anymore. And on the other side of the Atlantic Ocean, the French Canadians stubbornly insist on French as their official language, for the sole purpose of preserving their distinct cultural heritage. Even where no distinct language exists, people will invent one to gain a sense of cultural identity, as the emergence of the distinct Ebonic cant among today's African Americans aptly illustrates. In short, people resist language assimilation because of a basic human need to be part of a distinct cultural group.

Another important reason to prevent the extinction of a language is to preserve the distinct ideas that only that particular language can convey. Certain Native American and Oriental languages, for instance, contain words symbolizing spiritual and other abstract concepts that only these cultures embrace. Thus, in some cases to lose a language would be to abandon cherished beliefs and ideas that can be conveyed only through language.

On the other hand, in today's high-tech world of satellite communications, global mobility, and especially the Internet, language barriers serve primarily to impede cross-cultural communication, which in turn impedes international commerce and trade. Moreover, language barriers naturally breed misunderstanding, a certain distrust and, as a result, discord and even war among nations. Moreover, in my view the extinction of all but a few major languages is inexorable—as supported by the fact that the Internet has adopted English as its official language. Thus, by intervening to preserve a dying language a government might be deploying its resources to fight a losing battle, rather than to combat more pressing social problems—such as hunger, homelessness, disease, and ignorance—that plague nearly every society today.

In sum, preserving indigenous languages is, admittedly, a worthy goal; maintaining its own distinct language affords a people a sense of pride, dignity, and self-worth. Moreover, by preserving languages we honor a people's heritage, enhance our understanding of history, and preserve certain ideas that only some languages properly convey. Nevertheless, the economic and political drawbacks of language barriers outweigh the benefits of preserving a dying language. In the final analysis, government should devote its time and resources elsewhere, and leave it to the people themselves to take whatever steps are needed to preserve their own distinct languages.

Issue 16 Do **luxuries** prevent our becoming **strong and independent**?

Do modern luxuries serve to undermine our true strength and independence as individuals? The speaker believes so, and I tend to agree. Consider the automobile, for example. Most people consider the automobile a necessity rather than a luxury; yet it is for this very reason that the automobile so aptly supports the speaker's point. To the extent that we depend on cars as crutches, they prevent us from becoming truly independent and strong in character as individuals.

Consider first the effect of the automobile on our independence as individuals. In some respects the automobile serves to enhance such independence. For example, cars make it possible for people in isolated and depressed areas without public transportation to become more independent by pursing gainful employment outside their communities. And teenagers discover that owning a car, or even borrowing one on occasion, affords them a needed sense of independence from their parents.

However, cars have diminished our independence in a number of more significant respects. We've grown dependent on our cars for commuting to work. We rely on them like crutches for short trips to the corner store, and for carting our children to and from school. Moreover, the car has become a means not only to our assorted physical destinations but also to the attainment of our socioeconomic goals, insofar as the automobile has become a symbol of status. In fact, in my observation many, if not most, working professionals willingly undermine their financial security for the sake of being seen driving this year's new SW or luxury sedan. In short, we've become slaves to the automobile.

Consider next the overall impact of the automobile on our strength as individuals, by which I mean strength of character, or mettle. I would be hard pressed to list one way in which the automobile enhances one's strength of character. Driving a powerful SUV might afford a person a feeling and appearance of strength, or machismo. But this feeling has nothing to do with a person's true character.

In contrast, there is a certain strength of character that comes with eschewing modern conveniences such as cars, and with the knowledge that one is contributing to a cleaner and quieter environment, a safer neighborhood, and arguably a more genteel society. Also, alternative modes of transportation such as bicycling and walking are forms of exercise that require and promote the virtue of self-discipline. Finally, in my observation people who have forsaken the automobile spend more time at home, where they are more inclined to prepare and even grow their own food, and to spend more time with their families. The former enhances one's independence; the latter enhances the integrity of one's values and the strength of one's family.

To sum up, the automobile helps illustrate that when a luxury becomes a necessity it can sap our independence and strength as individuals. Perhaps our society is better off, on balance, with such "luxuries"; after all, the automobile industry has created countless jobs, raised our standard of living, and made the world more interesting. However, by becoming slaves to the automobile we trade off a certain independence and inner strength.

Issue 25　Does it require **effort and courage** to make things simple?

Whether making things simple requires greater effort and courage than making them bigger and more complex depends on the sort of effort and courage. Indisputably, the many complex technological marvels that are part-and-parcel of our lives today are the result of the extraordinary cumulative efforts of our engineers, entrepreneurs, and others. And, such achievements always call for the courage to risk failing in a large way. Yet, humans seem naturally driven to make things bigger and more complex; thus, refraining from doing so, or reversing this natural process, takes considerable effort and courage of a different sort, as discussed below.

The statement brings immediately to mind the ever-growing and increasingly complex digital world. Today's high-tech firms seem compelled to boldly go to whatever effort is required to devise increasingly complex products, for the ostensible purpose of staying ahead of their competitors. Yet, the sort of effort and courage to which the statement refers is a different one—bred of vision, imagination, and a willingness to forego near-term profits for the prospect of making lasting contributions. Surely, a number of entrepreneurs and engineers today are mustering that courage, and are making the effort to create far simpler, yet more elegant, technologies and applications, which will truly make our lives simpler—in sharp contrast to what computer technology has delivered to us so far.

Lending even more credence to the statement is the so-called "big government" phenomenon. Human societies have a natural tendency to create unwieldy bureaucracies, a fitting example of which is the U.S. tax-law system. The Internal Revenue Code and its accompanying Treasury Regulations have grown so voluminous and complex that many certified accountants and tax attorneys admit that they cannot begin to understand it all. Admittedly, this system has grown only through considerable effort on the part of all three branches of the federal government, not to mention the efforts of many special-interest groups. Yet, therein lies the statement's credibility. It requires great effort and courage on the part of a legislator to risk alienating special interest groups, thereby risking reelection prospects, by standing on principle for a simpler tax system that is less costly to administer and better serves the interests of most taxpayers.

Adding further credibility to the statement is the tendency of most people to complicate their personal lives—a tendency that seems especially strong in today's age of technology and consumerism. The greater our mobility, the greater our number of destinations each day; the more time-saving gadgets we use, the more activities we try to pack into our day; and with readier access to information we try to assimilate more of it each day. I am hard-pressed to think of one person who has ever exclaimed to me how much effort and courage it has taken to complicate his or her life in these respects. In contrast, a certain self-restraint and courage of conviction are both required to eschew modern conveniences, to simplify one's daily schedule, and to establish and adhere to a simple plan for the use of one's time and money.

In sum, whether we are building computer networks, government agencies, or personal lifestyles, great effort and courage are required to make things simple, or to keep them that way. Moreover, because humans naturally tend to make things big and complex, it arguably requires more effort and courage to move in the opposite direction. In the final analysis, making things simple—or keeping them that way—takes a brand of effort born of reflection and restraint rather than sheer exertion, and a courageous character and conviction rather than unbridled ambition.

Issue 28 Should students learn concepts before they **memorize facts**?

The speaker makes a threshold claim that students who learn only facts learn very little, then concludes that students should always learn about concepts, ideas, and trends before they memorize facts. While I wholeheartedly agree with the threshold claim, the conclusion unfairly generalizes about the learning process. In fact, following the speaker's advice would actually impede the learning of concepts and ideas, as well as impeding the development of insightful and useful new ones.

Turning first to the speaker's threshold claim, I strongly agree that if we learn only facts we learn very little. Consider the task of memorizing the periodic table of elements, which any student can memorize without any knowledge of chemistry, or that the table relates to chemistry. Rote memorization of the table amounts to a bit of mental exercise—an opportunity to practice memorization techniques and perhaps learn some new ones. Otherwise, the student has learned very little about chemical elements, or about anything for that matter.

As for the speaker's ultimate claim, I concede that postponing the memorization of facts until after one learns ideas and concepts holds certain advantages. With a conceptual framework already in place, a student is better able to understand the meaning of a fact and to appreciate its significance. As a result, the student is more likely to memorize the fact to begin with, and less likely to forget it as time passes. Moreover, in my observation students whose first goal is to memorize facts tend to stop there—for whatever reason. It seems that by focusing on facts first students risk equating the learning process with the assimilation of trivia; in turn, students risk learning nothing of much use in solving real-world problems.

Conceding that students must learn ideas and concepts, as well as facts relating to them, in order to learn anything meaningful, I nevertheless disagree that the former should always precede the latter—for three reasons. In the first place, I see no reason why memorizing a fact cannot precede learning about its meaning and significance—as long as the student does not stop at rote memorization. Consider once again our hypothetical chemistry student. The speaker might advise this student to first learn about the historical trends leading to the discovery of the elements, or to learn about the concepts of altering chemical compounds to achieve certain reactions—before studying the periodic table. Having no familiarity with the basic vocabulary of chemistry, which includes the information in the periodic table, this student would come away from the first two lessons bewildered and confused in other words, having learned little.

In the second place, the speaker misunderstands the process by which we learn ideas and concepts, and by which we develop new ones. Consider, for example, how economics students learn about the relationship between supply and demand, and the resulting concept of market equilibrium, and of surplus and shortage. Learning about the dynamics of supply and demand involves: (1) entertaining a theory, and perhaps even formulating a new one; (2) testing hypothetical scenarios against the theory; and (3) examining real-world facts for the purpose of confirming, refuting, modifying, or qualifying the theory. But which step should come first? The speaker would have us follow steps 1 through 3 in that order. Yet, theories, concepts, and ideas rarely materialize out of thin air; they generally emerge from empirical observations—i.e., facts. Thus, the speaker's notion about how we should learn concepts and ideas gets the learning process backward.

In the third place, strict adherence to the speaker's advice would surely lead to ill-conceived ideas, concepts, and theories. Why? An idea or concept conjured up without the benefit of data amounts to little more than the conjurer's hopes and desires. Accordingly, conjurers will tend to seek out facts that support their prejudices and opinions, and overlook or avoid facts that refute them. One telling example involves theories about the center of the universe. Understandably, we ego-driven humans would prefer that the universe revolve around us. Early theories presumed so for this reason, and facts that ran contrary to this ego-driven theory were ignored, while observers of these facts were scorned and even vilified. In short, students who strictly follow the speaker's prescription are unlikely to contribute significantly to the advancement of knowledge.

To sum up, in a vacuum facts are meaningless, and only by filling that vacuum with ideas and concepts can students learn, by gaining useful perspectives and insights about facts. Yet, since facts are the very stuff from which ideas, concepts, and trends spring, without some facts students cannot learn much of anything. In the final analysis, then, students should learn facts right along with concepts, ideas, and trends.

Issue 29 Should **public figures** expect to lose their privacy?

This statement is fundamentally correct; public figures should indeed expect to lose their privacy. After all, we are a society of voyeurs wishing to transform our mundane lives; and one way to do so is to live vicariously through the experiences of others whose lives appear more interesting than our own. Moreover, the media recognize this societal foible and exploit it at every opportunity. Nevertheless, a more accurate statement would draw a distinction between political figures and other public figures; the former have even less reason than the latter to expect to be left alone, for the reason that their duty as public servants legitimizes public scrutiny of their private lives.

The chief reason why I generally agree with the statement is that, for better or worse, intense media attention to the lives of public figures raises a presumption in the collective mind of the viewing or reading public that our public figures' lives are far more interesting than our own. This presumption is understandable. After all, I think most people would agree that given the opportunity for even fleeting fame they would embrace it without hesitation. Peering into the private lives of those who have achieved our dreams allows us to live vicariously through those lives.

Another reason why I generally agree with the statement has to do with the forces that motivate the media. For the most part, the media consist of large corporations whose chief objective is to maximize shareholder profits. In pursuit of that objective the media are simply giving the public what they demand—a voyeuristic look into the private lives of public figures. One need look no further than a newsstand, local-television news broadcast, or talk show to find ample evidence that this is so. For better or worse, we love to peer at people on public pedestals, and we love to watch them fall off. The media know this all too well, and exploit our obsession at every opportunity.

Nevertheless, the statement should be qualified in that a political figure has less reason to expect privacy than other public figures. Why? The private affairs of public servants become our business when those affairs adversely affect our servants' ability to serve us effectively, or when our servants betray our trust. For example, several years ago the chancellor of a university located in my city was expelled from office for misusing university funds to renovate his posh personal residence. The scandal became front-page news in the campus newspaper and prompted a useful system-wide reform. Also consider the Clinton sex scandal, which sparked a debate about the powers and duties of legal prosecutors vis-a-vis the chief executive. Also, the court rulings about executive privilege and immunity, and even the impeachment proceedings, all of which resulted from the scandal, might serve as useful legal precedents for the future.

Admittedly, intense public scrutiny of the personal lives of public figures can carry harmful consequences, for the public figure as well as the society. For instance, the Clinton scandal resulted in enormous financial costs to taxpayers, and it harmed many individuals caught up in the legal process. And for more than a year the scandal served chiefly to distract us from our most pressing national and global problems. Yet, until as a society we come to appreciate the potentially harmful effects of our preoccupation with the lives of public figures, they can expect to remain the cynosures of our attention.

Issue 30   The primary goal of **technological advancement**

The speaker contends that technology's primary goal should be to increase our efficiency for the purpose of affording us more leisure time. I concede that technology has enhanced our efficiency as we go about our everyday lives. Productivity software helps us plan and coordinate projects; intranets, the Internet, and satellite technology make us more efficient messengers; and technology even helps us prepare our food and access entertainment more efficiently. Beyond this concession, however, I find the speaker's contention indefensible from both an empirical and a normative standpoint.

The chief reason for my disagreement lies in the empirical proof. with technological advancement comes diminished leisure time. In 1960, the average U.S. family included only one breadwinner, who worked just over 40 hours per week. Since then the average work week has increased steadily to nearly 60 hours today; and in most families there are now two breadwinners. What explains this decline in leisure despite increasing efficiency that new technologies have brought about? I contend that technology itself is the culprit behind the decline. We use the additional free time that technology affords us not for leisure but rather for work. As computer technology enables greater and greater office productivity, it also raises our employers' expectations—or demands—for production. Further technological advances breed still greater efficiency and, in turn, expectations. Our spiraling workload is only exacerbated by the competitive business environment in which nearly all of us work today. Moreover, every technological advance demands our time and attention—in order to learn how to use the new technology. Time devoted to keeping pace with technology depletes time for leisure activities.

I disagree with the speaker for another reason as well: the suggestion that technology's chief goal should be to facilitate leisure is simply wrongheaded. There are far more vital concerns that technology can and should address. Advances in biotechnology can help cure and prevent diseases; advances in medical technology can allow for safer, less invasive diagnosis and treatment; advances in genetics can help prevent birth defects; advances in engineering and chemistry can improve the structural integrity of our buildings, roads, bridges, and vehicles; information technology enables education while communication technology facilitates global participation in the democratic process. In short, health, safety, education, and freedom—and not leisure—are the proper final objectives of technology. Admittedly, advances in these areas sometimes involve improved efficiency; yet efficiency is merely a means to these more important ends.

In sum, I find indefensible the speaker's suggestion that technology's value lies chiefly in the efficiency and resulting leisure time it can afford us. The suggestion runs contrary to the overwhelming evidence that technology diminishes leisure time, and it wrongly places leisure ahead of goals such as health, safety, education, and freedom as technology's ultimate aims.

Issue 38　Does **television** render books obsolete?

The speaker contends that people learn just as much from watching television as by reading books, and therefore that reading books is not as important for learning as it once was. I strongly disagree. I concede that in a few respects television, including video, can be a more efficient and effective means of learning. In most respects, however, these newer media serve as poor substitutes for books when it comes to learning.

Admittedly, television holds certain advantages over books for imparting certain types of knowledge. For the purpose of documenting and conveying temporal, spatial events and experiences, film and video generally provide a more accurate and convincing record than a book or other written account. For example, it is impossible for anyone, no matter how keen an observer and skilled a journalist, to recount in complete and objective detail such events as a Ballanchine ballet, or the scene at the intersection of Florence and Normandy streets during the 1992 Los Angeles riots. Besides, since the world is becoming an increasingly eventful place, with each passing day it becomes a more onerous task for journalists, authors, and book publishers to recount these events, and disseminate them in printed form. Producers of televised broadcasts and videos have an inherent advantage in this respect. Thus, the speaker's claim has some merit when it comes to arts education and to learning about modern and current events.

However, the speaker overlooks several respects in which books are inherently superior to television as a medium for learning. Watching television or a video is no indication that any significant learning is taking place; the comparatively passive nature of these media can render them ineffectual in the learning process. Also, books are far more portable than television sets. Moreover, books do not break, and they do not depend on electricity, batteries, or access to airwaves or cable connections—all of which may or may not be available in a given place. Finally, the effort required to read actively imparts a certain discipline that serves any person well throughout a lifetime of learning.

The speaker also ignores the decided tendency on the part of owners and managers of television media to filter information in order to appeal to the widest viewing audience, and thereby maximize profit. And casting the widest possible net seems to involve focusing on the sensational—that is, an appeal to our emotions and basic instincts rather than our intellect and reasonableness. The end result is that viewers do not receive complete, unfiltered, and balanced information, and therefore cannot rely on television to develop informed and intelligent opinions about important social and political issues.

Another compelling argument against the speaker's claim has to do with how well books and television serve their respective archival functions. Books readily enable readers to review and cross-reference material, while televised broadcasts do not. Even the selective review of videotape is far more trouble than it is worth, especially if a printed resource is also available. Moreover, the speaker's claim carries the implication that all printed works, fiction and non-fiction alike, not transferred to a medium capable of being televised, are less significant as a result. This implication serves to discredit the invaluable contributions of all the philosophers, scientists, poets, and others of the past, upon whose immense shoulders society stands today.

A final argument that books are made no less useful by television has to do with the experience of perusing the stacks in a library, or even a bookstore. Switching television channels, or even scanning a video library, simply cannot duplicate this experience. Why not? Browsing among books allows for serendipity—unexpectedly coming across an interesting and informative book while searching for something else, or for nothing in particular. Moreover, browsing through a library or bookstore is a pleasurable sensory experience for many people—an experience that the speaker would have us forego forever.

In sum, television and video can be more efficient than books as a means of staying abreast of current affairs, and for education in the arts that involve moving imagery. However, books facilitate learning in certain ways that television does not and cannot. In the final analysis, the optimal approach is to use both media side by side-television to keep us informed and to provide moving imagery, along with books to provide perspective and insight on that information and imagery.

Issue 40   Scholars and academic inquiry and research

Should academic scholars and researchers be free to pursue whatever avenues of inquiry and research interest them, no matter how unusual or idiosyncratic, as the speaker asserts? Or should they strive instead to focus on those areas that are most likely to benefit society? I strongly agree with the speaker, for three reasons.

First of all, who is to decide which areas of academic inquiry are worthwhile? Scholars cannot be left to decide. Given a choice they will pursue their own idiosyncratic areas of interest, and it is highly unlikely that all scholars could reach a fully informed consensus as to what research areas would be most worthwhile. Nor can these decisions be left to regulators and legislators, who would bring to bear their own quirky notions about what would be worthwhile, and whose susceptibility to influence renders them untrustworthy in any event.

Secondly, by human nature we are motivated to pursue those activities in which we excel. To compel scholars to focus only on certain areas would be to force many to waste their true talents. For example, imagine relegating today's preeminent astrophysicist Stephen Hawking to research the effectiveness of affirmative-action legislation in reducing workplace discrimination. Admittedly, this example borders on hyperbole. Yet the aggregate effect of realistic cases would be to waste the intellectual talents of our world's scholars and researchers. Moreover, lacking genuine interest or motivation, a scholar would be unlikely to contribute meaningfully to his or her "assigned" field of study.

Thirdly, it is "idiosyncratic" and "unusual" avenues of inquiry that lead to the greatest contributions to society. Avenues of intellectual and scientific inquiry that break no new ground amount to wasted time, talent, and other resources. History is laden with unusual claims by scholars and researchers that turned out stunningly significant—that the sun lies at the center of our universe, that time and space are relative concepts, that matter consists of discrete particles, that humans evolved from other life-forms, to name a few. One current area of unusual research is terraforming—creating biological life and a habitable atmosphere where none existed before. This unusual research area does not immediately address society's pressing social problems. Yet, in the longer term, it might be necessary to colonize other planets in order to ensure the survival of the human race; and after all, what could be a more significant contribution to society than preventing its extinction?

Those who would oppose the speaker's assertion might point out that public universities should not allow their faculty to indulge their personal intellectual fantasies at taxpayer expense. Yet as long as our universities maintain strict procedures for peer review, pure quackery cannot persist for very long. Other detractors might argue that in certain academic areas, particularly the arts and humanities, research and intellectually inquiry amount to little more than a personal quest for happiness or pleasure. This specious argument overlooks the societal benefits afforded by appreciating and cultivating the arts. And, earnest study in the humanities affords us wisdom to know what is best for society, and helps us understand and approach societal problems more critically, creatively, and effectively. Thus, despite the lack of a tangible nexus between certain areas of intellectual inquiry and societal benefit, the nexus is there nonetheless.

In sum, I agree that we should allow academic scholars nearly unfettered freedom of intellectual inquiry and research—within reasonable limits as determined by peer review. Engaging one's individual talents in one's particular area of fascination is most likely to yield advances, discoveries, and innovations that serve to make the world a better and more interesting place in which to live.

Issue 43 Ethical and moral standards and successful leadership

Whether successful leadership requires that a leader follow high ethical and moral standards is a complex issue—one that is fraught with the problems of defining ethics, morality, and successful leadership in the first place. In addressing the issue it is helpful to consider in turn three distinct forms of leadership: business, political, and social-spiritual.

In the business realm, successful leadership is generally defined as that which achieves the goal of profit maximization for a firm's shareholders or other owners. Moreover, the prevailing view in Western corporate culture is that by maximizing profits a business leader fulfills his or her highest moral or ethical obligation. Many disagree, however, that these two obligations are the same. Some detractors claim, for example, that business leaders have a duty to do no intentional harm to their customers or to the society in which they operate—for example, by providing safe products and by implementing pollution control measures. Other detractors go further—to impose on business leaders an affirmative obligation to protect consumers, preserve the natural environment, promote education, and otherwise take steps to help alleviate society's problems.

Whether our most successful business leaders are the ones who embrace these additional obligations depends, of course, on one's own definition of business success. In my observation, as business leaders become subject to closer scrutiny by the media and by social activists, business leaders will maximize profits in the long term only by taking reasonable steps to minimize the social and environmental harm their businesses cause. This observation also accords with my personal view of a business leader's ethical and moral obligation.

In the political realm the issue is no less complex. Definitions of successful political leadership and of ethical or moral leadership are tied up in the means a leader uses to wield his or her power and to obtain that power in the first place. One useful approach is to draw a distinction between personal morality and public morality. In my observation, personal morality is unrelated to effective political leadership. Modern politics is replete with examples of what most people would consider personal ethical failings: the marital indiscretions of President Kennedy, for instance. Yet few would agree that these personal moral choices adversely affected his ability to lead.

In contrast, public morality and successful leadership are more closely connected. Consider the many leaders, such as Hitler, whom most people would agree were egregious violators of public morality. Ultimately, such leaders forfeit their leadership as a result of the immoral means by which they obtained or wielded their power. Or consider less egregious examples such as President Nixon, whose contempt for the very legal system that afforded him his leadership led to his forfeiture of it. It seems that in the short term unethical public behavior might serve a political leader's interest in preserving his or her power; yet in the long term such behavior invariably results in that leader's downfall—that is, in failure.

One must also consider a third type of leadership: social-spiritual. Consider notable figures such as Gandhi and Martin Luther King, whom few would disagree were eminently successful in leading others to practice the high ethical and moral standards which they advocated. However, I would be hard-pressed to name one successful social or spiritual leader whose leadership was predicated on the advocacy of patently unethical or immoral behavior. The reason for this is simple: high standards for one's own public morality are prerequisites for successful social-spiritual leadership.

In sum, history informs us that effective political and social-spiritual leadership requires adherence to high standards of public morality. However, when it comes to business leadership the relationship is less clear—successful business leaders must strike a balance between achieving profit maximization and fulfilling their broader obligation to the society, which comes with the burden of such leadership.

Issue 47　Should society place more **emphasis on the intellect**?

The speaker asserts that society should place more emphasis on intellect and cognition. While the speaker might overlook the benefits of nurturing certain emotions and feelings, on balance I agree that it is by way of our heads rather than our hearts that we can best ensure the well-being of our society.

I concede that undue emphasis on cultivating the intellect at the expense of healthy emotions can harm an individual psychologically. Undue suppression of legitimate and healthy desires and emotions can result in depression, dysfunction, and even physical illness. In fact, the intellect can mask such problems, thereby exacerbating them. To the extent they occur on a mass scale these problems become societal ones—lowering our economic productivity, burdening our health-care and social-welfare systems, and so forth. I also concede that by encouraging and cultivating certain positive emotions and feelings—such as compassion and empathy—society clearly stands to benefit.

In many other respects, however, emphasizing emotions and de-emphasizing intellect can carry negative, even dangerous, consequences for any society. Our collective sense of fairness, equity, and justice can easily give way to base instincts like hate, greed, and lust for power and domination. Thus, on balance any society is better off quelling or at least tempering these sorts of instincts, by nurturing reason, judgment, tolerance, fairness, and understanding—all of witch are products of the intellect.

The empirical evidence supporting this position is overwhelming; yet one need look no further than a television set. Most of us have been witness to the current trend in trashy talk shows, which eschew anything approaching intellectual discourse in favor of pandering to our baser urges and instincts—like jealousy, lust, and hate. Episodes often devolve into anti-social, sometimes violent, behavior on the part of participants and observers alike. And any ostensible "lessons learned" from such shows hardly justify the anti-social outbursts that the producers and audiences of these shows hope for.

The dangers of a de-emphasis on intellect are all too evident in contemporary America. The incidence of hate crimes is increasing at a startling rate; gang warfare is at an all-time high; the level of distrust between African Americans and white America seems to be growing. Moreover, taken to an extreme and on a mass scale, appeal to the emotions rather than the intellect has resulted in humanity's most horrific atrocities, like the Jewish holocaust, as well as in nearly every holy war ever waged throughout history. Indeed, suppressing reason is how demagogues and despots gain and hold their power over their citizen-victims. In contrast, reason and better judgment are effective deterrents to despotism, demagoguery, and especially to war.

Those opposed to the speaker's position might argue that stressing cognition and intellect at the expense of emotion and feeling would have a chilling effect on artistic creativity, which would work a harm to the society. However, even in the arts students must learn theories and techniques, which they then apply to their craft—whether it be music performance, dance, or acting. And creative writing requires the cognitive ability to understand how language is used and how to best communicate ideas. Besides, creative ability is itself partly a function of intellect; that is, creative expression is a marriage between cognitive ability and the expression of feelings and emotions.

In sum, emotions and feelings can serve as important catalysts for compassion and for creativity. Yet behaviors that are most harmful to any society are also born of emotions and instincts, which the intellect can serve to override. The inescapable conclusion, then, is that the speaker is fundamentally correct.

Issue 48　Does the study of history overemphasize "**the famous few**"?

The speaker claims that significant historical events and trends are made possible by groups of people rather than individuals, and that the study of history should emphasize the former instead of the latter. I tend to disagree with both aspects of this claim. To begin with, learning about key historical figures inspires us to achieve great things ourselves-far more so than learning about the contributions of groups of people. Moreover, history informs us that it is almost always a key individual who provides the necessary impetus for what otherwise might be a group effort, as discussed below.

Admittedly, at times distinct groups of people have played a more pivotal role than key individuals in important historical developments. For example, history and art appreciation courses that study the Middle Ages tend to focus on the artistic achievements of particular artists such as Fra Angelico, a Benedictine monk of that period. However, Western civilization owes its very existence not to a few famous painters but rather to a group of Benedictine nuns of that period. Just prior to and during the decline of the Roman Empire, many women fled to join Benedictine monasteries, bringing with them substantial dowries which they used to acquire artifacts, art works, and manuscripts. As a result, their monasteries became centers for the preservation of Western culture and knowledge which would otherwise have been lost forever with the fall of the Roman Empire.

However, equally influential was Johannes Gutenberg, whose invention of the printing press several centuries later rendered Western knowledge and culture accessible to every class of people throughout the known world. Admittedly, Gutenberg was not single-handedly responsible for the outcomes of his invention. Without the support of paper manufacturers, publishers, and distributors, and without a sufficient demand for printed books, Gutenberg would never have become one of "the famous few." However, I think any historian would agree that studying the groups of people who rode the wave of Gutenberg's invention is secondary in understanding history to learning about the root historical cause of that wave. Generally speaking, then, undue attention to the efforts and contributions of various groups tends to obscure the cause-and-effect relationships with which the study of history is chiefly concerned.

Gutenberg is just one example of a historical pattern in which it is individuals who have been ultimately responsible for the most significant developments in human history. Profound scientific inventions and discoveries of the past are nearly all attributable not to forgettable groups of people but to certain key individuals—for example, Copernicus, Newton, Edison, Einstein, Curie, and of course Gutenberg. Moreover, when it comes to seminal sociopolitical events, the speaker's claim finds even less support from the historical record. Admittedly, sweeping social changes and political reforms require the participation of large groups of people. However, I would be hard pressed to identify any watershed sociopolitical event attributable to a leaderless group. History informs us that groups rally only when incited and inspired by key individuals.

The speaker might claim that important long-term sociological trends are often instigated not by key individuals but rather by the masses. I concede that gradual shifts in demography, in cultural traditions and mores, and in societal attitudes and values can carry just as significant an historical impact as the words and deeds of "the famous few" Yet, it seems that key individuals almost invariably provide the initial spark for those trends. For instance, prevailing attitudes about sexual morality stem from the ideas of key religious leaders; and a culture's prevailing values concerning human life are often rooted in the policies and prejudices of political leaders. The speaker might also point out that history's greatest architectural and engineering feats—such as the Taj Mahal and the Great Wall—came about only through the efforts of large groups of workers. Again, however, it was the famous few— monarchs in these cases—whose whims and egos were the driving force behind these accomplishments.

To sum up, with few historical exceptions, history is shaped by key individuals, not by nameless, faceless groups. It is the famous few that provide visions of the future, visions that groups then bring to fruition. Perhaps the speaker's claim will have more merit at the close of the next millennium—since politics and science are being conducted increasingly by consortiums and committees. Yet, today it behooves us to continue drawing inspiration from "the famous few," and to continue understanding history chiefly in terms of their influence.

Issue 50   Should college faculty also work **outside the academic world**?

Whether college faculty should also work outside academia, in professional work related to their academic fields, depends primarily on the specific academic area. With respect to fields in which outside work is appropriate, I strongly agree with the statement; students and faculty all stand to gain in a variety of respects when a professor complements academic duties with real-world experience.

As a threshold matter, the statement requires qualification in two respects. First, in certain academic areas there is no profession to speak of outside academia. This is especially true in the humanities; after all, what work outside academia is there for professors of literature or philosophy? Secondly, the statement fails to consider that in certain other academic areas a professor's academic duties typically involve practical work of the sort that occurs outside academia. This is especially true in the fine and performing arts, where faculty actively engage in the craft by demonstrating techniques and styles for their students.

Aside from these two qualifications, I strongly agree that it is worthwhile for college faculty to work outside academia in professional positions related to their field. There are three clear benefits of doing so. First, in my experience as a student, faculty who are actively engaged in their fields come to class with fresh insights and a contagious excitement about the subject at hand. Moreover, they bring to their students practical, real-world examples of the principles and theories discussed in textbooks, thereby sparking interest, and even motivating some students to pursue the field as a career.

Secondly, by keeping abreast with the changing demands of work as a professional, professors can help students who are serious about pursuing a career in that field to make more informed career decisions. The professor with field experience is better able to impart useful, up-to-date information about what work in the field entails, and even about the current job market. After all, college career-planning staff are neither equipped nor sufficiently experienced to provide such specific advice to students.

A third benefit has to do with faculty research and publication in their areas of specialty. Experience in the field can help a professor ferret out cutting-edge and controversial issues—which might be appropriate subjects for research and publication. Moreover, practical experience can boost a professor's credibility as an expert in the field. For example, each year a certain sociology professor at my college combined teaching with undercover work investigating various cults. Not only did the students benefit from the many interesting stories this professor had to tell about his experiences, the professor's publications about cults catapulted him to international prominence as an expert on the subject, and justifiably so.

In sum, aside from certain academic areas in which outside work is either unavailable or unnecessary, students and faculty alike stand everything to gain when faculty enrich their careers by interspersing field work with academic work.

Issue 92　Recognizing the limits of our knowledge

Does recognizing the limits of our knowledge and understanding serve us equally well as acquiring new facts and information, as the speaker asserts? While our everyday experience might lend credence to this assertion, further reflection reveals its fundamental inconsistency with our Western view of how we acquire knowledge. Nevertheless, a careful and thoughtful definition of knowledge can serve to reconcile the two.

On the one hand, the speaker's assertion accords with the everyday experience of working professionals. For example, the sort of "book" knowledge that medical, law, and business students acquire, no matter how extensive, is of little use unless these students also learn to accept the uncertainties and risks inherent in professional practice and in the business world. Any successful doctor, lawyer, or entrepreneur would undoubtedly agree that new precedents and challenges in their fields compel them to acknowledge the limitations of their knowledge, and that learning to accommodate these limitations is just as important in their professional success as knowledge itself.

Moreover, the additional knowledge we gain by collecting more information often diminishes— sometimes to the point where marginal gains turn to marginal losses. Consider, for instance, the collection of financial-investment information. No amount of knowledge can eliminate the uncertainty and risk inherent in financial investing. Also, information overload can result in confusion, which in turn can diminish one's ability to assimilate information and apply it usefully. Thus, by recognizing the limits of their knowledge, and by accounting for those limits when making decisions, investment advisers can more effectively serve their clients.

On the other hand, the speaker's assertion seems self-contradictory, for how can we know the limits of our knowledge until we've thoroughly tested those limits through exhaustive empirical observation—that is, by acquiring facts and information. For example, it would be tempting to concede that we can never understand the basic forces that govern all matter in the universe. Yet due to increasingly precise and extensive fact-finding efforts of scientists, we might now be within striking distance of understanding the key laws by which all physical matter behaves. Put another way, the speaker's assertion flies in the face of the scientific method, whose fundamental tenet is that we humans can truly know only that which we observe. Thus Francis Bacon, who first formulated the method, might assert that the speaker is fundamentally incorrect.

How can we reconcile our experience in everyday endeavors with the basic assumption underlying the scientific method? Perhaps the answer lies in a distinction between two types of knowledge—one that amounts to a mere collection of observations (i.e., facts and information), the other that is deeper and includes a realization of principles and truths underlying those observations. At this deeper level "knowledge" equals "understanding": how we interpret, make sense of, and find meaning in the information we collect by way of observation.

In the final analysis, evaluating the speaker's assertion requires that we define "knowledge" which in turn requires that we address complex epistemological issues best left to philosophers and theologians. Yet perhaps this is the speaker's point: that we can never truly know either ourselves or the world, and that by recognizing this limitation we set ourselves free to accomplish what no amount of mere information could ever permit.

Issue 93　The concept of individual responsibility

I fundamentally agree with the speaker's first contention, for unless we embrace the concept of "individual responsibility" our notions of moral accountability and human equality, both crucial to the survival of any democratic society, will whither. However, I strongly disagree with the second contention—that our individual actions are determined largely by external forces. Although this claim is not entirely without support, it runs contrary to common sense and everyday human experience.

The primary reason that individual responsibility is a necessary fiction is that a society where individuals are not held accountable for their actions and choices is a lawless one, devoid of any order whatsoever. Admittedly, under some circumstances a society of laws should carve out exceptions to the rule of individual responsibility—for example, for the hopeless psychotic who has no control over his or her thoughts or actions. Yet to extend forgiveness much further would be to endanger the social order upon which any civil and democratic society depends.

A correlative argument for individual responsibility involves the fact that lawless, or anarchist, states give way to despotic rule by strong individuals who seize power. History informs us that monarchs and dictators often justify their authority by claiming that they are preordained to assume it—and that as a result they are not morally responsible for their oppressive actions. Thus, any person abhorring despotism must embrace the concept of individual responsibility.

As for the speaker's second claim, it flies in the face of our everyday experiences in making choices and decisions. Although people often claim that life's circumstances have "forced" them to take certain actions, we all have an infinite number of choices; it's just that many of our choices are unappealing, even self-defeating. Thus, the complete absence of free will would seem to be possible only in the case of severe psychosis, coma, or death.

Admittedly, the speaker's second contention finds support from "strict determinist" philosophers, who maintain that every event, including human actions and choices, is physically necessary, given the laws of nature. Recent advances in molecular biology and genetics lend some credence to this position, by suggesting that these determining physical forces include our own individual genetic makeup. But, the notion of scientific determinism opens the door for genetic engineering, which might threaten equality in socioeconomic opportunity, and even precipitate the development of a "master race." Besides, since neither free will nor determinism has been proven to be the correct position, the former is to be preferred by any humanist and in any democratic society.

In sum, without the notion of individual responsibility a civilized, democratic society would soon devolve into an anarchist. state, vulnerable to despotic rule. Yet, this notion is more than a mere fiction. The idea that our actions spring primarily from our free will accords with common sense and everyday experience. I concede that science might eventually vindicate the speaker and show that our actions are largely determined by forces beyond our conscious control. Until that time, however, I'll trust my intuition that we humans should be, and in fact are, responsible for our own choices and actions.

Issue 94   What is required to become "truly educated"?

I fundamentally agree with the proposition that students must take courses outside their major field of study to become "truly educated." A contrary position would reflect a too-narrow view of higher education and its proper objectives. Nevertheless, I would caution that extending the proposition too far might risk undermining those objectives.

The primary reason why I agree with the proposition is that "true" education amounts to far more than gaining the knowledge and ability to excel in one's major course of study and in one's professional career. True education also facilitates an understanding of oneself, and tolerance and respect for the viewpoints of others. Courses in psychology, sociology, and anthropology all serve these ends. "True" education also provides insight and perspective regarding one's place in society and in the physical and metaphysical worlds. Courses in political science, philosophy, theology, and even sciences such as astronomy and physics can help a student gain this insight and perspective. Finally, no student can be truly educated without having gained an aesthetic appreciation of the world around us—through course work in literature, the fine arts, and the performing arts.

Becoming truly educated also requires sufficient mastery of one academic area to permit a student to contribute meaningfully to society later in life. Yet, mastery of any specific area requires some knowledge about a variety of others. For example, a political-science student can fully understand that field only by understanding the various psychological, sociological, and historical forces that shape political ideology. An anthropologist cannot excel without understanding the social and political events that shape cultures, and without some knowledge of chemistry and geology for performing field work. Even computer engineering is intrinsically tied to other fields, even non-technical ones such as business, communications, and media.

Nevertheless, the call for a broad educational experience as the path to becoming truly educated comes with one important caveat. A student who merely dabbles in a hodge-podge of academic offerings, without special emphasis on any one, becomes a dilettante—lacking enough knowledge or experience in any single area to come away with anything valuable to offer. Thus, in the pursuit of true education students must be careful not to overextend themselves—or risk defeating an important objective of education.

In the final analysis, to become truly educated one must strike a proper balance in one's educational pursuits. Certainly, students should strive to excel in the specific requirements of their major course of study. However, they should complement those efforts by pursuing course work in a variety of other areas as well. By earnestly pursuing a broad education one gains the capacity not only to succeed in a career, but also to find purpose and meaning in that career as well as to understand and appreciate the world and its peoples. To gain these capacities is to become "truly educated."

Issue 95   Teamwork as the key to productivity

The speaker asserts that because teamwork requires cooperative effort, people are more motivated and therefore more productive working in teams than working individually as competitors. My view is that this assertion is true only in some cases. If one examines the business world, for example, it becomes clear that which approach is more effective in motivating people and in achieving productivity depends on the specific job.

In some jobs productivity clearly depends on the ability of coworkers to cooperate as members of a team. For businesses involved in the production of products through complex processes, all departments and divisions must work in lock-step fashion toward product roll-out. Cooperative interaction is even essential in jobs performed in relative isolation and in jobs in which technical knowledge or ability, not the ability to work with others, would seem to be most important. For example, scientists, researchers, and even computer programmers must collaborate to establish common goals, coordinate efforts, and meet time lines. Moreover, the kinds of people attracted to these jobs in the first place are likely to be motivated by a sense of common purpose rather than by individual ambition.

In other types of jobs individual competition, tenacity, and ambition are the keys to productivity. For example, a commissioned salesperson's compensation, and sometimes tenure and potential for promotion as well, is based on comparative sales performance of coworkers. Working as competitors a firm's individual salespeople maximize productivity—in terms of profit—both for themselves and for their firm. Key leadership positions also call, above all, for a certain tenacity and competitive spirit. A firm's founding entrepreneur must maintain this spirit in order for the firm to survive, let alone to maximize productivity. Moreover, in my observation the kinds of people inclined toward entrepreneurship and sales in the first place are those who are competitive by nature, not those who are motivated primarily by a sense of common purpose.

On balance, however, my view is that cooperation is more crucial for an organization's long-term productivity than individual competition. Even in jobs where individual competitiveness is part-and-parcel of the job, the importance of cooperation should not be underestimated. Competition among sales people can quickly grow into jealousy, back-stabbing, and unethical behavior—all of which are counterproductive. And even the most successful entrepreneurs would no doubt admit that without the cooperative efforts of their subordinates, partners, and colleagues, their personal visions would never become reality.

In sum, individual competitiveness and ambition are essential motivating forces for certain types of jobs, while in other jobs it is a common sense of mission that motivates workers to achieve maximum productivity. In the final analysis, however, the overall productivity of almost every organization depends ultimately on the ability of its members to cooperate as a team.

Issue 98　Should colleges emphasize courses in **popular** culture?

The speaker asserts that the curriculum of colleges and universities should emphasize popular culture—music, media, literature, and so forth—rather than literature and art of the past, for the reason that the former is more relevant to students. I strongly disagree. Although courses in popular culture do play a legitimate role in higher education, formal study of the present culture at the expense of studying past cultures can undermine the function of higher education, and ultimately provide a disservice to students and to society.

Admittedly, course work in popular culture is legitimate and valuable for three reasons. First, popular culture is a mirror of society's impulses and values. Thus, any serious student of the social sciences, as well as students of media and communications, should take seriously the literature and art of the present. Secondly, in every age and culture some worthwhile art and literature emerges from the mediocrity. Few would disagree, for example, that the great modern-jazz pioneers such as Charlie Parker and Thelonius Monk, and more recently Lennon and McCartney, and Stevie Wonder, have made just as lasting a contribution to music as some of the great classical musicians of previous centuries. Thirdly, knowledge of popular films, music, and art enables a person to find common ground to relate to other people. This leads to better communication between different subcultures.

Nevertheless, emphasizing the study of popular culture at the expense of studying classical art and literature can carry harmful consequences for students, as well as for society. Without the benefit of historical perspective gained through the earnest study of the art and literature of the past, it is impossible to fully understand, appreciate, and critique literature and art of the present. Moreover, by approaching popular culture without any yardstick for quality it is impossible to distinguish mediocre art from worthwhile art. Only by studying the classics can an individual develop fair standards for judging popular works. Besides, emphasis on the formal study of popular culture is unnecessary. Education in popular culture is readily available outside the classroom—on the Internet, through educational television programming, and through the sorts of everyday conversations and cross-talk that occur at water coolers and in the coffee houses of any college campus.

In sum, while the study of popular literature and art can be worthwhile, it has to be undertaken in conjunction with an even greater effort to learn about the literature and art of the past. In the absence of the latter, our universities will produce a society of people with no cultural perspective, and without any standards for determining what merits our attention and nurtures society.

Issue 104   How does a culture **perpetuate** its prevailing ideas?

The speaker asserts that a culture perpetuates the ideas it favors while discrediting those it fears primarily through formal education. I agree that grade-school, and even highschool, education involves cultural indoctrination. Otherwise, I think the speaker misunderstands the role of higher education and overlooks other means by which a culture achieves these ends.

I agree with the speaker with respect to formal grade-school and even high-school education—which to some extent amount to indoctrination with the values, ideas, and principles of mainstream society. In my observation, young students are not taught to question authority, to take issue with what they are taught, or to think critically for themselves. Yet, this indoctrination is actually desirable to an extent. Sole emphasis on rote learning of facts and figures is entirely appropriate for grade-school children, who have not yet gained the intellectual capacity and real-world experience to move up to higher, more complex levels of thinking. Nevertheless, the degree to which our grade schools and high schools emphasize indoctrination should not be overstated. After all, cultural mores, values, and biases have little to do with education in the natural sciences, mathematics, and specific language skills such as reading and writing.

Although the speaker's assertion has some merit when it comes to the education of young people, I find it erroneous when it comes to higher education. The mission of our colleges and universities is to afford students cultural perspective and a capacity for understanding opposing viewpoints, and to encourage and nurture the skills of critical analysis and skepticism—not to indoctrinate students with certain ideas while quashing others. Admittedly, colleges and universities are bureaucracies and therefore not immune to political influence over what is taught and what is not. Thus, to some extent a college's curriculum is vulnerable to wealthy and otherwise influential benefactors, trustees, and government agencies—who by advancing the prevailing cultural agenda serve to diminish a college's effectiveness in carrying out its true mission. Yet, my intuition is that such influences are minor ones, especially in public university systems.

The speaker's assertion is also problematic in that it ignores two significant other means by which our culture perpetuates ideas it favors and discredits ideas it fears. One such means is our system of laws, by which legislators and jurists formulate and then impose so-called "public policy." Legislation and judicial decisions carry the weight of law and the threat of punishment for those who deviate from that law. As a result, they are highly effective means of forcing on us official notions of what is good for society and for quashing ideas that are deemed threatening to the social fabric, and to the safety and security of the government and the governed. A second such means is the mainstream media. By mirroring the culture's prevailing ideas and values, broadcast and print media serve to perpetuate them. It is important to distinguish here between mainstream media—such as broadcast television—and alternative media such as documentary films and non-commercial Web sites, whose typical aims are to call into question the status quo, expose the hypocrisy and unfair bias behind mainstream ideas, and bring to light ideas that the powers-that-be most fear. Yet, the influence of alternative media pales in comparison to that of mainstream media.

In sum, the speaker's assertion is not without merit when it comes to the role of grade schools and high schools. However, the speaker over-generalizes about what students are taught—especially at colleges and universities. Moreover, the speaker's assertion ignores other effective ways in which mainstream culture perpetuates its agenda.

Issue 108   The benefits of televising **government proceedings**

I strongly agree that the more government proceedings—debates, meeting, and so forth—that are televised, the more society will benefit overall. Nevertheless, undue emphasis on this means of informing a constituency has the potential for harm—which any society must take care not to allow.

Access to government proceedings via television carries several significant benefits. The main benefit lies in two useful archival functions of videotaped proceedings. First, videotapes are valuable supplements to conventional means of record keeping. Although written transcripts and audiotapes might provide an accurate record of what is said, only videotapes can convey the body language and other visual clues that help us understand what people say, whether they are being disingenuous, sarcastic, or sincere. Secondly, videotape archives provide a useful catalogue for documentary journalists.

Televised proceedings also provide three other useful functions. First, for shut-ins and people who live in remote regions, it might be impracticable, or even impossible, to view government proceedings in person. Secondly, with satellite television systems it is possible to witness the governments of other cities, states, and even nations at work. This sort of exposure provides the viewer a valuable sense of perspective, an appreciation for other forms of government, and so forth. Thirdly, in high schools and universities, television proceedings can be useful curriculum supplements for students of government, public policy, law, and even public speaking.

Nevertheless, televising more and more government proceedings carries certain risks that should not be ignored. Watching televised government proceedings is inherently a rather passive experience. The viewer cannot voice his or her opinions, objections, or otherwise contribute to what is being viewed. Watching televised proceedings as a substitute for active participation in the political process can, on a mass scale, undermine the democratic process by way of its chilling effect on participation. Undue emphasis on telegovernment poses the risk that government proceedings will become mere displays, or shows, for the public, intended as public relations ploys and so-called "photo opportunities," while the true business of government is moved behind closed doors.

In sum, readier access to the day-to-day business of a government can only serve to inform and educate. Although undue reliance on televised proceedings for information can quell active involvement and serve as a censor for people being televised, I think these are risks worth taking in the interest of disclosure.

Issue 109   Ads portraying people we want to "**be like**"

The speaker asserts that the many ads that make consumers want to "be like" the person portrayed in the ad are effective not only in selling products but also in helping consumers feel better about themselves. This assertion actually consists of two claims: that this advertising technique is used effectively in selling many products, and that consumers who succumb to this technique actually feel better about themselves as a result. While I agree with the first claim, I strongly disagree with the second one.

Turning first to the statement's threshold claim, do many ads actually use this technique to sell products in the first place? Consider ads like the wildly popular Budweiser commercial featuring talking frogs. There's nothing in that ad to emulate; its purpose is merely to call attention to itself. Notwithstanding this type of ad, in my observation the majority of ads provide some sort of model that most consumers in the target market would want to emulate, or "be like." While some ads actually portray people who are the opposite of what the viewer would want to "be like," these ads invariably convey the explicit message that to avoid being like the person in the ad the consumer must buy the advertised product. As for whether the many, many ads portraying models are effective in selling products, I am not privy to the sort of statistical information required to answer this question with complete certainty. However, my intuition is that this technique does help sell products; otherwise, advertisers would not use it so persistently.

Turning next to the statement's ultimate claim that these ads are effective because they help people who buy the advertised products feel better about themselves, I find this claim to be specious. Consumers lured by the hope of "being like" the person in an ad might experience some initial measure of satisfaction in the form of an ego boost. We have all experienced a certain optimism immediately after acquiring something we've wanted—a good feeling that we're one step closer to becoming who we want to be. However, in my experience this sense of optimism is ephemeral, invariably giving way to disappointment that the purchase did not live up to its implicit promise.

One informative example of this false hope involves the dizzying array of diet aids, skin creams, and fitness machines available today. The people in ads for these products are youthful, fit, and attractive—what we all want to "be like." And the ads are effective in selling these products; today's health-and-beauty market feeds a multibillion dollar industry. But the end result for the consumer is an unhealthy preoccupation with physical appearance and youth, which often leads to low self-esteem, eating disorders, injuries from over-exercise, and so forth. And these problems are sure signs of consumers who feel worse, not better, about themselves as a result of having relied on the false hope that they will "be like" the model in the ad.

Another informative example involves products that pander to our desire for socioeconomic status. Ads for luxury cars and upscale clothing typically portray people with lucrative careers living in exclusive neighborhoods. Yet, I would wager that no person whose lifestyle actually resembles these portrayals could honestly claim that purchasing certain consumer products contributed one iota to his or her socioeconomic success. The end result for the consumer is envy of others that can afford even more expensive possessions, and ultimately low self-esteem based on feelings of socioeconomic inadequacy.

In sum, while ads portraying people we want to "be like" are undoubtedly effective in selling products, they are equally ineffective in helping consumers feel better about themselves. In fact, the result is a sense of false hope, leading ultimately to disappointment and a sense of failure and inadequacy—in other words, feeling worse about ourselves.

Issue 110　Historians as **storytellers**

Are all historians essentially storytellers, for the reasons that the speaker cites? In asserting that we can never know the past directly, the speaker implies that we truly "know" only what we experience first-hand. Granting this premise, I agree that it is the proper and necessary role of historians to "construct" history by interpreting evidence. Nevertheless, the speaker's characterization of this role as "storytelling" carries certain unfair implications, which should be addressed.

One reason why I agree with the speaker's fundamental claim lies in the distinction between the role of historian and the roles of archivist and journalist. By "archivist" I refer generally to any person whose task is to document and preserve evidence of past events. And by "journalist" I mean any person whose task is to record, by writing, film, or some other media, factual events as they occur—for the purpose of creating evidence of those events. It is not the proper function of either the journalist or the archivist to tell a story. Rather, it is their function to provide evidence to the historian, who then pieces together the evidence to construct history, as the speaker suggests. In other words, unless we grant to the historian a license to "construct" history by interpreting evidence, we relegate the historian to the role of mere archivist or journalist.

Another reason why I agree with the speaker's characterization of the historian's proper function is that our understanding of history is richer and fuller as a result. By granting the historian license to interpret evidence—to "construct" history—we allow for differing viewpoints among historians. Based on the same essential evidence, two historians might disagree about such things as the contributing causes of a certain event, the extent of influence or impact of one event on subsequent events, the reasons and motives for the words and actions of important persons in history, and so forth. The inexorable result of disagreement, debate, and divergent interpretations among historians is a fuller and more incisive understanding of history.

However, we should be careful not to confuse this license to interpret history, which is needed for any historian to contribute meaningfully to our understanding of it, with artistic license. The latter should be reserved for dramatists, novelists, and poets. It is one thing to attempt to explain historical evidence; it is quite another to invent evidence for the sake of creating a more interesting story or to bolster one's own point of view. A recently released biography of Ronald Reagan demonstrates that the line that historians should not cross is a fine one indeed. Reagan's biographer invented a fictional character who provided commentary as a witness to key episodes during Reagan's life. Many critics charge that the biographer overstepped his bounds as historian; the biographer claims, however, that the accounts in the biography were otherwise entirely factual, and that the fictional narrator was merely a literary device to aid the reader in understanding and appreciating the historical Reagan.

In sum, I strongly agree that the historian's proper function is to assemble evidence into plausible constructs of history, and that an element of interpretation and even creativity is properly involved in doing so. And if the speaker wishes to call these constructs "story-telling," that's fine. This does not mean, however, that historians can or should abandon scholarship for the sake of an interesting story.

Issue 115   Monitoring our progress with **the use of logic** and measurement

Do we need careful measurements and logic to determine whether and to what extent we are progressing or regressing? I agree that in certain endeavors quantitative measurements and logical analysis of data are essential for this purpose. However, in other realms objective data provide little guidance for determining progress. My view applies to individuals as well as society as a whole.

As for monitoring individual progress, the extent to which careful measurement and logical analysis of data are required depends on the specific endeavor. In the area of personal finance, objective measurements are critical. We might feel that we are advancing financially when we buy a new car or a better home, or when our salary increases. Yet these signs of personal economic success can be deceptive. Cars depreciate quickly in value, and residential real estate must appreciate steadily to offset ownership expenses. Even a pay raise is no sure sign of personal financial progress; if the raise fails to keep pace with the cost of living then the real salary is actually in decline.

In the area of one's physical well-being, however, quantitative measurement might be useful yet insufficient. Quantitative data such as blood pressure, cholesterol level, and body weight are useful objective indicators of physical health. Yet quantitative measurement and logic can only take us so far when it comes to physical well-being. Levels of physical discomfort and pain, the most reliable indicators of physical well-being, cannot be quantified. And of course our emotional and psychological well-being, which can have a profound impact on our physical health, defy objective measurement altogether.

On a societal level, as on a personal level, the extent to which careful measurement and logic are needed to determine progress depends on the endeavor. In macroeconomics, as in personal finance, objective measurements are critical. For example, a municipality, state, or nation might sense that things are improving economically when its rate of unemployment declines. Yet, if new jobs are in poor-paying positions involving unskilled labor, this apparent advance might actually be a retreat. And, a boom in retail sales might amount to regress if the goods sold are manufactured by foreign firms, who benefit from the boom at the expense of domestic business expansion. Technological progress also requires careful measurement. Advances in computer technology can only be determined by such factors as processing and transfer speeds, numbers of installations and users, amounts of data accessed, and so forth. And, advances in biotechnology are determined by statistical measurements of the effectiveness of new drugs and other treatments, and by demographic statistics regarding the incidence of the ailments that the technology seeks to ameliorate.

In contrast, socio-political progress is less susceptible to objective measurement. For instance, progress in social welfare might be measured by the number of homeless people, incidence of domestic violence, or juvenile crime rate. Yet, would an increase in the number of single mothers on welfare indicate that our society is becoming more compassionate and effective in helping its victims, or would it indicate regress by showing that our private sector and education systems are failing? Moreover, when it comes to our legal system and to politics, progress has little to do with numbers, or even logic. For example, to what extent, if any, would more lenient gun ownership laws indicate progress, considering the competing interests of individual freedom and pubic safety? Do anti-abortion laws indicate a sociological advance or retreat? Or, when a political party gains greater control of a legislature by sweeping a particular election, is this progress or regress?

In sum, although the statement has merit, it unfairly generalizes. In areas such as finance, economics, and computing technology, all of which involve nothing but quantifiable data, nothing but careful measurement and logic suffice to determine the extent of progress. In other areas, such as health care and social welfare, determining progress requires both objective measurement and subjective judgment. Finally, progress in politics and law is an entirely subjective matter—depending on each individual's values, priorities, and interests.

Issue 116　The beneficiaries of **global networks**

I agree that the globalization of economic and communication networks will heighten international influences in all four of the areas listed. However, while those influences will no doubt benefit education and the sciences, the nature of those influences on the arts and on politics will probably be a mixed one—beneficial in some respects yet detrimental in others.

The clearest and most immediate beneficiaries of international influences are students. When students learn more about other cultures, systems of government, religions, and so forth, they advance their knowledge and grow in their understanding of humanity—which is, after all, the final objective of education. Emerging distance-learning technologies, made practicable now by the Internet, will no doubt carry an especially profound international influence on education. Distance learning will permit a class of students located all over the world to video-conference simultaneously with a teacher and with one other, thereby enlivening and enriching educational experiences.

The sciences clearly benefit from international influences as well. After all, principles of physics, chemistry, and mathematics know no political boundaries; thus, a useful insight or discovery can come from a researcher or theorist anywhere in the world. Accordingly, any technology that enhances global communication can only serve to advance scientific knowledge. For example, astronomers can now transmit observational data to other scientists throughout the world the instant they receive that data, so that the entire global community of astronomers can begin interpreting that data together—in a global brain-storming session. The sciences also benefit from multinational economic cooperation. Consider, for instance, the multi-national program to establish a human colony on the Moon. This ambitious project is possible only because participating nations are pooling their economic resources as well as scientific talents.

With respect to the arts, however, the speaker's claim is far less convincing. It might seem that if artists broaden their cultural exposure and real-world experience their art works would become richer and more diverse. However, the logical consequence of increasing international influence on the arts is a homogenous global culture in which art becomes increasingly the same. The end result is not only a chilling effect on artistic creativity, but also a loss of cultural identity, which seems to be an important sociological and psychological need.

The impact of global networking on political relations might turn out to be a mixed one as well. Consider, for instance, the current unification of Europe's various monetary systems. Since Europe's countries are becoming economically interdependent, it would seem that it would be in their best interests to cooperate politically with one another. However, discord over monetary policy might result in member countries withdrawing from the Community, and in a political schism or other falling out. Consider also the burgeoning global communications network. On the one hand, it would seem that instant face-to-face communication between diplomats and world leaders would help avert and quell political and military crises. By the same token, however, global networking renders any nation's security system more vulnerable. This point is aptly illustrated by a recent incident involving a high-ranking Pentagon official who stored top-secret files on his home computer, which was connected to the Internet without any firewall precautions. Incidents such as this one might prompt the world's governments to become more protective of their sovereignty, more insular, and even paranoid.

In sum, growing international influences that result naturally from global communications and economic networks can only serve to facilitate education and to advance scientific knowledge. However, although the same influences no doubt will have an impact on the arts and on international politics, the speaker's claim that those influences will be beneficial is dubious, or at least premature, given that global networking is still in its nascent stages.

Issue 119　Setting research priorities

Should researchers focus on areas that are likely to result in the greatest benefit to the most people, as the speaker suggests? I agree insofar as areas of research certain to result in immediate and significant benefits for society should continue to be a priority. Yet, strictly followed, the speaker's recommendation would have a harmful chilling effect on research and new knowledge. This is particularly true in the physical sciences, as discussed below.

Admittedly, scientific research whose societal benefits are immediate, predictable, and profound should continue to be a high priority. For example, biotechnology research is proven to help cure and prevent diseases; advances in medical technology allow for safer, less invasive diagnosis and treatment; advances in genetics help prevent birth defects; advances in engineering and chemistry improve the structural integrity of our buildings, roads, bridges, and vehicles; information technology enables education; and communication technology facilitates global peace and participation in the democratic process. To demote any of these research areas to a lower priority would be patently foolhardy, considering their proven benefits to so many people. However, this is not to say that research whose benefits are less immediate or clear should be given lower priority. For three reasons, all avenues of scientific research should be afforded equal priority.

First of all, if we strictly follow the speaker's suggestion, who would decide which areas of research are more worthwhile than others? Researchers cannot be left to decide. Given a choice, they will pursue their own special areas of interest, and it is highly unlikely that all researchers could reach a fully informed consensus as to what areas are most likely to help the most people. Nor can these decisions be left to regulators and legislators, who would bring to bear their own quirky notions about what is worthwhile, and whose susceptibility to influence-peddlers renders them untrustworthy in any event.

A telling example of the inherent danger of setting "official" research priorities involves the Soviet government's attempts during the 1920s to not only control the direction and the goals of its scientists' research but also to distort the outcome of that research—ostensibly for the greatest good of the greatest number of people. During the 1920s, the Soviet government quashed certain areas of scientific inquiry, destroyed entire research facilities and libraries, and caused the sudden disappearance of many scientists who were viewed as threats to the state's authority. Not surprisingly, during this time period no significant scientific advances occurred under the auspices of the Soviet government.

Secondly, to compel all researchers to focus only on certain areas would be to force many to waste their true talents. For example, imagine relegating today's preeminent astrophysicist Stephen Hawking to research the effectiveness of behavioral modification techniques in the reform of violent criminals. Admittedly, this example borders on hyperbole. Yet the aggregate effect of realistic cases would be to waste the intellectual talents of our world's researchers. Moreover, lacking genuine interest or motivation a researcher would be unlikely to contribute meaningfully to his or her "assigned" field.

Thirdly, it is difficult to predict which research avenues will ultimately lead to the greatest contributions to society. Research areas whose benefits are certain often break little new ground, and in the long term so-called "cutting-edge" research whose potential benefits are unknown often prove most useful to society. One current example involves terraforming—creating biological life and a habitable atmosphere where none existed before. This unusual research area does not immediately address society's pressing social problems. Yet, in the longer term, it might be necessary to colonize other planets in order to ensure the survival of the human race; and after all, what could be a more significant contribution to society than preventing its extinction?

In sum, when it comes to setting priorities for research, at least in the sciences, the speaker goes too far by implying that research whose benefits are unknown are not worth pursuing. After all, any research worth doing delves into the unknown. In the final analysis, the only objective of research should be to discover truths, whatever they might be—not to implement social policy.

Issue 124　The impact of technology on our **leisure time**

The speaker contends that technological advances that improve our efficiency have ironically resulted in less leisure time, and a pace of life that seems more hurried and frantic than ever. While I agree that leisure time is declining as a result of efficiencies that technology has brought about, whether the irony to which the speaker refers is real or imagined depends on what one considers to be the chief aim of technology.

Few would disagree that technology has enhanced the speed and efficiency with which we travel, prepare our food, plan and coordinate projects, and communicate with one another. And the empirical evidence that as a society we are more pressed for time than ever before is convincing indeed. In 1960, the average U.S. family included only one breadwinner, who worked just over 40 hours per week. Since then the average work week has increased steadily to nearly 60 hours today. In fact, in most families there are now two breadwinners who, for lack of leisure time, must delegate food preparation to fast-food workers and child care to professional day-care facilities. Even single, childless professionals today are so harried that they have no time to seek out romance, and must rely instead on matchmaker services.

What explains the irony—this decline in leisure despite increasing efficiency that new technologies have brought about? I agree that technology itself is the culprit. We use the additional free time that technology affords us not for leisure but rather for work. As computer technology enables greater and greater office productivity it also raises our employers' expectations—or demands—for production. Further technological advances breed still greater efficiency and, in turn, expectations. Our spiraling work load is only exacerbated by the competitive business environment in which nearly all of us work today. Moreover, every technological advance demands our time and attention—in order to learn how to use the new technology. Time devoted to keeping pace with technology depletes time for leisure activities.

Yet, upon further reflection this apparent irony does not seem so ironic after all. The final objectives of technology have little to do with affording us more leisure time. Rather, there are far more vital concerns that technology seeks to address. Advances in biotechnology can help cure and prevent diseases; advances in medical technology can allow for safer, less invasive diagnosis and treatment; advances in genetics can help prevent birth defects; advances in engineering and chemistry can improve the structural integrity of our buildings, roads, bridges, and vehicles; information technology enables education; and communications technology facilitates global participation in the democratic process.

In sum, the claim that the same technology that breeds efficiency also robs us of our leisure is simply wrongheaded. At the end of our hectic day, we have not been robbed at all. Instead, we've ultimately chosen our frantic pace—trading off leisure in pursuit of our health, our safety, our education, and our freedom.

Issue 130   Have we learned how to **raise children** who can **better society**?

I find the speaker's dual claim to be specious on both counts. The claim that society's destiny hinges on how children are socialized, while appealing in some respects, is an over-statement at best. And the claim that we have not yet learned how to raise children who can better society is poorly supported by empirical evidence.

Consider first the speaker's assertion that society's destiny depends on how children are socialized. I concede that unless a child is allowed sufficient opportunities for healthy interaction with peers, that child is likely to grow into an ineffectual, perhaps even an anti-social, adult. To witness healthy socialization in action, one need look no further than the school playground, where children learn to negotiate, cooperate, and assert themselves in a respectful manner, and where they learn about the harmful results of bullying and other anti-social behavior. These lessons help children grow up to be good citizens and effective leaders, as well as tolerant and respectful members of society.

However, socialization is only one factor influencing the extent to which an individual will ultimately contribute to a better society. And in my observation it is not the most important one. Consider certain prominent leaders who have contributed profoundly to a better society. Mahatma Gandhi's contributions sprang primarily from the courage of his inner convictions, in spite of his proper socialization among genteel Indian society and, as a law student, among British society. Martin Luther King's contribution was primarily the result of his strong religious upbringing, which had more to do with parental influence than with socialization. An even more remarkable modern example was

Theodore Roosevelt, whose social and physical development were both stunted by life-threatening physical infirmities during his childhood. In spite of his isolation, odd manner and aloofness throughout his early life, Roosevelt ascended to a social-activist presidency by means of his will to overcome physical infirmities, his voracious appetite for knowledge, and his raw intellect.

Consider next the speaker's claim that we have not yet learned how to raise children who can better society. If we define a "better" society as one characterized by greater tolerance of differing viewpoints and people who are different from ourselves, greater respect for individual rights, and greater cooperation across cultural and national boundaries, then the children of the most recent half-century are creating a better society. The most recent quarter-century has seen an increasing sensitivity in our society toward ensuring public health by policing the food and drug industries and by protecting our natural environment. We're becoming more sensitive to, and respectful of, the rights of women, various ethnic and racial groups, homosexuals, and mentally-and physically-challenged individuals. The reemergence of political third parties with decidedly libertarian ideals demonstrates an increasing concern for individual freedoms. And there is ample evidence of increasing international cooperation. The former Soviet Union and the U.S. have worked collaboratively in space research and exploration since the 1970s; peace-keeping missions are now largely multinational efforts; and nations are now tackling public health problems collaboratively through joint research programs. In short, the speaker's second claim flies in the face of the empirical evidence, as I see it.

In sum, when it comes to whether a child grows up to contribute to a better society, the key determinant is not socialization but rather some other factor—such as a seminal childhood event, parental influence, raw intelligence, or personal conviction. And, while reasonable people with differing political and social viewpoints might disagree about what makes for a "better" society, in my observation our society is steadily evolving into a more civilized, respectful, and tolerant one. In the final analysis, then, I fundamentally disagree with both aspects of the speaker's dual claim.

Issue 140　Do great achievements often lead to the **greatest discontent**?

I strongly agree that great achievements often lead to great discontent. In fact, I would assert more specifically that great individual achievements can cause discontent for the individual achiever or for the society impacted by the achievement, or both. Nevertheless, it is important to acknowledge that whether a great achievement causes great discontent can depend on one's personal perspective, as well as the perspective of time.

With respect to individual achievements, great achievers are by nature ambitious people and therefore tend to be dissatisfied and discontent with their accomplishments—no matter how great. Great athletes are compelled to try to better their record-breaking performances; great artists and musicians typically claim that their greatest work will be their next one With respect to individual achievements, great achievers are by nature ambitious people and therefore tend to be dissatisfied and discontent with their accomplishments—no matter how great. Great athletes are compelled to try to better their record-breaking performances; great artists and musicians typically claim that their greatest work will be their next one—a sign of personal discontent. And many child protégés, especially those who achieve some measure of fame early in life, later suffer psychological discontent for having "peaked" so early. Perhaps the paradigmatic modern example of a great achiever's discontent was Einstein, whose theoretical breakthroughs in physics only raised new theoretical conundrums which Einstein himself recognized and spent the last twenty years of his life struggling unsuccessfully to solve.

Individual achievements can often result in discontent on a societal level. The great achievement of the individual scientists responsible for the success of the Manhattan Project resulted in worldwide anxiety over the threat of nuclear annihilation—a form of discontent with which the world's denizens will forever be forced to cope. Even individual achievements that at first glance would appear to have benefited society turn out to be causes of great discontent. Consider the invention of the automobile, along with the innovations in manufacturing processes and materials that made mass production possible. As a result we have become a society enslaved to our cars, relying on them as crutches not only for transportation but also for affording us a false sense of socioeconomic status. Moreover, the development of assembly-line manufacturing has served to alienate workers from their work, which many psychologists agree causes a great deal of personal discontent.

Turning from individual achievements to societal, including political, achievements, the extent to which great achievements have caused great discontent often depends on one's perspective. Consider, for example, America's spirit of Manifest Destiny during the nineteenth century, or British Imperialism over the span of several centuries. From the perspective of an Imperialist, conquering other lands and peoples might be viewed as an unqualified success. However, from the viewpoint of the indigenous peoples who suffer at the hands of Imperialists, these so-called "achievements" are the source of widespread oppression and misery, and in turn discontent, to which any observant Native American or South African native could attest.

The extent to which great socio-political achievements have caused great discontent also depends on the perspective of time. For example, F.D.R.'s New Deal was and still is considered by many to be one of the greatest social achievements of the twentieth century. However, we are just now beginning to realize that the social-security system that was an integral part of F.D.R.'s social program will soon result in great discontent among those workers currently paying into the system but unlikely to see any benefits after they retire.

To sum up, I agree that great achievements, both individual and socio-political, often result in great discontent. Moreover, great individual achievements can result in discontent for both the individual achiever and the society impacted by the achievement. Nevertheless, in measuring the extent of discontent, we must account for varying personal and political perspectives as well as different time perspectives.

Issue 141　Does **personal economic success** require **conformity**?

Personal economic success might be due either to one's investment strategy or to one's work or career. With respect to the former, non-conformists with enough risk tolerance and patience invariably achieve more success than conformists. With respect to the latter, while non-conformists are more likely to succeed in newer industries where markets and technology are in constant flux, conformists are more likely to succeed in traditional service industries ensconced in systems and regulations.

Regarding the sort of economic success that results from investing one's wealth, the principles of investing dictate that those who seek risky investments in areas that are out of favor with the majority of investors ultimately reap higher returns than those who follow the crowd. It is conformists who invest, along with most other investors, in areas that are currently the most profitable, and popular.

However, popular investments tend to be overpriced, and in the long run their values will come down to reasonable levels. As a result, given enough time conformists tend to reap lower rewards from their investments than nonconformists do.

Turning to the sort of economic success that one achieves by way of one's work, neither conformists nor non-conformists necessarily achieve greater success than the other group. In consumer-driven industries, where innovation, product differentiation, and creativity are crucial to lasting success, non-conformists who take unique approaches tend to recognize emerging trends and to rise above their peers. For example, Ted Turner's departure from the traditional format of the other television networks, and the responsiveness of Amazon's Jeff Bezos to burgeoning Internet commerce, propelled these two non-conformists into leadership positions in their industries. Particularly in technology industries, where there are no conventional practices or ways of thinking to begin with, people who cling to last year's paradigm, or to the status quo in general, are soon left behind by coworkers and competing firms.

However, in traditional service industries—such as finance, accounting, insurance, legal services, and health care—personal economic success comes not to nonconformists but rather to those who can work most effectively within the constraints of established practices, policies and regulations. Of course, a clever idea for structuring a deal, or a creative legal maneuver, might play a role in winning smaller battles along the way. But such tactics are those of conformists who are playing by the same ground rules as their peers; winners are just better at the game.

In conclusion, non-conformists with sufficient risk tolerance and patience are invariably the most successful investors in the long run. When it comes to careers, however, while non-conformists tend to be more successful in technology and consumer-driven industries, traditionalists are the winners in system-driven industries pervaded by policy, regulation, and bureaucracy.

Issue 142 Is society better off when many **people question authority**?

The speaker asserts that when many people question authority society is better off. While I contend that certain forms of disobedience can be harmful to any society, I agree with the speaker otherwise. In fact, I would go further by contending that society's well-being depends on challenges to authority, and that when it comes to political and legal authority, these challenges must come from many people.

Admittedly, when many people question authority some societal harm might result, even if a social cause is worthy. Mass resistance to authority can escalate to violent protest and rioting, during which innocent people are hurt and their property damaged and destroyed. The fallout from the 1992 Los Angeles riots aptly illustrates this point. The "authority" that the rioters sought to challenge was that of the legal justice system, which acquitted police officers in the beating of Rodney King. The means of challenging that authority amounted to flagrant disregard for criminal law on a mass scale—by way of looting, arson, and even deadly assault. This violent challenge to authority resulted in a financially crippled community and, more broadly, a turning back of the clock with respect to racial tensions across America.

While violence is rarely justifiable as a means of questioning authority, peaceful challenges to political and legal authority, by many people, are not only justifiable but actually necessary when it comes to enhancing and even preserving society's well-being. In particular, progress in human rights depends on popular dissension. It is not enough for a charismatic visionary like Gandhi or King to call for change in the name of justice and humanity; they must have the support of many people in order to effect change. Similarly, in a democracy citizens must respect timeless legal doctrines and principles, yet at the same time question the fairness and relevance of current laws. Otherwise, our laws would not evolve to reflect changing societal values. It is not enough for a handful of legislators to challenge the legal status quo; ultimately, it is up to the electorate at large to call for change when change is needed for the well-being of society.

Questioning authority is also essential for advances in the sciences. Passive acceptance of prevailing principles quells innovation, invention, and discovery, all of which clearly benefit any society. In fact, the very notion of scientific progress is predicated on rigorous scientific inquiry—in other words, questioning of authority. History is replete with scientific discoveries that posed challenges to political, religious, and scientific authority. For example, the theories of a sun-centered solar system, of humankind's evolution from other life-forms, and of the relativity of time and space, clearly flew in the face of "authoritative" scientific as well as religious doctrine of their time. Moreover, when it comes to science a successful challenge to authority need not come from a large number of people. The key contributions of a few individuals—like Copernicus, Kepler, Newton, Darwin, Einstein, and Hawking—often suffice.

Similarly, in the arts, people must challenge established styles and forms rather than imitate them; otherwise, no genuinely new art would ever emerge, and society would be worse off. And again, it is not necessary that a large number of people pose such challenges; a few key individuals can have a profound impact. For instance, modern ballet owes much of what is new and exciting to George Ballanchine, who by way of his improvisational techniques posed a successful challenge to established traditions. And modern architecture arguably owes its existence to the founders of Germany's Bauhaus School of Architecture, which challenged certain "authoritative" notions about the proper objective, and resulting design, of public buildings.

To sum up, in general I agree that when many people question authority the well-being of society is enhanced. Indeed, advances in government and law depend on challenges to the status quo by many people. Nevertheless, to ensure a net benefit rather than harm, the means of such challenges must be peaceful ones.

Issue 146   Can a person be committed to an idea yet be **critical of it**?

The speaker claims that people who are the most firmly committed to an idea or policy are the same people who are most critical of that idea or policy. While I find this claim paradoxical on its face, the paradox is explainable, and the explanation is well supported empirically. Nevertheless, the claim is an unfair generalization in that it fails to account for other empirical evidence serving to discredit it.

A threshold problem with the speaker's claim is that its internal logic is questionable. At first impression it would seem that firm commitment to an idea or policy necessarily requires the utmost confidence in it, and yet one cannot have a great deal of confidence in an idea or policy if one recognizes its flaws, drawbacks, or other problems. Thus, commitment and criticism would seem to be mutually exclusive. But are they? One possible explanation for the paradox is that individuals most firmly committed to an idea or policy are often the same people who are most knowledgeable on the subject, and therefore are in the best position to understand and appreciate the problems with the idea or policy.

Lending credence to this explanation for the paradoxical nature of the speaker's claim are the many historical cases of uneasy marriages between commitment to and criticism of the same idea or policy. For example, Edward Teller, the so-called "father of the atom bomb," was firmly committed to America's policy of gaining military superiority over the Japanese and the Germans; yet at the same time he attempted fervently to dissuade the U.S. military from employing his technology for destruction, while becoming the most visible advocate for various peaceful and productive applications of atomic energy. Another example is George Washington, who was quoted as saying that all the world's denizens "should abhor war wherever they may find it "Yet this was the same military general who played a key role in the Revolutionary War between Britain and the States. A third example was Einstein, who while committed to the mathematical soundness of his theories about relativity could not reconcile them with the equally compelling quantum theory that emerged later in Einstein's life. In fact, Einstein spent the last twenty years of his life criticizing his own theories and struggling to determine how to reconcile them with newer theories.

In the face of historical examples supporting the speaker's claim are innumerable influential individuals who were zealously committed to certain ideas and policies but who were not critical of them, at least not outwardly. Could anyone honestly claim, for instance, that Elizabeth Stanton and Susan B. Anthony, who in the late nineteenth century paved the way for the women's rights movement by way of their fervent advocacy, were at the same time highly critical or suspicious of the notion that women deserve equal rights under the law? Also, would it not be absurd to claim that Mahatma Gandhi and Martin Luther King, history's two leading advocates of civil disobedience as a means to social reform, had serious doubts about the ideals to which they were so demonstrably committed? Finally, consider the two ideologues and revolutionaries Lenin and Mussolini. Is it even plausible that their demonstrated commitment to their own Communist and Fascist policies, respectively, belied some deep personal suspicion about the merits of these policies? To my knowledge, no private writing of any of these historical figures lends any support to the claim that these leaders were particularly critical of their own ideas or policies.

To sum up, while at first glance a deep commitment to and incisive criticism of the same idea or policy would seem mutually exclusive, it appears they are not. Thus the speaker's claim has some merit. Nevertheless, for every historical case supporting the speaker's claim are many others serving to refute it. In the final analysis, then, the correctness of the speaker's assertion must be determined on a case-by-case basis.

Issue 147　Must we choose between **tradition and modernization**?

Must we choose between tradition and modernization, as the speaker contends? I agree that in certain cases the two are mutually exclusive. For the most part, however, modernization does not reject tradition; in fact, in many cases the former can and does embrace the latter.

Oftentimes, so-called "modernization" is actually an extension or new iteration of tradition, or a variation on it. This is especially true in language and in law. The modern English language, in spite of its many words that are unique to modern Western culture, is derived from, and builds upon, a variety of linguistic traditions—and ultimately from the ancient Greek and Latin languages. Were we to insist on rejecting traditional in favor of purely modern language, we would have essentially nothing to say. Perhaps an even more striking marriage of modernization and tradition is our system of laws in the U.S., which is deeply rooted in English common-law principles of equity and justice. Our system requires that new, so-called "modern" laws be consistent with, and in fact build upon, those principles.

In other areas modernization departs from tradition in some respects, while embracing it in others. In the visual arts, for example, "modern" designs, forms, and elements are based on certain timeless aesthetic ideals—such as symmetry, balance, and harmony. Modern art that violates these principles might hold ephemeral appeal due to its novelty and brashness, but its appeal lacks staying power. An even better example from the arts is modern rock-and-roll music, which upon first listening might seem to bear no resemblance to classical music traditions. Yet, both genres rely on the same twelve-note scale, the same notions of what harmonies are pleasing to the ear, the same forms, the same rhythmic meters, and even many of the same melodies.

I concede that in certain instances, tradition must yield entirely to the utilitarian needs of modern life. This is true especially when it comes to architectural traditions and the value of historic and archeological artifacts. A building of great historic value might be located in the only place available to a hospital desperately needing additional parking area. An old school that is a prime example of a certain architectural style might be so structurally unsafe that the only practicable way to remedy the problem would be to raze the building to make way for a modern, structurally sound one. And when it comes to bridges whose structural integrity is paramount to public safety, modernization often requires no less than replacement of the bridge altogether. However, in other such cases architecturally appropriate retrofits can solve structural problems without sacrificing history and tradition, and alternative locations for new buildings and bridges can be found in order to preserve tradition associated with our historic structures. Thus, even in architecture, tradition and modernization are not necessarily mutually exclusive options.

To sum up, in no area of human endeavor need modernization supplant, reject, or otherwise exclude tradition. In fact, in our modern structures, architecture and other art, and especially languages and law, tradition is embraced, not shunned.

Issue 150   Will **computer connections** make tourism obsolete?

The speaker asserts that television and computer connectivity will soon render tourism obsolete. I agree that these technologies might eventually serve to reduce travel for certain purposes other than tourism. However, I strongly disagree that tourism will become obsolete, or that it will even decline, as a result.

As for the claim that television will render tourism obsolete, we already have sufficient empirical evidence that this will simply not happen. For nearly a half-century we have been peering through our television sets at other countries and cultures; yet tourism is as popular today as ever. In fact, tourism has been increasing sharply during the last decade, which has seen the advent of television channels catering exclusively to our interest in other cultures and countries. The more reasonable conclusion is that television has actually served to spark our interest in visiting other places.

It is somewhat more tempting to accept the speaker's further claim that computer connectivity will render tourism obsolete. However, the speaker unfairly assumes that the purpose of tourism is simply to obtain information about other people and places. Were this the case, I would entirely agree that the current information explosion spells the demise of tourism. But, tourism is not primarily about gathering information. Instead, it is about sensory experience—seeing and hearing firsthand, even touching and smelling. Could anyone honestly claim that seeing a picture or even an enhanced 3-D movie of the Swiss Alps serves as a suitable substitute for riding a touring motorcycle along narrow roads traversing those mountains? Surely not. The physical world is laden with a host of such delights that we humans are compelled to experience firsthand—as tourists.

Moreover, in my view tourism will continue to thrive for the same reason that people still go out for dinner or to the movies: we all need to "get away" from our familiar routines and surroundings from time to time. Will computer connectivity alter this basic need? Certainly not. In short, tourism is a manifestation of a basic human need for variety and for exploration. This basic need is why humans have come to inhabit every corner of the earth, and will just as surely inhabit other planets of the solar system.

In fact, computer connectivity might actually provide a boon for tourism. The costs of travel and accommodations are likely to decrease due to Internet price competition. Even more significantly, to the extent that the Internet enhances communication among the world's denizens, our level of comfort and trust when it comes to dealing with people from other cultures will only increase. As a result, many people who previously would not have felt safe or secure traveling to strange lands will soon venture abroad with a new sense of confidence.

Admittedly, travel for purposes other than tourism might eventually decline, as the business world becomes increasingly dependent on the Internet. Products that can be reduced to digital "bits and bites" can now be shipped anywhere in the world without any human travel. And the volume of business-related trips will surely decline in the future, as teleconferencing becomes more readily available. To the extent that business travelers "play tourist" during business trips, tourism will decline as a result. Yet it would be absurd to claim that these phenomena alone will render tourism obsolete.

In sum, while business travel might decline as a result of global connectivity, tourism is likely to increase as a result. Global connectivity, especially the Internet, can only pique our curiosity about other peoples, cultures, and places. Tourism helps satisfy that curiosity, as well as satisfying a fundamental human need to experience new things first-hand and to explore the world.

Issue 151　The effects of high-speed **communications media**

Do high-speed means of communication, particularly television and computers, tend to prevent meaningful and thoughtful communication, as the speaker suggests? Although ample empirical evidence suggests so with respect to television, the answer is far less clear when it comes to communication via computers.

Few would argue that since its inception broadcast television has greatly enhanced communication to the masses. The circulation of even the most widely read newspapers pales compared to the number of viewers of popular television news programs. Yet traditional television is a one-way communications medium, affording viewers no opportunity to engage those so-called "talking heads" in dialogue or respond. Of course, there is nothing inherent about television that prevents us from meaningful and thoughtful communication with each other. In fact, in television's early days it was a fairly common occurrence for a family to gather around the television together for their favorite show, then afterward discuss among themselves what they had seen and heard. Yet, over time television has proven itself to serve primarily as a baby-sitter for busy parents, and as an means of escape for those who wish to avoid communicating with the people around them. Moreover, in the pursuit of profit, network executives have determined over time that the most effective uses of the medium are for fast-paced entertainment and advertising—whose messages are neither thoughtful nor meaningful.

Do computers offer greater promise for thoughtful and reflective communication than television? Emphatically, yes. After all, media such as e-mail and the Web are interactive by design. And the opportunity for two-way communication enhances the chances of meaningful and thoughtful communication. Yet their potential begs the question: Do these media in fact serve those ends? It is tempting to hasten that the answer is "yes" with respect to e-mail; after are, we've all heard stories about how e-mail has facilitated reunions of families and old friends, and new long-distance friendships and romances. Moreover, it would seem that two-way written communication requires far more thought and reflection than verbal conversation. Nevertheless, e-mail is often used to avoid face-to-face encounters, and in practice is used as a means of distributing quick memos. Thus, on balance it appears that e-mail serves as an impediment, not an aide, to thoughtful and reflective communication.

With respect to Web-based communication, the myriad of educational sites, interactive and otherwise, is strong evidence that the Web tends to enhance, rather than prevent, meaningful communication. Distance-learning courses made possible by the Web lend further credence to this assertion. Nonetheless, by all accounts it appears that the Web will ultimately devolve into a mass medium for entertainment and for ecommerce, just like traditional television. Meaningful personal interactivity is already yielding to advertising, requests for product information, buy-sell orders, and titillating adult-oriented content.

Thus, on balance these high-speed electronic media do indeed tend to prevent rather than facilitate meaningful and thoughtful communication. In the final analysis, any mass medium carries the potential for uplifting us, enlightening us, and helping us to communicate with and understand one another. However, by all accounts, television has not fulfilled that potential; and whether the Web will serve us any better is ultimately up to us as a society.

Issue 152   The limits of the responsibility of **corporate executives**

Should the only responsibility of a business executive be to maximize business profits, within the bounds of the law? In several respects this position has considerable merit; yet it ignores certain compelling arguments for imposing on businesses additional obligations to the society in which they operate.

On the one hand are two convincing arguments that profit maximization within the bounds of the law should be a business executive's sole responsibility. First, imposing on businesses additional duties to the society in which they operate can, paradoxically, harm that society. Compliance with higher ethical standards than the law requires—in such areas as environmental impact and workplace conditions—adds to business expenses and lowers immediate profits. In turn, lower profits can prevent the socially conscious business from creating more jobs, and from keeping its prices low and the quality of its products and services high. Thus, if businesses go further than their legal duties in serving their communities, the end result might be a net disservice to those communities.

Secondly, by affirming that profit maximization within legal bounds is the most ethical behavior possible for business, we encourage private enterprise, and more individuals enter the marketplace in the quest of profits. The inevitable result of increased competition is lower prices and better products, both of which serve the interests of consumers. Moreover, since maximizing profits enhances the wealth of a company's stakeholders, broad participation in private enterprise raises the wealth of a nation, expands its economy, and raises its overall standard of living and quality of life.

On the other hand are three compelling arguments for holding business executives to certain responsibilities in addition to profit maximization and to compliance with the letter of the law. First, a growing percentage of businesses are related to technology, and laws often lag behind advances in technology. As a result, new technology-based products and services might pose potential harm to consumers even though they conform to current laws. For example, Internet commerce is still largely unregulated because our lawmakers are slow to react to the paradigm shift from brick-and-mortar commerce to e-commerce. As a result, unethical marketing practices, privacy invasion, and violations of intellectual-property rights are going unchecked for lack of regulations that would clearly prohibit them.

Secondly, since a nation's laws do not extend beyond its borders, compliance with those laws does not prevent a business from doing harm elsewhere. Consider, for example, the trend among U.S. businesses in exploiting workers in countries where labor laws are virtually non-existent—in order to avoid the costs of complying with U.S. labor laws. Thirdly, a philosophical argument can be made that every business enters into an implied social contract with the community that permits it to do business, and that this social contract, although not legally enforceable, places a moral duty on the business to refrain from acting in ways that will harm that community.

In sum, I agree with the statement insofar as in seeking to maximize profits a business serves not only itself but also its employees, customers, and the overall economy. Yet, today's rapidly changing business environment and increasing globalization call for certain affirmative obligations beyond the pursuit of profit and mere compliance with enforceable rules and regulations. Moreover, in the final analysis any business is indebted to the society in which it operates for its very existence, and thus has a moral duty, regardless of any legal obligations, to pay that debt.

Issue 153　Should students be skeptical about **what they are taught**?

The speaker contends that students should be skeptical in their studies, and should not accept passively whatever they are taught. In my view, although undue skepticism might be counterproductive for a young child's education, I strongly agree with the speaker otherwise. If we were all to accept on blind faith all that we are taught, our society would never progress or evolve.

Skepticism is perhaps most important in the physical sciences. Passive acceptance of prevailing principles quells innovation, invention, and discovery. In fact, the very notion of scientific progress is predicated on rigorous scientific inquiry—in other words, skepticism. And history is replete with examples of students of science who challenged what they had been taught, thereby paving the way for scientific progress. For example, in challenging the notion that the Earth was in a fixed position at the center of the universe, Copernicus paved the way for the corroborating observations of Galileo a century later, and ultimately for Newton's principles of gravity upon which all modern science is based. The staggering cumulative impact of Copernicus' rejection of what he had been taught is proof enough of the value of skepticism.

The value of skepticism is not limited to the physical sciences, of course. In the fields of sociology and political science, students must think critically about the assumptions underlying the status quo; otherwise, oppression, tyranny, and prejudice go unchecked. Similarly, while students of the law must learn to appreciate timeless legal doctrines and principles, they must continually question the fairness and relevance of current laws. Otherwise, our laws would not evolve to reflect changing societal values and to address new legal issues arising from our ever-evolving technologies.

Even in the arts, students must challenge established styles and forms rather than learn to imitate them; otherwise, no genuinely new art would ever emerge. Bee-bop musicians such as Charlie Parker demonstrated through their wildly innovative harmonies and melodies their skepticism about established rules for harmony and melody. In the area of dance, Ballanchine showed by way of his improvisational techniques his skepticism about established rules for choreography. And Germany's Bauhaus School of Architecture, to which modern architecture owes its existence, was rooted in skepticism about the proper objective, and resulting design, of public buildings.

Admittedly, undue skepticism might be counterproductive in educating young children. I am not an expert in developmental psychology; yet observation and common sense informs me that youngsters must first develop a foundation of experiential knowledge before they can begin to think critically about what they are learning. Even so, in my view no student, no matter how young, should be discouraged from asking "Why?" and "Why not?"

To sum up, skepticism is the very stuff that progress is made of, whether it be in science, sociology, politics, the law, or the arts. Therefore, skepticism should be encouraged at all but the most basic levels of education.

Issue 154　Should **parents and communities** participate in education?

Should parents and communities participate in local education because education is too important to leave to professional educators, as the speaker asserts? It might be tempting to agree with the speaker, based on a parent's legal authority over, familiarity with, and interest in his or her own children. However, a far more compelling argument can be made that, except for major decisions such as choice of school, a child's education is best left to professional educators.

Communities of parents concerned about their children's education rely on three arguments for active parental and community participation in that process. The first argument, and the one expressed most often and vociferously, is that parents hold the ultimately legal authority to make key decisions about what and how their own children learn—including choice of curriculum and text books, pace and schedule for learning, and the extent to which their child should learn alongside other children. The second argument is that only a parent can truly know the unique needs of a child—including what educational choices are best suited for the child. The third argument is that parents are more motivated—by pride and ego—than any other person to take whatever measures are needed to ensure their children receive the best possible education.

Careful examination of these three arguments, however, reveals that they are specious at best. As for the first one, were we to allow parents the right to make all major decisions regarding the education of their children, many children would go with little or no education. In a perfect world parents would always make their children's education one of their highest priorities. Yet, in fact many parents do not. As for the second argument, parents are not necessarily best equipped to know what is best for their child when it comes to education. Although most parents might think they are sufficiently expert by virtue of having gone through formal education themselves, parents lack the specialized training to appreciate what pedagogical methods are most effective, what constitutes a balanced education, how developmental psychology affects a child's capacity for learning at different levels and at different stages of childhood. Professional educators, by virtue of their specialized training in these areas, are far better able to ensure that a child receives a balanced, properly paced education.

There are two additional compelling arguments against the speaker's contention. First, parents are too subjective to always know what is truly best for their children. For example, many parents try to overcome their own shortcomings and failed self-expectations vicariously through their children's accomplishments. Most of us have known parents who push their child to excel in certain areas—to the emotional and psychological detriment of the child. Secondly, if too many parties become involved in making decisions about day-to-day instruction, the end result might be infighting, legal battles, boycotts, and other protests, all of which impede the educational process; and the ultimate victims are the children themselves. Finally, in many jurisdictions parents now have the option of schooling their children at home, as long as certain state requirements are met. In my observation, home schooling allows parents who prefer it great control over a child's education, while allowing the professional educators to discharge their responsibilities as effectively as possible—unfettered by gadfly parents who constantly interfere and intervene.

In sum, while parents might seem better able and better motivated to make key decisions about their child's education, in many cases they are not. With the possible exceptions of responsible home-schoolers, a child's intellectual, social, and psychological development is at risk when communities of parents dominate the decision-making process involving education.

Issue 157　Are all observations **subjective**?

The speaker claims that all observation is subjective—colored by desire and expectation. While it would be tempting to concede that we all see things differently, careful scrutiny of the speaker's claim reveals that it confuses observation with interpretation. In fact, in the end the speaker's claim relies entirely on the further claim that there is no such thing as truth and that we cannot truly know anything. While this notion might appeal to certain existentialists and epistemologists, it runs against the grain of all scientific discovery and knowledge gained over the last 500 years.

It would be tempting to afford the speaker's claim greater merit than it deserves. After all, our everyday experience as humans informs us that we often disagree about what we observe around us. We've all uttered and heard uttered many times the phase "That's not the way I see it!" Indeed, everyday observations—for example, about whether a football player was out of bounds, or about which car involved in an accident ran the red light—vary depending not only on one's spatial perspective but also on one's expectations or desires. If I'm rooting for one football team, or if the player is well-known for his ability to make great plays while barely staying in bounds, my desires or expectations might influence what I think I observe. Or if I am driving one of the cars in the accident, or if one car is a souped-up sports car, then my desires or expectations will in all likelihood color my perception of the accident's events.

However, these sorts of subjective "observations" are actually subjective "interpretations" of what we observe. Visitors to an art museum might disagree about the beauty of a particular work, or even about which color predominates in that work. In a court trial several jurors might view the same videotape evidence many times, yet some jurors might "observe" an incident of police brutality, while others "observe" the appropriate use of force to restrain a dangerous individual. Thus, when it comes to making judgments about what we observe and about remembering what we observe, each person's individual perspective, values, and even emotions help form these judgments and recollections. It is crucial to distinguish between interpretations such as these and observation, which is nothing more than a sensory experience. Given the same spatial perspective and sensory acuity and awareness, it seems to me that our observations would all be essentially in accord—that is, observation can be objective.

Lending credence to my position is Francis Bacon's scientific method, according to which we can know only that which we observe, and thus all truth must be based on empirical observation. This profoundly important principle serves to expose and strip away all subjective interpretation of observation, thereby revealing objective scientific truths. For example, up until Bacon's time the Earth was "observed" to he at the center of the Universe, in accordance with the prevailing religious notion that man (humankind) was the center of God's creation. Applying Bacon's scientific method Galileo exposed the biased nature of this claim. Similarly, before Einstein time and space were assumed to be linear, in accordance with our "observation." Einstein's mathematical formulas suggested otherwise, and his theories have been proven empirically to be true. Thus, it was our subjective interpretation of time and space that led to our misguided notions about them. Einstein, like history's other most influential scientists, simply refused to accept conventional interpretations of what we all observe.

In sum, the speaker confuses observation with interpretation and recollection. It is how we make sense of what we observe, not observation itself, that is colored by our perspective, expectations, and desires. The gifted individuals who can set aside their subjectivity and delve deeper into empirical evidence, employing Bacon's scientific method, are the ones who reveal that observation not only can be objective but must be objective if we are to embrace the more fundamental notion that knowledge and truth exist.

Issue 160　Effective leadership and commitment to **particular principles**

Whether effective leadership requires that a leader consistently follow his or her principles and objectives is a complex issue—one that is tied up in the problem of defining effective leadership in the first place. In addressing the issue it is helpful to consider, in turn, three distinct forms of leadership: business, political, and social-spiritual.

In the business realm, effective leadership is generally defined, at least in our corporate culture, as that which achieves the goal of profit maximization for a firm's shareholders or other owners. Many disagree, however, that profit is the appropriate measure of a business leader's effectiveness. Some detractors claim, for example, that a truly effective business leader must also fulfill additional duties—for example, to do no intentional harm to their customers or to the society in which they operate. Other detractors go further-to impose on business leaders an affirmative obligation to yield to popular will, by protecting consumers, preserving the natural environment, promoting education, and otherwise taking steps to help alleviate society's problems.

Whether our most effective business leaders are the ones who remain consistently committed to maximizing profits or the ones who appease the general populace by contributing to popular social causes depends, of course, on one's own definition of business success. In my observation, as business leaders become subject to closer scrutiny by the media and by social activists, business leaders will maximize profits in the long term only by taking reasonable steps to minimize the social and environmental harm their businesses cause. Thus, the two definitions merge, and the statement at issue is ultimately correct.

In the political realm the issue is no less complex. Definitions of effective political leadership are tied up in the means a leader uses to wield his or her power and to obtain that power in the first place. Consider history's most infamous tyrants and despots—such as Genghis Khan, Stalin, Mao, and Hitler. No historian would disagree that these individuals were remarkably effective leaders, and that each one remained consistently committed to his tyrannical objectives and Machiavellian principles. Ironically, it was stubborn commitment to objectives that ultimately defeated all except Khan. Thus, in the short term, stubborn adherence to one's objectives might serve a political leader's interest in preserving his or her power; yet, in the long term such behavior invariably results in that leader's downfall—if the principles are not in accord with those of the leader's would-be followers.

Finally, consider social-spiritual leadership. Few would disagree that through their ability to inspire others and lift the human spirit Mahatma Gandhi and Martin Luther King were eminently effective in leading others to effect social change through civil disobedience. It seems to me that this brand of leadership, in order to be effective, inherently requires that the leader remain steadfastly committed to principle. Why? It is commitment to principle that is the basis for this brand of leadership in the first place. For example, had Gandhi advocated civil disobedience yet been persuaded by close advisors that an occasional violent protest might be effective in gaining India's independence from Britain, no doubt the result would have been immediate forfeiture of that leadership. In short, social-spiritual leaders must not be hypocrites; otherwise, they will lose all credibility and effectiveness.

In sum, strict adherence to principles and objectives is a prerequisite for effective social-spiritual leadership-both in the short and long term. In contrast, political leadership wanes in the long term unless the leader ultimately yields to the will of the followers. Finally, when it comes to business, leaders must strike a balance between the objective of profit maximization—the traditional measure of effectiveness—and yielding to certain broader obligations that society is now imposing on them.

Issue 165　From whom do our **leading voices come**?

I agree with the statement insofar as our leading voices tend to come from people whose ideas depart from the status quo. However, I do not agree that what motivates these iconoclasts is a mere desire to be different; in my view they are driven primarily by their personal convictions. Supporting examples abound in all areas of human endeavor—including politics, the arts, and the physical sciences.

When it comes to political power, I would admit that a deep-seated psychological need to be noticed or to be different sometimes lies at the heart of a person's drive to political power and fame. For instance, some astute presidential historians have described Clinton as a man motivated more by a desire to be great than to accomplish great things. And many psychologists attribute Napoleon's and Mussolini's insatiable lust for power to a so-called "short-man complex"—a need to be noticed and admired in spite of one's small physical stature.

Nevertheless, for every leading political voice driven to new ideas by a desire to be noticed or to be different, one can cite many other political leaders clearly driven instead by the courage of their convictions. Iconoclasts Mahatma Gandhi and Martin Luther King, for example, secured prominent places in history by challenging the status quo through civil disobedience. Yet, no reasonable person could doubt that it was the conviction of their ideas that drove these two leaders to their respective places.

Turning to the arts, mavericks such as Dali, Picasso, and Warhol, who departed from established rules of composition, ultimately emerge as the leading artists. And our most influential popular musicians are the ones who are flagrantly "different." Consider, for example, jazz pioneers Thelonius Monk and Miles Davis, who broke all the harmonic rules, or folk musician-poet Bob Dylan, who established a new standard for lyricism. Were all these leading voices driven simply by a desire to be different? Perhaps; but my intuition is that creative urges are born not of ego but rather of some intensely personal commitment to an aesthetic ideal.

As for the physical sciences, innovation and progress can only result from challenging conventional theories—that is, the status quo. Newton and Einstein, for example, both refused to blindly accept what were perceived at their time as certain rules of physics. As a result, both men redefined those rules. Yet it would be patently absurd to assert that these two scientists were driven by a mere desire to conjure up "different" theories than those of their contemporaries or predecessors. Surely it was a conviction that their theories were better that drove these geniuses to their places in history.

To sum up, when one examines history's leading voices it does appear that they typically bring to the world something radically different than the status quo. Yet, in most cases, this sort of iconoclasm is a byproduct of personal conviction, not iconoclasm for its own sake.

Issue 167   Is **complete honesty** a useful virtue in politics?

Is complete honesty a useful virtue in politics? The speaker contends that it is not, for the reason that political leaders must sometimes lie to be effective. In order to evaluate this contention it is necessary to examine the nature of politics and to distinguish between short-term and long-term effectiveness.

On the one hand are three compelling arguments that a political leader must sometimes be less than truthful in order to be effective in that leadership. The first argument lies in the fact that politics is a game played among politicians—and that to succeed in the game one must use the tools that are part-and-parcel of it. Complete forthrightness is a sign of vulnerability and naivete, neither of which will earn a politician respect among his or her opponents, and which those opponents will use to every advantage against the honest politician.

Secondly, it is crucial to distinguish between misrepresentations of fact—in other words, lies—and mere political rhetoric. The rhetoric of a successful politician eschews rigorous factual inquiry and indisputable fact while appealing to emotions, ideals, and subjective interpretation and characterizations. Consider, for example, a hypothetical candidate for political office who attacks the incumbent opponent by pointing out only certain portions of that opponent's legislative voting record. The candidate might use a vote against a bill eliminating certain incentives for local businesses as "clear evidence" that the opponent is "anti-business," "bad for the economy," or "out of touch with what voters want." None of these allegations are outright lies; they are simply the rhetorical cant of the effective politician.

Thirdly, politics is a business born not only of idealism but also of pragmatism; after all, in order to be effective a politician must gain and hold onto political power, which means winning elections. In my observation, some degree of pandering to the electorate and to those who might lend financial support in reelection efforts is necessary to maintain that position. Modern politics is replete with candidates who refused to pander, thereby ruining their own chance to exercise effective leadership.

Although in the short term being less-than-truthful with the public might serve a political leader's interest in preserving power, would-be political leaders who lack requisite integrity ultimately forfeit their leadership. Consider Richard Nixon, whose leadership seemed born not of ideology but of personal ambition, which bred contempt of the very people who sanctioned his leadership in the first place; the ultimate result was his forfeiture of that leadership. In contrast, Ronald Reagan was a highly effective leader largely because he honestly, and deeply, believed in the core principles that he espoused and advocated during his presidency—and his constituency sensed that genuineness and responded favorably to it. Moreover, certain types of sociopolitical leadership inherently require the utmost integrity and honesty. Consider notable figures such as Gandhi and King, both of whom were eminently effective in leading others to practice the high ethical and moral standards which they themselves advocated. The reason for this is simple: A high standard for one's own personal integrity is a prerequisite for effective moral leadership.

To sum up, I concede that the game of politics calls for a certain measure of posturing and disingenuousness. Yet, at the end of the game, without a countervailing measure of integrity, political game-playing will serve to diminish a political leader's effectiveness—perhaps to the point where the politician forfeits the game.

Issue 168　Can only inside experts judge **work in any given field**?

The speaker's assertion that work in any field can be judged only by experts in that field amounts to an unfair generalization, in my view. I would concur with the speaker when it comes to judging the work of social scientists, although I would strongly disagree when it comes to work in the pure physical sciences, as explained in the following discussion.

With respect to the social sciences, the social world presents a seamless web of not only anthropogenic but also physical forces, which interact in ways that can be understood only in the context of a variety of disciplines. Thus, experts from various fields must collectively determine the merit of work in the social sciences. For example, consider the field of cultural anthropology. The merits of researcher's findings and conclusions about an ancient civilization must be scrutinized by biochemists, geologists, linguists, and even astronomers.

Specifically, by analyzing the hair, nails, blood, and bones of mummified bodies, biochemists and forensic scientists can pass judgment on the anthropologist's conjectures about the life expectancy, general well-being, and common causes of death of the population. Geologists are needed to identify the source and age of the materials used for tools, weapons, and structures—thereby determining whether the anthropologist extrapolated correctly about the civilization's economy, trades and work habits, lifestyles, extent of travel and mobility, and so forth. Linguists are needed to interpret hieroglyphics and extrapolate from found fragments of writings. And, astronomers are sometimes needed to determine whether the anthropologist's explanations for the layout of an ancient city or the design, structure and position of monuments, tombs, and temples is convincing—because ancients often looked to the stars for guidance in building cities and structures.

In contrast, the work of researchers in the purely physical sciences can be judged only by their peers. The reason for this is that scientific theories and observations are either meritorious or not, depending solely on whether they can be proved or disproved by way of the scientific method. For example, consider the complex equations that physicists rely upon to draw conclusions about the nature of matter, time, and space, or the origins and future of the universe. Only other physicists in these specialties can understand, let alone judge, this type of theoretical work. Similarly, empirical observations in astrophysics and molecular physics require extremely sophisticated equipment and processes, which only experts in these fields have access to and who know how to use reliably.

Those who disagree that only inside experts can judge scientific work might point out that the expertise of economists and pubic-policy makers is required to determine whether the work is worthwhile from a more mundane economic or political viewpoint. Detractors might also point out that ultimately it is our philosophers who are best equipped to judge the ultimate import of ostensibly profound scientific discoveries. Yet, these detractors miss the point of what I take to be the speaker's more narrow claim: that the integrity and quality of work—disregarding its socioeconomic utility—can be judged only by experts in the work's field.

In sum, in the social sciences no area of inquiry operates in a vacuum. Because fields such as anthropology, sociology, and history are so closely intertwined and even dependent on the physical sciences, experts from various fields must collectively determine the integrity and quality of work in these fields. However, in the purely physical sciences the quality and integrity of work can be adequately judged only by inside experts, who are the only ones equipped with sufficient technical knowledge to pass judgment.

Issue 169   Are politics and morality mutually exclusive?

Should politics and morality be treated as though they are mutually exclusive? I strongly agree with the speaker that any person claiming so fails to understand either the one or the other. An overly narrow definition of morality might require complete forthrightness and candidness in dealings with others. However, the morality of public politics embraces far broader concerns involving the welfare of society, and recognizes compromise as a necessary, and legitimate, means of addressing those concerns.

It is wrong-headed to equate moral behavior in politics with the simple notions of honesty and putting the other fellow's needs ahead of one's own—or other ways that we typically measure the morality of an individual's private behavior. Public politics is a game played among professional politicians—and to succeed in the game one must use the tools that are part-and-parcel of it. Complete forthrightness is a sign of vulnerability and naiveté, neither of which will earn a politician respect among his or her opponents, and that opponents will use to every advantage against the honest politician. Moreover, the rhetoric of a successful politician eschews rigorous factual inquiry and indisputable fact while appealing to emotions, ideals, and subjective interpretation and characterizations. For example, the politician who claims his opponent is "anti-business," "bad for the economy," or "out of touch with what voters want" is not necessarily behaving immorally. We must understand that this sort of rhetoric is part-and-parcel of public politics, and thus kept in perspective does not harm the society—as long as it does not escalate to outright lying.

Those who disagree with the statement also fail to understand that in order to gain the opportunity for moral leadership politicians must engage in certain compromises along the way. Politics is a business born not only of idealism but also of pragmatism—insofar as in order to be effective a politician must gain and hold onto political power. In my observation, some degree of pandering to the electorate and to those who might lend financial support for reelection efforts is necessary to maintain that position. Modern politics is replete with candidates who refused to pander, thereby ruining their own chance to exercise effective leadership.

Finally, those who claim that effective politicians need not concern themselves with morality fail to appreciate that successful political leadership, if it is to endure, ultimately requires a certain measure of public morality—that is, serving the society with its best interests as the leader's overriding concern. Consider the many leaders, such as Hitler, whom most people would agree were egregious violators of public morality. Ultimately, such leaders forfeit their leadership as a result of the immoral means by which they obtain or wield their power. Or consider less egregious examples such as President Nixon, whose contempt for the very legal system that afforded him his leadership led to his forfeiture of that leadership. It seems to me that in the short term amoral or immoral public behavior might serve a political leader's interest in preserving power; yet in the long term such behavior invariably results in that leader's downfall.

In sum, I fundamentally agree with the statement. It recognizes that the "game" of politics calls for a certain amount of disingenuousness that we might associate with dubious private morality. And it recognizes that such behavior is a necessary means to the final objective of moral political leadership. Besides, at the end of the political game any politician failing to exercise moral leadership ultimately forfeits the game.

Issue 170　The **surest indicator of a great nation**

Does a nation's greatness lie in the general welfare of its people rather than in the achievements of its artists, rulers, and scientists, as the speaker claims? I find this claim problematic in two respects. First, it fails to define "general welfare." Second, it assumes that the sorts of achievements that the speaker cites have little to do with a nation's general welfare—when in fact they have everything to do with it.

At first blush the speaker's claim might appear to have considerable merit. After all, the overriding imperative for any democratic state is to enhance the general welfare of its citizenry. Yet the speaker fails to provide a clear litmus test for measuring that welfare. When we speak of "promoting the general welfare," the following aims come to mind: public health and safety, security against military invasions, individual autonomy and freedom, cultural richness, and overall comfort—that is, a high standard of living. Curiously, it is our scientists, artists, and political leaders—or so-called "rulers"—who by way of their achievements bring these aims into fruition. Thus, in order to determine what makes a nation great it is necessary to examine the different sorts of individual achievements that ostensibly promote these aims.

Few would disagree that many scientific achievements serve to enhance a nation's general welfare. Advances in the health sciences have enhanced our physical well-being, comfort, and life span. Advances in technology have enabled us to travel to more places, communicate with more people from different walks of life, and learn about the world from our desktops. Advances in physics and engineering make our abodes and other buildings safer, and enable us to travel to more places, and to travel to more distant places, with greater safety and speed. Artistic achievement is also needed to make a nation a better place for humans overall. Art provides inspiration, lifts the human spirit, and incites our creativity and imagination, all of which spur us on to greater accomplishments and help us appreciate our own humanity. Yet the achievements of scientists and artists, while integral, do not suffice to ensure the welfare of a nation's citizens. In order to survive, let alone be great, a nation must be able to defend its borders and to live peaceably with other nations. Thus, the military and diplomatic accomplishments of a nation's leaders provide an integral contribution to the general welfare of any nation's populace.

Notwithstanding the evidence that, in the aggregate, individual achievements of the sorts listed above are what promote a nation's general welfare, we should be careful not to hastily assume that a nation is necessarily great merely by virtue of the achievements of individual citizens. Once having secured the safety and security of its citizens, political rulers must not exploit or oppress those citizens. Also, the populace must embrace and learn to appreciate artistic accomplishment, and to use rather than misuse or abuse scientific knowledge. Of particular concern are the many ways in which scientific achievements have served to diminish our quality of life, thereby impeding the general welfare. It is through scientific "achievements" that chemicals in our food, water, and air increase the incidence and variety of cancers; that our very existence as a species is jeopardized by the threat of nuclear warfare; and that greenhouse gases which deplete our ozone layer and heat the Earth's atmosphere threaten civilization itself.

In sum, in asserting that general welfare—and neither the scientific, artistic, nor political achievements of individuals—provides the yardstick for measuring a nation's greatness, the speaker misses the point that general welfare is the end product of individual achievements. Besides, achievements of artists, scientists, and political leaders rarely inure only to one particular nation. Rather, these achievements benefit people the world over. Accordingly, by way of these achievements the world, not just one nation, grows in its greatness.

Issue 171   What avenues of intellectual inquiry best serve **the public good**?

Are people who make the greatest contributions to society those who pursue their personal intellectual interests, as the speaker asserts? Or are they the ones who focus instead on areas that are most likely to benefit society? I strongly agree with the speaker, for three reasons.

First of all, by human nature we are motivated to pursue activities in which we excel. To compel people to focus their intellectual interests only on certain areas would be to force many to waste their true talents. For example, imagine relegating today's preeminent astrophysicist Stephen Hawking to researching the effectiveness of affirmative-action legislation in reducing workplace discrimination. Admittedly, this example borders on hyperbole. Yet the aggregate effect of realistic cases would be to waste the intellectual talents of our world's scholars and researchers.

Secondly, it is unusual avenues of personal interest that most often lead to the greatest contributions to society. Intellectual and scientific inquiry that breaks no new ground amount to wasted time, talent, and other resources. History is laden with quirky claims of scholars and researchers that turned out stunningly significant—that the sun lies at the center of our universe, that time and space are relative concepts, that matter consists of discrete particles, that humans evolved from other life-forms, to name a few. One current area of unusual research is terraforming—creating biological life and a habitable atmosphere where none existed before. This unusual research area does not immediately address society's pressing social problems. Yet, in the longer term it might be necessary to colonize other planets in order to ensure the survival of the human race; and after all, what could be a more significant contribution to society than preventing its extinction?

Thirdly, to adopt a view that runs contrary to the speaker's position would be to sanction certain intellectual pursuits while proscribing others—which smacks of thought control and political oppression. It is dangerous to afford ultimate decision-making power about what intellectual pursuits are worthwhile to a handful of regulators, legislators, or elitists, since they bring to bear their own quirky notions about what is worthwhile, and since they are notoriously susceptible to influence-peddling, which renders them untrustworthy in any event. Besides, history informs us well of the danger inherent in setting official research priorities. A telling modern example involves the Soviet government's attempts during the 1920s to not only control the direction and the goals of its scientists' research but also to distort the outcome of that research—ostensibly for the greatest good of the greatest number of people. During the 1920s the Soviet government quashed certain areas of scientific inquiry, destroyed entire research facilities and libraries, and caused the sudden disappearance of many scientists who were viewed as threats to the state's authority. Not surprisingly, during this time period no significant scientific advances occurred under the auspices of the Soviet government.

Those who would oppose the speaker's assertion might argue that intellectual inquiry in certain areas, particularly the arts and humanities, amounts to little more than a personal quest for happiness or pleasure, and therefore is of little benefit to anyone but the inquirer. This specious argument overlooks the palpable benefits of cultivating the arts. It also ignores the fact that earnest study in the humanities affords us wisdom to know what is best for society, and helps us understand and approach societal problems more critically, creatively, and effectively. Thus, despite the lack of a tangible nexus between certain areas of intellectual inquiry and societal benefit, the nexus is there nonetheless.

In sum, I agree that society is best served when people are allowed unfettered freedom of intellectual inquiry and research, and use that freedom to pursue their own personal interests. Engaging one's individual talents in one's particular area of fascination is most likely to yield advances, discoveries, and a heightened aesthetic appreciation that serve to make the world a better and more interesting place in which to live.

Issue 175　The **impetus for innovation**: individual enterprise or teamwork?

The speaker claims that individual enterprise, energy, and commitment, and not teamwork, provide the impetus for innovation in every case. In my view, although the claim is not without merit, especially when it comes to business innovation, it overlooks the synergistic relationship between individual effort and teamwork, particularly with respect to scientific innovations.

With respect to business innovation, I agree that it is the vision and commitment of key individuals—such as a firm's founder or chief executive—from which businesses burgeon and innovative products, services, and marketing and management strategies emerge. One notable example involves the Apple Computer debacle following the departure of its founding visionary Steve Jobs. It wasn't until jobs reassumed the helm, once again injecting his unique perception, insight, and infectious fervor, that the ailing Apple was able to resume its innovative ways, thereby regaining its former stature in the computer industry. Admittedly, the chief executives of our most successful corporations would no doubt concede that without the cooperative efforts of their subordinates, their personal visions would never become reality. Yet, these efforts are merely the carrying out of the visionary's marching orders.

Nevertheless, the speaker would have us accept a too-narrow and distorted view of how innovation comes about, particularly in today's world. Teamwork and individual enterprise are not necessarily inconsistent, as the speaker would have us believe. Admittedly, if exercised in a self-serving manner—for example, through pilfering or back stabbing—individual enterprise and energy can serve to thwart a business organization's efforts to innovate. However, if directed toward the firm's goals these traits can motivate other team members, thereby facilitating innovation. In other words, teamwork and individual enterprise can operate synergistically to bring about innovation.

We must be especially careful not to understate the role of teamwork in scientific innovation, especially today. Important scientific innovations of the previous millennium might very well have been products of the epiphanies and obsessions of individual geniuses. When we think of the process of inventing something great we naturally conjure up a vision of the lone inventor hidden away in a laboratory for months on end, in dogged pursuit of a breakthrough. And this image is not entirely without empirical support. For example, Thomas Edison's early innovations—including the light bulb, the television, and the phonograph—came about in relative isolation, and solely through his individual persistence and commitment.

However, in today's world, scientific innovation requires both considerable capital and extensive teams of researchers. Admittedly, in all likelihood we will continue to encounter the exceptional case—like Hewlett and Packard, or jobs and Wozniak, whose innovations sprang from two-man operations. But for the most part, scientific breakthroughs today typically occur only after years of trial-and-error by large research teams. Even Thomas Edison relied more and more on a team of researchers to develop new innovations as his career progressed. Thus the statement flies in the face of how most modern scientific innovations actually come about today.

To sum up, I agree that, when it comes to the world of business, true innovation is possible only through the imagination of the individual visionary, and his or her commitment to see the vision through to its fruition. However, when it comes to scientific innovation, yesterday's enterprising individuals have yielded to today's cooperative research teams—a trend that will no doubt continue as scientific research becomes an increasingly expensive and complex undertaking.

Issue 177 Does our education change how **we perceive the world**?

I strongly agree that by studying any particular academic discipline we alter the way we perceive the world. As intellectual neophytes we tend to polarize what we see as either right or wrong, or as either good or bad. We also tend to interpret what we see by way of our emotions. Once educated, we gain the capacity to see a broader spectrum of opinion and perspective, and to see our own culture and even ourselves as a tapestry-like product of history.

Through the earnest pursuit of knowledge—particularly in history and literature—we reveal to ourselves the flaws and foibles of other humans whose lives we study and read about. History teaches us, for example, that demagogues whom society places on pedestals often fall under the weight of their own prejudices, jealousies, and other character flaws. And, any serious student of Shakespeare comes away from reading *King Lear* and *Hamlet* with a heightened awareness of the tragically flawed ironic hero, and of the arbitrariness by which we distinguish our heroes from our villains.

Through education we begin to see flaws not only in people but also in ideologies that we had previously embraced on pure faith. A student of government and public policy learns that many of the so-called "solutions" which our legislatures and jurists hand down to us from atop their pedestals are actually Band-Aid compromises designed to appease opponents and pander to the electorate. A philosophy student learns to recognize logical fallacies of popular ideas and the rhetoric of our political parties, religious denominations, and social extremists. And, a law student learns that our system of laws is not a monolithic set of truths but rather an ever-changing reflection of whatever the society's current mores, values, and attitudes happen to be.

While education helps us see the flawed nature of our previously cherished ideas, paradoxically it also helps us see ideas we previously rejected out of hand in a different light—as having some merit after all. Through education in public policy and law, once-oppressive rules, regulations, and restrictions appear reasonable constraints on freedom in light of legitimate competing interests. Through the objective study of different religious institutions, customs, and faiths, a student learns to see the merits of different belief systems, and to see the cultural and philosophical traditions in which they are rooted.

Education also helps us see our own culture through different eyes. As cultural neophytes we participate unwittingly in our culture's own customs, rituals, and ceremonies—because we see them as somehow sacrosanct. A student of sociology or cultural anthropology comes to see those same customs, rituals, and ceremonies as tools which serve our psychological need to belong to a distinct social group, and to reinforce that sense of belonging by honoring the group's traditions. And, by reading the literary works of writers from bygone eras, a literature student comes to see his or her own culture as a potential treasure trove of fodder for the creative literary mind. For example, by studying Twain's works a student learns that Twain saw nineteenth-century life along the Mississippi not as a mundane existence but as a framework for the quintessential adventure story, and that we can similarly transform the way we see our own culture.

Finally, education in the arts alters forever the way we perceive the aesthetic world around us. Prior to education we respond instinctively, emotionally, and viscerally to the forms, colors, and sounds of art. Post education we respond intellectually. We seek to appreciate what art reveals about our culture and about humanity. We also seek to understand the aesthetic principles upon which true art is founded. For instance, an earnest art student learns to see not just pigments and shapes but also historical influences and aesthetic principles. An informed listener of popular music hears not just the same pleasing sounds and pulsating rhythms as their naive counterparts, but also the rhythmic meters, harmonic structure, and compositional forms used by the great classical composers of previous centuries, and which provided the foundation of modern music.

To sum up, through education we no longer see our heroes, leaders, and idols through the same credulous eyes, nor do we see other humans and their ideas through the black-and-white lens of our own point of view. In the final analysis, through education we come not only to perceive the world differently but also to understand the subjective, and therefore changeable, nature of our own perceptions.

Issue 180　Can **moral behavior** be legislated?

The speaker asserts that many laws are ineffective in solving society's problems because moral behavior cannot be legislated. I agree with this assertion insofar as it relates to constraints on certain personal freedoms. However, when it comes to the conduct of businesses, I think that moral behavior not only can but must be legislated for the purpose of alleviating societal problems.

Morality laws that impinge upon freedom of choice about our personal lives—to control what we do with and to ourselves—simply do not work in a democratic society. People always find ways to circumvent such laws, which ultimately give way to more lenient laws that acknowledge personal freedom of choice. The failed Prohibition experiment of the 1930s is perhaps the paradigmatic example of this. And we are slowly learning history's lesson, as aptly demonstrated by the recognition of equal rights for same-sex partners, and current trends toward legalization of physician-assisted suicide and the medicinal use of marijuana. In short, history informs us that legislating morality merely for morality's sake simply does not work.

Morality laws impinging on personal freedoms are not made any more useful or effective by purporting to serve the greater good of society, because on balance their costs far outweigh their benefits. For instance, those who defend the criminalization of drug use cite a variety of harms that result from widespread addiction: increased incidence of domestic violence, increased burden on our health-care and social-welfare systems, and diminished productivity of addicts. However, these defenders overlook the fact that outlawing addictive substances does not prevent, or even deter, people from obtaining and using them. It only compels users to resort to theft and even violent means of procuring drugs, adding to the economic costs of enforcement, prosecution, and punishment. In short, the costs of proscription outweigh the benefits.

In sharp contrast to personal behavior, the behavior of businesses can and must be controlled through legislation. Left unfettered, businesses tend to act on behalf of their own financial interest, not on behalf of the society at large. And when excessive business profits accrue at the expense of public health and safety, in my view business has behaved immorally.

Examples of large-scale immoral behavior on the part of businesses abound. For example, although technology makes possible the complete elimination of polluting emissions from automobiles, auto manufacturers are unwilling to voluntarily make the short-term sacrifices necessary to accomplish this goal. Tobacco companies have long known about the health hazards of smoking cigarettes; yet they weigh the costs of defending law suits against the profit from cigarette sales, and continue to cater to nicotine addicts. And when given the chance, many manufacturers will exploit underage or underprivileged workers to reduce labor costs, thereby enhancing profits. In short, only government holds the regulatory and enforcement power to impose the standards needed to ensure moral business behavior.

In sum, whether legislating morality is effective or even appropriate depends on whether the behavior at issue involves personal freedom or public duty. Legislating personal moral behavior is neither practicable nor proper in a democratic society. On the other hand, legislating business morality is necessary to ensure public health and safety.

Issue 181　What influences how **students and scholars interpret** materials?

I strongly disagree that personality is the key to how a student or scholar interprets the material with which he or she works. Whether those materials be facts, events, data, or observations, in my view the key factor in their interpretation is a person's training and educational background.

Assuming that by personality the speaker embraces such personal attributes as individual temperament, disposition and general mood, and outlook, it seems to me that personality has little bearing on how students and scholars interpret the materials with which they work. Admittedly, whether an individual tends to be an optimist or a pessimist might have some bearing on interpretation. For instance, an archeology student with a generally sanguine outlook toward life might respond to a lengthy yet unsuccessful search for certain artifacts as discovery and progress—insofar as certain possibilities have been eliminated, bringing us closer to affirmative discoveries. In contrast, an archeology student with a generally pessimistic outlook might conclude that the same effort was in vain and that nothing has been learned or otherwise gained. Yet it strikes me that these reactions are emotional ones that have nothing to do with intellectual interpretation.

In sharp contrast, one's educational background and training can serve as a strong influence on how one interprets historical events involving human affairs, statistical data, and especially art. With respect to human affairs, consider the centuries-old imperialist policies of Great Britain. A student of political science might interpret British imperialism as a manifestation of that nation's desire for political power and domination over others. A student of economics might see it as a strategy to gain control over economic resources and distribution channels for goods. A sociology or anthropology student might see it as an assimilation of culture. And, a student of theology or religion might interpret the same phenomenon as an attempt, well intentioned or otherwise, to proselytize and to impose certain beliefs, rituals, and customs on others.

Educational training and background also affects how students and scholars interpret seemingly objective statistical data. It is crucial here to distinguish between numbers themselves, which are not subject to varying interpretations, from what the numbers signify—that is, what conclusions, prescriptions, or lessons we might come away with. Consider, for example, a hypothetical increase in the rate of juvenile crime in a particular city. Although the percent change itself might be subject to only one reasonable meaning, what the change signifies is open to various interpretations. A sociologist might interpret this data as an indication of deteriorating family unit or community. A student of public policy or government might see this statistic as an indication that current legislation fails to implement public policy as effectively as it could. And a student of law or criminal justice might interpret the same statistic as a sign of overburdened courts or juvenile-detention facilities.

Finally, when it comes to how students and scholars interpret art, training and educational background play an especially significant role. After all, while facts and figures are to some extent objective, the meaning of art is an inherently subjective, and highly personal, matter. A business student might interpret a series of art works as attempts by the artist to produce viable products for sale in the marketplace. However, a theology student might eschew such a cold and cynical interpretation, seeing instead an expression of praise, a celebration of life, a plea for grace, or a struggle to come to terms with mortality. (Even art students and scholars can interpret the same art differently, depending on their training. A student of art history might see a particular work as the product of certain artistic influences, while a student of art theory, composition, and technique might view the same work as an attempt to combine color for visual impact, or as an experiment with certain brush-stroke techniques.)

To sum up, I concede that as students and scholars our working "materials"—facts, data, objects, and events—are open to subjective interpretation in terms of what they teach us. However, what our materials teach us is a function of what we've already learned, and has little if anything to do with our personal basket of emotions and moods called "personality."

Issue 185　Are **scandals** useful?

Are scandals useful in calling our attention to important problems, as this statement suggests? I agree that in many cases scandals can serve to reveal larger problems that a community or society should address. On the other hand, scandals can sometimes distract us from more important societal issues.

On the one hand, scandals can sometimes serve to call our attention to pervasive social or political problems that we would otherwise neglect. Perhaps the paradigmatic modern example is the Watergate scandal. Early in that scandal it would have been tempting to dismiss it as involving one isolated incidence of underhanded campaign tactics. But, in retrospect the scandal forever increased the level of scrutiny and accountability to which our public officials are held, thereby working a significant and lasting benefit to our society. More recently, the Clinton-Gore fundraising scandal sparked a renewed call for campaign-finance reform. In fact the scandal might result in the passage of a congressional bill outlawing private campaign contributions altogether, thereby rendering presidential candidates far less susceptible to undue influence of special-interest groups. Our society would be the clear beneficiary of such reform. Surely, no public speaker or reformer could have called our nation's collective attention to the problem of presidential misconduct unless these two scandals had surfaced.

On the other hand, scandals can sometimes serve chiefly to distract us from more pressing community or societal problems. At the community level, for example, several years ago the chancellor of a university located in my city was expelled from office for misusing university funds to renovate his posh personal residence. Every new development during the scandal became front-page news in the campus newspaper. But did this scandal serve any useful purpose? No. The scandal did not reveal any pervasive problem with university accounting practices. It did not result in any sort of useful system-wide reform. Rather, it was merely one incidence of petty misappropriation. Moreover, the scandal distracted the university community from far more important issues, such as affirmative action and campus safety, which were relegated to the second page of the campus newspaper during the scandal.

Even on a societal level, scandals can serve chiefly to distract us from more important matters. For example, time will tell whether the Clinton sex scandal will benefit our political, social, or legal system. Admittedly, the scandal did call our attention to certain issues of federal law. It sparked a debate about the powers and duties of legal prosecutors, under the Independent Counsel Act, vis-à-vis the chief executive while in and out of office. And the various court rulings about executive privilege and immunity will serve useful legal precedents for the future. Even the impeachment proceedings will no doubt provide useful procedural precedent at some future time. Yet on balance, it seems to me that the deleterious effects of the scandal—in terms of the financial expense to taxpayers and the various harms to the many individuals caught up in the legal process—outweigh these benefits. More importantly, for more that a year the scandal served chiefly to distract us from our most pressing national and global problems, such as the Kosovo crisis, our social-security crisis, and health-care reform, to name just a few.

In sum, I agree that scandals often serve to flag important socio-political problems more effectively than any speaker or reformer can. However, whether a scandal works more benefit than harm to a community or society must be addressed on a case-by-case basis.

Issue 187　Accepting **innovations** and **new ideas**

The speaker maintains that it is easy to accept innovation and new ideas, yet difficult to accept how they are put to use. In my view the speaker has it backward when it comes to socio-political ideas, at least in our democratic society. Nevertheless, I tend to agree with the speaker insofar as scientific innovation is concerned.

In the areas of politics and law, new ideas are not often easily accepted. More often than not, the status quo affords people a measure of security and predictability in terms of what they can expect from their government and what rights and duties they have under the law The civil-rights movement of the 1960s aptly illustrates this point. The personal freedoms and rights championed by leading civil-rights leaders of that era threatened the status quo, which tolerated discrimination based on race and gender, thereby sanctioning prejudice of all kinds. The resulting civil unrest, especially the protests and riots that characterized the late 1960s, was clear evidence that new ideas were not welcome. And today those who advocate gay and lesbian rights are encountering substantial resistance as well, this time primarily from certain religious quarters.

Yet once society grows to accept these new ideas, it seems that it has an easier time accepting how they are put into practice. The explanation for this lies in the fact that our system of laws is based on legal precedent. New ideas must past muster among the government's legislative, judicial, and executive branches, and ultimately the voters, before these ideas can be codified, implemented and enforced. Once they've passed the test of our democratic and legal systems, they are more readily welcomed by the citizenry at large.

In contrast, consider innovations in the natural sciences. It seems that we universally embrace any new technology in the name of progress. Of course there are always informed dissenters with legitimate concerns. For example, many scientists strongly opposed the Manhattan Project, by which nuclear warfare was made possible. Innovations involving alternative energy sources meet with resistance from those who rely on and profit from fossil fuels. Some sociologists and psychologists claim that advances in Internet technology will alienate society's members from one another. And opponents of genetic engineering predict certain deleterious social and political consequences.

Yet the reasons why these dissenters oppose certain innovations have to do with their potential applications and uses, not with the innovations themselves. Edward Teller, the father of the atom bomb, foresaw the benefits of atomic energy, yet understood the grave consequences of applying the technology instead for destruction. Innovations involving alternative energy sources meet with resistance from many businesses because of their potential application in ways that will threaten the financial interests of these businesses. And those who would impede advances in Internet technology fear that consumers and businesses will use the technology for crass commercialism, exploitation, and white-collar crime, rather than for the sorts of educational and communication purposes for which it was originally designed. Finally, opponents of genetic engineering fear that, rather than using it to cure birth defects and prevent disease, the technology will be used instead by the wealthy elite to breed superior offspring, thereby causing society's socioeconomic gap to widen even further, even resulting in the creation of a master race.

In sum, when it comes to new social and political ideas, the power and security afforded by the status quo impedes initial acceptance, yet by the same token ensures that the ideas will be applied in ways that will be welcome by our society. On the other hand, it seems that scientific innovation is readily embraced yet meets stronger resistance when it comes to applying the innovation.

Issue 188   Success: the **ability to survive** in and adapt and alter one's environment

Do academic and professional success both involve surviving in a new environment and eventually changing it, as the speaker claims? Regarding academic success, in my view the speaker overstates the significance of environment. Regarding professional success the speaker's threshold claim that adaptation is necessary has considerable merit; however, the extent to which professional success also entails shaping the environment in which the professional operates depends on the type of profession under consideration.

Turning first to academic success, I concede that as students advance from grade school to high school, then to college, they must accustom themselves not just to new curricula but also to new environments—comprised of campuses, classmates, teachers, and teaching methods. The last item among this list is proving particularly significant in separating successful students from less successful ones. As computers and the Internet are becoming increasing important tools for learning academic skills and for research, they are in effect transforming our learning environment—at every educational level. Students who fail to adapt to this change will find themselves falling behind the pace of their peers.

Otherwise, the speaker's prescription for academic success makes little sense. Aside from the environmental variables listed above, academia is a relatively staid environment over time. The key ingredients of academic success have always been, and will always be, a student's innate abilities and the effort the student exerts in applying those abilities to increasingly advanced course work. Besides, to assert that academic success involves changing one's environment is tantamount to requiring that students alter their school's teaching methods or physical surroundings in order to be successful students—an assertion that nonsensically equates academic study with educational reform.

Turning next to professional success, consider the two traditional professions of law and medicine. A practicing lawyer must stay abreast of new developments and changes in the law, and a physician must adapt to new and improved medical devices, and keep pace with new and better ways to treat and prevent diseases. Otherwise, those professionals risk losing their competency, and even their professional licenses. However, this is not to say that success in either profession also requires that the practitioner help shape the legal, medical, technological, or ethical environment within which these professions operate. To the contrary, undue time and energy devoted to advancing the profession can diminish a practitioner's effectiveness as such. In other words, legal and medical reform is best left to former practitioners, and to legislators, jurists, scientists, and academicians. Thus the speaker's claim unfairly overrates the ability to change one's professional environment as a key ingredient of professional success.

In contrast, when it comes to certain other professions, such as business and scientific research, the speaker's claim is far more compelling. Our most successful business leaders are not those who merely maximize shareholder profits, but rather those who envision a lasting contribution to the business environment and to society, and realize that vision. The industrial barons and information-age visionaries of the late nineteenth and twentieth centuries, respectively, did not merely adapt to the winds of business and technological change imposed upon them. They altered the direction of those winds, and to some extent were the fans that blew those winds. Similarly, ultimate success in scientific research lies not in reacting to new environments but in shaping future ones—by preventing disease, inventing products that transform the ways in which we live and work, and so forth. Perhaps the most apt example is the field of space exploration, which has nothing to do with adapting to new environments, and everything to do with discovering them and making them available to us in the first place.

To sum up, the speaker's claim has merit insofar as any individual must adapt to new environments to progress in life and to survive in a dynamic, ever-changing world. However, the speaker's sweeping definition of success overlooks certain crucial distinctions between academics and the professions, and between some professions and others.

Issue 191 Should education devote itself to **enriching** our personal lives?

Should educators focus equally on enriching students' personal lives and on job preparation, as the speaker contends? In my view, preparing students for the mundane aspects of work should be secondary to providing a broader education that equips students with historical and cultural perspective, as well as thoughtful and principled personal value systems and priorities. Paradoxically, it is through the liberal studies, which provide these forms of personal enrichment, that students can also best prepare for the world of work.

One reason why educators should emphasize personal enrichment over job preparation is that rote technical knowledge and skill do not help a student determine which goals in life are worthwhile and whether the means of attaining those goals are ethically or morally acceptable. Liberal studies such as philosophy, history, and comparative sociology enable students to develop thoughtful and consistent value systems and ethical standards, by which students can determine how they can best put their technical knowledge and skills to use in the working world. Thus, by nurturing the development of thoughtful personal value systems, educators actually help prepare students for their jobs and careers.

Another reason why educators should emphasize personal enrichment over job preparation is that specific knowledge and skills needed for jobs are changing more and more quickly. Thus it would be a waste of our education system to focus on specific knowledge and skills that will soon become obsolete—at the expense of providing a lasting and personally satisfying educational experience. It seems more appropriate today for employers to provide the training our workforce needs to perform their jobs, freeing up our educators to help enrich students' lives in ways that will serve them in any walk of life.

A third reason why educators should emphasize personally enriching course work—particularly anthropology, sociology, history, and political philosophy—is that these courses help students understand, appreciate, and respect other people and their viewpoints. As these students grow into working adults they will be better able to cooperate, compromise, understand various viewpoints, and appreciate the rights and duties of coworkers, supervisors, and subordinates. Rote technical knowledge and skill do little to help us get along with other people.

Admittedly, certain aspects of personal enrichment, especially spirituality and religion, should be left for parents and churches to provide; after all, by advocating teachings of any particular religion, public educators undermine our basic freedom of religion. Yet it is perfectly appropriate, and useful, to inform students about various religious beliefs, customs and institutions. Learning about different religions instills respect, tolerance, and understanding. Moreover, students grow to appreciate certain fundamental virtues, such as compassion, virtue, and humility, which all major religions share. Through this appreciation students grow into adults who can work well together toward mutually a-greed-upon goals.

In sum, it is chiefly through the more personally enriching liberal studies that educators help students fully blossom into well-rounded adults and successful workers. There will always be a need to train people for specific jobs, of course. However, since knowledge is advancing so rapidly, employers and job-training programs are better equipped to provide this function, leaving formal educators free to provide a broader, more personally enriching education that will serve students throughout their lives and in any job or career.

Issue 195　Politics—pursuing ideals vs. pursuing **a reasonable consensus**

Is the proper goal of politics to pursue not an ideal but rather a reasonable consensus, as the speaker maintains? I concede that pursuing consensus is to be preferred over pursuing illegitimate ideals. Otherwise, I find the speaker's position troubling. It ignores the fact that a political ideal might be consensus itself, or require some measure of consensus, and it flies in the face of the nature or politics and of human nature.

The primary reason for my disagreement with the speaker's position is that reasonable consensus and a political ideal need not be mutually exclusive. In the first place, if one adopts the view that the ultimate goal of public politics should be to achieve the ideal of peace among nations, then attaining a reasonable consensus among nations on issues germane to world peace would be, in essence, to achieve this ideal—at least tentatively. In the second place, in order to gain the opportunity to pursue their ideals politicians must build some measure of consensus along the way. Politics is a business born not only of idealism but also of pragmatism. In order to be effective a politician must gain and hold onto political power, which in turn requires some degree of pandering and compromising to build a consensus of support for the politician's agendas. Modern politics is replete with ideal-promoters who refused to find common ground upon which most people can agree, thereby never affording themselves the chance to pursue their ideals in a way that might make a difference.

Another reason why I tend to disagree with the speaker's position is that it flies in the face of human nature and the nature of politics. History informs us that, for better or worse, it is human nature to disagree, and to dominate or be dominated. The harsh truth is that achieving consensus is just as illusory as other ideals that politicians typically espouse. Moreover, politics inherently involves a tug-of-war between conflicting interests. Those inclined to achieve complete consensus are not true political animals. True politicians thrive instead on conflict and on advocating certain agendas while fighting to quash others. Thus to assert the politics should strive for consensus is to deny the nature of politics and of politicians.

A third problem with the speaker's position is that it begs the question: What are the proper ideals for politicians? The have little to do with justice and fairness. It is idealists—not consensus seekers—who sway the masses, incite revolutions, and make political ideology reality. Consider idealists such as America's founders, or Mahatma Gandhi, or Martin Luther King. Had these idealists concerned themselves with consensus building rather than with their notions of an ideal society, the United States and India might still be British colonies, and African Americans might still be relegated to the backs of buses. This is not to say that pursuing idealism is necessarily preferable to pursuing consensus. After all, legitimate ideals require a certain measure of morality—that is, they must further humanity's best interests. Consider the many idealists, such as Hitler, who most people would agree were egregious violators of human rights. Ultimately such leaders forfeit their leadership as a result of their illegitimate ideals and means of pursuing those ideals.

Finally, lacking idealism a political leader will tend to seek compromise and reasonable consensus for its own sake. It seems that pure pragmatism breeds a sort of unprincipled self-serving that unfortunately pervades contemporary politics. Most politicians seem driven today by their interest in being elected and reelected—that is, in short-term survival—rather than by any sense of mission, or even obligation to their constituency or country. All too often, diplomatic and legal maneuverings and negotiations are intended to meet the practical needs of the parties involved: minimizing costs, preserving options, and so forth. Idealists are better able to steer clear of short-term thinking, nearsighted goals, and self-serving maneuverings.

In sum, the speaker's call for consensus is ill-conceived. It ignores the fact that consensus is a necessary means to achieving political ideals, if not part-and-parcel of those ideals. Moreover, politicians are not by nature consensus seekers, nor are humans by nature inclined to consensus. In the final analysis, the statement is wrongheaded; what politics is about, and should be about, is the pursuit of ideals that accord with the shared interests of all humanity.

Issue 197　Are nations **necessarily connected** when it comes to their well-being?

I strongly agree that each nation's progress and well-being are now tied to the progress and well-being of other nations. In the pursuit of its citizens' economic and social welfare, as well as their safety, security, and health, each nation today creates a ripple effect—sometimes beneficial and sometimes detrimental—felt around the globe. And, although I disagree that our global interconnectedness is necessary, in all likelihood it is with us to stay.

Turning first to economic progress and well-being, the economic pursuits of any nation today are not merely connected to but actually interwoven with those of other nations. In some cases one nation's progress is another's problem. For instance, strong economic growth in the U.S. Attracts investment in U.S. equities from foreign investors, to the detriment of foreign business investments, which become less attractive by comparison. Or consider the global repercussions of developed nations' over-consumption of natural resources mined from emerging nations. Having been exploited once for the sake of fueling the high standard of living in the developed world, emerging nations are now being pressured to comply with the same energy conservation policies as their exploiters—even though they did not contribute to the problems giving rise to these policies, and cannot afford to make the sacrifices involved. Finally, although international drug trafficking provides an economic boon for the rogue nations supplying the drugs, it carries deleterious economic, social, and public-health consequences for user nations.

In other cases the economic connection between nations is synergistic—either mutually beneficial or detrimental. A financial crisis—or a political crisis or natural disaster—in one country can spell trouble for foreign companies, many of which are now multinational in that they rely on the labor forces, equipment, and raw materials of other nations. And, as trade barriers and the virtual distance between nations collapse, the result is economic synergies among all trading nations. For instance, the economic well-being of Middle East nations relies almost entirely on demand from oil-consuming nations such as the United States, which depend on a steady supply from the Middle East.

Nations have also become interconnected in the pursuit of scientific and technological progress. And while it might be tempting to hasten that the ripples generally benefit other nations, often one nation's pursuit of progress spells trouble for other nations. For example, the development of nuclear weapons and biological and chemical agents affords the nation possessing them political and military leverage over other nations. And, global computer connectivity has served to heighten national-security concerns of all connected nations—who can easily fall prey to Internet espionage.

Finally, the world's nations have become especially interconnected in terms of their public health. Prior to the modem industrial age, no nation had the capacity to inflict lasting environmental damage on other nations. But, as that age draws to a close it is evident that so-called industrial "progress" has carried deleterious environmental consequences worldwide. Consider, for instance, the depletion of atmospheric ozone, which has warmed the earth to the point that it threatens the very survival of the human species. And, we are now learning that dear-cutting the world's rainforests can set into motion a chain of animal extinction that threatens the delicate balance upon which all animals—including humans—depend.

In closing, I take exception to the statement only insofar as a nation can still pursue progress and the well-being of its own citizens in relative isolation from other nations. And I concede that in the future the world's nations might respond to the health and security risks of the ripple effect that I've described by adopting isolationist trade, communications, and military policies. Yet, having benefited from the economic synergies which free trade and global financial markets afford, and having seen the potential for progress technological revolution has brought about, I think that the world's nations will be willing to assume those risks.

Issue 203   Do a society's **heroes or its heroines** reflect its character?

The speaker claims that the character of a society's heroes and heroines ("heroes" hereafter) reflects the character of that society. I tend to disagree. In my observation a society chooses as its heroes not people who mirror the society but rather people whose character society's members wish they could emulate but cannot—for want of character. Nevertheless, I concede that one particular type of hero—the sociopolitical hero—by definition mirrors the character of the society whose causes the hero champions.

First consider the sports hero, whom in my observation society chooses not merely by virtue of athletic prowess. Some accomplished athletes we consider heroes because they have overcome significant obstacles to achieve their goals. For example, Lance Armstrong was not the first Tour de France cycling champion from the U.S.; yet he was the first to overcome a life-threatening illness to win the race. Other accomplished athletes we consider heroes because they give back to the society which lionizes them. As Mohammed Ali fought not just for boxing titles but also for racial equality, so baseball hero Mark McGuire fights now for disadvantaged children, while basketball hero Magic Johnson fights for AIDS research and awareness. Yet, do the character traits and resulting charitable efforts of sports heroes reflect similar traits and efforts among our society at large? No; they simply reveal that we admire these traits and efforts in other people, and wish we could emulate them—but for our own personal failings.

Next consider the military hero, who gains heroic stature by way of courage in battle, or by otherwise facing certain defeat and emerging victorious. Former presidential hopeful John McCain, whom even his political opponents laud as a war hero for having not only endured years of torture as a prisoner of war but also for continuing to serve his country afterward. Do his patriotism and mettle reveal our society's true character? Certainly not. They reveal only that we admire his courage, fortitude, and strength.

On the other hand, consider a third type of hero: the champion of social causes who inspires and incites society to meaningful political and social change. Such luminaries as India's Mahatma Gandhi, America's Martin Luther King, South Africa's Nelson Mandela, and Poland's Lech Lawesa come immediately to mind. This unique brand of hero does reflect, and indeed must reflect, the character of the hero's society. After all, it is the function of the social champion to call attention to the character of society, which having viewed its reflection in the hero is incited to act bravely—in accordance with its collective character.

In sum, I agree with the speaker's claim only with respect to champions of society's social causes. Otherwise, what society deems heroic reflects instead a basic, and universal, human need for paragons—to whom we can refer as metaphors for the sorts of virtues that for lack of character we cannot ourselves reflect.

Issue 208 Do people's appearance and behavior reveal **society's ideas and values**?

This statement generalizes unfairly that the way people look, dress, and act reveals their attitudes and their society's values. In my view, while in certain respects the habits and customs of a people are accurate indicators of their attitudes and values, in other respects they are not.

Turning first to the way people look and dress, certain aspects of the outward appearance of a culture's people do inform us of their ideas, attitudes, and values. A society whose members tend to be obese might place a high value on indulgence and pleasure, and a low value on physical health. A general preference for readymade, inexpensive clothing might indicate a preference for practicality or for saving rather than spending. And, a society whose members prefer to wear clothing that is traditional and distinct to that society is one that values tradition over modernization. In other respects, however, the way people look and dress is not a function of their attitudes and values but rather their climatic and work environment. In harsh climates people bundle up, while in hot, humid climates they go with few clothes. In developed nations people dress for indoor work and their skin appears pink and supple, while in agrarian cultures people dress for outdoor work and appear weather-beaten.

I turn next to the way people act. The habits, rituals and lifestyles of a culture often do provide accurate signals about its values. For instance, a society characterized by over-consumption is clearly one that values comfort and convenience over a healthy environment. And, a society whose members behave in a genteel, respectful, and courteous manner toward one another is one which values human dignity, while a society of people who act in a hateful manner toward others clearly places a low value on respect for others and on tolerance of other people's opinions and beliefs. In other respects, however, the way people behave can belie their attitudes and values. For instance, a society whose members tend to work long hours might appear to place a high value on work for its own sake, when in reality these work habits might be born of financial necessity for these people, who would prefer more leisure time if they could afford it.

Finally, the statement overlooks a crucial distinction between free societies and oppressed ones. Free societies, such as contemporary America, are characterized by a panoply of rituals, behaviors, and manners of dress among its members. Such diversity in appearances surely indicates a society that places a high value on individual freedoms and cultural diversity. Accordingly, it might seem that a society whose members share similar rituals, ways of dressing, and public behaviors places a low value on individual freedoms and cultural diversity. However, any student of Fascism would recognize cultural homogeneity as an imposition on society's members, who would happily display their preference for individuality and diversity but for their oppressors.

To sum up, while the statement has merit, it amounts to an unfair generalization. The way that people look, dress, and act is often bred of necessity, not of attitude or values. And in oppressed societies people's customs and habits belie their true attitudes and values in any event.

Issue 209   Progress through discourse among people

The speaker contends that progress is best made through discourse among people with opposing opinions and viewpoints. I strongly agree with this contention. In all realms of human endeavor, including the behavioral and natural sciences as well as government and law, debate and disagreement form the foundation for progress.

Regarding the physical sciences, our scientific method is essentially a call for progress through opposition. Any new theory must withstand rigorous scientific scrutiny. Moreover, the history of theoretical science is essentially a history of opposing theories. A current example involves two contrary theories of physics: wave theory and quantum theory. During the last 20 years or so scientists have been struggling to disprove one or the other, or to reconcile them. By way of this intense debate, theorists have developed a new so-called "string" theory which indeed reconciles them—at least mathematically.

Although "strings" have yet to be confirmed empirically, string theory might turn out to provide the unifying laws that all matter in the universe obeys.

The importance of opposing theories is not limited to the purely physical sciences. Researchers interested in human behavior have for some time been embroiled in the so-called "nature-nurture" debate, which involves whether behavioral traits are a function of genetic disposition and brain chemistry ("nature") or of learning and environment ("nurture"). Not surprisingly, psychologists and psychiatrists have traditionally adopted sharply opposing stances in this debate. And it is this very debate that has sparked researchers to discover that many behavioral traits are largely a function of the unique neurological structure of each individual's brain, and not a function of nurture. These and further discoveries certainly will lead to progress in dealing effectively with pressing social issues in the fields of education, juvenile delinquency, criminal reform, and mental illness. The outcomes of the debate also carry important implications about culpability and accountability in the eyes of the law. In short, the nature-nurture debate will continue to serve as a catalyst for progress across the entire social spectrum.

The value of discourse between people with opposing viewpoints is not limited to the physical and behavioral sciences. In government and politics, progress in human rights comes typically through dissension from and challenges to the status quo; in fact, without disagreement among factions with opposing viewpoints, political oppression and tyranny would go unchecked. Similarly, in the fields of civil and criminal law, jurists and legislators who uphold and defend legal precedent must face continual opposition from those who question the fairness and relevance of current laws. This ongoing debate is critical to the vitality and relevance of our system of laws.

History informs us of the chilling effect suppression of free discourse and debate can have on progress. Consider the Soviet Refusenik movement of the 1920s. During this time period the Soviet government, attempted not only to control the direction and the goals of scientific research but also to distort the outcomes of that research. During the 1920s the Soviet government quashed certain areas of scientific inquiry, destroyed research facilities and libraries, and caused the sudden disappearance of scientists who were engaged in research that the state viewed as a potential threat. Not surprisingly, during this time period no significant advances in scientific knowledge occurred under the auspices of the Soviet government.

In sum, the speaker correctly asserts that it is through discourse, disagreement, and debate between opposing viewpoints that true progress can best be made. Indeed, advances in science, social welfare, government and law depend on the debate.

Issue 214　Society's duty to identify children with special talents

I agree that we should attempt to identify and cultivate our children's talents. However, in my view the statement goes too far, by suggesting that selected children receive special attention. If followed to the letter, this suggestion carries certain social, psychological, and human-rights implications that might turn out to be more harmful than beneficial—not just to children but to the entire society.

At first blush the statement appears compelling. Although I am not a student of developmental psychology, my understanding is that unless certain innate talents are nurtured and cultivated during early childhood those talents can remain forever dormant; and both the child and the society stand to lose as a result. After all, how can a child who is musically gifted ever see those gifts come to fruition without access to a musical instrument? Or, how can a child who has a gift for linguistics ever learn a foreign language without at least some exposure to it? Thus I agree with the statement insofar as any society that values its own future well-being must be attentive to its children's talents.

Beyond this concession, however, I disagree with the statement because it seems to recommend that certain children receive special attention at the expense of other children—a recommendation that I find troubling in three respects. First, this policy would require that a society of parents make choices that they surely will never agree upon to begin with—for example, how and on what basis each child's talents should be determined, and what sorts of talents are most worth society's time, attention, and resources. While society's parents would never reach a reasonable consensus on these issues, it would be irresponsible to leave these choices to a handful of legislators and bureaucrats. After all, they are unlikely to have the best interests of our children in mind, and their choices would be tainted by their own quirky, biased, and otherwise wrongheaded notions of what constitutes worthwhile talent. Thus the unanswerable question becomes: Who is to make these choices to begin with?

Secondly, a public policy whereby some children receive preferential treatment carries dangerous sociological implications. The sort of selectivity that the statement recommends might tend to split society into two factions: talented elitists and all others. In my view any democratic society should abhor a policy that breeds or exacerbates socioeconomic disparities.

Thirdly, in suggesting that it is in society's best interest to identify especially talented children, the statement assumes that talented children are the ones who are most likely to contribute greatly to the society as adults. I find this assumption somewhat dubious, for I see no reason why a talented child, having received the benefit of special attention, might nevertheless be unmotivated to ply those talents in useful ways as an adult. In fact, in my observation many talented people who misuse their talents—in ways that harm the very society that helped nurture those talents.

Finally, the statement ignores the psychological damage that a preferential policy might inflict on all children. While children selected for special treatment grow to deem themselves superior, those left out feel that they are worthless as a result. I think any astute child psychologist would warn that both types of cases portend psychological trouble later in life. In my view we should favor policies that affirm the self-worth of every child, regardless of his or her talents—or lack thereof. Otherwise, we will quickly devolve into a society of people who cheapen their own humanity.

In the final analysis, when we help our children identify and develop their talents we are all better off. But if we help only some children to develop only some talents, I fear that on balance we will all be worse off.

Issue 216 Are **most important discoveries** and creations accidental?

The speaker contends that most important discoveries and creations are accidental—that they come about when we are seeking answers to other questions. I concede that this contention finds considerable support from important discoveries of the past. However, the contention overstates the role of accident, or serendipity, when it comes to modern-day discoveries—and when it comes to creations.

Turning first to discoveries, I agree that discovery often occurs when we unexpectedly happen upon something in our quest for something else—such as an answer to an unrelated question or a solution to an unrelated problem. A variety of geographical, scientific, and anthropological discoveries aptly illustrate this point. In search of a trade route to the West Indies Columbus discovered instead an inhabited continent unknown to Europeans; and during the course of an unrelated experiment Fleming accidentally discovered penicillin. In search of answers to questions about marine organisms, oceanographers often happen upon previously undiscovered, and important, archeological artifacts and geological phenomena; conversely, in their quest to understand the earth's structure and history geologists often stumble upon important human artifacts.

In light of the foregoing examples, "intentional discovery" might seem an oxymoron; yet in fact it is not. Many important discoveries are anticipated and sought out purposefully. For instance, in their efforts to find new celestial bodies astronomers using increasingly powerful telescopes do indeed find them. Biochemists often discover important new vaccines and other biological and chemical agents for the curing, preventing, and treating of diseases not by stumbling upon them in search of something else but rather through methodical search for these discoveries. In fact, in today's world discovery is becoming increasingly an anticipated result of careful planning and methodical research, for the reason that scientific advancement now requires significant resources that only large corporations and governments possess. These entities are accountable to their shareholders and constituents, who demand clear strategies and objectives so that they can see a return on their investments.

Turning next to how our creations typically come about, in marked contrast to discoveries, creations are by nature products of their creators' purposeful designs. Consider humankind's key creations, such as the printing press, the internal combustion engine, and semi-conductor technology. Each of these inventions sprung quite intentionally from the inventor's imagination and objectives. It is crucial to distinguish here between a creation and the spin-offs from that creation, which the original creator may or may not foresee. For instance, the engineers at a handful of universities who originally created the ARPAnet as a means to transfer data amongst themselves certainly intended to create that network for that purpose. What these engineers did not intend to create, however, was what would eventually grow to become the infrastructure for mass media and communications, and even commerce. Yet the ARPAnet itself was no accident, nor are the many creations that it spawned, such as the World Wide Web and the countless creations that the Web has in turned spawned.

In sum, the speaker has overlooked a crucial distinction between the nature of discovery and the nature of creation. Although serendipity has always played a key role in many important discoveries, at least up until now, purposeful intent is necessarily the key to human creation.

Issue 218　Must art be widely understood **to have merit**?

The speaker's assertion that art must be widely understood to have merit is wrongheaded. The speaker misunderstands the final objective of art, which has little to do with cognitive "understanding."

First consider the musical art form. The fact that the listener must "understand" the composer's artistic expression without the benefit of words or visual images forces us to ask: "What is there to understand in the first place?" Of course, the listener can always struggle to appreciate how the musical piece employs various harmonic, melodic, and rhythmic principles. Yet it would be absurd to assert that the objective of music is to challenge the listener's knowledge of music theory. In fact, listening to music is simply an encounter—an experience to be accepted at face value for its aural impact on our spirit and our emotions.

Next consider the art forms of painting and sculpture. In the context of these art forms, the speaker seems to suggest that if we cannot all understand what the work is supposed to represent, then we should dismiss the work as worthless. Again, however, the speaker misses the point of art. Only by provoking and challenging us, and inciting our emotions, imagination, and wonder do paintings and sculpture hold merit. Put another way, if the test for meritorious art were its ability to be clearly understood by every observer, then our most valuable art would simply imitate the mundane physical world around us. A Polaroid picture taken by a monkey would be considered great art, while the abstract works of Pollock and Picasso would be worth no more than the salvage value of the materials used to create them.

Finally, consider art forms such as poetry, song, and prose, where the use of language is part-and-parcel of the art. It is easy to assume that where words are involved they must be strung together in understandable phrases in order for the art to have any merit. Moreover, if the writer-artist resorts exclusively to obscure words that people simply do not know, then the art can convey nothing beyond the alliterative or onomatopoeic impact that the words might have when uttered aloud. However, in poetry and song the writer-artist often uses words as imagery—to conjure up feelings and evoke visceral reactions in the reader or listener. In these cases stanzas and verses need not be "understood" to have merit, as much as they need be experienced for the images and emotions they evoke.

When it comes to prose, admittedly the writer-artist must use words to convey cognitive ideas—for example, to help the reader follow the plot of a novel. In these cases the art must truly be "understood" on a linguistic and cognitive level; otherwise it is mere gibberish—without merit except perhaps as a doorstop. Nevertheless, the final objective even of literature is to move the reader emotionally and spiritually—not simply to inform. Thus, even though a reader might understand the twists and turns of a novel's plot intellectually, what's the point if the reader has come away unaffected in emotion or spirit?

In the final analysis, whether art must be understood by most people, or by any person, in order for it to have merit begs the question. To "understand" art a person need only have eyes to see or ears to hear, and a soul to feel.

Issue 225   Our tendency to look for similarities between **different things**

Do people too often look for similarities between things, regardless of whether it is helpful or harmful to do so, and not often enough evaluate things on their own individual merits? The speaker believes so. I agree to an extent, especially when it comes to making determinations about people. However, the speaker overlooks a fundamental and compelling reason why people must always try to find similarities between things.

I agree with the speaker insofar as insisting on finding similarities between things can often result in unfair, and sometimes harmful, comparisons. By focusing on the similarities among all big cities, for example, we overlook the distinctive character, architecture, ethnic diversity, and culture of each one. Without evaluating an individual company on its own merits before buying stock in that company, an investor runs the risk of choosing a poor performer in an otherwise attractive product sector or geographic region. And schools tend to group students according to their performance on general intelligence tests and academic exams. By doing so, schools overlook more specific forms of intelligence which should be identified and nurtured on a more individualized basis so that each student can fulfill his or her potential.

As the final example above illustrates, we should be especially careful when looking for similarities between people. We humans have a tendency to draw arbitrary conclusions about one another based on gender, race, and superficial characteristics. Each individual should be evaluated instead on the basis of his or her own merit—in terms of character, accomplishment, and so forth. Otherwise, we run the risk of unfair bias and even prejudice, which manifest themselves in various forms of discrimination and oppression. Yet prejudice can result from looking too hard for differences as well, while overlooking the things that all people share. Thus while partly correct, the speaker's assertion doesn't go far enough—to account for the potential harm in drawing false distinctions between types of people.

Yet, in another sense the speaker goes too far—by overlooking a fundamental, even philosophical, reason why we should always look for similarities between things. Specifically, it is the only way humans can truly learn anything and communicate with one another. Any astute developmental psychologist, epistemologist, or even parent would agree that we come to understand each new thing we encounter by comparing it to something with which we are already familiar. For example, if a child first associates the concept of blue with the sky's color, then the next blue thing the child encounters—a ball, for instance—the child recognizes as blue only by way of its similarity to the sky. Furthermore, without this association and a label for the concept of blue the child cannot possibly convey the concept to another person. Thus looking for similarities between things is how we make sense of our world, as well as communicate with one another.

To sum up, I agree that finding false similarities and drawing false analogies can be harmful, especially when reaching conclusions about people. Nevertheless, from a philosophical and linguistic point of view, humans must look for similarities between things in order to learn and to communicate.

Issue 230   Should colleges allow students to **make their own decisions**?

The speaker asserts that people prefer following directions to making their own decisions, and therefore colleges should make as many decisions as possible for their students. In my view, the speaker's threshold and ultimate claims are both specious. It might appear that people often prefer others to make decisions for them, and that colleges know what's best for their students. However, upon further reflection it becomes evident that following the speaker's advice would on balance do disservice to students and to society.

As for the speaker's threshold claim, I concede that under certain circumstances people prefer to take direction from others. For instance, when members of a football team heed their coach's directions, they are preferring not to make their own calls. Moreover, many people are natural followers who know that they function best when other people make decisions for them. Nevertheless, I find this threshold claim internally illogical. Yielding voluntarily to the direction of others for the purpose of serving one's own interests—such as winning the game or obtaining a useful college degree—is itself an expression of one's free preference to decide what is best for oneself. Accordingly, I find the speaker's threshold claim suspect.

I turn next to the speaker's ultimate claim that colleges should make as many decisions as possible for their students. I agree that when it comes to particular tasks in which college professors are more experienced and knowledgeable, following their directions is to be preferred, for failing to do so can result in costly mistakes. For instance, chemistry students must strictly follow proper laboratory procedures—or risk tainting experimental results, damaging equipment, or wasting their lab partners' time. Language students must follow the pedagogical lead of their teachers, or risk coming away without the linguistic foundation needed to master their new language. And, students who are free to disregard homework assignments find themselves unable to follow class discussions, let alone participate meaningfully in them.

However, when it comes to decisions about major and minor fields of study, curriculum choices, and other broad decisions, for the most part students themselves—and not college administrators—should be the final decision-makers. Admittedly, a college that requires exposure to a breadth of academic disciplines ensures that its graduates will be uniformly well-rounded. And students are generally well-served in the long term as a result. Nevertheless, I think it is a mistake to take too many curriculum choices away from students. If they are not free to choose course work that most interests them, students are likely to be unmotivated in their studies. Moreover, these students will not have learned to assume responsibility for the consequences of their own decisions. Thus a curriculum which includes certain core requirements along with a broad array of electives provides an optimal balance of discipline and choice for most students.

The speaker might retort that many college students respond to freedom of choice regarding curriculum by enrolling in as few courses as possible, in courses that are most enjoyable, and in courses whose instructors are lenient graders. Yet, students who misuse their freedom in these ways will ultimately fall by the wayside, freeing up our educational resources for more committed students who are more likely to contribute meaningfully to society later in life. Besides, by allowing students to experience the consequences of their youthful misjudgments colleges can teach students life lessons that are just as valuable, if not more so, than the lessons taught in the classroom.

In sum, my intuition is that by nature people prefer autonomy, and reach their full potential, only if they steer their own ship. When colleges take away too much of that autonomy in the name of quality assurance, they breed legions of graduates incapable of handling their incipient autonomy responsibly. In the final analysis, while some curriculum guidelines might be appropriate in the interest of ensuring a breadth of educational experience, on balance a policy of student choice is to be preferred.

Issue 231   Is **moderation in all things** poor advice?

Should we strive for moderation in all things, as the adage suggests? I tend to agree with the speaker that worthwhile endeavors sometimes require, or at least call for, intense focus at the expense of moderation.

The virtues of moderation are undeniable. Moderation in all things affords us the time and energy to sample more of what life and the world have to offer. In contrast, lack of moderation leads to a life out of balance. As a society we are slowly coming to realize what many astute psychologists and medical practitioners have known all along: we are at our best as humans only when we strike a proper balance between the mind, body, and spirit. The call for a balanced life is essentially a call for moderation in all things.

For instance, while moderate exercise improves our health and sense of well-being, over-exercise and intense exercise can cause injury or psychological burnout, either of which defeat our purpose by requiring us to discontinue exercise altogether. Lack of moderation in diet can cause obesity at one extreme or anorexia at the other, either of which endangers one's health, and even life. And when it comes to potentially addictive substances—alcohol, tobacco, and the like—the deleterious effects of over-consumption are clear enough.

The virtues of moderation apply to work as well. Stress associated with a high-pressure job increases one's vulnerability to heart disease and other physical disorders. And over-work can result in psychological burnout, thereby jeopardizing one's job and career. Overwork can even kill, as demonstrated by the alarmingly high death rate among young Japanese men, many of whom work 100 or more hours each week.

Having acknowledged the wisdom of the old adage, I nevertheless agree that under some circumstances, and for some people, abandoning moderation might be well justified. Query how many of the world's great artistic creations—in the visual arts, music, and even literature—would have come to fruition without intense, focused efforts on the part of their creators. Creative work necessarily involves a large measure of intense focus—a single-minded, obsessive pursuit of aesthetic perfection.

Or, consider athletic performance. Admittedly, intensity can be counterproductive when it results in burnout or injury. Yet who could disagree that a great athletic performance necessarily requires great focus and intensity—both in preparation and in the performance itself? In short, when it comes to athletics, moderation breeds mediocrity, while intensity breeds excellence and victory. Finally, consider the increasingly competitive world of business. An intense, focused company-wide effort is sometimes needed to ensure a company's competitiveness, and even survival. This is particularly true in today's technology-driven industries where keeping up with frantic pace of change is essential for almost any high-tech firm's survival.

In sum, the old adage amounts to sound advice for most people under most circumstances. Nevertheless, when it comes to creative accomplishment, and to competitive success in areas such as athletics and business, I agree with the speaker that abandoning or suspending moderation is often appropriate, and sometimes necessary, in the interest of achieving worthwhile goals.

Issue 233   Do **technologies** interfere with "real" learning?

The speaker asserts that innovations such as videos, computers, and the Internet too often distract from "real" learning in the classroom. I strongly agree that these tools can be counterproductive in some instances, and ineffectual for certain types of learning. Nevertheless, the speaker's assertion places too little value on the ways in which these innovations can facilitate the learning process.

In several respects, I find the statement compelling. First of all, in my observation and experience, computers and videos are misused most often for education when teachers rely on them as surrogates, or baby-sitters. Teachers must use the time during which students are watching videos or are at their computer stations productively—helping other students, preparing lesson plans, and so forth. Otherwise, these tools can indeed impede the learning process.

Secondly, passive viewing of videos or of Web pages is no indication that any significant learning is taking place. Thus teachers must carefully select Internet resources that provide a true interactive learning experience, or are highly informative otherwise. And, in selecting videos teachers must be sure to follow up with lively class discussions. Otherwise, the comparatively passive nature of these media can render them ineffectual in the learning process.

Thirdly, some types of learning occur best during face-to-face encounters between teacher and student, and between students. Only by way of a live encounter can a language teacher recognize and immediately correct subtle problems in pronunciation and inflection. And, there is no suitable substitute for a live encounter when it comes to teaching techniques in painting, sculpture, music performance, and acting. Moreover, certain types of learning are facilitated when students interact as a group. Many grade-school teachers, for example, find that reading together aloud is the most effective way for students to learn this skill.

Fourth, with technology-based learning tools, especially computers and the Internet, learning how to use the technology can rob the teacher of valuable time that could be spent accomplishing the teacher's ultimate educational objectives. Besides, any technology-based learning tool carries the risk of technical problems. Students whose teachers fail to plan for productive use of unexpected downtime can lose opportunities for real learning.

Finally, we must not overlook the non-quantifiable benefit that personal attention can afford. A human teacher can provide meaningful personal encouragement and support, and can identify and help to solve a student's social or psychological problems that might be impeding the learning process. No video, computer program, or Web site can begin to serve these invaluable functions.

Acknowledging the many ways that technological innovations can impede "real" learning, these innovations nevertheless can facilitate "real" learning, if employed judicially and for appropriate purposes. Specifically, when it comes to learning rote facts and figures, personal interaction with a teacher is unnecessary, and can even result in fatigue and burnout for the teacher. Computers are an ideal tool for the sorts of learning that occur only through repetition—typing skills, basic arithmetical calculations, and so forth. Computers also make possible visual effects that aid uniquely in the learning of spatial concepts. Finally, computers, videos and the Internet are ideal for imparting basic textbook information to students, thereby freeing up the teacher's time to give students individualized attention.

In sum, computers and videos can indeed distract from learning—when teachers misuse them as substitutes for personal attention, or when the technology itself becomes the focus of attention. Nevertheless, if judicially used as primers, as supplements, and where repetition and rote learning are appropriate, these tools can serve to liberate teachers to focus on individual needs of students—needs that only "real" teachers can recognize and meet.

Issue 234   Do people prefer constraints on **absolute freedom**?

Do people prefer constraints on absolute freedom of choice, regardless of what they might claim? I believe so, because in order for any democratic society to thrive it must strike a balance between freedom and order.

History informs us that attempts to quell basic individual freedoms—of expression, of opinion and belief, and to come and go as we please—invariably fail. People ultimately rise up against unreasonable constraints on freedom of choice. The desire for freedom seems to spring from our fundamental nature as human beings. But does this mean that people would prefer absolute freedom of choice to any constraints whatsoever? No. Reasonable constraints on freedom are needed to protect freedom—and to prevent a society from devolving into a state of anarchy where life is short and brutish.

To appreciate our preference for constraining our own freedom of choice, one need look no further than the neighborhood playground. Even without any adult supervision, a group of youngsters at play invariably establish mutually agreed-upon rules for conduct—whether or not a sport or game is involved. Children learn at an early age that without any rules for behavior the playground bully usually prevails. And short of beating up on others, bullies enjoy taking prisoners—i.e., restricting the freedom of choice of others. Thus our preference for constraining our freedom of choice stems from our desire to protect and preserve that freedom.

Our preference for constraining our own freedom of choice continues into our adult lives. We freely enter into exclusive pair-bonding relationships; during our teens we agree to "go steady," then as adults we voluntarily enter into marriage contracts. Most of us eagerly enter into exclusive employment relationships—preferring the security of steady income to the "freedom" of not knowing where our next paycheck will come from. Even people who prefer self-employment to job security quickly learn that the only way to preserve their "autonomy" is to constrain themselves in terms of their agreements with clients and customers, and especially in terms of how they use their time. Admittedly, our self-inflicted job constraints are born largely of economic necessity. Yet even the wealthiest individuals usually choose to constrain their freedom by devoting most of their time and attention to a few pet projects.

Our preference for constraining our own freedom of choice is evident on a societal level as well. Just as children at a playground recognize the need for self-imposed rules and regulations, as a society we recognize the same need. After all, in a democratic society our system of laws is an invention of the people. For example, we insist on being bound by rules for operating motor vehicles, for buying and selling both real and personal property, and for making public statements about other people. Without these rules, we would live in continual fear for our physical safety, the security of our property, and our personal reputation and dignity.

In sum, I agree with the fundamental assertion that people prefer reasonable constraints on their freedom of choice. In fact, in a democratic society we insist on imposing these constraints on ourselves in order to preserve that freedom.

Issue 235　Is loyalty always a **positive force**?

Is loyalty all too often a destructive force, rather than a virtue, as the speaker contends? To answer this question it is crucial to draw a distinction between loyalty as an abstract concept and its application. Apart from its consequences, loyalty is clearly a virtue that all humans should strive to develop. Loyalty is part of a universal ethos that we commonly refer to as the golden rule: Do unto others as you would have others do unto you. However, whether loyalty in its application amounts to virtue depends on its extent and its object.

First consider the ways in which loyalty, if exercised in proper measure and direction, can be a positive force. Relationships between spouses and other exclusive pairs require some degree of trust in order to endure; and loyalty is part-and-parcel of that trust. Similarly, employment relationships depend on some measure of mutual loyalty, without which job attrition would run so rampant that society's economic productivity would virtually come to a halt. And, without some mutual loyalty between a sovereign state and its citizenry there can be no security or safety from either revolt or invasion. The world would quickly devolve into anarchy or into a despotic state ordered by brute force.

On the other hand, misguided or overextended loyalty can amount to a divisive and even destructive force. In school, undue loyalty to popular social cliques often leads to insulting and abusive language or behavior toward students outside these cliques. Undue loyalty amongst friends can turn them into an antisocial, even warring, gang of miscreants. And, undue loyalty to a spouse or other partner can lead to acquiescence in abusive treatment by that partner, and abuse of oneself by continuing to be loyal despite the abuse.

Misguided loyalty can also occur between people and their institutions. Undue loyalty to college alma maters often leads to job discrimination—for example, when a job candidate with the same alma mater as that of the person making the hiring decision is chosen over a more qualified candidate from a different school. Loyalty to one's employer can also become a destructive force, if it leads to deceptive business practices and disregard for regulations designed to protect public health and safety. By way of undue loyalty to their employers, employees sometimes harm themselves as well. Specifically, many employees fail to advance their own careers by moving on to another place of work, or type of work altogether, because of a misplaced sense of loyalty to one company. Finally, and perhaps foremost in terms of destructive potential, is misguided loyalty to one's country or political leaders. History shows all too well that crossing the fine line between patriotism and irrational jingoism can lead to such atrocities as persecution, genocide, and war.

To sum up, without loyalty there can be no basis for trust between two people, or between people and their institutions. A world devoid of loyalty would be a paranoid, if not anarchical, one. Nevertheless, loyalty must be tempered by other virtues, such as fairness, tolerance, and respect for other people and for oneself. Otherwise, I agree that it can serve to divide, damage, and even destroy.

Issue 238   Does conformity stifle **creativity and energy**?

This statement about the impact of conformity on individual energy and creativity actually involves two distinct issues. In my view, the extent to which conformity stifles a person's energy depends primarily on the temperament of each individual, as well as on the goals toward which the person's energy is directed. However, I am in full agreement that conformity stifles creativity; indeed, in my view the two phenomena are mutually exclusive.

Whether conformity stifles individual energy depends on the individual person involved. Some people are conformists by nature. By this I mean that they function best in an environment where their role is dearly defined and where teamwork is key in meeting group objectives. For conformists individual energy comes from sharing a common purpose, or mission, with a group that must work in lock-step fashion to achieve that mission. In the military and in team sports, for example, the group's common mission is dearly understood, and group members conform to the same dress code, drill regimen, and so forth. And rather than quelling energy, this conformity breeds camaraderie, as well as enthusiasm and even fervor for winning the battle or the game. Besides, nonconforming behavior in these environments only serves to undermine success; if game plans or battle strategies were left to each individual team member, the results would dearly be disastrous.

Conformists find enhanced energy in certain corners of the business world as well, particularly in traditional service industries such as finance, accounting, insurance, legal services, and health care. In these businesses it is not the iconoclasts who revel and thrive but rather those who can work most effectively within the constraints of established practices, policies, and regulations. Of course, a clever idea for structuring a deal, or a creative legal maneuver, might play a role in winning smaller battles along the way. But such tactics are those of conformists who are playing by the same ground rules as their peers.

In sharp contrast, other people are nonconformists by nature. These people are motivated more often by the personal satisfaction that comes with creativity, invention, and innovation. For these people a highly structured, bureaucratic environment only serves to quell motivation and energy. Artists and musicians typically find such environments stifling, even noxious. Entrepreneurial business people who thrive on innovation and differentiation are often driven to self-employment because they feel stifled and frustrated, even offended, by a bureaucracy which requires conformity.

As for whether conformity stifles individual creativity, one need only look around at the individuals whom we consider highly creative to conclude that this is indeed the case. Our most creative people are highly eccentric in their personal appearance, lifestyle, and so forth. In fact, they seem to eschew any sort of established norms and mores. Bee-bop music pioneer Thelonius Monk was renowned for his eccentric manner of speech, dress, and behavior. Even as a young student, Frank Lloyd Wright took to carrying a cane and wearing a top hat and a cape. And who could argue that musicians

Prince and Michael Jackson, two of the most creative forces in popular music, are nothing if not non-conforming in every way. Besides, by definition creativity requires nonconformity. In other words, any creative act is necessarily in nonconformance with what already exists.

To sum up, conformists find their energy by conforming, nonconformists by not conforming. And creativity is the exclusive domain of the nonconformist.

Issue 243　The comparative value of artistic and **scientific accomplishments**

I find the speaker's claim that a civilization's value lies more in its artistic accomplishments than its scientific ones to be problematic insofar as the speaker fails to adequately define the term "value." Nonetheless, assuming that by "value" the speaker means the extent to which an accomplishment enhances and improves the quality of our lives as humans, on balance I agree with the claim.

A threshold problem with the speaker's claim is that the comparative value of art and science lies largely in the eye of the individual beholder. A person who is more emotional, or who has heightened aesthetic sensibilities, will tend to agree with the speaker. On the other hand, a person who is more analytical or cognitive by nature might tend to disagree. Thus the speaker's claim seems an unfair generalization, which ignores its own vulnerability to subjectivity.

Aside from the highly subjective nature of the claim, if the value of a civilization's accomplishments is determined by the civilization itself, then the speaker's claim begs the question. If a civilization chooses to concern itself primarily with science, as our modern Western civilization does, then by definition scientific accomplishments must be of greater value to the civilization than artistic accomplishments. Of course, the reverse would be true for any culture that stresses artistic accomplishment over scientific inquiry.

Assuming that by "value" the speaker means the extent to which later civilizations depend on earlier artistic and scientific accomplishments, I strongly disagree with the speaker's claim. We speak of scientific accomplishments in terms of "progress" and "setback," or "advances" and "retreat." The reason for this is clear enough. With few historical exceptions great scientific accomplishments build on prior ones. Even where new discoveries disprove old theories, scientists would not be challenged and incited in the first place without the benefit of their predecessor's efforts. In sharp contrast, artistic accomplishment has little to do with either advances or retreats. Art is timeless—independent of prior art. Artists draw inspiration not from other art but from the world around them, the essence of which artists attempt to capture and convey. In short, if the value of an accomplishment lies simply in the extent to which subsequent accomplishments depend on it, then the speaker's claim is fundamentally wrong.

However, if by "value" the speaker means something more—the extent to which a scientific or an artistic accomplishment makes the world a better place for humans overall—then the speaker's claim has far more merit. Although it would be tempting to embrace the popular notion that better living is achieved primarily through science, on balance I disagree with this notion. Admittedly, advances in the health sciences serve to enhance our physical well-being, our comfort, and our life span. However, in a myriad of other respects scientific accomplishments have diminished our quality of life. After all, it is through scientific accomplishment that chemicals in our food, water, and air increase the incidence and variety of cancers; that our very existence as a species is jeopardized by the threat of nuclear warfare; and that greenhouse gases which deplete our ozone layer and heat the Earth threaten civilization itself.

In sharp contrast, no great artistic accomplishment has brought about war, disease or any threat to the quality of life for any civilization. To the contrary, great art only serves to lift the human spirit in the face of the so-called "progress" that scientific accomplishments bring about. Therefore, on balance I agree with the speaker that the value of a civilization—in the long term—lies more in its artistic than scientific accomplishments.

第四章　Argument 范文精讲

Argument 中的逻辑错误及应对策略

　　Argument 的题目中设置了一些推论或论据方面的漏洞，使其有懈可击。一般而言每篇 Argument 里都有三四个明显的错误供考生批评。（在本章和第五章的范文中，大多数的论证部分都由三四个段落构成，每一段里都有一个明显的错误可供批评。）

　　我们来研究一下 Argument 中最常见的逻辑或推论方面的错误。每个问题都配有相应的一篇模拟 Argument 来提供错误的详情，并附有标准的应对范文。这些例子并非 GRE 真题中的 Argument，而是很逼真的模拟题。另外，这些 Argument 因为各自只针对一个具体的推理问题，所以比 Argument 真题的长度稍短一些。

False Analogy and comparison

一、经不起推敲的类推

　　在 GRE 的 Arguments 中可能出现由一个事物（如城市、学校或公司）对另一事物进行类推的情况。这就意味着，作者认为两件事物因为在某些方面相似，那么它们在其他所有方面就一定都相似。除非文章中提供了充分证据支持这种假设，否则其论述就可以受到置疑。下面的例子中有两处经不起推敲的类推：

Argument：

The following appeared in a memo from the manager of Cutters, a hair salon located in suburban Apton:

"...In order to boost Cutters' sagging profits we should relocate our hair salon from its current suburban—mall location to downtown Apton. After all, Hair-Dooz, our chief competitor at the rnall, has relocated downtown and is prospering in its new location. ...Besides, in neighboring Brainard the most successful hair salon is located in that city's downtown district. By emulating these two successful salons we'll surely succeed as well."

范文：

Can not achieve its goals by following xx's example

The argument relies on what might be a false analogy between Cutters and the Brainard and Hair-Dooz salons. In order for the last two salons to serve as models that Cutters should emulate, the manager must assume that all relevant circumstances involving the business are essentially the same. However, this assumption is *未证实为正当 不合情理* unwarranted. For example, the argument overlooks the poss-

assumes that similar incentives will carry a similar result for

ibility that the Hair-Dooz _ move was motivated by other concerns besides profitability. Perhaps the owner of Hair-Dooz relocated the salon to cater to a certain clientele that Cutters would not attract. As for the Brainard salon, perhaps the demographic trends in Brainard are quite different than those in Apton, and therefore Cutters is likely to fail in downtown Al even though the other salon prospers in downtown Brainard. Or, perhaps the Brainard salon thrives only because it is long-established in its current downtown location, while Cutters would flounder without an immediate customer base in downtown Apton.

二、将因果关系与单纯的关联关系或时间关系混淆起来

很多 Argument 的论述基于这样的思路：一件事情的发生是由另一件事情引起的。这种因果关系的推理也许是基于以下的原因：

1．两件事的发生有明显联系（两件事情总是一起出现）。

2．两件事的发生在时间上有关系（一件事出现在另一件事之后）。

两件事很明显的相关性或时间上的关联有可能意味着两者之间有因果关系，但仅此一点并不足以保证这种因果关系的存在。除非 Argument 提到并且排除其他可能的、且合乎情理的原因（顺便一提，该 Argument 不能排除），否则其论述就存在漏洞。下面的例子中含有上述两种情况：

Argument：

The following appeared in the editorial section of a newspaper.

"Many states have enacted laws prohibiting environmental emissions of nitrocarbon byproducts, on the basis that these byproducts have been shown to cause Urkin's Disease in humans. These laws have clearly been effective in preventing the disease. After all, in every state that has enacted such a law the incidence of Urkin's disease is lower than in any state that has not enacted a similar taw ..."

范文：

The argument concludes based on a known correlation between laws prohibiting certain emissions and the low incidence of Urkin's Disease that the latter is attributable, at least partly, to the former. Yet the correlation alone amounts to scant evidence of the claimed cause-and-effect relationship. Perhaps Urkin's disease can be caused by other factors as well, which are absent in these particular states but present in all others. Moreover, the argument overlooks the fact that it is the level of compliance with a law, not its enactment, that determines its effectiveness. The editorial's author has not accounted for the possibility that the laws prohibiting the emissions were never enforced or complied with, and that the emissions have continued unabated. If this is the case, then the conclusion that the laws are effective in preventing Urkin's Disease would lack any merit whatsoever.

Hasty Generalization

三、认为一个群体的特征适用于该群体的所有成员

Argument 中常把群体的特征延伸到个体。除非 Argument 有力地证明这一个体的确具有那一群体的典型特征（顺便一提，该 Argument 不能证明），否则其论述就有懈可击。请看：

Argument：

The following appeared in a memo from the president of Cutters, a regional chain of hair salons：

"It is a well-established fact that in today's society more and more people are moving from the suburbs to downtown areas. So in order to boost Cutters' sagging profits we should relocate each of our hair salons currently located in a suburban mall to the downtown area nearest to it ..."

范文：

The argument assumes that the demographic trend in the specific region where Cutters operates reflects the general trend upon which the argument relies. Yet, Cutters' president fails to offer any evidence to substantiate this crucial assumption. Absent such evidence, it is just as likely that in the region where Cutters operates people are not moving from the suburbs to downtown areas; for that matter, perhaps in this region the demographic trend is in the opposite direction, in which event the president's recommendation would amount to especially poor advice.

Necessity and Sufficiency

四、认为某条件是某结果的必要和／或充足条件

Argument 会出现基于下面两种思路而推荐某行为的情况：

1. 要想取得理想的结果就必须按照这种（推荐的）行为去做。
2. 按照这种（推荐的）行为去做就足以取得理想的结果。

附：如果个衬动机跳顺
与句 in order.？

以上两种思路常常出现在同一篇 Argument 中。这两个思路都易受到置疑。就第一条思路而言，Argument 必须提供证据证明，除了这个行为之外就没有其他能达到同样结果的行为了（顺便一提，它不能提供）。就第二条思路而言，Argument 也必须提供有力的证据证明，所建议的行为足以保证理想效果的获得（顺便一提，它不能提供）。如果缺少这些证据，文章作者就不应该用以上两个思路来支持所提的行为建议。下面的范文由两个段落组成。第一段针对思路一，第二段针对思路二。

Argument：

The following appeared in a uremo from the superintendent of the Cutter County school district：

"In order to raise the level of reading skills of our district's elementary-school students to a level that at least represents the national average, we should adopt the 'Back to Basics' reading program, After all, this reading program has a superior record for improving reading skills among youngsters nationwide. By adopting Back to Basics the parents of our young students would be assured that their children will develop the reading skills they will need throughout their lives . . ."

范文：

The recommendation depends on the assumption that no alternative means of improving the students' reading skills are available. Yet no evidence is offered to substantiate this assumption. Admittedly, the superior record of the Back to Basics (BTB) program is some evidence that no other program is as likely to achieve the desired result. However, it is entirely possible that means other than this or any other reading program would also achieve the desired result. Perhaps the desired improvement could be achieved if the schools instead hired special reading instructors, or encouraged parents to read with their children, or simply devoted more time during school to reading. Without considering and ruling out these and other alternative means of improving reading skills, the superintendent cannot confidently conclude that the schools must adopt the BTB program-or for that matter any reading program-in order to achieve the district's goal.

The recommendation depends on the additional unsubstantiated assumption that adopting BTB would by itself improve students' reading skills to the desired extent. Absent evidence that this is the case, it is equally possible that adopting the program would not suffice by itself. Students must be sufficiently attentive and motivated, and teachers must be sufficiently competent: otherwise, the program will not be effective. In short, unless the superintendent can show that the program will be effectively implemented and received. I cannot accept the recommendation.

五、基于可能不具代表性的统计数据

　　Argument 会引用一些对抽样组进行研究、调查或民意测验而得出的统计数据，并由此得出针对更多人或物的结论。但是，要确保这样做的正确性，抽样组必须具备以下两个条件：

　　1. 作为整体中的一部分，抽样组必须具有一定的规模。

　　2. 抽样组在相关的特点方面必须能代表整体。　其实不可能的，HeHe

这两个要求 Argument 往往都没有满足。当然，这是出题者故意为之，目的是提供给考生进行评判的机会。下面的例子为你演示如何在范文中用一个段落处理这两个问题。

Argument：

The following is taken from the editorial section of Urbanville's local newspaper: "Today's undergraduate college students in this state will have better success obtaining jobs in this state if they do not pursue advanced degrees after graduation. After all, more than 90 percent of Urbanville University's undergraduate students are employed full-time within one year after they graduate. However, less than half of the University's graduate students find employment within one year after receiving their graduate-level degrees . . ."

范文：

One problem with the argument involves the cited statistics about Urbanville graduates. It is unreasonable to draw any conclusions about graduates of all colleges in the state based on statistics about graduates of only one institution. Depending on the total number of colleges and college students in the state, it is entirely possible that Urbanville University (UU), or its students, are not representative of the state's colleges, or college students, generally. For example, perhaps UU's undergraduate students are particularly outstanding academically due to comparatively high admission standards, while the admission standards of UU's graduate programs are low compared to those of other graduate programs in the state. If so, then the editorial's recommendation might amount to poor advice for students at other coifeges.

六、基于不准确的调查或民意测验结果 调查吊受精误

正如以上所述，Argument 中会根据不具代表性且不充足的抽样组得出针对整体的结论。潜在的问题不仅在此。数据资料搜集过程（方法学）的不妥也可能导致所搜集的资料有问题，而不能用作下结论的依据。为使调查或民意测验可靠，必须注意以下两点：

1. 调查或民意测验的结果必须可信（真实而准确）。如果被调查者有提供不准确回答的可能，调查结果就应被认定为不可靠。

2. 搜集资料的方法必须公正，不带倾向性。如果调查表的设计有引导被调查者做出某种回答的嫌疑，那么调查结果就是不可靠的。

下面的 Argument 就存在这两个问题。范文在同一段落里评判了这两个问题。

Argument:

The following appeared in a memo from the director of human resources at Webco:

"Among Webco employees participating in our department's most recent survey, about half indicated that they are happy with our current four-day work week. These survey results show that the most effective way to improve overall productivity at Webco is to allow each employee to choose for himself or herself either a four-day or five-day work week."

范文：

The, survey methodology might be problematic in two respects: First, we are not informed whether the survey required that respondents choose their work-week preference between alternatives: If it did, then the results might distort the preferences of the respondents, who might very well prefer a work-schedule choice not provided for in the survey. Secondly, we are not informed whether survey responses were anonymous, or even confidential. If they were not. then respondents might have provided responses that they believed their superiors would approve of, regardless of whether the responses were truthful. In either event, the survey results would be unreliable for the purpose of drawing any conclusions about Webco employee preferences, let alone about how to improve overall productivity at Webco.

七、认为一切事情都是永恒不变的

Argument 可能会利用以前得出的某个结论作为依据，对目前或将来的事物做出结论（或提出建议）。除非作者提供了有力的证据来证明现在和过去在一些关键的方面是相似的（顺便一提，他不能提供），否则其论点就有懈可击。请看例证：

Argument:

> The following appeared in an advertisement for United Motors trucks:
>
> "United Motors trucks are clearly the safest trucks on the market ... Last year the local television-news program In Focus reported in its annual truck-safety survey that over the course of the last 10 years United Motors trucks were involved in at least 30 percent fewer fatalities to vehicle occupants than trucks built by any other single manufacturer ..."

范文:

> The ad's claim unfairly infers from United's comparatively strong safety record in the past that United's new trucks this year must also be comparatively safe: Absent evidence to support this inference, it is just as likely that the safety of competing trucks has improved recently: or that the safety of United trucks has diminished recently: For that matter, perhaps United's truck fatality record during the most recent few years is no better or perhaps even worse than those of its competitors. Any of these scenarios, if true. would serve to undermine the ad's claim that United's new trucks this year are comparatively safe:

Argument 1   Should **Nature's Way** open a store in **Plainesville**?

The following appeared in a memorandum written by the vice president of Nature's Way, a chain of stores selling health food and other health-related products.

"Previous experience has shown that our stores are most profitable in areas where residents are highly concerned with leading healthy lives. We should therefore build our next new store in Plainsville, which has many such residents. Plainsville merchants report that sales of running shoes and exercise clothing are at all-time highs. The local health club, which nearly closed five years ago due to lack of business, has more members than ever, and the weight training and aerobics classes are always full. We can even anticipate a new generation of customers: Plainsville's schoolchildren are required to participate in a 'fitness for life' program, which emphasizes the benefits of regular exercise at an early age."

【参考译文】以前的经验表明，我们的商店在那些居民对健康生活高度关注的地区是赢利最多的。因此我们应该把下一家连锁店开设在普兰斯维尔，那里有很多这样的居民。普兰斯维尔的商家报告说，运动鞋和运动衣的销售处于历史最高点。当地那家五年前因缺乏客源而濒临倒闭的康体俱乐部现在的会员比以往任何时候都多，减肥训练和体操班总是满员。我们还可以预料会有一批新生代的顾客：普兰斯维尔的小学生被要求参加一个叫做"终生健康"的项目，它强调从小开始经常锻炼的好处。

In this memo the **vice president** of Nature's Way (NW), a chain of stores selling health food and health-related products, **recommends** opening a store in Plainesville. To support this recommendation the vice president **cites the following facts** about Plainesville: (1) sales of exercise shoes and clothing are at all-time highs; (2) the local health club is more popular than ever; and (3) the city's schoolchildren are required to participate in a fitness program. **Close scrutiny of each of these facts, however, reveals that none of them lend credible support to the recommendation.**

First, strong sales of exercise apparel **do not necessarily indicate that** Plainesville residents would be interested in NW's products, or that these residents are interested in exercising. **Perhaps** exercise apparel happens to be fashionable at the moment, or inexpensive compared to other types of clothing. For that matter, perhaps the stronger-than-usual sales are due to increasing sales to tourists. In short, **without ruling out other possible reasons for** the strong sales **the vice president cannot convince me on the basis of them that** Plainesville residents are exercising regularly, let alone that they would be interested in buying the sorts of food and other products that NW sells.

Secondly, even if exercise is more popular among Plainesville residents than ever before, the vice president **assumes further that** people who exercise regularly are also interested in buying health food and health-related products. **Yet the memo contains no evidence to support this assumption. Lacking such evidence it is equally possible that** *aside from exercising* Plainesville residents *have little interest in* leading a healthy lifestyle. In fact, perhaps as a result of regular exercise they believe they are sufficiently fit and healthy and do not need a healthy diet.

Thirdly, the popularity of the local health club **is little indication that** NW will earn a profit from a store in Plainesville. Perhaps club members live in an area of Plainesville nowhere near feasible sites for a NW store. Or perhaps the club's primary appeal is as a singles meeting place, and that members actually have little interest in a healthy lifestyle. Besides, even if the club's members would patronize a NW store these members might be insufficient in number to ensure a profit for the store, especially considering that this health club is the only one in Plainesville.

Fourth, the fact that a certain fitness program is mandatory for Plainesville's schoolchildren **accomplishes nothing toward bolstering the recommendation.** Many years must pass before these children will be old enough to make buying decisions when it comes to food and health-related products. Their habits and interests might change radically over time. **Besides**, mandatory participation is no indication of genuine interest in health or fitness. Moreover, when these children grow older it is entirely possible that they will favor an unhealthy lifestyle—as a reaction to the healthful habits imposed upon them now.

Finally, even assuming that Plainesville residents are strongly interested in eating health foods and health-related products, the recommendation rests on two additional assumptions: (1) that this interest will continue in the foreseeable future, and (2) that Plainesville residents will prefer NW over other merchants that sell similar products. **Until the vice president substantiates both assumptions I remain unconvinced that** a NW store in Plainesville would be profitable.

In sum, the recommendation relies on certain doubtful assumptions that render it unconvincing as it stands. To bolster the recommendation the vice president must provide clear evidence—perhaps by way of a local survey or study—that Plainesville residents who buy and wear exercise apparel, and especially the health club's members, do in fact exercise regularly, and that these exercisers are likely to buy health foods and health-related products at a NW store. To better assess the recommendation, I would need to know why Plainesville's health club is popular, and why Plainesville does not contain more health clubs. I would also need to know what competition NW might face in Plainesville.

【参考译文】

自然方式（NW）公司的副总裁在其备忘录里建议在普兰斯维尔开一家商店。自然方式（NW）公司是一家连锁公司，其旗下的商店出售保健食品和与健康有关的产品。为了支持这个建议，副总裁引用了以下有关普兰斯维尔的事实：（1）运动鞋和运动服的销售额达到空前的高峰；（2）当地的健身俱乐部受到了前所未有的欢迎；（3）该市要求小学生参加一个健康计划。然而，仔细谨慎地研究上述事实后，我发现没有一条对有效支持其建议起作用。

首先，运动服饰的巨大销售额并不一定意味着普兰斯维尔居民会对 NW 的产品感兴趣，也不一定意味着这些居民对运动感兴趣。有可能是因为运动服饰时下正流行，或者与其他类型的衣服相比比较廉价。同样，也有可能因为出售给游客的销售额增长了，所以才出现了比平时要高得多的销售业绩。简而言之，在没有排除其他可能带来高销售额的原因前，副总裁要根据这个销售额使我相信普兰斯维尔居民经常运动是不可能的，更别说让我相信他们会有兴趣买 NW 出售的各类食品和其他产品。

第二，即使普兰斯维尔居民现在比以往任何时候都更喜欢运动了，副总裁也不能进而假设说那些经常运动的人也有兴趣购买保健食品和与健康有关的产品。然而备忘录里并没有任何证据来证实这一假定。由于缺乏这样的证据，便同样有可能出现这样的情况，即除了运动外，普兰斯维尔居民对过一种健康的生活方式没有什么兴趣。实际上，也许因为有经常运动的习惯，所以他们便认为自己已经足够健康结实，不再需要健康的饮食了。

第三，当地健身俱乐部大受欢迎并不意味着 NW 在普兰斯维尔开一家商店就可以赢利。可能俱乐部成员居住的普兰斯维尔地区离适合 NW 开店的地方很远。又或许该俱乐部以作为一个单身会场为主要魅力，而事实上其成员对健康的生活方式并没有兴趣。此外，即使俱乐部的成员会经常光顾一家 NW 商店，这些成员的数量也不足以保证商店会赢利，特别是考虑到普兰斯维尔只有那么一家健身俱乐部。

第四，某个健康计划对普兰斯维尔的小学生们来说是一个强制性措施这一事实，对支持该建议也起不了什么作用。要等这些孩子长大，能够就购买食品及与健康有关的产品做出决定，还要过许多年。随着时间的流逝，他们的习惯和兴趣可能发生彻底的改变。此外，强制性的参与不表明学生们对健康和保健真的有兴趣。而且，这些孩子们长大后，完全有可能因为对现在强加在他们身上的健康习惯反感了，所以反而喜欢过不健康的生活方式。

最后，即使假设普兰斯维尔居民对吃保健食品和使用与健康有关的产品有着强烈的兴趣，该建议还依据另外两个假定：（1）这种兴趣在可预知的将来还将继续存在；（2）和其他出售类似产品的商家相比，普兰斯维尔居民更喜欢 NW。在证明两个假定都属实之前，副总裁无法说服我相信在普兰斯维尔开的 NW 商店会赢利。

总之，该建议建立在某些值得怀疑的假设上面，以致它事实上是不能让人信服的。为支持他的建议，这位副总裁必须提供明确的证据——也许可以通过在当地做一个调查或研究——证明普兰斯维尔当地购买并穿着运动服的人，特别是那些健身俱乐部的成员们，确实经常运动，并且这些运动的人很可能到 NW 的商店购买健康食品和与健康相关的产品。为了更好地评价这个建议，我有必要知道普兰斯维尔的健身俱乐部为什么受欢迎，为什么普兰斯维尔没有更多的健身俱乐部。我还有必要知道 NW 在普兰斯维尔可能面临什么竞争。

【逻辑问题提纲】

本文作者一共攻击了原文的六处缺陷：

1. 运动服销量增加并不一定意味着普兰斯维尔的居民喜欢运动，或是喜欢 NW 的产品。

2. 喜欢运动并不一定意味着他们也会倾向于以健康食品和其他产品为代表的所谓健康生活方式。

3. 健康俱乐部的流行并不能说明健康产品一定流行。

4. 在校儿童参加强制性锻炼不能说明 NW 产品销量就会增加。

5. 普兰斯维尔居民现在的喜好和习惯在将来可能改变。

6. 没有考虑 NW 可能面对的市场竞争。

● 逻辑思路提示：从逻辑提纲我们可以发现，作者所攻击的六点中有四条都是在攻击原文所出现的差异概念的错误，比如运动服销量与居民对运动态度的差异概念，锻炼和健康生活方式的差异概念等等。实际上差异概念是非常普遍的一种错误，如果你觉得无法找出更加具体的逻辑缺陷，那就看一看文章前后论据和结论是否存在不能直接挂钩的概念 A 和 B，然后用诸如 A does not necessarily indicate that B 的句式连接起来，不失为一种简便的攻击思路。

另外，如果你对某一种逻辑错误认识比较深刻，掌握比较纯熟，也可以在同一道题中多次攻击同一类错误，但要注意语言的变化。

● 没有考试时间变化的错误：本文论证的第五个错误就是作者没有考虑情况会随着时间而变化，或简单地说就是作者没有"与时俱进"。本文并没有针对这个错误过多展开，但在其他一些题目中这也是一个经常可以拿来批判的点。当作者就以往或现在的情况、信息推测未来的趋势时，就要注意这个时间的桥梁，想一想情况有没有可能随时间而变化。

【开头方式】

本文是经典的三段式开头：(1) 复述结论；(2) 复述论据；(3) 指出原文存在缺陷。注意当题目论据过于复杂冗长时，也可以和本文一样用 (1)、(2)、(3) 来罗列。

【论证展开】

大部分论证的展开都是段首句 + 推测 / 假设 / 列举 + 段落小总结的结构，如果你觉得论证不好展开，可以先学习一下这个基本套路。用一个 topic sentence 指出要攻击的错误，然后用推测法、假设法或例举法展开，最后用一个句型作小总结。

● 推测法：推测法是最基本的展开思路，本文多次使用 perhaps 来引导推测。拿到一道题目，你可以试着先不看作者的结论，而对作者在文中提出作为论据的那些事实和现象做自己的另一番推测，然后把它们整理一下用适当的句型和语言串起来就行了。

【结尾方式】

经典的两段式结尾：(1) 指出作者未能支持结论；(2) 指出我们还需要哪些信息来完善论证。请注意开头和结尾的黑体字部分，如果你将要使用经典开头和结尾模式，把这些句子的结构和词汇稍加改动即可为我所用。

【语言提示】

● 用于开头段引导结论的词汇：recommend / suggest / advice / propose

● 用于攻击差异概念的句式：(1) A does not necessarily indicate that B. (2) A is little indication that B. (3) A accomplishes nothing toward bolstering the recommendation that ...

● 其他句式：(1) Without ruling out other possible reasons for A the vice president cannot convince me on the basis of them that B. (2) Yet the memo contains no evidence to support this assumption. (3) Lacking such evidence it is equally possible that ...

● 增强逻辑关系的词汇：段落乃至文章的整体逻辑性是影响文章质量很重要的因素，但很多同学自己写论证段落时对句子间的逻辑关系不够注意。事实上，句子的逻辑关系和层次很容易体现，学习和积累一下这些词汇及其使用：

(1) 让步：even if ...　(2) 递进：besides / moreover / additionally

Argument 3　Hiring new **law school graduates**

The following appeared in a newspaper article about law firms in the city of Megalopolis.

"In Megalopolis, the number of law school graduates who went to work for large, corporate firms declined by 15 percent over the last three years, whereas an increasing number of graduates took jobs at small, general practice firms. Even though large firms usually offer much higher salaries, law school graduates are choosing to work for the smaller firms most likely because they experience greater job satisfaction at smaller firms. In a survey of first-year students at a leading law school, most agreed with the statement that earning a high salary was less important to them than job satisfaction. This finding suggests that the large, corporate firms of Megalopolis will need to offer graduates more benefits and incentives and reduce the number of hours they must work."

【参考译文】在梅加洛波利斯，过去三年间在大型合伙事务所就职的法学院毕业生数量下降了15%，而在小型、一般性事务所就职的毕业生数量则在增加。尽管大型事务所通常提供高得多的薪水，但是法学院毕业生选择在小型事务所工作，主要是因为他们在那儿感受到更高的工作满足感。一项对于顶尖法学院一年级学生的调查显示，多数人同意工作满足感比挣更多的钱更重要。这一调查结果表明，梅加洛波利斯的大型合伙事务所应该给毕业生提供更多的福利和激励，并减少他们的工作时间。

This article concludes that despite the relatively high salaries at Megalopolis' large law firms, these firms must begin offering more benefits and incentives to new law-school graduates, while requiring them to work fewer hours, in order to reverse a three-year 15% decline in the number of graduates going to work for these firms. To justify this conclusion the article's author notes that during the last three years the number of new law-school graduates going to work for small firms has risen. The author also cites a survey at one leading law school in which most first-year students indicated that job satisfaction was more important than salary. I find this argument logically unconvincing in several respects.

First of all, the 15% decline that the author cites is not necessarily due to the vocational preferences of new law-school graduates. It is entirely possible that the number of new graduates preferring to work for large firms has not declined, but that during the last three years Megalopolis' large firms have had fewer and fewer job openings for these graduates. Since the article fails to account for this alternative explanation for the 15% decline, the article's author cannot make any sound recommendations to law firms based on that decline.

As for the survey that the article cites, the vocational goals of first-year law students do not necessarily reflect those of graduating students; after all, a law student's vocational goals can change over a three-year period. Moreover, the goals of students at one law school do not necessarily reflect those of the overall pool of graduates that might seek employment with Megalopolis law firms. In fact, given that the school whose students participated in the survey was a "leading" school, it is entirely

possible that the vast majority of the school's graduates may choose among offers from many large firms in many cities. If so, this fact would further undermine the survey's relevance in prescribing any course of action for Megalopolis' law firms.

Finally, the author **falsely equates** the proposed tangible incentives **with** job satisfaction, which is an intangible reward based on the nature of one's work. Moreover, enhanced job benefits can be tantamount to an enhanced salary, and shorter working hours amount to a higher hourly wage. Thus if new law-school graduates seeking jobs in Megalopolis are less interested in monetary rewards than in job satisfaction, then the proposed incentives are not likely to entice these graduates.

In sum, the argument is logically flawed and therefore unconvincing as it stands. To strengthen it the author must either modify the proposal to provide incentives for those seeking job satisfaction over monetary rewards, or provide better evidence that new law school graduates seeking jobs in Megalopolis would find the proposed incentives enticing.

【参考译文】

　　这篇文章得出结论说，尽管在梅加洛波利斯的大型法律事务所的薪金都相对较高，但三年来前来这些事务所效力的大学毕业生数量下跌了15%，为了扭转这一局面，对新的法律学院毕业生，这些事务所必须在缩短工时的同时，为他们提供更多的福利和奖励。为了证明这个结论是正确的，文章的作者特别提到在最近三年里到小型事务所去上班的新的法律学院毕业生数量已经增多。作者还引用了一项在一所重点法律学院进行的调查。该调查显示，大部分该校的一年级学生都表明对工作的满意度要比薪水重要得多。我认为这个论证在逻辑上存在着几个不能让人信服的方面。

　　首先，并不一定是因为新的法律学院毕业生的职业偏爱，才导致了作者所提到的15%的下跌。很可能喜欢到大型事务所工作的新毕业生的数量并没有下降，只是在最近的三年里梅加洛波利斯的大型事务所为这些毕业生提供的职位越来越少。这篇文章既然没有考虑到对这15%的下跌的这一种解释，那么文章的作者也就无法基于下跌的数据为律师事务所提出任何可靠的建议。

　　至于文章中所引用的调查，一年级的法律专业学生的职业目标并不一定就能够反映出毕业生的职业目标；毕竟，经过三年，学生的职业目标可能会改变。而且，一所法律学院的学生的目标并不一定能够反映出那些可能到梅加洛波利斯的律师事务所求职的整个毕业生群体的职业目标。事实上，鉴于参与该调查的学生所在的学院是一所"重点"学院，大多数该校的毕业生很可能是从许多城市的大型事务所提供的职位中做出选择。如果是这样的话，这一事实将削弱这个调查对梅加洛波利斯的律师事务所提出的行动方针的适用性。

　　最后，作者错误地把他所提议的有形的奖励等同于对工作的满意度，而对工作的满意度本身却是一种建立在一个人的工作性质基础上的无形奖励。而且，增加工作福利可以等同于加薪，而缩短工作时间就相当于涨每小时的工资。这么一来，如果在梅加洛波利斯找工作的新的法律学院毕业生对货币报酬的兴趣比对工作满意度的兴趣小，那么，作者提议的奖励就不大可能吸引这些毕业生了。

　　总之，就目前情况看，这篇论证本身在逻辑上有缺陷，因此也就不能使人信服。为了加强论证，作者必须修改建议，给那些寻找对工作的满意度超过货币报酬的人提供奖励，或者提供更好的证据证明在梅加洛波利斯找工作的新的法律学院毕业生会认为他提议的奖励很诱人。

【逻辑问题提纲】

本文作者一共攻击了原文的三处缺陷：

1. 法学院毕业生就业倾向与大型事务所就业人员数量下降之间未必有因果关系。

2. 一年级法学院学生的观点并不能代表毕业生的就业观念。

3. 福利和缩短工作时间等有形激励与工作满意度之间的差异概念。

● 逻辑思路提示：本文所攻击的第一点为因果关系错误，这是一个在 Argument 题库中出现非常频繁的错误。在具体展开论证时，可以先用一个句型作为段首句指出作者所认为的因果关系未必存在，然后对于结果的产生做其他推测，也就是列举导致该结果的其他可能原因。

【开头方式】

相对论证段而言本文开头略显冗长。原文有些论据可以简化合并，有时有些次要的或是你在论证段中不想攻击的论据可以略去不写。

【论证展开】

● 推测法在攻击因果关系错误中的应用：第一论证段论证因果关系错误时用的仍然是推测法。攻击因果关系错最基本的思路就是列举其他原因，在找到题目中出现的可疑的因果关系后，你可以对于作者提出的结果推测一些其他的可能原因，但要保证你的推测是符合常识和逻辑的，然后把这些推测罗列出来就可以独立成段了。

● 递进法：如果说推测和列举法是一种并行的论证方式的话，递进法（或让步法）就是一种串行的论证方式。本文攻击第二、第三点时所用的都是递进法。有些时候有的逻辑错误不是很好展开，这时就可以把几个相关的小错误放在一起用递进法进行论证。以第三段为例，作者首先说明学生的就业观念会随时间而变化，然后用 moreover 过渡，进一步指出一个学校学生的观点不能代表全市就业毕业生的情况。接着作者又用一个让步句式 given that ... it is entirely possible that 来递进到这个问题的第三个层次：毕业生仍然有可能选择在其他城市的大型事务所就业。这三点的每一点作者都只用了一句话而没有做过多展开，但这一段论证仍然很圆满，这要归功于递进法以及维系递进逻辑结构的词汇和句式的使用。

【语言提示】

● 表达"为了支持自己的结论"的词汇：support / justify / validate / substantiate

● 用于攻击差异概念的句式：The author falsely equates A with B.

● 攻击因果关系的句式：The article fails to account for the alternative explanation(s) for ..., thus the article's author cannot make any sound recommendations to ...

● 增强逻辑关系的句式：让步：given that ..., it is entirely possible that ...

Argument 6　A jazz club for **Monroe**

The following was written as a part of an application for a small business loan by a group of developers in the city of Monroe.

"A jazz music club in Monroe would be a tremendously profitable enterprise. Currently, the nearest jazz club is 65 miles away; thus, our proposed club, the C-Note, would have the local market all to itself. Plus, jazz is extremely popular in Monroe: over 100,000 people attended Monroe's jazz festival last summer, several well-known jazz musicians live in Monroe, and the highest-rated radio program in Monroe is 'Jazz Nightly,' which airs every weeknight. Finally, a nationwide study indicates that the typical jazz fan spends close to $1,000 per year on jazz entertainment. It is clear that the

C-Note cannot help but make money."

【参考译文】在门罗建立爵士乐俱乐部将会是非常赢利的产业。当前，最近的爵士俱乐部也在65英里以外；因此，我们筹建的俱乐部 C-Note 将会占有全部的本地市场。而且，爵士乐在门罗非常流行：去年夏天，10 万多人参加了门罗的爵士音乐节，若干知名爵士音乐家居住在门罗，门罗获评价最高的广播节目是周一至周五每天播出的"每晚爵士"。最后，一项全国性研究表明，典型的爵士爱好者每年花费近 1000 美元用于爵士娱乐。显然，C-Note 必然会赚钱。

This loan applicant claims that a jazz club in Monroe would be a profitable venture. To support this claim the applicant points out that Monroe has no other jazz clubs. He also cites various other evidence that jazz is popular among Monroe residents. Careful examination of this supporting evidence, however, reveals that it lends little credible support to the applicant's claim.

First of all, if the demand for a live jazz club in Monroe were as great as the applicant claims, it seems that Monroe would already have one or more such clubs. The fact that the closest jazz club is 65 miles away suggests a lack of interest among Monroe residents in a local jazz club. Since the applicant has not adequately responded to this concern, his claim that the proposed club would be profitable is untenable. The popularity of Monroe's annual jazz festival and of its nightly jazz radio show might appear to lend support to the applicant's claim. However, it is entirely possible that the vast majority of festival attendees are out-of-town visitors. Moreover, the author provides no evidence that radio listeners would be interested in going out to hear live jazz. For that matter, the radio program might actually pose competition for the C-Note club, especially considering that the program airs during the evening. Nor does the mere fact that several well-known jazz musicians live in Monroe lend significant support to the applicant's claim. It is entirely possible that these musicians perform elsewhere, perhaps at the club located 65 miles away. This would go a long way toward explaining why Monroe does not currently have a jazz club, and it would weaken the applicant's assertion that the C-Note would be profitable. Finally, the nationwide study showing that the average jazz fan spends $1,000 each year on jazz entertainment would lend support to the applicant's claim only if Monroe residents typify jazz fans nationwide. However, the applicant provides no credible evidence that this is the case.

In conclusion, the loan applicant's argument is not persuasive. To bolster it he must provide clearer evidence that Monroe residents would patronize the C-Note on a regular basis. Such evidence might include the following: statistics showing that a significant number of Monroe residents attend the jazz festival each year; a survey showing that fans of Monroe's jazz radio program would go out to hear live jazz if they had the chance; and assurances from well-known local jazz musicians that they would play at the C-Note if given the opportunity.

【参考译文】

这位贷款申请人声称，在门罗地区建一所爵士乐俱乐部将会是一个有利可图的企业。为了支持自己的观点，这位申请人指出门罗地区没有其他爵士乐俱乐部。他还援引爵士乐在门罗地区居民中很受欢迎的其他各种各样的证据。但是，如果仔细检查这用来作为支持的证据，我们会发现它并不能够给申请人的观点提供多少可信的支持。

首先，如果门罗地区对一个现场爵士乐俱乐部的需求真的像这位贷款申请人声称的那样大，当地似乎应该已经有一所或几所这样的俱乐部了。而事实是最近的爵士乐俱乐部也在65英里以外。这一点表明，即便在当地建一所爵士乐俱乐部，居民们也不会有多大的兴趣。由于这位贷款申请人对于这一点没有给出充分的回应，他所说的建一所爵士乐俱乐部将会有利可图的观点也是站不住脚的。门罗地区每年爵士音乐节和每晚爵士乐广播的流行似乎可以支持这位贷款申请人的观点。但是，完全有可能出现这种情况，即大多数参加音乐节的人是来自镇外的游客。而且，作者也没有提供任何证据证明收音机听众将有兴趣走出家门去听现场爵士乐。而且那些广播节目完全可能与 C-Note 俱乐部形成竞争，尤其是考虑到节目在晚间播出。几位著名爵士乐音乐家在门罗地区居住这一事实也不能给这位贷款申请人的观点提供重要的支持。这些音乐家完全有可能在别处表演，或许就在离门罗地区 65 英里的俱乐部里表演，而这正可以解释门罗地区为什么到目前为止还没有一个爵士乐俱乐部，并且它将减弱这位贷款申请人提出的 C-Note 将会赚钱这一断言的可信性。最后，那份全国性的调查研究显示，普通的爵士乐爱好者每年花费 1000 美元用于爵士乐娱乐消费，只有在门罗地区居民能够代表全国爵士乐爱好者的前提下，它才能支持这位贷款申请人的主张。但是，这位贷款申请人也没有提供任何可信的证据证明情况确实如此。

总之，这位贷款申请人的论证没有说服力。为了支持自己的观点，他必须提供更加清楚的证据来证明门罗地区居民将会定期光顾 C-Note。这样的证据可以包括如下方面的内容：一张统计表显示，每年有大量门罗地区居民参加爵士音乐节；一份调查，表明门罗地区爵士乐广播节目爱好者，如果他们有机会的话，愿意出去听现场爵士乐；以及那些著名的当地爵士乐音乐家的保证，保证如果有机会，他们愿意在 C-Note 演出。

【逻辑问题提纲】

本文作者一共攻击了原文的四处缺陷：

1．本地没有爵士乐俱乐部的事实正好作为反例说明在这个地方爵士乐并不流行。
2．爵士音乐节和广播节目受欢迎并不说明本地居民将会欢迎爵士乐俱乐部。
3．很多爵士音乐家住在门罗也不能证明我们就应该在这里发展俱乐部。
4．全国调查的结果不能简单地用于说明门罗的居民也愿意在爵士乐方面花很多的钱。

● 逻辑思路提示：本文所攻击的第一点比较奇特，可以叫做反证法，即指出原作者提出的论据实际上直接反对他的结论。这种论证方式在 argument 题目中的使用不是很广泛，而且使用不当的话会削弱文章的逻辑论证力度，所以使用时要慎重。

● 以多推少的草率推广：第四个缺陷就是差异范围的草率推广，简单地说，某个整体发生了某种现象和趋势并不能表明整体中的每个个体和部分都会发生同样的现象和趋势。同样，作者也不能把某些个体的现象和特点作为一般性的原则推广到个体所在的整体中去。当看到题库中出现"全国性的调查说明…"之类的词句时，往往会出现以整体推局部的草率推广。

【开头方式】

He also cites various other evidence that …在开头段列举论据的方式多种多样，当论据过于繁杂或不想用过多笔墨复述时即可用这个句型。也可以把它进一步简化为：The author cites various other evidence to justify the claim that …，这样就可以用一句话把复述论据的工作一笔带过，同时完成了复述结论的工作。

【论证展开】

CAUTION：本文论证段落只有一段，而且攻击的四个错误都没有充分展开，而是作为几个层次的递进组合成了论证段。这种展开方式在真正的考场上要慎用。一般而言这种论证结构除非语言和逻辑非常严密得当，否则很难得到较高分数。最好把要攻击的每个错误独立成段，并且有一定的语言展开。

【结尾方式】

结尾段用了一个有趣的句式：**To bolster it he must provide clearer evidence that … Such evidence might include the following.** 一般在结尾段我们需要指出作者还必须补充哪些工作才能使他的推论更加完善，有说服力，在指出这些方面时，我们可以用几个句子来表达，也可以用这个句型，把原文所缺乏的论据用 such evidence might include the following 引领起来。

【语言提示】

● 表达作者没有考虑某些情况的句式：Since the applicant has not adequately responded to this concern, his claim that … is untenable.

● 攻击论据不支持结论的句式：Nor does the mere fact that … lend significant support to …

● 攻击差异范围时表达 A 代表 B 的词汇：typify / be representative of

Argument 7　**Clearview**'s city-council election

The following appeared in a letter to the editor of the Clearview newspaper.

"In the next mayoral election, residents of Clearview should vote for Ann Green, who is a member of the Good Earth Coalition, rather than for Frank Braun, a member of the Clearview town council, because the current members are not protecting our environment. For example, during the past year the number of factories in Clearview has doubled, air pollution levels have increased, and the local hospital has treated 25 percent more patients with respiratory illnesses. If we elect Ann Green, the environmental problems in Clearview will certainly be solved."

【参考译文】在下一次市长选举中，克里尔威市的市民应投美好地球联盟成员安·格林的票，而不是投克里尔威市市政会成员弗兰克·布朗恩的票，因为现任的市政会成员没有保护我们的环境。举例来说，去年克里尔威市的工厂数量翻了一番，空气污染水平提高了，而且当地医院因呼吸道疾病就诊的病人数量增加了 25％。如果我们选举安·格林，克里尔威市的环境问题肯定将得到解决。

　　This editorial recommends that Clearview residents vote to replace city-council member Frank Braun with Ann Green, a member of the Good Earth Coalition. **To support this recommendation the editorial cites a** significant increase during the last year in the number of Clearview factories and in the number of Clearview hospital patients treated for respiratory illnesses. **On the basis of this evidence the author infers that** the current council members are not protecting the city's environment and that electing Green will solve the city's environmental problems. **This argument is logically flawed in several critical respects.**

　　To begin with, the argument unfairly assumes that last year's increase in the number of factories was due to the city council's decisions—rather than to some other phenomenon—and that this increase poses environmental problems for Clearview. **The editorial provides no evidence to substantiate these assumptions. Lacking such evidence it is entirely possible that** the council actually opposed the increase but lacked adequate authority to prevent it, or that the new factories do not in fact harm Clearview's environment.

　　The argument also assumes unfairly that last year's increase in the number of patients reporting respiratory problems indicates worsening environmental problems in Clearview. **Perhaps** the actual incidence of such health problems has not increased, and the reported increase is due to increasing awareness among Clearview residents of respiratory problems. **Even if** the incidence of respiratory problems has in fact increased, the increase might be due to an influx of people with pre-existing such problems, or to more effective cigarette marketing. **Since the editorial fails to rule out these and other possible explanations for** the increase, **I cannot accept any conclusions about** Clearview's environment—let alone about who voters should elect to city council—based on last year's hospital records.

Even if the two cited increases do indicate a worsening of Clearview's environment due to the city council's decisions, **the argument rests on the further assumption that** Braun was a factor in those decisions. **But, since the editorial provides no evidence to substantiate this assumption it is equally possible that** Braun actually opposed the decisions that were responsible for these increases. **Thus, without better evidence that** Braun contributed to key decisions adversely effecting Clearview's environment, **the editorial remains unconvincing.**

Even assuming that Braun was at least partially responsible for the two increases, and that those increases indicate a worsening environment, **the editorial provides no clear evidence that** Green would be effective in reversing that trend—let alone more effective than Braun. **The mere fact that** Green is a member of the Good Earth Coalition **hardly suffices to prove** her willingness and ability to help solve Clearview's environmental problems, at least not without more information about that coalition and Green's involvement in it.

Finally, even if Green would in fact be more effective than Braun in solving Clearview's environmental problems, **the author provides no firm evidence that** electing Green is necessary to solve those problems, or that electing Green would suffice. **Perhaps** another candidate, or another course of action, would be more effective. **Even if** Green does everything in her power as city-council member to solve these problems, **perhaps** additional measures—such as replacing other council members, state legislators, or even the state's governor—would also be required in order to achieve Clearview's environmental objectives.

In sum, the editorial's author cannot justify his or her voting recommendation on the basis of the scant evidence provided in the editorial. To bolster the recommendation the author must provide better evidence that (1) Clearview has environmental problems to begin with, (2) Green would be more effective than either Braun or any other candidate in solving those problems, and (3) electing Green would suffice to solve those problems. **To better assess the argument I would need to know** the scope of the city council's authority respecting environmental decisions. **I would also need to know** Braun's voting record on environmental issues, Green's experience and position on those issues, and the voters' other choices—besides Green and Braun.

【参考译文】

这篇社论建议克里尔威市市民投票支持由安·格林——美好地球联盟的一员——代替市政会成员弗兰克·布朗恩的位置。为了支持这个建议，社论引用了在过去一年里两个有显著增长的数据，一是克里尔威市工厂数量大量增加，二是克里尔威市接受呼吸道疾病治疗的病人数量也大幅上升。作者根据以上证据，推断现任政务委员会成员没有保护该城市的环境，而选择格林将会解决这一城市的环境问题。这篇论证在几个关键方面都犯了逻辑上的错误。

首先，论证有失偏颇地假定去年工厂数量的增加是由于市政会的决定——而不是其他原因——造成的，而且工厂数量的增加造成了克里尔威市的环境问题。这篇社论并没有提供任何证据来证实这些假设。由于缺乏这样的证据，完全可能是这样的情况：政务委员会实际上反对增加工厂数量，但却没有足够的权力来阻止这种情况，或者新建的工厂根本没有对克里尔威市的环境造成危害。

这篇论证还片面地认定去年报告得呼吸疾病人数的增加就表明了克里尔威市环境问题加剧了。可能实际上这种疾病的发病率并未提高，报告的病人数量增加也只是因为克里尔威市的市民对于呼吸疾病越来越重视和警觉了。即使这种呼吸疾病的发病率的确提高了，也可能是因为已有这种疾病的人员流入，或是由于香烟营销更加有效。由于这篇社论没有排除可以解释这种增长的各种原因，仅仅以去年医院的记录做依据，我无法接受由此得出的任何关于克里尔威市环境问题的结论，更不用说让选民选谁做城市委员会委员的结论。

即使这里提到的两个数量的增加的确能够表明由于城市委员会的决定导致了克里尔威市环境的恶化，这篇论证又在进一步的假设上展开，这个假设就是，布朗恩是促使做出那些决定的一个因素。然而，由于这篇社论也没有提供证据来证明这一假设，很可能布朗恩是对这些造成数量增加的决定持反对意见的。因此，如果这篇社论没有更好的证据来证明布朗恩对那些损害克里尔威市环境的关键决定起了促进作用，就仍然没有说服力。

即使我们假设布朗恩确实至少对这两个数量的增加负有部分责任，而且那些数量的增加确实说明环境的恶化，这篇社论还是没有提供清楚的证据来证实格林会在扭转这一趋势方面有什么回天之术，更没有证明她会比布朗恩做得更好。单单凭格林是美好地球联盟一员这一点并不足以证明她愿意并且有能力帮助解决克里尔威市的环境问题，至少如果没有提供有关这一联盟以及格林在其中的表现的更多信息，就不能证明。

最后，即使格林在解决克里尔威市环境问题上的确能比布朗恩更有办法，作者还是没有提供有力的证据证明选择格林是解决那些问题必需的，或者选择格林能满足解决那些问题的需要。也许其他候选人，或其他行动方针会更有效。即使格林作为委员会一员会尽全力来解决这些问题，可能还要采取其他的措施，比如替换别的委员会成员、州立法委员，甚至州长，才能达到克里尔威市的环境目标。

总之，社论作者不能通过社论中少量的证据证明他或她提出的选举建议是恰当的。要支持自己的建议，作者必须能够提供更好的证据来说明（1）克里尔威市的确有环境问题待解决，（2）在解决那些问题方面，格林会比布朗恩或其他候选人更有办法，（3）选择格林就足以解决那些问题。要想更好地评价这篇论证的优劣，我需要知道在环境决策方面，城市委员会的权限有多大。我还需要知道布朗恩在环境问题上的投票记录，格林在那些问题上的立场和经验，以及除他们二人以外，选民的其他选择。

【逻辑问题提纲】

本文作者一共攻击了原文的五处缺陷：

1. 去年工厂数量的增加未必和市委的决策有关系，以及工厂的增加未必对环境带来负面影响。

2. 去年呼吸道疾病患者的增加也未必是环境恶化所导致的，而可能另有其他原因。

3. 即使作者所提到的现象确实表明环境恶化，也不能认为布朗恩在其中起主要作用。

4. 即使布朗恩确实是导致文中所述现象的部分原因，我们也没有理由认为格林在这方面就一定能够做得更好。

5. 即使格林在改善环境问题方面确实能够比布朗恩做得更好，作者还忽略了其他可能更好地解决该问题的途径，换言之，选举格林未必是解决这一问题的惟一方案。

● 逻辑思路提示：

本文攻击的出发点从根本来说有两条：

1) 作者在文中暗示的 more factories→air pollution→more patients with respiratory illnesses 的因果关系链条。

2) 市委成员以及候选人与以上因果关系的联系。

总体攻击思路也就是论证作者所设想的联系未必存在，布朗恩未必造成工厂的增加，工厂增加未必导致环境恶化，环境问题未必是呼吸道疾病的诱因。如果想再攻击具体一些的错误，本题还可以论证一下数据模糊性的问题：

作者所说的工厂数量翻了一番以及呼吸道疾病患者增加了 25% 的信息未必说明这是一个值得担忧的现象，因为我们不知道两者的基数，即工厂和呼吸道疾病患者的数量原来有多少？在没有这个信息的情况下，作者所说的现象不一定能够说明环境问题的严重性。

【开头方式】

开头段简要罗列完作者的论据后，我们可以像本文一样用 On the basis of this evidence the author infers that ... 这样的句型来引导复述结论的内容，然后把作者的结论整理放在 that 引导的宾语从句中去就行了，其中 infer 这个词汇还可以用其他很多表达得出结论的词汇代替，比如 claim, indicate, imply 等等。

【语言提示】

● 开头段句式：(1) On the basis of this evidence the author infers that ... (2) This argument is logically flawed in several critical respects.

● 论证段句式：(1) Since the editorial fails to rule out these and other possible explanations for ..., I cannot accept any conclusions about ... (2) But, since the editorial provides no evidence to substantiate this assumption it is equally possible that ... (3) Thus, without better evidence that ..., the editorial remains unconvincing. (4) The mere fact that ... hardly suffices to prove ...

● 结尾段句式：In sum, the editorial's author cannot justify his or her voting recommendation on the basis of the scant evidence provided in the editorial.

Argument 8　Mesa Foods: a profitable investment?

The following appeared in a memorandum issued by the strategic planning department at Omni Inc.

"Mesa Foods, a manufacturer of snack foods that currently markets its products within a relatively small region of the country, has strong growth potential. Mesa enjoyed a 20 percent increase in profits last year, and its best-selling product, Diabolique Salsa, has had increased sales over each of the past three years. Since Omni Inc. is interested in reaching 14-to-25-year olds, the age group that consumes the most snack food, we should buy Mesa Foods, and concentrate in particular on marketing Diabolique Salsa throughout the country."

【参考译文】台地食品是一家当前仅在本国相对较小区域销售其产品的快餐食品生产商，具有很强的增长潜力。去年台地食品的利润上升了 20%，其最畅销产品迪亚波利克调味汁连续三年销量增加。由于奥姆尼股份有限公司对 14～25 岁这一消费快餐食品最多的年龄群体感兴趣，我们应该收购台地食品，并集中力量在全国推广迪亚波利克调味汁。

This Omni, Inc. memorandum recommends that Omni buy snack-food manufacturer Mesa Foods and aggressively promote its brand of salsa nationwide. **To support this recommendation the memo relies on** the exceptional profitability of Mesa's salsa during the last three years, along with the fact that Mesa's overall profits were up last year. **However, the recommendation relies on a series of unsubstantiated assumptions, which render it unconvincing as it stands.**

First of all, the memo indicates that Omni is interested in selling to 14-to-25-year-olds. **Accordingly, the argument rests on the assumption that** Mesa's snack foods appeal to this age group. **Yet, we are not informed** what types of snack foods Mesa manufactures, aside from its salsa. **It is entirely possible that** Mesa's foods, including its salsa, appeal primarily to other age groups. **If this is the case, the recommended acquisition would not** serve Omni's goal.

Secondly, the argument rests on the assumption that in the region where Mesa's products are sold the preferences of consumers between the ages of 14 and 25 typify nationwide preferences among this age group. **If this is not the case, then it is entirely possible that** Omni would not sell enough Mesa snack foods, including its salsa, to earn a profit from its Mesa operation. **Thus, without more marketing information about** the snack-food tastes of 14-to-25-year-olds nationwide **it is difficult to assess the merit of the memo's recommendation.**

Even if the memo's author can substantiate the foregoing assumptions, the author overlooks the possibility that last year's 20% increase in Mesa's profits was an aberration, and that in most other years Mesa has not been profitable. **Also,** the 20% increase **might have been due entirely to** sales of Mesa's salsa, and aside from the profit from salsa sales Mesa's profitability is actually declining. **If either is the case, and if** Mesa's salsa does not turn out to be popular among 14-to-25-year-olds across the nation, **then** Omni is unlikely to profit from the recommended course of action.

In conclusion, the recommendation is not well supported. To convince me that the Mesa Foods acquisition **would be profitable Omni would need to provide clear statistical evidence that** Mesa's snack foods, and its salsa in particular, would appeal to 14-to-25-year-olds nationwide. **To better evaluate the recommendation, I would need more information about** Mesa's profitability over a longer time period, **and about** the extent to which Mesa's salsa accounts for any such profitability.

【参考译文】

这个奥姆尼股份有限公司备忘录建议奥姆尼购买快餐食品制造商——台地食品，并且在全国积极推广它的调味汁品牌。为了支持这个建议，备忘录以过去三年间台地调味汁的出色的收益额，以及台地产业总利润去年上升这一事实为依据。但是这篇论证却是以一连串没有确实根据的假定为前提展开的，这一点使它的论证不那么可信。

首先，备忘录表明奥姆尼把14～25岁的孩子作为他们的消费群。相应地，论证假定台地快餐食品能够吸引这个年龄段的人。然而，我们不知道除了它的调味汁，台地还生产什么类型的快餐食品。完全可能，台地食品包括它的调味汁，主要是适合其他年龄段人群的。如果情况确实如此，建议的收购行动将不能达到奥姆尼的目标。

第二，论证假定，在台地产品出售的地区，在14～25岁之间的消费者的偏好能代表全国在这个年龄段的人的偏好。如果情况不是如此，完全有可能奥姆尼将不能售出足够的台地快餐食品，包括它的调味汁，从而通过收购台地食品这项交易获得利润。因此，如果没有更多的市场信息，反映全国范围内14～25岁的人对快餐食品的喜好，很难评价备忘录里建议的价值有多大。

即使备忘录的作者能证明上述的假定，作者还忽略了一个可能性，即台地去年的利润增加

20％是市场失常的结果，而且在大多数其他年份里台地并不赢利。此外，20％的增加可能完全由于台地调味汁的出售，除了调味汁销售获得的利润外，台地的收益实际是在下降的。如果是其中任何一种情况，并且台地的调味汁在全国 14～25 岁的人中结果并不受欢迎，那么奥姆尼将不能从建议的这一举动中受益。

　　总之，这份建议没有得到很好的支持。要使我确信买进台地食品将会赚钱，奥姆尼需要提供清楚的统计证据证明台地快餐食品，尤其是它的调味汁，将吸引全国 14～25 岁的人。要想更好地评价这项建议，我需要了解在一个更长的时间段内，关于台地盈利的更多信息，以及台地的调味汁对赢利有多大的贡献。

【逻辑问题提纲】

本文作者一共攻击了原文的三处缺陷：

1. 文中没有提供证据表明台地的快餐食品能够吸引 14～25 岁的青少年人群。

2. 台地的产品在小范围内销售成功并不表明它在全国范围内也能赢利（以少推多的差异范围）。

3. 台地去年的利润增长可能是一个特例，或是仅仅因为 Diabolique Salsa 的销售成功，而在其他年份、其他产品的销售可能是下降的。

【论证展开】

本文论证第一个问题时所用的语言结构完整，逻辑严密，值得学习：

First of all, the memo indicates that ... 首先用这句话引出作者有缺陷的观点；

Accordingly, the argument rests on the assumption that ... 然后用本句型指出以上观点所基于的假设；

Yet, we are not informed ... 接着用这个句型转折，指出这个假设是没有依据的；

It is entirely possible that ... 展开对文中所述现象的其他可能推测；

If this is the case, the recommended acquisition would not serve Omni's goal. 在推测法的基础上进行推理，从而对原文作者的观点构成质疑，同时做段落小总结。

【语言提示】

● 论证句式：（1）If this is the case, the recommended acquisition would not ... （2）Thus, without more marketing information about ... it is difficult to assess the merit of the memo's recommendation.

● 结尾段句式：To convince me that ... Omni would need to provide clear statistical evidence that ...

Argument 9 Grade inflation at **Omega University**

The following appeared in a memorandum from a dean at Omega University.

"Fifteen years ago, Omega University implemented a new procedure that encouraged students to evaluate the teaching effectiveness of all their professors. Since that time, Omega professors have begun to assign higher grades in their classes, and overall student grade averages at Omega have risen by thirty percent. Potential employers apparently believe the grades at Omega are inflated; this would explain why Omega graduates have not been as successful at getting jobs as have graduates from nearby Alpha University. To enable its graduates to secure better jobs, Omega University should now terminate student evaluation of professors."

【参考译文】 15年前，欧米加大学实施了一项新措施，鼓励学生对所有教授的教学效果进行评价。从那以后，欧米加的教授开始给予学生更高的分数，欧米加的学生成绩平均分总体上升了30%。未来的雇主显然认为欧米加的分数贬值了；这可以解释为什么欧米加的毕业生找工作时没有邻近的爱尔法大学毕业生成功。为使欧米加毕业生找到好工作，欧米加大学应立即停止学生对教授的评价。

　　In this memo Omega University's dean points out that Omega graduates are less successful in getting jobs than Alpha University graduates, despite the fact that during the past 15 years the overall grade average of Omega students has risen by 30%. **The dean also points out that** during the past 15 years Omega has encouraged its students, by way of a particular procedure, to evaluate the effectiveness of their professors. **The dean reasons that** this procedure explains the grade-average increase, which in turn has created a perception among employers that Omega graduates are less qualified for jobs. **On the basis of this line of reasoning the dean concludes that** to enable Omega graduates to find better jobs Omega must terminate its professor-evaluation procedure. **This argument contains several logical flaws, which render it unconvincing.**

　　A threshold problem with the argument involves the voluntary nature of the evaluation procedure. **The dean provides no evidence about** the number or percentage of Omega students who participate in the procedure. **Lacking such evidence it is entirely possible that** those numbers are insignificant, in which case terminating the procedure is unlikely to have any effect on the grade average of Omega students or their success in getting jobs after graduation.

　　The argument also assumes unfairly that the grade-average increase is the result of the evaluation procedure—rather than some other phenomenon. **The dean ignores a host of other possible explanations for** the increase—such as a trend at Omega toward higher admission standards, or higher quality instruction or facilities. **Without ruling out all other possible explanations for** the grade-average increase, **the dean cannot convince me that** by terminating the evaluation procedure Omega would curb its perceived grade inflation—let alone help its graduates get jobs.

　　Even if the evaluation procedure has resulted in grade inflation at Omega, **the dean's claim that** grade inflation explains why Omega graduates are less successful than Alpha graduates in getting jobs **is unjustified**. **The dean overlooks a myriad of other possible reasons for** Omega's comparatively poor job-placement record. **Perhaps** Omega's career services are inadequate; or perhaps Omega's curriculum does not prepare students for the job market as effectively as Alpha's. **In short, without accounting for other factors that might contribute to** Omega graduates' comparative lack of success in getting jobs, **the dean cannot justify the claim that** if Omega curbs its grade inflation employers will be more likely to hire Omega graduates.

　　Finally, even if the dean can substantiate all of the foregoing assumptions, the dean's assertion that Omega must terminate its evaluation procedure to enable its graduates to find better jobs **is still unwarranted**, in two respects. First, **the dean ignores other possible ways** by which Omega can increase its job-placement record—for example, by improving its public relations or career-counseling services. **Second, the dean unfairly equates** "more" jobs with "better" jobs. **In other words, even if** more Omega graduates are able to find jobs as a result of the dean's recommended course of action, the kinds of jobs Omega graduates find would not necessarily be better ones.

　　In sum, the dean's argument is unpersuasive as it stands. To strengthen it the dean must provide

better evidence that the increase in grade average is attributable to Omega's professor-evaluation procedure, and that the end result is a perception on the part of employers that Omega graduates are less qualified for jobs than Alpha graduates. **To better assess the argument I would need to analyze** 15-year trends in (1) the percentage of Omega students participating in the evaluation procedure, (2) Omega's admission standards and quality of education, and (3) Omega's emphasis on job training and career preparation. **I would also need to know** what other means are available to Omega for enabling its graduates to find better jobs.

【参考译文】

在这份备忘录里，欧米加大学院长指出，尽管在过去15年里欧米加大学学生的平均成绩提高了30%，在获得工作方面欧米加大学毕业生还是没有爱尔法大学毕业生成功。院长还指出，在过去15年里，欧米加大学鼓励它的学生通过一个特别的程序来评价他们教授的教学质量。院长认为这一程序可以解释平均分增加的原因，反过来已经给雇主一种印象，认为欧米加大学毕业生不那么能胜任工作。根据这种推理方法，院长断定为了使欧米加大学毕业生找到好工作，欧米加大学必须结束现在的教授评估程序。这份论证包含着几处逻辑上的缺陷，这使得它不能让人信服。

论证首先存在的一个问题与评估程序的自愿性实质有关。院长没有提供关于参加这一程序的欧米加大学学生的数目或者百分比的证据。由于缺乏这样的证据，完全可能那些数目是很微小的或无意义的，在这种情况下，终止程序不可能对欧米加大学学生的平均成绩，或者他们在毕业之后能否成功获得工作有任何影响。

这篇论证还有失偏颇地假定平均分的增加是评估程序而不是一些其他因素导致的结果。院长忽视了许多其他可能解释这一增加的因素，例如欧米加大学的入学标准越来越高，教学和设备质量越来越好。由于没有排除所有其他可能的对平均分增加的解释，院长不能使我确信通过终止评估程序，欧米加大学将会控制这种成绩的浮夸，更不用说会帮助毕业生找到工作。

即使评估程序确实导致了欧米加大学的成绩浮夸，院长认为欧米加大学毕业生在找工作过程中没有爱尔法毕业生成功是成绩浮夸所造成的，这也还是无法解释的。院长忽略了造成欧米加大学的就业安置记录不太好的其他无数可能的原因。或许欧米加大学的职业服务不够完善；或许欧米加大学的课程不像爱尔法大学那样能够有效地使学生适应就业市场的需要。简而言之，由于没有说明其他可以解释欧米加大学毕业生不能成功地找到工作的因素，院长不能证明如果欧米加大学控制住分数的浮夸，雇主就更可能雇用欧米加大学毕业生。

最后，即使院长能够证明所有上述的假定，他的断言从两方面看仍然没有根据，他认为欧米加大学必须结束它的评估程序，使它的毕业生能够找到更好的工作。首先，院长忽视了欧米加大学能通过其他可能的方式增加它的就业安置记录，比如，通过改进它的公共关系或者职业咨询服务。其次，院长错误地将"更好"的工作等同于"更多"的工作。换句话说，即使由于院长建议的举动，更多的欧米加大学毕业生能找到工作，毕业生找到的工作也不见得是更好的。

总之，就此看来，院长的论证没有说服力。为了加强论证，院长必须提供更好的证据证明平均分的增加可归因于欧米加大学的教授评估程序，并且这造成的结果是使雇主方形成欧米加大学毕业生不如爱尔法毕业生更胜任工作的印象。要更好地评价这篇论证，我需要分析15年来在以下方面的趋势：(1) 参加评估程序的欧米加大学学生的百分比，(2) 欧米加大学的入学标准和教育质量，(3) 欧米加大学对岗位培训和职业准备的重视程度。我还需要知道有哪些其他办法可供欧米加大学选择，能使毕业生找到更好的工作。

【逻辑问题提纲】

本文作者一共攻击了原文的四处缺陷：

1. 原文作者没有指出参与评价教授活动的学生的数量，因而无法评价该制度对学生成绩的影响。

2. 作者没有考虑导致学生成绩上升的其他可能原因。

3. 作者也没有考虑导致欧米加学生就业情况不如爱尔法的其他可能原因。

4. 停止现行的评价制度未必能保证更好的就业情况。

【开头方式】

On the basis of this line of reasoning the dean concludes ... 这是在罗列完作者的假设之后引导结论的又一句式，注意词汇词组的使用和替换。

【语言提示】

● 开头段句式：(1) On the basis of this line of reasoning the dean concludes that ... (2) This argument contains several logical flaws, which render it unconvincing.

● 论证段句式：(1) A threshold problem with the argument involves... (2) The dean overlooks a myriad of other possible reasons for ... (3) In short, without accounting for other factors that might contribute to ..., the dean cannot justify the claim that ... (4) Finally, even if the dean can substantiate all of the foregoing assumptions, the dean's assertion that ... is still unwarranted ... the dean unfairly equates ... with ...

Argument 10　The **price of milk**

The following appeared in a letter to the editor of a Batavia newspaper.

"The department of agriculture in Batavia reports that the number of dairy farms throughout the country is now 25 percent greater than it was 10 years ago. During this same time period, however, the price of milk at the local Excello Food Market has increased from $1.50 to over $3.00 per gallon. To prevent farmers from continuing to receive excessive profits on an apparently increased supply of milk, the Batavia government should begin to regulate retail milk prices. Such regulation is necessary to ensure both lower prices and an adequate supply of milk for consumers."

【参考译文】巴达维亚的农业部门报告说全国奶牛场的数量比10年前增加了25%。然而就在同一时期，当地爱克塞罗食品市场牛奶的价格从每加仑$1.5上涨到了$3.0。为防止农场主在牛奶供应量明显增加的情况下获取过多的利润，巴达维亚的政府应该开始管制牛奶的零售价。这种管制对于保证更低的牛奶价格和充足的供应是必需的。

This editorial recommends that Batavia's government regulate milk prices because profits from milk sales are excessive given the apparently adequate supply. The editorial also claims that price regulation would help ensure an adequate supply of milk. To support these **assertions** the author cites the fact that over the past ten years the number of dairy farms in Batavia has increased by 25% while at Excello Food Market milk prices have increased by 100%. **However, the argument relies on a series of unsubstantiated assumptions, which render it unconvincing as it stands.**

First of all, the author assumes that Excello's milk prices reflect those throughout Batavia. However, **the author provides no evidence that this is the case. To the extent that** Excello's milk prices currently exceed nationwide averages the author's argument for government regulation of milk prices would be undermined.

In the second place, **even if** Excello's milk prices reflect those in Batavia generally, in claiming that milk prices are particularly "excessive" the author assumes that milk-sale profits exceed profits from the sale of other goods in Batavia to a significant degree. But the author provides no evidence to substantiate this assumption. Perhaps other prices have risen commensurably, or perhaps even more on a percentage basis, during the same time period. Moreover, perhaps profit margins from the sale of other goods are even greater than profits from milk sales. **In either event, the author could not justifiably rely on the mere fact that** milk prices have increased by 100% **to support the claim that** milk-sale profits are excessive.

In the third place, the author assumes that an increase in milk prices results in increased profits. However, this is not necessarily the case. It is entirely possible that the costs associated with producing and delivering milk have increased as well over the last ten years. Thus, the strength of the author's claim of excessive milk-sale profits depends on **a cost benefit analysis** that the author does not provide.

In the fourth place, based on the fact that the number of dairy farms has increased the author infers that the supply of milk has also increased. However, this is not necessarily the case. It is possible that dairy farm production has shifted away from milk to other dairy products, and that the supply of milk has actually declined over this time period. To the extent that this is the case, then the author's supply-and-demand argument that milk prices are excessive is unconvincing.

Finally, in asserting that price regulation would help ensure an adequate supply of milk **the author overlooks the possibility that** milk producers would respond to the regulation by producing less milk, depending on the extent to which demand increases as a result of lower milk prices. If regulation has the effect of lowering profits, then common sense tells me that milk producers might be less inclined to produce milk. **Without ruling out this possible scenario, the author cannot convince me that** the recommendation would help ensure an adequate supply of milk.

In conclusion, the recommendation for regulation of milk prices is not well supported. To convince me that the proposed regulation is needed to ensure a reasonably priced milk supply, **the author must provide clear statistical evidence that** Excello's milk prices reflect nationwide milk prices and that profits from milk sales are in fact excessive. **To better evaluate the recommendation, I would need more information about** how the proposed regulation would effect both the supply of milk and the demand for milk in Batavia.

【参考译文】

这篇社论建议巴达维亚政府对牛奶实行价格管制，因为在现有供给明显充足的情况下，所得到的利润是超额的。这篇社论还提出价格管制有利于确保充足的牛奶供应量。为了支持这些论断，作者陈述了这样一个事实：在过去十年中，巴达维亚奶牛场的数量增加了 25%，然而，在爱克塞罗食品市场，牛奶价格翻了整整一番。但是，这篇论证却是以一连串没有确实根据的假定为前提展开的，这一点使它的论证不那么可信。

首先，作者假定爱克塞罗食品市场的牛奶价格反映了整个巴达维亚的情况。但是，作者并没有提供任何证据证明情况确实如此。如果爱克塞罗食品市场的牛奶价格目前超过了全国的平均水平，那作者关于政府对牛奶价格管制的这篇论证就肯定不成功了。

其次，即使爱克塞罗食品市场牛奶价格能够反映巴达维亚的整体水平，在提出牛奶价格过高时，作者假定在巴达维亚牛奶销售所得利润大大超过了其他物品销售能够带来的利润。但是作者没有提供任何证据来证明这一假设。也许同期其他产品的价格百分比也有等幅甚至更大幅的增长。也许从其他产品销售所获得的利润率比从牛奶销售中所获得的更高。对于任何一种情况，作者都不能很有说服力地以牛奶价格翻了一番的事实来支持牛奶销售利润超额这一论点。

再次，作者假定牛奶价格的提高导致了利润的增加。然而，情况并不一定如此。完全有可能与生产、运送牛奶相关的成本也在过去十年中有所提高。因此，作者关于牛奶销售利润过量的论证是否有说服力取决于一份成本利润分析，然而，作者并没有给出。

第四，作者根据奶牛场数量增加这一点来推断牛奶的供应也增加了。但是，事情也并不一定就是这样。可能奶牛场从生产牛奶转为生产其他乳制品，牛奶供应在这一时期实际是减少了的。如果是这种情况，那作者关于牛奶价格过高的供求论证也是不可信服的。

最后，在主张价格管制有利于保证充足的牛奶供应方面，作者忽视了一个可能性，即牛奶生产商会降低牛奶产量以应对管制，这取决于较低的牛奶价格对增加牛奶需求的影响程度。如果管制使利润降低，凭常识我们也知道牛奶生产商生产牛奶的积极性会降低。因为没有排除这些可能的情况，作者无法让我信服这一建议会有利于确保充足的牛奶供应。

总之，这篇关于牛奶价格管制的建议论证并不充分。要想让我深信建议进行的管制是确保具有合理价格的牛奶供应所必须的，作者必须提供清楚的统计信息证明爱克塞罗食品市场牛奶价格能够反映全国的牛奶价格，而且牛奶销售利润确实是超额的。要更好地评价这项建议，我需要知道更详尽的信息，包括所提到的管制会怎样影响巴达维亚牛奶的供应和需求。

【逻辑问题提纲】

本文作者一共攻击了原文的五处缺陷：
1. Excello Food Market 一个地方的牛奶价格并不能代表全国奶价的变化情况。
2. 没有考虑整体物价的波动情况，因而无法证实奶价的变化是否异常。
3. 奶价上涨未必带来收益的增加。
4. 牛奶农场数量的增加不能表明牛奶供应量一定增加。
5. 没有考虑出台限价政策对牛奶市场带来的可能影响。

- 逻辑思路提示：本文攻击的五个错误可以分为三类：

  攻击的第一点是取样不具有代表性的错误，也可以认为是以个体推整体的草率推广；

  第二、五两点是作者没有考虑其他相关因素，考虑问题不全面的错误；

  第三、四两点是差异概念：即 the price of milk ≠ the profits of farmers 和 the number of dairy farms ≠ the supply of milk。

- 没有考虑相关因素的错误：这也是 argument 题目中经常可以拿来攻击的错误，即作者在进行论述时思维过于局限和片面，只看到问题的某个方面而忽视了其他因素。在本节的语言总结中大家可以看到攻击这类错误时可以使用的一些句型范例。

【论证展开】

论证段落的引导词：也就是引领每个论证段的第一、第二、第三这些词汇。这些词汇虽然看似有些模式化，但他们在增强全文逻辑性方面的作用是不可忽视的，而且如果觉得词汇过于单调，也可以用一些引导句式来构成论证骨架。大家平时应注意多方面积累这类引导词汇和句式，在自己写作时方能游刃有余。

【语言提示】

- 开头段引导结论的词汇：assert / conclude / claim / advocate / state / reason / assume
- 表达作者没有考虑相关因素的句式：(1) In either event, the author could not justifiably rely

on the mere fact that ... to support the claim that ... (2) Without ruling out this possible scenario, the author cannot convince me that ...

　　在论证段列举了作者所忽视的相关因素后即可用这些句型作为段落结尾，另外还有一些表达此类缺陷的常用句式如：(1) The author ignores other relevant factors that may also influence ... (2) The author fails to take into account / consider the possibility that ...

● 引导论证段落的词汇和句式：(1) First / second / finally; (2) First of all (In the first place)/ in the second place / last but not least; (3) The major problem with this argument is that ... / Another point worth considering is that... / Before I come to my conclusion, it is necessary to point out another flaw appeared in the argument.

Argument 11　The recycling habits of **West Egg**'s residents

The following appeared in a memo from the mayor of the town of West Egg.

"Two years ago, our consultants predicted that West Egg's landfill, which is used for garbage disposal, would be completely filled within five years. During the past two years, however, town residents have been recycling twice as much aluminum and paper as they did in previous years. Next month the amount of material recycled should further increase, since charges for garbage pickup will double. Furthermore, over ninety percent of the respondents to a recent survey said that they would do more recycling in the future. Because of our residents' strong commitment to recycling, the available space in our landfill should last for considerably longer than predicted."

【参考译文】两年前，我们的顾问预言西蛋用于投放垃圾的填埋地将在五年内完全充满。然而在过去两年间，市民对于铝和纸张的循环再生的数量比以前翻了一番。由于垃圾收集的收费在下个月将会加倍，循环再生的材料数量将进一步增加。而且，最近一次调查超过 90% 的回应者表示他们将会在未来做更多的循环再生工作。由于居民对循环再生的有力支持，我们的填埋地可利用空间的使用时间将比预期的长得多。

In this memo West Egg's mayor **reasons** that West Egg's residents are now strongly committed to recycling, and **projects** that the city's landfill will not be filled to capacity until considerably later than anticipated two years ago. To support this projection the mayor cites (1) a twofold increase in aluminum and paper recycling by West Egg residents over the last two years, (2) an impending twofold increase in charges for trash pickup, and (3) a recent survey in which 90% of respondents indicated that they intend to do more recycling in the future. **For several reasons, I am not convinced that the mayor's projection is accurate.**

To begin with, in all likelihood aluminum and paper account for only some of the materials West Egg's residents can recycle. Perhaps recycling of other recyclable materials—such as plastic and glass—has declined to the point that the total amount of recycled materials has also declined. If so, then the mayor could hardly justify the claim that West Egg's residents are becoming more committed to recycling. **Another problem with the argument is that** an increase in the amount of recycled materials does not necessarily indicate a decrease in the total amount of trash deposited in the city's landfill. Admittedly, if West Egg residents previously disposed of certain recyclable materials that they now recycle instead, then this shift from disposal to recycling would serve to reduce the amount of trash going to the landfill. However, the mayor provides no evidence of such a shift.

Moreover, the argument overlooks the strong possibility that the recycling habits of West Egg residents are not the only factor affecting how quickly the landfill will reach capacity. **Other such factors might include** population and demographic shifts, the habits of people from outside West Egg whose trash also feeds the landfill, and the availability of alternative disposal methods such as burning. Thus, regardless of the recycling efforts of West Egg residents the landfill might nevertheless reach full capacity by the date originally forecast.

Yet another problem with the argument involves the mayor's implicit claim that increased charges for trash pickup will serve to slow the rate at which the landfill is reaching capacity. This claim relies on the unlikely assumption that West Egg residents have the option of recycling—or disposing in some other way—much of what they would otherwise send to the landfill. However, it is likely these residents have no practical choice but to send some refuse to the landfill. The greater the amount, the less likely higher trash charges would have any effect on how quickly the landfill reaches capacity.

Finally, the mayor provides no evidence that the survey's respondents are representative of the overall group of people whose trash goes to the city's landfill. Lacking such evidence, **it is entirely possible that people inclined to** recycle **were more willing to respond to the survey than other people were. In short, without better evidence that the survey is statistically reliable the mayor cannot rely on it to draw any firm conclusions about** the overall recycling commitment of West Egg residents—let alone about how quickly the landfill will reach capacity.

In sum, the mayor's projection is simply not credible, at least based on the memo. Rather than relying solely on questionable recycling statistics, **the mayor should provide direct evidence that** the amount of trash going to the landfill is declining and that this trend will not reverse itself anytime soon. **To better assess the accuracy of the mayor's projection it would be useful to know** who besides West Egg residents contributes trash to the landfill, and whether the amount of trash those people contribute is declining or is likely to decline in the near future.

【参考译文】

在这份备忘录里，西蛋市市长陈述说西蛋居民现在很热衷于回收废物，并推断该城市的垃圾填埋地会在很久以后才会达到饱和状态，比两年前预期的要晚得多。为了支持他的这一说法，市长陈述了以下理由：(1) 过去两年里西蛋居民回收铝和纸张的双倍增长，(2) 垃圾处理费用即将加倍，(3) 一份近期问卷显示回答者中90％的人表示有意今后会做更多的废物再利用。由于几点原因，我认为这位市长的说法并不准确。

首先，很可能铝和纸张只能代表西蛋居民能回收利用的部分材料。可能像塑料、玻璃等其他可回收物的回收数量下降了，导致回收物的总量也减少了。如果是这样，这位市长就很难证实自己所说的西蛋居民更热衷于废物回收再利用。论证中的另一个问题是回收物数量的增加并不一定表明投放到城市垃圾填埋场的垃圾总量的减少。诚然，如果西蛋居民以前丢弃某些可回收物，而现在开始回收利用，那这种由弃置到回收利用的变化将会减少垃圾掩埋数量。然而，市长并没有提供证据来证明这一转变。

而且，这篇论证忽视了一个很大的可能性，即西蛋居民的回收废物再利用的习惯并不是影响垃圾掩埋地达到允许峰值早或晚的惟一因素。其他的影响因素可能包括人口、人口移动，西蛋以外也在同一填埋地丢弃垃圾的人的习惯，以及是否有其他垃圾处理方式可供选择。因此，不考虑西蛋居民在回收废物方面的进步，垃圾填埋场可能仍然会在早先预计的时间达到饱和。

然而论证中的另一个问题是市长暗示垃圾处理费用的提高会减缓掩埋数量达到最大容量的

速度。这一提法建立在一个不太可靠的假设基础上，即西蛋居民可以选择对很多原本会送到垃圾填埋场的垃圾进行回收再利用或采用其他办法处理。然而，可能这些居民没有其他可行的选择，只能把一些垃圾扔到填埋地。这些垃圾的数量越大，更高额的垃圾处理费对垃圾填埋场达到饱和的时间长短的影响就会越小。

最后，市长没有提供证据证明问卷回答者能够代表所有向当地填埋地投放垃圾的人。由于缺乏这样的证据，完全有可能倾向于废物回收利用的人比其他人更愿意对这项调查做出回答。简而言之，由于这篇论证没有提供证据证明这项调查的统计是可靠的，这位市长并不能够仅凭这些来得出任何肯定的结论，认为全体西蛋居民都承诺废物再利用——更不用说垃圾掩埋量会以怎样的速度达到最大量。

总之，市长的说法是完全不可信的，至少从这份备忘录来看是这样。这位市长不应该仅依靠一些有疑问的与回收循环有关的数字，而是应该提供直接证据证明送往掩埋区的垃圾数量在减少，而且这种减少趋势不会在近期逆转。要想更好地评定这位市长的说法是否准确，我们需要知道除了西蛋居民以外还有哪些人在往掩埋区弃置垃圾，以及那些人丢弃垃圾的数量是否减少或可能在不远的未来有所减少。

【逻辑问题提纲】

本文作者一共攻击了原文的四处缺陷：

1. 铝和纸品垃圾的循环利用并不说明整体垃圾循环利用水平；而且循环垃圾的增加也并不能说明投放在填埋地的垃圾就会减少。

2. 作者没有考虑影响填埋地使用的其他因素，比如人口变化和周边使用同一填埋地的居民习惯。

3. 对于垃圾收集的高收费不一定能减少投放在填埋地的垃圾数量——有些垃圾除了投放在填埋地可能别无选择。

4. 回答调查的回应者的情况未必有代表性。

● 逻辑思路提示：样本代表性的问题：很多题目都会使用调查结果作为论据，这就会出现调查所取样本的代表性的问题。比如，取样是否完整和符合随机性的要求？有没有本该调查的某些群体没被调查到？没回答调查的群体情况如何？这些都是针对调查取样需要质疑的因素。而且，对于调查的结果有时会出现这样一个问题，就是那些对所调查的事件本身感兴趣的人可能更倾向于回答调查，而那些不感兴趣的可能对调查置之不理。这就会导致调查结果不具有代表性。本文攻击的第四点就是针对这一点展开的论证，其中的语言值得学习和参考。

【论证展开】

● 展开论证的基本套路：在 Argument 1 的讲解中我们说过段首句＋推测／假设＋段落小结是展开论证的基本形式，这里我们把这个套路补充完善一下。如果要对一个问题展开完整严密的论证，可以使用以下结构：

主题句（指出存在逻辑错误的点）＋（指出作者得出这个有问题结论所依赖的假设）＋用推测或假设法列举影响结论的其他可能或指出该假设的不合理因素＋（小让步指出作者结论某种程度的合理性）＋转折作段落小总结

● 列举法：在攻击因果关系错误、作者没有考虑相关因素错误时，往往需要用到列举法这一基本的论证方式，这也是用于段落展开的简单方法之一。用一些句式和词组比如 for example，for instance 等等来把导致结果的其他原因、作者所忽视的其他可能等列举出来也可以构成完整的论证段落。

【语言提示】

● 用于开头段引导结论的词汇：predict / project / forecast / expect /

● 引导论证段落的句式：To begin with / Another problem with this argument is that / Moreover / Yet another problem with the argument involves ...

● 攻击调查样本代表性的句式：It is entirely possible that people inclined to recycle were more willing to respond to the survey than other people were.

● 结尾段可以使用的句式：（1）Rather than relying solely on questionable..., the mayor should provide direct evidence that ... （2）To better assess the accuracy of the mayor's projection it would be useful to know ... （3）To evaluate the author's conclusion more efficiently, we would need more information concerning ... （4）To strengthen the conclusion the owner must provide more convincing evidence that ...

● 用于列举法的句式：For example / For instance / e.g. / Other relevant factors might include ...

Argument 14　**Green Thumb** Gardening Center

The following appeared in a memo from the owner of Green Thumb Gardening Center, a small business serving a suburban town.

"There is evidence that consumers are becoming more and more interested in growing their own vegetables. A national survey conducted last month indicated that many consumers were dissatisfied with the quality of fresh vegetables available in supermarkets. And locally, the gardening magazine Great Gardens has sold out at the Village News stand three months in a row. Thus, we at Green Thumb Gardening Center can increase our profits by greatly expanding the variety of vegetable seeds we stock for gardeners this coming spring."

【参考译文】 有证据表明消费者对于自己种植蔬菜越来越感兴趣。上个月举行的一项全国性调查显示，很多消费者对于超市上供应的新鲜蔬菜的质量不满意。在本地，园艺杂志《大花园》在乡村新闻报亭连续三个月售罄。因此，我们园艺能手园艺中心可以通过大量增加今春为园艺爱好者准备的蔬菜种子的种类而增加赢利。

In this memo, the owner of Green Thumb Gardening Center (GT) concludes that GT could increase its profits by expanding its stock of vegetable seeds. **The owner cites a national survey showing** growing dissatisfaction with supermarket vegetables, **and points out that** a certain gardening magazine has sold out at one local newsstand three months in a row. **I find the owner's argument weak, for three reasons.**

First, **by relying on** the national survey **to support its conclusion the argument depends on the assumption that** the level of satisfaction locally with store-bought groceries reflects national levels. Yet the owner provides no evidence to support this assumption. It is possible that residents of this town are quite satisfied with these vegetables. **Without eliminating this possibility, the owner cannot rely on the national survey to conclude that** this town's residents would be interested in buying vegetable seeds from GT.

Secondly, by relying on the survey the argument assumes that consumers who are dissatisfied with store-bought groceries are likely to grow their own vegetables instead. **However, the owner fails** to provide any evidence to support this assumption. Perhaps consumers are continuing to buy vegetables from grocery stores despite their dissatisfaction. Or perhaps this dissatisfaction is leading consumers to buy their vegetables from special produce markets and vegetable stands instead of supermarkets. **Since the owner has failed to consider and rule out these possibilities, the owner's assertion that** this town's dissatisfied consumers would be eager to buy vegetable seeds from GT to grow their own vegetables **cannot be taken seriously.**

Thirdly, **the mere fact that** a certain gardening magazine has recently sold out at one newsstand in this town **is scant evidence that** the town's residents would be eager to buy vegetable seeds from GT. Perhaps three months ago this newsstand decreased the number of copies it stocks; or perhaps the magazine does not even concern itself with vegetable gardening; or perhaps the only reason for this apparent increase in sales is that other newsstands in town have stopped stocking the magazine. **Given these possible scenarios, the fact that** one newsstand has sold every copy of the last three monthly issues **proves nothing about** local trends in vegetable gardening.

In conclusion, the owner's argument is unpersuasive. To strengthen it the owner must provide more convincing evidence that consumers in this town are actually becoming less satisfied with supermarket vegetables, and that as a result they are buying fewer such vegetables. **To better evaluate the argument we would need more information about** alternative sources of vegetables for local consumers—for example, the number and quality of produce stands. We would also need to know why the newsstand's copies of the gardening magazine sold out.

【参考译文】

在这个备忘录里，园艺能手园艺中心（GT）的所有者断定，通过增加对蔬菜种子的存储，园艺能手园艺中心（GT）就能够增加它的利润。该所有者引用了一项全国性调查来表明人们对超级市场卖的蔬菜日益不满，并且指出某园艺杂志在一个当地报亭已经连续三个月销售一空。出于三个原因，我认为该所有者的论证缺乏说服力。

首先，在引用全国性调查来支持结论时，该论证基于如下假设：当地对从商店购买的食品杂货的满意程度反映了全国的水平。然而所有者没有提供任何证据来证实这个假设。有可能这个镇的居民对这些蔬菜是相当满意的。没有消除这种可能性，这个所有者就不能依赖这个全国性调查断定该镇居民会有兴趣从园艺能手园艺中心（GT）购买蔬菜种子。

第二，基于这个调查，该论证假设对从商店购买的食品杂货感到不满的消费者很可能转为自己种植蔬菜。但是，该所有者不能提供任何证据证明这个假定。也许尽管消费者感到不满，但是他们还是继续从杂货店买蔬菜。或者也有可能这种不满就导致消费者不去超级市场而转而去特产市场和蔬菜摊位购买蔬菜。因为该所有者并没有考虑并排除这些可能性，所以他所做的关于该镇的不满消费者会有渴望从园艺能手园艺中心（GT）买到蔬菜种子来自己种植蔬菜的断言是不能信以为真的。

第三，仅凭某种园艺杂志最近在这个镇的一个报亭销售一空这个事实是难以成为充分的证据证明该镇的居民会渴望从园艺能手园艺中心（GT）购买蔬菜种子。或许三个月之前，这个报亭减少了杂志的储备量；或者也许该杂志甚至和蔬菜园艺风马牛不相及；又或者也许造成这种显著的销售增长的惟一原因是该镇的其他报亭停止销售这种杂志。鉴于这些可能出现的情况，一个报亭在最近三个月卖出了该杂志的每一份月刊的事实并不能证明蔬菜园艺在当地的发展趋势。

总之，这个所有者的论点是不能说服人的。为了加强该论证的力度，这个所有者必须提供更多有力的证据来证明这个镇的消费者确实对超级市场卖的蔬菜越来越不满意，并且他们也因此越来越少购买这种蔬菜。为了更好地评价这个论证，我们需要了解更多有关当地消费者可以选择去购买蔬菜的地方的信息——比如，农产品供应摊点的数量和质量。我们还有必要知道为什么这个报亭的这份园艺杂志会销售一空。

【逻辑问题提纲】

本文作者一共攻击了原文的三处缺陷：

1. 调查取样代表性的问题：全国调查的结果并不能说明本地居民的消费行为和倾向。
2. 对超市供应的蔬菜不满意的消费者未必会自己种植蔬菜。
3. 某种园艺杂志在某一处书报亭连续售罄并不能说明人们对于自己种植蔬菜的倾向性。

【论证展开】

推测和假设的合理性：在论证段落展开论证使用推测法和假设法时，一定要注意自己对原文现象的其他方面的推测和假设应该是符合常识和逻辑的。在本文论证第二、第三点时使用的都是推测法。比如，对超市蔬菜不满意的消费者可能会继续在超市或其他商店购买蔬菜而不是自己种菜，杂志售罄有可能是因为进货量减少或其他书报亭停止出售这种杂志等。有些人在 Argument 论证过程中联想过于丰富，进行推测和假设时天马行空浮想联翩，以至于推测离题太远或不符合逻辑，这是一定要避免的。Argument 进行的是逻辑论证，它不需要过多的修辞和文学手法，只要晓之以理，不要动之以情。

【语言提示】

● 用于描述作者忽视其他可能的句式：(1) Without eliminating this possibility, the owner cannot rely on the national survey to conclude that . . . (2) Since the owner has failed to consider and rule out these possibilities, the owner's assertion that . . . cannot be taken seriously. (3) Given these possible scenarios, the fact that . . . proves nothing about . . .

● 其他句式：(1) by relying on the national survey to support its conclusion the argument depends on the assumption that . . . (2) However, the owner fails to provide any evidence to support this assumption. (3) the mere fact that . . . is scant evidence that . . .

Argument 18　Speed limits in **Prunty County**

The following appeared in an editorial in a Prunty County newspaper.

"In an attempt to improve highway safety, Prunty County recently lowered its speed limit from 55 miles per hour to 45 on all major county roads. But the 55 mph limit should be restored, because this safety effort has failed. Most drivers are exceeding the new speed limit and the accident rate throughout Prunty County has decreased only slightly. If we want to improve the safety of our roads, we should instead undertake the same kind of road improvement project that Butler County completed five years ago: increasing lane widths and resurfacing rough roads. Today, major Butler County roads still have a 55 mph speed limit, yet there were 25 percent fewer reported accidents in Butler County this past year than there were five years ago."

【参考译文】 为提高高速公路的安全性，布朗特县最近把县上所有主要路段的最高限速从55mph降到了45mph。但我们应该回复到55mph的限速，因为这种保障安全的努力已经失败了。多数司机都超过了新的限速，而且布朗特县的事故率仅有微量下降。如果我们要提高公路安全性应该采取巴特勒县在五年前完成的同样的道路改善计划：增加车道宽度和重新铺装现在，巴特勒县的主要道路仍然使用 55mph 限速，而那里近年间上报的事故发生率比五年前减少了 25%。

This editorial **argues** that a recent reduction in Prunty County's speed limit on its major roads, from 55 to 45 miles per hour (mph), has proven ineffective, and that the county should therefore restore its 55-mph speed limit and improve its roads. **To support this argument the editorial's author points out that** the accident rate has decreased only "slightly" since the speed limit was reduced. The author **also points out that** in nearby Butler County, which has maintained a 55-mph limit while widening and resurfacing its roads, the accident rate has decreased by 25% over the last 5 years. **The editorial suffers from several problems, which render it unconvincing as it stands.**

First of all, Prunty only "recently" reduced its speed limit, and only for "major" roads. Perhaps not enough time has passed to determine the effectiveness of this change in reducing the accident rate—especially if the new speed limit remains untested during a season of the year in which better driving conditions prevail. **Additionally**, the editorial refers only to the overall accident rate countywide. Perhaps the accident rate on the county's major roads has decreased while on minor roads not subject to the speed-limit reduction it has increased. **Thus, lacking reliable evidence of the effectiveness of** the new speed limit **it is difficult to accept the conclusion that** Prunty's safety effort has failed.

Secondly, the argument assumes that all other factors affecting highway accident rates have remained unchanged since the county lowered its speed limit. Yet the author fails to provide evidence to support this assumption. **It is entirely possible that** the lower speed limit does in fact serve to reduce the accident rate, while some other factor, such as unseasonably poor weather, reduced law enforcement measures, or even an influx of teenage drivers to the area, has served to increase the accident rate. **Without considering and ruling out these and other factors that might have served to** increase the accident rate since the speed limit was lowered, **the author cannot justifiably conclude that** this safety effort has failed.

Thirdly, the author unfairly implies that the higher speed limit in Butler County has not served to increase the incidence of road accidents in that county. **It is entirely possible that** the 55-mph speed limit actually serves to increase the accident rate on Butler's highways, **but that other factors**, such as stricter law enforcement measures or improved driver education, have served to decrease the accident rate to a greater extent. **Without considering and ruling out these and other factors that might have served to** decrease the accident rate in Butler County, **the author cannot confidently recommend that** Prunty County emulate Butler's speed-limit policy. **Moreover**, the cited statistic involves only "reported" accidents in Butler County. **It is possible that** an increasingly large percentage of accidents are going unreported in that county.

In conclusion, the editorial fails to convince me that Prunty County should emulate Butler[...] [...]ety measures. **To strengthen the argument the author must account for all other fac[...]** [...]uence the accident rate on roads in both counties. **To better assess the impact of** the [...] road safety, **I would need more statistical information about** the accident rate on [...]ls, collected over a longer time period. I would also need to know what percent[...] [...]s in Butler County go unreported.

【参考译文】

这篇社论认为，布朗特县最近在其主要道路上施行的把车速限制从 55 英里/小时降到 45 英里/小时的措施，已被证明无效；因此该县应恢复其 55 英里/小时的速度限制并着手改善其道路。为论证其观点，这篇社论的作者指出，自速度限制降低后，事故发生率仅有"稍微"减少。作者还指出，邻近的巴特勒县在加宽路宽并重铺路面的同时保持 55 英里/小时的速度限制，结果在过去的五年里其事故发生率降低了 25%。该社论存在若干问题，从而令人难以信服。

首先，布朗特"最近"才降低其速度限制，范围也只限于其"主要"道路。或许实施时间还不够，特别是如果因处于每年驾驶状况较好的那一季度而致使新施行的速度限制未得到测验，那么将无法确定该措施在降低事故发生率上的实际效力。此外，社论只提及全县范围内的总事故发生率。那么，也许在该县的主要道路上事故发生率已经降低，而在未执行速度限制降低措施的次要道路上其事故发生率却增加了。因此，缺乏检验新速度限制的有效性的可靠证据，就草率做出布朗特县所做的确保行车安全的努力已经失败的结论是难以让人接受的。

第二，社论中作者做了这么一个假设：自从该县降低其速度限制后，影响交通事故发生率的所有其他因素均保持不变。然而作者未能提供证据证明这个假定。降低了的速度限制实际上可能降低事故发生率，但有一些其他因素发生，例如不合时令的坏天气、宽松的法律强制措施，甚至是一群青少年司机流入该地区，都足以提高事故发生率。没有考虑并排除降低速度限制后可能发生的导致事故发生率上升的各种因素，作者就没有理由做出该县为确保行车安全而做的努力已经失败的结论。

第三，作者做了一个不合理的暗示：巴特勒县内较高的速度限制没有对其境内的事故发生率的上升产生任何影响。实际上 55 英里/小时的速度限制使巴特勒县的公路上的事故发生率上升是完全可能的，但是其他因素，例如更为严格的法律强制措施或者司机培训水平的提高，可能在更大的程度上降低事故发生率。没有考虑并排除各种可能降低巴特勒县的事故发生率的因素，作者就不能大胆地建议布朗特县仿效巴特勒的速度限制政策。此外，作者在文中引用的有关巴特勒县的统计数字只包含"报告"了的事故，而该县发生的越来越大比例的事故可能都没有报告。

总之，这篇社论未能使我确信布朗特县仿效巴特勒县的公路安全措放的建议的可行性。为加强其论证，作者必须充分考虑到可能影响两县交通事故发生率的所有其他因素。为了更好地评价新施行的速度限制对交通安全的影响，我需要更多有关布朗特县的主要道路上的事故发生率的统计信息，而这些信息必须是经过一段较长时期的积累得到的。我还有必要知道在巴特勒县发生的车祸中有多大比例没有报告。

【逻辑问题提纲】

本文作者一共攻击了原文的三处缺陷：

1. 布朗特县只是刚刚在主要路段实施了限速，因而现在总体事故率的变化还不足以判断限速政策是否有效。

2. 作者没有考虑其他可能导致事故率增加的因素，诸如天气、执法力度、青少年驾驶员数量增加等。

3. 作者没有考虑导致巴特勒县事故下降的其他可能因素。

● 逻辑思路提示：信息不完整的错误（incomplete information）：在有些题目中，作者只提供了一些局部的、只言片语的信息来说明自己的观点，而这些信息可能不足以判断作者结论的合理性。

在题目中作者仅仅简单提到布朗特县的事故率没有显著下降，但要想判断限速是否真的无效，我们需要的是在实行限速的路段事故率变化的信息。因此，对于作者所提供的调查结果统计数据，要记得问一句：Is the result complete?

【论证展开】

"指出作者假设 + 指出作者未能支持该假设 + 列举其他可能 + 指出在没有排除这些可能的情况下作者的假设不合理"的论证套路。

这也是展开论证经常用到的经典套路。首先找出作者的推论所依据的假设，然后用 the author fails to provide evidence to support this assumption 这类的句子过渡，接着用列举法指出作者有哪些可能没有考虑到，最后用 Without considering and ruling out these and other factors that might have served to ..., the author cannot justifiably conclude that...这样的句式作为段落结尾。

【语言提示】

● 用于表达作者做了某种假设的语言和词汇：the author unfairly / falsely assumes / implies / infers / reasons

● 引导推测的句式：(1) It is (entirely / equally / quite) possible that ... (2) Another possibility is that ... (3) Perhaps / Possibly / Maybe

● 表达 A 导致 B 的因果关系的词汇：cause / explain / serve to / account for / be due to / be responsible for / lead to / result in (from) / contribute to

Argument 19   Promoting the rock band **Double Rice**

The following appeared in a letter from the manager of a rock band named Double Rice.

"One year ago, tickets for Double Rice's concerts in stadiums around the country took, on average, at least 24 hours to sell out, if they sold out at all. But the band has been enjoying a surge in nationwide popularity among 14 to 25 year olds, and the 30,000 tickets for a recent concert in Megalopolis sold out in 12 minutes. Clearly the ticket sales in Megalopolis are a result both of the band's increased popularity and of the advertising campaign run in Megalopolis by the Ad Lib advertising agency. Thus, in order to ensure that the band's success in Megalopolis is repeated across the country, the band should hire Ad Lib to duplicate the Megalopolis ad campaign on a nationwide scale."

【参考译文】一年前，Double Rice 在全国体育场举行的音乐会门票如果能卖完的话，也平均至少需要 24 小时。但乐队现在在全国 14~25 岁的人中间的受欢迎程度大大提高，最近在梅加洛波利斯的一次音乐会的 30000 张门票在 12 分钟内就售完了。显然梅加洛波利斯的门票热销得益于乐队日益增加的人气度和由 Ad Lib 广告公司在梅加洛波利斯所做的广告宣传。因此，为保证乐队在梅加洛波利斯的成功能够在全国再现，乐队应雇用 Ad Lib 在全国范围内重复他们在梅加洛波利斯所做的广告宣传。

The manager of the rock band Double Rice (DR) concludes that the band should hire the advertising agency Ad Lib to promote the band throughout the country. **To justify this conclusion the manager cites** Ad Lib's campaign to promote a recent DR concert at a large venue in Megalopolis. Tickets for this concert sold out in 12 minutes, whereas one year ago tickets for DR concerts at large venues rarely sold out in less than 24 hours—if at all. **The manager reasons that** the Megalopolis success must have been attributable to both Ad Lib's efforts and DR's popularity. **The manager's argument is flawed in several critical respects.**

To begin with, assuming that the Megalopolis success was in fact due to DR's popularity there, **the manager overlooks the possibility that** Ad Lib's campaign had nothing to do with that popularity. **Perhaps** the band recently became overwhelmingly popular due to a new hit song or to a revival of the type of music DR plays. **Either scenario, if true, would serve to undermine the manager's claim that** Ad Lib's efforts are to be credited for the Megalopolis success.

The manager also overlooks the possibility that one or more factors other than Ad Lib's efforts or DR's popularity **were instead responsible for** the Megalopolis success. **For instance, perhaps** DR shared the bill at the concert with another band, whose appearance was the actual reason for the concert's success. **If so, this fact would seriously weaken the manager's claim that** the Megalopolis success is attributable to Ad Lib's efforts and to DR's popularity in Megalopolis—whether or not that popularity resulted from Ad Lib's campaign.

Even assuming that either DR's popularity **or** Ad Lib's campaign, **or both, were responsible for** the Megalopolis success, **the manager's claim that** this success can be repeated elsewhere **might nevertheless be unwarranted**. Megalopolis **might not be representative of** most cities in which DR plans to appear—in any one of various ways that would adversely impact ticket sales in other cities. **For instance, perhaps** DR hails from Megalopolis and has far more fans in Megalopolis than any other city. **Or, perhaps** the kind of ad campaign that is Ad Lib's specialty, although effective in Megalopolis, would not be effective in most cities.

Finally, in concluding that DR must hire Ad Lib in order to ensure similar success throughout the country, **the manager assumes that** Ad Lib's services **are both necessary and sufficient for this purpose**. **Yet the manager has not provided any evidence to substantiate either assumption. Lacking such evidence, it is just as likely that** some other ad agency would be equally or more effective. **Even if** Ad Lib's services are necessary to achieve the manager's goal, **it is entirely possible that** Ad Lib's services **would not suffice to ensure** similar success elsewhere—**due to the sort of factors mentioned above that might have contributed to** the Megalopolis success but would not come into play in other cities.

In sum, the manager has not convinced me that DR's interests would be well served if and only if it hires Ad Lib to promote the band throughout the country. **To bolster the argument the manager must rule out all other possible reasons for** the success of the Megalopolis concert, **and must show that** Ad Lib is capable of achieving similar success in other cities.

【参考译文】

　　Double Rice（DR）的经理断定，应该雇用 Ad Lib 广告公司在整个国家宣传他们。为证明这一论断是正确的，经理引用近期 Ad Lib 在梅加洛波利斯成功宣传了 DR 的一场大型音乐会的这一事实。音乐会的票在 12 分钟内卖完，而一年以前 DR 在大型场所举办的音乐会的票如果能卖完，也很少能在 24 个小时之内售完。经理认为在梅加洛波利斯的成功一定可归因于 Ad Lib 的努力和 DR 的流行。经理的论证在几个关键的方面都有缺陷。

　　首先，假设在梅加洛波利斯举办音乐会的成功是因为 DR 的流行，经理忽略了 Ad Lib 的宣传活动根本与 DR 的流行无关这种可能性。或许由于一首新的热门歌曲或者 DR 演奏的风格又重新流行，所以乐队最近变得空前受欢迎。只要是其中任何一种情况，就能破坏经理关于 Ad Lib 的工作导致了乐队在梅加洛波利斯取得成功这一说法的可信性。

　　经理还忽视了除了 Ad Lib 的努力或者 DR 的流行以外的其他一个或更多因素也可能导致在梅加洛波利斯的成功的可能性。例如，或许 DR 与另一个乐队共同出演音乐会，而另一乐队的出席才是音乐会成功的真正原因。如果是这样，这个事实将严重地削弱经理的论断，即他们在梅加洛波利斯的成功可归因于 Ad Lib 的努力和 DR 的流行，无论这种流行是否源于 Ad Lib 的广告宣传。

即使假定 Ad Lib 的努力或者 DR 的流行，或者两个兼有，导致了他们在梅加洛波利斯的成功，经理声明这次的成功在别处可被重复还是没有保证的。梅加洛波利斯也许不能代表 DR 计划演出的大多数城市。无论其中任何一种情况，都将在其他城市影响票的出售。比如，或许 DR 来自梅加洛波利斯，与其他城市相比较，在梅加洛波利斯有更多的歌迷。或许，Ad Lib 在广告推广方面的专长虽然在梅加洛波利斯很有效，但在其他大多数城市内是不会奏效的。

最后，在做出为了确保 DR 音乐在整个国家内取得相似的成功，而必须雇用 Ad Lib 这一结论时，经理假定 Ad Lib 的服务对于实现这一目标既必要又充分。然而，经理没有提供任何证据证明两种假定中的任意一种。由于缺乏这样的证据，一些其他广告代理将同样或者更加有用。即使 Ad Lib 的服务对于实现那些目标是必要的，也完全可能 Ad Lib 的服务不能够保证在别处获得相似的成功，因为上述这些可能导致梅加洛波利斯成功的因素在其他城市可能并不具备。

总之，该经理没能使我确信雇用，甚至只有雇用 Ad Lib 在全国来宣传 DR 才能很好地为 DR 的利益服务。要支持这篇论证，经理必须排除所有其他可以解释梅加洛波利斯音乐会成功的可能的原因，并且必须表明 Ad Lib 能在其他城市取得相似的成功。

【逻辑问题提纲】

本文作者一共攻击了原文的四处缺陷：

1. 乐队在 Megalopolis 的成功可能与 Ad Lib 的广告活动并无关系。
2. 可能有其他因素导致了乐队在 Megalopolis 的成功而并非其本身的人气度。
3. Megalopolis 的情况未必能够代表其他地区对乐队的态度（以特殊推一般的草率推广）。
4. Ad Lib 的广告宣传对于乐队在其他地区的成功可能并不是必要的。

● 逻辑思路提示：本文论证的第一和第二个错误从本质上说是同一个错误，就是乐队在 Megalopolis 的成功可能有其他原因而不是由于乐队本身受欢迎或是由于广告公司的策略。虽然在一篇文章中可以对一个现象做不同角度的论述和攻击，但本文论证的这两段很大程度上都是类似的，包括语言、论证手法，很多语言重复出现，所用的论证思路也都是有其他可能原因的方式：在第二段是指出可能是 DR 的某一首主打歌曲或是其演奏的音乐类型导致其成功，在第三段则是指出可能是其他乐队的共同出演导致了音乐会的成功（这个推测本身就有点离题过远）。因此本文的第二、三两段并不是很好的论证思路，在这种情况下完全可以把这两点合并为一点用一段来进行论述。

【论证展开】

● 某某措施对于某结果既非充分又非必要的论述：

当作者在原文的结论中做了"我们应该采取 A 措施来达到 B 结果"，或是"A 措施是实现 B 的惟一途径"等比较绝对的论述的时候，我们就可以指出 A 对于实现 B 可能并不是必要的，其他手段和措施可能也能，甚至更有效地保证 B 的实现。这时可以用本文的句型 the manager assumes that ... are both necessary and sufficient for this purpose, yet the manager has not provided any evidence to substantiate either assumption. 来指出 A 对于 B 既非充分又非必要。

● 攻击错误类比和草率推广的论证句式：攻击错误类比和草率推广的语言往往是可以通用的。本文所出现的这个句子：

It is entirely possible that ... (the experiences / measures / policy in A) would not suffice to ensure similar ... (the result in B) elsewhere—due to the sort of factors mentioned above that might have contributed to ... (the result in A) but would not come into play in other cities. 就是一个攻击这两类错误的很好的句式，具有一定的复杂度，而且语言规范严密。论证 A 与 B 不能类比或 A 的情况不能推广到 B 时，可以把 A 的情况和措施填到第一个空格处，指出它不能保证同样的措施也会在 B 产生同样的效果（把 B 的效果填入第二个空格），接着论证由于上文所指出的导致 A 的结果的因素未必在其他地方同样有效。

【语言提示】

● 论证句式：(1) The manager also overlooks the possibility that ... were instead responsible for ... (2) If so, this fact would seriously weaken the manager's claim that ... (3) Finally, in concluding that ... the manager assumes that ... are both necessary and sufficient for this purpose. (4) Lacking such evidence, it is just as likely that ... (5) It is entirely possible that ... would not suffice to ensure similar success elsewhere—due to the sort of factors mentioned above that might have contributed to ...

Argument 23　A seafood restaurant for **Bay City**

"A recent sales study indicated that consumption of seafood dishes in Bay City restaurants has increased by 30 percent over the past five years. Yet there are no currently operating city restaurants that specialize in seafood. Moreover, the majority of families in Bay City are two-income families, and a nationwide study has shown that such families eat significantly fewer home-cooked meals than they did a decade ago but at the same time express more concern about eating healthily. Therefore, a new Bay City restaurant specializing in seafood will be quite popular and profitable."

【参考译文】 最近的销量调查显示，海湾城市餐馆的海鲜菜肴的消费量比过去五年增加了 30％。而现在该市还没有专门经营海鲜菜的餐厅。而且，海湾城市的大多数家庭是双收入家庭，一次全国性调查显示，这类家庭在家做饭的数量比十年前显著减少，同时他们更关注健康饮食。因此，在海湾城市开设一家新的专营海鲜食品的餐馆将会非常受欢迎，而且有利可图。

This argument's conclusion is that a new Bay City restaurant specializing in seafood would be both popular and profitable. **To justify this conclusion the argument points out that** seafood consumption in Bay City's restaurants has risen by 30％ during the last five years. **Also, the argument points out that** most Bay City families are two-income families, and cites a national survey showing that two-income families eat out more often and express more concern about eating healthily than they did ten years ago. **I find the argument unpersuasive, for several reasons.**

First, a 30％ increase in seafood consumption at Bay City restaurants **does not necessarily indicate** a sufficient demand for a new Bay City restaurant serving seafood dishes only. **Although** a 30％ increase seems significant, the actual level of consumption might nevertheless be very low. **This scenario is quite possible, especially considering that** there are currently no seafood restaurants in Bay City. **Lacking evidence that** a significant number of the city's restaurant patrons are ordering seafood, **the argument's conclusion that** a new seafood restaurant would be popular and profitable **is unjustified.**

Secondly, even if current demand would otherwise support an increase in the availability of seafood at Bay City's restaurants, **the argument unfairly assumes that** Bay City's restaurant patrons who order seafood would frequent the new restaurant. Perhaps the vast majority of these patrons would remain loyal to their favorite restaurant. **Thus, lacking evidence that** these patrons would be willing to try the new restaurant **the argument's claim that** a new seafood restaurant would be popular **is dubious.**

Thirdly, the nationwide study showing clear trends among two-income families toward dining out and eating healthily **does not necessarily apply to** Bay City. **It is quite possible that** Bay City's two-income families do not follow these general trends. For that matter, in Bay City the trend might be just the opposite. Thus, the nationwide trends that the argument cites amount to scant evidence that Bay City residents in particular would frequent a new seafood restaurant in their city.

Fourth, even if most of Bay City's families are following the nationwide trends indicated above, **it is unreasonable to infer that** these families will necessarily patronize a new seafood restaurant in Bay City. For all we know Bay City might boast a variety of health-oriented restaurants that do not specialize in seafood. For that matter, perhaps Bay City's existing restaurants are responding to the trends by providing more healthful dishes. **Moreover, perhaps** either or both of these trends will soon reverse themselves—at least in Bay City—for whatever reason. **Any of these scenarios, if true, would cast considerable doubt on the argument's conclusion that** a new seafood restaurant in Bay City would be popular and profitable.

Finally, even if Bay City families flock to the new seafood restaurant, the restaurant would not necessarily be profitable as a result. **Profitability is a function of both revenue and expense.** Thus, it is entirely possible that the restaurant's costs of obtaining high-quality, healthful seafood, or of promoting the new restaurant, might render it unprofitable despite its popularity. **Without weighing revenue against expenses the argument's conclusion is premature at best.**

In sum, the argument is unpersuasive as it stands. To bolster it the argument's author must show—perhaps by way of a reliable citywide study—**that** the demand among restaurant patrons for seafood is sufficient to support a new seafood restaurant, and that a sufficient number of people who order fish at Bay City restaurants will be able and willing to at least try the new restaurant. **The author would also bolster the argument by providing reliable evidence that** Bay City reflects the nationwide trends cited, and that these trends will continue in the foreseeable future—in Bay City. **Finally, to better assess the argument I would need** detailed cost and revenue estimates for a new Bay City seafood restaurant—to determine the likelihood that even a popular such restaurant would turn a profit.

【参考译文】

本文论证的结论是一家新开张的主营海鲜的海湾城市餐厅将会宾客满门，财源广进。为了证明这个结论的正确性，文章指出海湾城市的餐厅里的海鲜消费在过去五年期间已经提高了30％。此外，文章还指出大多数海湾城市家庭是双职工家庭，而据一项全国范围内的调查显示双职工家庭比十年前更经常到餐馆用餐，更关注健康饮食。基于以下几个原因，我发现该论证不具说服力。

首先，在海湾城市的餐厅里的海鲜消费增加了30％并不一定表明海湾城市的人们对新开一家专供海鲜的餐厅有着迫切要求。虽然30％的增长看起来似乎很显著，但是实际消费水平可能仍然非常低。这种假设是十分可能的，特别是考虑到海湾城市目前还没有海鲜馆。由于缺乏证据证明该城市有大量的餐厅顾客常吃海鲜，那么该文章做出的新开一家海鲜馆将宾客满门、财源广进的结论是不足为信的。

第二，即使当今的市场需求以其他方式促使海湾城市餐厅的海鲜供应增长，本文不合理地假定常吃海鲜的海湾城市餐厅的顾客会频繁光顾这家新开张的餐厅。也许这些常客中的大多数人会一贯忠于他们最喜欢的餐厅。然而，缺乏证据证明这些常客也乐于尝试一下光顾新餐厅，该论证就断定新开一家海鲜馆会大受欢迎，这是值得怀疑的。

第三，那项表明双职工家庭有到餐厅就餐和健康饮食的明显趋势的全国范围内的研究，并不一定适用于海湾城市。很可能海湾城市的双职工家庭并不随这个大流。因而本城市双收入家庭不遵循这些一般的趋势是十分可能的。就此而言，海湾城市的流行趋势可能正好相反。因此，本文引用的全国性的趋势实际上并不能证明海湾城市居民会时常光顾他们的城市新开的一家海鲜馆。

第四，即使大多数海湾城市家庭也跟随上面表明的全国性趋势，就此推断这些家庭必定光顾在海湾城市新开张的一家海鲜馆是不合理的。因为就我们所知，海湾城市也会以拥有各种非专营海鲜而提供健康食品的餐厅而自豪，所以从这点来说，或许海湾城市的现有的餐厅会提供更多有益于健康的饭菜，以应对这种趋势。而且，也许这两个趋势其中之一，甚至是这两个趋势都很快由于某种原因转向相反的方向发展——至少在海湾城市有这种可能。如果这些假想中的任何一条证明属实的话，那么本文所做的在海湾城市新开一家海鲜馆会宾客满门、财源广进的结论是相当值得怀疑的。

最后，即使海湾城市的家庭都蜂拥去那家新开的海鲜馆就餐，那家餐厅也不一定就会因此而财源广进。赢利随着收入和支出的变化而变化。因此，完全可能尽管餐厅很受欢迎，但是因为餐厅购进了高质量、有益于健康的海鲜，并对新餐厅进行积极宣传，从而陷入亏损的境地。没有权衡收入与支出，只能说论证的结论下得太早了。

总之，就目前情况看，这一论证是不具说服力的。为支持其论点，作者也许可以通过做一个城市范围内的可靠的研究方式来表明，餐厅的常客对海鲜的需求量足以支持一家新开张的海鲜馆，而且在海湾城市的餐厅吃鱼的顾客中有足够数量的人至少可能并且乐于尝试新的餐厅。为支持其论点，作者也应提供可靠证据来证明海湾城市的情况也反映出所引用的全国性的趋势，而这些趋势在可预知的将来里还会在海湾城市继续存在。最后，为了更好地评价这个论证，我需要一份在海湾城市新开一家海鲜馆的详尽收入和支出预算，以确定使这么一家受欢迎的餐厅能够赢利的可能性。

【逻辑问题提纲】

本文作者一共攻击了原文的五处缺陷：

1. 海鲜食品消费量增加 30% 这一百分比数值并不能说明居民对于海鲜有很大的需求量。

2. 就算海湾城市的海鲜需求量很大，消费者也未必光顾新开的餐厅。

3. 对于双收入家庭饮食习惯的全国性调查结果不一定适用于海湾城市的情况（整体不能代表局部）。

4. 即使海湾城市的家庭饮食习惯符合全国潮流，他们也不一定去新的海鲜餐馆就餐。

5. 作者没有考虑开设新餐馆的成本与收益之比，过高的采购与宣传成本可能导致餐馆无利可图。

● 逻辑思路提示：没有全面衡量正负得失的错误：很多题目中，在作者判断某种行为、制定某种决策的时候，只看到了事物好的或者坏的一方面，然后就根据一方面的信息下结论，这是一种不理性的思路，也是一个我们可以批判的点。这种缺陷在一些题目中的具体体现就是：作者认为某种行为和措施必然赢利的时候，没有考虑实行这种行为和措施所必须的投入，即没有计算投入与产出之比。所以当看到作者单方面鼓吹某某事物一定赢利的时候，要想一想：你考虑成本了吗？本文第五点攻击的就是这类错误，作者只看到海鲜餐厅可能有需求，就认为开设这样一个餐馆能赚钱，但我们还必须考虑开餐馆所必须的诸如场地、原材料、人力、宣传等投入，只有在全面衡量了投入与产出，也就是得与失之后我们才能下结论。

【开头方式】

This argument's conclusion is that...开头段列举原文结论的时候，我们既可以像前面很多题目那样，用the author concludes that...这类的宾语从句表达，也可以换一换形式，用这个表语从句引出结论。

【论证展开】

整体递进的论证结构：前面说过在一个论证段之中的不同句子可以使用递进关系联系起来，而全文的不同论证段之间也可以用递进关系来维系，这样可以使文章的逻辑非常紧凑，整体性很强。在这篇范文中，作者在论证第二、第四、第五三个错误时都使用了 even if 的让步句式作为开头，观察一下即可发现，让步的内容就是前一段所攻击的错误。像这种环环相扣的论证系统是值得学习和使用的，先攻击第一个最明显的错误，然后在第二段让步，就算我们认为第一个错误不存在，这里还有第二个缺陷；然后再递进，就算第二个错误我们可以忽略，还存在第三个错误，等等。当然让步的语言不一定都用 even if，可以积累很多可用于让步的句式。

【语言提示】

● 用于推测其他可能的句式：This scenario is quite possible, especially considering that ...

● 用于论证段落小总结的句式：(1) Lacking evidence that ..., the argument's conclusion that ... is unjustified. (2) Thus, lacking evidence that ... the argument's claim that ... is dubious. (3) Any of these scenarios, if true, would cast considerable doubt on the argument's conclusion that...

● 用于描述整体调查结果不能用于个体的句式：the nationwide study showing ... does not necessarily apply to ...

● 用于表达作者没有考虑成本与收益之比的句式：(1) Profitability is a function of both revenue and expense. (2) Without weighing revenue against expenses the argument's conclusion is premature at best.

● 结尾句式：(1) To bolster it the argument's author must show—perhaps by way of a reliable citywide study—that ... (2) The author would also bolster the argument by providing reliable evidence that ... (3) To better assess the argument I would need detailed cost and revenue estimates for ...

Argument 26　Improving a school district's **music education programs**

The following appeared in a memo from the chairperson of the school board in the town of Saluda.

"For the past five years, Mr. Charles Schade has been the music director at Steel City High School, and during that time the school band from Steel City High has won three regional band competitions. In addition, the quality of the music rehearsal facilities and musical instruments at Steel City High has improved markedly over the past five years. Because of such successes at Steel City High, the Saluda school board should hire Mr. Schade to plan and direct the general music education programs for the entire Saluda school system."

【参考译文】过去五年中，查尔斯·谢德先生担任了钢铁城市高中的音乐指挥，在那期间学校乐队在三次地区乐队比赛中获胜。而且，钢铁城市高中的音乐排练设备和乐器在过去五年中明显得到改善。由于钢铁城市高中所获得的这些成功，撒露达地方教育董事会应该雇用谢德先生来为整个撒露达学校系统规划和指导总体音乐教育计划。

    In this memo the chairperson of the Saluda school board recommends hiring Schade, Steel City High's music director for the past five years, to plan and direct the school district's general music-education programs. **To support this recommendation the chairperson points out that** over the past five years Steel's band has won three regional awards and that the school's facilities and instruments have improved markedly. **However, close scrutiny of this evidence reveals that it lends little support for the recommendation.**

    First of all, the chairperson unfairly assumes that the three band awards **were attributable to** Schade's abilities and efforts. **Lacking evidence to confirm this assumption, it is entirely possible that** Schade was not the school's band instructor when the band won these awards. **Or, perhaps** the band won all three awards early in Schade's tenure, and his predecessor is to be credited. **For that matter, perhaps** it was the improved quality of the band's musical instruments that should be credited for the awards. **After all, the chairperson provides no evidence that** Schade **was actually responsible for** this improvement. **Without considering and ruling out other possible reasons why** the band won the awards **the chairperson cannot convince me of** Schade's abilities or, in turn, that he should be appointed to the district job.

    Even if Schade is to be credited for the band's awards, **it is possible that** the skills that Schade possesses and that resulted in the band's winning these awards are not the same skills required for the district position. **For example, perhaps** Schade's music-conducting ability or his ability to motivate individual students was responsible for the band's award-winning performances. **If so, then the fact that** Steel's band won these awards **would amount to scant evidence at best that** Schade would make an effective administrator for the district.

    Next, the chairperson unfairly assumes that improvements in the school's music facilities and instruments **are attributable to** Schade's efforts. **If they are, then I would agree that** Schade might possess valuable administrative skills that would serve the district well. **Yet, just because** these improvements occurred during Schade's tenure **it is unreasonable to assume that** Schade is to be credited for them. **It is entirely possible that** the improvements were the result of another administrator's efforts, or even the efforts of parents. **Without showing clearly that** Schade, and not some other person, **was responsible for** the improvements, **the chairperson cannot convince me that** Schade possesses the administrative abilities needed for the district job.

    Finally, in recommending Schade for the job **the chairperson fails to consider other possible job** candidates. **Even if all the evidence shows that** Schade is well qualified, **perhaps** one or more other individuals would be even more suitable for the job. **Without addressing this possibility the chairperson cannot convince me that** the district should hire Schade.

    In conclusion, the argument is unpersuasive as it stands. To convince me that Schade would be effective in the new job, **the chairperson must provide clear evidence that** the band's awards and especially the improvements cited are attributable to Schade's abilities and efforts, **and that** these abilities would translate directly to those required for the district position. **Finally, to better evaluate the argument I would need to** compare Schade's qualifications with those of other possible job candidates.

【参考译文】

在这个备忘录里，撒露达（Saluda）地方教育董事会的主席推荐聘用谢德，钢铁城市高中（Steel City High）最近五年的音乐指挥，来策划并指导这个学区的总体音乐教育规划。为了支持这个建议，该主席指出在最近的五年里，钢铁城市高中的乐队已经赢得了三次地区奖项，而且这个学校的设备和乐器有了显著的改善。但是，进一步仔细分析这个证据会发现它对支持这个建议一点帮助也没有。

首先，主席不合理地认为乐队所得的三个奖项归功于谢德的能力和努力。由于缺乏证据来确认这个假定，这个学校的乐队赢得这些奖项的时候谢德完全有可能不是这个学校乐队的指导老师。或者，有可能这个乐队是在谢德就职早期赢得所有三个奖项的，那么功劳就应该属于谢德的前任了。同样，也有可能是因为这个乐队的乐器质量提高了，所以才赢得了那些奖项。毕竟，主席并没有提供任何证据证明这个进步是谢德的功劳。没有考虑到并排除这个乐队获奖的其他可能的原因，这个主席就不能使我信服谢德的能力，甚至进而聘他担任地区工作。

即使对于乐队获奖，谢德确实有功劳，但是有可能谢德所拥有并促成乐队获奖的那些技能与地区职位所要求的技能并不相同。例如，也许谢德的音乐指挥能力和他激励学生个人的能力使得这个乐队在演出中获奖。如果是这样的话，钢铁城市高中的乐队获奖的事实很难证明谢德能够在这个地区担当一个杰出的管理者。

其次，这个主席想当然地认为这所学校的音乐设备和乐器方面的改进都归功于谢德的努力。如果事实确实是如此，那么我将同意谢德可能具备可以很好地为该地区服务的可贵的管理技巧。然而，光凭这些改进发生在谢德的任期内就想当然地认为这是他的功劳是不合理的。这些改进完全有可能是另一个管理者，或者甚至是学校的学生父母努力的结果。没有明确的证明正是谢德，而不是其他人，有助于这些改进，这个主席就不能使我确信谢德拥有为该地区工作所需要的管理能力。

最后，在推荐谢德来担当这项工作的同时，这个主席没有考虑其他可能的工作候选人。即使全部证据都证明谢德相当合格，或许也还有其他一个或更多人会更适合这项工作。没有考虑到这种可能性，主席就不能使我信服这个地区应该雇用谢德。

总之，就目前情况看，这个论证不能说服人。要让我相信谢德将在新工作里表现出色，这个主席就必须提供可靠的证据证明乐队获奖，特别是上面说的改进都归功于谢德的能力和努力，而这些能力都将会直接转化为该地区的职位所要求的能力。最后，为了更好地评价这个论证，我有必要把谢德的条件和其他可能的工作候选人进行一番比较。

【逻辑问题提纲】

本文作者一共攻击了原文的四处缺陷：

1. 学校乐队的三次获胜未必都是谢德的功劳。
2. 谢德领导乐队获胜的能力对于指导全区学校音乐教学未必有用。
3. 学校音乐排练设备和乐器的改善未必是谢德带来的。
4. 作者没有考虑其他候选人的可能情况，而认定谢德是惟一适合的人选。

【语言提示】

● 开头段句式：However, close scrutiny of this evidence reveals that it lends little support for the recommendation.

● 论证段句式：(1) For that matter, perhaps ... (2) After all, the chairperson provides no evidence that Schade was actually responsible for ... (3) If they are, then I would agree that ... (4) Yet, just because... it is unreasonable to assume that ... (5) Without addressing this possibility the chairperson cannot convince me that . . .

Argument 28　Breakfast for students in the **Mylar school district**

The following is a memo from the superintendent of the Mylar school district.

"A recent six-month study, in which breakfast was made available at school for 100 schoolchildren ages five to twelve, found that children on the breakfast plan were less likely than other children to be absent from or late for school. Clearly, eating breakfast before school plays a role in reducing student absenteeism and tardiness. It is also well known that children who regularly eat a healthful breakfast tend to perform better in school. Therefore, in order to reduce absenteeism and tardiness and to improve academic performance in all of Mylar's elementary and secondary schools, we should provide breakfasts for all students before each school day."

【参考译文】在最近一项为期六个月的研究中，我们为 100 名 5～12 岁的小学生在学校提供早餐；研究发现参加早餐计划的儿童比其他儿童更不容易缺席或迟到。显然，上学前吃早餐对于减少学生的缺席和迟到作用很大。而且众所周知，经常吃健康早餐的儿童一般在学校的表现也更好。因此，为减少迈拉地区所有小学和初中的缺席和迟到的现象，以及提高学习成绩，我们应该在每天上课前为所有学生提供早餐。

　　In this memo, **the superintendent of the Mylar school district concludes** that by providing breakfast to all its students the district would reduce tardiness and absenteeism as well as improve the overall academic performance of its students. **To support this conclusion the superintendent points out that** during a 6-month trial program involving 100 students ranging in age from 5 to 12, these students were less likely to be tardy or absent than other students. **The superintendent also cites the well-known fact that** eating healthful breakfasts on a regular basis improves academic performance. **The superintendent's argument is problematic in several respects, rendering the argument unconvincing as it stands.**

　　The argument's chief problem is that it relies on numerous unsubstantiated assumptions about the 6-month study. **One such assumption is that** the participants' regular and punctual attendance was attributable to the fact that breakfasts were provided. **Yet logic and common sense inform me that the results might have been due instead to one or more other factors. Perhaps** these particular students were compelled to show up punctually and regularly for some other reason. **Perhaps** the 100 participants were comparatively reliable and disciplined children who are less likely in any event to be late for school. **Or perhaps** the participants are relatively healthy and therefore less likely to be absent from school than the average student. **Moreover, it is uncertain whether** the program's participants even ate the breakfasts that the trial program provided. **In short, without considering and ruling out alternative explanations for the study's results, the superintendent cannot justifiably conclude that** the results are due to the fact that breakfasts were provided to participating students.

　　Even if the participants' punctual and regular attendance was due to the breakfasts provided to them, **the statistical reliability of the trial program's results is questionable. The number of participants, 100, might constitute an insufficiently small sample to draw any reliable conclusions about** how district students 5 – 12 years of age would behave under similar conditions—as a group. The larger this group compared to the sample of 100 participants, the less reliable the study's results. **Also, the sample might be unrepresentative of** district students **as a group. For example, perhaps** the 100 participants happened to be children who eat small dinners and are therefore hungry for breakfast.

Even if the 100 participants are statistically representative of district students who are 5 – 12 years of age, **one cannot infer that** older, secondary-school students would behave similarly under similar conditions. **Yet by concluding that the** district should implement the program for its secondary-school students as well, **the superintendent seems to assume without supporting evidence that this is the case.** **In short, lacking assurances that** the 100 participants are statistically representative of all district students, **the superintendent cannot draw any reliable conclusions based on the study.**

Aside from the problems involving the 6-month study, **the superintendent's conclusion that** the overall academic performance of district students would improve under the proposed program **is unwarranted. By relying on the fact that** eating healthful breakfasts on a regular basis improves academic performance, **the superintendent assumes that** the district's breakfasts would be healthful and that students would eat them on a regular basis. **Yet no evidence is offered to substantiate these crucial assumptions. It is entirely possible that** the district's breakfasts would not be sufficiently healthful, or that district students would not eat these breakfasts regularly. **In fact, the superintendent has not shown either that** the trial program's participants **or that** the broader population of district students would eat healthful breakfasts, or any breakfast at all, under any circumstances.

In conclusion, the superintendent's argument is specious. To bolster it she must provide clear evidence that the 100 participants in the trial program actually attended school regularly and punctually because of the breakfasts provided, **and that** these 100 students are statistically representative not only of other 5 – 12 year-olds but of older students as well—as a group. **Finally, to better evaluate the claim that** the program would improve academic performance **I would need more information about** the healthfulness of the breakfasts provided under the proposed program.

【参考译文】

　　在这份备忘录里，迈拉学区的主管人认为，通过给所有学生提供早餐，该地区学生的拖拉迟到和缺勤情况将有所好转，并且学生的总的学业成绩也将有所提高。为了支持这个结论，主管人指出在一个长达六个月，涉及从5~12岁的100个学生的试行计划里，这些学生比起其他学生，很少有迟到和缺勤的情况。主管人也引用了人所共知的事实，即定时吃有益于健康的早餐会提高学生的学业成绩。就目前情况看，主管人的论证在以下几个方面是有疑问的，使得这篇论证不足以让人信服。

　　论证的主要问题是关于那六个月的研究所做的许多无确实根据的假定。假定之一是参加者定时和准时出席可归因于提供了早餐。然而逻辑和常识告诉我，结果可能是由其他一种或多种因素造成的。或许这些学生因为其他一些原因而被迫准时并且正常到校。或许这100个参加者相对而言是可信赖的，并且是遵守纪律的，他们不论在什么情况下都不太可能上课迟到。或者也许那些参加者比一般学生较为健康，因此不太可能缺勤。此外，甚至计划的参加者是否吃了试行计划所提供的早餐也是不确定的。简而言之，如果没有考虑到并排除其他的对研究结果的解释，主管人不能无可非议地断定该结果是因为向参加的学生提供了早餐而引起的。

　　即使参加者准时和正常到校是由于向他们提供了早餐，试行计划的结果在统计上的可靠性也是有疑问的。参加者的数量是100，这能不能作为一个充分的样本，从而得出任何有关本学区5~12岁的学生作为一个整体在相似的条件下会有怎样的表现的可靠结论。这个整体与100个参加者的样本相差越大，研究的结果就越不可靠。同样，这个样本可能不能代表学区学生这个整体。例如，或许100个参加者碰巧是因晚餐吃少了因而在早晨很饿。

即使在统计学上这100个参加者可以代表学区5～12岁的学生，我们也不能由此推断出更大一些的中学生在相似的状况下将有类似的表现。主管人似乎断定情况确实如此，因为他得出结论，认为该地区也应该为中学生实施该项计划，然而，对此没有提出证据来支持。简而言之，在不能保证100个参加者在统计学上能够代表全部地区的学生的情况下，主管人不能基于此研究得出任何可靠的结论。

除了与六个月的研究有关的那些问题，主管人关于执行了建议后学生的总成绩将会有所提高的结论也是没有根据的。在引述定时吃有益于健康的早餐能够提高学业成绩的事实时，主管人假定本地区的早餐将是有益于健康的，而且学生将会定时吃早餐。但是他没有提供证据证明这些至关紧要的假定。完全可能地区的早餐不够健康，或者学区的学生不会定时吃这些早餐。实际上，主管人没有证实试行计划的参加者和学区的更多的学生不管在任何情况下都将会吃有益于健康的早餐，或者吃早餐。

总之，主管人的论证是可疑的。为了支持此论证，她必须提供清楚的证据证明试行计划的100个参加者正常而准时到校确实是因为提供了早餐而导致，并且这100个学生作为一个整体在统计上不仅可以代表5～12岁的学生，也可以代表年龄更大的学生。最后，为了更好地评价该计划能够提高学业成绩的这一主张，我需要更多的关于提议的计划中所提供的早餐对健康的有益程度的信息。

【逻辑问题提纲】

本文作者一共攻击了原文的四处缺陷：

1. 参加调查的儿童准时到校未必是因为被提供了早餐而导致的，在这一段中作者用了三个perhaps来引导这些学生不迟到的其他可能原因。

2. 参加调查的100个样本未必能够代表全体学生的情况（取样代表性的问题）。

3. 即使早餐计划对于5～12岁的小学生确实有效，我们也不能认为它对于中学生也同样起作用（以少推多的差异范围草率推广）。

4. 作者没有提供任何信息表明本地区学生的早餐一定会是"健康"的，或者他们一定经常按时吃早餐。

● 逻辑思路提示：

1）本文论述的第一个问题是早餐计划和学生出勤之间的因果关系，这一点还可以从调查的角度做其他两方面的展开：首先，作者没有告诉我们这些样本是如何确定的，因而代表性值得怀疑；另一方面，还是对于调查参加者的经典质疑套路：那些本来就不太迟到的儿童可能更愿意，或有条件参加早餐计划，因为作者提到早餐是在学校提供的，因此也只有不迟到的学生才能够吃到早餐，这实际是一个因果倒置的错误。

2）以少推多的草率推广：一般在题目中如果出现了诸如 all / every / any 这类词汇的时候，都会出现以少推多的差异范围。如本文就是作者仅从100名小学生的调查出发就简单推出所有的中小学生都可以从早餐计划获益。

【语言提示】

● 开头段句式：The superintendent also cites the well-known fact that ...

● 论证段句式：（1）The argument's chief problem is that it relies o numerous unsubstantiated assumptions about... （2）Yet logic and common sense inform me that the results might have been due instead to one or more other factors. （3）Moreover, it is uncertain whether ... （4）the statistical reliability of the trial program's results is questionable. （5）The number of participants might constitute an insufficiently small sample to draw any reliable conclusions about ... (6) Also, the sample might be unrepresentative of ... as a group. (7) Yet by concluding that ..., the superintendent seems to assume without supporting evidence that this is the case. (8) In short, lacking assurances that ..., the superintendent cannot draw any reliable conclusions based on the study. (9) Aside from the problems involving ..., the superintendent's conclusion that ... is unwarranted. (10) Yet no evidence is offered to substantiate these crucial assumptions. (11) In fact, the superintendent has not shown either that ... or that ...

Argument 141   The environmental impact of copper **mining**

The following appeared in a newsletter distributed at a recent political rally.

"Over the past year, the Consolidated Copper Company (CCC) has purchased over one million square miles of land in the tropical nation of West Fredonia. Mining copper on this land will inevitably result in pollution and environmental disaster, since West Fredonia is home to several endangered animal species. But such disaster can be prevented if consumers simply refuse to purchase products that are made with CCC's copper until the company abandons its mining plans."

【参考译文】去年, 统一铜公司 (CCC) 在热带国家西弗莱德尼亚购买了上百万平方英里的土地。在这些地方采矿将会不可避免地导致污染和环境灾害, 因为西弗莱德尼亚是很多濒危物种的栖居地。但如果消费者完全拒绝购买用 CCC 所生产的铜而制造的产品, 直到 CCC 放弃它的采矿计划, 就可以避免这种灾害。

The author of this newsletter excerpt concludes that if consumers refuse to buy products made with Consolidated Copper Company (CCC) copper the company will eventually abandon its mining plans in the nation of West Fredonia, thereby preventing pollution and an "environmental disaster" in that country. **To justify this conclusion the author points out that** CCC has recently bought more than a million square miles of land in West Fredonia, and that West Fredonia is home to several endangered animal species. **I find this argument specious on several grounds.**

First, the author provides no evidence that the West Fredonia land that CCC has acquired amounts to a significant portion of land inhabited by endangered animal species, or that CCC's land is inhabited by endangered animal species at all. **Nor does the author provide clear evidence that** CCC's mining activities are of the type that might cause pollution, the extinction of animal species, or any other environmental damage. **Lacking such evidence the author simply cannot convince me that** CCC must abandon its plans in order that such damage be prevented.

Secondly, even assuming CCC's planned mining activities in West Fredonia will cause pollution and will endanger several animal species, **it is nevertheless impossible to assess the author's broader contention that** CCC's activities will result in "environmental disaster," at least without an agreed-upon definition of that term. If by "environmental disaster" the author simply means some pollution and the extinction of several animal species, then the claim would have merit; otherwise, it would not. **Absent either a clear definition of the term or clear evidence that** CCC's activities would carry grave environmental consequences by any reasonable definition, **the author's contention that** CCC's activities will result in environmental disaster **is simply unjustified.**

Thirdly, the author's position that environmental disaster is "inevitable" absent the prescribed boycott precludes the possibility that other measures can be taken to prevent CCC from carrying out its plans, or to offset any harm that CCC causes should it carry out its plans. **Yet the author fails to provide assurances that** no other means of preventing the predicted disaster are available. **Lacking such evidence the author cannot reasonably conclude that** the proposed boycott is needed to prevent that disaster.

Finally, even if the prescribed boycott is needed to prevent pollution and environmental disaster in West Fredonia, **the author assumes too hastily that** the boycott will suffice for these purposes. Perhaps additional measures would be required as well. For instance, perhaps consumers would also need to boycott other companies that pollute West Fredonia's environment. **In short, without any evidence that** the recommended course of action will be enough to prevent the predicted problems, **the author's conclusion remains dubious at best.**

In sum, as it stands the argument is wholly unpersuasive. To bolster it the author must show that CCC's planned mining activities on its newly acquired land will pollute and will threaten endangered animal species. **The author must also** define "environmental disaster" and show that the inevitable results of CCC's activities, absent the proposed boycott, would meet that definition. **To better assess the argument it would be useful to know** what other means are available for preventing CCC from mining in West Fredonia or, in the alternative, for mitigating the environmental impact of those mining activities. **Also useful would be any information about** the likelihood that the boycott would be effective in accomplishing its intended objectives.

【参考译文】

这篇通讯摘录的作者断定，如果消费者拒绝购买用统一铜公司（CCC）的铜生产的铜产品，该公司将最终放弃它在西弗莱德尼亚国的采矿计划，而那个国家也将因此免受污染并避开一场"环境灾难"。为了证明这个结论是正确的，作者指出统一铜公司（CCC）已于近期在西弗莱德尼亚买下100多万平方英里的土地，而西弗莱德尼亚栖息着几种濒危动物。我发现本文在若干方面是可疑的。

首先，作者没有提供证据证明统一铜公司（CCC）已购入的西弗莱德尼亚的土地就是濒危动物种类所栖息的土地的重要组成部分，或者濒危动物种类确实就栖息在统一铜公司（CCC）的土地上。作者也未明确证明统一铜公司（CCC）进行的采矿活动是属于会引起污染，导致动物种类灭绝，或其他环境破坏的那一类活动。缺乏这些证据，作者根本无法使我相信，为了防止这种破坏，统一铜公司（CCC）必须放弃它的计划。

第二，即使假设统一铜公司（CCC）已计划的采矿活动确实将在西弗莱德尼亚引起污染并危及数种动物，作者关于统一铜公司（CCC）的活动将最终导致"环境灾难"的论点更加宽泛得让人不可能对其进行准确的评价。至少如果对"环境灾难"这个术语没有一致的定义，就不可能对其进行准确的评价。如果作者所谓的"环境灾难"仅仅表示一些污染和几种动物的灭绝，那么其主张还有一些价值；否则，它将是可疑的。缺乏对该术语的明确定义，或者未能通过清晰证据证实统一铜公司（CCC）的活动确实将导致严重的环境后果，并且对严重的环境后果做出合理的定义，那么作者所做的关于统一铜公司（CCC）的活动将导致环境灾难的论点是完全不合理的。

第三，作者认为如果人们不进行联合抵制，那么环境灾难是"不可避免"的。其实，除了作者指定的办法，人们可以采用其他措施来阻止统一铜公司（CCC）开展计划，或者如果计划已被实施，人们也有办法来弥补其造成的损害，但作者的观点排除了这种可能性。然而作者未能提供确切保证证实没有其他可采用的方法来阻止预计可能发生的灾难。缺乏这样的证据，作者不能合理地断定人们必须用他提议的联合抵制的方法来防止那个灾难的发生。

最后，即使人们确实需要采取指定的联合抵制的方法来防止将在西弗莱德尼亚产生的污染和环境灾难，作者认为联合抵制就可以达到上述目的也太轻率了。也许还需要加上别的措施才能达到目的。例如，或许消费者也需要联合抵制污染西弗莱德尼亚环境的其他公司。简而言之，如果没有任何证据证明作者所建议的行动方式足以解决预计的问题，那么无论如何作者的结论都是可疑的。

总之，就目前情况看，这个论点是完全不具有说服性的。为了支持其论点，作者必须说明统一铜公司（CCC）所计划的采矿活动将对它新购得的土地产生污染，并威胁到濒危的动物种类。作者还必须确定"环境灾难"的定义，并说明如果不进行他提议的联合抵制，他所定义的"环境灾难"也将成为统一铜公司（CCC）的活动不可避免的后果。了解还有什么方法可以阻止统一铜公司（CCC）在西弗莱德尼亚进行开采，或者有什么办法可以减轻那些采矿活动对环境的影响，对更好地评价这个论证都是很有用的。此外，任何关于通过联合抵制达成原定目标的可能性的信息也都是很有用的。

【逻辑问题提纲】

本文作者一共攻击了原文的四处缺陷：

1. 缺乏 CCC 所购买土地具体位置，以及这些土地与所谓的濒危动物栖居地关系的信息（信息不完整的错误）；也没有说明 CCC 的采矿方式就会导致污染、环境危害和物种灭绝。

2. 作者对于"环境灾难"一词没有具体定义，因而作者的预言没有说服力。

3. 作者没有考虑到除了抵制 CCC 的产品之外还有其他可能措施也可以用来防止和减少可能的环境危害。

4. 关于抵制行动一定能达到防止 CCC 所导致的环境危害的效果的假设未必成立。

● 逻辑思路提示：结论可行性的问题：实际上，本文还有一个可以攻击的缺陷，就是作者所提倡的抵制行为本身在客观上的可行性。请考虑一下，如果消费者真的想要响应作者的号召抵制由 CCC 所生产的铜而制造的产品的话，还需要一个前提条件，就是消费者必须能够区分出哪些产品是由 CCC 的铜生产的，哪些是由其他公司的铜生产的。这就是结论的客观可行性的问题。对于结论明显不太可能实现的题目可以从这个点进行攻击。

【论证展开】

针对作者定义模糊的概念进行论证：

本文论证的第二点就是作者对"environmental disaster"一词定义不清。如果作者的论证中使用了过于危言耸听、概念模糊的语言，也可以抓住这一点进行攻击。严格的说，这实际上还是差异概念的错误。论证时可以结合其他论证手法，比如本文，先让步说就算 CCC 的采矿过程可能导致污染，但这也不表明一定会产生作者所说的环境灾难。然后对环境灾难一词的定义展开论证，指出如果它指的是污染和危害一些物种，那就还说的过去，但从一般的意义来说还够不上"灾难"的程度。

【结尾方式】

本文结尾所用句式值得借鉴：（1）To better assess the argument it would be useful to know ...（2）Also useful would be any information about... 用这两句来指出作者还需要做的工作，整体感很强。注意积累不同的结尾语言和句式以避免僵化和雷同。

【语言提示】

● 开头段承上启下的语言：I find this argument specious on several grounds.

● 用于攻击作者所用概念模糊不清的句式：(1) Even assuming ..., it is nevertheless impossible to assess the author's broader contention that ... (2) Absent either a clear definition of the term or clear evidence that ..., the author's contention that ... is simply unjustified.

● 其他句式：(1) Yet the author fails to provide assurances that ... (2) Lacking such evidence the author cannot reasonably conclude that ... (3) The author assumes too hastily that ... (4) In short, without any evidence that ..., the author's conclusion remains dubious at best.

● 结尾句式：(1) In sum, as it stands the argument is wholly unpersuasive. (2) To bolster it the author must show that ... (3) The author must also ... (4) To better assess the argument it would be useful to know ... (5) Also useful would be any information about ...

Argument 142　The link between **iron in the diet** and heart disease

The article entitled "Eating Iron" in last month's issue of Eating for Health reported that a recent study found a correlation between high levels of iron in the diet and an increased risk of heart disease. Further, it is well established that there is a link between large amounts of red meat in the diet and heart disease, and red meat is high in iron. On the basis of the study and the well-established link between red meat and heart disease, we can conclude that the correlation between high iron levels and heart disease, then, is most probably a function of the correlation between red meat and heart disease.

【参考译文】上一期的《健康饮食》杂志上刊登的题为《食铁》的文章报道说，最近一项研究发现饮食中铁的含量过高与心脏病发病率增加有关联。而且，我们已经知道饮食中含大量的牛羊肉和心脏病是有联系的，牛羊肉中铁的含量很高。基于以上研究和牛羊肉与心脏病之间的已知联系，我们可以得出结论，铁含量高与心脏病之间的关联最有可能是牛羊肉与心脏病之间关联的作用。

In this argument, the author cites a study correlating the amount of iron in a person's diet with the person's risk of heart disease. The author also cites a well-established correlation between diets that include large amounts of red meat, which is high in iron, and the incidence of heart disease. The author concludes that the correlation observed in the study is a function of the correlation between red meat and heart disease. This argument suffers from a series of poor assumptions, which render it wholly unpersuasive as it stands.

To begin with, the author provides no evidence that the study's results are statistically reliable. In order to establish a strong correlation between dietary iron and heart disease, the study's sample must be sufficient in size and representative of the overall population of heart-disease victims. Lacking evidence of a sufficiently representative sample, the author cannot justifiably rely on the study to draw any conclusion whatsoever.

Even assuming that the study is statistically reliable, a direct correlation between a high-iron diet and heart disease does not necessarily prove that the former causes the latter. While a high correlation is strong evidence of a causal relationship, in itself it is not sufficient. The author must also account for all other possible factors leading to heart disease, such as genetic propensity, amount of exercise, and so forth. Lacking evidence that the heart-disease sufferers whom the study observed were similar in all such respects, **the author cannot justifiably conclude that** a high-iron diet is the primary cause, or even a contributing cause, of heart disease.

　　Similarly, a correlation between a diet that includes large amounts of red meat and heart disease **does not necessarily infer a causal relationship. Lacking evidence to the contrary, it is possible** that red-meat eaters are comparatively likely to incur heart disease due to factors that have nothing to do with the amount of red meat in their diet. Perhaps red-meat eaters are the same people who generally overeat, and it is obesity rather the consumption of red meat specifically that causes heart attacks. **The author must consider and eliminate this and other possible reasons** why red-meat eaters are more likely than other people to suffer from heart disease. **Otherwise, I cannot accept the author's implicit claim that** eating red meat is any more likely to cause heart disease than eating other foods.

　　Even assuming that a high-iron diet, including a diet high in red meat, promotes heart disease, **the author cannot reasonably conclude that** this causal relationship fully explains the study's results. **The author overlooks the possibility that** other foods are also high in iron, and that the study's participants ate these other foods as well as, or instead of, red meat. **Without accounting for this possibility the author cannot convincingly conclude from the study that** red meat is the chief cause of heart disease.

　　In conclusion, the argument unfairly assumes that correlation is tantamount to causation. To strengthen the argument, the author must provide clear evidence that a high-iron diet contributes to heart disease. **The author must also provide clear evidence that** people who eat red meat are more likely to incur heart disease because of the amount of red meat in their diet, rather than some other factor. **To better evaluate the reliability of the study upon which the author's conclusion depends, I would need more information about** the size and makeup of the study's sample. **I would also need to know** whether other foods are also high in iron and, if so, which high-iron foods the study's participants ate on a regular basis.

【参考译文】

　　在本文论证中，作者引用了一项讨论一个人的饮食中所含铁质的量与这个人患心脏病的几率之间的关系的研究。作者还引用了一个已经被确认的联系，即食物中包括大量铁含量很高的牛羊肉类与心脏病患病率之间的联系。作者就此断定，该研究所观察到的相互关系是牛羊肉类和心脏病之间的相互关系的作用。这个论证做了一系列拙劣的假定，以致出现了现在完全没有说服力的状况。

　　首先，作者没有提供证据证明这项研究的结果在统计上是可靠的。为了确定一个令人信服的关于饮食中的铁和心脏病之间的联系，这个研究必须抽取足够数量的样本，并且抽取的样本能代表心脏病患者这个群体。缺乏一个具有充分代表性的抽样调查作证据，作者无论如何也不可能依赖这个研究合理地做出任何结论。

　　即使假设该研究在统计上是可靠的，含铁量高的饮食和心脏病之间的直接联系也不一定就能证明前者必定导致后者。尽管两者间的高度相关可作为因果关系的有力证据，但其本身还不足以确定它们间的因果关系。作者还必须考虑所有其他可能导致心脏病的因素，如遗传倾向、运动量等等。缺乏证据证明该研究所观察的心脏病患者在所有这些方面都是相似的，作者就不能合理地断定含铁量高的饮食就是导致心脏病的主要原因，甚至是起作用的原因。

　　同理，包含大量牛羊肉类的饮食和心脏病之间有关系并不一定就意味着它们之间必有因果关系。缺乏证据证明情况正好与之相反，那么就有可能出现这样的情况，即吃牛羊肉类的人患心脏病也相当可能是出于其他与他们的饮食中所含牛羊肉类的量毫无关系的因素。或许正好那些吃牛羊肉类的人都是平时总是暴食的人，而导致心脏病的确切原因是肥胖而不是食用牛羊肉类的量。作者必须考虑并排除能够说明为什么吃牛羊肉类的人比其他人患心脏病的几率要高的各种可能的原因。否则，作者含蓄地声称吃牛羊肉类比吃其他食物更容易导致心脏病的观点是我所不能接受的。

即使假设含铁量高的饮食，包括含大量牛羊肉类的饮食，确实会提高心脏病的发病率，作者也不能合理断定这种因果关系就能完整地解释该研究的结果。作者忽略了这么一种情况，即其他食物含铁量也很高，该研究的参与者可能既吃牛羊肉类，同时也吃其他食物，或者干脆吃其他食物代替牛羊肉类。没有解释这种可能性，作者就不能令人信服地断定牛羊肉类是导致心脏病的主要原因。

总之，本文不合理地认为相关性就等价于因果关系。为了使本文更加有力，作者必须提供明确的证据证明含铁量高的饮食导致人们患心脏病。作者还必须提供明确的证据证明吃牛羊肉类的人更容易得心脏病确实是因为他们饮食中所含牛羊肉类的量，而不是因为其他因素所导致。为了更好的评价作者做结论所依赖的研究的可靠性，我需要更多有关该研究的抽样调查的规模和组成的信息。我还需要知道是否有其他食品含铁量也很高，如果是，那么该研究的参与者定期吃了哪种含铁量高的食物。

【逻辑问题提纲】

本文作者一共攻击了原文的四处缺陷：
1. 指出作者所引用的调查对于调查对象的描述不够清晰，因而其样本的代表性值得怀疑。
2. 含铁量高的饮食与心脏病之间有相关性，但这并不能用来证明两者之间的因果关系。
3. 同样，过多食用牛羊肉与心脏病之间也仅仅具有相关性而不一定是前者导致后者。
4. 作者没有考虑导致心脏病的其他食品和其他因素。
- 逻辑思路提示：把相关性混同为因果关系的错误：有些事件之间只有相关性，也就是它们之间是有关联的，但是相关性不能作为证明两者间有因果关系的证据。有相关性的两件事可能都是由某种第三事件共同导致，也可能仅仅是巧合。本文攻击了两处相关性混同为因果性的错误，很多句式和语言值得学习。

【论证展开】

对调查样本的质疑方式：本文第一点攻击的就是作者引用的调查样本值得怀疑。但仔细观察原题我们可以发现，在题目中几乎对于调查所采取的样本没有做任何说明。有些同学觉得无法攻击，但实际上正好是一个有机可乘的突破口。本文在论证这一点时几乎全部使用抽象的逻辑描述语言进行攻击，首先指出调查结果并不一定可信，然后用一句抽象笼统的语言指出调查对象必须具备一定的数量和代表性，最后说在缺乏充分代表性的证据的情况下，作者不能简单依据这些调查来得出结论。这些语言既可单独使用，也可整体组成论证，稍加改动和变化即可同样用于其他没有具体指出调查样本的题目。

【语言提示】

- 用于攻击调查样本未必有代表性的句式：（1）The author provides no evidence that the study's results are statistically reliable.（2）In order to establish a strong correlation between ..., the study's sample must be sufficient in size and representative of ...（3）Lacking evidence of a sufficiently representative sample, the author cannot justifiably rely on the study to draw any conclusion whatsoever.
- 用于攻击相关性混同为因果性错误的句式：（1）A direct correlation between ... does not

necessarily prove that the former causes the latter. (2) While a high correlation is strong evidence of a causal relationship, in itself it is not sufficient. (3) The author must also account for all other possible factors leading ..., such as ... (4) A correlation between ... does not necessarily infer a causal relationship.

● 其他句式: The author must consider and eliminate this and other possible reasons why ... Otherwise, I cannot accept the author's implicit claim that ...

● 结尾句式: (1) In conclusion, the argument unfairly assumes that correlation is tantamount to causation. (2) To better evaluate the reliability of the study upon which the author's conclusion depends, I would need more information about the size and makeup of the study's sample. I would also need to know ...

Argument 144 Rates of **charitable** donations

According to a poll of 200 charitable organizations, donations of money to nonprofit groups increased by nearly 25 percent last year, though not all charities gained equally. Religious groups gained the most (30 percent), followed by environmental groups (23 percent), whereas educational institutions experienced only a very small increase in donations (3 percent). This poll indicates that more people are willing and able to give money to charities but that funding for education is not a priority for most people. These differences in donation rates must result from the perception that educational institutions are less in need of donations than are other kinds of institutions.

【参考译文】根据一项针对200个慈善组织的调查，去年对于非赢利团体的捐款上升了将近25%，而并不是所有组织都获得了同样的增幅。宗教团体增幅最大（30%），其次为环保组织（23%），而教育机构所获捐款仅有少量增长（3%）。这一调查说明有更多的人愿意而且有能力为慈善组织捐款，但资助教育并不是大多数人的首选。这种捐款比率上的差异一定是由于人们认为教育机构没有其他组织更需要资助的观念而导致的。

In this argument the author cites a poll showing that the amount of charitable donations increased last year, but that the increase to educational institutions was far less than to either religious or environmental groups. **Based on this evidence the author concludes that** more people are willing and able to make charitable donations, but that education is not a priority for most people. **The author also concludes that** the discrepancy among donation rates is the result of a general perception that educational institutions are in less need of money than other institutions are. **This argument depends on several unsubstantiated assumptions and is therefore unpersuasive as it stands.**

First of all, the author's conclusions about people's willingness to donate to the three types of charities listed **depend on the assumption that the poll results are statistically reliable. Yet, the author offers no evidence to substantiate this assumption. The author must show that** the 200 charitable organizations polled constitute a sufficiently large sample of religious, environmental, and educational charities, and that this sample is representative of all such charities. **Otherwise, the author cannot confidently draw any general conclusions about** the willingness of people to donate to these three types of institutions, or about general perceptions regarding the needs of any such institutions.

Similarly, the author's sweeping claim that "more people are willing and able to give money to charities" **depends on the assumption that** the poll results are sufficiently representative of charitable giving in general. **Yet, the author offers no evidence to substantiate this assumption. The author must show that** the 25% total increase in the rate of donations to the three types of institutions polled is representative of the increase in donations to all types of charities. **The author must also show that** the total number of donors actually increased last year; **as it stands the argument leaves open the possibility that** the total number of donors decreased last year while the average amount given by each donor increased. **Absent evidence to support these assumptions, the author's broad conclusion that** "more people are willing and able" to make charitable donations **is dubious at best.**

Additionally, the author provides no evidence whatsoever for the claim that educational institutions are perceived as less needy than other institutions, or that this perception explains the lower donation rate to educational institutions. **Lacking such evidence, there are many other possible explanations for** the discrepancy in donation rates. Perhaps people's perception is that educational institutions are more likely than the other types to squander or misuse donated money; or perhaps most donors are simply more interested in advocating religions or environmental protection than in subsidizing education. For that matter, perhaps among all charitable organizations educational institutions ranked third last year in terms of gifts received—bettered only by religious and environmental charities. **Such evidence would serve to undermine the author's claim that** funding for education is "not a priority for most people."

In conclusion, the argument is indefensible as it stands. To strengthen it the author must assure me that the poll results accurately reflect donation rates not only to all religious, environmental, and educational institutions but also to the broader group of all charitable institutions. **The author must also provide clear evidence for the claimed perception about** the need of educational institutions and that this perception, and not some other factor, explains the comparatively low donation rate to these institutions.

【参考译文】

在这篇论证中，作者引用了一次民意调查，显示去年的慈善捐款数量增加了，然而给教育机构的捐款增长率远比不上给宗教或环保组织的。根据这一现象，作者推断越来越多的人愿意并且有能力进行慈善捐款，但是对大多数人来说给教育捐款不是首选。作者还推断，人们普遍认为教育机构不像其他机构那么需要钱，这种观念导致了给不同机构的慈善捐款增长率的差异。这篇论证建立在若干个没有确实根据的假设上，以致就目前情况看，本文不具说服力。

首先，只有先假设民意调查的结果是经过统计可以信赖的，作者才能做出人们更愿意给所列的三类慈善机构中的哪种捐款的结论。然而，作者没有提供任何证据证明这一假设。作者必须说明被调查的 200 个慈善团体分成宗教、环保和教育慈善机构三类，组成一个规模足够大的样本，而这个样本必须能代表所有这些慈善机构。否则，作者不能可信地做出任何有关人们更愿意给这三种机构中的哪种捐款，或者人们普遍认为哪种机构更需要钱的结论。

与此类似，作者的空泛声明"越来越多的人愿意并且有能力进行慈善捐款"有赖于民意调查的结果足以代表普遍的慈善捐赠的假定。然而，作者没有提供证据证明这个假定。作者必须证明给这三种参与调查的机构其捐款的 25% 的总增长率可以代表给所有类型慈善机构捐款的增长。作者还必须证明去年捐赠人的总数确实增加了；然而事实是这篇论证忽略了这种可能性，即去年的捐赠人总数减少了，而每个捐赠人平均捐赠的款数却增加了。缺乏证据支持这些假设，作者就妄断"越来越多的人愿意并且有能力进行慈善捐款"，这个结论无论如何都是值得怀疑的。

另外，作者声称人们认为教育机构不像其他机构那么需要钱，及人们的这种观念解释了为什么给教育机构的捐款增长率比较低，但是对这两个推断作者没有提供任何证据来证明。缺乏这些证据，我们就可能有许多其他理由来解释捐款增长率的差异。或许人们觉得教育机构比其他类机构更可能浪费或者滥用捐款；又或许与资助教育相比，大多数的捐赠人只是对宣扬宗教或者提倡环境保护更感兴趣。而且，在去年所有慈善团体所得的捐赠多寡方面，教育机构可能位居第三，仅次于宗教和环保机构。这样的证据就能削弱作者做的关于教育经费捐赠"对大多数人来说不是首选"的论断的力度。

　　总之，就目前情况看，这篇论证的论点是站不住脚的。为了加强其力度，作者必须保证，民意调查的结果精确地反映的不仅是所有宗教、环保和教育机构所得捐款的增长率，还包括所有慈善机构组成的更广泛的组织。作者还必须提供明确的证据证明，他所声称的人们对教育机构的需求的普遍观念属实，以及正是这种观念而不是其他因素导致这些机构的捐款增长率较低。

【逻辑问题提纲】

　　本文作者一共攻击了原文的三处缺陷：

　　1. 对于慈善组织捐款数额的调查样本的代表性值得怀疑。

　　2. 对于文中所提到的三种慈善组织的捐款并不能表明人们对于所有慈善团体总体的态度，也不能说明"有更多的人"愿意捐款。

　　3. 未必是人们关于教育组织不如其他组织需要捐款的观念导致了捐款数额的差异。

　　● 逻辑思路提示：本文攻击的前两点仍然是调查取样代表性的问题，对于没有指出具体调查对象的题目攻击样本代表性一般只用一个段落就可以了，对于本题我们还可以攻击数据模糊性的缺陷。题目中提到每个组织所收到捐款的增幅时，仅仅提到百分比的数值。而很多时候仅有增幅比例是不够的，我们必须知道这些增幅的基数才能判断各机构真正的增幅大小。比如，如果教育组织在前一年所获得的捐款是1000万，那么今年的增幅就是 1000万 × 3% = 30万，这并不是一个小数目；同样，宗教和环保组织虽然增幅比例比较大，但结合基数来看就有可能是很小的增长。

【开头方式】

　　开头段落复述论据和结论的语言语序都是可以发挥、变化的，比如可以像本文一样，先用In this argument the author cites a poll showing that … 的句式来引述原文论据，然后进一步用Based on this evidence the author concludes that … 的句式来引导结论，过渡自然、联系紧密，同学们可以在此基础上做一些变化和发挥来形成自己的、有特色的开头模式。

【论证展开】

　　指出作者所做假设的语言：在指出作者的推论所基于的假设时，既可以直接用the author assumes that … 之类的简单句式来引导，也可以学习使用本文的方式：用the author's conclusions about … depend on the assumption that … Yet, the author offers no evidence to substantiate this assumption 这样的句式结构来复述假设并引出论证。

【语言提示】

　　● 开头段句式：(1) In this argument the author cites a poll showing that … Based on this evidence the author concludes that … (2) This argument depends on several unsubstantiated assumptions and is therefore unpersuasive as it stands.

　　● 用于攻击调查样本代表性的句式：(1) The author's conclusions about … depend on the assumption that the poll results are statistically reliable. (2) The author must show that … Otherwise, the author cannot confidently draw any general conclusions about …

　　● 其他句式：(1) The author must also show that … ; as it stands the argument leaves open the possibility that ... (2) Absent evidence to support these assumptions, the author's broad conclusion that ... is dubious at best. (3) Lacking such evidence, there are many other possible explanations for ... (4) Such evidence would serve to undermine the author's claim that ...

● 结尾段句式: (1) In conclusion, the argument is indefensible as it stands. (2) To strengthen it the author must assure me that ... (3) The author must also provide clear evidence for the claimed perception about ...

Argument 148　Monroetown's election between **Brown** and **Greene**

The following appeared in the editorial section of Monroetown's local newspaper.

"Mayor Brown was recently re-elected by a clear majority of 52 percent of Monroetown's voters. Her re-election, however, does not show that most people in our town favored Mayor Brown's proposal for tax reduction over that of her opponent, Mr. Greene, who proposed raising taxes to improve education. It has been shown that voters nationwide tend to re-elect people already in office, regardless of candidates' proposals. In fact, a local survey after the election showed most people in Monroetown disagreed with Mayor Brown's proposal. Clearly most people in Monroetown favor improving education and therefore approve of Mr. Greene's proposal despite the fact that they did not vote for him."

【参考译文】布朗市长最近获得了门罗镇全体选民52%的明显多数票而再次当选市长。然而，她的再次当选并不表明我们城市的多数市民更喜欢布朗提出的减税提案，而不是其竞争对手格林先生提出的增加税收以促进教育的提案。已有证据表明，全国的选民都倾向于再次选举那些已经在位的官员，不论候选人的竞选提案是什么。实际上，这次选举后的一次地方调查显示，门罗镇的多数市民不赞同布朗市长的提案。显然，门罗镇的多数市民赞同改善教育，从而支持格林的提案，尽管他们并没有投他的票。

The author of this editorial concludes that most Monroetown residents favor Greene's proposal to raise taxes in order to improve education over Brown's proposal to cut taxes, even though incumbent Brown defeated Greene by way of a 52% majority vote in a recent mayoral election. **To support this conclusion the author points out** a nationwide tendency to reelect incumbent candidates regardless of their positions. **The author also points out that** a survey taken after the election showed that most Monroetown residents oppose Brown's proposal. **As the following discussion shows, the author's argument is not well supported by the evidence.**

First of all, the author unfairly assumes that the nationwide tendency applies specifically to Monroetown residents. **Lacking evidence that** Monroetown voters reflect this general tendency, **it is entirely possible that** Monroetown residents vote strictly according to their position on the issues. **For that matter, it is possible that** Monroetown voters tend strongly to vote against incumbents, **in which case the author's claim that** Monroetown residents oppose Brown's proposal would more flagrantly fly in the face of the election results.

Secondly, the author fails to indicate when the statistics showing this nationwide tendency were collected. The longer the time period between the collection of these statistics and the election, the greater the possibility that the tendency has changed over this time span, and the less justifiable the author's reliance on these statistics to support the claim that Monroetown residents oppose Brown's proposal.

Thirdly, the author fails to indicate how much time passed between the Brown-Greene election and the survey showing that most Monroetown residents oppose her proposal. If the survey was conducted immediately after the election, **then the fact that** the election results conflict with the survey results would cast considerable doubt on the reliability of either to indicate what proposals Monroetown residents truly support. However, if the survey occurred long after the election, then the conflict can readily be explained by changing opinions and demographics over time. **In either case, it is impossible to weigh the evidence without more specific information about** percentages. The larger the percentage of Monroetown residents participating in the election, the greater the extent to which the election results would cast doubt on the survey results. By the same token, the larger the percentage of Monroetown residents shown by the survey to oppose Brown's proposal the more clearly this evidence would support the author's argument.

Finally, the argument suffers from "either-or" reasoning. Based on the fact that Monroetown residents are opposed to Brown's proposed tax cut, **the author unfairly concludes that** they must be in favor of Greene's proposal. **However, the author overlooks the possibility that** Monroetown residents are not in favor of either proposal.

In sum, the author's argument that Monroetown residents oppose Brown's proposal and are in favor of the proposals set forth by Greene **is unconvincing. To strengthen the argument the author must provide clear evidence that** Monroetown residents voted contrary to their own positions on the issues when they reelected Brown. **To better evaluate the argument I would need to know** how much time passed between the collection of the statistics showing the national tendency cited by the author and the election. **I would also need to know** how much time passed between the election and the survey showing that Monroetown residents oppose Brown's proposal. **Finally, I would need to know** what portion of Monroetown's residents voted in the election, and what portion of these residents were shown by the survey to oppose Brown's policies.

【参考译文】

这篇社论的作者断言，比起布朗的减税建议，大多数门罗镇的居民会更支持格林提出的为了推进教育发展而提税的建议，尽管现任的布朗在一次新近的市长选举里以52%的多数票战胜了格林。为了支持这个结论，这个作者指出一种全国性的趋势，即全国的选民都倾向于再次选举那些已经在位的官员，不论候选人的立场是什么。作者还指出，一项在选举结束后所做的调查显示大多数门罗镇居民反对布朗的提议。正如以下的讨论显示的，作者的论证没有得到很好的支持。

首先，作者想当然地认为全国性的趋势也具体地适用于门罗镇的居民。缺乏证据证明门罗镇选民的情况也反映这种普遍的趋势，那么便完全有可能出现这种情况，门罗镇的居民在投票时是严格遵照他们对各种问题的立场做出决定。同样，也有可能门罗镇的居民强烈地倾向于不投现任者的票，这样的话，作者所做的关于门罗镇的居民反对布朗的提议的断言就会更明显地与选举结果大相径庭。

第二，作者未能表明显示这个全国性趋势的统计数据是什么时候被收集起来的。这些统计数据的收集和这次选举之间相隔的时间越久，这个趋势经过时间变换而产生变化的可能性就越大，作者就更没有正当理由利用这些统计数据来支持他所做的关于门罗镇的居民反对布朗的提议的断言。

第三，作者未能表明布朗—格林的竞选和那个表明大多数门罗镇居民反对布朗的提议的调查之间隔了多长的时间。如果该调查是在选举之后立即进行的，那么选举结果与调查结果互相冲突的事实会使人们对作者到底要表明门罗镇居民真正支持的提议是什么产生相当的怀疑。但是，如果调查是在选举结束很久之后才进行的，那么我们就可以用人们想法的改变和人口统计数据的改变来解释这个冲突。无论发生的是哪种情况，都不可能在没有更多有关比率的具体信息的情况下去估量这个证据。有更大比率的门罗镇居民参与到这次选举中的话，这次的选举结果会使人对调查结果产生更深的怀疑。同理，调查所显示的反对布朗的提议的门罗镇居民的比率越大，这个证据就会越忠实地支持作者的论证。

最后，这个论证犯了非此即彼的逻辑错误。基于门罗镇居民反对布朗提议的减税的事实，作者想当然地断定他们一定赞成格林的提议。然而，作者忽略了门罗镇居民对两个提议中的任一个都不赞成的可能性。

总之，作者所提出的关于门罗镇居民反对布朗的提议而赞成格林的提议的论点是不能使人信服的。为了加强这个论证，作者必须提供明确的证据证明门罗镇居民在重选布朗的时候确实是违背他们自己在各种问题上的立场进行投票的。为了更好地评价这个论证，我有必要知道收集作者提及的表明全国趋势的数据和竞选之间相隔多长时间。我还需要知道在这次竞选和证明门罗镇居民反对布朗的提议的调查之间相隔了多长时间。最后，我还有必要知道门罗镇居民中有多少人参加了这次选举的投票，以及这些居民中有多少人如调查所示反对布朗的政策。

【逻辑问题提纲】

本文作者一共攻击了原文的四处缺陷：

1. 全国性的选举行为倾向并不说明门罗镇的居民也是如此投票选举的（以整体推部分的差异范围草率推广）。

2. 作者没有指出文中提到的全国性倾向的发生时间，因而未必支持结论（信息时效性的问题）。

3. 作者也没有指出选举后进行的地方性调查与选举的时间间隔，因此两者可能并不矛盾。

4. 门罗镇的居民反对布朗的减税提案并不说明他们一定支持格林的增税方针（非此即彼的错误）。

● 逻辑思路提示：非此即彼的错误。这是一种作者的思维过于简单化的错误，作者把一个本来有很多种可能和解释的事件简单认为只存在两种截然对立的可能，比如在本题中，作者看到群众反对布朗的提案，马上就认为他们肯定支持格林的提案，就是这种错误的典型体现。这一情况可能有很多其他可能，也许门罗镇的居民两个提案都不支持，也许他们更倾向于除了布朗和格林以外的其他候选人的提案。因此当看到作者简单地认为某事件只有非此即彼的两种可能的时候就可以攻击这种错误。

【语言提示】

● 开头段句式：As the following discussion shows, the author's argument is not well supported by the evidence.

● 论证句式：(1)In either case, it is impossible to weigh the evidence without more specific information about ...(2)Based on the fact that ..., the author unfairly concludes that ...

Argument 150　**Yosemite**'s amphibian decline

The following is a letter to the editor of an environmental magazine.

"The decline in the numbers of amphibians worldwide clearly indicates the global pollution of water and air. Two studies of amphibians in Yosemite National Park in California confirm my conclusion. In 1915 there were seven species of amphibians in the park, and there were abundant numbers of each species. However, in 1992 there were only four species of amphibians observed in the park, and the numbers of each species were drastically reduced. The decline in Yosemite has been blamed on the introduction of trout into the park's waters, which began in 1920 (trout are known to eat amphibian eggs). But the introduction of trout cannot be the real reason for the Yosemite decline because it does not explain the worldwide decline."

【参考译文】全球两栖动物数量的下降清楚地说明全球空气和水质的污染。在加州约塞米提国家公园对于两栖动物所进行的两次研究证实了我的结论。1915 年，公园中有七种两栖动物，每种的数量都很丰富。然而到了 1992 年，在公园中只观察到四种两栖动物，并且每种动物的数量都显著下降。约塞米提公园两栖动物数量的下降一直被归因于始于 1920 年的在公园水域引入鲑鱼的行为（我们知道鲑鱼捕食两栖动物的卵）。但鲑鱼的引入不会是约塞米提两栖动物数量下降的真正原因，因为它并不能解释全球范围的数量下降。

The author of this letter concludes that a worldwide decline in the number of amphibians is an indication, or result, of global air and water pollution. **To support this assertion the author first notes** a decline in amphibians in Yosemite Park between 1915 and 1992, **and acknowledges that** trout, which eat amphibian eggs, were introduced there in 1925. But, **the author then claims that** the introduction of trout cannot be the reason for the decline in Yosemite because the introduction of trout in Yosemite does not explain the worldwide decline. **I find this argument logically unconvincing in three critical respects.**

First, the author fails to provide any evidence to refute the strong inference that the amphibian decline in Yosemite was indeed caused by trout. **Because the author provides no affirmative evidence that** pollution—or some other phenomenon—was instead the reason for the decline, **the author's broad assertion that** a worldwide decline in amphibians indicates global pollution **is entirely unconvincing.**

Secondly, even if I were to concede that the introduction of trout was not the cause of Yosemite's amphibian decline, **the author provides no evidence that** the decline was caused by pollution—rather than some other phenomenon. Perhaps some other environmental factor was instead the cause. **Without ruling out all other possible explanations the author cannot convince me that** pollution is the cause of the worldwide amphibian decline—or even the decline in Yosemite alone.

Thirdly, even if I were to concede that pollution caused Yosemite's amphibian decline, **this single sample is insufficient to draw any general conclusion about** the reason for a worldwide amphibian decline. **It is entirely possible that** the cause-and-effect relationships in Yosemite are not typical of the world in general. **Without additional samples from diverse geographic locations, I cannot accept the author's sweeping generalization about** the decline of amphibians and global pollution.

In sum, the scant evidence the author cites proves nothing about the reason for the general decline of amphibians worldwide; **in fact, this evidence only serves to refute the author's own argument. To strengthen the argument the author should** examine all changes occurring in Yosemite between 1915 and 1992 and show that air and water pollution have at least contributed to the park's amphibian decline. **In any event, the author must provide data about** amphibian population changes and pollution at diverse geographical locations; and this data must show a strong inverse correlation between levels of air and water pollution and amphibian populations worldwide.

【参考译文】

这封信的作者断定，世界范围内的两栖动物数量减少是全球空气和水质污染的一个反映或者结果。为证明其断言，作者首先特别提到了约塞米提国家公园的两栖动物的数量从 1915 年到 1992 年有所减少，并承认该公园于 1925 年引进了吃两栖动物下的卵的鲑鱼。不过，作者然后声称鲑鱼的引进不可能是约塞米提国家公园的两栖动物数量减少的原因，因为约塞米提国家公园引进鲑鱼无法解释全世界的两栖动物数量减少的原因。我认为这篇论证有三个关键方面在逻辑上不可信。

首先，作者未能提供任何证据来反驳约塞米提国家公园的两栖动物数量减少确实是由鲑鱼引起的这一有力的推断。因为作者没有提供有力的证据证明污染或者一些其他的现象才是引起数量减少的原因，所以作者宽泛地声明世界范围内的两栖动物数量减少表明全球遭污染是完全没有说服力的。

第二，即使我承认鲑鱼的引进不是约塞米提国家公园两栖动物数量减少的原因，作者也没有提供任何证据证明这次锐减是由污染而不是一些其他的现象引起的。原因也可能是其他的一些环境因素。没有排除所有其他可能的解释，作者就不能使我相信全世界的两栖动物数量减少，或者甚至是约塞米提国家公园方面的减少，是由污染引起的。

第三，即使我相信约塞米提国家公园的两栖动物数量减少是由污染引起的，由这个个例也不足以得出任何关于全世界的两栖动物数量锐减的原因的笼统结论。约塞米提国家公园出现的因果关系完全可能不代表世界的普遍现象。没有来自不同的地理位置的其他样例，我不能接受作者有关两栖动物数量减少和全球污染的笼统的论断。

总之，作者所引用的证据太少，根本不能证明全世界的两栖动物数量减少的原因是什么。实际上，他提供的证据反倒为别人反驳自己的论点提供了便利。为加强这篇论证的力度，作者应该调查分析 1915～1992 年间发生在约塞米提国家公园的所有变化，并证明空气和水质污染起码对公园两栖动物数量减少产生了影响。不论是哪种情况，作者必须提供有关不同的地理位置的两栖动物数量变动和所受污染的数据；并且这些数据必须显示空气和水质污染程度和全世界两栖动物的数量之间的强烈反差关系。

【逻辑问题提纲】

本文作者一共攻击了原文的三处缺陷：

1. 作者没有排除鲑鱼导致两栖动物数量下降的可能性。

2. 即使鲑鱼不是导致两栖动物数量下降的罪魁祸首，作者也没能证实就是污染而不是别的什么因素造成了这一数量的下降。

3. 即使在约塞米提公园确实是污染导致了两栖动物数量的下降，这也不能用于证实全球范围的数量下降都是因为污染而导致的。

● 逻辑思路提示：以少推多的差异范围草率推广：本文攻击的第三点就是以少推多，以偏概全，以部分推整体的草率推广。前面我们介绍过不能从整体现象推知局部特征，即不能以多推少，同样，也不能以少推多。当作者仅就某些个体的、特殊的现象推出整体的、更大范围的现象和趋势时，就犯了这种错误。

【开头方式】

列举论据的语言。本文作者用了两个句子来列举原文论据：

To support this assertion the author first notes ..., and acknowledges that ...

【论证展开】

对于以少推多的草率推广的论证：对于这类错误，我们往往可以先做一个让步，指出作者的结论对于一些个体或局部可能确实是成立的有效的，然后再转折指出不能把这一结论草率推广到更大的概念范畴。本文使用了 even if ..., this single sample is insufficient to draw any general conclusion about ...这样的句式来表达这种论证关系，我们也可以用其他句型来引导让步，比如although it is true that ... / although it is true in some cases / granted that ...等等。

【语言提示】

● 开头段句式：(1) To support this assertion the author first notes ..., and acknowledges that ... (2) I find this argument logically unconvincing in three critical respects.

● 描述以少推多的草率推广的句式：(1) The author's broad assertion that ... is entirely unconvincing. (2) This single sample is insufficient to draw any general conclusion about ... (3) Without additional samples from diverse geographic locations, I cannot accept the author's sweeping generalization about ...

● 其他句式：(1) Because the author provides no affirmative evidence that ... (2) Without ruling out all other possible explanations the author cannot convince me that ...

● 结尾句式：(1) In sum, the scant evidence the author cites proves nothing about ... (2) In fact, this evidence only serves to refute the author's own argument. (3) To strengthen the argument the author should examine ... (4) In any event, the author must provide data about ...

Argument 152　Saving **Tria**'s beach sand and its tourist industry

The following is a letter to the head of the tourism bureau on the island of Tria.

"Erosion of beach sand along the shores of Tria Island is a serious threat to our island and our tourist industry. In order to stop the erosion, we should charge people for using the beaches. Although this solution may annoy a few tourists in the short term, it will reduce the number of people using the beaches and will raise money for replenishing the sand. Replenishing the sand, as was done to protect buildings on the nearby island of Batia, will help protect buildings along our shores, thereby reducing these buildings' risk of additional damage from severe storms. And since the areas along the shore will be more attractive as a result, the beaches will be preserved and the area's tourist industry will improve over the long term."

【参考译文】 特蒂亚岛海岸沙滩的侵蚀对于我们岛和我们的旅游业是个严重的威胁。为阻止侵蚀，我们应该对使用海滩的人收费。尽管这一解决方案会在短期内触怒少量游客，它将会减少使用海滩的人数并增加补充沙子的资金。像邻近的巴蒂亚岛为了保护岛上的房子一样补充沙子将会有助于对我们沿岸建筑的保护，从而减少这些房屋在大风暴中受损的危险。并且由于这会导致沿岸地区更具吸引力，海滩将会受到保护，本地区的旅游业将会在长远得到发展。

This letter's author recommends charging fees for public access to Tria's beaches as an effective means of raising funds for the purpose of saving Tria's tourist industry. **The author reasons that** beach-access fees would reduce the number of beachgoers while providing revenue for replenishing beach sand needed to protect nearby buildings, thereby enhancing the area's attractiveness to tourists. **To support this argument the author points out that** beach sand was replenished on the nearby island of Batia, thereby reducing the risk of storm damage to buildings there. **I find the argument unconvincing for several reasons.**

　　First of all, the author makes certain dubious assumptions about the impact of beach-access fees. On the one hand, the author ignores the possibility that charging fees might deter so many tourists that Tria would be worse off overall. **On the other hand, perhaps** the vast majority of Tria's tourists and residents alike would happily pay for beach access, in which case Tria's beaches would continue to be no less crowded than they are now. **Under either scenario, adopting the author's proposal might harm, rather than benefit, Tria's tourist industry in the long run.**

　　Secondly, the mere fact that on nearby Batia replenishing beach sand has served to protect shoreline buildings **is scant evidence that** Tria would achieve its goals by following Batia's example. **Perhaps** the same course of action would be ineffective on Tria **due to geological differences between the two islands. Or perhaps** Batia is in a far better position than Tria financially to replenish its sand on a continual basis. **In short, lacking evidence that conditions on the two islands are relevantly similar, the author cannot convince me on the basis of Batia's experience that** the proposed course of action would be effective in attaining Tria's goals.

　　Thirdly, even if replenishing Tria's beach sand is financially feasible and would protect nearby buildings, **the author provides no evidence that** Tria's tourist industry would be saved thereby. **Perhaps** Tria's tourist appeal has little to do with the beach and nearby buildings; for that matter, perhaps Tria's tourist appeal would be greater with fewer buildings along the coast. **Since the author provides no firm evidence that** replenishing sand and protecting nearby buildings would be more beneficial to Tria's tourist industry than allowing nature to take its course, **I do not find the author's argument the least bit compelling.**

　　In sum, the argument is unconvincing as it stands. To strengthen it the author must show that charging beach-access fees would reduce the number of beachgoers, but not to the extent of undermining the goal of raising sufficient funds to maintain an attractive coastal area. **The author must also provide better evidence that** replenishing sand would indeed protect nearby buildings, and that the net result would be the enhancement of Tria's tourist industry.

【参考译文】

　　这封信的作者建议在公众进入海滩时要收取海滩使用费，这可以作为有效的方法来为挽救特蒂亚的旅游业筹款。作者推论道海滩进入费将减少去海滩的人的数量，与此同时，所提供的收入用于补充保护附近大楼所需要的海滩沙，从而提高该地区对游客的吸引力。为了支持这一论点，作者指出附近巴蒂亚岛的海滩沙得以补充，因此那里风暴对大楼的损害的危险程度得以降低。我认为这一论点由于以下几个原因不足以令人信服。

　　首先，作者做出了关于收取海滩使用费影响的不确定的假定。一方面，收费可能阻止很多游客而使特蒂亚总的情况恶化，而这一可能性被作者所忽视。另一方面，也许大多数特蒂亚的游客和居民会愉快地支付海滩使用费，在这种情况下，特蒂亚海滩将仍旧如同现在一样拥挤。在其中任意一种情况下，采用作者的提议归根结底可能损害特蒂亚的旅游业，而不是有益于特蒂亚的旅游业。

　　其次，本文仅提出在附近巴蒂亚岛上补充海滩沙对保护海岸沿线大楼有用的极个别事实，而缺乏足够的证据能够证明特蒂亚通过效仿巴蒂亚，也可以达到这样的目的。或许由于在这两座岛之间的地质差别，相同的行动对于特蒂亚将是无效的。或者，在持续提供海滩沙方面，巴蒂亚比特蒂亚在经济上处于更好的处境。简而言之，缺乏证据表明这两座岛的条件有很大程度上相似，作者不能使我信服根据巴蒂亚的经验提议的行动方针将对特蒂亚达到目的有效。

第三，即使补充特蒂亚海滩沙在财政上可行并且能够保护附近大楼，作者并没有提供证据表明特蒂亚的旅游业将会因此而得到挽救。或许，特蒂亚对游客的吸引力与海滩和海滩附近的大楼没有什么相关性；而且也许随着海岸大楼的减少，特蒂亚游客的兴趣反而更高。因为作者没有提供强有力的证据表明，比起顺其自然，补充海滩沙并且保护附近大楼将更有利于特蒂亚的旅游业，我认为作者的论断一点儿也不能令人信服。

总之，就目前情况看，论点并不令人信服。为了加强说服力，作者必须说明收取海滩使用费将减少海滩游客的数量，但以不影响筹集足够的资金来维持一个有吸引力的沿海地区为限。作者也必须提供更好的证据证明补充海滩沙确实能够保护附近的大楼，并且最终结果是特蒂亚的旅游业得以发展。

【逻辑问题提纲】

本文作者一共攻击了原文的三处缺陷：

1. 海滩收费政策可能会带来意想不到的恶果（攻击后果）。
2. 在特蒂亚照搬巴蒂亚的经验未必同样有效（错误类比）。
3. 作者所做的关于补充沙子的措施一定能够带来旅游业繁荣的假设是可疑的。

● 逻辑思路提示：错误类比的错误：这是 Argument 题目中又一类出现频率很高的缺陷，其特征是作者在用 A 事物的情况类比类推 B 事物时，只看到 A 和 B 表层的相似性，而忽略了它们之间可能存在的其他深层次差异。本文所攻击的第二点就是特蒂亚和巴蒂亚之间错误类比的错误。

对于错误类比，最基本的论证展开套路就是指出作者进行类比的双方有哪些可能不一样的地方；比如本文在论证时就列举了地质特征、补充沙子的方便程度等可能的不同点。

【论证展开】

● 对错误类比的论证展开：对于错误类比的错误，我们可以用以下套路进行论证：

　　1）用 Topic Sentence 指出错误类比。
　　2）用推测法和列举法指出作者进行类比的双方有什么可能的差异。
　　3）用小总结句型作段落结尾。

● 推测法展开的其他语言方式：用推测法展开论证除了使用最基本的 perhaps、possibly、it is possible that 等句式外，也可以学习参考本文所用的"一方面……另一方面"的句型。

【语言提示】

● 指出作者所做假设不可靠的：The author makes certain dubious assumptions about ...

● 引导推测法的句式：On the one hand, the author ignores the possibility that ... On the other hand, perhaps ...

● 用于攻击错误类比的句式：In short, lacking evidence that conditions on the two islands are relevantly similar, the author cannot convince me on the basis of Batia's experience that ...

● 其他句式：Under either scenario, adopting the author's proposal might...

Argument 155　Learning to read by listening to **books on tape**

The following appeared in a letter to the editor of a local newspaper.

"Too much emphasis is placed on the development of reading skills in elementary school. Many

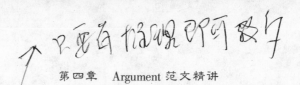

students who are discouraged by the lonely activity of reading turn away from schoolwork merely because they are poor readers. But books recorded on audiocassette tape provide an important alternative for students at this crucial stage in their education, one the school board should not reject merely because of the expense involved. After all, many studies attest to the value of allowing students to hear books read aloud; there is even evidence that students whose parents read to them are even more likely to become able readers. Thus, hearing books on tape can only make students more eager to read and to learn. Therefore, the school board should encourage schools to buy books on tape and to use them in elementary education."

【参考译文】小学教育过分强调了对于阅读能力的培养。很多对单调的阅读活动不感兴趣的学生仅仅因为他们阅读能力欠佳而放弃学习。但录制在盒式磁带上的教材为学生在教育的关键阶段提供了重要的补充，地方教育董事会不应该仅仅因为其所需的花费而拒绝它。无论如何，很多研究证实了让学生听大声朗读的教材的作用；甚至还有证据表明，那些由家长为他们朗读的学生阅读能力更容易提高。因此，听录制教材只会让学生更乐意阅读和学习。所以，地方教育董事会应该鼓励学校购买录制的教材，并把它们用于小学教育。

This editorial concludes that the school board should invest in audiocassettes because listening to audiocassettes makes elementary students more eager to learn and to read. **To support this conclusion the editorial cites studies showing** the value of listening to someone else read. **However, close scrutiny of this evidence and of the editorial's line of reasoning reveals that they provide little credible support for the editorial's conclusion.**

To begin with, the argument claims that for a poor reader the isolation of reading will provide a general disincentive to do schoolwork. **However, the author provides no evidence to support this claim. It is just as possible that** a child who has difficulty reading might excel at other subjects that do not require much reading, such as mathematics or music. **Besides, this argument assumes that** learning to read must be an isolated activity. **Experience informs us, however, that this is not the case, especially for** elementary school students who typically learn to read in a group environment.

The editorial goes on to cite studies which "attest to the value" of allowing students to hear books read aloud. **However, as it stands this evidence is far too vague to support the editorial's conclusion;** we are not informed whether the "value" relates specifically to reading skills. **Common sense tells me that** while audiocassettes can help any person learn facts and understand concepts, a skill such as reading can only be learned by practicing the skill itself.

Nor are we informed about the manner in which books were read aloud in the study; were they read directly by parents or were they recorded on audiocassettes? **Absent additional information about the cited studies, these studies lend no credible support to the conclusion that** audiocassettes will help elementary school students to read and to learn.

The editorial continues by claiming that listening to audiocassettes will make children better readers because when parents read aloud to their children these children become better readers. **This argument by analogy is wholly unpersuasive.** The latter allows for interaction between parent and child, while the former does not. The latter allows for the child to view written words as the parent reads—that is, to read—while the former does not. Besides, common sense and experience tell us that audiocassettes, which provide for passive listening, are likely to serve as crutches that dissuade children from active reading—instead of encouraging them to read.

In conclusion, the editorial is unconvincing as it stands. To strengthen the argument, the editorial's author must provide more compelling evidence that listening to audiocassettes will actually help and encourage elementary school students to read, not just to learn in general. **In order to better evaluate the argument, we would need more information about** whether the cited studies refer specifically to the value of audiocassettes and specifically to their value in terms of the reading and learning processes.

【参考译文】

　　这篇社论做出结论：地方教育董事会应该投资盒式录音磁带，因为听盒式录音磁带将使小学生更渴望学习和阅读。为了支持这个结论，社论引用了几项研究。这些研究显示出听别人朗读的价值。但是，对于论据及推理过程的详细审查，发现它们对社论的结论提供了不可信的支持。

　　首先，论点声称，对于阅读能力差的学生，阅读的孤立性通常将阻碍他做学校作业。然而，作者并没有为此提供证据。很可能一个孩子在阅读方面有困难，却可能擅长于不要求大量阅读的科目，例如数学或者音乐。此外，这个论点假定学习阅读一定是一项孤立的活动。然而，经验告诉我们情况并不是如此，特别是对于通常在集体环境中学习阅读的小学生。

　　社论接着引用研究"证明"允许学生听大声朗读的书的"价值"。但是，如它所述，这个证据太含糊而不能支持社论的结论；我们没被告知是否该"价值"明确地与阅读技能相关。常识告诉我，盒式录音磁带能帮助任何人了解事实并且理解概念，但一项技能，如阅读，只能从实践该项技能中习得。

　　同样，我们也没被告知在研究中，书被以高声朗读的方式是由父母直接读的，还是被录在盒式录音磁带上的？缺少关于所引用研究的附加说明，这些研究没有给予可信的证据证明盒式录音磁带将帮助小学生阅读和学习。

　　社论继而声称，通过听盒式录音磁带将使孩子成为更好的读者，因为当父母高声读给他们的孩子听时，这些孩子成了更好的读者。这个基于类比提出的论点是完全没有说服力的。后者考虑到父母和孩子之间的相互作用，而前者却没有。后者使孩子可以看到父母读的字词——换句话说，他们可以阅读——而前者却没有。而且，常识和经验告诉我们，盒式录音磁带是为被动的听而做准备的，很可能成为阻碍孩子不去主动阅读的工具，而不是鼓励他们阅读。

　　总之，就目前情况看，社论并不能使人信服。为了加强说服力，社论的作者必须提供更强有力的证据证明听盒式录音磁带实际上将帮助并且鼓励小学生阅读，而不仅仅是为了一般性的学习。为了更好地评价论点，我们将需要更多的信息。这些信息包括被引用的研究是否明确地与盒式录音磁带的价值有关，以及明确地与它们在阅读和学习过程中的价值有关。

【逻辑问题提纲】

　　本文作者一共攻击了原文的四处缺陷：

1. 阅读能力欠佳的学生未必对学校学业不感兴趣，他们可能在不需要阅读的学科另有所长。
2. 原文所提供的关于磁带教学的研究信息不能表明其价值就在于促进阅读能力。
3. 由于信息的缺乏，我们不知道文中所提到的研究中大声朗读文章的形式，也就无法判断这一信息对结论的支持作用。
4. 听父母朗读和听磁带是两种不同的形式，不能进行类比。

● 逻辑思路提示：本文攻击的主要错误主要还是常见的两类——调查信息不完整和错误类比。

1) 文中所提到的研究调查结果的叙述过于模糊不够具体，我们既没有被告知研究所得到

的听磁带的 "价值" 对于提高阅读能力的作用，也不知道研究中朗读的具体形式，这种模糊的数据是无法给予结论以有力支持的。

2）听父母朗读和听磁带的过程有很大的差异，前者对儿童提高阅读能力有益的事实不能说明后者也同样可以促进学生的阅读能力。

【论证展开】

论证段落中的小转折：在进行论证段落的论述时，我们既可以一上来就以 Topic sentence 直接指出作者所犯的错误，也可以先用 the argument claims that... 这类的句型引述想要批判的论据或假设，然后再转折，用 However, the author provides no evidence to support this claim 这样的句型引出批判的内容。

可用于转折的词汇：

however / but / yet / nevertheless / nonetheless / unfortunately

【语言提示】

● 用于开头段的句式：However, close scrutiny of this evidence and of the editorial's line of reasoning reveals that they provide little credible support for the editorial's conclusion.

● 用于攻击信息不完整的句式：（1）As it stands this evidence is far too vague to support the editorial's conclusion. （2）Absent additional information about the cited studies, these studies lend no credible support to the conclusion that ...

● 用于攻击错误类比的句式：This argument by analogy is wholly unpersuasive.

● 其他句式：Experience informs us, however, that this is not the case, especially for ...

Argument 156　**Dickens Academy**'s interpersonal-skills seminars

The following is taken from an advertisement placed in a weekly business magazine by the Dickens Academy.

"We distributed a survey to senior management at International Mega-Publishing, Inc. The result of the survey clearly indicates that many employees were well prepared in business knowledge and computer skills, but lacked interpersonal skills to interact gracefully with customers. International Mega-Publishing decided to improve customer satisfaction by sending their newly hired employees to our one-day seminars. Since taking advantage of our program, International Mega-Publishing has seen a sharp increase in sales, an indication that the number of their disgruntled customers has declined significantly. Your company should hire Dickens and let us turn every employee into an ambassador for your company."

【参考译文】 我们对米加国际出版公司的高层管理人员进行了一次调查。调查结果清楚地显示很多员工在商业知识和计算机技能方面准备充足，但是缺乏与客户得体沟通的人际交往能力。米加国际出版公司决定通过让他们的新员工参加我们为期一天的研讨会来提高客户满意度。在参加了我们的课程之后，米加国际出版公司的销量急剧上升，这表明不满意的顾客数量显著下降。你们公司应该聘用 Dickens，来让我们把每名员工变成你们公司的大使。

This Dickens Academy ad claims that any company wanting to improve customer relations will benefit from enrolling its employees in Dickens' one-day seminars. **To support this claim the ad cites** Mega-Publishing's improved sales after its new employees attended Dickens' seminar **as an indication of** improved customer relations. **As it stands the ad rests on a series of dubious assumptions, and is**

therefore unconvincing.

In the first place, the ad relies on the unsubstantiated assumption that the Mega employees attending the seminar are positioned to influence Mega's sales and its customer relations. **Perhaps** these new employees were hired for production, editorial, or personnel positions that have nothing to do with customer relations and that have only an indirect and negligible impact on sales. **Without providing evidence that** these new employees directly influence Mega's customer relations and sales, **I cannot accept the argument that** the Dickens seminar was responsible for any of Mega's sales or customer-relations improvements subsequent to the seminar.

Even if Mega's seminar attendees are involved in sales and customer relations, **the ad unfairly assumes that** the improvement in Mega's sales must be attributable to the seminar. **Perhaps** the improvement in sales was the result of increasing product demand, new pricing policies, decreased competition, or any one of a myriad of other possible developments. **For that matter, perhaps** Mega's new employees as a group already possessed exceptional interpersonal skills, and therefore Mega's sales and customer relations would have improved during the ensuing months regardless of the seminar. **Since the ad fails to consider and rule out these and other alternative explanations for** the improvements at Mega, **I find the ad's claim that** the Dickens seminar should receive credit unconvincing.

Even if the Dickens seminar was responsible for improved sales and customer relations at Mega, **the ad's claim that** all other businesses would benefit similarly from a Dickens seminar **is unjustified. It is entirely possible that** the techniques and skills that participants in Dickens' seminars learn are effective for the kind of business in which Mega engages, but not for other types of businesses. **Although it is possible that** Dickens' training methods would be equally effective for other types of businesses, **since Dickens has not provided evidence that this is the case I remain unconvinced by the ad's claim.**

In sum, this ad fails to provide key evidence needed to support its claim. To strengthen that claim Dickens must show that Mega's seminar attendees—and not other employees or other occurrences—were indeed responsible for the subsequent improvement in sales, **and that** customer relations also improved as a result of their attending the seminar. **Dickens must also provide additional** success stories—about other types of businesses—**to convince me that** Dickens' training methods will work for any business.

【参考译文】

这个狄更斯学校的广告声称想要改进顾客关系的任何公司将受益于雇员在狄更斯的为期一天的研究班的学习。为了支持这一论断，广告引用了一个例子，在米加出版社的新雇员参加狄更斯的讨论会之后，销售额提高，而这可以作为一个顾客关系改进的迹象。就目前情况来看，广告以一系列可疑的假定为基础，因此不能让人信服。

首先，广告建立在无确实根据的假定上。这个假定是参加讨论会的雇员所处的职位会影响米加的销售额及其顾客关系。或许这些新雇员受雇于生产、编辑或者人力资源部门，而与顾客关系无关，对销售额只有间接和可以忽略的影响。在没有提供证据证明这些新雇员直接影响米加的顾客关系和销售额的情况下，我不能接受狄更斯讨论会是随后米加的销售额增加或者顾客关系改进的原因的观点。

即使米加的讨论会参加者涉及销售和顾客关系，广告不公平地认为米加销售额的增加一定可归因于讨论会。或许，销售额的增加是由于产品需求增加、新定价政策出台、竞争减少，或者其他无数原因中的任何一个。除此之外，或许米加的新雇员作为一个团队已经拥有非同寻常的人际关系技能，因此不管是否有这个讨论会，米加的销售和顾客关系都可能在接下来的几个月内改进。因为关于米加的改进，这个广告没有考虑和排除这些和其他的可供选择的解释，我认为这一广告声称狄更斯讨论会有功劳是不足以使人信服的。

即使米加销售和顾客关系的改进源于狄更斯讨论会，广告声称所有其他公司将会同样受益于狄更斯讨论会是不合理的。完全可能狄更斯讨论会的参与者所习得的那些技术和技能对于米加所从事的那种工作是有效的，但对于其他类型的公司却是无效的。尽管狄更斯的训练方法对于其他类型的公司可能同样有效，但因为狄更斯并未提供证据证明情况确实如此，我仍然不能相信广告所宣称的。

总之，这个广告没有成功地提供关键证据来支持它的论断。为了加强此论断，狄更斯必须说明随后销售的改进是因为米加的讨论会参与者，而不是因为其他的雇员或者其他事件所导致的，并且顾客关系的改进也是他们参加讨论会的结果。狄更斯也必须提供一些附加的关于其他类型的公司成功的例子，使我确信狄更斯的训练方法将适合任何公司。

【逻辑问题提纲】

本文作者一共攻击了原文的三处缺陷：

1. 没有证据表明是参加了狄更斯培训的米加雇员促进了公司销量和客户满意度，因而参加培训与销量增加之间未必有因果关系。

2. 米加的销量增加可能由其他原因导致，比如市场需求增加、新的价格政策等等。

3. 即便承认米加确实从狄更斯的培训课程受益，我们也不能草率认为其他公司也能从培训中获得同样的好处。

● 逻辑思路提示：本文攻击的第一点和第二点从本质上说是同一个问题，即狄更斯的培训与米加业绩的上升之间不一定存在因果关系，但作者从两个不同角度进行展开：第一段作者论述的是原文的论据和信息不够充分，没有提出直接证据证实就是狄更斯的培训导致了业绩上升；第二段作者又从业绩上升可能有其他原因的角度展开批驳。如果有些题目中的逻辑缺陷实在太少，写的时候担心攻击的出发点不够多的话，也可以学习本文的方法，针对同一个问题从不同的角度展开论证。

【语言提示】

● 开头段句式：As it stands the ad rests on a series of dubious assumptions, and is therefore unconvincing.

● 论证段句式：(1) the ad relies on the unsubstantiated assumption that ... (2) since Dickens has not provided evidence that this is the case I remain unconvinced by the ad's claim.

● 结尾段句式：(1) In sum, this ad fails to provide key evidence needed to support its claim. (2) Dickens must also provide ... to convince me that ...

Argument 158　Garbage sites and the health of nearby residents

The Trash-Site Safety Council has recently conducted a statewide study of possible harmful effects of garbage sites on the health of people living near the sites. A total of five sites and 300 people were examined. The study revealed, on average, only a small statistical correlation between the proximity of homes to garbage sites and the incidence of unexplained rashes among people living in these homes. Furthermore, although it is true that people living near the largest trash sites had a slightly higher incidence of the rashes, there was otherwise no correlation between the size of the garbage sites and people's health. Therefore, the council is pleased to announce that the current system of garbage sites does not pose a significant health hazard. We see no need to restrict the size of such sites in our state or to place any restrictions on the number of homes built near the sites.

【参考译文】垃圾场安全委员会最近就垃圾场对住在附近的居民的健康可能造成的危害进行了一次调查。调查一共检测了五个垃圾场，调查了300位居民。研究发现，平均而言，在垃圾场附近居住和这些居民中未查明原因的皮炎的发病率之间只有很小的相关性。而且，尽管住在最大的垃圾场附近的居民患皮炎的比例确实要高一些，但是除此之外，垃圾场的规模和人们的健康之间是没有关联的。因此，委员会很高兴地宣布，现有的垃圾场系统不会对健康产生严重的危害。我们认为没有必要限制本州这类垃圾场的规模，或对于在垃圾场周围建造的住宅的数量加以任何限制。

The Trash-Site Safety Council concludes here that there is no public-health reason to restrict the size of trash sites or their proximity to homes. **The Council cites its recent statewide study involving** five sites and 300 people; in the study the Council observed only a small correlation between the residents' proximity to a trash site and unexplained rashes, and only a "slightly higher incidence" of rashes among people living near larger sites. **The study suffers from certain statistical and other problems, which render the Council's argument based upon it unpersuasive.**

First, the Council has not convinced me that the five sites in the survey are representative of trash sites in general throughout the state—in terms of their impact on the health of nearby residents. Admittedly, the study was a "statewide" one. Nevertheless, **it is entirely possible that** the five sites studied are characterized by certain environmental conditions that are not typical of most sites in the state and that render nearby residents either more or less susceptible to rashes and other health problems.

Secondly, the 300 people in the study are not necessarily representative of the state's general population—in terms of their susceptibility to health problems. **For example, perhaps** nearly all of these people are adults, while most of the health problems associated with trash sites occur among children. **Or perhaps** preventative healthcare programs in these particular communities are unusually effective in preventing health problems. **In short, lacking evidence that** these 300 people are typical in terms of their vulnerability to health problems **the Council cannot convince me that** no statewide trash-site regulations are needed.

Thirdly, the Council's conclusion that the five sites studied pose no serious health hazards to nearby residents **seems premature.** Common sense informs me that a serious health problem might become apparent only after a long period of exposure to the environmental cause of the problem. **The Council fails to take into account** the length of time these residents have been exposed to the conditions created by the trash sites; and **in any event,** one "recent" study **amounts to scant evidence that** the sites pose no significant long-term public-health hazards.

In sum, the Council's argument is unconvincing as it stands. To strengthen it the Council must provide better evidence that the environmental conditions at the five sites studied represent conditions at trash sites throughout the state, and that the 300 people studied are representative of state residents generally in terms of vulnerability to health problems. **To better assess the argument I would need more information** comparing the health of the 300 people studied before and after continual exposure to the environmental conditions associated with the trash sites. **I would also need to know** the length of the study to determine whether it adequately accounted for latent health problems.

【参考译文】

　　垃圾场安全委员会在这里做出结论：没有公共健康理由去限制垃圾场的大小或者与居民住所的接近程度。委员会引用了其新近在全州范围内的研究，此次研究涉及五个垃圾场和300个人；在研究中，委员会注意到居民毗邻垃圾场和未查明原因的发疹之间只有微小的相互关系，以及居住在大垃圾场周围的居民"稍微有点高的发疹率"。研究由于一些统计和其他问题的缘故，致使委员会的论断没有说服力。

　　首先，委员会没能使我确信，就它们对附近居民的健康的影响而言，调查中的五个地点可以代表整个州的垃圾场。研究确实是"全州范围"的，但尽管如此，完全可能研究的五个地点存在某些环境特点，而这些环境特点在全州的大多数地方不是典型的，并且致使附近居民或多或少容易感染皮疹或其他健康问题。

　　其次，研究中的300人就易患疾病性而言，不一定就是州内一般人的代表。例如，也许这300人都是成年人，而大多数与垃圾场相关的健康问题都发生在儿童之中。或者也许在这些特定的社区里，预防保健方案防止健康问题异常有效。简而言之，在缺乏证据表明这300人在疾病的易感性方面具有典型性的情况下，委员会不能使我信服不需要在全州范围内制定有关垃圾场的规定。

　　再次，委员会关于研究的五个地点不会对附近居民的健康造成严重危害的结论下得为时过早。常识告诉我，环境原因所引起的严重的健康问题只能在很长一段时间后才可能变得明显。委员会没有考虑到这些居民暴露于由垃圾场所造成的环境下的时间的长短；无论如何，一项"新近"的研究缺少证据表明垃圾场不会造成显著的长期的公众健康危害。

　　总之，就目前情况看，委员会的论点并不能使人信服。为了使之加强，委员会必须提供更好的证据，即研究的五个地点的环境状况可代表整个州的垃圾场的环境状况，并且在疾病易感性方面所研究的300人可代表全州居民。为了更好地评价这一论断，我需要更多的信息。这些信息是关于所研究的300人长期暴露于与垃圾场相关的环境状况下之前和之后的健康状况的比较。我也需要知道研究的时间长度，来确定它是否能充分地解释潜在的健康问题。

【逻辑问题提纲】

　　本文作者一共攻击了原文的三处缺陷：

　　1. 由于不知道文中所提到调查的取样过程，被调查的五个垃圾场未必能代表整个州垃圾场的总体情况。

　　2. 同样，调查所研究的居民从年龄、体质、生活环境等方面也未必能代表整个州的情况。

　　3. 有些疾病和危害是需要一定时间才能显现的，因而委员会基于最近的一次调查就断言垃圾场没有危害过于草率。

　　● 逻辑思路提示：本文攻击的前两点都是调查取样代表性的问题，就这道题来说这确实是一个比较主要的缺陷，但在同一篇文章中用两个段落论证这一问题不是很恰当，而且文章攻击的第三点的论证也有些差强人意，原文所说的"recent study"只是表达调查是最近进行的，而不能由此认为调查周期一定不够。要想把本文论述改进得更完善，我们可以把第一、二点也就是调查样本的代表性问题归在一段里进行论述，第二段可以论证调查本身的意义问题：委员会所做的调查仅仅研究了 rashes 这样一种无关痛痒的小毛病，却就此认为现有垃圾场不会导致任何重大健康危害，显然调查内容对于所要说明的结论并没有直接的支持意义。另外，就算承认 rashes 的研究足以体现垃圾场的健康危害，原文所提供的调查结果也正好说明垃圾场规模和人们的发病率是成正比的，可以用反证法来对这一问题展开论述。

【语言提示】

● 开头段句式：The study suffers from certain statistical and other problems, which render the Council's argument based upon it unpersuasive.

● 论证句式：(1) the Council's conclusion that ... seems premature. (2) in any event, ... amounts to scant evidence that ...

Argument 160　Improving **learning and memory**

As people grow older, an enzyme known as PEP increasingly breaks down the neuropeptide chemicals involved in learning and memory. But now, researchers have found compounds that prevent PEP from breaking neuropeptides apart. In tests, these compounds almost completely restored lost memory in rats. The use of these compounds should be extended to students who have poor memory and difficulty in concentrating-and therefore serious problems in school performance. Science finally has a solution for problems neither parents nor teachers could solve.

【参考译文】随着人们的衰老，一种叫做 PEP 的酶不断地分解与学习和记忆有关的神经肽化学物质。但现在研究人员已经发现了一些阻止 PEP 分解神经肽的化合物。在试验中，这些化合物几乎完全恢复了老鼠失去的记忆。这些化合物的使用可以扩展到那些因记忆力较差和注意力不能集中而在学习中存在严重问题的学生。科学最终能够解决家长和教师都无法解决的问题。

This argument concludes that certain compounds should be administered to students with poor memory and concentration to improve their performance in school. **The argument cites an experiment involving** rats in which the same compounds prevented the enzyme PEP from breaking down chemicals involved in learning and memory. **The argument suffers from several flaws, which render it unconvincing.**

A threshold problem with the argument is that it assumes that what improves memory and learning in rats will also improve memory and learning in humans. **Although this is entirely possible, the argument provides no evidence to support this assumption. Without such evidence the argument can be rejected out of hand.**

A second problem involves the fact that PEP increasingly breaks down the chemicals needed for learning and memory as humans age—as the argument points out. **Yet the argument seems to claim that** inhibiting PEP will be effective in improving learning and memory in young people. (The argument refers to students' "parents," implying that proposed human subjects are young people rather than adults.) Thus, the effectiveness of the compounds is likely to be far less significant than it would be for older people.

A third problem with the argument is that it assumes that learning and memory are the only significant factors affecting performance in school. **Common sense and experience tells us this is not the case, and that a variety of other factors**, such as motivation and natural ability, **also play major roles.** Thus, the compounds might very well turn out to be largely ineffective.

A final problem with the argument is that it asserts that the compounds will improve concentration, **yet it makes no claim that** the same compounds improved concentration in rats—only that they improved the rats' learning and memory. **Thus, the argument's conclusion is indefensible to this extent.**

In sum, the argument is weak on several grounds. To strengthen it the argument's proponent must provide clear evidence that the same compounds that improved learning and memory in rats will do so in young humans. **Moreover, the argument's proponent must show that** poor academic performance is due primarily to learning and memory problems, rather than to poor concentration, motivation, or other factors.

【参考译文】

这篇论证断定应该给予那些记忆力和注意力比较差的学生某些化合物，使其在学校内的表现得以改善。此篇论证引用了在老鼠身上做的一个实验，实验证明相同的化合物会防止 PEP 酶分解学习和记忆所需的化学物质。论证存在若干缺陷，使其不能令人信服。

此论证的第一个问题是假定能改进老鼠的记忆和学习的方式和物质也可以改进人类的记忆和学习。虽然这是完全可能的，但此论证并未提供证据来支持这一假定。如果没有这样的证据，此论证可以被立即否决。

第二个问题涉及作者所引用的事实，即 PEP 酶是在人类衰老的情况下日益分解学习和记忆所需的化学物质——如同此论证所指出的那样。然而此论证似乎主张抑制 PEP 酶对于年轻人改进学习和记忆将是有效的（论断谈到学生的"父母"，暗示被建议的对象是青年人而不是成年人）。因此，化合物的效力很可能远不及对老年人那样显著。

此论证的第三个问题是它假定学习和记忆是影响学校里表现的惟一重要因素。常识和经验告诉我们情况并不是如此，事实上有多种其他因素，例如积极性和天生的能力也起了主要的作用。因此，化合物可能在很大程度上会被证明是无效的。

此论证的最后一个问题是它断言化合物将改善注意力，然而，此论断并没有确定指出相同的化合物改善了老鼠的注意力——它仅仅改善了老鼠的学习和记忆。因此，在这个范围内，论断的结论是站不住脚的。

总之，论断在这几点上很薄弱。为了使之加强，论断的支持者必须提供更好的证据来表明改善老鼠学习和记忆的化合物也能改善年轻人的学习和记忆。而且，论证的支持者必须说明学业成绩较差主要是由于学习和记忆的问题，而不是由于注意力不集中、能动性或者其他因素。

【逻辑问题提纲】

本文作者一共攻击了原文的四处缺陷：
1. 用 PEP 对于老鼠的试验效果来类推对人类的效果不一定可行，错误类比。
2. 原文的信息只表明 PEP 在人们衰老时起作用，因而它对于青少年的作用有待进一步证实。
3. 作者简单假定学习和记忆是决定在校表现的惟一因素。
4. 原文没有提供任何证据来表明所提到的化合物能够起到集中注意力的作用。
- 逻辑思路提示：信息和证据缺乏的错误：有些题目的作者会在结论中提出一些根本没有论据支持的观点，比如本题，本来在论据的信息中提到的都是化合物以及 PEP 对于学习和记忆的作用，但作者却在结论中又突然提到抑制 PEP 的这种化合物也能起到集中注意力的作用，这是没有依据的。这类错误往往比较隐蔽而且容易被忽视，因此在读题时一定要对一些细节留有足够的警惕。

【论证展开】

本文用了一系列引导句式来引导四个论证段落：(1) A threshold problem with the argument is that it ... (2) A second problem involves the fact that ... (3) A third problem with the argument is that ... (4) A final problem with the argument is that ...

这些句式可以学习，但另一方面，最好注意一下语言的变化，比如最后一个段落我们可以用 Last but not least 或是 the last problem worth considering is that 等其他引导句型来增加语言的多样性。

- 引导推测法的句式：在本文论证第二、三个问题时，作者使用了 Although this is entirely possible, the argument provides no evidence to support this assumption. Common sense and experience tells us this is not the case, and that a variety of other factors, such as ..., also play major roles. 这样的句型来引导推测。在具体展开推测、假设、列举之前，我们也可以使用类似的句式来把推测的内容统领起来。
- 本文的论证段落每段都没有做具体展开，仅仅使用一些抽象的逻辑描述句式来指出错误，这是行文的缺陷，在自己练习写作时要注意保证每个论证段的完整性和丰满度。

【语言提示】

- 引导论证段的句式：(1) A threshold problem with the argument is that it ... (2) A second problem involves the fact that ... (3) A third problem with the argument is that ... (4) A final problem with the argument is that ...
- 引导推测法的句式：(1) Although this is entirely possible, the argument provides no evidence to support this assumption. (2) Common sense and experience tells us this is not the case, and that a variety of other factors, such as ..., also play major roles.
- 论证小总结句式：(1) Without such evidence the argument can be rejected out of hand. (2) Thus, the argument's conclusion is indefensible to this extent.

Argument 161　　The reading habits of **Leeville citizens**

In a study of reading habits of Leeville citizens conducted by the University of Leeville, most respondents said they preferred literary classics as reading material. However, a follow-up study conducted by the same researchers found that the type of book most frequently checked out of each of the public libraries in Leeville was the mystery novel. Therefore, it can be concluded that the respondents in the first study had misrepresented their reading habits.

【参考译文】 在一次由利维勒大学所举行的关于利维勒居民阅读习惯的调查中，多数被访者说他们倾向于阅读古典文学。然而，由相同的研究人员进行的跟踪调查发现利维勒所有公共图书馆中最经常被借阅的书是神秘小说。因此，我们可以得出结论，第一次调查的被访者错误地表达了他们的阅读习惯。

This argument concludes that in a certain study about reading habits Leeville citizens misrepresented their true reading habits. **To justify this conclusion, the argument points out** an apparent discrepancy between their representations and the results of a follow-up study showing that a different type of book is the one most frequently checked out from Leeville's public libraries. **However, the argument fails to account for several other possible explanations for this apparent discrepancy.**

First of all, the argument does not indicate how much time passed between the two studies. During a sufficiently long interim period the demographic makeup of Leeville might have changed, or the reading habits of the first study's respondents might have changed. In other words, the longer the time between studies the less reliable the conclusion that respondents in the first study misrepresented their reading habits.

Secondly, the argument fails to account for the possibility that the respondents in the first study constitute a different population than public library patrons. Admittedly, both groups are comprised of Leeville citizens. **However, it is entirely possible that** more highly educated citizens who frequent the University library rather than public libraries, or who purchase books rather than borrow them, are the ones who responded to the first study.

Thirdly, the argument fails to account for the possibility that literary classics, the book type that the first study's respondents indicated they preferred, are not readily available at Leeville's public libraries—or at least not as readily available as mystery novels. Experience informs me that this is likely, because mystery novels are in greater supply and are cheaper for libraries to acquire than literary classics. **If this is the case, it provides an alternative explanation for the fact that** more mystery novels than literary classics are checked out from Leeville's public libraries.

Finally, the reliability of the first study rests on its statistical integrity. The argument fails to indicate what portion of the people surveyed actually responded; the smaller this portion, the less reliable the results. **Nor does the argument indicate** how many people were surveyed, or whether the sample was representative of Leeville's general population. Again, the smaller the sample, the less reliable the results.

In conclusion, the assertion that respondents in the first study misrepresented their reading habits **is untenable, in light of a variety of alternative explanations for the apparent discrepancy between the two studies. To strengthen the argument, its proponent must show that** the respondents in the first study are representative of Leeville citizens generally, and that both groups are equally likely to check out books from Leeville's public libraries. **To better evaluate the argument, we would need to know** the length of time between the two studies, and whether any significant demographic changes occurred during this time. **We would also need to know** the availability of literary classics compared to mystery novels at Leeville's public libraries.

【参考译文】

这篇论证断定，在某次关于读书习惯的研究中，利维勒居民没有如实叙述他们真实的读书习惯。为了证明这个结论是正确的，论证指出了他们的表述与后续的一个研究的结果之间有一处明显的差异。后续的研究显示利维勒公共图书馆里查阅频率最高的书是和调查结果不同的另外一类。但是，对于这处明显的差异，论证没能说明其他几种可能的解释。

首先，论证没有表明两项研究之间的时间间隔。在足够长的过渡期内，利维勒的人口结构可能改变，或者第一项研究的回答者的读书习惯可能改变。换句话说，两项研究之间的时间间隔越长，回答者在第一个研究里不如实地叙述了他们的读书习惯的结论的可信度就越低。

第二，论证没能解释与公共图书馆的光顾者相比较，在第一个研究里的那些回答者组成了不同人群的可能性。不可否认，两组都是由利维勒居民组成的。但是，完全可能教育程度更高的居民经常去大学图书馆而不是公共图书馆，或者购买书籍而不是借阅书籍，而这些人是在第一个研究中做出回答的人。

第三，论证没能解释文学经典作品，即第一项研究的回答者表明他们所喜欢的这种类型的图书，在利维勒公共图书馆可能是不容易获得的，或者至少不像神秘小说一样容易获得。经验告诉我这是可能的，因为神秘小说供应量更大，并且对于图书馆来说，比获得文学经典作品更便宜一些。如果情况如此，它也能解释为什么图书馆中被借阅的神秘小说比文学经典作品要多。

最后，第一个研究的可靠性建立在其统计完整的基础上。论证没能表明有多少比例的被访者实际回答了问卷；这个比例越小，结果越不可靠。论证也没能表明多少人被调查，或者所取样本是否能够代表利维勒的一般人口。这个样本越小，结果越不可靠。

　　总之，由于存在多种对这两项研究之间明显差异的其他解释，关于第一个研究中的回答者没有如实叙述他们的读书习惯的断言是站不住脚的。为了加强论证，它的支持者必须表明在第一个研究里的那些回答者是利维勒居民的典型代表，并且这两组被访者都同样可能从利维勒的公共图书馆办理借书手续。为了更好地评价论证，我们需要知道两项研究之间的时间间隔，并且这段时间内，是否有任何显著的人口统计的变化发生。我们也需要知道在利维勒的公共图书馆里文学经典作品与神秘小说相比是否同样容易获得。

【逻辑问题提纲】

本文作者一共攻击了原文的四处缺陷：

1. 作者没有考虑两次调查之间的时间间隔，因而在此期间人们的阅读习惯可能发生变化（没有与时俱进的错误）。

2. 作者没有指出参加第一次调查的对象具体情况，因而其调查结果未必有代表性。

3. 作者没有具体分析第二次调查的结果，因而公共图书馆借出的书的类型未必能代表市民的阅读倾向性。

4. 作者没有指出回答调查的人占所有调查者的比例，因而样本未必有代表性。

● 逻辑思路提示：本文的论据就是两个调查，因而本文的论证也完全围绕调查所需要注意的方方面面展开。其中攻击的第二、四点是样本的代表性的问题，指出看古典文学的人群和看神秘小说的人群可能不是同一群体；以及样本的大小和比例的问题。对于第四点要想进一步展开，我们还可以借鉴以前介绍过的思路和语言，指出那些对古典文学感兴趣的人可能更倾向于回应调查从而导致调查结果的局限性。

【论证展开】

攻击因果关系错误段落的小总结：If this is the case, it provides an alternative explanation for the fact that ... 我们说过对于因果关系的错误，最基本的论证思路是指出结果的产生可能有其他原因。在这些段落，我们就可以用上面所列的句型作为段落小总结。

【语言提示】

● 开头段句式：However, the argument fails to account for several other possible explanations for this apparent discrepancy.

● 论证段句式：(1) If this is the case, it provides an alternative explanation for the fact that ... (2) Finally, the reliability of the first study rests on its statistical integrity. (3) The argument fails to indicate what portion of the people surveyed actually responded; the smaller this portion, the less reliable the results. (4) Nor does the argument indicate ...

● 结尾段句式：In conclusion, the assertion that ... is untenable, in light of a variety of alternative explanations for the apparent discrepancy between the two studies.

Argument 162　Eating soy to prevent fatigue and depression

A recent study shows that people living on the continent of North America suffer 9 times more chronic fatigue and 31 times more chronic depression than do people living on the continent of Asia. Interestingly, Asians, on average, eat 20 grams of soy per day, whereas North Americans eat virtually none. It turns out that soy contains phytochemicals called isoflavones, which have been found to possess disease-preventing properties. Thus, North Americans should consider eating soy on a regular basis as a way of preventing fatigue and depression.

【参考译文】最近一次研究显示，居住在北美大陆的人患慢性疲劳和慢性抑郁症的数量分别为居住在亚洲大陆居民的 9 倍和 31 倍。有趣的是，亚洲人平均每天食用 20 克大豆，而北美人几乎不吃。原来大豆含有一种植物化合物异黄酮，人们发现它具有抗病功效。因此，北美人应该考虑经常食用大豆，把它作为预防疲劳和抑郁的一种方法。

This argument concludes that North Americans should eat soy on a regular basis as a means of preventing fatigue and depression. **The argument cites a recent study showing that** North Americans suffer far greater from these problems than people in Asia do, that Asians eat soy regularly whereas North Americans do not, and that soy is known to possess disease preventing properties. **The argument relies on several doubtful assumptions, and is therefore unconvincing.**

First, the argument assumes that depression and fatigue are just as readily diagnosed in Asia as in North America. **However, it is entirely possible that** Asians suffering from these problems do not complain about them or otherwise admit them. **For that matter, perhaps** Asian medical doctors view certain symptoms that North Americans would consider signs of fatigue and depression as signs of some other problem.

Secondly, the argument assumes that the difference in soy consumption **is the only possible explanation for** this disparity in the occurrence of fatigue and depression. **Yet the argument fails to substantiate this assumption. Common sense informs me that** any one of a myriad of other differences—environmental, dietary, and genetic—might explain why North Americans suffer from these problems to a greater extent than Asians do. **Without considering and ruling out alternative reasons for** this disparity, **the argument's conclusion that** soy is the key to the disparity **is indefensible.**

Thirdly, the argument unfairly infers from the fact that soy is known to possess disease-preventing properties that these properties help prevent fatigue and depression specifically. **The argument supplies no evidence to substantiate this assumption. Moreover,** whether fatigue and depression are appropriately classified as diseases in the first place is questionable.

Finally, even if the properties in soy can be shown to prevent fatigue and depression, **the argument unfairly assumes that** eating soy is the only means of ingesting the key substances. **It is entirely possible that** these same properties are found in other forms, and therefore that North Americans need not increase soy consumption to help prevent fatigue and depression.

In sum, the argument is dubious at best. Before I can accept its conclusion, the argument's proponent must provide better evidence that people in Asia in fact suffer less from fatigue and depression than North Americans do. **To better evaluate the argument I would need to know** what kinds of diseases the properties of soy are known to help prevent, and whether they relate at all to fatigue and depression. **I would also need to know what** other foods contain the same properties as soy—to determine what alternatives, if any, are available for preventing fatigue and depression.

【参考译文】

　　这篇论证断定北美人应该经常吃大豆，把它作为防止疲劳和抑郁的一种方法。论证引用了一个新近的研究，该研究显示北美人比亚洲人存在更多这类健康问题，而亚洲人经常吃大豆，但北美人没有这样做；并且人们知道大豆拥有防止疾病的性质。该论证基于几个可疑的假定，从而导致它缺乏可信度。

首先，论证假定抑郁和疲劳在亚洲如同在北美洲那样容易诊断。但是完全可能存在这些问题的亚洲人不抱怨这些问题或者不以其他方式承认这些问题。而且，或许对于某些北美人会认为是疲劳和抑郁征兆的现象，亚洲的医生只会看成是一些其他问题的征兆。

第二，论证假定食用大豆的差别是对疲劳和抑郁发生率差异的惟一的可能解释。然而论证没能证实这个假定。常识告诉我，很多其他的差别，例如环境、饮食、遗传，都可以解释为什么北美人比亚洲人在更大程度上存在这些问题。如果没有考虑到并排除其他可能的原因，大豆是导致患病率差异的原因的结论是站不住脚的。

第三，众所周知，大豆拥有防止疾病的性质，但论证不公平地以此事实为依据推断出这些性质也能帮助防止疲劳和抑郁。论证没有提供证据证明这个假定。而且，疲劳和抑郁是否可以恰当地归类为疾病是可疑的。

最后，即使大豆的这些性质可以防止疲劳和抑郁，该论证还不公平地假定吃大豆是摄取这些关键物质的惟一方法。完全可能同类物质可以通过其他形式得到，因此北美人不必增加大豆消费量来帮助防止疲劳和抑郁。

总之，本文论证充其量是可疑的。在我能接受它的结论之前，论证的支持者必须提供更好的证据证明在亚洲的人们确实比北美人较少忍受疲劳和抑郁之苦。为了更好地评价论证，我需要知道，大豆那种为人所知的所含的物质可以帮助防止哪种疾病，它们是否确实与疲劳和抑郁相关。我也需要知道和大豆一样含有这一物质的其他食品——来确定如果有可选择的食品的话，哪些食品可以防止疲劳和抑郁。

【逻辑问题提纲】

本文作者一共攻击了原文的四处缺陷：

1. 亚洲地区对于抑郁和疲劳的定义及诊断可能和北美不一样，从而导致两地区患病人数的差异（另有其他原因的攻击方式）。

2. 作者没有考虑导致抑郁和疲劳的其他诱因（仍然是另有其他原因的本质）。

3. 文中信息不能说明大豆中所含的抗病物质就能用于防止疲劳和抑郁。

4. 即使承认大豆中所含的物质可以防止疲劳和抑郁，作者也没有考虑其他同样能够获取此类物质的食物和方式。

● 逻辑思路提示：这道题目的论证过程即使用了类比又做了因果关系的假设，因而在范文中作者把攻击错误类比与攻击因果关系的方式结合使用：一方面指出北美居民和亚洲居民有什么其他可能差异，诸如对于疾病的诊断和定义、基因、环境等，这是攻击错误类比的典型方式；另一方面指出这些可能差异也同样会导致患病人数的差异这一结果，这是指出有其他原因来攻击因果关系的典型方式。从这道题我们可以看到，逻辑错误之间并不是泾渭分明的，有时会结合出现，这时就需要同学们综合运用针对不同错误的论证方式展开论证。

【论证展开】

the argument assumes that ... is the only possible explanation for ...作者攻击第一个错误时所用的这个句型是指出因果关系错误的典型句式，接下来我们就可以自然而然地使用推测法、列举法展开论证，指出作者忽略了哪些其他可能的解释。这个句式可以和我们在 Argument 161 中介绍过的另一句式 If this is the case, it provides an alternative explanation for the fact that ...结合使用，作为这个段落的小总结。

【语言提示】

● 论证段句式：the argument assumes that ... is the only possible explanation for ...

● 结尾段句式：Before I can accept its conclusion, the argument's proponent must provide better evidence that ...

Argument 166　Comparing **cold medications**

The following appeared in a local newspaper.

"People should not be misled by the advertising competition between Coldex and Cold-Away, both popular over-the-counter cold medications that anyone can purchase without a doctor's prescription. Each brand is accusing the other of causing some well-known, unwanted side effect: Coldex is known to contribute to existing high blood pressure and Cold-Away is known to cause drowsiness. But the choice should be clear for most health-conscious people: Cold-Away has been on the market for much longer and is used by more hospitals than is Coldex. Clearly, Cold-Away is more effective."

【参考译文】人们不应该被两类非处方类感冒药 Coldex 和 Cold-Away 之间的广告战所误导。每个牌子都指责另一种药会导致某种众所周知的不良副作用：Coldex 导致血压升高，而 Cold-Away 导致嗜睡。但对于多数关心健康的人来说，选择是明显的：Cold-Away 比 Coldex 上市时间更长，而且被更多的医院所使用。显然，Cold-Away 效果更好。

This argument concludes that Cold-Away is a more effective non-prescription cold medication than Coldex. **The argument points out that** each one has a distinct unwanted side effect: Cold-Away causes drowsiness, while Coldex contributes to existing high blood pressure. **To support its conclusion, the argument points out that** Cold-Away has been on the market considerably longer, and that it is used by more hospitals than Coldex. **I find the argument unconvincing for three reasons.**

First, the mere fact that Cold-Away has been on the market longer than Coldex **is scant evidence of** their comparative effectiveness. Well-established products are not necessarily better than newer ones. **Moreover,** in my observation newer medicines often make use of newer pharmaceutical developments than competing products; **thus it can be argued that** since Cold-Away has been on the market longer than Coldex it is likely to be less, not more, effective than Coldex.

Secondly, the argument unfairly assumes that hospitals prefer Cold-Away because of its comparative effectiveness as a cold medication. **It is entirely possible that** hospitals do not consider drowsiness an undesirable side effect for their patients. **For that matter, perhaps** hospitals use Cold Away primarily for this effect rather than as a cold medication.

A third problem with the argument involves Coldex's side effect: high blood pressure. **Admittedly,** people who already have a serious blood pressure problem would probably be well advised to use Cold-Away instead. **However,** only those people are susceptible to this side effect. Thus, for all other people—the vast majority of cold-medicine users—Coldex's side effect is irrelevant in choosing between the two products. **Moreover, if** a person without high blood pressure wishes to avoid drowsiness, Coldex would seem to be the preferable medication.

In sum, the argument is unconvincing as it stands. To strengthen it, the argument's proponent must provide clear evidence that hospitals prefer Cold-Away because of its effectiveness in treating colds. **To better assess the argument, I would need better evidence** comparing the effectiveness of the two products—perhaps through clinical studies or reliable surveys of the general population.

【参考译文】

这个论证断定 Cold-Away 是一种比 Coldex 更为有效的非处方感冒药。该论证指出，以上两种感冒药都伴随明显的不良副作用。Cold-Away 会导致昏睡，而 Coldex 则使已经有的高血压更加严重。为支持这个结论，该论证指出 Cold-Away 上市的时间要长得多，并比 Coldex 被更多的医院使用。我认为这个论证由于三个原因不能使人信服。

首先，Cold-Away 比 Coldex 的上市时间要长这一事实无法作为比较它们之间的药效的充分证据。已经占据市场的产品并不一定就比新产品要好。而且，据我的观察，新出的药品经常都比竞争产品更好地利用更新的医学发展成果；因此，这倒可能表明 Cold-Away 并不比 Coldex 更有效，而是效果更差，因为它的上市时间比 Coldex 长。

第二，该论证还理所当然地认为医院更喜欢用 Cold-Away，是因为作为感冒药，它的效果比较好。医院完全有可能不把昏睡作为他们的病人的一种不良的副作用来考虑。同样，也有可能医院用 Cold-Away 就是要利用它的这种效果，而不是把它作为一种感冒药来用的。

这个论证的第三个问题与 Coldex 的副作用高血压有关。无可否认，对于已经患有严重的高血压的人，可能最好还是建议他们使用 Cold-Away。然而，也只有那些人才容易受这种副作用的影响。因此，对于其他所有人——广大感冒药服用者——在从两种产品中做选择的时候，Coldex 的副作用是毫无关系的。而且，如果一个没有高血压的人想要避免昏睡，Coldex 看来会是更好的药物。

总之，就目前情况看，这个论证不能使人信服。为了加强它，这个论证的支持者必须提供明确的证据证明医院是因为 Cold-Away 治疗感冒的效果才更喜欢 Cold-Away。为了更好地评价这个论证，我需要更多的证据比较两种产品的效果——也许可以通过对普通人的临床研究或者可靠调查得到。

【逻辑问题提纲】

本文作者一共攻击了原文的三处缺陷：

1. 上市时间长的药品未必疗效更好，新的药可能会采用一些新的有效成分、配方和加工工艺从而更加有效。

2. 医院采用 Cold-Away 未必是因为它作为感冒药疗效更好，而可能看重它的其他方面。

3. Coldex 的不良副作用对于血压正常的患者来说不成问题，而且那些想避免嗜睡的患者刚好可以选择 Coldex。

● 逻辑思路提示：本题是一道不太容易展开的题目，其最主要的问题就集中在最后一条论据：Cold-Away 上市时间更长且被很多医院采用。对于这条论据可以参考本文攻击的头两点展开论证。

【论证展开】

Moreover, in my observation ...在 argument 的论证中，最好避免出现此类句子和词汇。因为个人的观察、观点和经验不免带有主观性和片面性，从而论证的力度并不很强。这里我们可以用诸如 as we know, we all know that ...之类的句式来代替。

Argument 167　Lavender as a cure for insomnia

A folk remedy* for insomnia, the scent in lavender flowers, has now been proved effective. In a recent study, 30 volunteers with chronic insomnia slept each night for three weeks on lavender-scented pillows in a controlled room where their sleep was monitored. During the first week, volunteers continued to take their usual sleeping medication. They slept soundly but wakened feeling tired. During the second week, the volunteers discontinued their medication. As a result, they slept less soundly than the previous week and felt even more tired. During the third week, the volunteers slept longer and more soundly than in the previous two weeks. This shows that over a short period of time lavender cures insomnia.

A folk remedy is usually a plant-based form of treatment common to traditional forms of medicine, ones that developed before the advent of modern medical services and technology.

【参考译文】一种治疗失眠的偏方*——薰衣草花香，现在被证明是有效的。在一次最近的调查中，30 名患有慢性失眠的志愿者在三周之内每晚都在一个受监视的控制室内睡在带薰衣草花香的枕头上。在第一周，志愿者继续服用他们常用的安眠药。他们睡得很沉，但醒来时很累。在第二周，他们不服用药物。结果与前一周相比，他们睡得不那么沉，并且感觉更累。在第三周，他们睡得比前两周时间长，而且睡眠效果更好。这表明薰衣草在短时间内治愈了失眠。

* 偏方通常是一种在传统医药中常见的以植物为基础的治疗形式，这些传统医药是在现代医药服务和科技出现之前发展起来的。

The speaker concludes that the scent of lavender provides an effective short-term cure for insomnia. **To support this conclusion the speaker cites** a three-week experiment in which researchers monitored the apparent effects of lavender on 30 insomniacs, who slept on lavender-scented pillows each night of the experiment. **The speaker's account of** the experiment **reveals several critical problems with it. Together, these problems serve to undermine the speaker's argument.**

A threshold problem involves the definition of insomnia. **The speaker fails to** define this critical term. If insomnia is defined as an inability to fall asleep, then how soundly or long a person sleeps, or how tired a person feels after sleep, **is irrelevant to whether** the person suffers from insomnia. **In short, without a clear definition of** insomnia **it is impossible to assess the strength of the argument.**

Another fundamental problem is that the speaker omits to inform us about the test subjects' sleep patterns just prior to the experiment. **It is impossible to conclude with any confidence that** the subjects benefited from sleeping on lavender-scented pillows without comparing how they slept with the pillows to how they sleep without them.

Yet another problem involves the fact that subjects slept more soundly and awakened less tired the first week than the second, and that they used their regular sleep medication the first week but not the second. **This evidence tends to show only that** the subjects' other sleep medications were effective; it proves nothing about the effectiveness of lavender.

A fourth problem involves the speaker's account of the experiment's third week, during which the speaker reports only that the subjects slept longer and more soundly than in the previous two weeks. **We are not informed whether** the subjects took any medication during the third week. **Assuming they** did not, any one of a variety of factors other than the lavender-scented pillows might explain the third week's results. **Perhaps** the subjects were simply making up for sleep they lost the previous week when they discontinued their regular medication. **Or perhaps** the subjects were finally becoming accustomed to the lavender-scented pillows, which actually disturbed sleep initially. **In short, without ruling out other explanations for** the third week's results, **the speaker cannot confidently identify** what caused the subjects to sleep longer and more soundly that week.

Two final problems with the argument involve the experimental process. The experiment's results are reliable only if all other factors that might affect sleep patterns remained constant during the three-week period, and if the number of experimental subjects is statistically significant. Without evidence of the experiment's methodological and statistical reliability, the speaker's conclusion is unjustifiable.

In conclusion, the argument is unconvincing as it stands. To strengthen the assertion that lavender-scented pillows provide a short-term cure for insomnia, the author must provide evidence that the test subjects' insomnia was worse just prior to the experiment than at the conclusion of the experiment, and that the number of subjects is statistically sufficient to warrant the conclusion. To better assess the argument, we would need a clear definition of insomnia, as well as more information about whether the researchers conducted the experiment in a controlled environment.

【参考译文】

这位发言者断定熏衣草的气味对于有效地治疗失眠可以起到短期的作用。发言者引用了一个为期三周的实验来证实这个结论。在实验期间的每个夜晚，30名失眠症患者都睡在带有熏衣草香味的枕头上。在这个过程中，研究人员严密监视着熏衣草对这些人的显著影响。发言者对这个实验的解释暴露出该实验的若干个严重的问题。正是这些问题一起削弱了发言者的论证。

最开始的问题出在失眠的定义上。对这个关键的术语，发言者没有做解释。如果将失眠定义为无法入睡，那么一个人睡多么香或者多么久，以及这个人睡醒之后感觉多累，都与这个人是否受到失眠的困扰毫无关系。简而言之，不对失眠下一个确切的定义，是不可能评价这个论证的力度的。

另一个重要的问题是发言者由于疏忽，没有告诉我们那些实验对象在参加这个实验之前都是采取何种方式睡觉的。这样，研究人员就无法比较实验对象枕与不枕熏衣草枕头的睡眠状况，也便不能可信地断定实验对象使用带熏衣草香味的枕头后一定是有效的。

而另一个问题涉及这么一个事实，即实验对象第一周比第二周睡得更香，醒后没有那么累，而这些人在第一周服用了他们一直在用的安眠药，但在第二周没有服用。这个证据只能表明实验对象使用的其他药物治疗很有效；这对于证明熏衣草的效用一点儿作用也没有。

第四个问题与发言者对实验进行到第三周的情况叙述有关，发言者只是报道了这期间实验对象比前两周的睡眠时间更长，睡得也更香了。发言者没有告诉我们在第三周实验对象是否服用了任何药物。假如他们没有，那么不用带熏衣草香味的枕头，而是随便从各种因素中挑一个就可以解释第三周的实验结果。或许那些实验对象由于前一周停止服用他们一直用的药物而导致睡眠不足，所以这周他们只是在弥补他们上周的睡眠时间。又或许带熏衣草香味的枕头实际上一开始是干扰睡眠的，但实验对象最终开始习惯了。简而言之，没有排除其他可能导致第三周的实验结果的因素，发言者不能有把握地确定是什么导致实验对象在那周睡得更长、更香。

这个论述的最后两个问题与实验过程有关。只有当可能影响睡眠方式的所有其他因素在这三周的时间里保持不变，并且实验对象的人数具有统计意义时，这个实验的结果才具有可信性。没有证据证明该实验具有方法学和统计学上的可靠性，发言者的结论就不能被认为是合理的。

总之，就目前情况看，这个论证不能使人不信服。要证实其带熏衣草香味的枕头对治疗失眠有短期作用的声明，作者必须提供证据证明，在参加实验之前，实验对象的失眠症比参加完实验之后要糟糕得多；另外，实验对象的人数从统计角度来说足够证明这个结论。为了更好地评价这个论证，我们需要对失眠下一个明确的定义，同时需要掌握更多信息，了解研究人员是不是在一个受控的环境里进行这个实验的。

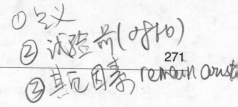

【逻辑问题提纲】

本文作者一共攻击了原文的五处缺陷:

1. 作者并没有明确"失眠"一词的确切定义,因而试验中所观察到的现象是否与治疗失眠有关仍然值得怀疑(差异概念)。

2. 作者没有告诉我们参加试验的失眠者在试验之前的睡眠情况,因而无法判断试验结果是否真的有效(信息缺乏的错误/缺乏比较)。

3. 试验对象在第二周的睡眠情况恰恰说明薰衣草影响了他们的睡眠。

4. 作者没有告诉我们试验对象在第三周是否继续服用安眠药,如果不服,则可能有其他因素导致他们的睡眠改善。

5. 作者没有提供证据表明在试验中其他影响睡眠的因素是保持不变的。

● 逻辑思路提示:

1)对比试验:在科学研究中,经常使用对比试验的形式来验证两个事件间是否存在因果关系。比如要想验证 A 因素是否导致 B 结果,那么就取两组试验对比参照物(称之为 counterparts),使其中一组受到 A 的影响,另一组不受,然后观察两组试验参照物 B 结果的产生情况,通过对比来验证 A 与 B 之间是否存在因果关系。对比试验结果的有效性基于两个主要前提:a)进行试验的两组参照物在受试前情况应该是相同的;b)试验过程中除了 A 因素外,其他条件和情况没有发生变化。

2)缺乏比较的错误:本题的主要论据就是一个试验,而这个试验本身从科学角度来讲是非常不严密的。要验证薰衣草是否真的对治疗失眠有效,最科学的办法是做一个对比试验,取两组病情相似的失眠人群,让其中一组人睡在有薰衣草花香的枕头上,另一组人睡普通枕头,一段时间后再去对比两组人的睡眠状况,这样才能比较可信地确定薰衣草对失眠的作用;原文作者并没有做这样的对比,因而其试验并不具有说服力,此是其一;第二,即使作者的试验方法和步骤是可行的,他也没有提供给我们失眠者参加试验之前的初始睡眠情况,因而我们也无从判断试验结果的意义,这就是上文论证的第二点;第三,作者也没有提供证据保证在试验中除了薰衣草和安眠药以外,其他影响睡眠的因素都保持不变,这是上文论证的第五点,这一点在别的题目中也会遇到,我们可以借鉴本文攻击这一问题的语言:The experiment's results are reliable only if all other factors that might affect ... remained constant during the experiment, and if the number of experimental subjects is statistically significant. 来描述对比试验所必需的这一前提。

【论证展开】

● 攻击词汇定义的方式:有时作者对某一关键词汇定义不清,或根本没有定义,从而导致偷换概念的错误。这时我们可以参考本文攻击第一点所用的论证结构:先用 A threshold problem involves the definition of A; the speaker fails to define this critical term. 这样的句型指出作者对 A 概念的定义不清;然后用 If A is defined as ..., then ... is irrelevant to whether ... 这类句式展开论证和推测,最后用 In short, without a clear definition of A it is impossible to assess the strength of the argument. 来做段落小总结。

● 攻击缺乏对比的方式:攻击作者没有提供试验前的初始状态从而缺乏对比的错误时,我们可以先用 Another fundamental problem is that the speaker omits to inform us about the test subjects' ... (initial condition) just prior to the experiment. 指出这个错误,然后用 It is impossible to conclude with any confidence that ... without any information about the initial condition before the experiment.之类的句型展开论述。

【语言提示】

● 开头段句式：The speaker's argument reveals several critical problems with it. Together, these problems serve to undermine the speaker's argument.

● 论证段句式：攻击关键词汇定义不清：（1）In short, without a clear definition of insomnia it is impossible to assess the strength of the argument ... （2）It is impossible to conclude with any confidence that ... （3）The experiment's results are reliable only if all other factors that might affect ... remained constant during the experiment, and if the number of experimental subjects is statistically significant. （4）Without evidence of the experiment's methodological and statistical reliability, the speaker's conclusion is unjustifiable.

Argument 168　Vitamin D, calcium, and bone mass in older people

Typically, as people age, their bone mass decreases, making them more vulnerable to bone fractures. A recent study concludes that the most effective way to reduce the risk of fractures in later life is to take twice the recommended dose of vitamin D and calcium daily. The three-year study followed a group of French women in their eighties who were nursing-home residents. The women were given daily supplements of twice the recommended dose of vitamin D and calcium. In addition, the women participated in a light weightlifting program. After three years, these women showed a much lower rate of hip fractures than is average for their age.

【参考译文】通常当人们衰老的时候，他们的骨质减少，使他们容易骨折。最近一项研究认为，在老年减少骨折危险的最好办法就是每天加倍服用推荐用量的维生素 D 和钙。这项为期三年的研究跟踪了一组在养老院生活的 80 多岁的法国妇女。她们每天被给予两倍于推荐用量的维生素 D 和钙。而且，这些妇女参加了轻微的举重活动。三年之后，这些妇女髋关节骨折的发生率低于同龄人的平均水平。

This argument concludes that elderly people should take twice the recommended dosage of vitamin D and calcium in order to minimize loss of bone mass, and therefore the risk of bone fractures. **To support this conclusion the argument's proponent cites** a 3-year study involving a group of French female nursing-home residents in their eighties. After three years of weight training, along with taking the indicated dosages of vitamin D and calcium, these women as a group were observed to suffer far fewer hip fractures than is average for their age. **This argument suffers from several critical flaws and is therefore unconvincing.**

First and foremost, the argument assumes unfairly that the additional vitamin D and calcium, rather than the weight training, **were responsible for** the lower-than-average incidence of hip fractures among this group of women. **It is entirely possible that** the weight training, not the supplements, was responsible for preserving bone mass. **Also,** weight training is known to improve muscular strength, coordination, and flexibility, which in turn might reduce the likelihood of accidental falls and other injuries. **Thus,** the weight training could also have been responsible in this respect.

The argument also overlooks many other possible explanations for the comparatively low incidence of hip fractures among this group of women. **For example, perhaps** these women were more physically fit than average to begin with. **Or perhaps** the nursing homes where the group resided provided special safeguards against accidental injuries that are not ordinarily available for most elderly people. **Or perhaps French people are less susceptible to bone loss than other people are**—due perhaps to cultural dietary habits or genetic predisposition. For that matter, **perhaps** women are genetically less disposed to lose bone mass than men are. **Any of these scenarios, if true, would undermine the conclusion that** the lower incidence of hip fractures was attributable to the additional vitamin D and calcium.

Finally, even if we accept that taking twice the recommended dosages of vitamin D and calcium significantly reduces the risk of bone fractures for older people, **the argument ignores the possibility that** some other dosage—perhaps three times the recommended dosage—would reduce the risk of bone fractures even more. **Without ruling out this possibility, the argument's proponent cannot justifiably conclude that** twice the recommended dosage provides the optimal reduction of risk.

In sum, this is a weak argument. To strengthen it, the argument's proponent must consider and eliminate all other possible explanations for the comparatively low incidence of hip fractures among this group of women. **The proponent must also provide evidence that** this group of women are representative of older people generally in ways that might affect the incidence of hip fractures—aside from their vitamin D and calcium intake. **To better assess the argument, I would need more information about** other means of preventing bone loss in older adults, and whether such other means are more or less effective than taking twice the recommended dosage of vitamin D and calcium.

【参考译文】

这个论述做出了一个结论：为了最大限度地减少老人体内的骨质流失及因此而导致骨折的危险，老人应该服用双倍于一般建议的维生素 D 和钙的剂量。为证实这个结论，该论点的支持者引用了一个针对一群住在疗养院里的 80 多岁的法国女性做的为期三年的研究。经过三年的举重锻炼并服用上面所说剂量的维生素 D 和钙后，据观察发现，这群妇女患髋骨骨折的几率比她们的同龄人要少。这个论点存在着几处缺陷，因此不能使人信服。

首先，论证不合理地假设造成这群妇女比同龄人患髋骨骨折几率小的原因是那些额外的维生素 D 和钙，而不是举重锻炼。其实完全有可能是举重锻炼而不是那些增补剂起了保持骨质含量的作用。此外，众所周知，举重锻炼可以加强肌肉力量，提高协调性和灵活性，这些反过来可以降低意外跌倒和其他创伤的可能性。因此，举重锻炼也可以在这方面做出解释。

这个论证还忽视了许多其他可能可以用来解释这群妇女患髋骨骨折的几率比较小的原因。例如，也许一开始这些妇女的身体就比她们的同龄人要结实。或者也许这群人所住的疗养院提供了特殊保障以防意外受伤，而大多数老人通常是得不到这种特殊待遇的。又或者可能因为饮食文化习惯或遗传体质的不同，法国人不像其他人那么容易患骨质流失。同理，也有可能妇女本身就比男人不容易患骨质流失。如果以上任何假设成立的话，将削弱那个结论，即髋骨骨折几率的降低归功于添加的维生素 D 和钙。

最后，即使我们同意加倍服用建议剂量的维生素 D 和钙对降低老人骨折的危险效果显著，本文忽视了这样一种可能，即某些其他剂量——或许三倍于一般建议服用的剂量——更能降低骨折的危险。没有排除这种可能性，论点的支持者就不能无可非议地断定加倍服用一般建议的剂量能达到降低危险的最佳效果。

总之，这是一个没有力度的论证。为了加强其效力，论点的支持者必须考虑到所有其他可能解释这群妇女患骨折的几率相对较低的因素，并对它们进行排除。支持者还必须提供证据证明，除了她们服用维生素 D 和钙的剂量以外，在可能影响髋骨骨折发病率的其他方面，这群妇女可以代表一般的老年人。为了更好评价这个论证，我需要了解更多其他可以防止老年人骨质流失的方法的信息，以及这些其他的方法和加倍服用一般建议的维生素 D 和钙的剂量相比效果如何。

【逻辑问题提纲】

本文作者一共攻击了原文的三处缺陷：

1. 试验结果未必说明是 Vd 和钙导致骨折发生率的减少，也有可能是举重活动产生了效果。

2. 作者没有考虑试验对象在其他方面诸如饮食、体质、基因等的差异。

3. 作者没有考虑除了文中所推荐的治疗方案以外的其他可能更有效减少骨折的方法。

● 逻辑思路提示：本文所依据的论据又是一个典型的对比试验，试验者通过让一组法国妇女服用大剂量的 Vd 和钙来验证这种方法是否能预防骨折。如上一题所述，这一试验结果的有效性基于两条前提：

1) 试验的对比参照物初始状态相同，或没有其他差别，也就是这些法国妇女在参加试验前的身体状况应该和一般人群没有显著差异，但很明显这一前提不一定能保证，比如有可能这些妇女的体质本来就好于一般水平因而本来就不容易骨折，本文论证的第二点就是从这一前提出发，指出可能是这些妇女的基因、饮食，以及养老院的安全措施导致骨折发生率低。

2) 试验过程中除了要验证的因素以外，其他条件没有发生变化。但本文试验很明显不能保证这一前提，因为试验对象在服用 Vd 和钙的同时，还参加举重运动，因而我们也就无从判断到底是 Vd 和钙还是举重导致骨折减少，这是本文论证的第一点。

本文的试验还有一个缺陷就是试验对象只有女性，因而文中所提到的预防骨折的方法对于男性是否有效是值得怀疑的。

Argument 172　The **Mozart School of Music**

The Mozart School of Music should obviously be the first choice of any music student aware of its reputation. First of all, the Mozart School stresses intensive practice and training, so that students typically begin their training at a very young age. Second, the school has ample facilities and up-to-date professional equipment, and its faculty includes some of the most distinguished music teachers in the world. Finally, many Mozart graduates have gone on to be the best known and most highly paid musicians in the nation.

【参考译文】 莫扎特音乐学校显然应该是所有知道其声誉的学音乐学生的第一选择。首先，莫扎特学校强调强化的练习和训练，因而学生通常在很小的时候就开始接受训练。其次，学校拥有充足的设备和最先进的专业器具，其员工包括一些全球最著名的音乐教师。最后，很多莫扎特学校的毕业生已经成为全国最有名而且收入最高的音乐家。

This argument concludes that the Mozart School should be the first choice of any music student aware of its reputation **for** (1) its intensive practice requirements for students of all ages; (2) its outstanding facilities, up-to-date equipment, and distinguished faculty; and (3) the accomplishments of its graduates. **Although the evidence provided strongly suggests that** this school would be an excellent choice for certain prospective students, **the conclusion that** it should be the first choice for any prospective music student **is indefensible**—in three respects.

First, the fact that the Mozart School is known for its intensive practice and training regimen for even the youngest students **suggests that** the school might be suitable for certain child proteges, **but**

perhaps not for children for whom a more balanced education would be more prudent. **For that matter**, many older students with other interests and activities would no doubt find the intensity and time commitment that the Mozart program requires unfeasible or undesirable.

Secondly, in all likelihood the outstanding facilities, equipment, and faculty come at a considerable price to students—in the form of high tuition. **Thus, the argument seems to assume that** for all prospective music students money is no object when it comes to musical training. **Yet common sense informs me that** many students would place a higher priority on affordable training than on the specific features that the argument touts.

Thirdly, although the fact that many famous performers and highly-paid performers are among the school's graduates **might be relevant to** students with the requisite natural talent and motivation to attain these lofty goals, **for others this feature would not be relevant. For example**, some prospective students would no doubt wish to focus their study on musicology, theory, composition, or even performance—not to become famous or highly-paid performers but rather to prepare for careers in music education. Other prospective students might not aspire to make music their eventual vocation at all. Thus, some other school—one with a less rigorous performance-oriented approach—might be a better choice for less-gifted students and for those with other aspirations.

In sum, the Mozart School's features **do not justify the argument's sweeping conclusion that** the school should be the first choice for every music student. **To strengthen the argument, its proponent must show at the very least that** the school would be affordable to any prospective student. **To better assess the argument I would need more information about** what non-performance music programs the school offers, and whether Mozart students of various ages have any choice in how intensely they are required to practice and train.

【参考译文】

　　这篇论证断定莫扎特学校应该是任何知道其声誉的学音乐的学生的首选，因为：（1）对各个年龄段的学生的强化练习的要求；（2）先进的设备、最新式的器材和卓越的教职工；以及（3）毕业生的成就。虽然所提供的证据能够证明这所学校将是某些未来的学生的极佳选择，但是它将是任何未来的学音乐的学生的第一选择的结论在三个方面是站不住脚的。

　　首先，莫扎特学校以其强化练习和常规训练而闻名，对于最小的学生也是如此。这暗示了这所学校适于某些受保护的儿童，但是，对于一些想得到更加均衡的教育的孩子来讲，这所学校也许并不适合。而且有其他兴趣和活动的很多更年长的学生无疑将发现莫扎特课程所要求的强度和时间承诺是不现实的或不受欢迎的。

　　第二，很可能先进的设备、器材和教职工是一笔相当大的花费，并且以高额学费的形式平摊到了学生头上。因此，这篇论证似乎假定当涉及音乐训练时，对于所有未来的学音乐的学生来讲，金钱是不成问题的。然而常识告诉我很多学生把可承受的学费放在首位，而不是论证所吹捧的具体的特征。

　　第三，虽然很多著名表演者和高额收入的表演者是这个学校的毕业生这一事实可能对于一些学生来说是有重要意义的，这些学生具备必不可少的自然禀赋和取得极高目标的动机，但对于其他人来讲这个事实并没有意义。例如，一些未来的学生可能想把他们的研究集中于音乐学、理论、作曲，甚至是表演，他们并不希望成为著名表演者或有着高额收入的表演者，而是希望为音乐教育工作做准备。其他未来的学生可能根本就没有立志将音乐作为他们最终的职业。因此，一些其他在表演教学方面不那么严格的学校可能是那些天分低一些和那些有其他目标学生的更好选择。

总之，莫扎特学校的这些特征没有有力支持莫扎特学校应该是每个学音乐学生的第一选择的结论。为了加强此论证，它的支持者必须至少说明学校学费对于任何未来的学生都是可承受的。为了更好地评价此论证，我需要更多的信息，包括学校提供了哪些非表演性的音乐课程，以及莫扎特学校各年龄段的学生是否可以选择他们练习和训练的强度。

【逻辑问题提纲】

本文作者一共攻击了原文的三处缺陷：

1. 莫扎特学校在音乐方面进行强化训练的事实对于那些希望在其他学科也全面发展的学生来说并没有吸引力。

2. 学校的先进设备和师资有可能导致高昂的学费，从而使很多学生无法负担。

3. 该学校很多毕业生成为知名演奏家的事实对于那些希望成为作曲家、音乐教育家的学生来说同样没有吸引力。

● 逻辑思路提示：原题目的论证表面上看无懈可击，作者提出的论据似乎确实说明莫扎特学校是一流的音乐学校，但当我们把这些看似有力的论据和他的结论结合起来的时候就能发现其中的问题。这篇范文所攻击的三点究其根本是从题目第一句话结论的一个绝对化词汇 any 展开的。确实莫扎特学校可能在音乐教育方面有一些独到之处，但不能草率认为所有学生都应该选择它，因为每个学生的目标、经济状况可能不一样。本题还有一个可以攻击的点是最后一句论据，这里暗含了一个因果关系错误，即作者没有证据表明是莫扎特学校的音乐教育导致了这些知名演奏家的成功，而可能有其他因素，比如天分、机遇等造成了他们的出名。

【语言提示】

● 开头段句式：Although the evidence provided strongly suggests that ..., the conclusion that ... is indefensible.

● 论证段句式：Thirdly, although the fact that ... might be relevant to ..., for others this feature would not be relevant.

● 结尾段句式：In sum, ... do not justify the argument's sweeping conclusion that ...

Argument 173　International **cover stories** and magazine sales

The following is a memorandum issued by the publisher of a newsmagazine, Newsbeat, in the country of Dinn.

"Our poorest-selling magazine issues over the past three years were those that featured international news stories on their front covers. Over the same period, competing news-magazines have significantly decreased the number of cover stories that they devote to international news. Moreover, the cost of maintaining our foreign bureaus to report on international news is increasing. Therefore, we should decrease our emphasis on international news and refrain from displaying such stories on our magazine covers."

【参考译文】过去三年中，我们销量最低的几期杂志是在封面上刊登了国际新闻报道的那几期。在同一时期，与我们竞争的几种新闻刊物显著减少了与国际新闻有关的封面文章的数量。而且，我们用于维持国外部报道国际新闻的费用正在增加。因此，我们应该降低对于国际新闻的强调程度，并且避免把这类消息刊登在杂志封面上。

In this memo, the publisher of the magazine *Newsbeat* claims that to maximize sales the magazine should decrease its emphasis on international news and refrain from displaying such stories on its covers. To support this conclusion the publisher points out that the magazine's poorest-selling issues during the last three years have been those with cover stories about international events, and that during this same period the number of international cover stories appearing in other news magazines has decreased. On several grounds, this evidence lends little credible support for the memo's conclusion.

First of all, the fact that the magazine's poorest-selling issues were the ones with international cover stories might be explained by a variety of factors. Perhaps international events themselves were not as interesting during those periods. If so, it might be a mistake to refrain from emphasizing international events when those events are interesting enough to stimulate sales. Or perhaps the news magazine business is seasonal, or cyclical, and those particular issues would have sold more poorly regardless of the cover story. In short, without ruling out other possible explanations for the relatively poor sales of those particular issues the publisher cannot justifiably conclude that international cover stories were the cause of the relatively poor sales.

Secondly, the memo fails to indicate whether other magazines experienced an increase or a decrease in sales by reducing their emphasis on international news. It is possible, for instance, that the other magazines experienced declining sales even for issues focusing only on domestic news. If so, then the publisher's recommendation would make little sense. On the other hand, if other magazines experienced the same correlation between cover story and sales volume, this fact would lend considerable support to the publisher's conclusion that international cover stories were responsible for poor sales.

Thirdly, the memo cites increasing costs of maintaining international news bureaus as an additional reason to de-emphasize international news. While this fact does lend support to the publisher's suggestion, the publisher overlooks the possibility that if other news magazines de-emphasize international coverage due to increasing bureau costs, *Newsbeat* might turn out to be the only magazine covering international news, which in turn might actually stimulate sales. It would be hasty to implement the publisher's suggestion without acknowledging and exploring this possible scenario.

In conclusion, the memo is unconvincing as it stands. To strengthen the argument, the ～～～～ must show that it was the international covers of *Newsbeat*, and not some oth～～ ～～～～ ～～～ ～～ sponsible for the relatively poor sales of issues with those covers. To ～～～ ～～～～ ～～～ ommendation that *Newsbeat* should de-emphasize international ne～～ ～～～～ ～～～ changes in sales volume other news magazines experienced by d～～ ～～～～ ～～～ would also need more information about the impact that increas～～ ～～～～ presently competing with *Newsbeat* in the area of internatio～～

【参考译文】

在这份备忘录里,《新闻采访区》杂志的出版商声称, ～～～～
对国际新闻的重视度, 并且避免在封面上刊登此类报道。 ～～～
三年期间, 杂志销售额最低的几期是那些以国际事件为封面 ～～～
志里出现国际封面报道的数量已经减少。由于以下几个理由 ～～～
乏可信度。

Argument ～～
The followi～
lege, a private inst～
"We recommend～
ther than admit men in～
education, arguing that i～

首先，杂志销售额最低的几期是以国际事件为封面的那几期这个事实可以由多种因素解释。或许在那段时期国际事件本身就不是那么有趣。如果是这样的话，当那些事件变得有趣并足以刺激销售时，不关注国际事件可能是一个错误。或者也许新闻杂志的销售是季节性的，或是周期性的，并且不管封面报道如何，那特别的几期可能更不好出售。简而言之，如果没有排除对这特别的几期销售额相对较低的其他可能的解释，出版商不能无可辩驳地断定国际性的封面报道是导致销售额相对较低的原因。

第二，备忘录没能指出其他杂志是否通过降低对国际新闻的关注度，使得销售额增多或减少。例如，很可能其他杂志仅仅关注国内新闻的那几期的销售额也下降了。如果是这样的话，那么出版商的建议就没有多大的意义了。另一方面，如果其他杂志的封面报道和销售量之间也有同样的相互关系，这个事实将给予出版商的结论相当大的支持，即国际性封面报道是低销售额的起因。

第三，备忘录把维持国外部所需的逐渐增长的开销作为减少对国际新闻的关注度的另外一个原因。这个事实确实在一定程度上支持出版商的建议，但出版商忽视了一个可能性，即如果其他新闻杂志由于办公费的增加而减少国际报道范围，《新闻采访区》可能最终是报道国际新闻的惟一的一份杂志，这反过来实际上可能刺激销路。如果没有考虑和研究这种可能的情况，执行出版商的建议将是草率的。

总之，就目前情况看，备忘录不能令人信服。为了加强此论证，出版商必须说明是由于新闻独家报道的国际封面，而非其他一些因素，使得有着这些封面的那几期杂志销售额相对较低。为了更好地评价出版商关于《新闻采访区》应降低对国际新闻的关注度的建议，我们需要知道其他新闻杂志降低对国际新闻的关注度后销售额有何变化。我们也需要更多的信息，了解逐渐增长的办公费用对目前在国际新闻领域与《新闻采访区》相竞争的其他杂志的影响。

【逻辑问题提纲】

本文作者一共攻击了原文的三处缺陷：

1. 文中所提到的杂志销量下降有可能是其他方面原因导致的，而并非因为在封面刊登了国际新闻（把同时性混淆为因果性的错误）。

2. 作者没有指出那些减少了以国际新闻为封面的杂志销量的变化（缺乏比较的错误）。

3. 作者没有考虑到保留国际新闻可能带来的好处。

【语言提示】

● 开头段句式：On several grounds, this evidence lends little credible support for the memo's conclusion.

● 论证段句式：(1) If so, then the publisher's recommendation would make little sense. (2) While this fact does lend support to the publisher's suggestion, the publisher overlooks the possibility that ... (3) It would be hasty to implement the publisher's suggestion without acknowledging and exploring this possible scenario.

174　Should **Grove College** adopt a coeducational policy?

　　　　ng recommendation was made by the president and administrative staff of Grove Col-
　　　　itution, to the college's governing committee.

　　　　that Grove College preserve its century-old tradition of all-female education
　　　　to its programs. It is true that a majority of faculty members voted in favor of
　　　　would encourage more students to apply to Grove. But eighty percent of

the students responding to a survey conducted by the student government wanted the school to remain all female, and over half of the alumni who answered a separate survey also opposed coeducation. Keeping the college all-female, therefore, will improve morale among students and convince alumni to keep supporting the college financially."

【参考译文】我们建议格罗夫学院保留其已有百年历史的女校传统，而不是允许录取男性。确实有大部分教职工投票赞成男女同校，认为这会使更多的学生申请格罗夫。但由学生自治会所组织的一次调查中，有80％给予反馈的学生要求学校维持女校形式，并且在回应了一次单独调查的校友中超过一半的人也反对男女同校。因此，维持女校形式将促进学生的精神状态，并且让校友继续对学院进行财政资助。

In this memo, Grove College's administration recommends preserving its tradition of admitting only female students. **The administration admits that** most faculty members are in favor of a co-educational policy as a means of encouraging more students to apply to Grove. **But the administration defends its recommendation by citing** a student government survey in which 80％ of student respondents and more than 50％ of alumni respondents reported that they favor the status quo. **The administration reasons that** preserving the status quo would improve student morale and help ensure continued alumni donations to Grove. **This argument is flawed in several critical respects.**

First, the memo provides no evidence that the results of either of the two surveys are statistically reliable. For example, suppose newer students tend to be content with the all-female policy while students who have attended Grove for a longer time would prefer a co-educational policy. **If** a disproportionate number of the survey's respondents were newer students, then the survey results would distort the student body's opinion as a group. **With respect to** the alumni survey, perhaps fewer alumni who donate substantial sums to Grove responded to the survey than other alumni did. **If so, then the survey results would distort the comparison between** the total amount of future donations under the two scenarios. **Besides, the memo provides no information about what percentage of** Grove's students and alumni responded to the surveys; **the lower the percentages, the less reliable the results of the surveys.**

Secondly, the administration hastily assumes that Grove's alumni as a group would be less inclined to donate money merely if Grove begins admitting male students. This aspect of Grove's admission policy **is only one of many factors that might affect** alumni donations. **For example, since** Grove's faculty are generally in favor of changing the policy, **perhaps** the change would improve faculty morale and therefore the quality of instruction, in turn having a positive impact on alumni donations. **And, if** the particular alumni who are in a position to make the largest contributions recognize faculty morale as important, an increase in donations by these individuals might very well offset a decline in smaller donations by other alumni.

Finally, the administration's argument that student morale would improve under the status quo **is logically unsound** in two respects. **First, the administration provides no reason why** morale would improve, as opposed to remaining at its current level, if the status quo is simply maintained. **Second, the administration cannot logically determine** how the morale of the student body would be affected under a co-educational policy until it implements that policy and takes into account the morale of the new male students along with that of all female students.

In sum, the administration has failed to convince me that maintaining Grove's all-female policy would be more likely to improve student morale and help ensure continued alumni donations than moving to a co-educational policy. **To better assess the argument I would need detailed information about** the two surveys to determine whether the respondents as groups were representative of their respective populations. **To bolster its recommendation the administration must provide better evidence—** perhaps by way of a reliable alumni survey that takes into account respondents' financial status and history of donations—**that** prospective donor alumni would be strongly opposed to a co-educational policy and would be less inclined to donate money were Grove to implement such a policy.

【参考译文】

在这篇备忘录里，格罗夫学院的管理部门建议保留只接纳女学生的传统。管理部门承认大多数教职工赞成把男女同校的政策作为鼓励更多的学生申请格罗夫的方法。但是管理部门通过引用学生自治会的调查为它的建议辩护，该调查表明 80％ 做出回答的学生和超过 50％ 做出回答的校友表示他们喜欢维持现状。管理部门推论道，保留现状可以提高学生的士气，并且有助于保证校友对格罗夫进行源源不断的捐款。这篇论证在以下几个关键的方面有缺陷。

首先，备忘录没有提供证据证明这两次调查的结果根据统计是可靠的。例如，假定新学生倾向于满足纯女子学校的政策，而已入学很久的学生更喜欢男女同校的政策。如果调查的回答者中新生的比例较多，那么调查结果将可能歪曲学生作为一个整体的意见。对于文中提到的校友调查，或许比起其他校友，给格罗夫大量捐款的校友中对此调查做出反应的人要少一些。如果是这样的话，调查结果将会使这两种情况下捐款总量之间的比较不符合现实。而且，备忘录没有提供关于回答调查的格罗夫的学生和校友的百分比的信息；百分比越低，调查的结果就越不可靠。

第二，管理部门轻率地假定要是格罗夫开始招收男学生，格罗夫的校友作为一个整体将不太倾向于对其捐款。格罗夫的招生政策只是可以影响校友捐款的很多因素之一。例如，也许因为格罗夫的教员大多数赞成改变政策，这一变化将提高教员的士气，并且教育质量因此得以提高，转而对校友捐款产生积极的影响。并且，如果某些能提供最多捐款的校友认为教员的士气很重要，那么这些个人捐款的增加就可能弥补其他校友的小笔捐款的减少。

最后，管理部门关于维持现状学生的士气将提高的论点在以下两方面在逻辑上没有根据。首先，管理部门没有提供论据说明如果仅仅保持现状的话，为什么士气将会提高，而不是维持现有水平。第二，管理部门在贯彻那个政策并且连同新入校男生的士气一起考虑之前，不能合乎逻辑地确定学生整体的士气将会受到怎样的影响。

总之，管理部门没能使我确信与实行男女同校的政策相比较，保留格罗夫学院的纯女子学校的政策将可能提高学生的士气，并且有助于保证校友继续捐款。为了更好地评价这篇论证，我需要关于这两次调查的详细信息，以确定那些回答者作为整体是否能代表他们各自的群体。为了支持这篇论证，管理部门应当提供更好的证据——也许通过可靠的考虑了回答者的经济状况和捐赠历史的校友调查——来证明那些有望捐款的校友将强烈反对男女同校政策，并且当格罗夫学院贯彻此项政策时，更加不愿捐款。

【逻辑问题提纲】

本文作者一共攻击了原文的三处缺陷：

1. 文中提到的两次调查的代表性值得怀疑。
2. Grove 的校友不一定会仅仅因为男女同校这一政策变化而减少资助。
3. 作者没有提出证据说明维持现有状态将会促进学生的精神状态。

● 逻辑思路提示：本题的论据中出现了两个调查，但这两个调查的样本都有疑问：首先，在第一个调查中作者并没有指出被访学生的范围，因而他们的观点未必有代表性；其次，在第二个调查中又出现了对调查对象的经典质疑：完全有可能是那些反对同校政策的校友更愿意回答问卷，因而其结果仍不一定具有代表性，另外，作者也没有调查那些反对同校政策的校友所提供的财政资助的数额，或者那些提供资助较多的校友对于同校政策的态度，因而同校政策会影响资助的看法是站不住脚的。本文还有一个可以攻击的错误是没有全面理性衡量一个行为措施的正负得失，即没有考虑男女同校所可能带来的好处，比如使学生更加活跃，在各方面能够更全面地发展等。

【论证展开】

攻击调查样本代表性的方式：在攻击样本数量不一定足够，调查结果不一定有代表性的时候，我们可以使用本文的论证语言：先用 First, the memo provides no evidence that the results of either of the two surveys are statistically reliable 指出样本的缺陷，然后用 the memo provides no information about what percentage of ... responded to the surveys; the lower the percentages, the less reliable the results of the surveys 指出作者没有告诉我们样本是否有覆盖面、代表性和随机性，接着可以用推测法展开。

【语言提示】

● 开头段句式：the administration defends its recommendation by citing ...

● 论证段句式：(1) First, the memo provides no evidence that the results of either of the two surveys are statistically reliable. (2) Besides, the memo provides no information about what percentage of ... responded to the surveys; the lower the percentages, the less reliable the results of the surveys. (3) ... is only one of many factors that might affect ...

Argument 176 The health benefits of **Venadial**

The following is a memorandum from the sales director to the president of the Healthy-and-Good food company.

"A recent study indicates that Venadial, a new margarine currently produced only in the country of Alta, actually reduces cholesterol levels. Derived from the resin of pine trees, Venadial works by activating a metabolic response that is not yet well understood. However, cholesterol levels fell ten to fifteen percent among participants in the study who consumed Venadial daily, and the risk of heart attack by one-third. In addition, the new margarine is so popular that stores in Alta are unable to keep it on their shelves. Therefore, if our company obtains the exclusive right to sell Venadial internationally, our profits are sure to increase substantially within a very short time."

【参考译文】 最近一次研究表明，当前仅在阿尔塔生产的新的人造黄油维纳戴尔实际可以降低胆固醇指标。维纳戴尔从松树树脂中提炼而来，它通过激活一种现在还未完全明确的代谢反应发生作用。然而，在那些每天食用维纳戴尔的研究对象中，胆固醇指标下降了 10～15%，心脏病发病率下降了三分之一。而且，这种新的人造黄油非常受欢迎，以至于在阿尔塔的商店中往往一抢而光。因此，如果本公司取得维纳戴尔的全球独家代理权，我们的利润肯定能够在很短的时间内显著增长。

In this memo, the sales director of Healthy-and-Good food company recommends obtaining the exclusive right to sell the new margarine Venadial internationally in order to increase company profits substantially and quickly. **To support this recommendation the director points out that**, in a recent study, participants who consumed Venadial daily experienced a decrease in their cholesterol level and in their risk of heart attack. **The director also points out that** in Alta, the only country where Venadial is currently produced, this margarine is extremely popular among consumers. **This argument contains several critical flaws, which render it unpersuasive.**

First of all, the memo lacks sufficient information about how the study was conducted to determine what conclusions, if any, can be drawn from it. Unless all other conditions potentially affecting cholesterol level and heart-attack risk remained constant during the study, and unless the study included a statistically significant number of participants, **any conclusions from the study are simply unreliable.** **Moreover, the memo fails to indicate** whether the study also included a distinct group of participants who did not consume Venadial daily. **If it did, then the comparison of** cholesterol levels and heart attacks between the two groups **would help us to assess the strength of the memo's claims** about the health benefits of Venadial.

Secondly, the memo unfairly assumes that since Venadial is popular in Alta it will also be popular in other countries. Consumer tastes in foods like margarine, as well as concerns about health matters such as cholesterol level, vary widely from country to country. **It is quite possible that** consumers in Alta enjoy the taste of Venadial more than other consumers would, or that consumers in Alta are more concerned than the average person about cholesterol level and heart attacks. **Since the memo provides no evidence that** tastes and health concerns of Alta consumers are representative of those of people generally, **the sales director's conclusion that** Venadial will be popular elsewhere **is unjustifiable**, at least based on the memo.

Thirdly, even if Venadial is shown conclusively to carry the touted health benefits and to be popular worldwide, Healthy-and-Good will not necessarily earn a substantial profit by acquiring international rights to sell Venadial. **The memo provides no information about** the costs involved in manufacturing and distributing Venadial—only that it is derived from pine-tree resin and has been produced only in Alta. **Perhaps** Venadial can be derived only from certain pine trees located in Alta and surrounding regions. **If so**, then the costs of procuring Venadial might prevent the company from earning a profit. **In short, without more information about supply, demand, and production costs, it is impossible to determine whether the company can earn a profit from** acquiring international rights to sell Venadial.

In sum, the memo's recommendation is not well supported. Before I can accept it, the sales director must supply clearer evidence that (1) Venadial contributes to lower cholesterol level and decreased heart-attack risk, (2) consumers outside of Alta would prefer Venadial over alternative products, and (3) the revenue from sales of Venadial would significantly outweigh the costs of producing and distributing the product.

【参考译文】

　　在这个备忘录里，康好食品公司（Healthy-and-Good food company）的销售主管建议公司购买新产品维纳戴尔（Venadial）人造黄油在国际市场上的专销权，这样可以显著并迅速地增加公司的利润。为了支持这个建议，主管指出，一项新近的研究发现，参与该研究的每天都食用维纳戴尔的人的胆固醇含量减少了，心脏病发作的几率也降低了。这个主管还指出，在阿尔塔这个目前惟一一个生产维纳戴尔的国家里，这种人造黄油在消费者中极其受欢迎。这个论证包含几处严重错误，导致它没有说服力。

　　首先，这个备忘录缺乏足够的关于那个研究是怎么进行的信息，以确定可以从中总结出什么结论，如果有的话。除非所有其他可能影响胆固醇含量和心脏病发作危险的潜在条件在研究进行期间都保持不变，并且该研究包括有统计学意义的参加者的数量，否则根据这个研究得出的任何结论都是不可靠的。而且，备忘录也没有表明该研究是否也包括另外一组人，这些人没有每天食用维纳戴尔。如果有的话，那么在两个组中进行胆固醇含量和心脏病发作危险的比较，将有助于我们确定备忘录的关于维纳戴尔对健康的好处的断言的说服力。

第二，这个备忘录还想当然地认为，维纳戴尔既然在阿尔塔受欢迎，那么它在其他国家也将受欢迎。消费者对人造黄油等食物的口味，以及对胆固醇含量等健康问题的关注度，都会因国家不同而有很大的差异。有可能阿尔塔的消费者比其他国家的消费者要喜欢维纳戴尔的味道，或者阿尔塔的消费者比普通人要关心胆固醇含量和心脏病发作危险。因为这个备忘录没有提供任何证据证明阿尔塔的消费者的口味及对健康的关心度可以代表普通人，所以该销售主管所做的关于维纳戴尔在别的地方也会受欢迎的结论就是不合理的，至少根据这个备忘录上的东西做出这个结论是不合理的。

第三，即使事实最终证明维纳戴尔确实如销售主管所说对健康有好处，并且确实在世界范围内广受欢迎，康好食品公司就算得到了维纳戴尔在国际市场上的专销权，也不一定就可以赚到相当可观的利润。这个备忘录没有提供有关生产和配送维纳戴尔所需成本的信息——仅提到这种人造黄油来源于松树的树脂，并且只在阿尔塔生产。或许维纳戴尔只能从位于阿尔塔和周边地区的某种松树中提取。这样的话，为获得维纳戴尔而支出的费用可能会妨碍公司挣得利润。简而言之，如果没有更多有关产品的供应、需求以及生产成本的信息，那么就不可能确定该公司获得维纳戴尔在国际市场上的专销权后是否能够赢利。

总之，该主管没有很好地运用证据支持这个备忘录里写的建议。要使我接受它，这个销售主管必须提供如下更加详实的证据：(1) 维纳戴尔有助于降低胆固醇含量以及减少心脏病发作危险；(2) 与其他同类产品相比，阿尔塔之外的其他国家的消费者会更喜欢维纳戴尔；(3) 销售维纳戴尔的收入会明显地多于生产和配送这种产品的费用。

【逻辑问题提纲】

本文作者一共攻击了原文的三处缺陷：

1. 作者没有告诉我们文中提到的调查的具体过程，因而其结果是否有效值得怀疑；另外作者也没有把食用维纳戴尔和不食用的人群做相应的比较来确定吃这种黄油和降低发病率之间的关系。

2. 由于口味和对健康的关注点不同，维纳戴尔在阿尔塔受欢迎未必保证它在其他地方也有很大销量。

3. 作者没有考虑维纳戴尔的生产和分销成本，过高的成本可能导致公司无利可图。

● 逻辑思路提示：

本文作者所攻击的是三个最经典、最常见的 Argument 论证点：

1) 调查的过程与样本代表性问题，以及在建立两事物间因果联系时缺乏相应的对比的错误。

2) 以特殊推一般，以局部推整体的差异范围的草率推广。

3) 没有全面衡量某措施的正负得失，没有比较成本与收益。

【论证展开】

论证作者没有全面衡量投入与产出的语言。我们可以参照本文攻击第三点的语言来论述其他题目中出现的类似问题：首先用 A will not necessarily earn a substantial profit by ... 的句型指出作者所说的措施未必为 A 带来巨额利润，然后用 The memo provides no information about the costs involved in ... 来引导具体分析，用推测和列举法指出该措施可能需要那些额外成本，接着指出 If so, then the costs of ... might prevent the company from earning a profit. 最后用 In short, without more information about supply, demand, and production costs, it is impossible to determine whether the company can earn a profit from ... 来作为段落小总结。

【语言提示】

● 论证段句式：(1) First of all, the memo lacks sufficient information about how the study was conducted to determine what conclusions, if any, can be drawn from it. (2) Unless all other conditions potentially affecting ... remained constant during the study, and unless the study included a statistically significant number of participants, any conclusions from the study are simply unreliable. (3) If it did, then the comparison of ... would help us to assess the strength of the memo's claims about ... (4) In short, without more information about supply, demand, and production costs, it is impossible to determine whether the company can earn a profit from ...

● 结尾段句式：Before I can accept it, the sales director must supply clearer evidence that ...

Argument 178　Employee compensation at **National Brush Company**

The following appeared in the annual report from the president of the National Brush Company.

"In order to save money, we at the National Brush Company have decided to pay our employees for each brush they produce instead of for the time they spend producing brushes. We believe that this policy will lead to the production of more and better brushes, will allow us to reduce our staff size, and will enable the company factories to operate for fewer hours-resulting in savings on electricity and security costs. These changes will ensure that the best workers keep their jobs and that the company will earn a profit in the coming year."

【参考译文】为节省开支，我们国家刷子公司决定不再按员工生产刷子的工时支付工资，而是按他们生产刷子的数量来支付。我们相信这一政策将会导致刷子产量和质量的提高，将会减少我们的员工数量，并将会使工厂能够减少运营时间从而导致电费和保安费用的节省。这些改革将保证那些最好的工人留在这里工作，公司将会在来年有赢利。

In this report, the president of National Brush Company (NBC) concludes that the best way to ensure that NBC will earn a profit next year is for the company to pay its workers according to the number of brushes they produce—rather than hourly. **To support this conclusion, the president claims that** the new policy will result in the production of more and better brushes, which in turn will allow NBC to reduce its staff size and operating hours, thereby cutting expenses. **This argument is fraught with dubious assumptions, which render it entirely unconvincing.**

First of all, the argument relies on the unsubstantiated assumption that the new policy will motivate workers to produce brushes more quickly. Whether this is the case will depend, of course, on the amount earned per brush and the rate at which workers can produce brushes. It will also depend on the extent to which NBC workers are content with their current income level. **Lacking evidence that** the new policy would result in the production of more brushes, **the president cannot convince me that** this policy would be an effective means to ensure a profit for NBC in the coming year.

Even if the new policy does motivate NBC workers to produce more brushes, **the president's ar-**

gument depends on the additional assumption that producing brushes more quickly can be accomplished without sacrificing quality. In fact, the president goes further by predicting an increase in quality. Yet, common sense informs me that, if the production process otherwise remains the same, quicker production is likely to reduce quality—and in any event certainly not increase it. And a decline in quality might serve to diminish the value of NBC's brushes in the marketplace. Thus, the ultimate result of the new policy might be to reduce NBC's revenue and, in turn, profits.

Even assuming that as the result of the new policy NBC's current workforce produces more brushes without sacrificing quality, reducing the size of the workforce and the number of operating hours would serve to offset those production gains. Admittedly, by keeping the most efficient employees NBC would minimize the extent of this offset. Nevertheless, the president provides no evidence that the result would be a net gain in production. Without any such evidence the president's argument that the new policy will help ensure profitability is highly suspect.

In sum, the president has failed to provide adequate evidence to support his claim that the new policy would serve to ensure a profit for NBC in the coming year. To strengthen the argument, NBC should conduct a survey or other study to demonstrate not only its workers' willingness to work more quickly but also their ability to maintain quality at a quicker pace. To better assess the argument I would need detailed financial projections comparing current payroll and other operating costs with projected costs under the new policy—in order to determine whether NBC is likely to be more profitable under the proposed scheme.

【参考译文】

在这份报告里，国家刷子公司（NBC）的总裁断定要保证公司明年将赢利的最好方法就是改变支付公司工人的标准，即把原来以工作小时为标准变为根据他们所生产的刷子的数量为标准。为了支持这个结论，总裁声称这个新政策将导致刷子的产量增多、质量提高，而这反过来也将使国家刷子公司（NBC）能够裁减员工、减少工作时间，并因此削减支出。这个论证充满了可疑假定，致使它完全不能使人信服。

首先，这个论证依赖于一个无确实根据的假定，即新政策将激励工人更迅速地生产刷子。事实是否如此当然取决于从每把刷子上可挣得多少钱，以及工人生产刷子的效率；还将取决于国家刷子公司（NBC）的工人对他们目前的收入水平的满意度。在缺乏证据证实新政策会导致刷子产量增多的情况下，这位总裁不能让我相信这个政策是保证国家刷子公司（NBC）来年赢利的一个有效的方法。

即使新政策确实可以激励国家刷子公司（NBC）的工人生产更多的刷子，这位总裁的论证还依据另一个假定，即达到更加迅速地生产刷子的目标的同时不会以牺牲质量为代价。实际上，这位总裁进一步预测刷子质量会提高。然而，常识告诉我，如果生产程序等其他因素保持不变的话，那么加快生产速度就很可能降低质量——总之无论如何是不会提高质量的。而质量下降可能致使国家刷子公司（NBC）的刷子的市场价值削减。因此，这个新政策的最终结果可能就是降低国家刷子公司（NBC）的收入，进而减少利润。

即使假设新政策的结果是导致国家刷子公司（NBC）现有的劳动力在没有牺牲质量的同时生产了更多的刷子，但是削减劳动力数量和减少工作小时则将抵消那些生产所得。不可否认，国家刷子公司（NBC）通过保留生产效率最高的雇员就可以使这种抵消的程度减到最小。虽然如此，那位总裁也并没有提供任何证据证明结果将是生产的净增长。如果没有任何这种证据，那么该总裁所做的关于新政策将保证获得利润的论证就非常值得怀疑。

总之，这位总裁未能提供足够的证据来支持他的断言，即新政策可以保证国家刷子公司（NBC）来年会赢利。为了加强论证的力度，国家刷子公司（NBC）应该进行一次调查来证明公司的工人不仅愿意提高工作速度，而且也具备在提高速度的同时保证质量的能力。为了更好地评价这个论证，我需要一份详细的财务预算，比较现在的薪水总额和其他运营成本以及在新政策实施后的预测成本——以确定国家刷子公司（NBC）在实行该总裁提议的方案后赢利是否可能更多。

【逻辑问题提纲】

本文作者一共攻击了原文的三处缺陷：

1. 新的政策未必带来更大的产量。

2. 单个工人产量的增加往往伴随着质量的下降，从而导致 NBC 利润的下降。

3. 减少员工人数和工作时间的措施尽管能够节约成本，但也同时导致总产量以及利润的下降，与所节约的成本相抵消。

● 逻辑思路提示：本文攻击的第一点的论述实际上并不很具有说服力，一般来说如果采取计件付酬的形式肯定会导致产量的增加，无论员工以前的收入情况如何以及单件工资是多少。但这样做一般会带来质量的下降，在论证时可以把重点放在这一问题上。

本文另一可以攻击的缺陷是在最后一句话，作者认为这种措施能使最好的工人留下而淘汰能力差一些的，但这是没有根据的。如果作者对于好员工的定义是产量高的员工的话，这一结论还可以成立，但显然我们不能仅仅考虑产量，还需要考虑产品的质量等因素。

【语言提示】

● 开头段句式：This argument is fraught with dubious assumptions, which render it entirely unconvincing.

● 论证段句式：(1) In fact, the president goes further by predicting ... (2) Without any such evidence the president's argument that ... is highly suspect.

● 结尾段句式：(1) In sum, the president has failed to provide adequate evidence to support his claim that ... (2) To strengthen the argument, NBC should conduct a survey or other study to demonstrate ...

Argument 181   Sleep and **academic performance**

From a letter to the editor of a city newspaper.

"One recent research study has indicated that many adolescents need more sleep than they are getting, and another study has shown that many high school students in our city are actually dissatisfied with their own academic performance. As a way of combating these problems, the high schools in our city should begin classes at 8:30 A.M. instead of 7:30 A.M., and end the school day an hour later. This arrangement will give students an extra hour of sleep in the morning, thereby making them more alert and more productive. Consequently, the students will perform better on tests and other assignments, and their academic skills will improve significantly."

【参考译文】最近一项研究表明，很多青少年需要更多的睡眠，另外一项研究表明，我们市很多中学生对于自己的学习成绩不满意。作为解决这些问题的途径，我市的中学应该在早上 8:30 开始上课，而不是 7:30，并且推迟一小时放学。这种安排将允许学生在早上多睡一个小时，从而使他们更加清醒和高效。因此，学生在测验和其他作业中将表现得更好，他们的学习能力将会显著提高。

This letter concludes that the academic performance of local high school students would improve if the daily school schedule were to begin and end one hour later. **To support this recommendation the letter's author cites** two studies, one showing that adolescents generally do not get enough sleep, the other showing that many local high school students are dissatisfied with their academic performance. **The recommendation relies on a series of unsubstantiated assumptions about** the habits of high school students and about the studies themselves. **As a result, the letter is not convincing.**

First of all, the letter's recommendation depends on the doubtful assumption that by beginning classes one hour later students will sleep one hour longer each night. **Experience tells us, however, that this will not necessarily be the case. Just as likely,** students will adjust to the new schedule by falling asleep one hour later. **Moreover,** by staying up one hour later at night students might very well engage in the sort of late-night social or even delinquent activities that would disrupt their productivity at school.

Secondly, the letter's conclusion relies on the assumption that one additional hour of sleep would in fact result in improved academic performance. **While this might be the case, the letter provides no evidence to substantiate this assumption. It is entirely possible that** one hour of additional sleep would not suffice. **Moreover, the letter provides no evidence that** the students who are dissatisfied with their academic performance are also the ones who would benefit from the new schedule. **It is entirely possible that** these particular students already sleep longer than most other students, or that their academic performance is already optimal. **Conversely, it is entirely possible that** those students whose academic performance could stand the greatest improvement would be unmotivated to become better students regardless of how much they sleep each night.

A final problem with the argument involves the two studies themselves. **The letter provides no information about** how either study was conducted. **Without knowing whether the sample of** adolescents studied **was representative of the overall** high school **population** in the city, **it is impossible to confidently apply the studies' results to that population. Moreover, we are not informed about the size of the sample in either study; the smaller the sample, the less reliable the study's conclusion.**

In conclusion, this letter's recommendation for beginning and ending the high school day one hour later **is not well justified. To strengthen the argument, the author must provide clear evidence that** adjusting the schedule will in fact result in the students' sleeping longer each night, and that this additional sleep will in fact improve their academic performance. **To better assess the author's recommendation, we would need more information about** the sampling method used in the two studies.

【参考译文】

　　这封信断定如果学校每日的时间表整个往后推移一个小时的话，那么当地中学生的学习成绩将提高。为了支持这个建议，这封信的作者引用了两项研究，一项研究显示青少年普遍睡眠不足，另一项研究显示很多当地中学生都对他们的学习成绩感到不满。这个建议依赖于一系列有关中学生的习惯和这两项研究本身的无确实根据的假定。因此，这封信不能令人信服。

　　首先，这封信的建议依据这么一个值得怀疑的假定，即晚一个小时开始上课，学生每天晚上将多睡一个小时。然而，经验告诉我们，事实并不一定就是这样的。学生同样可能根据这个新的时间表调整自己的习惯，而晚一个小时睡觉。而且，晚一个小时睡觉，学生可能参与一些在夜里进行的交际甚至是违法活动，而这些活动将妨碍他们在学校的学习效率。

第二，这封信的结论还建立在这个假设的基础上，即多睡一个小时确实将导致学习成绩的提高。虽然事实也有可能是这样的，但是这封信并没有提供任何证据来证明这个假设。多一个小时的睡眠时间完全可能还是不够。而且，这封信也没有提供证据证明那些对自己的学习成绩不满意的学生就是那些会因为这个新的时间表而受益的学生。完全有可能出现这种情况，也就是上面说到的这些学生已经比大部分其他学生的睡眠时间都要长，或者他们的学习成绩其实已经是他们的最佳成绩了。相反，对于那些学习成绩可能得到最大程度的提高的学生们，不管他们每天晚上睡多少个小时，都无法促使他们变成更好的学生。

这个论证的最后一个问题与两项研究本身有关。这封信没有提供任何有关这两项研究中的任何一项如何进行的信息。不知道参与研究的青少年是否能够代表城市里的整个中学生群体，我们就不可能自信地把这两个研究的结果应用于那个群体。而且，信里也没告诉我们两个研究中任何一个的样本规模；样本规模越小，研究结果的可信度就越小。

总之，这封信关于把中学的时间表整个往后推移一个小时的建议没有得到很好的论证。为了加强这个论证的力度，作者必须提供坚实的证据证明调整时间表确实可以导致学生每晚的睡眠时间延长，并且延长了睡眠时间后他们的学习成绩确实会提高。为了更好地评价作者的建议，我们还需要了解更多有关这两项研究进行取样的方法的信息。

【逻辑问题提纲】

本文作者一共攻击了原文的三处缺陷：

1. 文中提到的作息制度的改变未必保证学生有更多的睡眠，而可能使他们在晚间推迟入睡时间。

2. 增加睡眠时间未必能带来学习成绩的提高。

3. 文中提到的调查信息过于模糊，关于样本的数量和代表性都无法确认。

● 逻辑思路提示：对于本文所攻击的第二点我们也可以从因果关系的角度进行论证，即有些学生成绩不够满意未必是由于睡眠不足而导致，而是可能有其他原因。或者换句话说，作者没有直接证据能够证实延长睡眠时间对于提高学习成绩是有帮助的。

【论证展开】

论证调查样本代表性问题的语言：在阐述某些样本的情况不能推广到整体时，可以使用本文的 Without knowing whether the sample studied was representative of the overall group, it is impossible to confidently apply the studies' results to that population. 以及 we are not informed about the size of the sample in either study; the smaller the sample, the less reliable the study's conclusion. 这样的句型来进行描述，指出调查对象不一定有代表性，以及样本的数量不确定。

【语言提示】

● 开头段句式：The recommendation relies on a series of unsubstantiated assumptions about ... and as a result, the letter is not convincing.

● 论证段句式：(1) Experience tells us, however, that this will not necessarily be the case. (2) While this might be the case, the letter provides no evidence to substantiate this assumption. (3) Without knowing whether the sample studied was representative of the overall population, it is impossible to confidently apply the results to that population. (4) Moreover, we are not informed about the size of the sample in either study; the smaller the sample, the less reliable the study's conclusion.

Argument 186　**Automobile factory workers** age and productivity

The following is a recommendation from the director of personnel to the president of Professional Printing Company.

"In a recent telephone survey of automobile factory workers, older employees were less likely to report that having a supervisor present increases their productivity. Among workers aged 18 to 29, 27 percent said that they are more productive in the presence of their immediate supervisor, compared to 12 percent for those aged 30 or over, and only 8 percent for those aged 50 or over. Clearly, if our printing company hires mainly older employees, we will increase productivity and save money because of the reduced need for supervisors."

【参考译文】在最近一次对汽车工厂工人的电话调查中，年纪大一些的员工更少报告说有管理员在场会提高他们的生产效率。在 18～29 岁的员工中，27％的人说，当他们的顶头上司在场时，他们更有效率，相比之下，30 岁及以上的工人只有 12％，50 岁及以上的工人只有 8％这样认为。显然，如果我们印刷公司主要雇用年纪大一些的员工的话，我们的劳动生产率将会提高，并且将会节省开支，因为对于管理员的需求将会减少。

In this argument, the personnel director of Professional Printing Company (PPC) recommends hiring older workers in order to increase productivity, as well as to save money by reducing costs of supervision. **To support this recommendation, the director cites** an auto-industry telephone survey ostensibly showing that older workers are generally less productive under close supervision than otherwise, whereas younger workers are generally more productive under close supervision than otherwise. **This argument is flawed in several critical respects.**

A threshold problem with the argument involves the statistical reliability of the survey. The director provides no evidence that the number of respondents is statistically significant or that the respondents were representative of auto workers **in general. Lacking information about the randomness and size of the survey's sample, the director cannot make a convincing argument based on that survey.**

Even if the survey's respondents are representative of the entire population of auto workers, **the argument relies on the assumption that** the responses themselves are reliable. **Yet the director ignores the possibility that** a young, inexperienced worker is less likely to be forthright about the value of supervision—for fear of retaliation by that supervisor. **For that matter,** younger workers might not have enough experience working without supervision to determine when they are most productive. **Lacking evidence that the respondents' reports were both truthful and meaningful, the director cannot confidently draw any conclusions about** worker productivity from them.

Even assuming that the survey data accurately reflect the auto industry, **the argument unfairly assumes that** supervision affects worker productivity similarly at PPC. **Perhaps** PPC employs certain unique equipment or processes that require close worker supervision—even for older, more experienced workers. **For that matter, perhaps** youth or inexperience is an advantage in working productively at PPC, whereas in the auto industry either is a disadvantage. **In short, without accounting for possible differences between** PPC **and** auto manufacturers **the director cannot convince me that his recommendation for PPC is sound.**

The argument also assumes that older people are more experienced, and thus less likely to benefit from supervision, than younger people. **Although this assumption might generally be sound, it never-**

theless might not hold true for workers at PPC specifically. **In other words, despite** their age many younger PPC workers might be more experienced at their jobs, and therefore more productive without supervision, than many older PPC workers.

Finally, even if hiring older workers will reduce the need for supervision, **the director concludes too hastily that** PPC will save money as a result. **It is possible that** older workers command a higher wage than younger workers do. **If so**, these higher wages might offset production gains and payroll savings accruing from reduced supervision.

In sum, the survey's statistical reliability and its relevance to PPC **is questionable. To strengthen the recommendation the director must provide clear evidence that** in the printing industry, and especially at PPC, older workers are more experienced or otherwise can work more productively without supervision than younger workers. **To better assess the argument, I would need** a detailed cost-benefit analysis that accounts not only for gains in productivity but also for the possible impact of hiring only older workers on total payroll costs.

【参考译文】

在这个论述中，专业印刷公司（PPC）的人事主管建议公司聘用年龄较长的工人以提高生产率，同时可以通过减少管理费用来节约资金。为了支持这个建议，该主管引用了一个有关汽车工业的电话调查。这个调查从表面上显示，年长的工人在比较严格的监督下普遍比用不同的方式管理时生产效率要低；与此相反，年轻的工人在严格的监督下普遍比用不同的方式管理时生产效率要高。这个论述在几个关键的方面存在着缺陷。

这个论证里首先出现的问题涉及这个调查在统计意义上的可靠性。该主管没有提供任何证据证明回应者的人数达到统计学要求的足够数量，并且那些回应者能代表汽车工业的全体工人。缺乏关于这个调查的样本的随机性和规模的任何信息，该主管就无法基于那个调查做出令人信服的论证。

即使调查的回答者是整个汽车工人群体的代表，这个论证也依赖于这么一个假设，即调查的回答本身是可信的。然而该主管忽视了这个可能性，就是缺乏经验的年轻工人因生怕监督人的报复，所以在评价监督的价值时就很可能不够直截了当。同样，年轻的工人可能缺少关于在没有监督的情况下工作的足够的经验，不能确定他们在什么时候工作效率最高。在缺乏证据证实回答者的回答都是真实而有意义的情况下，该主管就不能自信地从这些回答中做出任何有关工人的生产效率的结论来。

即使假设调查数据确实准确地反映了汽车工业的状况，该论证就此认为监督对专业印刷公司（PPC）的工人生产效率也有类似的影响是不合理的。可能专业印刷公司（PPC）采用了某些要求对工人进行严格监督的独特的设备或者过程——即使对经验丰富的年长工人也是如此。同样，也有可能在专业印刷公司（PPC）年轻或者缺乏经验对高效地工作都是一种优势，尽管在汽车工业里它们中的任何一个都是一种不足。简而言之，在没有说明专业印刷公司（PPC）和汽车制造厂商之间可能存在的不同之前，该主管就不能使我确信他对专业印刷公司（PPC）的建议是合理的。

该论证还认为年长的人更有经验，因此与年轻人相比，就不太可能受益于监督。虽然这种假定在一般情况下都可能是合理的，但是仍有可能偏偏不适用于专业印刷公司（PPC）的工人。换句话说，尽管他们的年龄不大，但是许多年轻的专业印刷公司（PPC）工人可能在工作上更加熟练，因此在没有监督的情况下，生产效率比许多年长的专业印刷公司（PPC）工人更高。

最后，即使雇用年长的工人将降低对监督的需要，主管断定专业印刷公司（PPC）一定会因此而节约资金也太轻率了。可能年长的工人所索求的工资会比年轻的工人要高。如果是这样的话，那么更高的工资就可能正好抵消了增加生产所得的利润，以及因为减少监督而节省下来的薪金存款。

总之，这个调查在统计学意义上的可靠性和它与专业印刷公司（PPC）的关联性是可疑的。为了加强这个建议的说服力，该主管必须提供明确的证据证实在印刷工业领域，特别是在专业印刷公司（PPC），年长的工人经验确实更丰富，或者说在没有监督的时候比年轻的工人工作效率更高。为了更好地评价这个论证，我需要一个详细的成本效益分析，分析里不仅应该说明从生产效率上所得的利润，还应该包括只雇用年长的工人对应发的工资总额可能造成的影响。

【逻辑问题提纲】

本文作者一共攻击了原文的五处缺陷：

1. 文中所提到的调查的样本大小、代表性与随机性都没有保证，因而无法判断其对于结论的意义。

2. 年轻员工对于管理人员的作用可能的看法可能有偏差，从而导致调查结果不可信。

3. 汽车工业的情况未必能同样用于印刷出版业（错误类比的错误）。

4. 年纪大的员工一定更有经验、劳动生产率更高的假设不一定站得住脚。

5. 老员工所要求的薪酬往往也较高，因而雇用老员工未必达到作者所设想的减少成本的目的。

● 逻辑思路提示：攻击原因与攻击后果；某一事件的发生往往符合以下因果关系的联系：cause→FACT→result，即一件事既有其原因，又会造成一定后果。在 Argument 的论述中，对于作者所提出的事实、现象我们既可以攻击作者所认为的原因，也可以攻击作者基于某事实、某措施而推测预见的后果。攻击原因时即可使用我们以前提到过的用推测法、列举法列举其他可能原因的论证思路；而攻击后果时往往使用推理法、演绎法来推导出作者所没有预见到的可能后果，比如 Argument 185 中对于减少水压可能导致的恶果的推理，本题中对于雇用老员工对成本的影响的推理都属于这一论证方式，请大家学习使用。

【论证展开】

● 攻击调查样本与过程：本文攻击的第一点几乎完全用抽象的语言攻击调查，这类语言我们在前面也总结过一些，这里我们再来看看还有哪些语言形式可以使用：（1）A threshold problem with the argument involves the statistical reliability of the survey. 指出调查的可信度值得怀疑；（2）The director provides no evidence that the number of respondents is statistically significant or that the respondents were representative of . . . in general. 指出作者没有提供关于样本数量和代表性的保证；（3）Lacking information about the randomness and size of the survey's sample, the director cannot make a convincing argument based on that survey. 段落小总结，指出在不知道调查样本的数量与随机性的情况下，作者的结论是不可靠的。

● 攻击调查结果的真实性：有时调查对象对于调查问题的回答是否反映真实情况也是一个可以质疑的点。在本题中，年轻员工对于管理人员的作用的看法就值得怀疑，可能出于某种原因这些员工没有表达真实看法，或者他们对于自己的 productivity 的判断有偏差。我们可以用本文中的 Even if the survey's respondents are representative of the entire population of . . . , the argument relies on the assumption that the responses themselves are reliable. 来指出这类错误，再用推测法指出调查对象在哪些方面的回答可能出现问题，最后用 Lacking evidence that the respondents' reports were both truthful and meaningful, the director cannot confidently draw any conclusions about ... from them. 来做段落小总结。

● 攻击错误类比的方式：本文攻击的第三点是错误类比，它为我们攻击此类错误的语言又提出了一些参考：首先用 Even assuming that the survey data accurately reflect A, the argument unfairly assumes that the situation at A is similar at B. 指出 A 的情况未必能够用于类推 B；然后用推测法或列举法指出 A 与 B 之间的可能差异；最后用 In short, without accounting for possible differences between A and B the director cannot convince me that his recommendation for B is sound. 来做段落小总结。

【语言提示】

● 论证段句式：(1) A threshold problem with the argument involves the statistical reliability of the survey. (2) The director provides no evidence that ... (3) Lacking information about ... (4) Lacking evidence that ..., the director cannot confidently draw any conclusions about ... from them. (5) Even assuming that the survey data accurately reflect ..., the argument unfairly assumes that ... (6) In short, without accounting for possible differences between ... and ... the director cannot convince me that his recommendation for ... is sound. (7) Although this assumption might generally be sound, it nevertheless might not hold true for ...

● 结尾段句式：In sum, the survey's statistical reliability and its relevance to ... is questionable.

Argument 188　　The effectiveness of **pain medication**

A new report suggests that men and women experience pain very differently from one another, and that doctors should consider these differences when prescribing pain medications. When researchers administered the same dosage of kappa opioids—a painkiller—to 28 men and 20 women who were having their wisdom teeth extracted, the women reported feeling much less pain than the men, and the easing of pain lasted considerably longer in women. This research suggests that kappa opioids should be prescribed for women whenever pain medication is required, whereas men should be given other kinds of pain medication. In addition, researchers should reevaluate the effects of all medications on men versus women.

【参考译文】一项新报告表明，男性和女性对于疼痛的感受是有显著差异的，医生在开止痛药方的时候应该考虑到这种差异。当研究者把相同剂量的卡帕麻醉药——一种止痛药——分发给智齿刚刚被拔除的 28 名男子和 20 名女子的时候，女性报告她们感受的痛楚要比男性小得多，而且止痛的时间更长。这一研究说明当需要止痛药时，应该给女性服用卡帕麻醉药，而应该给男性服用其他的止痛药。而且，研究人员应该重新评估所有药品对于男性以及女性的效用。

This argument concludes that the pain medication kappa opioids（KO）should be prescribed for women but not for men. **To support this conclusion the speaker cites** a recent study involving 28 men and 20 women who took KO when having wisdom teeth removed; according to these patients' reports, the women felt less pain than the men, and for the women the easing of pain lasted longer. **The argument is flawed in several important respects.**

One problem with the argument is that since the study involved only 48 people **it is impossible to confidently draw any conclusions about the general population from it. Specifically, the argument overlooks other possible reasons why** these particular women reported less pain than the men did. The women in the study might have a higher-than-average pain threshold; conversely, the men in the study might have a lower-than-average pain threshold. **Or perhaps** this group of women are less prone to complain about pain than this group of men—due to their unusually stoical nature or their experience with painful medical procedures.

Another problem with the argument is that it overlooks other factors that might have contributed to the amount of pain these patients experienced. **Perhaps** the women's wisdom teeth were not as impacted as the men's teeth generally, so that for the women the surgery was not as invasive and painful. **Perhaps** some of the women took other medications as well to help relieve the pain. **For that matter**, some of the men might have taken certain foods or medications that counteracted the effects of KO. **In short, unless the experiment was conducted in a controlled environment in which all factors were the same for** the men as for the women, **it is impossible to draw any firm conclusions about** the comparative effectiveness of KO for the two sexes.

Even if KO is more effective for women than for men, **the argument's conclusion that** men should take another pain medication instead **is unwarranted. It is entirely possible that** KO is still the most effective pain medication for men. **Without** comparing the effectiveness of KO to that of other pain medications, **the speaker simply cannot justify his recommendation that** men avoid KO.

In sum, the argument has not convinced me that men should take a medication other than KO for pain. **To strengthen the argument the speaker must assure me that** the men and women in the study are representative of men and women generally—in terms of their dental profile, experience in handling pain, and willingness to recognize and report pain. **The speaker must also assure me that the study was performed in a controlled environment where all other factors possibly affecting** pain **remained constant. To better assess the argument I would need to know** how effective KO is compared to other medications in reducing pain for men.

【参考译文】

这个论证断定，医生在给病人开止痛药卡帕麻醉药（KO）时，应该只给妇女开而不应该给男人开。为了支持这个结论，发言者引用了一项最近对在拔智齿时服用了 KO 的 28 个男士和 20 个女士进行的研究；根据这些病人的报告，女士比男士所感觉到的疼痛要轻，并且止痛的时间也长。这个论证在几个重要的方面犯了错误。

这个论证中出现的一个问题是既然这个研究只涉及 48 个人，那么就不可能从中得出任何有关全体人口的可靠结论来，尤其是这个论证忽略了其他可能导致这些女士比男士感觉到疼痛要小得多的原因。这个研究中的女士可能具有比普通人要高的疼痛忍受阈限；相反，这个研究中的男士的疼痛忍受阈限比普通人要低。又或者可能比起那些男士，这群妇女更少抱怨疼痛——因为她们平常本性坚忍，或者对使人疼痛的医疗过程有经验。

这个论证的另一个问题是它忽略了其他可能影响这些病人所受痛苦的程度的因素。或许妇女的智齿所受的挤压力一般没有男人的牙齿那么重，因此对那些妇女来说手术没有那么大、那么痛。又或许这些妇女中的某些人还服用了其他的药物来帮助缓解疼痛。同样，也有可能是这些男人中的某些人吃了某些会削弱 KO 的药效的食物或者药物。简而言之，除非实验是在一个对于这些男人和女人所有因素都是一样的受控环境中进行的，否则就不可能总结出任何有关 KO 对两性的相对效果的强有力的结论来。

即使 KO 的效果确实对女人比对男人更显著，这篇论证也没有理由做出让男人服用其他止痛药来代替 KO 的结论。对于男人，KO 完全可能仍然是效果最好的止痛药。没有比较 KO 和其他止痛药的药效，发言者就绝对不能证明他建议男人别用 KO 是正确的。

总之，这个论证没能使我确信男人应该服用其他止痛药来代替 KO。为了加强这个论证的力度，发言者必须保证这个研究中的男人和妇女可以代表广大的男性和女性——在牙齿的情况、止痛经历及是否愿意承认并报告疼痛等方面。发言者还必须保证该研究是在一个所有其他可能影响疼痛的因素都保持不变的受控环境中进行的。为了更好地评价这个论证，我需要知道在缓解男性所受的疼痛上，KO 和其他的药物相比效果如何。

【逻辑问题提纲】

本文作者一共攻击了原文的三处缺陷：

1. 文中调查的样本数量太少，未必有代表性；而且参加试验的女性可能在性格、体质等某些方面与男性参加者不同。

2. 可能有其他因素导致女性感到的痛楚较少，而作者没有考虑这些因素。

3. 由于没有做和其他止痛药止痛效果的比较，KO 仍然有可能是对于男性来说最有效的止痛药。

● 逻辑思路提示：

1) 样本的数量（the quantity of the sample）：在很多题目中我们都攻击过样本数量的问题。作为调查，样本必须有代表性，而保证代表性的首要因素就是一定要保证足够的样本数量。本题明确指出作者只调查了 48 个样本，这对于一般性的调查显然是不充分的。

2) 本题还可以有以下攻击出发点：

 a. 拔牙所带来的痛楚的感觉和一般意义的 pain 可能是有差异的，因而 KO 对于拔牙后疼痛的作用未必能够表明它在其他情况下的疗效（差异概念的草率推广）。

 b. 对于女性应该使用 KO 作为止痛药的结论，作者也没有进行相应的比较，也许有其他的药物对于女性疼痛比 KO 更加有效（缺乏比较的错误）。

 c. 最后一句结论中"我们应该重新评估所有药物"中的绝对化词汇 all 值得怀疑。就算 KO 对于男女的效果是不同的，我们也没有理由认为其他所有药品都存在这种差异（差异范围的草率推广）。

【论证展开】

● 攻击调查样本数量不足的方式：在指出样本数量太少不足以代表整体时，我们可以用文中的句型：Since the study involved only N samples, it is impossible to confidently draw any conclusions about the general population from it. 或者把它改换成 It is impossible to draw any conclusion about the general subject from the study because the sample is too limited.

● 攻击对比试验的缺陷的方式：本题所用的试验形式是对比试验（controlled experiment），对于对比试验，我们一定要保证除了想要验证的试验因素以外的所有其他条件都是确定不变的。在攻击这一点时我们可以用这样的句型来描述：In short, unless the experiment was conducted in a controlled environment in which all factors were the same for A as for B, it is impossible to draw any firm conclusions about the comparative effectiveness of . . . for the two counterparts. 或者 The speaker must also assure me that the study was performed in a controlled environment where all other factors possibly affecting . . . remained constant.

【语言提示】

● 论证句式：

  One problem with the argument is that since the study involved only . . . it is impossible to confidently draw any conclusions about the general population from it.

Another problem with the argument is that it overlooks other factors that might have contributed to ...

In short, unless the experiment was conducted in a controlled environment in which all factors were the same for ... as for..., it is impossible to draw any firm conclusions about ...

Without ..., the speaker simply cannot justify his recommendation that ...

The speaker must also assure me that the study was performed in a controlled environment where all other factors possibly affecting ... remained constant.

Argument 192　The benefits of merging two **townships**

The following is a letter to the editor of the Roseville Gazette.

"Despite opposition from some residents of West Roseville, the arguments in favor of merging the townships of Roseville and West Roseville are overwhelming. First, residents in both townships are confused about which authority to contact when they need a service; for example, the police department in Roseville receives many calls from residents of West Roseville. This sort of confusion would be eliminated with the merger. Second, the savings in administrative costs would be enormous, since services would no longer be duplicated: we would have only one fire chief, one tax department, one mayor, and so on. And no jobs in city government would be lost—employees could simply be reassigned. Most importantly, the merger will undoubtedly attract business investments as it did when the townships of Hamden and North Hamden merged ten years ago."

【参考译文】尽管西罗斯维尔的一些居民持反对意见，支持合并罗斯维尔和西罗斯维尔的呼声还是占了上风。首先，两地区的居民经常搞不清在需要服务的时候应该和哪个机关联系；举例来说，罗斯维尔的警署接到过很多西罗斯维尔居民的电话。这种混乱可以通过合并来消除。其次，管理开支将会得到很大节省，因为服务性机构不再重复设置：我们将只有一个消防局局长、一个税务局、一个市长等等。在市政府的工作并不会失去，雇员可以被重新委任。最重要的是，合并无疑会吸引更多的商务投资，就像哈姆丹和北哈姆丹在十年前合并时所发生的那样。

This editorial recommends the merger of Roseville and West Roseville. **The author claims that** the merger would (1) eliminate confusion among both townships' residents about which authority to call for services, (2) reduce aggregate administrative costs by eliminating duplicative jobs and services, and (3) attract business investment as did the merger of Hamden and North Hamden ten years ago. **The author claims further that** the merger would result in certain job reassignments but not in the loss of any jobs for current municipal employees. **I find these claims problematic in several respects.**

First, although a merger might be necessary to eliminate current confusion about which authority to contact for services, **the editorial overlooks the possibility that** the merger will not in itself suffice to eliminate this confusion. **Specifically, until** the residents of both communities are apprised of the change and learn how to respond appropriately, confusion will continue—and perhaps even increase in the short term. **Thus,** some measure of community awareness and responsiveness might also be required for the elimination of confusion.

Secondly, the editorial seems to make two irreconcilable claims. One is that the merger will result in the elimination of certain duplicative jobs; **the other is that** no current municipal employee will become unemployed as a result of the merger. **The editorial fails to consider that** eliminating duplicative jobs would decrease the aggregate number of current municipal employees unless enough new jobs are created to offset the decrease, and that new jobs would in turn add to administrative costs. **Thus, as it stands the argument is self-contradictory, and the author must either modify it by** choosing between two competing objectives—preserving current employment levels and cutting costs—**or somehow reconcile these two objectives**.

Thirdly, the author's claim that the merger will attract business investment **relies on the hasty assumption that** the newly merged Roseville would be similar to Hamden in every way, affecting their attractiveness to business investment. **Perhaps** Hamden's business tax rates, labor pool, or even climate are more attractive than the newly merged Roseville's would be. **If so, then** the proposed merger in itself might accomplish little toward attracting business investment to Roseville. **In other words, without evidence that** Hamden and the newly merged Roseville would be equally attractive to business investments I **cannot accept the author's conclusion that** a merger will carry the same result for Roseville as for Hamden.

In sum, the editorial not only is logically unsound but also relies on several doubtful assumptions. To strengthen the argument the author must modify the recommendation to account for other measures needed to eliminate the confusion mentioned in the editorial. **The author must also provide a cost-benefit analysis that accounts for** the costs of creating new jobs to offset the elimination of duplicative jobs. **Finally, the author must show that** the new Roseville would be just as attractive to business investment as the new Hamden has been.

【参考译文】

这篇社论建议将罗斯维尔（Roseville）和西罗斯维尔（West Roseville）合并。作者声称合并将：（1）消除两镇居民在需要政府服务时不知道要找哪个机关的混乱；（2）通过削减重复的工作和服务来降低总的行政支出；（3）就像十年前合并的哈姆丹（Hamden）和北哈姆丹（North Hamden）一样吸引商业投资。作者更进一步声称，这次合并将导致某些工作重新分配，但并不会导致现在的政府雇员失业。我认为这些断言在几个方面很值得怀疑。

首先，虽然合并可能对消除在寻求哪个机关来服务时产生的困惑是必需的，但是这篇社论忽略了光凭这个合并本身并不足以消除这种混乱的可能性。尤其是要等到两个镇区的居民都被告知了这个变化并且已经学会如何适当地响应，这种混乱才会消除——否则，混乱甚至可能在短期内还会加重。因此，为了消除混乱，公众需要对变化有一定程度的认识和反应。

第二，这篇社论好像做了两个互相矛盾的声言。一是合并将导致某些重复的工作的消除；另一个是现在的政府雇员不会因合并而失业。社论没有考虑到削减重复的工作必然减少现在政府雇员的总需求数，除非设置足够的新工作岗位来抵消这种减少，然而增加新职位必然反过来增加行政支出。因此，就此看来，这个论证是自相矛盾的。作者必须对这个论证进行修改，可以从两个互相抵触的目标（保留现有的雇用水平或者削减开支）中选择其一——或者采用任何可行办法来调解这两个目标的矛盾。

第三，作者做出的合并将吸引商业投资的断言依赖于这个草率的假设，即在影响商业投资吸引力的每一个方面，那个新合并的罗斯维尔都将和哈姆丹相似。或许哈姆丹的商业税率、劳动力资源或者甚至是气候都要比新合并的罗斯维尔更加吸引人。如果是这样的话，那么所提议的合并本身很难实现吸引商业投资到罗斯维尔的目标。换句话说，没有证据证明哈姆丹和新合并后的罗斯维尔在吸引商业投资上魅力相当的话，我无法接受作者所做的关于合并会给罗斯维尔带来和哈姆丹一样的结果的结论。

总之，这篇社论不仅逻辑上没有根据，而且所依赖的好几个假设都很可疑。为了加强这篇论证的力度，作者必须修改这个建议，说明其他用于消除社论中提到的混乱所需的措施。作者还必须提供一个成本效益分析，解释为了抵消削减重复职位而设置新职位所需的花费。最后，作者必须证明在吸引商业投资上，新成立后的罗斯维尔将会和刚成立时的哈姆丹一样具有诱惑力。

【逻辑问题提纲】

本文作者一共攻击了原文的三处缺陷：

1. 合并政府只是消除混乱的必要条件，而不是充分条件（攻击后果）。

2. 作者所描述的合并所带来的管理成本下降与就业岗位的稳定两个后果是自相矛盾的（攻击后果）。

3. Hamden 与 Roseville 地区的情况可能有所不同，因而合并给 Hamden 带来的良好后果未必在 Roseville 同样发生（错误类比）。

- 逻辑思路提示：本文作者的主要思路是攻击作者在文中提出的建议的可能后果。对于本题还有一个后果可以攻击，那就是合并以后可能会给居民带来极大的不便。假如 Roseville 和 West Roseville 的地域比较广阔，距离比较远的话，作者所描述的消防局、税务局等单位不论设于哪一地区，对于另外一个地区而言都将是不方便的。

【论证展开】

- 必要而非充分条件：有些措施对于实现某种结果是必要的，但仅有这一措施本身并不足以保证这种结果的发生。这时我们把这一措施称为实现这一结果的必要而非充分条件，换言之，除了该措施之外，我们还需要其他条件同时作用才能保证某结果的发生。要攻击这种错误，我们可以借鉴本文的句型：the editorial overlooks the possibility that the measure will not in itself suffice to ... 其中 in itself：就其本身而言，仅有该措施的情况下。介词 in / by + 反身代词一般都是就其本身而言的意思。

  或者也可以用以下句型描述：

  (1) The argument proceeds as if a condition which by itself is enough to guarantee a certain result is the only condition under which the result would occur.

  (2) The reasoning is flawed in that the argument treats evidence that a factor is necessary to bring about an event as if it were evidence that the factor is sufficient to bring about that event.

  (3) The argument takes a factor that might contribute to an explanation of the observed difference as a sufficient explanation for that difference.

- 自相矛盾的错误：有时作者在题目中提出的某些现象和假设是自相矛盾的，即两个条件或结果不可能同时保证。对于这类错误我们可以用本文的论证方式来加以攻击：先用 ... the editorial seems to make two irreconcilable claims. One is that ... ; the other is that ... 来指出作者自相矛盾的两条观点，然后用 The editorial fails to consider that... 来指出作者有哪些情况没有考虑到，最后用 Thus, as it stands the argument is self-contradictory, and the author must either modify it by ..., or somehow reconcile these two objectives. 来做段落小总结。

【语言提示】

- 论证段句式：(1) The editorial seems to make two irreconcilable claims, one is that ... ; the other is that ... (2) Thus, as it stands the argument is self-contradictory, and the author must either modify it by ... or somehow reconcile these two objectives. (3) The author's claim that ... relies on the hasty assumption that ... (4) In other words, without evidence that ... I cannot accept the author's conclusion that ...

● 结尾段句式：(1) In sum, the editorial not only is logically unsound but also relies on several doubtful assumptions. (2) To strengthen the argument the author must modify the recommendation to account for other measures needed to ... mentioned in the editorial. (3) The author must also provide a cost-benefit analysis that accounts for ...

Argument 194   Left-handed people and success in business

A recent study suggests that people who are left-handed are more likely to succeed in business than are right-handed people. Researchers studied photographs of 1,000 prominent business executives and found that 21 percent of these executives wrote with their left hand. So the percentage of prominent business executives who are left-handed (21 percent) is almost twice the percentage of people in the general population who are left-handed (11 percent). Thus, people who are left-handed would be well advised to pursue a career in business, whereas people who are right-handed would be well advised to imitate the business practices exhibited by left-handers.

【参考译文】最近一项研究发现左撇子比右撇子更可能在商业活动中取得成功。研究者研究了1000名著名商业管理者的照片，发现这些管理者有21%的人用左手写字。因而著名商业管理者中左撇子比例（21%）几乎是总体人群中左撇子比例（11%）的两倍。因此，左撇子应该被建议寻求商业方面的职业，而右撇子应该被建议模仿左撇子的商业行为。

This argument recommends the all left-handed people should pursue a career in business and that right-handed people should learn to imitate the business practices of left-handed people. **To support this recommendation the speaker cites a study** of 1,000 prominent business executives, among whom 21 percent were photographed while writing with their left hand. **The speaker then points out that** only 11 percent of the general population is left-handed. **The argument suffers from several logical flaws and is therefore unconvincing.**

First of all, the study amounts to scant evidence of the speaker's implicit conclusion that left-handedness contributes to business success. **Just because** photographs show a person writing with his or her left hand **does not necessarily mean that** the person is left-handed; many people are ambidextrous—using either hand to write or using one hand to write while using the other hand for other tasks. **Besides**, the 1,000 executives **from the study are not necessarily representative of the overall population of** prominent business executives. **Moreover**, many prominent executives might have risen to their status not by way of their achievements or business acumen but through other means—such as familial relationships. **In short**, the photographs in themselves **prove little about the causal relationship between** left-handedness **and** the ability to succeed in business.

Even if left-handed people are more likely to have an innate ability to succeed in business than right-handed people are, **the author's conclusion that** all left-handed people should pursue business careers **unfairly assumes that** all left-handed people are similar in terms of their talents, interests, and motivations. **Common sense informs me that** the best vocational choice for any person **depends on a va-**

riety of factors. **Thus, without clearer evidence that** left-handed people tend to be successful in business but unsuccessful in other vocations **the speaker cannot justify such a sweeping recommendation for** left-handed people.

Even if most left-handed people would be well advised to pursue business careers, **the speaker's recommendation for** right-handed people **is unwarranted. Common sense informs me that** any innate business acumen with which left-handed people might be endowed cannot be imitated. **Moreover, the speaker assumes without substantiation that** the way in which left-handed people conduct business is the only way to succeed in business. **It is entirely possible that** right-handed people have certain natural ways of thinking that lend themselves better to other business approaches. **Without considering and ruling out this possibility the speaker cannot convince me that** right-handed people should imitate the business practices of left-handed people.

In sum, the argument is logically unsound. To strengthen it the speaker must show that the 1,000 executives in the photos were in fact using their dominant hand, that they are representative of all prominent executives, and that prominence in business is generally the result of an executive's business practices. **To better assess the argument I would need to** compare the percentage of left-handed people who succeed in business with those who succeed in other vocations. **I would also need more information about** the business practices of left-handed people to determine whether they employ similar practices, and whether right-handed people who have succeeded in business employ different practices.

【参考译文】

这个论证建议所有左撇子应该以经商为职业，而惯用右手的人应该学习并模仿左撇子的经商之道。为支持这个建议，发言者引用了一个对 1000 名杰出商业管理者所做的研究，在这 1000 人中有 21% 的人在用左手写字的时候被拍了下来。发言者随后指出全体人口中只有 11% 的人是左撇子。这个论证有几处犯了逻辑上的错误，因此不能服人。

首先，发言者所引用的研究实际上无力证明他所做的左撇子有助于商业成功的暗示。光凭几张照片没有用，照片上的那个人用他或她的左手在写字并不一定就意味着那个人是左撇子；有许多人双手都很灵巧，有的两只手都可以写字，也有的可以一只手用来写字，而另一只手去做别的事。此外，研究中的那 1000 位管理者并不一定可以代表整体的杰出商业管理者群体。而且，有很多杰出的管理者达到今天的地位并不是通过他们个人的成就或者商业头脑，而是通过其他的方式——比如家族关系。简而言之，照片本身并不能证明左撇子和赢得商业成功的能力之间存在着因果关系。

即使左撇子的人比惯用右手的人更可能天生具有通往商业成功的能力，那作者所做的关于所有左撇子都应该从商的结论也是在不合理地认为所有左撇子在天资、兴趣和动机上都是相似的。常识使我明白任何人的最好的职业选择都取决于各种各样的因素。因此，如果没有更确切的证据证明左撇子比较容易在商业上取得成功，而在其他职业领域就不容易成功的话，那么发言者就不能证明他给左撇子所提的那个笼统的建议是正确的。

即使让大多数左撇子去从商是一个好建议，但发言者给惯用右手的人提的建议也是毫无根据的。常识告诉我赋予左撇子的与生俱来的商业头脑是无法被模仿的。而且，发言者毫无证据地认为左撇子经商的方法是在商业领域取得成功的惟一方式。惯用右手的人完全有可能通过某些自然的思维方式更好地帮助自己找到其他经商之道。没有考虑到并排除这种可能性，发言者就不能使我确信惯用右手的人们应该模仿左撇子的经商之道。

总之，这个论证逻辑不严密。为了加强论证，发言者必须说明照片里的 1000 位管理者在用的左手实际上正是他们的优势手，还要说明他们确实可以代表所有杰出的管理者，以及商业上的杰出成就通常都来源于管理者的经商之道。为了更好地评价这个论证，我有必要比较一下在商业领域成功的左撇子与在其他职业成功的左撇子的比率。我还需要更多有关左撇子的经商之道的信息，以确定他们是否采用相似的方法，以及在商业领域取得成功的惯用右手的人是否采用了不同的方法。

【逻辑问题提纲】

本文作者一共攻击了原文的三处缺陷：

1. 仅有照片并不能表明这些经理就是左撇子，而且这 1000 名经理也未必能够代表所有的知名经理，以及有些经理可能通过一些其他途径获得商业上的成功。

2. 由于天分、兴趣等诸多因素，左撇子可以有很多职业选择而未必都去参加商业活动。

3. 仅仅通过模仿左撇子的商业行为未必能够带来同样的商业成功，而且除了左撇子的商业模式以外还有很多可以取得成功的方法。

● 逻辑思路提示：本文所攻击的第一点其实包含了三个小点：照片不能说明这些人到底是左撇子还是右撇子；调查样本的代表性；获得商业成功的方式和原因可能是多种多样的。这三点的任意一点都可以单独成段展开论述。另外本题还可以攻击以下错误：作者没有提供切实证据表明左撇子这一现象与商业成功之间有因果联系，或者说作者没有具体分析导致这些经理人成功的真正原因。

【语言提示】

● 论证句式：(1) First of all, the study amounts to scant evidence of the speaker's implicit conclusion that … (2) Just because … does not necessarily mean that … (3) … from the study are not necessarily representative of the overall population of … (4) In short, … prove little about the causal relationship between … and … (5) Common sense informs me that … depends on a variety of factors. (6) Thus, without clearer evidence that … the speaker cannot justify such a sweeping recommendation for …

Argument 201   Have **Forsythe** citizens adopted healthier lifestyles?

The citizens of Forsythe have adopted healthier lifestyles. Their responses to a recent survey show that in their eating habits they conform more closely to government nutritional recommendations than they did ten years ago. Furthermore, there has been a fourfold increase in sales of food products containing kiran, a substance that a scientific study has shown reduces cholesterol. This trend is also evident in reduced sales of sulia, a food that few of the healthiest citizens regularly eat.

【参考译文】福赛思的居民选择了更健康的生活方式。他们对于最近一项调查的回答显示，他们的饮食习惯比十年前更加贴近政府的营养建议。而且，含有基伦的食品销量增长了四倍，在一次科学研究中发现基伦（kiran）是一种能够减少胆固醇的物质。素丽亚（sulia）的销量下降同样证实了这种趋势，素丽亚（sulia）是那些最健康的居民中极少有人经常食用的食品。

In this argument, the speaker concludes that Forsythe citizens have adopted healthier lifestyles. **To justify this conclusion the speaker cites a recent survey of** Forsythe citizens suggesting that their eating habits now conform more closely to government nutritional recommendations than they did ten years ago. **The speaker also points out that** sales of kiran, a substance known to reduce cholesterol, have increased fourfold, while sales of sulia, which few of Forsythe's healthiest citizens eat regularly, have been declining. **This argument is unpersuasive for several reasons.**

First, the survey must be shown to be reliable before I can accept any conclusions based upon it. Specifically, the responses must be accurate, and the respondents must be statistically significant in number and representative of the overall Forsythe citizenry in terms of eating habits. **Without evidence of the survey's reliability, it is impossible to draw any firm conclusions about** the current dietary habits of Forsythe citizens based on the survey.

Second, the argument relies on the dubious assumption that following the government's nutrition recommendations promotes health to a greater extent than following any other nutrition regime. **It is entirely possible that** the dietary habits of Forsythe citizens were healthier ten years ago than they are now. **Thus, without evidence to substantiate this assumption, the speaker cannot reasonably conclude that** the diet of Forsythe's citizens has become more nutritional.

Third, the speaker assumes too hastily that increasing sales of products with kiran indicates healthier eating habits. **Perhaps** Forsythe citizens are eating these foods in amounts or at intervals that undermine the health benefits of kiran. **Without ruling out this possibility the speaker cannot reasonably conclude with any** confidence that increased kiran consumption has resulted in improved health for Forsythe's citizens.

Fourth, the mere fact that few of Forsythe's healthiest citizens eat sulia regularly **does not mean that** sulia is detrimental to health—**as the speaker assumes. It is possible that** sulia has no effect on health, **or** that it actually promotes health. **Lacking firm evidence that** sulia affects health adversely, **and that** healthy people avoid sulia for this reason, **the speaker cannot justify any conclusions about the health of Forsythe's citizens from the mere fact that** sulia sales are declining.

Finally, even if the dietary changes to which the speaker refers are healthful ones, **the speaker overlooks the possibility that** Forsythe citizens have been making other changes in their dietary or other habits that offset these healthful changes. **Unless all other habits affecting health have remained unchanged, the speaker cannot justifiably conclude that** the overall lifestyle of Forsythe's citizenry has become healthier.

In sum, the argument is unconvincing as it stands. To strengthen it the speaker must show that the survey accurately reflects the dietary habits of Forsythe's citizens, **and that** by following the government's nutritional recommendations more closely these citizens are in fact healthier. **The speaker must also show that** Forsythe's citizens have not made other dietary or other lifestyle changes that offset healthful changes. **Finally, to better assess the argument I would need more information about** the manner and extent to which Forsythe's citizens now consume kiran and about the healthfulness of sulia.

【参考译文】

在这个论证里，发言者断定福赛思市民的生活方式已经变得更加健康了。为了证明这个结论是正确的，发言者引用了一项最近的调查，其中福赛思市民回答说他们现在的饮食习惯和十年前相比越来越和政府的营养建议趋于一致了。发言者还指出基伦（kiran）——一种可以分解胆固醇的物质——的销售额已经翻了四倍，而那些福赛思的最健康的市民很少有人经常吃的素丽亚（sulia）的销售额一直下降。这个论证由于几个原因显得很不具有说服力。

首先，要使我相信以这个调查为基础做出的任何结论，调查本身一定要是可信的。特别是回答一定要是准确的，并且回答者的人数应具备统计学上的意义，就饮食习惯而言，能代表全体福赛思市民。没有证据证明该调查的可信性，就不可能根据这个调查得出任何关于福赛思市民现在的饮食习惯的肯定结论。

其次，这个论证依赖于一个可疑的假定，即按照政府的营养建议比按照其他任何营养养生法能更好地促进健康。福赛思市民十年前的饮食习惯完全有可能比他们现在的要健康。因此，没有证据证明这个假设是正确的，发言者就不能想当然地断定福赛思市民的饮食已经变得更加营养了。

第三，发言者过于草率地认为含有基伦（kiran）的产品的销售额上升就表明了饮食习惯变得更加健康。或许福赛思市民正过量或者间歇地食用这些食物，以致破坏了基伦（kiran）对健康的好处。没有排除这种可能，发言者就不能理所当然地并有把握地得出结论，增长的基伦（kiran）消费已经产生了改善福赛思市民的健康的效果。

第四，福赛思的最健康的市民中很少有人常吃素丽亚（sulia）的这个事实并不意味着素丽亚（sulia）就如同发言者说的那样对健康有害。有可能素丽亚（sulia）对健康并没有影响，或者实际上它还能促进健康。缺乏有力的证据证明素丽亚（sulia）确实对健康有不良影响，并且健康的人们因此而排斥它，发言者就不能从素丽亚（sulia）的销售额在下降这个事实来证明他所做的关于福赛思市民的健康情况的结论是正确的。

最后，即使发言者提到的饮食变化确实是有益于健康的，但发言者也忽略了这种可能性，即福赛思市民的饮食或者其他习惯一直在变化，而这些变化正好抵消了有益于健康的饮食变化。除非影响健康的所有其他习惯均保持不变，否则发言者就不能无可非议地断定福赛思市民整体的生活方式已经变得更加健康。

总之，就目前情况看，论点不能令人信服。为了加强它的说服力，发言者必须证明那个调查能够准确地反映出福赛思市民的饮食习惯，以及通过更严格地遵循政府的营养建议，这些市民确实变得更加健康。发言者还必须证明福赛思市民没有在饮食或者生活方式上发生其他任何变化，会抵消有益于健康的变化。最后，为了更好地评价这个论证，我需要更多有关现在福赛思市民食用基伦（kiran）的方式与剂量的信息，以及素丽亚（sulia）是否有益于身体健康的信息。

【逻辑问题提纲】

本文作者一共攻击了原文的五处缺陷：

1. 调查样本的数量和代表性值得怀疑。
2. 政府推荐的营养建议未必比其他的饮食习惯更符合健康要求。
3. 含基伦食品销量的上升未必意味着人们的饮食习惯更加健康。
4. 素丽亚消费量少未必是因为它对健康有害。
5. 仅有饮食习惯的变化不足以判断人们的生活方式是否更健康，我们还需要考虑生活习惯的其他方面。

● 逻辑思路提示：本文攻击的出发点虽然比较多，但每个问题都没有做充分展开，而且使用了大量的抽象性逻辑描述语言来进行论证，这对于得分来说并不有利。因而本文主要以逻辑攻击点作为参考，同学们真正参加考试时可以选取其中的三到四点做更加充分的展开论证。

【语言提示】

● 攻击调查样本的语言：(1) The survey must be shown to be reliable before I can accept any conclusions based upon it. (2) Specifically, the responses must be accurate, and the respondents must be statistically significant in number and representative of the overall ... (3)

Without evidence of the survey's reliability, it is impossible to draw any firm conclusions about ... based on the survey.

● 其他论证句式：(1) Thus, without evidence to substantiate this assumption, the speaker cannot reasonably conclude that ... (2) Without ruling out this possibility the speaker cannot reasonably conclude with any confidence that ... (3) The mere fact that ... does not mean that ...—as the speaker assumes. (4) Lacking firm evidence that ..., and that ..., the speaker cannot justify any conclusions about ... from the mere fact that ...

Argument 202　Extinction of mammals in the **Kaliko islands**

Humans arrived in the Kaliko Islands about 7,000 years ago, and within 3,000 years most of the large mammal species that had lived in the forests of the Kaliko Islands had become extinct. Yet humans cannot have been a factor in the species' extinctions, because there is no evidence that the humans had any significant contact with the mammals. Further, archaeologists have discovered numerous sites where the bones of fish had been discarded, but they found no such areas containing the bones of large mammals, so the humans cannot have hunted the mammals. Therefore, some climate change or other environmental factor must have caused the species' extinctions.

【参考译文】大约 7000 年前，人类到达了卡里口岛，在 3000 年内曾经生活在卡里口岛的树林中的大型哺乳动物绝大多数已经灭绝了。然而人类并不是导致这些物种灭绝的因素，因为没有证据表明人类与这些哺乳动物有重要的接触。而且，考古学家发现一些有大量鱼骨被抛弃的场所，而他们并没有发现存在大型哺乳动物骨头的类似场所，因而人类并没有猎杀这些哺乳动物。因此，一定是一些气候上的变化或其他环境因素导致了这些物种的灭绝。

In this argument the speaker concludes that humans could not have been a factor in the extinction of large mammal species in the Kaliko islands 3,000 years ago. To justify this conclusion, the speaker points out that no evidence exists that humans hunted or had other significant contact with these mammals. The speaker also points out that while archeologists have found bones of discarded fish in the islands, they have not found any discarded mammal bones there. For three reasons, this evidence lends little credibility to the speaker's argument.

First, the argument concludes too hastily that humans could not have had any significant contact with these mammals. In relying on the lack of physical evidence such as bones, the speaker overlooks the possibility that humans exported mammals—particularly their bones—during this time period. Without ruling out this alternative explanation for the disappearance of these species from the islands, the speaker cannot justify the conclusion that humans were not a factor in their extinction from the islands.

Secondly, the argument relies on the assumption that without significant contact with these other species humans could not have been a factor in their extinction. But the speaker provides no evidence that this is the case. Moreover, perhaps humans drove these other species away from their natural habitat not by significant contact but merely by intruding on their territory. Or perhaps humans consumed the plants and animals on which these species relied for their subsistence. Either scenario would explain how humans could have been a factor in the extinction of these species despite a lack of significant contact.

　　Thirdly, the speaker assumes that the bones of fish that archeologists have found discarded on the island were discarded by humans, and not by some other large mammal. **However, the speaker provides no evidence to substantiate this assumption. Given other possible explanations for** these discarded fish bones, **this evidence in itself lends little credible support to the speaker's theory about** the extinction of large species of mammals.

　　In conclusion, the argument is unconvincing as it stands. To strengthen it, the speaker must rule out the possibility that humans exported the bones of these other species. **To better evaluate the argument, we would need more information about** the diet of humans and of the now-extinct mammals during that time period; **particularly, we would need to know** whether those other mammals also fed on the fish whose discarded bones have been found on the islands.

【参考译文】

　　在这篇论证里发言者断定，人类不是 3000 年以前卡里口岛上的大型哺乳动物物种灭绝的原因。为了证明这个结论是正确的，发言者指出没有证据表明人类捕猎这些哺乳动物，或者与这些哺乳动物有其他重要的接触。发言者也指出，考古学家已经在岛上找到丢掉的鱼骨头，而没在那里找到任何丢掉的哺乳动物的骨头。由于以下的三个原因，发言者的论证缺乏可信度。

　　首先，论证太轻率地断定人类不可能与这些哺乳动物有任何重要的接触。在缺乏例如骨头等物证的基础上，发言者忽略了一个可能发生的情况，这就是在这段时间内这些人出口哺乳动物，特别是骨头。如果没有排除这些物种从岛上消失的这另一种解释，发言者就不能证实人不是这些物种从岛上灭绝的一个因素的结论。

　　第二，论证基于这样一个假设，即如果与这些物种没有重要的接触，人就不可能是导致它们灭绝的一个因素。但是发言者没有提供证据证明情况确实如此。而且，或许人把这些物种从它们的天然栖息地驱逐走，不是通过直接的接触，而仅仅是通过侵入他们的领土。或者，也许人消耗了这些物种生存必需的植物和动物。尽管缺乏重要的接触，两假定中的任一假定都可以解释人是如何成为这些物种灭绝的一个因素的。

　　第三，发言者假定岛上考古学家找到的被丢掉的鱼骨头是被人丢掉的，而不是被其他一些大型哺乳动物丢掉的。但是，发言者没有提供证据证明这个假定。考虑到对这些被丢掉的鱼骨头的其他可能的解释，这个证据本身不能为发言者关于大型哺乳动物物种灭绝的理论提供可靠的支持。

　　总之，就目前情况来看，论证并不使人信服。为了加强其说服力，发言者必须排除人们出口这些物种的骨头的可能性。为了更好地评价此论证，我们需要更多的关于那段时期内人和现在已绝种的哺乳动物的饮食信息；我们尤其需要知道那些其它的哺乳动物是否也以鱼为食，那种鱼的骨头已在岛上被发现。

【逻辑问题提纲】

　　本文作者一共攻击了原文的三处缺陷：

　　1. 没有发现哺乳动物的骨头不能说明人类与这些动物没有接触。

　　2. 人类与这些动物不直接接触也有可能导致它们的灭绝。

　　3. 没有证据表明文中提到的鱼骨是被人类抛弃的。

【语言提示】

● 论证句式：(1) Without ruling out this alternative explanation for ..., the speaker cannot justify the conclusion that ... (2) However, the speaker provides no evidence to substantiate this assumption. (3) Given other possible explanations for ..., this evidence in itself lends little credible support to the speaker's theory about ...

Argument 203　Small **nonprofit hospitals** vs. large for-profit hospitals

The following appeared in a newspaper feature story.

"At the small, nonprofit hospital in the town of Saluda, the average length of a patient's stay is two days; at the large, for-profit hospital in the nearby city of Megaville, the average patient stay is six days. Also, the cure rate among patients in the Saluda hospital is about twice that of the Megaville hospital. The Saluda hospital has more employees per patient than the hospital in Megaville, and there are few complaints about service at the local hospital. Such data indicate that treatment in smaller, nonprofit hospitals is more economical and of better quality than treatment in larger, for-profit hospitals."

【参考译文】在撒路达镇的小型非赢利医院，患者平均逗留时间是两天；在邻近的麦哥维勒市的大型赢利医院，患者平均逗留时间为六天。而且，撒路达医院患者的治愈率大约是麦哥维勒医院的两倍。撒路达平均每个患者对应的医务人员的数量比麦哥维勒医院多，而且地方医院关于服务的投诉也较少。这些数据表明小型非赢利医院的治疗比大型赢利医院更加经济，质量更高。

This newspaper story concludes that the small, nonprofit hospital in Saluda provides more efficient, better-quality care than the for-profit hospital in Megaville. **To justify this conclusion the author cites the following comparisons between** the Saluda hospital and the Megaville hospital: At the Saluda hospital the average length of a patient's stay is shorter, the cure rate and employee-patient ratio are both higher, and the number of complaints from patients is lower. **However, careful consideration of these facts reveals that they fail to justify the author's conclusion.**

In the first place, the author unfairly assumes that a shorter hospital stay indicates a quicker recovery and therefore better care. **It is equally possible that** the Saluda hospital simply cannot afford to keep patients as long as it should to ensure proper care and recovery. **Perhaps** the hospital sends patients home prematurely for the purpose of freeing up beds for other patients. **Since the author has failed to rule out other possible explanations for** this shorter average stay, **I remain unconvinced based on this evidence that** the Saluda hospital provides better care than Megaville's hospital.

In the second place, the mere fact that the rate of cure at the Saluda hospital is higher than at Megaville's hospital **proves nothing about** the quality of care at either hospital. **It is entirely possible that** more Saluda patients suffer from curable problems than Megaville patients do. **Without considering this possibility the author cannot justifiably rely on** cure rates **to draw any conclusions about** comparative quality of care.

In the third place, a higher employee-patient ratio at Saluda **is weak evidence of** either better care or greater efficiency. **Common sense informs me that** it is the competence of each employee, not the number of employees, that determines overall quality of care. **Besides, it is entirely possible that** the comparatively large staff at Saluda is the result of organizational inefficiency, and that a smaller staff of more effective, better managed people would provide better care.

Finally, the mere fact that the Saluda hospital receives fewer patient complaints than Megaville's hospital **proves nothing about** either efficiency or quality of care. **Even though** the number of complaints is smaller, the percentage of patients complaining might be higher. **Also,** Megaville's staff might openly encourage patient feedback while Saluda's does not. **This scenario accords with my observation that** for-profit organizations are generally more concerned with customer satisfaction than non-profit organizations are.

　　In sum, the facts that the story cites **amount to weak evidence that** the Saluda hospital provides more efficient, better-quality care than Megaville's hospital. **To strengthen the argument, the author must provide clear evidence that** at the Saluda hospital patients are released earlier because they have received better care—rather than for some other reason. **To better assess the argument, I would need to** compare the percentage of Megaville's hospital patients who suffer from curable problems with the percentage of Saluda patients who suffer from similar problems. **Also, I would need more information** from each hospital **about** complaint procedures and the percentage of patients who lodge complaints.

【参考译文】

　　这篇报纸上的报道下结论说撒路达的非赢利的小医院比麦哥维勒的赢利的医院提供了更有效率、更优质的护理。为了证明这个结论是正确的，作者引用了在撒路达医院和麦哥维勒医院之间的以下比较：在撒路达医院，病人停留的平均时间更短，治愈比率以及护理员和病人的比率都更高，并且病人的抱怨也更少。但是，通过对这些事实的仔细考虑，我们会发现它们不能证明作者的结论是正确的。

　　首先，作者不公平地假定在一所医院停留时间越短就表明恢复得越快，因此得到了更好的护理。同样可能的是，撒路达医院只不过没有条件使病人呆在医院里足够长的时间，来保证适当的护理和恢复。或许医院为了为其他病人腾出床位，过早地送病人回家。因为作者没有排除对更短的平均停留时间的其他可能的解释，基于这个论据，作者不能使我信服，撒路达医院比麦哥维勒医院提供了更好的护理。

　　其次，仅凭撒路达医院的治愈率比麦哥维勒医院高这一事实并不能证明两所医院中的任一所的护理质量。完全可能与麦哥维勒的病人相比，更多撒路达的病人患的是可医治的病痛。如果没有考虑到这个可能性，作者不能无可辩驳地凭借治愈率来得出关于护理质量比较的任何结论。

　　再次，撒路达更高的医务人员和患者的比率既不能有力地证明它有更好的护理，也不能证明它有更高的效率。常识告诉我是每个雇员的能力，并非雇员的数量，决定着护理的总体质量。而且，完全可能的是，撒路达相对庞大的医务人员队伍是组织效率低下的结果，并且一个人数更少的，更有效的，管理得更好的医务人员队伍可以提供更好的护理。

　　最后，仅凭撒路达医院比麦哥维勒医院收到更少的来自病人的抱怨这一事实既不能证明它的效率，也不能证明它的护理质量。即使抱怨的数量较少，有抱怨的病人的百分比却可能更高。此外，麦哥维勒的人员可能公开地鼓励病人反馈，而撒路达的人员却不这么做。这种推测符合我所观察到的赢利组织通常比非赢利组织更关注客户的满意度的现象。

　　总之，报道所引用的事实不能有力地证明撒路达医院比麦哥维勒医院提供了更有效率、更优质的护理。为了加强此论证，作者应当提供清楚的证据来证明撒路达医院病人更早出院是因为他们受到更好的护理，而不是其他一些原因。为了更好地评价此论证，我需要比较患可治愈的疾病的麦哥维勒医院的病人的百分比与患相似疾病的撒路达的病人的百分比。此外，我需要来自每所医院的关于投诉程序和投诉的病人所占的百分比的更多的信息。

【逻辑问题提纲】

　　本文作者一共攻击了原文的四处缺陷：

1．患者在医院逗留的时间长短并不是治疗质量和效果的标志，可能有其他因素导致逗留时间的长短。

2．由于患者情况不同，治愈率的高低也不能说明医疗护理的质量。

3．医患比例的高低也不能说明医疗护理的质量。

4．撒路达医院受到的患者投诉较少可能由其他原因导致，而且投诉人数少并不能说明投诉的比例也一定小（比例与总量混淆，数据模糊性的错误）。

● 逻辑思路提示：本题所用的论据形式主要是对比（comparison），通过两家医院几方面的比较来说明其医护质量的高低。攻击对比和攻击类比（analogy）的方式类似，都是指出作者进行对比的双方在其他方面还有哪些被作者忽视的可能差异。本文作者即指出两家医院的设备条件、患者所患疾病情况、医院对于投诉的态度可能存在差异从而导致了文中的现象，而未必是医护质量的高低所致。

【语言提示】

● 开头段句式：However, careful consideration of these facts reveals that they fail to justify the author's conclusion.

● 论证段句式：(1) Since the author has failed to rule out other possible explanations for ..., I remain unconvinced based on this evidence that ... (2) Without considering this possibility the author cannot justifiably rely on ... to draw any conclusions about ... (3) This scenario accords with my observation that ...

● 结尾段句式：In sum, the facts that the story cites amount to weak evidence that ...

Argument 208　The need for more **electric generating plants**

The following appeared in a memorandum from the planning department of an electric power company.

"Several recent surveys indicate that homeowners are increasingly eager to conserve energy and manufacturers are now marketing many home appliances, such as refrigerators and air conditioners, that are almost twice as energy-efficient as those sold a decade ago. Also, new technologies for better home insulation and passive solar heating are readily available to reduce the energy needed for home heating. Therefore, we anticipate that the total demand for electricity in our area will not increase, and may decline slightly. Since our three electric generating plants in operation for the past 20 years have always met our needs, construction of new generating plants should not be necessary."

【参考译文】一些最近的调查表明，私房房主越来越强烈地希望节省能源，并且生产商现在正在推出很多比十年前的电器几乎节能两倍的家用电器，比如冰箱和空调。而且，更好的房屋隔热和被动式太阳能采暖的新技术已经可以用于减少家庭采暖所需的能源。因此，我们预计我们地区的用电需求总量不会增加，而可能有轻微下降。由于我们的已经运作了20年的三座发电站一直能够满足需求，我们无需建造新的发电厂。

The author of this memo concludes that there is no need for an additional electric power plant in the area because total electricity demand in the area is not likely to increase in the future. **To support this conclusion the author cites** the availability of new energy-efficient appliances and systems for homes, and the eagerness of area homeowners to conserve energy. **However, the argument relies on several doubtful assumptions, and is therefore unpersuasive as it stands.**

First, **the author's projection for** flat or declining total demand for electricity **ignores** business and commercial electricity usage. **It is entirely possible that** area businesses will increase their use of electricity in the future and that total electricity consumption will actually increase despite flat or declining residential demand. **The author's projection also ignores the possibility that** the number of area residents will increase in the future, thereby resulting in an increase in electricity usage regardless of whether more efficient appliances are used in area homes. **Without taking into account these possibilities, the author cannot persuade me that** total demand for electricity will not increase in the future.

Secondly, the author's conclusion relies on the assumption that area residents will actually purchase and install the energy-saving appliances and systems the author describes. **Admittedly, the author points out that** homeowners are "eager to conserve energy." **Nevertheless**, these homeowners might not be able to afford these new systems and appliances. **Moreover**, the energy-efficient insulation that the author mentions might be available only for new home construction, or it might be a gas system. **In either case, the mere** availability of this system **might have no effect on** total electric usage in existing homes.

A final problem involves the assertion that no new electric power plants are needed because the three existing plants, which are 20 years old, have always been adequate for the area's electric needs. **The author fails to account for the possibility that** the old plants are themselves less energy efficient than a new plant using new technology would be, **or that** the old plants need to be replaced due to their age, or for some other reason. **Besides, this assertion ignores the possible** influx of residents or businesses in the future, thereby increasing the demand for electricity beyond what the three existing plants can meet.

In conclusion, the argument is unconvincing as it stands. To strengthen it the author must show that area residents can afford the new energy-efficient appliances and systems, **and that** area commercial demand for electricity will not increase significantly in the foreseeable future. **In order to better evaluate the argument, we would need to know** whether the new energy-efficient technologies are available to businesses as well, and whether area businesses plan to use them. **We would also need more information about** expected changes in the area's population, and about the condition and energy-efficiency of the three current electric power plants.

【参考译文】

　　这个备忘录的作者断言没有必要再在这个地区建造另一个发电厂，因为将来该区的电力总需求量不可能增加。为了支持这个结论，作者引用了获得家用的节能电器具和系统的可能性，以及该区自己拥有住房的居民渴望节约能量的愿望。但是，这个论证依赖于几个可疑的假定，并因此变得没有说服力。

　　首先，作者在预测电力总需求量会持平或者下降的时候，忽视了商业和贸易用电。这个地区的商业用电将来完全有可能增加，那么尽管家庭用电量持平或者下滑，实际上总的电量消耗也会上升。作者的预测还忽略了这么一种可能性，即该区居民的人口数将来也会增长，那么不管该区的家庭里是不是有更多的节能电器，用电量也会增多的。没有考虑到这些可能性，作者不能让我相信将来对电力的总需求量不会上涨。

　　第二，作者的结论是建立在这个假设上的，即该区的居民确实会购买并安装作者所描述的节能电器和系统。无可否认，作者确实指出房主"渴望节约能量"。虽然如此，这些房主也可能无法承担这些新器具和系统的费用。而且，作者提到的节能隔热材料可能只适用于新的家庭建筑物，或者它也可能就是一个燃气系统。无论是上述哪种情况，这个系统的存在对现有家庭的总用电量可能毫无影响。

最后一个问题与这个断言有关：因为现有的三家有 20 年历史的发电厂一直能够满足这个地区的电力需求，所以没有必要再建新的发电厂。作者没有考虑到这种可能性，也就是旧的发电厂无法比使用新技术的发电厂更加节能，或者由于时间太长或其他什么原因，旧发电厂有必要被取代了。此外，这个断言忽略了将来有居民或者商业机构流入，致使原有的三家发电厂不能满足电力需求的可能性。

总之，就目前情况看，该论点不能使人信服。为了加强它的力度，作者必须证明这个地区的居民能够承担新式的节能器具和系统的费用，并且在可预见的将来该区的商业电力需求量不会有显著的增加。为了更好地评价这个论证，我们需要知道新式的节能技术是否也能应用于商业机构，并且该区的商业机构是否打算采用这些新式的节能技术。我们还将需要更多有关该地区人口的预期变化，以及有关现有的三家发电厂的条件和节能率的信息。

【逻辑问题提纲】

本文作者一共攻击了原文的三处缺陷：

1. 作者仅仅考虑了居民用电而没有考虑工业、商业用电（考虑问题不够全面的错误）；以及没有考虑本地区居民数量可能增加（没有与时俱进的错误）。

2. 作者仅仅提出现在已有节能电器和建筑，但没有考虑人们是否能够承受这些新技术的花费。

3. 作者没有考虑现有的三座老发电厂的能源效率可能不如新型电厂，也没有考虑这些老电厂可能在近期到达使用年限的情况（没有与时俱进的错误）。

● 逻辑思路提示：

1）没有与时俱进的错误：即作者忽视了时间变量的存在，仅仅看到现有情况就下结论，而没有考虑很多条件和情况会随着时间变化。

2）经济承受力的问题：在很多题目中都会出现类似的论证形式，即作者只看到现有某种措施、条件和设备可以解决某问题，但没有考虑它们所需费用的经济问题，从另一方面来说，这也可以看成是结论缺乏客观可行性。在本题中，作者就是只提出现有节能电器和建筑，而没有考虑有多少人买得起而选择它们。在缺乏使用节能设备的居民的确切比例的情况下是无法判断这些电器和技术的出现是否真的能减少用电量的。

【语言提示】

● 论证句式：In either case, the mere ... might have no effect on ...

Argument 210　Increasing factory efficiency by using **robots**

The following is a letter to the editor of a news magazine.

"Clearly, the successful use of robots on missions to explore outer space in the past 20 years demonstrates that robots could be increasingly used to perform factory work more effectively, efficiently, and profitably than human factory workers. The use of robots in factories would offer several advantages. First, robots never get sick, so absenteeism would be reduced. Second, robots do not make mistakes, so factories would increase their output. Finally, the use of robots would also improve the morale of factory workers, since factory work can be so boring that many workers would be glad to shift to more interesting kinds of tasks."

【参考译文】显然，过去 20 年中机器人在探索外层空间任务中的成功使用证明，机器人可以更多地用于工厂，它们工作起来比人类工作人员更有效、更有利可图。工厂中机器人的使用将带来若干好处。首先，机器人从不生病，从而旷工将会减少。其次，机器人不会出错，因此工厂产量将会增加。最后，使用机器人同样也会提高工厂工人的精神状态，因为工厂的工作有时如此枯燥，以至于很多工人将会乐于转换到更有趣的任务。

This editorial concludes that using robots for factory work would improve factory efficiency. To justify this conclusion the editorial's author cites the fact that robots have been used effectively in many space missions. Also, the author claims that the use of robots in factories would (1) reduce absenteeism because robots never get sick, (2) improve output because robots do not make errors, and (3) improve factory-worker morale because these workers could be reassigned to less boring jobs. However, the author's argument is problematic in several critical respects.

To begin with, the argument depends on the hasty assumption that the kinds of tasks robots perform in space are similar to the ones they would perform in factories, and that there are no differences between the two environments that would render robots less effective in factory jobs than in space missions. Perhaps the effectiveness of robots in space missions is due largely to the weightless environment of space. Or perhaps the average space-mission robot performs less work than a typical factory robot would be required to perform. In either case, the fact that robots are effective in space would amount to scant support for the author's argument.

As for the author's claim that the use of robots would decrease absenteeism, although robots clearly do not get sick, in all likelihood factory robots would break down from time to time—which is tantamount to absenteeism. Without accounting for this likelihood the author cannot rely on this claim to conclude that the use of robots would improve overall factory efficiency.

Also questionable is the author's claim that the use of robots would increase factory output because robots do not make errors. Unless the author can provide clear evidence that human errors result in a lower rate of factory output, and not just a lower quality of product, I cannot be convinced that using robots would in fact increase the rate of output.

Two final problems involve the author's claim that using robots would improve the morale of factory workers, thereby improving factory efficiency. First, the author provides no assurances that if factory workers are reassigned to other types of jobs their morale would improve as a result. Although the new jobs might be less boring, these jobs might pose other problems that would adversely affect worker morale. Secondly, even if the morale of the workers improves as a result of reassignment, overall factory efficiency will not necessarily improve as a result. These workers might be ill-suited for their new jobs and thus be extremely ineffective in them.

In sum, the editorial relies on a potentially weak analogy as well as on a series of unwarranted claims. To strengthen the argument that the use of robots would improve factory efficiency, the editorial's author must at the very least provide clear evidence that factory robots would perform the same types of tasks, and just as well, as the tasks robots have performed in space missions. To better assess the strength of each of the author's three unwarranted claims, respectively, I would need to know: (1) the expected downtime—i.e., absenteeism—for factory robots; (2) the extent to which human error decreases the rate of factory output; and (3) the extent to which human factory workers would be happy and effective in the new jobs to which they would be assigned.

【参考译文】

这篇社论断定在工厂工作中使用机器人将提高工厂效率。为了证明这个结论是正确的，社论的作者引用了机器人已经在很多太空任务中有效地使用的事实。此外，作者声称在工厂使用机器人将：(1) 减少缺勤，因为机器人从不会生病；(2) 增加产量，因为机器人不会犯错误；并且 (3) 提高工厂工人士气，因为这些工人可能被再分配去做不那么令人厌烦的工作。但是，作者的论证在几个关键的方面是有疑问的。

首先，论证所依靠的是草率的设想，即空间作业机器人在太空执行的任务与它们在工厂内将要执行的任务是类似的，而且两种环境之间没有任何能导致机器人在工厂工作没有在太空工作那么有效的差别。或许在太空执行任务的机器人之所以有效，主要是由于太空失重的环境所导致的。或者普通的太空作业机器人比一个典型的工厂机器人被要求执行更少的工作。无论是哪种情况，机器人在太空中有效的事实并不能成为对作者论证的支持。

至于作者认为使用机器人将减少缺勤，虽然很明显机器人不会生病，但是很可能，工厂机器人不时会出现故障，这等于缺勤。如果没有考虑这个可能性，作者就不能依靠这个论据来断定机器人的使用将提高工厂总的效率。

此外的可疑之处是作者声称因为机器人不会犯错误，使用机器人将增加工厂的产量。除非作者能够提供清楚的证据证明人的错误会导致更低的工厂产量，而并非次等产品，我不能确信使用机器人实际上将增加产量。

最后两个问题与作者主张使用机器人将提高工厂工人士气，从而改进工厂效率有关。首先，作者没有提供保证，如果再分配工厂工人做其他类型的工作，他们的士气将因此而得以提高。虽然新工作可能不那么令人厌烦，但是这些工作可能引起其他问题而对工人士气产生不好的影响。第二，即使那些工人的士气由于重新分配而提高，工厂总效率将不一定因此而改进。这些工人可能不适合他们的新工作，因此做这些工作时效率极低。

总之，社论所依据的是一个不太有说服力的类比以及一系列无根据的主张。为了加强使用机器人将提高工厂效率的论证，社论的作者必须至少提供清楚的证据证明工厂机器人将执行和太空任务相同类型的任务，并且表现也一样好。为了更好地评定作者这三个无根据的主张的力度，我将需要分别知道：(1) 工厂机器人的预期停工期，即缺勤的情况；(2) 因人的错误而减少的工厂产量的程度；以及 (3) 工厂工人将愉快、有效地从事他们被分配的新工作的程度。

【逻辑问题提纲】

本文作者一共攻击了原文的四处缺陷：

1．由于工作环境等种种条件的不同，在太空使用机器人获得成功未必说明在工厂使用机器人也同样有效（错误类比的错误）。

2．机器人可能会出现故障，不一定提高效率。

3．机器人的使用未必带来更高的产量（缺乏比较的错误）。

4．工人调换岗位后未必带来精神状态的提高，而且有可能因为不胜任新工作而导致工厂效率的下降。

● 逻辑思路提示：

本文还有以下缺陷可以攻击：

1) 作者没有考虑使用机器人的花费，没有考虑成本与收益的比较。

2) 使用机器人可能会导致大量工人失业，从而产生很多社会和其他问题。

3) 机器人出现故障以及日常的维修保养会大大增加成本。

【语言提示】
● 论证段句式：（1）Without accounting for this likelihood the author cannot rely on this claim to conclude that … （2）Also questionable is the author's claim that … （3）Unless the author can provide clear evidence that …, I cannot be convinced that …
● 结尾段句式：（1）In sum, the editorial relies on a potentially weak analogy as well as on a series of unwarranted claims. （2）To strengthen the argument that …, the editorial's author must at the very least provide clear evidence that …

Argument 214　Funding public schools in **Blue City** and **Parson City**

In each city in the region of Treehaven, the majority of the money spent on government-run public school education comes from taxes that each city government collects. The region's cities differ, however, in the value they place on public education. For example, Parson City typically budgets twice as much money per year as Blue City does for its public schools—even though both cities have about the same number of residents. It seems clear, therefore, that Parson City residents care more about public school education than do Blue City residents.

【参考译文】 在特里黑文地区的每个城市，政府用于公立学校教育的开支大部分都是从各市政府征收的税收而来的。然而，该地区不同城市对公共教育的重视程度是不同的。举例而言，帕森市每年用于公立学校的预算通常是布鲁市的两倍，尽管两城市居民数量基本相同。因此，帕森市的居民显然比布鲁市居民更关注公立学校教育。

This argument concludes that Parson City residents value public-school education more highly than Blue City residents do. **To justify this conclusion the argument points out that** in both cities the majority of funds for public schools comes from taxes, and that Blue City budgets only half as much money per year for its public schools as Parson City, even though the population in both cities is about the same. **The argument relies on a series of unsubstantiated assumptions, which considered together render the argument wholly unconvincing.**

One such assumption is that the total budget for the two cities is about the same. **It is entirely possible that** Blue City's total budget is no more than half that of Parson City. **If so, then the fact that** Blue City budgets only half as much as Parson City for its public schools **would suggest** at least the same degree of care about public-school education among Blue City's residents as among Parson City's residents.

Even if Parson City devotes a greater percentage of its budget each year for its schools, **the argument relies on the additional assumption that** this percentage is a reliable indicator of the value a city's residents place on public-school education. **Yet it is entirely possible, for example, that** Blue City's schools are already well funded, or that Blue City has some other, extremely urgent problem which requires additional funding despite a high level of concern among its residents about its public schools. **Absent evidence that** the two city's various needs are similar, **any comparison between** the level of concern about public schools among residents in the two cities based simply on funds spent for public schools **is dubious at best**.

A third assumption upon which the argument rests is that the percentage of residents who attend public schools is about the same in both cities. **The argument indicates only that** the total population of the two cities is about the same. **If a comparatively small percentage of Blue City residents attend public schools, then** the comparatively small amount of money Blue City devotes to those schools might be well justified despite an equal level of concern about the quality of public-school education among residents in the two cities.

Finally, although the argument states that in both cities "the majority" of money spent on public schools comes from taxes, perhaps the actual percentage is smaller in Blue City than in Parson City, and other such funds come from residents' donations, earmarked for public education. Compliance with tax laws **is scant evidence of** taxpayer support of public-school education, while voluntary giving is strong evidence. **Thus, it is possible that** Blue City residents donate more money per capita for public-school education than Parson City residents do. **If so, this fact would seriously weaken the argument that** Blue City residents place a comparatively low value on public-school education.

In sum, the argument is unpersuasive as it stands. To strengthen it the argument's proponent must provide clear evidence that the percentage of the budget allotted to public schools, as well as the percentage of money spent on public schools and derived from taxes, is about the same in both cities. **To better assess the argument I would need to** compare the neediness of Blue City's public schools with that of Parson's public schools. **I would also need more information about** other urgent financial needs in each city, and about the other sources of the money applied toward public-school education in each city.

【参考译文】

　　这个论证认为帕森市的居民比布鲁市的居民更重视公立学校教育。为了证明这个结论是正确的，这个论证指出两座城市的大部分公立学校的资金都来自税款，然而布鲁市每年预算投入它的公立学校的资金仅为帕森市的一半，尽管两座城市的人口大概相当。这个论证依赖于一系列无确实根据的假定，而这些假定合起来导致这个论证完全不能使人信服。

　　其中一个假定是假设两个城市的总预算大致都是一样的。布鲁市的总预算完全有可能不超过帕森市预算的一半。如果是这样的话，布鲁市投在公立学校的预算只是帕森市的一半那么多这个事实至少是在暗示布鲁市居民和帕森市居民一样关心公立学校教育。

　　即使帕森市每年都把它的预算中的更大份额投给了它的公立学校，这个论证还依靠另外一个假设，即这一份额就能可靠地显示出一个城市的居民对其公立学校教育的重视程度。然而，事实却完全有可能这样，例如，布鲁市的学校的资金已经充足，或者尽管它的居民非常关心公立学校，但是布鲁城市还有其他一些特别急迫的问题需要更多的资金。由于缺乏证据证明两个城市的各种需求是相似的，那么仅基于投在公立学校的资金多寡来对两个城市的居民关心公立学校的程度进行比较，无论如何是值得怀疑的。

　　该论证所依据的第三个假设是两个城市中就读于公立学校的居民比例几乎相同。这个论证只是表明两座城市的总人口几乎一样。如果相比之下布鲁市的居民中只有较小比例的人上公立学校，那么尽管两个城市的居民对公立学校的教育质量关心程度一样，布鲁城市投在那些学校的资金相对少一些也是有理由的。

　　最后，虽然论证说明两座城市投在公立学校的大部分资金都来自税款，但是有可能布鲁市所得的实际比例比帕森市要小，而这些资金的其他部分都来自居民专门为公立教育捐献的款项。因遵从纳税法而把资金投给公立学校无力证明纳税者对公立学校教育的支持，然而自愿支付才是更强有力的证据。因此，有可能按人口平均计算，布鲁市的居民为公立学校教育所捐的款比帕森市的居民多。如果是这样的话，它将严重削弱有关布鲁市的居民对公立学校教育的重视程度相对较低这一论点。

　　总之，就目前情况看，论证是不具有说服力的。为了加强它的力度，论证的支持者必须提供明确的证据证明两个城市分派给公立学校的预算资金份额，以及公立学校花费的资金份额和从税收所得的资金份额都是几乎一样的。为了更好地评价这个论证，我需要比较布鲁市和帕森市的公立学校对资金的需求量。我还需要了解更多有关各个城市的其他重要财政需求的消息，以及各个城市投给公立学校教育的资金的其他来源的信息。

【逻辑问题提纲】

　　本文作者一共攻击了原文的四处缺陷：

　　1. 两个城市的财政预算总额可能不同，从而教育经费在其中所占的比例即无从比较（总量与比例混淆，数据模糊性的错误）。

　　2. 教育经费在财政预算中所占的比例也并不是人们对于教育的关注程度的指标。

　　3. 两个城市参加公立学校的人数可能不同，因而所需的教育经费不同（错误类比的错误）。

　　4. 作者没有考虑除了政府预算以外的其他经费来源。

　　● 逻辑思路提示：

　　1) 比例与总量混淆的问题：本文有两个段落是攻击这个数据混淆的错误的，首先是指出在不知道财政预算总额这一基数（base amount）的情况下，我们无法判断每个城市教育经费在总额中所占的比例，因而不能仅从教育经费总量的多与少来衡量它们对于教育的重视程度；其次是指出两个城市尽管居民总量相近，但需要在公立学校受教育的人所占比例不同，因而受教育者人均教育经费的数值有可能仍然是相当的。

　　2) 逻辑错误的相通性：我们曾经提到过，不同的错误形式之间并不是截然对立非此即彼的，有些错误互相包含互相融合。比如本文攻击的第三点，从论证根本来说攻击的是两个城市的情况不同不存在类比关系的错误类比的错误，但在具体展开时使用的是总量与比例混淆的论据。因此，我们自己写作时也不必把错误分得那么绝对，有些错误是相互交织、本质共通的；有时同一个问题也可以从几个不同的方面来展开论证。

　　3) 本题还有一个可供攻击的点，就是在原文中仅仅提到公立学校的经费情况，而公共教育（public education）显然不仅仅包括公立学校教育（public school education），还要考虑私立学校的经费情况。

【语言提示】

　　● 开头段句式：The argument relies on a series of unsubstantiated assumptions, which considered together render the argument wholly unconvincing.

　　● 论证段句式：(1) Absent evidence that ..., any comparison between ... is dubious at best.

　　　　(2) A third assumption upon which the argument rests is that ...

Argument 217　　A fitness-gym **franchise** opportunity

　　The following appeared in a brochure promoting the purchase of local franchises for a national chain of gyms.

　　"Now is the time to invest in a franchise so that you can profit from opening one of our gyms in your town. Consider the current trends: Power-Lift Gyms are already popular among customers in 500 locations, and national surveys indicate increasing concern with weight loss and physical fitness. Furthermore, last year's sales of books and magazines on personal health totaled more than $50 million, and purchases of home exercise equipment almost doubled. Investing now in a Power-Lift Gym franchise will guarantee a quick profit."

【参考译文】现在是投资于力量举重体育馆特许权的良好时机，你可以在你们城市开设一家体育馆，从中赢利。考虑一下当前的潮流：力量举重体育馆已经在 500 个地点的消费者中相当流行，全国调查表明对于减肥和健身的关注越来越多。而且，去年关于个人健康的书籍和杂志销售总额超过了 5000 万美元，家庭健身器具的购买量几乎翻了一番。现在投资力量举重体育馆特许权将保证快速致富。

This brochure for Power-Lift Gym claims that by investing in a Power-Lift franchise an investor will earn a quick profit. **To support this claim the brochure cites** a variety of statistics about the current popularity of physical fitness and of Power-Lift Gyms in particular. **However, careful scrutiny of this evidence reveals that it lends no credible support to the claim.**

One problem with the brochure's claim involves its reliance on the bare fact that revenue from last year's sales of health books and magazines totaled $50 million. **This statistic in itself proves nothing.** Health magazines do not all focus on weightlifting or even physical fitness; **it is possible that** very few sales were of those that do. **Besides, it is entirely possible that** in previous years total sales were even higher and that sales are actually declining. **Either scenario, if true, would serve to weaken the brochure's claim rather than support it.**

Another problem with the brochure's claim involves the fact that more and more consumers are purchasing home gyms. **It is entirely possible that** consumers are using home gyms as a substitute for commercial gyms, and that the number of Power-Lift memberships will decline as a result. **Without ruling out this possibility, the brochure cannot convince me that** a new Power-Lift franchise would be profitable.

A third problem with the brochure's claim involves its reliance on the fact that 500 Power-Lift franchises are now in existence. **It is entirely possible that** the market has become saturated, **and that** additional Power-Lift Gyms will not be as successful as current ones. **Moreover, it is possible that** the number of competing gyms has also increased in tandem with the general interest in health and fitness. **Without addressing this supply-and-demand issue, the brochure cannot justify its conclusion that** a new Power-Lift franchise would be a sound investment.

In conclusion, the brochure is unpersuasive as it stands. To strengthen its claim that a new Power-Lift franchise would be profitable, **the brochure should provide stronger evidence that** the ~~____~~ est in physical fitness, and weightlifting in particular, will conti~~____~~ **The brochure must also provide evidence that** home gyms are no~~____~~ gyms. **Finally, to better evaluate the argument we would need** ~~____~~ which the fitness-gym market has become saturated, not only by ~~____~~ ing gyms as well.

【参考译文】

　　这个力量举重体育馆的小册子声称，投资力量举重特许权~~____~~ 这个主张，小册子引用了大量关于当前对身体健康的普遍关注~~____~~ 流行程度的统计数据。但是，通过对这个证据的细察，我们发~~____~~ 支持。

　　小册子的主张所涉及的第一个问题是它所依靠的事实，即去年健康书籍和杂志的销售收入共达 5000 万美元。这个统计本身没有证明任何东西。健康杂志并不全都关注举重或者身体健康；很可能那些关注这个问题的刊物销售量很少。而且，完全可能在前些年，总销售量甚至比这还要高，所以销售量实际上正在下降。如果两个假定中的任何一个成立的话，小册子的主张将被削弱，而不是被支持。

　　小册子主张的另一个问题与越来越多的消费者正在购买家庭健身房的事实有关。完全可能消费者把家庭健身房作为一种商业体育馆的代用品，并且力量举重的成员数量将因此下降。如果没有排除这种可能性，小册子不能使我信服新的力量举重特许权将是有利可图的。

　　小册子主张的第三个问题在于它依靠现在有 500 个力量举重特许权这一事实。完全可能市场已经变得饱和，新增加的力量举重体育馆将不会像当今的那样成功。而且，很可能为了迎合大众对健康的普遍兴趣，与它相竞争的体育馆的数量也有所增加。如果没有处理供应与需求的问题，小册子就不能证明新的力量举重特许权将是一项合理投资的结论是正确的。

　　总之，就目前情况看，小册子是没有说服力的。为了加强它的主张，即新的力量举重特许权将是有利可图的，小册子应该提供更强有力的证据证明对身体健康，尤其是举重的普遍兴趣将在可预知的将来继续保持而不衰退。小册子也必须提供证据证明家庭健身房不会作为商业体育馆的代用品。最后，为了更好地评价论证，我们将需要更多的信息。这些信息是关于健身房市场现有的饱和程度，包括力量举重体育馆以及其他与此竞争的场馆设施。

【逻辑问题提纲】

本文作者一共攻击了原文的三处缺陷：

1. 健康杂志和书籍的销售额并不能说明人们对于健身的关注程度。
2. 家庭健身器械购买量的增加有可能导致对于健身场馆的需求下降。
3. 现有的 500 家场馆可能已经造成市场的饱和，并且市场竞争将会越来越激烈。

● 逻辑思路提示：本题还有以下缺陷可以攻击：

1) 作者没有提供关于已开设的 500 家场馆所在城市的信息，也许这些场馆都集中于那些对健康和健身的热衷程度非常高的城市，这些城市的经营状况并不能说明 Power-Lift Gym 在所有城市都能取得成功（草率推广的错误）。

2) 全国性调查所得到的人们关注减肥和健身的结果未必适用于每一城市（草率推广的错误）。

3) 作者没有提供关于 Power-Lift Gym 具体功能的任何信息，因而就算城市居民有减肥和健身的要求，也不能认定这些场馆就能用于满足这些要求（信息不完整的错误）。

4) 作者没有告知投资于 Power-Lift Gym 所需的成本，因而我们无法判断通过这一途径是否能够致富（没有考虑成本与收益之比的错误）。

【语言提示】

● 开头段句式：However, careful scrutiny of this evidence reveals that it lends no credible support to the claim.

论证段句式：(1) One problem with the brochure's claim involves its reliance on the bare fact . . . (2) This statistic in itself proves nothing. (3) Either scenario, if true, would serve to ～ the brochure's claim rather than support it. (4) Without addressing this supply-and-～ue, the brochure cannot justify its conclusion that . . .

Argument 220　The rewards for book writers vs. **television** writers

The following appeared in an article in a magazine for writers.

"A recent study showed that in describing a typical day's conversation, people make an average of 23 references to watching television and only 1 reference to reading fiction. This result suggests that, compared with the television industry, the publishing and bookselling industries are likely to decline in profitability. Therefore, people who wish to have careers as writers should acquire training and experience in writing for television rather than for print media."

【参考译文】最近一次研究显示，当描述日常对话的时候，人们平均有23次提到看电视，而只有一次提到读小说。这一结果说明，与电视行业相比，出版和书籍销售行业的赢利能力可能会下降。因此，想要以作家为职业的人应该接受为电视而不是为印刷媒体写作的训练，并得到相关的经验。

This article cites a recent study showing that during a typical day people make an average of 23 references to watching television but only one reference to reading fiction. **From these statistics the author reasons that** the television industry must be far more profitable than the book-publishing industry, **then concludes that** people seeking careers in writing should acquire training and experience in television writing. **This argument is flawed in several critical respects.**

First of all, the article's author has not shown the study upon which the argument depends to be statistically reliable. The people studied must be representative of the overall population of people who buy books and watch television; **otherwise the author cannot draw any firm conclusions about** the comparative profitability of the television and book-publishing industries **based on the study's results.**

Secondly, the author's argument depends on the assumption that the frequency with which a person refers in conversation to television, or to fiction books, **is a good indication of** how much television a person watches, or how many fiction books a person reads. **Yet this is not necessarily the case. Perhaps** people tend to refer many times in daily conversation to the same television show. **If so, then the statistics cited would overstate** the amount of television people watch compared to the number of fiction books they read.

Thirdly, even if the statistics cited accurately reflect the amount of television people watch compared to the number of fiction books they read, **it would be hasty to infer based merely on this fact that** the television industry is more profitable than the book-publishing industry. **To begin with,** the study's results excluded any data about nonfiction books—a category that might very well constitute book publishers' main profit source. **Moreover, the author has not shown any correlation, let alone a cause-and-effect relationship, between** the number of hours a person spends watching television **and that** industry's profits. **In any event, lacking financial statistics about** the profitability of the two industries **the editorial's author cannot convince me that** writers should follow the author's recommendation.

Finally, even assuming that the television industry is more profitable than the book-publishing industry, **the author's implicit claim that** television writers enjoy more secure and lucrative careers than book writers **is without support. It is entirely possible that** television writers are paid comparatively low wages; **in fact,** low writer compensation might partially explain why the television industry is relatively profitable. **Without better evidence that** television writers are better off than book writers **it might be folly to follow the author's recommendation.**

In sum, the argument relies on several poor assumptions and is therefore unconvincing as it stands. To strengthen it the article's author must provide clear evidence that the study's subjects reflect the overall population, **and that** their conversational habits accurately reflect how much television they watch compared to how many books they read. **The author must also show that** the disparity between the two contributes to far greater financial rewards for the television industry, as well as for its writers, than for the book-publishing industry and its writers.

【参考译文】

这篇文章引用了一项新近的研究，该研究表明在日常谈话中，人们平均有23次提到看电视，只有一次提到读小说。根据这些统计数据，作者做出如下推论，电视行业一定比图书出版业更加有利可图，从而得出结论，欲从事作家这一职业的人应该获得电视写作的训练和经验。这篇论证在以下几个关键的方面是有缺陷的。

首先，文章的作者没有说明论证所依据的研究统计数据的可靠性。这项研究的对象必须能够代表全部买书和看电视的人；否则，作者不能基于研究的结果得出任何关于电视和图书出版业的赢利比较的可靠结论。

第二，作者的论证依据一个假设，即一个人在谈话中所提及的看电视或是读书的频率，可以说明他看了多少电视或者读了多少小说。但是情况并不一定是这样。或许人们倾向于在日常对话中多次提到相同的电视节目。如果是这样的话，那么所引用的统计可能夸大了人们看电视的数量与读小说的数量之比。

第三，即使所引用的统计准确地反映出人们看电视的数量与人们读的小说的数量的比较，仅仅基于这个事实推断出电视行业比图书出版业更加有利可图也是很草率的。首先，研究的结果没有考虑其他非小说类书籍的数据，而这类书籍可能是组成图书出版商利润的主要来源。而且，作者没有揭示在一个人看电视所花费的时间和那个行业的利润之间有任何相互关系，更不用说一种因果关系。无论如何，缺乏关于这两个行业赢利的财务统计，社论的作者不能使我信服作家应该遵循他的建议。

最后，即使假定电视行业比图书出版业更加有利可图，作者所暗示的电视剧作家这一职业比为出版业写作的作家的职业更安全，更有利可图的主张是缺乏支持的。完全可能电视剧作家获得相对较少的薪酬；而实际上，支付给作家低薪可以部分解释为什么电视行业会相对赚钱。如果没有更好的证据证明电视剧作家的经济状况比写书的作家更好，遵循作者的建议可能很愚蠢。

总之，就目前情况看，论证依据的是几个没有根据的假定，因此不具有说服力。为了加强论证，文章的作者必须提供清楚的证据表明研究的对象能够代表全部人口，并且他们的会话习惯准确反映出他们看电视与读书数量的比较。作者也必须证实，与图书出版业及其作家相比，人们看电视和读书所花时间的差异将会导致电视行业及其作家获得更多的经济报酬。

【逻辑问题提纲】

本文作者一共攻击了原文的四处缺陷：

1. 作者没有提供文中提到的调查所采取的样本的信息，因而样本的代表性值得怀疑。

2. 人们在日常谈话中提到电视和小说的频率并不是他们看电视和小说的真正数量的指标（差异概念的错误）。

3. 作者没有考虑除了小说以外的其他出版物的情况，也没有建立观众看电视的时间与电视行业赢利情况之间的因果关系。

4. 即使电视行业赢利确实更多，但为电视写作的作者的收入未必更高。

● 逻辑思路提示：本题还有一个可以攻击的错误，就是非此即彼的错误（either-or fallacy）：电视和印刷媒体并非互相排斥非此即彼的选择，为这两种媒体写作的训练和经验可能并不矛盾。另一方面，可选择的媒体也并非只有这两种，想以写作为职业的人也可以有其他选择，比如网络、电影等等。因此作者不能简单地认为不为出版业写作就只能为电视行业写作。

【论证展开】

　　攻击差异概念的方式：攻击差异概念的最基本思路是先指出作者所提出的哪两个概念不能划等号，然后再具体说明它们之间有那些不同。我们可以使用 The argument depends on the assumption that A is a good indication of B. 来指出 A 和 B 是差异概念，也可以使用 The author simply equates A with B. 这样的句子。

【语言提示】

● 论证段句式：攻击调查样本的句式：(1) The article's author has not shown the study upon which the argument depends to be statistically reliable. (2) The people studied must be representative of the overall population of people who ...; otherwise the author cannot draw any firm conclusions about ... based on the study's results. 攻击差异概念的句式：Secondly, the author's argument depends on the assumption that ... is a good indication of ...其他句式：(1) Even if ..., it would be hasty to infer based merely on this fact that ... (2) Moreover, the author has not shown any correlation, let alone a cause-and-effect relationship, between ... and ... (3) In any event, lacking financial statistics about ... the editorial's author cannot convince me that ... (4) Without better evidence that ... it might be folly to follow the author's recommendation.

● 结尾段句式：In sum, the argument relies on several poor assumptions and is therefore unconvincing as it stands.

Argument 221　Jobs for **Hooper**'s social science majors

The following article appeared in a recent issue of a college newspaper.

"Among all students who graduated from Hooper University over the past five years, more physical science majors than social science majors found permanent jobs within a year of graduation. In a survey of recent Hooper University graduates, most physical science majors said they believed that the prestige of Hooper University's physical science programs helped them significantly in finding a job. In contrast, social science majors who found permanent employment attributed their success to their own personal initiative. Therefore, to ensure that social science majors find permanent jobs, Hooper University should offer additional social science courses and hire several new faculty members who already have national reputations in the social sciences."

【参考译文】在过去五年，从胡珀大学毕业的所有学生中，自然科学专业的毕业生在毕业一年内找到固定工作的人数要多于社会科学的毕业生。在一次对于胡珀大学最近的毕业生的调查中，多数自然科学专业的学生说，他们认为胡珀大学自然科学学科的声望在他们找工作的过程中起到了极大的作用。相比之下，找到固定工作的社会科学毕业生则把他们的成功归因于他们自己的能动性。因此，为保证社科毕业生找到固定工作，胡珀大学应该提供更多的社科课程，并雇用一些已经在社科领域获得全国声誉的新教员。

This article concludes that in order to help its new social-science graduates find permanent jobs Hooper University should enhance its reputation in this field by adding courses and hiring eminent faculty. **To support this claim the letter points out that** more physical-science than social-science students find permanent jobs within a year after graduation. **The letter also cites a survey** in which the former group of graduates attributed their job finding success to the prestige of Hooper's physical-science department, while the latter group attributed their job-finding success to their own initiative. **However, careful scrutiny of the argument reveals various statistical and other logical problems, which render it unconvincing.**

To begin with, the survey that the argument cites is potentially problematic in three respects. First, we are not informed whether the survey's respondents were representative of the overall population of recent Hooper graduates in these two fields. **The smaller the sample, the greater the possibility for biased results, and the less reliable the survey. Second,** the survey reflects the graduates' subjective "beliefs" about why they obtained jobs; **yet it is entirely possible** these beliefs are not in accord with the true reason why they obtained jobs. **Third, we are informed that** the survey involved "recent" Hooper graduates; **however,** if the only graduates surveyed were those from last year's class, then the survey results would be less reliable than if the survey embraced a wider range of graduating classes. **The smaller the range the less reliable any general conclusions drawn from the survey.**

Even assuming the statistics that the letter cites are reliable, the letter's claim that the proposed course of action will achieve its intended result assumes a sufficient job market for social-science graduates. **However, it is entirely possible that** the number of jobs for physical-science graduates greatly exceeds the number of jobs for social-science graduates, and that this is the reason for the disparity in job-finding success between the two groups. **In fact, real-world observation suggests that** this is a reasonable explanation for the disparity. **Moreover, the letter fails to account for the possibility that** the latter group of graduates are less likely than the former group to be interested in immediate employment—electing instead to pursue graduate-level study. **Without accounting for these possibilities, the letter's author cannot justifiably conclude that** the proposed course of action will boost the employment rate of new social-science graduates.

A third problem with the argument is that it unfairly infers that the proposed course of action is the only means of achieving the desired result. **The letter's author overlooks other possible means of** ensuring that social-science students find immediate employment—such as co-op programs, job seminars, and so forth. **Without ruling out alternative means of** achieving the same goal, **the author cannot convince me that** the proposed course of action is needed.

In conclusion, as it stands the argument is unconvincing. To strengthen it the author must provide strong evidence that the survey's respondents were statistically representative of all recent Hooper graduates in these two fields of study. **The author must also rule out all other possible explanations for** the disparity between job-finding success between the two groups of Hooper graduates. **Finally, to better evaluate the argument I would need more information about** the portion of graduates in each field pursuing immediate employment, and what alternative means are available to help ensure that Hooper's new social-science graduates find permanent employment.

【参考译文】

　　这篇文章断定，为了帮助新的社会科学专业毕业生找到固定职业，胡珀大学应该通过增加课程和雇用有名气的教员来提高其在这个领域内的声望。为了支持这个主张，这封信指出与社会科学专业学生相比较，更多的自然科学专业学生在毕业后一年内找到了固定职业。那封信也引用了一个调查，在这个调查中，自然科学专业的学生将找到工作归功于胡珀自然科学院系的威望，而社会科学专业的学生将找到工作归功于他们自己的主动性。但是，通过对论证的细察，我们发现有很多统计和其他逻辑问题，使这篇文章不能令人信服。

首先，这篇论证所引用的调查在三个方面有潜在问题。第一，文章没有告诉我们调查的回答者是否能代表这两个领域内新近的胡珀毕业生的总群体。这个样本越小，结果有偏差的可能性越大，调查就越不可靠。其次，调查反映出毕业生关于他们为什么获得工作的主观的"看法"；然而完全可能这些看法并不与他们获得工作的真实原因相一致。第三，文章告诉我们调查是有关"新近"的胡珀毕业生的；但是，如果那些被调查的毕业生仅仅是去年那届的，那么比起调查对象包括更多几届的毕业生的调查，这个调查结果就更不可靠了。调查的范围越小，由调查得出的任何概括性的结论的可靠性就越差。

即使假定这封信所引用的统计是可靠的，它关于通过建议的行动方针将达到其预定目标的论断仍假定社会科学专业的毕业生就业市场足够广阔。但是，完全可能适合自然科学专业毕业生的岗位数量远远超过适合社会科学专业毕业生岗位数量，并且这是这两组毕业生就业状况有所不同的原因。实际上，现实社会观察表明这是对两者之间存在的差异的一个合理解释。而且，这封信没有考虑到社会科学专业毕业生比起自然科学专业毕业生来，立即就业的兴趣相对小一些，而有可能选择继续研究生的学习。如果没有解释这些可能性，这封信的作者不能无可非议地断定他所提倡的行动方针将提高新的社会科学专业毕业生的就业率。

此论证的第三个问题是它不公平地假定所提议的行动方针是取得预期效果的惟一方法。这封信的作者忽视了确保社会科学专业学生立即找到工作的其他可能的方法，例如合作计划，工作讨论会等等。如果没有排除其他可达到相同目标的方法，作者不能使我信服被提议的行动方针是必需的。

总之，就目前情况来看，这篇论证是不能令人信服的。为了加强论证，作者必须提供强有力的证据来证明调查的回答者是这两个学科领域所有新近的胡珀毕业生的代表。作者也必须排除有关这两组胡珀毕业生找工作的成功率不同的所有其他可能的解释。最后，为了更好地评价这篇论证，我需要更多的关于各个学科寻求立即就业的毕业生所占比例的信息，以及能够确保胡珀的社会科学专业的新毕业生找到固定工作的其他可能的方法的信息。

【逻辑问题提纲】

本文作者一共攻击了原文的三处缺陷：

1. 文中引用的调查样本的代表性、回答真实性和覆盖范围值得怀疑。
2. 增加作者所说的课程未必能增加就业，就业人数的差异可能由别的原因所导致。
3. 作者没有考虑除了文中提到的方式以外的其他增加就业率的手段。

● 逻辑思路提示：本文还有一个数据模糊性的错误可以攻击：作者没有提供关于两个系毕业生总数（基数）的信息，因而尽管自然科学系学生找到工作的总数大于社科系学生，但由于学生基数不同，就业比例的高低可能正好相反。

【语言提示】

● 开头段句式：However, careful scrutiny of the argument reveals various statistical and other logical problems, which render it unconvincing.

● 论证段句式：(1) The survey that the argument cites is potentially problematic in three respects. (2) We are not informed whether the survey's respondents were representative of the overall population of … (3) The smaller the sample, the greater the possibility for biased results, and the less reliable the survey. (4) The smaller the range the less reliable any general conclusions drawn from the survey.

Argument 224 Governor Riedeburg's candidacy

The following appeared as part of a letter to the editor of a local newspaper.

"During her three years in office, Governor Riedeburg has shown herself to be a worthy leader. Since she took office, crime has decreased, the number of jobs created per year has doubled, and the number of people choosing to live in our state has increased. These trends are likely to continue if she is reelected. In addition, Ms. Riedeburg has promised to take steps to keep big companies here, thereby providing jobs for any new residents. Anyone who looks at Ms. Riedeburg's record can tell that she is the best-qualified candidate for governor."

【参考译文】在州长瑞德勃格在位的三年中，她证明了自己是一个优秀的领导者。自从她就任以后，犯罪减少了，每年创造的就业机会数量翻了一番，选择在本州居住的人数也增加了。如果她再次当选，这种趋势很可能将会继续下去。而且，瑞德勃格承诺说要采取措施使大公司留在这里，从而为新居民提供就业机会。任何目睹了瑞德勃格工作成就的人都会认为她是州长的最佳人选。

This letter concludes that Governor Riedeburg is the best-qualified candidate for the job of state governor. To justify this conclusion the letter points out various statewide trends since the governor was elected, and the fact that she has promised to keep big companies in the state, thereby providing jobs for any new residents. However, close scrutiny of the argument reveals various logical problems, which render it unconvincing.

One problem with the argument is that the letter's author might be assigning a false cause to these statewide trends. The author provides no evidence that Riedeburg's policies and actions as governor were indeed the reason for these developments. Without such evidence, it is equally possible that other factors are instead responsible for the trends. For instance, perhaps the crime rate has declined due to legislative or judicial action over which Riedeburg had no control. Perhaps the rise in the state's population is the result of sociological trends that have nothing to do with Riedeburg's policies as governor. Or perhaps people are moving to the state for other reasons, such as the state's climate. Moreover, the argument assumes that an increase in population is a positive development in the first place; yet it is entirely possible that the state's residents properly view this trend as a negative one. If so, and if Riedeburg's policies have contributed to this trend, then the author cannot reasonably conclude based on this evidence that Riedeburg is the best-qualified candidate.

Another problem with the argument involves Riedeburg's promise to keep big companies in the state, thereby providing jobs for any new residents. Assuming that Riedeburg keeps her promise in the first place, the author provides no evidence that these employers would be either willing or able to hire new residents. Perhaps these employers plan to curtail new hiring in any event; or perhaps they plan to hire new employees only among current state residents. Moreover, whether these employers are able to hire new employees depends on a variety of extrinsic economic factors over which Riedeburg might have no control. Without accounting for these possibilities, the author cannot rely on

Riedeburg's promise **to conclude that** she is the best-qualified candidate for the job of state governor.

Finally, the author's conclusion that Riedeburg is "the best-qualified candidate" **raises two problems in itself. First,** regardless of Riedeburg's record as governor **it is entirely possible that** one or more other candidates are actually better qualified. **Second, the letter fails to adequately define** what makes a candidate for state governor qualified. **Without indicating** what the ideal qualifications would be **and ruling out the possibility that** another candidate better meets these qualifications, **the author cannot make a convincing case that** Riedeburg is the best-qualified candidate.

In conclusion, the argument is unpersuasive as it stands. To strengthen it the author must provide clear evidence that it was Riedeburg who was responsible for the currents trends, **and that** the current population trend is desirable in the first place. **The author must also show that** the state's major employers would be willing and able to hire new residents in the future. **Finally, to better evaluate the argument we would need more information about** what defines an ideal governor and how well other candidates meet that definition.

【参考译文】

　　这封信断定瑞德勃格州长是适合州长工作的最佳候选人。为了证明这个结论是正确的，这封信指出了州长当选后全州范围内的很多方面的趋势，并指出了她已经许诺留住州内的大公司，从而为新居民提供工作。但是，通过对论证的细察，我们发现它有很多方面的逻辑问题，使其不能令人信服。

　　这篇论证的一个问题是此信的作者对这些全州范围内的趋势所做的解释可能是错误的。作者没有提供证据证明瑞德勃格作为州长时的政策和行动的确是引起这些发展的原因。如果没有这样的证据，其他因素造成此趋势也是同样可能的。例如，或许犯罪率下降是由于瑞德勃格无法控制的立法或者司法举措。或许全州人口数量的升高与瑞德勃格作为州长所推行的政策无关，而是社会趋势变化的结果。或者也许人们由于其他原因而迁移到本州，例如，因为本州的气候。并且，论证首先假定人口的增加是一个积极的现象；但是，也可能那个州的居民实际上将这个趋势视为消极的发展。如果这样的话，并且如果瑞德勃格的政策导致了这个趋势，那么作者不能基于这个证据合理地做出瑞德勃格是最佳候选人的结论。

　　这篇论证涉及的另一个问题是瑞德勃格关于留住全州范围内的大公司，从而为新居民提供工作的许诺。首先假定瑞德勃格能够遵守她的诺言，作者也没有提供证据证明这些雇主将愿意或者能够雇用新居民。或许这些雇主计划无论如何要缩减新的招聘计划；或者也许他们计划只在目前全州范围内的居民中雇用新雇员。而且，这些雇主是否能够雇用新雇员取决于多种外部经济因素，而这些可能是瑞德勃格无法控制的。如果没有考虑这些可能性，作者就不能凭借瑞德勃格的许诺断定她是适合州长工作的最佳候选人。

　　最后，作者关于瑞德勃格是"最佳的候选人"的结论本身还存在两个问题。首先，尽管瑞德勃格曾有当州长的经历，但完全可能有其他候选人更具资格。其次，这封信没能充分地阐明州长候选人的资格定义。如果没有说明什么才是理想的资格，并且排除另一个候选人更好地具备这些资格的可能性，作者不能使人信服瑞德勃格是最佳候选人。

　　总之，就目前情况看，论证是不具有说服力的。为了加强论证，作者必须提供清楚的证据证实瑞德勃格是造成目前趋势的原因，并且当今的人口趋势正是人们想要的。作者也必须说明将来州内主要的雇主将愿意并且能够雇用新居民。最后，为了更好地评价这篇论证，我们需要更多的关于理想州长的定义和其他候选人是否适合那个定义的信息。

【逻辑问题提纲】

本文作者一共攻击了原文的三处缺陷：

1. 作者没有提出直接证据表明瑞德勃格的领导是产生文中所述现象的原因。

2. 留在本州的大公司未必雇用新居民。

3. 作者没有考虑到可能有其他比瑞德勃格更加胜任的候选人，也没有对于合格与否的条件做出明确定义。

【论证展开】

攻击因果关系错误的语言：在批判作者没能建立 A 与 B 两件事之间的因果联系时，我们可以使用最基本的 the author fails to establish the causal relationship between A and B 和 the author fails to convince us that A contribute to B，以及 the author provides no evidence that A is the reason for B；也可以使用本文的句型：One problem with the argument is that the letter's author might be assigning a false cause to ... 或 Without such evidence, it is equally possible that other factors are instead responsible for ...

【语言提示】

● 论证句式：(1) One problem with the argument is that the letter's author might be assigning a false cause to ... (2) The author provides no evidence that ... were indeed the reason for ... (3) Without such evidence, it is equally possible that other factors are instead responsible for... (4) If so, the author cannot reasonably conclude based on this evidence that ... (5) Without accounting for these possibilities, the author cannot rely on ... to conclude that ... (6) Finally, the author's conclusion that ... raises two problems in itself.

Argument 236　　Will business incentives help **Beauville**'s economy?

The following appeared as part of an article in a local Beauville newspaper.

"According to a government report, last year the city of Dillton reduced its corporate tax rate by 15 percent; at the same time, it began offering relocation grants and favorable rates on city utilities to any company that would relocate to Dillton. Within 18 months, two manufacturing companies moved to Dillton, where they employ a total of 300 people. Therefore, the fastest way for Beauville to stimulate economic development and hence reduce unemployment is to provide tax incentives and other financial inducements that encourage private companies to relocate here."

【参考译文】 根据一项政府报告，去年迪顿市把它的企业所得税率降低了 15%；同时，该市给予迁移至迪顿的公司一定的再安置费和相应城市设施使用费的优惠。在 18 个月内，两家生产制造公司搬迁到了迪顿，他们在那里一共雇用了 300 名工人。因此，宝维勒市刺激经济发展从而降低失业率最快的方法就是提供税率以及其他经济上的优惠来鼓励私有企业搬迁到本地。

This article argues that the fastest way for Beauville to stimulate its economic development and reduce unemployment would be to provide the same kinds of tax and financial incentives for business as the incentives which the city of Dillton began providing 18 months ago. Dillton's incentives included a reduced corporate tax rate as well as relocation grants and favorable utility rates for businesses willing to relocate to Dillton. **The article points out that** during the last 18 months two manufacturing companies, which together now employ 300 people, relocated to Dillton. **The argument is logically unconvincing in several respects.**

To begin with, the argument depends on the assumption that the two businesses moving to Dillton did so because of Dillton's new incentives—rather than for some other reason. **Yet lacking evidence to the contrary it is entirely possible that** the two businesses were motivated primarily by Dillton's climate, labor pool, or some other factor. **Without ruling out all other reasons why** the two businesses might have relocated to Dillton, **the argument that** Beauville can entice businesses to move to Beauville by offering similar incentives **is dubious at best.**

Even if it was Dillton's new incentives that enticed the two manufacturers to Dillton, **the argument relies on the further assumption that** the two firms' relocating to Dillton in fact had a beneficial impact on the city's economy. **Yet the only evidence the article offers to substantiate this assumption is that** the two manufacturers now employ 300 people. **Perhaps** those 300 employees left other jobs in Dillton to go to work for those two firms; **if so,** then the incentives had no positive impact on Dillton's employment rate. **Or perhaps** other businesses have left Dillton during the last 18 months, taking even more job opportunities with them. **For that matter, perhaps** on average more businesses relocated to Dillton each year prior to Dillton's establishing the new incentives than afterward. **In short, without more information about** Dillton's economic conditions and employment level both before and after the incentives were established **it is impossible to assess** whether those incentives had a positive or negative impact—or any impact at all—on Dillton's overall economy.

Even if Dillton's new incentives did in fact serve to help Dillton's economy, **the article unfairly assumes that** similar incentives will carry a similar result for Beauville. **It is entirely possible that** the two cities differ in ways that would undermine the effectiveness of similar incentives for Beauville. **For instance, perhaps** Beauville's labor pool is smaller; **or perhaps** unemployed Beauville residents would be less willing or able to go to work if offered the chance. **Without accounting for such differences any analogy between** the two cities **is premature, and any conclusion based on that analogy is unjustified.**

Furthermore, the author's inference that incentives which were effective in the past will also be effective in the future **rests on the poor assumption that** during the last 18 months all conditions upon which their effectiveness depend have remained unchanged. **Perhaps** the general economy is expected to turn down. **Or perhaps** other cities have recently begun to provide similar incentives. **Indeed, the fact that** Dillton is already providing these incentives might actually portend failure for Beauville, which might need to devise even stronger incentives to convince businesses to move to Beauville rather than Dillton.

Finally, the article fails to consider any other course of action that might help Beauville attain the same economic goals. **Perhaps** by improving its schools or hospitals, or by reducing its crime rate, Beauville can just as quickly and effectively attract new businesses and achieve its economic objectives. **In short, without weighing the proposal against alternatives, the article's claim that** the proposed incentives are the "best" means of achieving Beauville's objectives **is wholly unconvincing.**

To sum up, the article has not convinced me that the proposed incentives would be the best way for Beauville to achieve its economic goals. **To bolster the argument the article's author must provide clear evidence that** Dillton's incentives—and not some other phenomenon—were in fact responsible for stimulating Dillton's economy during the last 18 months. **To better assess the argument I would need to know** what other conditions in Beauville that were not present in Dillton might dissuade businesses from moving to Beauville—despite the proposed incentives. **I would also need to** compare near-term economic forecasts with economic conditions during the last 18 months. **Finally, I would need to consider** the proposed incentives in light of alternative courses of action.

【参考译文】

　　这篇文章认为，对于宝维勒来说，刺激经济发展和减少失业率的最快的方法是按照迪顿市18个月以前开始提供商业优惠政策那样为商业提供同种类型的税收和财政优惠。迪顿市的优惠政策包括降低企业所得税率，除此之外，还包括为愿意迁往迪顿市的企业提供再安置费和优惠的使用费用。文章指出，在过去的18个月里，有两家现在共雇用了300人的制造公司在迪顿市安置了下来。这篇文章的论证在以下几个方面逻辑上不具有说服力。

　　首先，论证所依据的假定是那两家企业迁移到迪顿市是因为迪顿市的新优惠政策，而不是因为其他一些原因。然而缺乏与之相反的证据，完全可能那两家企业主要是被迪顿市的气候、劳动力市场或者其他一些因素促使的。如果没有排除那两家企业迁往迪顿市的所有其他的原因，宝维勒通过提供类似的优惠政策可诱使企业迁往宝维勒的说法无论如何都是可疑的。

　　即使确实是迪顿市的新优惠政策诱使了两家制造公司迁往迪顿市，论证仍依据一个更进一步的假定，即那两家公司迁移到迪顿市实际上给这个城市的经济带来了有利的影响。然而文章所提供的惟一可证实这个假定的证据是这两家制造商现在雇用了300人。或许那300个雇员是离开迪顿市的其他工作岗位而到那两家公司去上班的；如果是这样的话，那么优惠政策没有对迪顿市的就业率产生积极的影响。或者也许其他企业在过去18个月期间离开了迪顿市，带走了更多的就业机会。同样，也许在迪顿市实行优惠政策之前平均每年迁往迪顿市的企业比实行优惠政策之后还要多。简而言之，如果没有更多关于优惠政策实行之前和之后迪顿市的经济状况和雇用人数的信息，就不可能判断那些优惠政策对迪顿市的整个经济是否有正面或负面的影响，还是根本就没有什么影响。

　　即使迪顿市的新优惠政策确实有助于迪顿市的经济，文章还不公平地认为相似的优惠政策将给宝维勒带来相似的结果。完全可能这两座城市在很多方面有所不同，以致相似的优惠政策的效力在宝维勒将会降低。比如，或许宝维勒的劳动力市场更小；或者即使有工作机会提供，失业的宝维勒居民也不愿意或者不能够去上班。如果没有考虑这些差异，任何这两座城市之间的类推都是为时过早的，并且任何基于那个类推的结论都无法被有效证实。

　　此外，作者关于这些在过去有效的优惠政策在将来也将有效的推论建立在一个没有根据的假定上，就是过去18个月中优惠政策的效力所依存的全部条件仍然保持不变。或许总体经济状况将会低迷，或者也许其他的城市最近已经开始提供相似的优惠政策了。其实，迪顿市已经提供这些优惠政策的事实实际上可能会导致宝维勒的失败，宝维勒可能需要制定更有吸引力的优惠政策来说服企业迁往宝维勒，而不是迪顿。

　　最后，文章没有考虑可能有助于宝维勒实现相同的经济目标的任何其他行动方针。或许通过改进它的学校或者医院，或者通过降低它的犯罪率，宝维勒一样能迅速而有效地吸引新的企业，并且达到它的经济目标。简而言之，在没有权衡文中建议和其他选择的情况下，文章主张建议的优惠政策是达到宝维勒目标的"最好"的办法，这是完全不能令人信服的。

　　总的来说，文章没能使我相信所建议的优惠政策是宝维勒达到其经济目标的最好的方式。为了支持论证，文章作者必须提供清楚的证据证实在过去18个月间，确实是迪顿市的优惠政策而不是一些其他现象刺激了迪顿市的经济。为了更好地评价论证，我需要知道在宝维勒还有哪些其他条件是迪顿市所不具备的，而这些条件会阻止企业迁往宝维勒，尽管它提供了建议的优惠措施。我也需要比较近期的经济预测与过去18个月的经济状况。最后，我需要参照其他的可选择的行动方针来考虑文中建议的优惠政策。

【逻辑问题提纲】:

本文作者一共攻击了原文的五处缺陷:

1. 两家企业搬到迪顿未必是因为文中所述政策的刺激而可能有别的原因。

2. 搬到迪顿的两家企业未必对该市的就业率等经济状况起到正面影响。

3. 迪顿的政策未必会在宝维勒起到相同的作用(错误类比的错误)。

4. 在过去18个月产生效果的政策和措施在将来未必同样有效(没有与时俱进的错误)。

5. 作者没有考虑其他能够帮助宝维勒市达到同样目标的途径。

【论证展开】

● 攻击作者没有与时俱进的错误的方式:在攻击作者没有考虑时间的变化,简单地从过去或现在的情况推断将来时,可以先用the author's inference that ... rests on the poor assumption that during the ... (the interim) all conditions upon which their effectiveness depend have remained unchanged.来指出作者的错误,然后用推测法和列举法例举有哪些情况和因素会随着时间而变化,最后用我们掌握的句型作段落小总结。

● 攻击作者没有考虑其他途径的方式:在攻击作者思路过于片面,只考虑某一种方案而没有考虑其他时,可以先用the article fails to consider any other ... that might help ... attain the same effect.来指出错误,再列举一下还有哪些其他途径和措施也可以达到相同的效果,最后用without weighing the proposal against alternatives, the article's claim that ... is the "best" means of achieving ... is wholly unconvincing.来作段落结尾。

【语言提示】

● 论证句式:(1) Yet lacking evidence to the contrary it is entirely possible that ... (2) Without ruling out all other reasons why ..., the argument that ... is dubious at best. (3) Without accounting for such differences any analogy between ... is premature, and any conclusion based on that analogy is unjustified. (4) Finally, the article fails to consider any other course of action that might ... (5) In short, without weighing the proposal against alternatives, the article's claim that ... is wholly unconvincing.

第五章　Argument 范文精选

Argument 2　Enhancing property values at **Deerhaven Acres**

In this letter, a committee of Deerhaven Acres homeowners recommends that in order to enhance Deerhaven property values homeowners should follow certain restrictions concerning their homes' exterior appearance. To support this recommendation the committee points out that in the seven years since Brookville adopted similar restrictions property values there have risen. This argument rests on a series of unsubstantiated assumptions, and is therefore unpersuasive as it stands.

A threshold assumption upon which the recommendation relies is that Brookville homeowners implemented Brookville's restrictions in the first place. The letter fails to substantiate this crucial assumption. If these restrictions were not implemented, then any change in Brookville's property values cannot be attributed to them. Accordingly, the committee cannot draw any firm conclusion about what effect similar restrictions would have on Deerhaven property values.

Even assuming that Brookville homeowners implemented these restrictions, the committee relies on the additional assumption that this course of action was responsible for the increase in Brookville property values. However, it is entirely possible that one or more other factors were instead responsible for the increase, especially since a considerable period of time has passed since Brookville adopted its restrictions. Property values are a function of supply and demand. Perhaps the demand for housing in the area has increased due to an influx of major employers. Or, perhaps the supply of housing has decreased. Either scenario would provide an alternative explanation for the increase in property values.

Even assuming that Brookville's rising property values are attributable to the implementation of these restrictions, the committee fails to consider possible differences between Brookville and Deerhaven that might help to bring about a different result for Deerhaven. For instance, potential Deerhaven homebuyers might be less interested in a home's exterior appearance than Brookville homebuyers. For that matter, perhaps Deerhaven homebuyers would find consistent exterior appearance a distasteful feature—in which case adopting these restrictions might actually tend to decrease Deerhaven property values. Without accounting for these and other possible dissimilarities, the committee cannot assume that what resulted in rising property values in Brookville would bring about the same result in Deerhaven.

In conclusion, to persuade me that Deerhaven should adopt the proposed restrictions the committee must supply clear evidence that the implementation of Brookville's restrictions, and not some other factor, was responsible for the rise in Brookville's property values. The committee must also provide evidence that other factors affecting home prices in the two areas are otherwise essentially the same.

Argument 4　Which **real estate firm** is better?

The author of this argument claims that Adams Realty is superior to Fitch Realty. To support this claim the author cites certain statistics about the number and working hours of the firms' agents, and the number and sales prices of homes sold by the two firms. The author also cites anecdotal evidence involving her own experience with Fitch and Adams. Close scrutiny of this evidence reveals that it lends little credible support for the author's assertion.

The author bases her claim partly on the fact that Adams has more agents than Fitch, and that many of Fitch's agents work only part-time. However, the author provides no evidence that the quality of a real estate firm is directly proportional to the number of its agents or the number of hours per week that its agents work. Lacking such evidence, it is equally possible that a smaller firm is more effective than a larger one, and that a part-time agent is more effective than a full-time agent. Besides, the author does not provide any information about how many Adams agents work part-time.

To further support her claim the author cites the fact that Adams sold more properties last year than Fitch. However, the author overlooks the possibility that last year's sales volume amounted to an aberration, and that in most other years Adams has actually sold fewer properties than Fitch. Moreover, the disparity in sales volume can readily be explained by factors other than the comparative quality of the two firms. Perhaps Adams serves a denser geographic area, or an area where turnover in homeownership is higher for reasons unrelated to Adams' effectiveness. Or perhaps sales volume is higher at Adams simply because it employs more agents, and each Adams agent actually sells fewer homes on average than each Fitch agent does. Without ruling out such alternative explanations for the disparity in sales volume, the author cannot defend the conclusion that based on this evidence Adams is superior to Fitch.

In further support of her claim, the author points out that the average sales price of a home sold by Adams is greater than the average price of a home sold by Fitch. However, this evidence shows only that the homes that Adams sells are more valuable on average than the ones that Fitch sells, not that Adams is more effective in selling homes than Fitch. Moreover, it is possible that a few relatively high-priced or low-priced properties skewed these averages, rendering any conclusions about the comparative quality of the two firms based on these averages unfair.

For additional support the author points out that it took Fitch Realty considerably longer to sell one of the author's homes than it took Adams Realty to sell another one of her homes ten years earlier. However, this disparity is explainable by other plausible factors, such as changing economic conditions during that ten-year period, or a difference in the desirability of the two properties. Without establishing that all other factors affecting the speed of a sale were essentially the same for the two homes, the author cannot rely on this limited anecdotal evidence to support her claim.

In conclusion, the author's evidence lends little credible support to her claim. To persuade me that Adams is better than Fitch, the author would need to provide clear evidence that individual Adams agents are more effective in selling homes than individual Fitch agents, and that the disparity in home sales and sales price is attributable to that difference. Finally, to better evaluate the author's claim we would need more information comparing the percentage of agents working part-time at Fitch versus Adams. We would also need more information about the comparative attractiveness of the author's two homes, and the extent to which the residential real estate market changed during the decade between the sale of these two homes.

Argument 12　Worker safety at **Alta Manufacturing**

This editorial recommends that Alta Manufacturing reduce its work shifts by one hour each in order to reduce its on-the-job accident rate and thereby increase Alta's productivity. To support this recommendation the author points out that last year the number of accidents at Alta was 30% greater than at Panoply Industries, where work shifts were one hour shorter. The author also cites certain experts who believe that many on-the-job accidents are caused by fatigue and sleep deprivation. I find this the argument unconvincing for several reasons.

First and foremost, the author provides absolutely no evidence that overall worker productivity is attributable in part to the number of on-the-job accidents. Although common sense informs me that such a relationship exists, the author must provide some evidence of this cause-and-effect relationship before I can accept the author's final conclusion that the proposed course of action would in fact increase Alta's productivity.

Secondly, the author assumes that some accidents at Alta are caused by fatigue or sleep deprivation. However, the author overlooks other possible causes, such as inadequate equipment maintenance or worker training, or the inherent hazards of Alta's manufacturing processes. By the same token, Panoply's comparatively low accident rate might be attributable not to the length of its work shifts but rather to other factors, such as superior equipment maintenance or worker training. In other words, without ruling out alternative causes of on-the-job accidents at both companies, the author cannot justifiably conclude that merely by emulating Panoply's work shift policy Alta would reduce the number of such accidents.

Thirdly, even assuming that Alta's workers are fatigued or sleep-deprived, and that this is the cause of some of Alta's on-the-job accidents, in order to accept the author's solution to this problem we must assume that Alta's workers would use the additional hour of free time to sleep or rest. However, the author provides no evidence that they would use the time in this manner. It is entirely possible that Alta's workers would use that extra hour to engage in some other fatiguing activity. Without ruling out this possibility the author cannot convincingly conclude that reducing Alta's work shifts by one hour would reduce Alta's accident rate.

Finally, a series of problems with the argument arise from the scant statistical information on which it relies. In comparing the number of accidents at Alta and Panoply, the author fails to consider that the per-worker accident rate might reveal that Alta is actually safer than Panoply, depending on the total number of workers at each company. Second, perhaps accident rates at the two companies last year were aberrations, and during other years Alta's accident rate was no greater, or even lower, than Panoply's rate. Or perhaps Panoply is not representative of industrial companies generally, and that other companies with shorter work shifts have even higher accident rates. In short, since the argument relies on very limited statistical information I cannot take the author's recommendation seriously.

In conclusion, the recommendation for emulating Panoply's work-shift policy is not well supported. To convince me that shorter work shifts would reduce Alta's on-the-job accident rate, the author must provide clear evidence that work-shift length is responsible for some of Alta's accidents. The author must also supply evidence to support her final conclusion that a lower accident rate would in fact increase overall worker productivity.

Argument 15 Investing in **Old Dairy** stock

This excerpt from an investment newsletter cites a recent study in which 80% of respondents indicated a desire to reduce their consumption of high-fat and high-cholesterol foods, then points out that food stores are well stocked with low-fat food products. Based on this evidence the newsletter predicts a significant decline in sales and profits for Old Dairy (OD), a producer of dairy products high in fat and cholesterol, and advises investors not to own OD stock. I find this advice specious, on several grounds.

First, the excerpt fails to assure me that the survey results accurately reflect the desires of most consumers, or that the results accurately predict consumer behavior. Without evidence that the respondents' desires are representative of those of the overall population where OD products are sold, it is hasty to draw any conclusions about future foodbuying habits from the survey. Moreover, common sense informs me that consumers do not necessarily make food-purchase decisions in strict accordance with their expressed desires. Thus, as it stands the statistic that the newsletter cites amounts to scant evidence that OD sales and profits will decline in the future.

Secondly, the fact that low-fat foods are in abundant supply in food stores does not necessarily indicate an increasing demand for low-fat dairy products or a diminishing demand for high-fat dairy products. Absent evidence to the contrary, it is quite possible that consumers are buying other types of low-fat foods but are still demanding high fat in their dairy products. For that matter, it is entirely possible that food stores are well stocked with low-fat foods because actual demand has not met the demand anticipated by the stores.

Thirdly, even assuming an indisputable consumer trend toward purchasing more low-fat dairy products and fewer high-fat dairy products, the newsletter concludes too hastily that OD profits will decline as a result. OD can always raise the price of its dairy products to offset declining sales, and given a sufficient demand OD might still turn a profit, despite the general consumer trend. Besides, profit is a function of not just revenue but also expenses. Perhaps OD expenses will decline by a greater amount than its revenue; if so, then OD profits will increase despite falling revenues.

In sum, without additional information prudent investors should refrain from following the newsletter's advice. To better assess the soundness of this advice it would be helpful to know the following: (1) the demographic profile of the survey's respondents; (2) the extent to which consumer desires regarding food intake accord with their subsequent behavior; (3) the extent of OD loyalty among its regular retail customers who might continue to prefer OD products over low-fat products even at higher prices; and (4) the extent to which OD might be able to reduce expenses to offset any revenue loss resulting from diminishing sales of OD products.

Argument 16 A lottery for **Impecunia**

In this editorial, the author concludes that by establishing a lottery the state of Impecunia could use the profits from it to improve the state's education and public health programs. To support this conclusion the author points out that the neighboring state of Lucria established a lottery two years ago, and that today Lucria spends more per pupil and treats more people through its health programs than Impecunia does. The editorial also cites a study showing that the average Impecunia resident now spends $50 per year on gambling. In several respects, however, the evidence lends little credible support for the argument.

First of all, the fact that Lucria now spends more than Impecunia per pupil, in itself, lends no support to the argument. Perhaps Lucria has always placed a high priority on education; or perhaps Lucria has always had more funds than Impecunia to spend on its programs, including education. Lacking clearer evidence that Lucria's lottery successfully raised revenues that were then used to increase the amount spent per pupil, the author cannot expect us to take seriously the claim that by establishing a similar lottery Impecunia would improve its education programs.

Similarly, the fact that Lucria's health programs treat more people than Impecunia's programs lends no support to the argument. Perhaps Lucria's population is greater than Impecunia's; or perhaps its residents are older, on average, than Impecunia's residents, and therefore require a greater measure of health care. Without considering and ruling out these and other possible explanations for the distinction cited, the author cannot justifiably conclude that Lucria's lottery was responsible for improved health care in that state or that a similar lottery in Impecunia would carry a similar result.

Moreover, the argument unfairly assumes that the lottery in Lucria has been profitable. The author provides no evidence that this is the case. It is entirely possible that the money used for education and health care in Lucria comes from sources other than the lottery. Without accounting for this possibility, the author cannot justify the conclusion that a lottery in Impecunia would be successful.

Finally, the fact that Impecunia's residents spend $50 per capita on gambling each year lends little support to the argument. Admittedly, this statistic amounts to some evidence of interest among Impecunia's residents in gambling, and therefore potential interest in a lottery. However, this evidence in itself does not suffice to prove that the lottery will in fact be popular. Perhaps Impecunia residents have no more discretionary income to participate in a lottery after spending $50 on other forms of gambling. Or perhaps Impecunia residents typically travel elsewhere to gamble as part of their vacations, and that they would not otherwise be interested in gambling. In short, without more convincing evidence of both an ability and a willingness on the part of Impecunia's residents to participate in a lottery the author cannot convince me that the lottery will be profitable.

In conclusion, the editorial has not convinced me that a lottery would be profitable and would serve to improve Impecunia's education and health programs. To better evaluate the argument I would need more information comparing Lucria's level of health care and education expenditures before and after the lottery was established. To strengthen the argument, the author must provide clear evidence that Lucria's lottery was profitable and that these profits contributed to improved education and health care in Lucria. The author must also provide dearer evidence of the willingness and ability of Impecunia residents to participate broadly in a lottery.

Argument 17　Walnut Grove's trash collection service

This letter recommends that Walnut Grove continue to contract with EZ Disposal, which has provided trash-collection services to Walnut Grove for ten years, rather than switching to ABC Waste. To justify this recommendation the letter's author notes that even though ABC's weekly fee is $500 less than EZ's, EZ collects twice per week whereas ABC would collect only once per week. The author also points out that, although both companies have the same number of trucks, EZ has ordered additional trucks. Finally, the author cites a recent survey in which 80% of respondents indicated that they were satisfied with EZ's service. I find this recommendation specious on several grounds.

First of all, the fact that EZ collects trash twice as often as ABC is significant only if the town would benefit from an additional collection each week. Yet the author provides no evidence that this is the case. For all we know, one collection per week suffices to dispose all of the town's trash. If so, then on the basis of frequency of collection it would make no sense to favor EZ's costlier service over ABC's less expensive one.

Secondly, the fact that EZ has ordered more trucks proves little in itself about which service would be the better choice for Walnut Grove. Perhaps EZ does not plan to use its new trucks for collecting Walnut Grove's trash. For that matter, perhaps EZ does not use its entire current fleet for this purpose, whereas ABC would. Besides, the author does not indicate when EZ will receive its new trucks; the later the delivery date, the less significant this factor should be in Walnut Grove's decision.

Thirdly, the mere fact that most respondents to a recent survey considered EZ's service satisfactory provides little support to the author's recommendation. The author fails to provide assurances that these respondents are representative of the overall population of people whose trash EZ collects. Moreover, even if that population is generally satisfied it is entirely possible that they would be even more satisfied with ABC's services.

In sum, the recommendation is not well supported. To bolster it the letter's author must provide specific evidence that Walnut Grove would benefit from an additional trash collection each week, and that the use of additional trucks would improve service to Walnut Grove. To better assess the strength of the recommendation I would need more information about the demographic profile of the survey's respondents. It would also be helpful to obtain opinions from municipalities and individuals that have some experience with both EZ and ABC.

Argument 20   Restricting moped rentals on **Balmer Island**

The author of this editorial recommends that to reduce accidents involving mopeds and pedestrians Balmer Island's city council should restrict moped rentals to 30 per day, down from 50, at each of the island's six rental outlets. To support this recommendation the author cites the fact that last year, when nearby Torseau Island's town council enforced similar measures, Torseau's rate of moped accidents fell by 50%. For several reasons, this evidence provides scant support for the author's recommendation.

To begin with, the author assumes that all other conditions in Balmer that might affect the rate of moped-pedestrian accidents will remain unchanged after the restrictions are enacted. However, with a restricted supply of rental mopeds people in Balmer might purchase mopeds instead. Also, the number of pedestrians might increase in the future; with more pedestrians, especially tourists, the risk of moped-pedestrian accidents would probably increase. For that matter, the number of rental outlets might increase to make up for the artificial supply restriction per outlet-a likely scenario assuming moped rental demand does not decline. Without considering and ruling out these and other possible changes that might contribute to a high incidence of moped-pedestrian accidents, the author cannot convince me that the proposed restrictions will necessarily have the desired effect.

Next, the author fails to consider other possible explanations for the 50% decline in Torseau's moped accident rate last year. Perhaps last year Torseau experienced unusually fair weather, during which moped accidents are less likely. Perhaps fewer tourists visited Torseau last year than during most years, thereby diminishing the demand for rental mopeds to below the allowed limits. Perhaps last year some of Torseau's moped rental outlets purchased new mopeds that are safer to drive. Or perhaps the restrictions were already in effect but were not enforced until last year. In any event, a decline in Torseau's moped accident rate during only one year is scarcely sufficient to draw any reliable conclusions about what might have caused the decline, or about what the accident rate will be in years ahead.

Additionally, in asserting that the same phenomenon that caused a 50% decline in moped accidents in Torseau would cause a similar decline in Balmer, the author relies on what might amount to an unfair analogy between Balmer and Torseau. Perhaps Balmer's ability to enforce moped-rental restrictions does not meet Torseau's ability; if not, then the mere enactment of similar restrictions in Balmer is no guarantee of a similar result. Or perhaps the demand for mopeds in Torseau is always greater than in Balmer. Specifically, if fewer than all available mopeds are currently rented per day from the average Balmer outlet, while in Torseau every available moped is rented each day, then the proposed restriction is likely to have less impact on the accident rate in Balmer than inTorseau.

Finally, the author provides no evidence that the same restrictions that served to reduce the incidence of all "moped accidents" by 50% would also serve to reduce the incidence of accidents involving "mopeds and pedestrians" by 50%. Lacking such evidence, it is entirely possible that the number of moped accidents not involving pedestrians decreased by a greater percentage, while the number of moped-pedestrian accidents decreased by a smaller percentage, or even increased. Since the author has not accounted for these possibilities, the editorial's recommendation cannot be taken seriously.

In conclusion, the recommendation is not well supported. To convince me that the proposed restriction would achieve the desired outcome, the author would have to assure me that no changes serving to increase Balmer's moped-pedestrian accident rate will occur in the foreseeable future. The author must also provide clear evidence that last year's decline in moped accidents in Torseau was attributable primarily to its moped rental restrictions rather than to one or more other factors. In order to better evaluate the recommendation, I would need more information comparing the supply of and demand for moped rentals on the two islands. I would also need to know the rate of moped-pedestrian accidents in Torseau both prior to and after the restrictions were enforced in Torseau.

Argument 21   The demand for **alpaca overcoats**

In this memo the vice president of Sartorian, a clothing manufacturer, argues that by resuming production of alpaca (wool) overcoats, after discontinuing production of these coats five years ago due to an unreliable alpaca supply, Sartorian would increase its profits. To support this argument the vice president points out that Sartorian now has a new fabric supplier, and reasons that since Sartorian's chief competitor has discontinued making these coats there must be pent-up consumer demand for them, which Sartorian would fill. The vice president also reasons that, since overall clothing prices have risen in each of the last five years, consumers will be willing to pay higher prices for Sartorian's alpaca coats. I find the argument specious in several respects.

To begin with, the argument relies on the assumption that the new fabric supplier will be a reliable supplier of alpaca. Yet the memo provides no substantiating evidence for this assumption. Perhaps the supply problems Sartorian experienced years earlier were attributable not to its supplier at the time but rather to factors beyond any supplier's control and that might render the alpaca supply unreliable today as well. Besides, without evidence to the contrary, it is entirely possible that Sartorian's new supplier will turn out to be unreliable and to be blameworthy for that unreliability.

Even if the new supplier turns out to be reliable, the memo assumes too hastily, on the basis of a competitor's discontinuing alpaca coat production, that consumer demand for alpaca coats made by Sartorian is now pent-up. Perhaps that competitor stopped making alpaca coats due to diminishing consumer demand for them. Or, perhaps other clothing manufacturers are now beginning to fill the market void by producing similar coats. Either of these scenarios, if true, would cast serious doubt on the vice president's claim that there is now pent-up alpaca coat demand from which Sartorian would profit.

Even if the vice president can substantiate the two foregoing assumptions, the argument relies on the additional assumption that consumers will be willing to pay whatever price Sartorian requires to turn a profit on its alpaca coat sales. Yet, perhaps Sartorian's costs for alpaca wool will be so high as to preclude any profit from alpaca coat sales. Also, the fact that clothing prices have been steadily increasing for five years suggests that consumers might have less disposable income for purchasing items such as alpaca coats, especially if consumers' income has not kept pace with escalating prices. Thus, without stronger evidence that consumers would be both willing and able to pay high prices for Sartorian's alpaca coats the vice president cannot convince me that the proposed course of action would be a profitable one.

Finally, even if Sartorian would turn a profit from the sale of its alpaca coats, the memo's claim that the company's overall profits would increase thereby is unwarranted. Sartorian's overall profitability is a function of revenue and expenses relating to all of Sartorian's products. Since the memo provides no evidence that Sartorian will continue to be profitable in other respects, I simply cannot take the vice president's argument seriously.

In sum, the argument is unpersuasive as it stands. To bolster it the vice president must provide assurances that the new supplier will be a reliable and affordable alpaca supplier, and that consumers will be able and willing to pay whatever prices Sartorian requires in order to turn a profit from selling its alpaca coats. To better assess the argument I would need to know whether consumers are demanding alpaca coats anymore, and if so whether new competitors entering the alpaca coat market would thwart Sartorian's efforts to profit from any pent-up demand for these coats. I would also need detailed financial projections for Sartorian to determine the likelihood that it will continue to be profitable overall, aside from its predicted profitability from alpaca coat sales.

Argument 22 The market for new houses in **Steel City**

In this memo, the president of a new-home construction firm in Steel City concludes that the firm can increase its profits by focusing on building expensive homes, priced above $150,000, rather than lower-priced homes, and by hiring additional workers to increase the number of homes the firm can build. To support this recommendation the president cites the fact that Steel City's population has increased by more than 20% over the last five years and that family income in Steel City is rising much faster than the nationwide average. The president also points out that nationwide sales of homes priced above $150,000 are rising faster than sales of lower-priced homes. In several respects, this evidence provides little credible support for the president's recommendation.

First, by citing Steel City's population increase in order to argue for a step-up in home construction, the speaker relies on certain unsubstantiated demographic assumptions. One such assumption is that area demand for new housing will support additional home construction in the foreseeable future. Yet lacking firm evidence that this will be the case, it is entirely possible that the area's population will stabilize, or even decrease, and that the firm will have trouble selling its new homes at profitable levels. Another unfair demographic assumption is that Steel City residents will be interested in purchasing more expensive single-family homes. Perhaps the population increase has been and will continue to be the result of an influx of retired people who regardless of their income level are interested in smaller, less expensive homes and condominiums, or even rental housing.

Secondly, by citing Steel City's fast-rising family-income levels to support the recommendation, the speaker relies on other tenuous assumptions. One such assumption is that area residents interested in buying new homes can afford homes priced over $150,000. It is entirely possible that in Steel City family-income levels are rising rapidly primarily among current homeowners who would not be in the market for new homes in the foreseeable future, or among only a handful of the area's wealthiest residents. It is also possible that despite the rapid increase the average family income in Steel City is still low compared to national averages—too low to justify the president's recommendation to shift focus to more expensive homes.

Thirdly, even if this firm builds and can sell expensive homes according to the president's proposal, the firm's profits would not necessarily increase as a result. Hiring additional workers adds to the expense of building a home, and of course the cost of materials will no doubt increase with the value of the homes that are built. Furthermore, in all likelihood the firm would not be able to build a greater number of expensive homes than cheaper homes. Moreover, given the scant evidence that area residents could actually afford expensive homes, it is entirely possible that the firm would have trouble selling these homes quickly and at profitable price levels. In short, without a detailed cost-benefit analysis the president cannot convince me that the proposed course of action would increase this firm's profits.

In conclusion, the president's argument is unpersuasive. To strengthen it the president must convince me that in the foreseeable future Steel City residents will actually demand and be able to afford houses costing more than $150,000. To better evaluate the argument I would need more information about Steel City's demographic trends and about the income of area residents interested in buying new homes in the foreseeable future. I would also need a detailed analysis comparing the costs and revenues associated with the proposed course of action with the costs and revenues associated with the construction and sale of the firm's less expensive homes.

Argument 24　The best location for **Viva-Tech**'s new plant

In this memo the president of Viva-Tech, a high-tech medical equipment firm, recommends closing its small assembly plants and centralizing its operations at one location—in the city of Grandview. To support this recommendation the president points out certain attractive demographic features, as well as the town's willingness to allow Viva-Tech to operate there without paying property taxes for the first three years. However, careful scrutiny of the evidence reveals that it provides little credible support for the president's recommendation.

To begin with, the fact that Grandview's adult population is larger than that of any other locale under consideration is scant evidence in itself that Grandview would be the best location for Viva-

Tech. Perhaps Grandview's adult residents are not skilled to work in the medical equipment industry. Or perhaps a large portion of its residents are retired. Or perhaps virtually all of its residents are already employed in jobs that they would be unwilling or unable to leave to work at Viva-Tech. Without considering and eliminating these and other possible reasons why Viva-Tech might have difficulty finding enough suitable employees in Grandview, the president cannot rely on the fact that Grandview has a large adult population to bolster the recommendation.

Furthermore, the fact that the earnings of the average Grandview worker are comparatively low does not necessarily mean that Viva-Tech could minimize labor costs by employing Grandview residents, as the president suggests. It is entirely possible that this low average wage is attributable to a high percentage of jobs requiring low-level skills. This scenario would be particularly likely if a large portion of Grandview's workers are teenagers and college students. In fact, the low average wage in Grandview is further evidence that Grandview residents do not possess the sorts of high-tech skills that would command a higher wage and that Viva-Tech might require among its workforce.

A final problem with the argument involves Grandview's willingness to forego payment of property taxes for the first three years. Admittedly, this evidence lends some measure of support to the recommendation. However, the president ignores the possibility that other cities under consideration would be willing to make similar concessions, or provide other equally attractive financial incentives. The president also overlooks the expense of property taxes over the longer term. Lacking evidence to the contrary, it is entirely possible that Grandview's property-tax rates are otherwise comparatively high, and that in the longer term Viva-Tech's property-tax liability would be greater in Grandview than in other locales. Until the president accounts for these two possibilities, I cannot be persuaded that Grandview is the best location for Viva-Tech from a property-tax standpoint.

In the final analysis, the recommendation of Viva-Tech's president is not well supported. To strengthen it the president must provide detailed demographic evidence showing that a sufficient number of Grandview residents would be able and willing to work in Viva-Tech's high-tech environment. A proper evaluation of the recommendation requires more information about Grandview's property-tax rates vis-a-vis those of other locales under consideration, and about the willingness of these other municipalities to provide their own financial or tax incentives to Viva-Tech.

Argument 25　A new golf course and resort hotel for **Hopewell**

In this memo, Hopewell's mayor recommends that in order to stimulate the town's economy and boost tax revenues Hopewell should build a new golf course and resort hotel, just as the town of Ocean View did two years ago. To support this recommendation the mayor points out that in Ocean View during the last two years tourism has increased, new businesses have opened, and tax revenues have increased by 30%. I find the mayor's argument unconvincing in several important respects.

First of all, it is possible that the mayor has confused cause with effect respecting the recent developments in Ocean View. Perhaps Ocean View's construction of a new golf course and hotel was a response to previous increases in tourism and business development—increases that have simply continued during the most recent two years. Since the mayor has failed to account for this possibility, the claim that Hopewell would boost its economy by also constructing a golf course and hotel is completely unwarranted.

Secondly, the mayor fails to account for other possible causes of the trends in Ocean View during the last two years. The increase in tourism might have been due to improving economic conditions nationwide, or to unusually pleasant weather in the region. The new businesses that have opened in Ocean View might have opened there irrespective of the new golf course and hotel. And, the 30% increase in tax revenues might have been the result of an increase in tax rates, or the addition of a new type of municipal tax. Without ruling out these and other alternative explanations for the three recent trends in Ocean View, the mayor cannot reasonably infer based on those trends that Hopewell's economy would benefit by following Ocean View's example.

Thirdly, even if the recent trends in Ocean View are attributable to the construction of the new golf course and hotel there, the mayor assumes too hastily that the golf course and hotel will continue to benefit that town's overall economy. The mayor has not accounted for the possibility that increased tourism will begin to drive residents away during tourist season, or that new business development will result in the town's losing its appeal as a place to visit or to live. Unless the mayor can convince me that these scenarios are unlikely I cannot accept the mayor's recommendation that Hopewell follow Ocean View's example.

Finally, the mayor's argument rests on the unsubstantiated assumption that Hopewell and Ocean View are sufficiently alike in ways that might affect the economic impact of a new golf course and hotel. Hopewell might lack the sort of natural environment that would attract more tourists and new businesses to the town—regardless of its new golf course and hotel. For that matter, perhaps Hopewell already contains several resort hotels and golf courses that are not utilized to their capacity. If so, building yet another golf course and hotel might amount to a misallocation of the town's resources—and actually harm the town's overall economy.

In sum, the mayor's recommendation is not well supported. To bolster it the mayor must provide better evidence that Ocean View's new golf course and hotel—and not some other phenomenon-has been responsible for boosting Ocean View's economy during the last two years. To better assess the recommendation I would need to know why Ocean View decided to construct its new golf course and hotel in the first place—specifically, what events prior to construction might have prompted that decision. I would also need to thoroughly compare Hopewell with Ocean View—especially in terms of their appeal to tourists and businesses—to determine whether the same course of action that appears to have boosted Ocean View's economy would also boost Hopewell's economy.

Argument 27　How **Automate** can retain its best workers

In this memo the president of Automate, an automobile manufacturer, concludes that to retain its best employees Automate must offer them salaries equal to those that Sparks automobile manufacturing pays its employees. To justify this conclusion the president points out that Sparks has just moved into the state and is now advertising job openings with salaries twice as high as those Automate pays its assembly-line workers, and that some Automate employees have already defected to Sparks. As further support for the argument, the president notes that Sparks plans to build additional plants in the state and will need to staff those plants. I find the argument unconvincing on several grounds.

First, the memo does not indicate what kinds of jobs Sparks is now advertising—the ones for which salaries are to be twice those paid to Automate's assembly-line workers. Those jobs might be top management positions or other jobs for which salaries are often significantly higher than those for assembly-line work. If so, this fact would serve to refute the president's assumption that Sparks is paying higher salaries than Automate for similar work.

Secondly, the president assumes that the reason why some Automate workers have defected to Sparks is that Sparks has offered them higher salaries. Yet, the president fails to provide evidence to substantiate this assumption. Lacking such evidence, those defectors might have gone to work for Sparks because the city where Sparks is located is a preferable place to live, or because Sparks offers other job incentives that Automate does not. And, if the defectors accepted jobs at Sparks before Sparks began offering higher salaries, then salary could not have been a factor in their decision to defect to Sparks. In short, until the president establishes a clear causal relationship between the advertised salaries and the defection of some Automate employees to Sparks, the president cannot reasonably conclude that Automate must increase its salaries in order to prevent additional employees from defecting to Sparks in the future.

Thirdly, even assuming that those defectors did leave Automate because Sparks offered higher salaries for similar work, the president's argument rests on the additional assumptions that the number of defectors is significant and that these defectors are valuable to Automate. Yet the president fails to substantiate either assumption. Perhaps only a very small percentage of Automate's worker's have defected; if so, the president's proposed salary increases might amount to an overreaction. Or, perhaps the defectors were among Automate's least valuable employees; for that matter, perhaps Automate's most valuable employees are the ones who are most loyal and would not leave Automate even if they were offered a higher salary elsewhere. Without substantiating both assumptions, the president cannot reasonably conclude that Automate must raise the salaries of its best workers in order to retain them.

Finally, the mere fact that Sparks plans to build additional new plants in the state amounts to scant evidence that Automate will continue to lose valuable employees unless it raises their salaries. Perhaps Sparks plans to staff those new plants with workers from its other plants, or from other sources besides Automate. Or, perhaps Sparks is advertising high salaries now simply to gain a foothold into the state's labor market, and that once Sparks is established in the state it will offer lower salaries for new jobs. Besides, Sparks' plan to build additional plants might amount to sheer speculation, in which case the president's proposed salary increases would seem hasty.

In sum, the president's recommendation seems ill conceived, at least lacking additional supporting evidence. To bolster the argument the president must provide clear evidence that a significant percentage of Automate's valuable employees have defected to Sparks because Sparks offered them higher salaries for similar work—rather than for some other reason. The president must also provide better evidence that this is a trend that is likely to continue and to harm Automate's operations unless Automate boosts the salaries of its best employees to match the salaries Sparks would pay those employees.

Argument 140　A salary raise and promotion for **Professor Thomas**

In this report, an Elm City University committee recommends increasing Professor Thomas' salary and promoting her to Department Chairperson because of her effectiveness as a teacher and researcher. To support this recommendation the report points out that Thomas' classes are among the University's most popular and that last year the amount of grant money she attracted to the University exceeded her $50,000 salary. The committee argues further that unless the University implements its recommendation Thomas is likely to defect to another school. For several reasons, the evidence offered in support of the recommendation provides little credible support for it.

First, the recommendation relies on the assumption that the popularity of Thomas' classes is attributable to her effectiveness as a teacher. Yet this assumption overlooks other possible reasons for the popularity of these classes. Perhaps Thomas is a comparatively lenient grader, or perhaps the classes she teaches are requirements for every science student. Without considering and eliminating these and other possible alternative explanations for the popularity of Thomas' classes, the committee cannot convincingly conclude based on that popularity that Thomas is an effective teacher and therefore should be granted a raise and a promotion.

Secondly, the mere fact that the amount of grant money Thomas attracted to the University last year exceeded her salary proves nothing about either her teaching abilities or her research abilities. Perhaps last year was an aberration, and in other years Thomas did not attract much grant money. For that matter, perhaps many—or even most—other professors at the University attracted even more grant money than Thomas, relative to their salary levels. Under either scenario, Thomas would appear undeserving of the recommended raise and promotion—based on this particular criterion.

Thirdly, the report provides no evidence whatsoever regarding the likelihood that Thomas would leave the University if she is not granted the proposed raise and promotion. Lacking such evidence, it is entirely possible that Thomas is quite content in her current position and at her current salary level. Thus, the committee cannot justifiably rely on this claim to bolster its recommendation.

In conclusion, the committee's recommendation is ill-founded. To strengthen it the committee must provide clear evidence that Thomas is in fact an effective teacher—perhaps by citing student or peer evaluations. The committee must also provide specific evidence of Thomas' research abilities—perhaps by listing scientific journals that have published the results of her work. Finally, to better evaluate the argument I would need more information about the degree to which Thomas is content in her current position and at her current salary, and whether any other University would be willing to offer her a more attractive employment package.

Argument 143   The effects of corporate **downsizing**

This editorial disagrees with a certain article's claim that as a result of widespread corporate downsizing many able workers have faced serious long-term economic hardship—due to their inability to find other suitable employment. To justify its disagreement with this claim the editorial cites the following three findings of a recent report: (1) There has been a net increase in the number of new jobs created since 1992, (2) many workers who lost their jobs have found other work, and (3) most newly created jobs are full-time positions in industries that tend to pay above-average wages. Careful scrutiny of these findings, however, reveals that they accomplish little toward refuting the article's claim.

Regarding the first finding, the editorial overlooks the possibility that most of the newly created jobs since 1992 are not suitable for job seekers downsized by corporations. Perhaps the vast majority of these jobs involve food serving, clerical assistance, cleaning and maintenance, and other tasks requiring a low level of skill and experience. At the same time, perhaps most downsized job seekers are highly educated middle-managers looking for the same type of work elsewhere. In short, lacking evidence that the newly created jobs match the skills, experience, and interests of the downsized corporate employees, the editorial's author cannot convincingly refute the article's claim.

As for the second finding, the term "many" is far too vague to allow for any meaningful conclusions; if "many" amounts to an insignificant percentage of downsized employees, then the finding is of little use in refuting the article's claim. Moreover, the workers to whom this finding refers to are not necessarily downsized corporate employees. To the extent that they are not, this second finding is irrelevant in drawing any conclusions about the impact of corporate downsizing on downsized employees.

The third finding would lend support to the author's position only under two assumptions: (1) that the newly created jobs in those high-paying industries are suitable for downsized corporate employees, and (2) that the new jobs are among the high-paying ones. Otherwise, downsized employees seeking jobs would be unlikely to regain their former economic status by applying for these newly created positions, whether or not these positions are full-time.

In sum, the author has not effectively refuted the article's claim that corporate downsizing has worked economic hardship on downsized corporate employees. To more effectively refute the claim the author should provide clear evidence that most of those job-seekers are able to fill the sorts of new jobs that have been created since 1992, and that these new positions are suitable for those job-seekers given their work experience, areas of interest, and former salaries.

Argument 145 The relationship between snoring and **weight** gain

In this argument, the speaker concludes that any person who snores should try to eat less and exercise more than the average person. To justify this conclusion the speaker points out that many snorers awaken frequently during sleep—often so briefly that they are unaware that they are awake—in order to catch their breath (a condition called sleep apnea), and as a result are too tired during normal waking hours to exercise. The speaker also cites data collected during a recent study, suggesting that snorers are more likely to gain weight than other people. This argument is flawed in several critical respects.

First, the speaker provides no assurances that the recently collected data suggesting a correlation between snoring and weight gain are statistically reliable. Perhaps the study's subjects were unrepresentative of the overall population—in terms of other traits and habits that might affect body weight. Lacking such evidence the speaker simply cannot draw any firm conclusions based on the study about the relationship between snoring and weight gain.

Even assuming a strong correlation between snoring and weight gain among the general population, the speaker has not adequately shown that sleep apnea causes weight gain. A correlation is one indication of a causal relationship, but in itself does not suffice to prove such a relationship. It is entirely possible that some other medical condition, or some other trait or habit, that causes snoring also causes weight gain. Without establishing clearly that snoring at least contributes to weight gain, the speaker cannot convince me that snorers should either eat less or exercise more than the average person.

Even if many snorers suffer from sleep apnea and tend to gain weight as a result, the speaker's advice that "anyone who snores" should try to eat less and to exercise is nevertheless unwarranted. It is entirely possible that some—or perhaps even most—snorers do not suffer from sleep apnea, or are not too tired to exercise, or do not in any event tend to gain weight. Without ruling out these possibilities, the speaker must expressly limit the advice to those snorers whose snoring causes weight gain.

Even if the speaker's advice were modified as indicated above, the advice to exercise would still be logically unsound. If a person with sleep apnea is too tired to exercise as a result, then simply advising that person to exercise begs the question: What should the person do to eliminate the cause of the tiredness? Thus, the speaker should determine the cause of sleep apnea and modify the advice so that it targets that cause. Of course, if it turns out that weight gain is one cause of snoring and sleep apnea, then the speaker's advice that snorers should try to eat less would have considerable merit. Yet, without any evidence that this is the case, the speaker's advice might be at least partially ineffective in counteracting a snorer's tendency to gain weight.

In sum, the speaker's advice for "any" snorer is ill conceived and poorly supported. To lend credibility to this advice the speaker should provide evidence that the recently collected data reflect the general population. To better assess the argument it would be useful to know all the possible causes of snoring and of sleep apnea.

Argument 146 Encouraging students to use school **libraries**

In this editorial the author claims that the town's students are reading less, and that by improving the atmosphere in the town's school libraries students would visit their school library more frequently and, in turn, would read more. To support these claims the author points out that the number of annual visits students make to their school library, on average, has decreased significantly in recent years. Specifically, the average seventh-grader paid five such visits last year, four of which were required for classes. Close inspection of the evidence reveals, however, that it lends little credible support for the proposed course of action.

First, the author unfairly assumes that since the number of library visits per student is declining the amount of reading on the part of students must also be declining. This poor assumption overlooks the possibility that students are doing more reading or checking out more reading materials during each library visit. It also ignores the possibility that more and more students are obtaining reading material elsewhere—for example, from public libraries or from the Internet. Without considering and ruling out these possibilities, the author cannot justifiably conclude that students are reading less merely because they are visiting their school library less often.

Secondly, the author assumes that the reason for the declining number of library visits is that the library is uncomfortable. Yet, the author offers no evidence to substantiate this assumption. Lacking such evidence, a variety of other factors might account for the decline. As noted above, perhaps students are becoming less dependent on the school library for obtaining reading material and information. Besides, lacking evidence to the contrary it is entirely possible that library atmosphere is completely insignificant to most students.

Thirdly, the author assumes that improving atmosphere and comfort is necessary to reverse the current trend. However, even if the surroundings go unchanged there might be other ways to attract students to their library. Perhaps increasing the number of computer terminals or the number of staff members would reverse the current trend. Or perhaps increasing the number of books and periodicals, or enhancing their variety, would be effective. In short, without ruling out all other possible means of achieving the desired results, the author cannot convince me that the proposed course of action is necessary.

Finally, the author assumes that improving the library's atmosphere would suffice to increase the frequency of student visits and the amount of reading on the part of students. Yet, the author offers no evidence that these improvements alone would suffice. In fact, a more comfortable library might actually discourage students from reading by creating a social rather than work atmosphere.

In sum, the recommendation is not well supported. To strengthen the argument the author must provide clear evidence that the school's students are in fact reading less and that if they visit the school library more frequently they will read more. The author must also provide evidence—perhaps by way of a student survey—that the library atmosphere is the chief determinant of the frequency with which students visit the library. Finally, to better evaluate the argument I would need to know what alternatives, if any, are available for increasing the frequency with which students visit their library, and for increasing the amount that students read.

Argument 147　The prospects for **Whirlwind** video-game sales

This editorial concludes that a two-year decline in sales of Whirlwind's video games is about to reverse itself, and that sales will increase dramatically in the next few months. To justify this conclusion the editorial's author cites a recent survey in which videogame players indicated a preference for games with realistic graphics requiring state-of-the art computers. The editorial then points out that Whirlwind has just introduced several such games, along with an extensive advertising campaign aimed at people 10 – 25 years old—the demographic group most likely to play video games. I find this argument specious on several grounds.

First, the author provides no assurances that the survey on which the argument depends is statistically reliable. Unless the survey's respondents are representative of the overall population of video-game enthusiasts, the author cannot rely on it to predict the success of Whirlwind's new games. For all we know a significant percentage of the respondents were not 10 – 25 years of age; for that matter, perhaps the number of respondents was too low to ensure that they are typical of video-game enthusiasts in that age group.

Secondly, the argument relies on the assumption that the two-year decline in Whirlwind's sales is attributable to a problem that Whirlwind's introduction of its new games and ad campaign will solve. Yet it is entirely possible that the decline was due to factors such as imprudent pricing and distribution strategies or poor management, and that these problems have not been remedied. In fact, perhaps the same advertising agency that is promoting Whirlwind's new games also promoted Whirlwind's earlier games, and it was the agency's inability to attract interest among the key demographic group that caused the decline. Since the author has not dearly identified the cause of the decline, I cannot be convinced that Whirlwind's new strategy will reverse that decline at all—let alone dramatically.

Thirdly, even if the ad campaign successfully attracts many 10 – 25 year-olds to Whirlwind's new games, the argument rests on the further assumption that this result will suffice to cause the predicted sales increase during the next few months. Yet this need not be the case. Perhaps Whirlwind's new state-of-the-art games are prohibitively expensive for the key demographic group. Or perhaps Whirlwind's competitors are now introducing similar games at lower prices or with additional features that render them more attractive to video-game enthusiasts than Whirlwind's new games. Unless the author can rule out such possibilities, I simply cannot be swayed by the prediction that Whirlwind is about to experience a dramatic increase in sales.

Finally, even if the author can substantiate the foregoing assumptions, I remain unconvinced that the impending increase in sales will occur within the next few months. Perhaps video-game sales are highly seasonal and Whirlwind will need to wait longer than two months to see the dramatic increase it expects. If so, the author must modify the prediction accordingly.

In sum, the argument is unconvincing as it stands. To strengthen it the author must provide clear evidence that video-game enthusiasts 10 – 25 years of age would be interested in Whirlwind's new games, and that they could afford to buy them. To better assess the argument I would need to know (1) what caused the two-year sales to decline to begin with, and whether Whirlwind's new strategy eliminates that cause; (2) what competing products might serve to diminish sales of Whirlwind's new games during the next few months; and (3) when Whirlwind's introduction of its new games has occurred in relation to the peak video-game sales season, if any.

Argument 149　Aircraft maintenance and **airline** profits

In this memorandum, Get Away Airline's personnel director asserts that Get-Away mechanics should enroll in the Quality Care Seminar on proper maintenance procedures in order to increase customer satisfaction and, in turn, profits. The director reasons that because the performance of auto-racing mechanics improves after the seminar, so will that of Get-Away's mechanics. The director's argument relies on a number of dubious assumptions and is therefore unconvincing.

First of all, the argument unfairly assumes that because the performance of auto-racing mechanics improves after the seminar so will the performance of aircraft mechanics. Common sense tells me that, even though aircraft and auto mechanics serve similar functions, aircraft repair and maintenance is far more involved than car repair and maintenance. Thus, a seminar that improves the performance of auto mechanics will not necessarily improve that of aircraft mechanics.

Secondly, the argument assumes that the performance of Get-Away mechanics is subject to improvement. However, it is entirely possible that their performance level is already very high and that the seminar will afford little or no improvement. Perhaps Get-Away's mechanics have already attended a similar seminar, or perhaps they meet higher standards than the ones imposed on auto-racing mechanics.

Thirdly, the argument concludes from the mere fact that the performance of auto-racing mechanics improved after the seminar that the seminar was responsible for this improvement. However, it is possible that some other factor, such as improved diagnostic technology or more stringent inspection requirements, was the reason for the improved performance. Without ruling out these and other such possibilities, I cannot accept the memo's final conclusion that enrolling in the seminar will improve the performance of Get-Away's mechanics as well.

Finally, the argument concludes without adequate evidence that improved performance on the part of Get-Away's mechanics will result in greater customer satisfaction and therefore greater profits for Get Away. Admittedly, if a low performance level results in accidents, customer satisfaction and profits will in all probability decrease. Otherwise, however, improved mechanic performance will in all likelihood have no bearing on customer satisfaction; in other words, customers are unlikely to be aware of the level of performance of an aircraft's mechanics unless accidents occur.

In conclusion, the argument is unconvincing as it stands. To strengthen it, the director must provide more convincing evidence that the performance of Get-Away's mechanics will actually improve as a result of the seminar—perhaps by pointing out other airlines whose mechanics benefited from the seminar. The director must also show a strong causal nexus between improved mechanic performance and profit. In order to better evaluate the argument, I would need more information about the cost of the seminar compared to its expected benefits, and about what factors other than the seminar might have been responsible for the improved performance of auto-racing mechanics.

Argument 151　Blaming the mayor for problems with **River Bridge**

This editorial concludes that Mayor Durant's approval of the River Bridge construction twenty years ago was the cause of current traffic and deterioration problems at the bridge. To support this conclusion, the editorial points out that a nearby bridge is not experiencing similar problems. However, the editorial relies on a number of doubtful assumptions and is therefore unconvincing.

First of all, since the bridge is 20 years old it is unfair to assign blame for recent traffic problems and deterioration to Durant or to anyone else involved in the initial bridge-building project. Given this time span it seems reasonable that these problems are due to ordinary wear and tear rather than to a design defect. Moreover, it is entirely possible that unforeseen developments during the last twenty years are partly responsible for the deterioration and traffic problems. For example, perhaps growth in the area's population, and therefore increased bridge traffic, has been greater than could have been anticipated twenty years ago.

Secondly, the editorial concludes without adequate evidence that if Durant had approved a wider and better-designed bridge none of the current problems would have occurred. This amounts to fallacious reasoning. Just because a bridge that Durant approved has experienced certain problems, one cannot reasonably conclude that without that particular bridge the same problems would not have occurred.

Thirdly, the editorial relies primarily on an analogy between River Bridge and Derby Bridge, yet provides no evidence that the two bridges are similar in ways that are relevant to the argument. Even assuming weather conditions are generally the same at both locations, a variety of other factors might explain why the River Bridge problems have not occurred at the Derby Bridge. Perhaps relatively few people traverse the Derby Bridge; or perhaps the Derby Bridge is relatively new; or perhaps the comparatively long span of the Derby Bridge places less structural stress on any given point. In short, without ruling out other factors that might explain why similar problems have not occurred at the Derby Bridge this argument by analogy is untenable.

Finally, the argument assumes that mere approval of the proposed bridge is tantamount to causation of traffic and deterioration problems. But the editorial fails to indicate why Durant approved the bridge in the first place. It is quite possible, for example, that it was the only feasible plan, and that Durant had no choice. Moreover, common sense tells me that deterioration and traffic problems are consequences of poor planning and engineering, and therefore more likely caused by negligence of engineers and planners than by politicians.

In conclusion, the editorial is unconvincing as it stands. To strengthen the argument, the editorial's author must provide evidence that conditions which might have contributed to the bridge's deterioration and to traffic problems were reasonably foreseeable 20 years ago, and that some other feasible bridge design would have avoided the current problems. In order to better evaluate the argument, we would need more information about what choices Durant had at the time, as well as more information about the age of the Derby Bridge and about how heavily that bridge is used compared to the River Bridge.

Argument 153　Violent **teenage crime** and television programming

This editorial concludes that increasingly violent television programming during prime time in the country of Alta is responsible for the steady increase in violent crime among Alta's teenagers. To support this conclusion the editorial cites various statistical studies about violence on television. However, this evidence provides little credible support for the editorial's conclusion.

To begin with, the editorial observes a correlation between violence on television and violent teenage crime, then concludes that the former is the cause of the latter. However, the editorial fails to rule out other possible explanations for the rise in violent crime among teenagers. For example, since the 1950s it is entirely possible that Alta has seen a large growth in its population, or a deterioration of its juvenile justice system or economy. Any of these factors, or other social, political or economic factors, might lead to an increase in violent crime among teenagers. Without ruling out all other such factors it is unfair to conclude that television programs are responsible for this increase.

Next, the editorial cites studies showing that young children exposed to violent images are more likely to behave violently in the home. This evidence would support the editorial's conclusion only if teenagers and younger children react similarly to television. However, common sense tells me that young children are more likely than teenagers to mimic observed behavior. Moreover, the editorial fails to provide any evidence that this sort of mimicry ultimately develops into violent criminal behavior.

The editorial then cites the *Observer* survey in which "90% of the respondents were parents" who would prefer less violent television programming during prime time. However, the editorial fails to provide any information about the survey population; therefore it is impossible to determine whether the survey results apply generally to the Alta population. In addition, we are not informed how many parents were surveyed but did not respond. The greater this number, the less reliable the survey. Thus, as it stands the *Observer* study is statistically unreliable and lends no credible support to the editorial's conclusion.

Aside from the survey's statistical unreliability, in citing the survey the editorial assumes that parents' preferences about television programming have some bearing on whether their teenage children will commit violent crimes. However, the editorial provides no evidence to link one with the other. Moreover, the survey is relevant only to the extent that teenagers watch television during prime time. However, the editorial provides no evidence about this extent.

In conclusion, the editorial is unconvincing as it stands. To strengthen the argument, the editorial's author must rule out all other possible factors contributing to the rise in teenage violence. The author must also show that teenagers react to violent television images similarly to how younger children react to the same images, and that Alta teenagers watch a significant amount of television programming during prime time. In order to better evaluate the argument, we would need more information about the *Observer* survey population, and about the percentage of those surveyed who responded.

Argument 154　Exercise and **longevity**

This editorial concludes that to maximize longevity people should engage in vigorous outdoor exercise on a daily basis. To support this conclusion the editorial cites a 20-year study of 500 middle-aged men in which, among subjects responding to an annual survey, those who followed this regimen lived longer, on average, than those who exercised mildly once or twice per week. A careful analysis of the study reveals several problems with the editorial's argument.

First of all, the excerpt provides no information about the number of respondents or their occupational or residential profiles. The fewer respondents, the less reliable the study's results. Also, the narrower the spectrum of occupations and geographic areas represented among respondents, the more likely that one of these two phenomena, rather than exercise, played the key role in the subjects' longevity. Moreover, once a subject dies it would be impossible for that subject to respond to the annual survey. Unless a sufficient number of subjects from diverse geographic areas and occupations responded accurately and on a regular basis, and unless accurate responses were made on behalf of deceased subjects, I simply cannot accept the editorial's conclusion.

Secondly, a 20-year time span might not be sufficient to gauge the longevity of the study's subjects; that is, until a significant number of subjects have died, it is impossible to determine with certainty the effect of exercise on the subjects' longevity as a group. Lacking information about how many deaths among the 500 subjects were reported by the end of the study, it is impossible to draw any reliable conclusion about the relationship between exercise and longevity..

Thirdly, the editorial fails to indicate how many or what percentage of the respondents engaged in vigorous outdoor exercise on a daily basis. Lacking this information, it is entirely possible that only a few subjects matched this profile and that those few subjects happened to live to an old age—due to some factor other than exercise habits. The longevity of a small number of respondents is scant evidence upon which to draw any broad conclusions about the effect of exercise on longevity.

Finally, even if we accept the reliability of the study as it relates to men, the study does not support the editorial's broad conclusion that doctors should recommend to all patients vigorous daily outdoor exercise. Since the study excluded women, it is entirely possible that a different exercise regime would maximize female longevity.

In sum, the evidence cited in this excerpt does not permit any reliable inference about the effect of exercise on longevity. To better assess the study's reliability I would need more information about the number of respondents and the number of deaths among them by the end of the 20-year period. I would also need information about the occupational and residential history of each respondent. To strengthen the argument the editorial should either limit its conclusion to men or provide evidence that its recommended exercise regimen also maximizes longevity for women.

Argument 157　Local merchants and a new **ski resort**

This editorial concludes that a new ski resort should be developed north of town because it would attract tourism and therefore be an economic boon to local merchants. To support this claim the author, a local merchant, points out that those opposed to the project do not live in the area and that a bank has agreed to fund the project. The argument suffers from several critical flaws and is therefore unpersuasive as it stands.

First of all, that mere fact that environmentalists who oppose the development do not live in the town lends no credible support to the editorial's conclusion. In essence, the author attempts to argue for one position by attacking his opponents based on potentially irrelevant considerations. We are not informed about the environmentalists' specific reasons for their position. Besides, although they do not live in the town they might operate businesses or own property in the area; thus, their opposition might be based on economic grounds entirely relevant to the argument.

Secondly, the editorial provides no firm evidence to justify the assertion that a new ski resort north of town will in fact benefit the town's merchants. It is entirely possible that the resort might have the opposite effect, by drawing business away from local merchants, especially if the resort includes facilities such as apparel shops, restaurants, and grocery stores. Besides, we are not informed how far from town the resort would be located or how tourists would reach the resort. It is possible, for example, that the resort would be situated where visitors would take a route that does not pass through the town. Without ruling out these possibilities the editorial cannot justify its assertion that the resort would be a boon for local merchants.

Thirdly, the editorial's conclusion relies partly on the fact that a bank has agreed to fund the resort's development. However, this fact alone does not lend support to the assertion that local merchants will benefit. Common sense tells me that the bank agreed to fund the project because it believes the resort will be profitable, not because it believes other local merchants will benefit. In fact, a profitable ski resort might very well draw business away from local merchants.

In conclusion, the argument is untenable as it stands. To strengthen it, the editorial's author must provide clear evidence that the resort would increase business for the town's merchants rather than drawing business away from these merchants. To better evaluate the argument, we would need more information about the bank's reasons for agreeing to fund the project—especially whether the bank also lends to existing local merchants whose interests would be affected by the resort.

Argument 159　How to **save money on electricity**

This argument recommends that all citizens of Claria should run fans as well as air conditioners, for the purpose of saving money on electricity. To support this recommendation, the argument's proponent points out that Claria citizens who run only fans incur higher electric costs than those who run only air conditioners, and that those who run both incur the lowest electric costs among the three groups. However, the argument depends on certain dubious assumptions about climate, electric costs, and the cited statistics. As a result, the recommendation is ill-conceived.

First, the argument relies on the assumption that climatic conditions are similar throughout all regions of Claria. Yet this is probably not the case, especially since the passage explicitly characterizes Claria as vast and widely diverse geographically. It is entirely possible that only fans are used in certain regions because the climate in these regions is comparatively cold year-round, and that electric heating costs are so high that they result in the highest overall electric costs in the country. If this is the case, implementing the proponent's suggestion would result in higher electric costs for citizens in these regions. Or perhaps people who run both fans and air conditioners live in regions where there is less need for artificial cooling. This would explain why total electric costs in these regions are comparatively low. If this is the case, then implementing the proponent's suggestion might still result in higher electric costs for citizens in other regions.

Secondly, the recommendation depends on the assumption that the cost of electricity is the same for all three groups. However, it is possible that people who use both fans and air conditioners incur the lowest total electric costs among the three groups simply because these people pay the least per unit of electricity. The fact that Claria is geographically diverse lends support to this notion; people who use both fans and air conditioners are likely to live in the same climatic region, and people in the same region are more likely to be subject to the same electricity usage rates.

Thirdly, the argument provides insufficient information about the study on which it relies. If the results were based on only one warm season then the argument would be less persuasive than if the results were based on more than one warm season; in other words, the larger the statistical sample the more reliable the results.

In conclusion, the recommendation for using both cooling methods is dubious at best. To bolster it, the argument's proponent must show that climatic conditions are similar in all regions. The proponent must also show that rates charged for electricity are similar in all regions. Finally, in order to better evaluate the extent to which the cited study supports the recommendation we would need more statistical information about the study's time span.

Argument 163　Replacing an **old town hall**

This editorial concludes that the town of Rockingham would save money by replacing its old town hall with a larger, more energy-efficient one. To support the argument the editorial's author cites the need for a larger building to comfortably accommodate employees, and the fact that the proposed building would cost less per cubic foot to heat and cool than the current building would. However, the editorial is unconvincing for several reasons.

First of all, even though it would cost less per cubic foot to heat and cool the new building, because the new building would be larger the total cooling and heating costs might actually be greater than they are now. Add to this possibility the initial cost of replacing the structure, and in all likelihood the new building would not save money for the town. Besides, the argument ignores other, potentially less expensive, means of reducing current heating and cooling costs—for example, retrofitting the building with a new climate control system.

Secondly, the editorial relies partly on the fact that the current building cannot comfortably accommodate all the people who work in it. However, this fact in itself is irrelevant to whether the town would save money by replacing the building. Besides, the editorial ignores other, potentially less expensive, solutions to the current comfort problem—for example, adding an annex to the current structure.

Thirdly, the editorial relies partly on the assertion that the town could generate income by renting out part of a larger new building. However, the author equivocates here—on the one hand claiming that a larger building is needed because the old one is too small to accommodate employees, while on the other hand proposing that the additional space not be used to solve this problem. The use of conflicting evidence to support the same conclusion renders the argument wholly unpersuasive.

In conclusion, the editorial is unconvincing as it stands. To strengthen the assertion that a new building would save the town money, the editorial's author must provide a detailed analysis comparing the cost of cooling and heating the current hall to the anticipated cost of cooling and heating the new hall. In this analysis, the author must factor in the initial cost of replacing the old hall, as well as the additional rental income that the larger hall might generate. Finally, the author must choose between two competing objectives: creating a more spacious environment for current employees or creating a larger hall for the purpose of generating rental income.

Argument 164　New housing for **Claitown University** students

This argument recommends commissioning a famous architect known for futuristic and experimental designs as the best means of providing new affordable housing for Claitown University students. The argument's line of reasoning is that the building will attract paying tourists, new students, and donations from alumni—all of which will help raise the funds needed for the project. However, the argument is problematic in several critical respects.

First of all, a famous architect might charge a substantial fee for the project, in which case the funds raised by charging tourists and through alumni donations might be offset to the point of rendering the entire project unfeasible financially. The argument's proponent must address this issue before I can accept the argument's conclusion.

Secondly, the argument relies on the tenuous assumption that tourists will be interested in paying for tours of a building used for a purpose as mundane as student housing. It is entirely possible that once the building **is** in use, tourists will not be willing to pay for tours. Besides, perhaps the appeal of this architect's buildings lies primarily in their exteriors, in which case tourists would be able to appreciate the new building's salient architectural features without paying for a tour. In either case, the argument's claim that the architect's notoriety and the building itself will generate the funds needed for its construction would be dubious at best.

Thirdly, the argument fails to explain how the University will be able to pay for construction when it will not begin to receive the revenue it needs until after construction is complete. Unless the architect and contractors agree to be paid later, the argument's proponent cannot convince me that the recommended course of action will achieve the University's goals.

Finally, the argument assumes without justification that a futuristic or experimental building will attract alumni donations and students. While this might be true, it is also possible that instead the University's alumni and students strongly prefer the architectural status quo at their campus; in fact, the appeal of the campus' predominant architectural styles might be one of the key attractions for students and alumni dollars. Thus, I would need some evidence to substantiate this assumption before I can accept the argument's conclusion.

In sum, as it stands the argument is not well supported. To strengthen it, the argument's proponent must supply dear evidence—perhaps involving other college buildings designed by famous architects—that tourists will be willing to pay for tours of the building once it is completed and is in use as student housing. To better assess the argument I would need detailed and realistic financial projections, accounting for the architect's fees, to determine the project's financial feasibility. I would also need to know—perhaps by way of a reliable survey—the extent to which students and alumni would be likely to support the project.

Argument 165　**Promofoods'** recall of its cans of tuna

This magazine article concludes that the 8 million cans of tuna Promofoods recalled, due to complaints about nausea and dizziness, do not after all contain any chemicals that pose a health risk. To support this conclusion the author cites the fact that five of eight chemicals commonly causing these symptoms were not found in the recalled cans, while the other three also occur naturally in other canned foods. For several reasons, this evidence lends little credible support to the author's conclusion.

To begin with, the author relies partly on the fact that, although three of the eight chemicals most commonly blamed for nausea and dizziness appeared in Promofoods' recalled tuna, these chemicals also occur naturally in other canned foods. However, this fact alone lends no support to the author's conclusion, for two reasons. First, the author might be ignoring an important distinction between "naturally occurring" chemicals and those not occurring naturally. It is entirely possible that these three chemicals do not occur naturally in Promofoods' tuna, and that it is for this reason that the chemicals cause nausea and dizziness. Secondly, it is entirely possible that even when they occur naturally these chemicals cause the same symptoms. Unless the author rules out both possibilities, he cannot reliably conclude that the recalled tuna would not cause these symptoms.

Another problem with the argument is that the author's conclusion is too broad. Based on evidence about certain chemicals that might cause two particular heath-related symptoms, the author concludes that the recalled tuna contains no chemicals that pose a health risk. However, the author fails to account for the myriad of other possible health risks that the recalled tuna might potentially pose. Without ruling out all other such risks, the author cannot justifiably reach his conclusion.

A third problem with the argument involves that fact that the eight particular chemicals with which the test was concerned are only the eight "most commonly blamed" for nausea and dizziness. It is entirely possibly that other chemicals might also cause these symptoms, and that one or more of these other chemicals actually caused the symptoms. Without ruling out this possibility, the author cannot justifiably conclude that the recalled tuna would not cause nausea and dizziness.

A final problem with the argument involves the testing procedure itself. The author provides no information about the number of recalled cans tested or the selection method used. Unless the number of cans is a sufficiently large sample and is statistically representative of all the recalled cans, the study's results are not statistically reliable.

In conclusion, the article is unconvincing as it stands. To strengthen the assertion that the recalled tuna would not cause nausea and dizziness, the author must provide evidence that the three chemicals mentioned that occur naturally in other canned foods also appear naturally in Promofoods' tuna. The author must also provide evidence that ingesting other canned foods containing these three chemicals does not cause these symptoms. To better evaluate the argument, we would need to know whether the sample used in the tests was statistically significant and representative of all the recalled tuna. We would also need to know what other chemicals in the recalled tuna might pose any health risk at all.

Argument 169　Attracting new faculty to **Pierce University**

In this letter, a department chairperson at Pierce University recommends that Pierce offer jobs to spouses of new faculty in order to attract the most gifted teachers and researchers. To support this recommendation, the chairperson cites certain Bronston University studies, which concluded that in small towns male as well as female faculty are happier when their spouses are employed in the same geographic area. However, the chairperson's argument relies on certain unsubstantiated assumptions about the similarity between Pierce faculty and the faculty involved in the Bronston study, and about how the most gifted teachers and researchers choose among jobs in the first place.

A threshold problem with the argument involves the Bronston studies themselves. The letter provides no information about the faculty in the study—specifically, whether they were representative of college faculty in general, and of potential Pierce faculty in particular. For example, if the study involved only Bronston faculty, then it would be less reliable than if it involved Pierce faculty as well. In any case, the smaller and more biased the survey's sample, the less reliable it is for the purpose of drawing any conclusions about how Pierce might attract new faculty.

Secondly, the argument relies on the assumption that faculty whose spouses work for the same employer are just as happy as faculty whose spouses work for other employers. However, since the letter fails to substantiate this assumption it is entirely possible that the spouses involved in the Bronston study and who worked in the same geographic area attribute their happiness to the fact that they work for different employers. If so, then the chairperson's recommendation that Pierce try to entice gifted teachers and researchers by offering jobs to their spouses as well would seem ill-advised.

Thirdly, the argument assumes that jobs for faculty spouses at Pierce would contribute to the happiness of Pierce faculty to at least as great an extent as the jobs in the geographical areas where the study's subjects resided. However, the letter provides no evidence to substantiate this assumption. Thus it is entirely possible that jobs in the areas where the study's faculty resided are higher-paying, offer better benefits, or otherwise contribute to the happiness of employees' spouses—college faculty—more so than a typical staff position at Pierce. In fact, the letter suggests that this might be the case. By admitting that Pierce job offers are not ideal, the letter implies that faculty candidates and their spouses might find a more attractive dual-employment package elsewhere.

Finally, the argument assumes that gifted teachers and researchers consider employment for spouses a key factor in choosing among job offers. However, the letter provides no evidence that this is the case. In fact, it is entirely possible that the faculty in the Bronston study are not exceptional teachers and researchers and therefore do not have as many job options as the kind of faculty Pierce hopes to attract. If this is the case, Pierce cannot justifiably expect the most exceptional teachers to accept positions at Pierce just because Pierce provides employment to faculty spouses.

In conclusion, the letter is unpersuasive as it stands. To strengthen the argument, the chairperson must show that jobs for spouses of faculty involved in the Bronston study are no more attractive than non-faculty jobs at Pierce. The chairperson must also provide clear evidence that the most gifted teachers and researchers find the sort of benefit that this letter proposes to be significantly attractive in choosing among job offers. Finally, to better assess the argument we would need more information about the faculty involved in the Bronston studies, so that we can determine the study's relevance to Pierce, as well as its statistical reliability.

Argument 170 The price of oysters

This argument points out that, ever since harmful bacteria were found in a few Gulf Coast oysters five years ago, California consumers have been willing to pay twice as much for northeastern Atlantic oysters as for Gulf oysters. The argument then notes that scientists have now developed a process for killing these bacteria. The argument concludes that once consumers become aware of this fact they will be willing to pay as much for these oysters as for Atlantic oysters, and that profits for Gulf oyster producers will thereby increase. The argument is flawed in three critical respects.

First, the argument assumes that the bacteria discovery is the reason for California consumers' unwillingness to pay as much for Gulf shrimp during the past five years. However, this is not necessarily so. Perhaps regional culinary tastes shifted during the last five years, and perhaps Atlantic oysters have a distinct taste, texture, size, or other quality that has made them more popular among California consumers. Since the argument fails to rule out this and other alternative explanations for the willingness of California consumers to pay more for Atlantic oysters, the argument's conclusion is unwarranted.

Secondly, the argument assumes too hastily that consumer awareness of the process that kills the bacteria will necessarily result in the behavior that the argument predicts. Perhaps after five years of favoring Atlantic oysters, consumer oyster tastes and habits have become so well entrenched that consumers will continue to favor Atlantic oysters and will happily pay a premium for them. Moreover, in my observation consumers often act unpredictably and irrationally, and therefore any prediction about consumer preferences is dubious at best. Besides, it is entirely possible that Gulf oyster producers will be unwilling to employ the new bacteria-killing process; if so, and if consumers are aware of this fact, then in all likelihood consumers will continue to favor Atlantic oysters.

Thirdly, even if consumers begin paying as much for Gulf oysters once they become aware of the bacteria-killing process, the argument's conclusion that Gulf oyster producers will enjoy increased profits as a result is unwarranted. Profit is a factor of not only revenue but also costs. It is entirely possible that the costs of employing this new process for killing bacteria, or other costs associated with producing Gulf oysters, will offset additional revenue. Besides, a myriad of other possible occurrences, such as unfavorable regional weather or economic conditions, might prevent the Gulf oyster producers from being as profitable in the foreseeable future as the argument predicts.

In sum, the argument is unpersuasive as it stands. To strengthen it the argument's proponent must consider and rule out all other possible explanations for the willingness of California consumers to pay a premium for Atlantic oysters, and must convince me that with consumer awareness of the bacteria-killing process Gulf oysters will become just as desirable as Atlantic oysters. To better assess the argument's claim that profits for Gulf oyster producers will increase as an end result, I would need to know whether Gulf oyster producers will incur the expenses involved in killing the bacteria and, if so, the extent to which these expenses will impinge on the producers' profits.

Argument 171　Bargain Brand Cereal profits

In this memo the marketing director of Bargain Brand Cereal claims that the company will continue to make a profit from sales of its cereal, and therefore that the company should expand its bargain priced product line to include other foods as well. To support these assertions, the memo points out that Bargain Brand is still earning a profit from its cereal sales, despite the fact that major competitors have lowered their cereal prices and plan to offer bargain-priced cereal brands. On several grounds, this evidence lends little credible support for the memo's conclusions.

First of all, the mere fact that Bargain Brand is still earning a profit from its cereal sales is not the key in determining whether its competitors are succeeding. The key instead is the extent to which Bargain Brand profits have diminished since other companies lowered their cereal prices. It is entirely possible that Bargain Brand has been less profitable since its competitors lowered their cereal prices, and that given a little more time these competitors will draw enough additional sales away from Bargain Brand to render it unprofitable. The fact that the other companies offer the "top brands" is strong evidence that these companies can survive a prolonged price war and ultimately prevail over Bargain

Brand.

Secondly, the memo states that several major competitors plan to offer their own special bargain brands to compete directly with Bargain Brand. Yet the memo fails to account for this fact in concluding that Bargain Brand will continue to be profitable. In all likelihood, after the introduction of competing brands Bargain Brand's profits will diminish even further. Without providing evidence that this will not occur, the director cannot convincingly conclude that Bargain Brand will continue to profit from its cereal sales.

Thirdly, based on the fact that Bargain Brand continues to profit from cereal sales, the memo concludes that Bargain Brand should expand its product line to include other food products. Yet the memo provides no evidence that Bargain Brand is likely to be profitable in other markets. Common sense suggests the contrary—that Bargain Brand is unlikely to succeed in markets in which it has no previous experience or exposure. Without providing evidence as to how Bargain Brand would overcome natural barriers to entry into other markets, the director's conclusion is weak at best.

In conclusion, the memo is unpersuasive as it stands. To strengthen the argument, the director must show that Bargain Brand will continue to profit from cereal sales even after its major competitors introduce their own bargain brands. To better assess the director's conclusion that Bargain Brand should expand its line of bargain-priced foods, we would need more information about the extent of competition and other barriers to entry in those other markets.

Argument 175   Driver's education at **Centerville High**

This letter recommends mandatory driver's education courses at Centerville High School. The author bases this recommendation on three facts: during the last two years several Centerville car accidents have involved teenage drivers; Centerville parents are too busy to teach driving to their children; and the two private driver-education courses in the area are expensive. As discussed below, the argument suffers from several critical flaws and is therefore unpersuasive.

First of all, the letter fails to indicate who or what caused the car accidents to which the letter refers. If Centerville High School students caused the accidents, and if those accidents would have been avoided had these students enrolled in the high school's driving course, then the argument would have merit. However, it is equally likely that the other drivers were at fault, or that no driver was at fault. Moreover, it is entirely possible that the teenage drivers had in fact taken the high school's driving course, or that they were not local high school students in the first place. The author must rule out all these possibilities in order to conclude confidently that a school-sponsored mandatory driving course would have prevented these accidents.

Secondly, whether the fact that several car accidents the last two years involved teenage drivers suggests a need for a mandatory driving course depends partly on the comparative accident rate during earlier years. It is entirely possible, for instance, that the rate of accidents involving teenagers has been steadily declining, and that this decline is due to the availability of the two private driving courses. Without ruling out this possibility, the letter's conclusion is not defensible.

The argument is problematic in certain other respects as well. It assumes that a mandatory school-sponsored course would be effective, yet provides no evidence to support this assumption. Similarly, the argument fails to substantiate its assumption that a significant percentage of Centerville's parents cannot afford private driving instruction for their teenage children. Absent substantiating evidence for either of these necessary assumptions, I cannot be convinced that Centerville should establish the proposed driving course.

In conclusion, the letter's author fails to adequately support the recommendation for a school-sponsored mandatory driving course. To strengthen the argument, the author must provide dear evidence that Centerville High School students caused the accidents in question, and that a mandatory driving course would have prevented them. To better evaluate the argument, I would need more information about the affordability of the two private driving courses and about the effectiveness of a mandatory school-sponsored course compared to that of the two private courses.

Argument 177　Membership in **Oak City's Civic Club**

This letter recommends that membership in Oak City's Civic Club, the primary objective of which is to discuss local issues, be limited to local residents. To support this recommendation, the author claims that since only residents pay local taxes they are the only people who sufficiently understand local business and political issues. The author also cites the fact that in the last ten years very few non-residents of Oak City who work in Oak City have joined nearby Elm City's Civic Club, which is open to any person. The argument suffers from two critical flaws and is therefore unpersuasive as it stands.

To begin with, the letter fails to adequately support the claim that since only residents pay local taxes only they truly understand local business and political issues. Even given the dubious assumption that being a local taxpayer affords one an understanding of local business and political issues, it is fallacious to conclude that being a local taxpayer is a necessary condition for understanding these issues. Moreover, common sense tells me that local business people, residents or not, would probably be more intimately involved in many such issues than local residents who do not have business interests in the town. Having failed to address this distinct possibility, the letter is wholly unconvincing.

In further support of the recommendation, the letter cites the fact that nearby Elm City's Civic Club is open to any person, yet very few Oak City business people who are not residents have joined Elm City's club in the last ten years. But this fact alone lends no support to the recommendation. It is possible, for instance, that these business people have no connection with Elm City whatsoever, or that these business people have been members of Elm City's Civic Club for longer than ten years. The author must eliminate these possibilities in order to rely justifiably on this evidence for his or her recommendation.

In conclusion, the letter's author fails to adequately support the recommendation that Oak City Civic Club membership be restricted to local residents. To strengthen the argument, the author must provide clear evidence that non-residents who work in Oak City do not understand local issues as well as residents do. To better evaluate the argument, we would need more information about why non-resident business people in Oak City have not joined Elm City's Civic Club during the last ten years.

Argument 179　Selecting a food service provider for an **employee cafeteria**

This memo recommends that Cedar Corporation replace its current food provider, Good-Taste, with Discount Foods. To support this recommendation, the memo's author cites Good-Taste's increasing fees, the fact that three Cedar employees refuse to eat in the cafeteria, and various features of Discount Foods. For several reasons, this evidence fails to provide adequate support for the recommendation.

The memo's reliance on the fact that three Cedar employees find eating in the company cafeteria "unbearable" presents two problems. First, the memo unfairly assumes that Good-Taste is responsible for these complaints. It is entirely possible that other conditions in the cafeteria are instead responsible. Second, the memo assumes that complaints by only three Cedar employees constitutes a statistically significant number which warrants replacing Good-Taste with another food / provider. However, the memo provides no evidence that this is the case.

Another problem with the recommendation is that it relies partly on the fact that Good-Taste has been increasing its fees and is now the second-most-expensive food provider available to Cedar. Yet the recommendation is based on what food provider would best satisfy Cedar's employees, not what provider would reduce Cedar's costs. In other words, this evidence is not directly relevant to the reasons for the author's recommendation. Even if expense were a legitimate factor, it is possible that Discount is even more expensive than Good-Taste.

Yet another problem with the recommendation is that it relies partly on the need to accommodate employees with special dietary needs. The memo provides no evidence that Good-Taste is any less capable than Discount of accommodating these employees. Rather, the memo merely provides that Discount offers "a varied menu of fish and poultry". Without a more detailed comparison between the offerings of the two companies, it is unfair to conclude that one would meet the needs of Cedar's employees better than the other would.

Finally, the recommendation relies partly on the fact that in one taste test the memo's author found Discount Foods to be "delicious". In all likelihood, however, the author's tastes do not represent the collective tastes of Cedar employees; accordingly, the author's report is patently insufficient to demonstrate that Cedar's employees would be more satisfied with Discount than with Good-Taste.

In conclusion, the letter's author fails to adequately support the recommendation that Cedar replace Good-Taste with Discount. To strengthen the argument, the author must provide clear evidence that Cedar employees are dissatisfied with Good-Taste's food and that they would be more satisfied with Discount's food. To better evaluate the argument, we would need more information comparing the two companies' menus to determine which is more varied and caters to those with special dietary needs.

Argument 180   The benefits of the **Easy Read Speed-Reading Course**

In this argument, the personnel director of Acme Publishing claims that Acme would benefit greatly from improved employee productivity if every employee takes the 3-week Easy-Read seminar at a cost of $ 500 per employee. To support this claim the director points out that many other companies have claimed to benefit from the seminar, that one student was able to read a long report very quickly afterward, and that another student saw his career advance significantly during the year after the seminar. However, close scrutiny of the evidence reveals that it accomplishes little toward supporting the director's claim, as discussed below.

First of all, the mere fact that many other companies benefited greatly from the course does not necessarily mean that Acme will benefit similarly from it. Perhaps the type of reading on which the course focuses is not the type in which Acme Publishing employees often engage at work. Moreover, since Acme is a publishing company its employees are likely to be excellent readers already, and therefore might stand to gain far less from the course than employees of other types of companies.

Secondly, the two individual success stories the argument cites amount to scant evidence at best of the course's effectiveness. Moreover, the director unfairly assumes that their accomplishments can be attributed to the course. Perhaps both individuals were outstanding readers before taking the course, and gained nothing from it. Regarding the individual whose career advanced after taking the course, any one of a myriad of other factors might explain that advancement. And the individual who was able to read a long report very quickly after the course did not necessarily absorb a great deal of the material.

Thirdly, the director assumes without warrant that the benefits of the course will outweigh its costs. While all of Acme's employees take the 3-week course, Acme's productivity might decline significantly. This decline, along with the substantial fee for the course, might very well outweigh the course's benefits. Without a complete cost-benefit analysis, it is unfair to conclude that Acme would benefit greatly should all its employees take the course.

In sum, the director's evidence does not warrant his conclusion. To support his recommendation he must first provide evidence that employees with similar reading skills as those that Acme employees possess have benefited significantly from the course; a survey of other publishing companies might be useful for this purpose. To better assess the argument I would need more information about the extent to which the course would disrupt Acme's operations. Specific information that would be useful would include the proximity of the seminar to Acme, the hours involved, and the percentage of Acme employees enrolled simultaneously.

Argument 182　Should **Happy Pancake House** serve margarine or butter?

In this argument the speaker recommends that, in order to save money, Happy Pancake House (HPH) should serve margarine instead of butter at all its restaurants. To support the argument, the speaker points out that HPH's Southwestern restaurants now serve margarine but not butter, and that only 2% of these restaurants' customers have complained about the change. The speaker also cites reports from many servers that a number of customers asking for butter have not complained when given margarine instead. This argument is unconvincing for several reasons.

First of all, the speaker does not indicate how long these restaurants have been refusing butter to customers. If the change is very recent, it is possible that insufficient data have been collected to draw any reliable conclusions. Lacking this information I cannot assess the reliability of the evidence for the purpose of showing that HPH customers in the Southwest are generally happy with the change.

Secondly, the speaker fails to indicate what portion of HPH customers order meals calling for either butter or margarine. Presumably, the vast majority of meals served at any pancake restaurant call for one or the other. Yet it is entirely possible that a significant percentage of HPH customers do not order pancakes, or prefer fruit or another topping instead. The greater this percentage, the less meaningful any statistic about the level of customer satisfaction among all of HPH's Southwestern customers as an indicator of preference for butter or margarine.

Thirdly, the speaker unfairly assumes that HPH customers unhappy with the change generally complain about it. Perhaps many such customers express their displeasure simply by not returning to the restaurant. The greater the percentage of such customers, the weaker the argument's evidence as a sign of customer satisfaction with the change.

Two additional problems specifically involve the reports from "many" servers that "a number" of customers asking for butter do not complain when served margarine instead. Since the speaker fails to indicate the percentage of servers reporting or customers who have not complained to servers, this evidence is far too vague to be meaningful. Also, the speaker omits any mention of reports from servers about customers who have complained. Since the anecdotal evidence is one-sided, it is inadequate to assess overall customer satisfaction with the change.

Finally, even if HPH's Southwest customers are happy with the change, the speaker unfairly assumes that customers in other regions will respond similarly to it. Perhaps Southwesterners are generally less concerned than other people about whether they eat margarine or butter. Or perhaps Southwesterners actually prefer margarine to butter, in contrast to prevailing tastes elsewhere. Or perhaps Southwesterners have relatively few choices when it comes to pancake restaurants.

In sum, the speaker's argument is weak. To better assess it I would need to know: (1) how long the change has been in effect in the Southwest, (2) what percentage of HPH servers and managers have received customer complaints about the change, and (3) the number of such complaints as a percentage of the total number of HPH customers who order meals calling for either butter or margarine. To strengthen the argument, the speaker must provide dear evidence—perhaps by way of a reliable survey—that HPH customers in other regions are likely to be happy with the change and continue to patronize HPH after the change.

Argument 183　Outlook for **new hires** and layoffs

The speaker concludes that employees of major U.S. corporations should not fear that they will lose their jobs in the near future. To support this conclusion the speaker cites the fact that most companies expect to hire new employees next year, while fewer plan to lay off employees. The speaker also cites the current proliferation of job-finding resources. The argument is problematic in several critical respects.

First of all, the argument depends on the assumption that the total number of expected hires exceeds the total number of expected layoffs. However, we are not informed whether this is the case. It is possible that, although more companies expect to hire than lay off employees, the total number of employees expected to be laid off exceeds the total number expected to be hired. If true, this fact would serve to refute the speaker's conclusion that employees of major U.S. corporations should not expect to be laid off.

Secondly, the argument assumes that the companies that expect to hire next year are major U.S. corporations. However, it is entirely possible that these are the firms that expect layoffs, while it is smaller companies that expect to hire. Common sense tells me that this is a reasonable possibility, because the number of small companies greatly exceeds the number of large U.S. corporations. Moreover, even if it is the major U.S. corporations that expect to do most of the hiring next year, it is entirely possible that it is these same companies that expect to do most of the laying off. Again, common sense informs me that this is entirely possible—that these employers intend to replace many current employees or job positions with new ones.

Thirdly, the argument rests on the dubious assumption that all conditions relevant to a company's decision to hire or lay off employees will remain unchanged in the near future. While this might be the case, it is equally possible that unexpected changes in general economic conditions will result in more layoffs among major U.S. corporations next year than these firms now anticipate.

Finally, the argument seems to rely partly on the proliferation of job-finding programs. While this fact might allay the worries of employees that they will not find new employment, it is irrelevant to whether these employees should expect to be laid off in the first place. In fact, it can even be argued that the proliferation of job-finding programs is evidence of increasing job attrition, and therefore evidence that these employees' fears are well founded.

In conclusion, the argument is unconvincing as it stands. To strengthen it the author must provide clear evidence that the number of expected hires exceeds the number of expected layoffs, and that major U.S. corporations are the companies planning to hire rather than to lay off employees.

Argument 184　Replacing **Bayhead Public Library**'s books

In this argument the speaker supports Bayhead Public Library's plan to replace books that are borrowed less frequently than once per year with additional copies of recent novels. In support of this position, the speaker suggests that seldom-borrowed books amount to wasted shelf space because people who want to read recent novels frequently find the library's only copy checked out. In further support of this position, the speaker points out that only thirty people have protested the plan. I find the speaker's position unjustified in several critical respects.

First of all, the speaker ignores the possibility that replacing less popular books with more copies of popular new novels will undermine the library's primary function as a repository of a wide variety of books for free public access. New books are available at bookstores, whereas older, less popular ones are not. Thus, the library might lose the patronage of a large percentage of the community should it adopt the plan.

Secondly, the speaker unfairly implies that the library has only two options: to maintain the status quo or to follow the proposed plan. Some other alternative—one that would appease protesters while preserving community support—might provide an optimal long-term solution. For example, perhaps the library can remove books that have not been borrowed for three years or for five years, rather than for one year. Although this alternate plan would free up less shelf space than the current plan, it would nevertheless make room for the most popular new books.

Finally, the mere fact that only thirty people have protested the plan accomplishes little toward supporting the speaker's argument—for two reasons. First, this statistic is scant evidence that the community at large would support the plan; it is entirely possible that many opponents have simply not voiced their opposition. Second, the thirty protesters might very well be in a position to influence many other people; or they might be among the library's most significant financial patrons. In either event, ignoring these protesters might result in the ultimate loss of community or financial support the library needs to thrive, or even survive.

In sum, the library's plan seems neither well-reasoned nor well-supported. To strengthen her position, the speaker must convince me that the plan is the only viable option to maintaining the status quo. To better assess the plan's impact on the library's value as a community resource, I would need to know what percentage of the library's current inventory would be replaced under the plan. I would also need to know the extent of influence among the thirty protesters, and the extent of support for the plan among the vast majority of community members who have not voiced their opinions about it.

Argument 185   Saving water at the **Sunnyside Towers**

In this letter, the owner of an apartment building concludes that low-flow shower heads should be installed in showers on all 20 floors of the building, for the purpose of saving money. To support this conclusion, the owner cites the fact that since installing low-flow heads in showers on the bottom five floors only a few tenants have complained about low water pressure, and that no other problems with showers have been reported. However, this evidence provides little credible support for the owner's argument, as discussed below.

In the first place, the argument depends on the assumption that installation of low-flow heads on the first five floors has resulted in lower water costs for the owner. However, this need not be the case. It is equally possible that tenants on these floors compensate for lower flow by either taking longer showers or by opening their shower valves further than they would otherwise. It is also possible that water pressure, and therefore water usage, on the remaining floors has increased as a result. It is even possible that during the month since installation many of the tenants on the bottom five floors have been absent from the building, and this fact explains why few tenants have complained.

In the second place, the owner ignores possible indirect consequences of installing low-flow shower heads on all 20 floors—consequences that in turn might adversely affect the owner's net operating income. For example, the more low-flow installations the more likely that one or more tenants will become disgruntled and vacate as a result. In fact, the owner has admitted that at least a few tenants have complained about these new shower heads. High tenant turnover might very well serve to increase the owner's overall operating costs.

In the third place, in order to reasonably conclude that low-flow heads will reduce total water usage in the building the owner must assume that other water uses will remain constant in the future. However, this will not necessarily be the case. Perhaps the water supplier will raise rates, or perhaps current tenants will be replaced by other tenants who use more water. Without ruling out such possibilities the owner cannot justifiably conclude that his total water costs will decrease after installing low-flow heads in every shower.

In conclusion, the argument is unconvincing as it stands. To strengthen it the owner must provide clear evidence that the use of a low-flow shower head in fact reduces total water usage. To better assess the argument we would need figures comparing water usage before and after installation. We would also need to know how many of the bottom five floors were occupied since the new heads were installed, and whether the tenants on these floors are likely to use more or less water than tenants on the upper floors.

Argument 187   Preventing depression by eating more **fish**

The author of this article asserts that people who live in the U.S. should increase their fish consumption in order to prevent depression. To support this assertion, the author cites the fact that our ancestors, who were less likely to experience depression than we are today, consumed more omega-3 fatty acids, which help prevent depression and are found in some fish and fish oils. The author also cites the fact that in modern societies where people eat more fish than we do the reported incidence of depression is comparatively low. However, the author's reasoning is problematic in several critical respects.

The first problem with the argument involves the comparatively low incidence of depression among our ancestors. The author assumes that no factor other than the ingestion of omega-3 is responsible for this lower incidence. However, it is entirely possible that environmental or other dietary factors are instead responsible for the lower incidence. For example, perhaps other substances common in the U.S. diet today, and which promote depression, were not part of our ancestors' diets.

Another problem with the argument involves the low incidence of depression reported among today's fish-eating societies. To reasonably infer a causal relationship between fish-eating and low rates of depression in these societies, two assumptions are required. The first is that the types of fish consumed in these societies in fact contain omega-3; however, the article provides no evidence that this is the case. The second assumption is that the reported incidence of depression accurately reflects the actual incidence. However, it is entirely possible that in those societies people generally do not report depression.

A third problem with the argument is that it assumes that omega-3 is only available in fish. However, the author provides no evidence to substantiate this crucial assumption.

Perhaps people can ingest omega-3 by taking fish oil capsules rather than eating fish. Or perhaps omega-3 is also found in other foods as well. In either case, the author cannot reasonably conclude that we must eat more fish to ingest omega-3 and thereby help prevent depression.

Finally, in concluding that people in the U.S. must ingest more omega-3 to prevent depression, the author infers that this is the only means of preventing depression. This reasoning is fallacious. There might be a myriad of alternative ways to prevent depression; moreover, experience and common sense informs me that this is indeed the case.

In conclusion, the argument is unconvincing as it stands. To strengthen it, the author must provide clear evidence that no other factors explain the comparatively low incidence of depression among our ancestors. The author must also show that in modern fish-eating societies people in fact ingest more omega-3 than people in the U.S. do, and that the incidence of depression is in fact lower in those societies. To better evaluate the argument, we would need more information about alternative methods of preventing depression and alternative sources of omega-3.

Argument 189　How to increase enrollment at Foley College

The dean of Foley College claims that by guaranteeing prospective students that they will obtain jobs immediately upon graduation Foley can increase its enrollment and more effectively compete against more prestigious schools. To support this assertion the dean claims that students who commit early to a course of study and are guaranteed eventual employment are more likely to complete that course work and will be better prepared for the future. On several grounds, however, the dean's argument is unconvincing.

First of all, the argument assumes that providing this guarantee will in fact result in increased enrollment. However, the dean provides no evidence that this will be the case. It is entirely possible that the sort of student attracted to Foley in the first place would not find such a guarantee a particularly enticing feature. In fact, since Foley is a liberal arts college its students are more likely to be interested in graduate-level study rather than immediate employment upon graduation.

Secondly, the dean provides no support for the claim that because of the proposed guarantee Foley students would be more likely to successfully complete the course work they choose as entering freshman. To the contrary, experience and common sense inform us that while in college students often change their minds about their best career direction. Accordingly, by requiring an early commitment to a course of study Foley might be doing its students a disservice in terms of helping them select the course of study that they are most likely to complete successfully.

Thirdly, the dean provides no support for the final conclusion that the earlier a student's commitment to a course of study the better prepared the student will be for the future. It is entirely possible that exploring diverse options during the first year or two of college is a better way to prepare for one's future—by providing the sort of well-rounded education that one might need for career flexibility. Without addressing this issue the dean cannot justifiably conclude that the proposed guarantee will better prepare Foley students for the future.

In conclusion, the argument is unconvincing as it stands. To strengthen it the dean must provide statistical evidence that college students who commit early to a course of study or who are promised eventual employment in that field are more likely than other college students to succeed in college and in their careers. Finally, to better evaluate the argument, we would need more information about why prospective students apply to Foley in the first place.

Argument 190   Advance ticket sales for **Glenville**'s concerts

This letter recommends that Glenville feature modern music, especially the music of Richerts, at its summer concerts in order to boost advance ticket sales and attendance. To support this recommendation the letter's author points out that advance ticket sales have declined over the past few years, but that unpredictable weather cannot be the reason for the decline because "many people attended the concerts even in bad weather". The author concludes that choice of music must be the reason for the decline, then reasons further that since Richerts' recordings are very popular among Glenville residents featuring Richerts' music at the concerts would boost ticket sales and attendance. I find this argument to be logically unconvincing in several respects.

As a threshold matter, the author unfairly equates the number of ticket purchasers with the number of tickets purchased. The author ignores the possibility that the average number of tickets sold to each purchaser is increasing and, as a result, the total number of tickets is not declining—or perhaps even increasing. Thus, the author cannot convincingly conclude that Glenville has a ticket-sale problem in the first place.

Even if the actual number of tickets sold in advance has been declining, the author concludes too hastily that unpredictable weather cannot be the reason for the decline. Perhaps concert attendees during the past few years have now learned from their experience with bad concert weather not to purchase advance tickets again. Besides, the mere fact that "many people" attended concerts in bad weather proves nothing unless the author can show that total attendance has been lower in bad weather than in good weather.

Even assuming unpredictable weather is not the reason for the decline in advance ticket sales, the author falsely assumes that the decline must be attributable to choice of music. This "either-or" argument is fallacious in that it ignores other possible causes of the decline. For example, perhaps during the last few years Glenville has begun its promotional efforts unusually late. Or perhaps the number of outlets where tickets are available in advance has declined. For that matter, perhaps Glenville's demographics are in flux so that the total number of residents willing and able to attend summer concerts is declining.

Finally, even assuming that choice of music is the true cause of the decline in advance ticket sales, the author fails to provide adequate evidence that choosing modern music, and Richerts' compositions in particular, will boost sales and attendance. The author unfairly assumes that people who purchase recordings are the same group that would be inclined to attend live concerts. Lacking evidence that this is the case, the author cannot convince me that the proposed course of action will bring about its intended result.

In sum, the argument is logically unconvincing as it stands. To strengthen it the author must first establish a clear causal relationship between the number of people buying advance tickets and actual concert attendance. The author must also provide evidence—perhaps by way of a reliable survey—that the "many people" who have attended the concerts in bad weather are likely to do so again despite their experience. The author must then consider and eliminate all other possible explanations for the decline. Finally, to better assess the argument I would need more information about the musical tastes of the Glenville residents who are most inclined to attend live concerts.

Argument 191　Distance-learning courses at **Xanadu College**

In this letter a Xanadu College professor asserts that the development of an extensive distance-learning program would enhance the college's reputation, as well as increase total enrollment and therefore total tuition income. To support this assertion the professor points out that in last year's trial program two traditional courses were easily adapted for distance learning. Next, the professor reasons that with more free time faculty could engage in extensive research, which in turn would enhance the college's reputation. The argument is flawed in several critical respects.

First of all, the professor's claim that an increase in enrollment would result in an increase in tuition income is warranted only if Xanadu students would be willing to pay a sufficiently high fee for distance-learning courses. However, it is entirely possible that Xanadu's distance-learning courses would not command as high a fee as its traditional courses, and that Xanadu's total tuition income would actually decline if this less-expensive alternative were available to Xanadu students.

Secondly, the professor's dual claims about distance learning—that it would enhance Xanadu's reputation and that it would increase enrollment and income—might very well be mutually exclusive alternatives. The availability of distance-learning courses might actually diminish Xanadu's overall reputation for quality education. Without addressing this issue the professor cannot justifiably conclude that the distance-learning alternative would achieve both goals.

A third problem with the argument involves last year's trial project. Despite the fact that two particular courses were easily adapted to distance learning, other courses might not be as adaptable. Common sense informs me that certain courses, especially in the arts, require hands-on learning to be effective. Thus, the professor cannot justify her claim on the basis of the trial project.

Finally, the professor's claim that distance learning would afford Xanadu faculty more free time to engage in extensive research raises two problems. First, it is possible that the time needed for faculty to adapt their courses for distance learning would equal or even exceed the time they would save by not teaching traditional classes. Second, even if a net time savings does result, the professor provides no evidence that Xanadu faculty would actually use this extra free time for research, or that additional research would in fact enhance Xanadu's reputation.

In conclusion, the argument is indefensible as it stands. To strengthen it the professor must provide specific information about Xanadu's current reputation, and provide dear evidence that distance learning would in fact enhance this reputation. The professor must also convince us that the two courses in the trial project were representative of Xanadu's other courses—in terms of the ease with which the faculty could adapt their courses to distance learning. Finally, to better assess the argument we would need a detailed analysis comparing loss in tuition from traditional-course enrollment with expected gains in tuition from distance-learning enrollment.

Argument 193   Homework assignments and academic performance

The speaker argues that if the state board of education required that homework be assigned to high school students no more than twice per week academic performance would improve. To support this assertion the speaker cites a statewide survey of math and science teachers. According to the survey, students in the Marlee district, who are assigned homework no more than once per week, achieve better grades and are less likely to repeat a school year than students in the Sanlee district, who are assigned homework every night. Close scrutiny reveals, however, that this evidence provides little credible support for the speaker's assertion.

To begin with, the survey appears to suffer from two statistical problems, either of which renders the survey's results unreliable. First, the speaker relies on statistics from only two districts; however, it is entirely possible that these two districts are not representative of the state's school districts overall. Second, the survey involved only math and science teachers. Yet the speaker draws a broad recommendation for **all** teachers based on the survey's results.

In addition, the speaker's recommendation relies on the assumption that the amount of homework assigned to students is the only possible reason for the comparative academic performance between students in the two districts. However, in all likelihood this is simply not the case. Perhaps Sanlee teachers are stricter graders then Marlee teachers. Or perhaps Sanlee teachers are less effective than Marlee teachers, and therefore Sanlee students would perform more poorly regardless of homework schedule. Or perhaps fewer Sanlee students than Marlee students actually do their assigned homework. In short, in order to properly conclude that fewer homework assignments results in better academic performance, the speaker must first rule out all other feasible explanations for the disparity in academic performance between the two districts.

Finally, the survey results as reported by the speaker are too vague to support any firm conclusion. The speaker reports that Sanlee students receive lower grades and are more likely to repeat a school year then Marlee students. Yet the speaker does not indicate whether this fact applies to Sanlee and Marlee students generally, or just to math and science students. The speaker's recommendation for all high school students might be defensible in the former case, but not in the latter case.

In conclusion, the recommendation that all high school students be assigned homework once per week at most is indefensible based on the evidence. To strengthen the argument, the speaker must show that the reported correlation in the areas of math and science is also found among most other academic subjects. The speaker must also rule out other factors that might determine the students' grades and their likelihood of repeating a year. Finally, to better assess the argument we would need to know whether the reported disparity in academic performance between Sanlee and Marlee students involved only math and science students or all students.

Argument 195   **Liber Publishing Company**'s waning profits

An editor at Liber Publishing contends here that Liber will become profitable again if and only if it returns to its original mission of publishing works primarily by small-town authors. To support this contention the editor cites the fact that since moving away from that mission Liber has become unprofitable. The editor's argument suffers from a series of logical problems, and is therefore wholly unpersuasive.

To begin with, the editor's recommendation depends on the assumption that no factors other than Liber's shift to big-city authors caused Liber's declining profits. However, common sense informs me that this assumption is a poor one. A myriad of other factors, including management and marketing problems, or shifting demand among book buyers, might just as likely be the cause of Liber's declining profits. Without ruling out these and other possible causes, the editor cannot justifiably conclude that by returning to its original mission Liber will return to profitability.

Even assuming Liber's move away from small-town authors was the cause of its declining profits, the editor's argument suffers from two classic fallacies that render the recommendation indefensible. First, the editor infers that the only way for Liber to return to profitability is to return to its original mission. Yet absent evidence to the contrary, other means of boosting its profits might also be available. Secondly, the editor infers that returning to its original mission is a sufficient condition for Liber's returning to profitability. This inference is also fallacious, at least without additional evidence to support it.

Finally, a careful reading of the argument reveals two additional problems. The editor indicates that 90% of Liber's novels are written by authors who maintain a residence in a big city. However, the editor fails to indicate whether these authors also maintain residences in small towns. If they do, then Liber has not in fact departed from its original mission, and the editor's argument is essentially moot. In addition, the editor fails to indicate what percentage of Liber's publications are novels; the lower the percentage the less likely that Liber has in fact departed from its original mission.

In conclusion, the editor's argument cannot be taken seriously as it stands. To strengthen it, the editor must show that Liber has in fact departed from its original mission, and that this departure was the actual cause of Liber's declining profits. To better evaluate the argument we would need to know what other means, if any, are available to Liber to help return the company to profitability.

Argument 200   **Dentists who advertise**

This argument contends that dentists' advertisements should target male patients, and should focus on assuaging distress about the pain associated with dental work. To support this assertion the argument cites statistics showing that three times more men than women faint while visiting dentists. The argument suffers from several logical problems, and is therefore unpersuasive.

To begin with, the argument depends on the assumption that men who faint while visiting the dentist do so because they are distressed about the sorts of factors that the proposed advertising aims to address. Yet the argument provides no evidence dearly establishing this causal relationship. It is equally likely that other factors are instead responsible for the fact that more men than women faint at the dentist's office. Perhaps on average men suffer from more painful dental problems than women, explaining why more men than women faint at dental offices. Without ruling out this and other alternative explanations, the speaker cannot convince me that any advertising technique will reduce either distress or fainting among male patients.

Another problem with the argument is that the speaker provides no evidence that the proposed advertising techniques will have the intended effect. Perhaps fewer men than women notice dental advertisements. Or perhaps the proposed advertising techniques will have the opposite effect—by calling attention to the very sorts of images that cause distress and fainting. The speaker must address these possibilities and rule them out before we can accept the recommendation.

Finally, the speaker's recommendation relies on two unsubstantiated assumptions about the statistics that the speaker cites. The first is that the patients contributing to these statistics are representative of all dental patients. It is entirely possible, for instance, that a disproportionate number of male patients contributed to the statistics, rendering them biased and therefore unreliable. The second unsubstantiated assumption is that the number of patients contributing to these statistics is large enough to be statistically significant. Unless the speaker can substantiate this assumption, he cannot justifiably rely on these statistics to draw any general inferences about dental patients.

In conclusion, the argument cannot be taken seriously as it stands. To strengthen it, the speaker must show why men become distressed and faint during visits to their dentists, and that the proposed advertising techniques would in fact achieve their intended result. To better evaluate the argument we would need more information about the statistics that the argument cites—specifically, how many patients contributed to these statistics and whether these patients are representative of dental patients in general.

Argument 204　Peanuts as a replacement for sugar crops

This letter concludes that to increase farm revenue this country's farmers should replace their sugar crops with peanuts. To support this assertion, the letter's author claims that demand for sugar is sure to decline due to a growing awareness of the health hazards of eating too much sugar. The author also cites the fact that in the nearby country of Palin increased peanut production has resulted in increased revenue for farmers. However, the author's argument relies on several poor assumptions, and is therefore unpersuasive as it stands.

A threshold problem with the letter involves the new research that the author cites to support his conclusion. The author fails to indicate whether consumers are in fact aware of the new research about the harmful effects of eating too much sugar, or whether consumers eat too much sugar in the first place. If consumers are unaware of the research, or if they do not currently eat too much sugar, then this research lends no support to the author's assertion that sugar consumption is likely to decline as a result of the new research.

Secondly, the argument unjustifiably assumes that growing consumer awareness of sugar's health hazards will cause consumers to not only decrease sugar consumption but also increase peanut consumption. Common sense informs me otherwise, especially considering the addictive quality of sugar. In fact, the author provides explicitly that peanuts are low in sugar, suggesting that peanuts are a poor substitute for sugar.

Thirdly, the author's claim that farm revenues will increase should farmers replace sugar crops with peanuts relies on certain dubious economic assumptions. One such assumption is that the market price of peanuts will be sufficiently high to compensate for lost revenue from current sugar sales. Another is that the supply of peanuts will suffice to provide farmers with sufficient revenue. Absent evidence comparing the market price of sugar to that of peanuts, as well as evidence about the capacity of this country's farms to grow peanut crops, it is impossible to assess the author's assertion that replacing sugar crops with peanuts will increase farm revenues.

Finally, the author's reliance on the fact that peanut-farming revenues in neighboring Palin have increased is problematic in two respects. First, the analogy depends on the assumption that dietary tastes of consumers in both countries are similar. However, it is entirely possible that consumer demand for peanuts in Palin would be higher than that in this country in any event. This would explain why, in Palin, demand has met increased production, and therefore why Pahn's peanut-farming revenues have increased. The analogy also depends on the assumption that environmental conditions in both countries equally support peanut crops. If they do not, then the author cannot justifiably rely on the profitability of Palin's peanut farms to conclude that peanut farms in the author's country would be just as profitable.

In conclusion, the argument is unconvincing as it stands. To strengthen it, the author must demonstrate that this country's consumers will in fact decrease their sugar consumption as a result of their growing awareness of its health risks. The author must also provide clear evidence that the demand for peanuts and the revenue from peanut production in this country are likely to match the current demand for sugar and farm revenue from sugar production, respectively. To better evaluate the argument we would need to compare the two countries' climatic and soil conditions; we would also need to compare consumer tastes in Palin with consumer tastes in the author's country.

Argument 205　Reducing crime in the city of **Amburg**

Amburg's Chamber-of-Commerce president has recommended high-intensity lighting throughout Amburg as the best means of reducing crime and revitalizing city neighborhoods. In support of this recommendation the president points out that when Belleville took similar action vandalism declined there almost immediately. The president also points out that since Amburg's police began patrolling on bicycles the incidence of vandalism has remained unchanged. The president's argument is flawed in several critical respects.

First, the argument rests on the unsupported assumption that in Belleville the immediate decline in vandalism was attributable to the lighting—rather than to some other phenomenon—and that the lighting has continued to serve as an effective deterrent there. Perhaps around the same time the city added police units or more after-school youth programs. Moreover, perhaps since the initial decline vandals have grown accustomed to the lighting and are no longer deterred by it. Without ruling out other feasible explanations for the decline and showing that the decline was a lasting one, the president cannot reasonably conclude on the basis of Belleville's experience that the same course of action would serve Amburg's objectives.

Secondly, the president assumes too hastily that Amburg's bicycle patrol has been ineffective in deterring vandalism. Perhaps other factors—such as a demographic shift or worsening economic conditions—have served to increase vandalism while the bicycle patrol has offset that increase. Thus, without showing that all other conditions affecting the incidence of vandalism have remained unchanged since the police began its bicycle patrol the president cannot convincingly conclude that high-intensity lighting would be a more effective means of preventing vandalism.

Thirdly, the president falsely assumes that high-intensity lighting and bicycle patrolling are Amburg's only possible means of reducing crime. In all likelihood Amburg has a myriad of other choices—such as social programs and juvenile legal-system reforms, to name just a few. Moreover, undoubtedly vandalism is not the only type of crime in Amburg. Thus, unless the president can show that high-intensity lighting will deter other types of crime as well I cannot take seriously the president's conclusion that installing high-intensity lighting would be the best way for Amburg to reduce its overall crime rate.

Finally, even if high-intensity lighting would be Amburg's best means of reducing crime in its central business district, the president's further assertion that reducing crime would result in a revitalization of city neighborhoods is unwarranted. Perhaps the decline of Amburg's city neighborhoods is attributable not to the crime rate in Amburg's central business district but rather to other factors—such as the availability of more attractive housing in the suburbs. And if the neighborhoods in decline are not located within the central business district the president's argument is even weaker.

In sum, the recommendation is not well-supported. To bolster it the president must show that Belleville's decline in vandalism is lasting and is attributable to the lighting. The president must also show that lighting would be more effective than any other means at Amburg's disposal to reduce not just vandalism but other crimes as well. To better assess the recommendation I would need to know whether Amburg's declining city neighborhoods are located within the central business district, and whether any other factors might have contributed to the decline.

Argument 206　Organized sports for **Parkville**'s children

This letter concludes that Parkville should not allow children under age nine to participate in organized competitive sports. To support this conclusion, the author points out the increasing number of children nationwide who become injured during athletic competitions. The author also cites the fact that in some big cities children report undue pressure from coaches and parents to win, and that long practice sessions take time away from a child's academic pursuits. However, the author's argument relies on a series of unsubstantiated assumptions, and is therefore unpersuasive as it stands.

One problem with the argument is that it assumes that the nationwide statistics about the incidence of sports injuries among youngsters applies equally to Parkville's children. Yet this might not be the case, for a variety of possible reasons. Perhaps Parkville maintains more stringent safety standards than the national norm; or perhaps children's sporting events in Parkville are better supervised by adults, or supervised by more adults. Without ruling out such possibilities, the author cannot justifiably conclude that Parkville has a sports-injury problem to begin with.

A second problem with the argument is that it unjustifiably assumes that in Parkville parents and coaches unduly pressure youngsters to win organized athletic competitions. The only evidence the author provides to substantiate this assumption are the reports from "big city" children. We are not informed whether Parkville is a big city. Perhaps people who live in big cities are generally more competitive than other people. If so, and if Parkville is not a big city, then the author cannot justifiably rely on these reports to conclude that the proposed course of action is necessary.

A third problem with the argument is that it unfairly assumes that children do not benefit academically from participating in competitive sports. It is entirely possible that such sports provide children with the sort of break from academics that helps them to be more productive academically. It is also possible that the competitive drive that these sports might instill in young children carries over to their academics and spurs them on to perform well in school. Without considering such potential academic benefits, the author cannot reasonably conclude that for young children the disadvantages of participating in athletic competition outweigh the benefits.

In conclusion, the argument is unconvincing as it stands. To better evaluate the argument we would need more information about the incidence of sports injuries among young children in Parkville. To strengthen the argument the author must demonstrate that Parkville's parents and coaches exert the kind of pressure on their children reported by "big city" children and, if so, that this pressure in fact contributes to the sort of problems with which the author is concerned.

Argument 207　The ozone layer and the **salamander** population

In this argument the speaker claims that increased ultraviolet radiation due to thinning of the earth's ozone layer is responsible for the significant decline in the number of salamanders who lay their eggs in mountain lakes, and that this thinning will cause population declines in other species. To justify these claims the speaker points out that salamander eggs lack a protective shell and thus their tissues are highly susceptible to radiation damage, then reasons that the increased radiation must damage these eggs and prevent them from hatching. The argument is problematic in several critical respects, which render it unconvincing.

To begin with, the argument assumes that the salamander population is in fact declining, yet this assumption is not born out by the mere fact that the number of salamanders laying eggs in mountain lakes is declining. It is entirely possible that in other locations the salamander population is increasing. For that matter, perhaps the number of eggs a salamander lays in a mountain lake is increasing on average. Either scenario, if true, would seriously call into question any prediction about population changes for salamanders or for other species.

Even if the total salamander population is declining, an inverse correlation between ultraviolet radiation and salamander population does not suffice in itself to prove that the former causes the latter. The speaker must account for the possibility that the number of eggs salamanders lay is declining in all areas—regardless of the amount of radiation reaching the surface. The speaker must also eliminate all other reasonable explanations for the decline. For example, if the population of species that prey on salamanders or eat their eggs is increasing, this would explain the population decline and therefore undermine the speaker's entire argument.

Even assuming that the total salamander population is declining as a result of increasing radiation, the speaker cannot reasonably infer that other species are equally vulnerable to a population decline as a result. Perhaps the absence of a shell, combined with its mountain-lake location, renders a salamander egg more vulnerable to ultraviolet radiation than any other type of egg. If so, this fact would cast considerable doubt on the speaker's prediction for other species.

Finally, the speaker's grave prediction relies on the assumption that the ozone-thinning process will not reverse in the future. Although this assumption might be born out, on the other hand it might not. Without providing some assurance that the ozone layer will at least continue to be as thin as it is now, the speaker cannot convince me that other species will experience a population decline as a result of radiation damage to eggs.

In sum, the speaker's argument depends on a series of doubtful assumptions, and is therefore weak. To strengthen it the speaker must supply better evidence that the total salamander population is declining, and must rule out all other possible explanations for that decline. The speaker must also provide clear evidence that the current level of radiation reaching the surface is as potentially damaging to the eggs of other species, and must account for why other species have not already experienced a declining population. Finally, to better assess the argument I would need a reliable prognosis for the earth's ozone layer.

Argument 209   A new president for the **Fancy Toy Company**

In this memo, a manager at Fancy Toy Company recommends replacing Pat Salvo, the company's current president, with Rosa Winnings, who is currently president of Starlight Jewelry. To support this recommendation the manager points out that Fancy's profits have declined during the last three quarters under Pat's leadership, while Starlight's profits have been increasing dramatically. The manager's argument is unconvincing for several reasons.

First, the manager's recommendation relies partly on the assumption that Pat was the cause of Fancy Toy's declining profits. However, this need not be the case. Perhaps the toy business is seasonal, and the coming quarter is always the most profitable one. Or perhaps the cost of materials or labor have increased, and Pat has had no control over these increases. Without taking into account such possibilities, the manager simply cannot reasonably conclude that Pat is responsible for Fancy's declining profits, and that replacing Pat will therefore enhance Fancy's profits.

Similarly, the manager's recommendation assumes that it is Rosa who has been primarily responsible for Starlight's profitability. However, the manager provides no evidence to affirm this assumption. It is entirely possible that all jewelry businesses have prospered recently, regardless of the abilities of the managers. Or perhaps the costs of precious metals and other materials have declined in recent years, thereby leading to increased profits for Starlight. Moreover, perhaps Rosa has only served as president of Starlight for a short while, and it was her predecessor who is to credit for Starlight's profitability. Without taking into account these possibilities, the manager cannot defend the conclusion that it is Rosa who is responsible for Starlight's increasing profitability.

Finally, the manager's recommendation to replace Pat with Rosa rests on the poor assumption that the two businesses are sufficiently similar that Rosa's experience and skill in one business will transfer to the other. Even if Starlight's increasing profitability is attributable to Rosa's leadership, she might nevertheless be unsuccessful leading a toy company, depending on how much experience in the toy business is required to successfully lead such a company.

In conclusion, the argument is unconvincing as it stands. To strengthen it the manager must show that Pat, and not some other factor beyond Pat's control, is responsible for Fancy's declining profits. Similarly, the manager must show that it is Rosa who is primarily responsible for Starlight's profitability, and that Rosa's abilities will transfer to the toy business. In order to better evaluate the argument, we would need more information about how long Pat and Rosa have served as presidents of their respective companies, and what their long-term record is for leading their respective companies to profitability.

Argument 211   A job-opportunity program for **Waymarsh University**

In this memo, a Waymarsh University administrator recommends that in order to achieve its academic goals Waymarsh should adopt the same "job-op" program currently offered at Plateau Technical

College. To support this recommendation, the administrator points out a high enrollment rate in the program at Plateau, high academic grades among Plateau students enrolled in the program compared to other Plateau students, and a high success rate among new Plateau graduates in finding jobs. The administrator's argument is unconvincing for several reasons.

First of all, the administrator does not inform us what Waymarsh's academic goals are. It is entirely possible that these goals have nothing to do with enrollment in job opportunity programs or in the job placement rate for new graduates. Although Plateau's goals are likely to depend on its job-placement rate, perhaps Waymarsh's primary goal is to prepare its students for graduate-level study. Even if Waymarsh's goals involve job placement, there might be alternative means of accomplishing those goals. In short, without identifying Waymarsh's goals and ruling out other possible means of attaining them, the administrator cannot justifiably conclude that Waymarsh should adopt the job-op program.

Secondly, the fact that a high percentage of Plateau students enroll in Plateau's job-op program does not mean that a large portion of Waymarsh students will also enroll in the program. Plateau students might be far more concerned about obtaining employment immediately after graduation than Waymarsh students are. The fact that Plateau is a two-year technical college while Waymarsh is a university supports this assertion.

Thirdly, the fact that Plateau students enrolled in the job-op program attain higher grades than other Plateau students does not necessarily mean that the job-op program is responsible for this phenomenon. Perhaps only the brighter, more competitive Plateau students enroll in the job-op program in the first place. Without ruling out this possibility, the administrator cannot convincingly conclude that Waymarsh students who enroll in the job-op program are more likely to attain better grades or find jobs upon graduation. In fact, a job-op program might actually thwart Waymarsh's efforts, by encouraging enrollees to quit school and take jobs for which a four-year degree is not needed.

Finally, the administrator overlooks the possibility that the job-op program is oriented toward the needs of students at technical schools. A job-op program that successfully places technical students might not be as successful in placing graduates of four-year universities, because the types of jobs the two groups of graduates typically seek and would qualify for are quite different.

In conclusion, the argument is unconvincing as it stands. To strengthen it the administrator must show that one of Waymarsh's academic goals is to place its new graduates in jobs. The administrator must also show that this job-op program is equally successful in placing university graduates as it is in placing technical school graduates. To better evaluate the argument we would need more information about the extent to which the job-op program is actually responsible for the successful job placement rate among Plateau's graduates.

Argument 212　Patriot car company's marketing strategy

In this memo, the president of Patriot car manufacturing argues that in order to increase its market share Patriot should (1) discontinue its older models, which look "old-fashioned" and have not been selling well, (2) begin manufacturing sporty models, and (3) hire Youth Advertising agency, which has successfully promoted the country's leading soft drink. To justify this recommendation the president points out that many regions report a rapid increase in the number of newly licensed drivers. However, this argument relies on several dubious assumptions, and is therefore unpersuasive.

To begin with, the president's argument relies on certain unproven assumptions about the reports of a sharp increase in the number of newly licensed drivers. First, the argument assumes that the reports are accurate, and that these regions account for a statistically significant portion of Patriot's potential buyers. Secondly, the president overlooks the possibility that in other regions that number is actually declining, so that there is no net increase at all.

Even assuming that the reports are accurate and the regions cited are representative of the overall territory in which Patriot cars are marketed, the president concludes too hastily that newly licensed drivers will tend to favor new cars over used ones, and to favor Patriot's sporty new cars over other manufacturers' new vehicles. The president ignores the likelihood that the vast majority of new drivers are teenagers who cannot afford new sports cars, or new cars of any kind. Even teenagers who can afford new sports cars might prefer other manufacturers' cars—perhaps due to Patriot's old-fashioned image. Lacking evidence that new drivers who buy cars will tend to buy Patriot sports cars, the president cannot convince me that the recommended course of action will increase Patriot's market share.

Finally, the fact that Youth has successfully promoted the country's leading soft drink amounts to scant evidence that Youth would also be successful in promoting Patriot cars.

Marketers that are effective in one industry are not necessarily effective in another. Besides, the president unfairly assumes that Patriot's current advertising agency is partly responsible for Patriot's relatively small market share. Perhaps some other factor—such as poor management, distribution, or pricing decisions—is the true reason for Patriot's market-share problem. Moreover, perhaps Youth would be less effective than Patriot's current ad agency. Thus, switching to Youth will not necessarily improve Patriot's market share—and might even result in a decline in that share.

In sum, the president's recommendation is weak. To strengthen it the president must show that the reports are a reliable indicator of the overall change in the number of newly licensed drivers. The president must also provide clear evidence—perhaps by way of a reliable survey—that a sufficient percentage and number of new drivers who are able and willing to buy new cars will choose Patriot's sports cars over other manufacturers' cars, so that Patriot's overall market share will increase. To better assess the recommendation that Patriot switch to Youth, I would need to know the extent to which Patriot's current ad strategy is responsible for Patriot's market-share problems; then I would need to know Youth's experience and success record in the car industry—relative to that of Patriot's current agency as well as other available agencies.

Argument 213 Boosting **Armchair Video**'s profits

In this memo, the owner of Armchair Video concludes that in order to boost sagging profits Armchair's stores should eliminate evening operating hours and should stock only movies that are less than 2 years old. To support this conclusion the owner points out that since Armchair's downtown Marston store implemented these changes, very few customers have complained. The owner's argument relies on several unsubstantiated assumptions, and is therefore unconvincing as it stands.

In the first place, implicit in the argument is the assumption that no other means of boosting profits is available to Armchair. While the owner has explicitly ruled out the option of raising its rental rates, the owner ignores other means, such as selling videos, or renting and selling compact discs, candy, and so forth. Without considering such alternatives, the owner cannot justifiably conclude that the proposed changes are the only ways Armchair can boost its profits.

A second problem with the argument is that it assumes that the proposed changes would in fact enhance profits. It is entirely possible that the lost revenue from reducing store hours would outweigh the savings in reduced operating costs. Perhaps Armchair customers are attracted to the stores' wide selection and variety of movies, and that Armchair would lose their patronage should it reduce its inventory. Moreover, common sense informs me that video rental stores do most of their business during evening hours, and therefore that the proposed action would actually result in a further decline in profits.

Two additional problems involve the downtown Marston store. First, the owner implicitly assumes that the store has increased its profits as a result of eliminating evening operating hours and stocking only newer movies. Yet the owner provides no evidence to support this assumption. One cannot infer from the mere fact that the store's patrons have not complained that the store's business, and in turn profits, have increased as a result of these changes.

A second problem with Marston is that the owner assumes this store is representative of Armchair outlets generally. It is entirely possible that, due to its downtown location, the Marston store attracts a daytime clientele more interested in new movies, whereas other outlets depend on an evening clientele with different or more diverse tastes in movies. Or perhaps downtown Marston lacks competing video stores or movie theaters, whereas Armchair's other stores are located in areas with many competitors. Without accounting for such possibilities, the owner cannot convince me that the profits of other Armchair outlets would increase by following Marston's example.

In conclusion, the argument is unconvincing as it stands. To strengthen it the owner must provide strong evidence that the cost savings of the proposed course of action would outweigh any loss in revenue, and that no other viable means of boosting its profits is available to Armchair. To better evaluate the argument we would need information enabling us to compare the Marston store's clientele and competition with that of other Armchair stores. We would also need more information about Marston's profitability before and after it implemented the new policies.

Argument 215　Water rationing and economic growth

In this letter, a Grandview City business leader concludes that in order to promote economic health the city must abolish the water-rationing rules it implemented during last year's drought. To support this conclusion the letter's author points out that since the city implemented these rules industrial growth in the area has declined. However, this argument contains several logical problems, which render it unconvincing as it stands.

First of all, the argument relies on two threshold assumptions: that people who use the city's water have complied with the rules, and that area industry is subject to the rules in the first place. Yet the author supplies no evidence to substantiate either assumption. In other words, if area industries have not in fact been rationing water, the author's conclusion that water rationing is a contributing cause of the recent decline in industry growth would be indefensible.

A second problem with the argument is that it overlooks other possible explanations for the decline in industry growth. Perhaps the decline is the result of a general economic recession that has also impacted businesses in areas not subject to water rationing. Or perhaps local or state regulations unrelated to water rationing are instead responsible for the slowdown. Without accounting for such possibilities, the author cannot justify the conclusion that the water rationing is the cause of the slowdown.

A third problem with the argument is that it unjustifiably assumes that stopping water rationing would help reverse the decline in industry growth. It is entirely possible that this course of action would actually exacerbate the decline. Specifically, perhaps the lack of water has been the primary factor in the slowdown. If so, and if the rationing stops, water might become even more scarce depending on current drought conditions, in which case the slowdown would worsen.

In conclusion, the argument is unconvincing as it stands. To strengthen it the business leader must provide strong evidence that no other factors were responsible for the slowdown in industry growth, and that industry has complied with the rules in the first place. Finally, to better evaluate the argument we would need more information about current water availability in the area, so that we can assess how stopping water rationing would affect this availability.

Argument 216   The benefits of retiring to **Clearview**

This article argues that anyone seeking a place to retire should choose Clearview. To support this argument the article cites Clearview's consistent climate and natural beauty; it's falling housing costs; its low property taxes compared to nearby towns; and the mayor's promise to improve schools, streets, and services. The article also claims that retirees can expect excellent health care because the number of physicians in Clearview greatly exceeds the national average. This argument is flawed in several critical respects.

To begin with, although consistent climate and natural beauty might be attractive to many retirees, these features are probably not important to all retirees. For many retirees it is probably more important to live near relatives, or even to enjoy changing seasons. Thus, I cannot accept the author's sweeping recommendation for all retirees on this basis.

Also, Clearview's declining housing costs do not necessarily make Clearview the best place to retire—for two reasons. First, despite the decline Clearview's housing costs might be high compared to housing costs in other cities. Secondly, for wealthier retirees housing costs are not likely to be a factor in choosing a place to retire. Thus, the mere fact that housing costs have been in decline lends scant support to the recommendation.

The article's reliance on Clearview's property-tax rates is also problematic in two respects. First, retirees obviously have innumerable choices about where to retire besides Clearview and nearby towns. Secondly, for retirees who are well-off financially property taxes are not likely to be an important concern in choosing a place to retire. Thus, it is unfair to infer from Clearview's property-tax rates that retirees would prefer Clearview.

Yet another problem with the argument involves the mayor's promises. In light of Clearview's low property-tax rates, whether the mayor can follow through on those promises is highly questionable. Absent any explanation of how the city can spend more money in the areas cited without raising property taxes, I simply cannot accept the editorial's recommendation on the basis of those promises. Besides, even if the city makes the improvements promised, those improvements—particularly the ones to schools—would not necessarily be important to retirees.

Finally, although the number of physicians in Clearview is relatively high, the per capita number might be relatively low. Moreover, it would be fairer to compare this per capita number with the per capita number for other attractive retirement townsrather than the national average. After all, retirees are likely to place a relatively heavy burden on health-care resources. Besides, the article provides no assurances that the number of physicians in Clearview will remain high in the foreseeable future.

In conclusion, the recommendation is poorly supported. To strengthen it the author must convince me—perhaps by way of a reliable survey—that the key features that the vast majority of retirees look for in choosing a place to live are consistent climate, natural beauty, and low housing costs. The author must also provide better evidence that Clearview's property taxes are lower than the those of cities in other areas. The author must also explain how the city can make its promised improvements without raising property taxes. Finally, to better assess the argument I would need to now how the per capita number of physicians in Clearview would compare to the national average in the future.

Argument 218　Maintaining profits at **Hyper-Go Toy Company**

In this memo, the president of Hyper-Go Toy Company (HG) argues that in order to maintain profitability the company should discontinue its complete line of action toys and focus exclusively on a new line of educational toys. To support this argument the president cites the dramatic decline in sales of HG's Fierce Fighter (FF) toy airplane, which during the previous three years had been a top seller, and an HG customer survey indicating increasing concern among parents about youth violence and for improving their children's education. The president also points out that several other toy companies have begun marketing educational toys and report a 200% increase in overall sales, and that the average family income is growing. The president's argument relies on several doubtful assumptions and is therefore unpersuasive.

First, the president's assumption that parental concern about youth violence is the cause of declining FF sales might be unwarranted. The decline might have been caused by one or more other factors—such as supply or distribution problems, new competing products from other toy companies, or a waning of interest in FF among children. Without ruling out these and other possible reasons for the decline, the president's argument seems ill-conceived.

Secondly, the results of HG's customer survey are not necessarily representative of the overall population of toy-buying parents. Perhaps HG's current customers are more concerned about youth violence and education than most parents. If so, then the president has overlooked the possibility that a substantial portion of HG's target market would not react favorably to the proposed changes.

Thirdly, perhaps sales of HG's other action toys remained stable or even increased last year. In fact, it is entirely possible that some of HG's other toys are becoming very popular and will soon replace FF as top sellers. If so, then discontinuing the entire line would be ill-advised indeed.

Fourth, assuming the toy companies that saw a 200% sales increase last year are statistically representative of toy companies in general, that increase might be due to action-toy sales rather than to educational-toy sales. If so, then the statistic would amount to scant support for the proposed course of action.

Finally, the mere fact that average family income is growing provides little assurance that the proposed changes would increase HG's sales. Perhaps the average income of families without young children is growing, but for families with young children who buy toys it is shrinking. For that matter, perhaps average family expenses are also growing, so that families have even less discretionary income than before. Without ruling out these possibilities, the president cannot justify the proposed changes on the basis of the growth of average family income.

In sum, the president's argument is unconvincing as it stands. To strengthen it the president must show that parents in general, not just HG customers, are concerned about youth violence and e-ducation, and that these concerns are the reason for declining FF sales. To better assess the argument I would need more information about sales trends of HG's other action toys, and about the types of toys that have contributed to the 200% increase in sales for the other toy companies.

Argument 219   Megamart's leisure-activity product lines

In this memo, the vice president of Megamart concludes that Megamart should expand its line of products related to leisure activities. To support this claim the memo points out that for three years in a row the average household income nationwide has risen. However, close inspection of the argument reveals several logical problems, which render it unconvincing as it stands.

First of all, the claim relies on two threshold assumptions about rising income. One is that this trend will continue in the future; if it does not then the proposed course of action is unlikely to result in increased profits for Megamart. The other threshold assumption is that the cost of living is not also increasing at least at a commensurate rate. Yet it is entirely possible that living costs have risen to meet or even exceed the rise in income. If so, Megamart would in all likelihood sell fewer leisure products than otherwise.

Even assuming that discretionary income is rising and will continue to rise, the argument relies on the additional assumption that people will spend this discretionary income on leisure products. However, the memo provides no evidence to substantiate this assumption. Perhaps people are in-creasing their savings rather than spending their additional income. If so, this fact would significantly undermine the vice president's claim that demand for leisure products is increasing, and therefore that Megamart would benefit by offering more such products.

Yet another problem with the argument involves the reason why average income has risen in the first place. It is entirely possible that income has risen because people have been working more hours. If so, then in all likelihood people have less leisure time, in which case they will not spend more mon-ey on leisure products—simply because they have less time for leisure pursuits. Without addressing this issue, the vice president cannot convince me that Megamart should expand its line of leisure prod-ucts.

In conclusion, the vice president's argument is unconvincing as it stands. To strengthen it the vice president must provide strong evidence that discretionary income is rising and will continue to rise. The vice president must also show that people will in fact choose to spend this income on leisure products, and that people have enough free time for leisure pursuits in the first place.

Argument 223   How to increase profitability at ABC Cereal Company

This ABC Cereal Company memo concludes that to increase its profitability ABC must lower both the sugar content and price of its Better Bran (BB) cereal. To justify this conclusion the memo cites the fact that sales of BB have declined in recent years. The memo attributes this decline to a concern among most consumers about the amount of sugar in their cereals, and to the 5% increase in the price of BB during each of the last three years. The memo is unconvincing for several reasons.

First, the mere fact that most consumers are concerned about sugar in cereal amounts to scant evidence that the decline in BB sales is due to that concern. The level of concern, or the amount of sugar in BB, might not be sufficiently high to cause consumers to stop buying BB cereal on either ba-sis. Moreover, unless the level of concern has grown during recent years I cannot take seriously the claim that declining BB sales in recent years is due to that concern—rather than to some other event or trend.

Secondly, assuming that the 5% price increases have contributed to the decline in BB sales, it would be premature to conclude that profits from BB sales have also declined as a result. Perhaps the additional revenue from the price increases more than offset the decline in revenue due to the dimin-ishing number of units sold. Thus, ABC cannot convince me on the basis of the price increases and the sales decline that lowering BB's price would serve to improve ABC's overall profitability.

Thirdly, the memo's recommendation rests on the dubious assumption that the proposed actions are the only two means of increasing ABC's overall profitability. In all likelihood, ABC's profits are a function not only of how many boxes of BB it sells but also of its costs and its revenue from other products. Perhaps ABC can improve its profits by other means—such as expanding its cereal line, marketing BB to health-conscious consumers and raising the price of BB, or cutting costs in other ar-eas. For that matter, if other cereal companies raise their prices, consumers might begin to consider BB a bargain at its current price—or perhaps even at a somewhat higher price. In short, since the memo has not ruled out all other possible scenarios that might serve to improve ABC's overall prof-itability I simply cannot take the memo's recommendation seriously.

Finally, even in the unlikely event that one of the two proposed changes is necessary to increase ABC's overall profitability, the memo's assertion that both changes are necessary might nevertheless be unwarranted. Perhaps only one of the two changes will suffice. Since the memo ignores this possi-bility the strength of its recommendation remains questionable at best.

In sum, ABC might be ill-advised to follow the memo's advice. To strengthen the argument that ABC must lower BB's price and sugar content to improve profitability ABC's planners must provide dear evidence that consumer concern about sugar in cereals is the primary reason for declining BB sales, and that this decline has diminished BB's profitability. To better assess ABC's claim that the proposed course of action is necessary to improve ABC's profitability, I would need to know what other alternatives, if any, are available to ABC for cutting costs and for increasing revenue.

Argument 225 Meeting consumer demand for **automobiles**

In this memo, the manager of a car manufacturing company argues that the company must add a second plant in order to continue to thrive. To support this argument the manager points out that its existing plant can only produce 40 million cars, but that according to company projections 80 million people will want to buy the company's cars. The manager claims that the company can achieve its objective by operating the new plant on a part-time basis using workers from the existing plant on a rotational basis. To support this claim the manager points out that a certain airplane manufacturing company employed this strategy successfully five years ago. The manager's argument is problematic in several critical respects.

First of all, the manager assumes that no course of action other than the proposed one will en-sure that the company continues to thrive; yet the manager fails to substantiate this assumption. Since demand is expected to be very high, perhaps the company can continue to thrive simply by raising the price of its cars. For that matter, perhaps the company can continue to thrive if it makes no changes at all. Without accounting for either possibility the manager cannot convince me that building a second plant is necessary.

Secondly, even if building a second plant is necessary for the company to continue to thrive, in itself this course of action might not suffice. After all, how can the manager reasonably expect that a second plant will produce as many cars as the existing one if it operates on only a part-time basis? And if the new plant borrows labor from the existing plant then production at the existing plant might decline. Thus, unless the manager can convince me that the new plant will be far more efficient than the current plant I do not see any way that operating a new plant on a part-time basis can double the company's production.

Finally, the mere fact that one certain airplane manufacturer adopted a similar plan with some success is scant evidence that this car company will succeed if it follows the manager's plan. The memo provides no information about how many airplanes the airplane manufacturer produced. Nor does the memo identify what constituted "success" for the airplane manufacturer. Perhaps that company considered itself successful by producing only an additional 10% more airplanes, or by merely managing to avoid bankruptcy. In short, as it stands the anecdotal evidence about the airplane company is far too vague to lend meaningful support to the manager's argument.

In sum, the manager's plan seems ill-conceived. To strengthen the argument that the company must add a second plant to continue to thrive, the manager must at the very least convince me that the company has no alternative means of achieving this objective. The manager should also provide evidence that operating a new plant on only a part-time basis would suffice to double production—perhaps by showing that the new plant would employ newer, more efficient equipment than the existing plant. To better assess the argument it would be useful to know what constituted "success" for the airplane manufacturer and, more specifically, the percentage by which that company increased production as a result of adding a second plant.

Argument 226   Improving **Central Plaza**'s attractiveness

This editorial concludes that the city should ban skateboarding from its downtown Central Plaza in order to attract visitors to that area, to return the area to its "former glory", and to make it "a place where people can congregate for fun and relaxation". To justify this conclusion the editorial points out that skateboarders are nearly the only people one sees anymore at Central Plaza, and that the Plaza is littered and its property defaced. The editorial also points out that the majority of downtown merchants support the skateboarding ban. This argument is flawed in several critical respects.

First, the editorial's author falsely assumes that a ban on skateboarding is both necessary and sufficient to achieve the three stated objectives. Perhaps the city can achieve those objectives by other means as well—for example, by creating a new mall that incorporates an attractive new skateboard park. Even if banning skateboarders altogether is necessary to meet the city's goals, the author has not shown that this action by itself would suffice. Assuming that the Plaza's reputation is now tarnished, restoring that reputation and, in turn, enticing people back to the Plaza might require additional measures—such as removing litter and graffiti, promoting the Plaza to the public, or enticing popular restaurant or retail chains to the Plaza.

Secondly, the editorial assumes too hastily that the Plaza's decline is attributable to the skateboarders—rather than to some other phenomenon. Perhaps the Plaza's primary appeal in its glory days had to do with particular shops or eateries, which were eventually replaced by less appealing ones. Or perhaps the crime rate in surrounding areas has risen dramatically, for reasons unrelated to the skateboarders' presence at the Plaza. Without ruling out these and other alternative explanations for the Plaza's decline, the editorial's author cannot convince me that a skateboard ban would reverse that decline.

Thirdly, the editorial's author might be confusing cause with effect—by assuming that the skateboarders caused the abandonment of the Plaza, rather than vice versa. It is entirely possible that skateboarders did not frequent the Plaza until it was largely abandoned—and because it had been abandoned. In fact this scenario makes good sense, since skateboarding is most enjoyable where there are few pedestrians or motorists to get in the way.

Fourth, it is unreasonable to infer from the mere fact that most merchants favor the ban that the ban would be effective in achieving the city's objectives. Admittedly, perhaps these merchants would be more likely to help clean up the Plaza area and promote their businesses were the city to act in accordance with their preference. Yet lacking any supporting evidence the author cannot convince me of this. Thus, the survey amounts to scant evidence at best that the proposed ban would carry the intended result.

Finally, the author recommends a course of action that might actually defeat the city's objective of providing a fun and relaxing place for people to congregate. In my experience skateboarding contributes to an atmosphere of fun and relaxation, for adults and children alike, more so than many other types of ambiance. Without considering that continuing to allow skateboarding—or even encouraging this activity—might achieve the city's goal more effectively than banning the activity, the author cannot convincingly conclude that the ban would be in the city's best interests.

In sum, the argument is a specious one. To strengthen it, the editorial's author must provide clear evidence that skateboarding, and not some other factor, is responsible for the conditions marking the Plaza's decline. The author must also convince me that no alternative means of restoring the Plaza are available to the city, and that the proposed ban by itself would suffice to attract tourists and restore the Plaza to its former glory. Finally, to better assess the argument it would be useful to know the circumstances under which the downtown merchants would be willing to help the city achieve its objectives.

Argument 227 The benefits of a **new expressway**

In this newsletter the author concludes that, in order to promote the economic health of the city's downtown area, voters should approve the construction of an expressway linking downtown to outlying suburbs. To support this conclusion the author claims that the expressway would alleviate shortages of stock and materials among downtown businesses and manufacturers, and would attract workers from elsewhere in the state. However, the argument relies on a series of unsubstantiated assumptions, which render it unconvincing.

The first problem with the argument involves the author's claim that the expressway would help prevent downtown merchants and manufacturers from experiencing shortages in stock and materials. This claim depends on three assumptions. One assumption is that such a problem exists in the first place. A second assumption is that the absence of an expressway is the cause of such shortages; yet common sense tells me that the availability of these commodities is probably the primary such factor.

A third assumption is that stock and materials would be delivered primarily via the expressway. Yet it is entirely possible that these commodities are delivered directly to the downtown area by other means, such as rail or air transport. Without substantiating these assumptions the author cannot justifiably conclude that the expressway would help prevent shortages of stock and materials.

Another problem with the argument involves the author's dual claim that because of the new expressway workers from elsewhere in the state will be lured to work in this city's downtown area and at the same time will choose to live in the suburbs. The author provides no evidence that the existence of an expressway would suffice to entice people to work in this city's downtown area. Moreover, the author ignores the possibility that people who might want to work in the city's downtown area would generally prefer to live in that area as well. In this case, the expressway would be of no help in attracting qualified workers to this city's downtown area.

A third problem with the argument is that it unfairly assumes that the expressway will result in a net influx, rather than outflow, of workers to the downtown area. In fact, the expressway might make it easier for people who currently live and work downtown to commute to jobs in other areas or even relocate their businesses to outlying areas. Either scenario would serve to undermine the author's claim that the expressway would provide a boon to the downtown economy.

Finally, the argument rests on the assumption that funds used to build the expressway and to create jobs for construction workers cannot be applied to some other program instead—one that would be even more effective in promoting the health of the downtown economy. Without identifying and weighing such alternatives, the author cannot defend the conclusion that voters should approve the expressway project.

In conclusion, the argument is unconvincing as it stands. To strengthen it the author must provide strong evidence that the expressway would help alleviate shortages of supply and materials among downtown businesses and manufacturers. The author must also show that the expressway would in fact result in a net influx of workers who would change jobs because of the availability of the expressway. Finally, to better evaluate the argument we would need more information about possible alternatives to the proposal, and whether any such alternative would be more effective in promoting the health of the downtown economy.

Argument 229　Transopolis' urban renewal plan

The planning department for the city of Transopolis recommends, as part of its urban renewal plan, that the city convert a certain residential area for industrial use and relocate residents from that area to nearby unoccupied housing. To support this recommendation, the planners point out that ten years ago the city converted an area of substandard housing on the other side of town, near a freeway, for industrial use, and that afterward that area's crime rate declined while the city's overall property-tax revenue increased. I find the recommendation specious on several grounds.

To begin with, the recommendation relies on two poor assumptions about the effects of the freeway-area conversion. One such assumption is that the freeway-area conversion caused the decline in that area's crime rate. The mere fact that the conversion occurred before the decline does not suffice to prove that the conversion caused the decline. Perhaps the true cause was some unrelated development—such as a new city-wide "tough-on-crime" policy or improvements in police training. Another such assumption is that the increase in overall property-tax revenue indicates an increase in tax revenue from properties in the freeway area. Perhaps property-tax revenue from the converted properties remained the same, or even declined, after the conversion, and that the city's overall property-tax revenue increase was attributable to properties located elsewhere in the city. For that matter, perhaps the city raised its property-tax rates shortly after the conversion. In short, without ruling out alternative explanations for the developments that came after the freeway-area conversion, the planners cannot convince me that the conversion was responsible for those developments.

Even if the evidence turns out to substantiate the two foregoing assumptions, the recommendation further assumes that the proposed conversion would carry the same results as the freeway-area conversion. Yet key differences between the two areas might undermine the analogy. For example, perhaps the properties surrounding the ones converted in the freeway area were not residential. Common sense informs me that crimes such as burglary and robbery are less likely in areas where few people reside. Since at least some nearby housing is available for residents displaced by the proposed conversion, this conversion might not result in any significant decline in the area's crime rate. At the same time, unless unoccupied nearby housing can accommodate all displaced residents, the conversion might create a homelessness problem, thereby undermining the city's objectives.

Finally, the recommendation assumes that all conditions bearing on whether residential-to-industrial conversions would help renew Transopolis have remained unchanged over the past ten years—and will continue unchanged in the foreseeable future. Yet, perhaps Transopolis had more and better housing for displaced residents ten years ago than today. Or perhaps Transopolis would have more trouble finding occupants for additional industrial buildings today than it did ten years ago. Indeed, a myriad of factors—including the regional and national economy, demographic shifts, and political influences—might explain why an urban-renewal program that had a salutary impact on Transopolis' crime rate and property-tax revenues in the past might nevertheless not revitalize the city today, or in the future.

In sum, the planners' recommendation is largely unfounded. To bolster it they must provide clear evidence that the freeway-area conversion contributed to the decline in that area's crime rate and to the city's overall property-tax revenue increase. To better assess the argument I would need to know what other changes have occurred in the city that might explain those developments. Finally, to better assess the proposed plan's chances of success I would need to compare the circumstances surrounding the decline in the area slated for conversion with the decline in the freeway area prior to its conversion.

Argument 230　Should the **school board**'s members be reelected?

This editorial argues that the town's school board members are unconcerned about promoting high-quality arts education in local schools, and therefore should not be reelected. To support this argument the editorial's author points out that student participation in high-school drama programs has been declining steadily, and that the board recently refused to renew the high-school drama director's contract, despite the fact that he has written several award-winning plays. The author also cites the fact that $300,000 of the high school budget is allotted to athletic programs, and that the head football coach is the highest paid teacher. This argument is unpersuasive for a variety of reasons.

First and foremost, the editorial indicates neither how long the current board members have occupied their board positions nor the scope of their authority. Perhaps they are new members and the facts that the editorial cites are attributable to events and decisions occurring before the current board members assumed their positions. If so, and if the current board either has not had adequate opportunity or does not have adequate authority to reverse these developments, then any claim regarding their level of concern about arts education is unjustifiable—at least based on the evidence cited.

Even assuming adequate authority and tenure on the part of the current board members, they are not necessarily responsible for the declining student participation in drama programs. The decline might be due to some other factor. For instance, perhaps students generally dislike the current drama director. If so, then the board's refusal to renew his contract would indicate that the board is attempting to reverse the decline, and that the board is in fact concerned about facilitating arts education.

As for the fact that $300,000 is devoted to athletic programs, the editorial does not indicate the school's total budget. It is entirely possible that $300,000 accounts for a small portion of that budget compared to the amount budgeted for the arts. If so, and if the current school board is at least partly responsible for the current budget, these facts would cast considerable doubt on the editorial's claim that the board is unconcerned about promoting arts education.

Admittedly, the fact that the head football coach is the highest paid teacher provides some support for the editorial's claim—assuming that the current board members are at least partially responsible for that salary. However, this fact in itself is insufficient to show that the board members are unconcerned about promoting arts education. Perhaps the football coach carries additional duties that warrant the high salary; in fact, perhaps he also teaches drama or music. Or perhaps his salary is high simply because he has been a teaching-staff member longer than nearly any other local school teacher.

Finally, the editorial's claim overlooks the fact that local arts education embraces not just high-school drama but also drama programs at lower levels, and music, dance, and visual-and graphic-arts programs. Thus, even if the board's decisions indicate that they place a low priority on high-school drama education, it is entirely possible that the board is real-locating resources from that program to other arts programs. If so, then the editorial's claim is wrong, and the proper conclusion is that the board is actively concerned about promoting arts education as a whole in local schools.

In sum, the argument is unconvincing as it stands. To strengthen it the editorial's author must at the very least assure me that the current board members have been on the board long enough to have adequate opportunity to demonstrate their level of concern for arts education, and that they have the authority to do so. The author should also provide clear evidence that the decisions of these board members were responsible for the declining student participation in drama programs. To better assess the argument I would need to know the reason why the board has not renewed the current drama director's contract. I would also need to know what percentage of the high school's current budget is allocated not just to drama programs but to arts education generally, so that I could compare that percentage with the percentages allocated to other programs.

Argument 231　Advertising **Eco-Power** tools and appliances

In this memo, Eco-Power's sales manager recommends that the company switch from print ads to ads with catchy songs in order to reverse its declining profits. To support this recommendation the memo cites the fact that most high-school students easily recognize tunes used to advertise leading soft-drinks and fast-food restaurants. However, the argument is unconvincing in light of several problems.

A threshold problem with the argument is that the author assumes that the current ad strategy is the cause of Eco-Power's declining profits. The author provides no evidence that this is the case. It is entirely possible that other factors are responsible for the decline. Perhaps the demand for all tools and home appliances generally has slowed; or perhaps Eco-Power's management or pricing policies are to blame. Without ruling out such possibilities, the author cannot persuade me that switching ad strategies would reverse Eco-Power's declining profits.

Another problem with the argument involves the memo's reliance on the high rate of tune-recognition among teenagers. For two reasons, this evidence lends little credible support for the recommended strategy. First, even if Eco-Power were to achieve a high rate of tune-recognition among teenagers, this demographic group is not the same group that purchases tools and home appliances. Secondly, even assuming Eco-Power can achieve a high tune-recognition rate among its target demographic group, this fact alone is no guarantee that these consumers would be more likely to buy Eco-Power products as a result of recognizing the company's tunes.

A third problem with the argument is that it assumes that the increased sales due to a high tune-recognition rate would outweigh the costs of achieving this rate. However, a tune can be communicated only via such media as radio and television; and real-world experience informs us that these advertising media are more costly than print media. Although leading soft-drink and fast-food companies can well afford the costs of producing effective tunes and of ensuring that these tunes are heard again and again by many, many consumers, Eco-Power might lack the resources to ensure the sort of tune recognition which these other companies have achieved. Unless the sales manager can convince us that the proposed ad strategy will be cost effective, his conclusion that this strategy will result in increased profits for Eco-Power is untenable.

In conclusion, the sales manager has not provided a convincing argument for the proposed ad strategy. To strengthen the argument the manager must show that the current ad strategy is in fact the cause of Eco-Power's declining profits. The manager must also provide strong evidence that the people who buy the kinds of tools Eco-Power sells would hear the company's tunes frequently enough to immediately associate the tune with the company, and that this association would cause these listeners to buy Eco-Power products. Finally, to better evaluate the argument we would need a detailed cost-benefit analysis of the proposed ad strategy.

Argument 232　Choosing a **paving** contractor

The vice president of a company that builds shopping malls argues here that the company should hire Appian rather than McAdam to build access roads for the company. To support this argument the vice president points out that a certain area of Route 101 that McAdam repaved two years ago has deteriorated significantly, while a certain stretch of Route 66 that Appian repaved four years ago remains in good condition. The vice president also points out that Appian recently acquired new state-of-the-art paving equipment and hired a new quality-control manager. I find the vice president's argument logically unconvincing—in several respects.

First of all, it is unfair to infer based solely on the comparison between the two stretches of highway that Appian does better work than McAdam. The inference relies on the poor assumption that the comparative quality of two contractors' work, rather than some other phenomenon, was responsible for the comparative condition of the two stretches of pavement. Perhaps the stretch that McAdam repaved is located in an area whose extremes in climate or high traffic volume serve to erode and damage pavement very quickly. For that matter, perhaps soil or other geological conditions in that area were primarily responsible for deterioration of the pavement along that stretch. In short, without showing that all other conditions in the two areas have been essentially the same, the vice president cannot convince me that the quality of McAdam's and Appian's repaving work was responsible for the difference in how well the two stretches of pavement have held up.

Secondly, it is unfair to conclude based on Appian's recent equipment acquisition and personnel decision that Appian will do a better job than McAdam. Perhaps McAdam has also acquired the same type of equipment. Moreover, perhaps McAdam's quality-control manager is far more experienced than Appian's new manager, and as a result McAdam's product is likely to be better than Appian's. Besides, equipment and on-site management are only two of many factors affecting the quality of a pavement job. other such factors include the experience and competence of other workers, and the paving material used. Without showing that the two firms are similar in these and other respects, the vice president cannot justify his recommendation of Appian over McAdam.

Finally, the vice president's recommendation rests on the unlikely assumption that the company has only two alternatives—McAdam and Appian. In all likelihood the company can engage one of many other paving contractors instead. Thus, to the extent the vice president recommends Appian over not just McAdam but over any other contractor the recommendation is unwarranted.

In sum, the vice president has not convinced me that the company should hire Appian. To strengthen the argument the vice president must provide clear evidence that it was the quality of McAdam's and Appian's work—rather than one or more other factors—that resulted in the difference between how well the two stretches of pavement have held up over time. The vice president must also provide better evidence that Appian's new equipment and new manager will enhance, or at least maintain, the quality of Appian's overall work—at a higher level than McAdam's overall work. Finally, to better assess the argument I would need to know what other paving contractors the company could hire, and the quality of those contractors' work compared to McAdam's and Appian's.

Argument 233   Does small-town life promote **better health and greater longevity**?

This newspaper story concludes that living in a small town promotes health and longevity. The story's author bases this conclusion on a comparison between the small town of Leeville and nearby Mason City, a much larger town. However, careful scrutiny of the author's evidence reveals that it lends no credible support to the author's conclusion.

A threshold problem with the argument is that the author draws a general conclusion about the effect of a town's size on the health and longevity of its residents based only on characteristics of two towns. The author provides no evidence that these two towns (or their residents) are representative of other towns their size. In other words, this limited sample simply does not warrant any general conclusions about the effect of a town's size on the health and longevity of its residents.

Next, the author cites the fact that the incidence of sick leave in Leeville is less than in Mason City. This evidence would lend support to the argument only if the portion of local residents employed by local businesses were nearly the same in both towns, and only if the portion of employees who are local residents were nearly the same in both towns. Moreover, in relying on this evidence the author assumes that the portion of sick employees who actually take sick leave is nearly the same in both towns. In short, without showing that the two towns are similar in these ways, the author cannot draw any reliable comparisons about the overall health of the towns' residents—or about the impact of town size on health.

The author also cites the fact that Mason City has five times as many physicians per resident than Leeville. However, any number of factors besides the health of the towns' residents might explain this disparity. For example, perhaps Leeville residents choose to travel to Mason City for physician visits. Without ruling out such explanations, these physician-resident ratios prove nothing about the comparative health of Leeville and Mason City residents—or about the impact of town size on health.

Finally, the author cites the fact that the average age of Leeville residents is higher than that of Mason City residents. However, any number of factors might explain this disparity. For example, perhaps Leeville is a retirement community, while Mason City attracts younger working people. For that matter, perhaps Leeville is comprised mainly of former Mason City residents whose longevity is attributable chiefly to their former lifestyle in Mason City. In any event, the author cannot justify the conclusion that this disparity in average age is due to the difference in size between the two towns.

In conclusion, the argument that small-town living promotes good health and longevity is unpersuasive as it stands. To strengthen the argument the author must provide clear evidence that the overall population of Leeville, not just employees in Leeville, is healthier than that of Mason City. The author must also provide strong evidence that Leeville and Mason City residents visit local physicians whenever they become sick. Finally, to better evaluate the argument we would need more information about why the average age of Leeville residents exceeds that of Mason City residents.

Argument 234　A change in programming format for **KNOW radio station**

This memo recommends that KNOW radio station shift from rock-and-roll (R&R) music programming to all-news programming. To support this recommendation the manager points out that the number of KNOW listeners is decreasing while the number of older people in KNOW's listening area is increasing. The manager also points out that area sales of music recordings are in decline, and that a recent survey suggests that local residents are becoming better informed about politics. Finally, the manager cites the success of all-news stations in nearby cities. Careful scrutiny of the manager's argument reveals several unproven assumptions, which render it unconvincing.

First, the manager unfairly assumes that the decline in the number of KNOW listeners is attributable to the station's current format. Perhaps the decline is due instead to KNOW's specific mix of R&R music, or to transmission problems at the station. Without ruling out these and other feasible reasons for the decline, the manager cannot convince me that changing the format would reverse the trend.

Secondly, the manager's assumption that older people favor all-news programming is unsupported. Perhaps KNOW listeners are dedicated R&R fans who will continue to prefer this type of programming as they grow older. Or perhaps as KNOW's regular audience ages it will prefer a mix of R&R and news programming—rather than one format to the total exclusion of the other. Besides, the number of young people in the listening area might be increasing as well. In short, the mere fact that the number of older people in KNOW's listening area is increasing suggests nothing about KNOW's best programming strategy.

Thirdly, a decrease in local music recording sales is scant evidence that KNOW should eschew music in favor of an all-news format. Although overall music sales are in decline, perhaps sales of R&R recordings are actually increasing while sales of all other types of music recordings are decreasing. For that matter, perhaps people who buy music recordings are generally not the same people who listen to music on the radio. Either scenario, if true, would seriously undermine the manager's contention that KNOW should discontinue R&R programming.

Fourth, it is unfair to conclude from one survey suggesting that local residents are becoming better informed about politics that they are becoming less interested in listening to R&R music, or that they are becoming more interested in listening to news. After all, news embraces many topics in addition to politics. Besides, there is no reason why people interested in politics cannot also be interested in listening to R&R music. Moreover, a single survey taken just prior to an election is poor evidence that local residents' piqued interest in politics is sustainable.

Finally, it is unwarranted to infer from the success of all-news stations in nearby cities that KNOW will also succeed by following the same format. Those stations might owe their success to their powerful transmitters, popular newscasters, or other factors. Besides, the very success of these stations suggests that the area's radio listeners might favor those well-established news providers over the fledgling all-news KNOW.

In sum, the manager's evidence accomplishes little toward supporting the manager's argument for the proposed format shift. To further bolster the argument the manager must provide better evidence, perhaps by way of a reliable survey, that people within KNOW's listening area are becoming more interested in news and less interested in R&R music—or any other kind of music. The manager must also show that an all-news format would be more popular than a mixed format of music and news, and that a significant number of people would prefer KNOW's all-news programming over that of other stations in the listening area.

Argument 235　Solano's music education programs

This letter concludes that Solano school district should discontinue its music programs altogether. To justify this conclusion the author points out that only 20% of Solano's students enroll in music classes and that few Solano students pursue music as a major course of study in college. The author also points out that in nearby Rutherford student grades increased the year after that district discontinued music education. This argument is problematic in several critical respects.

A threshold problem with the argument is that it relies on certain implicit assumptions about the value of music education. Specifically, the author assumes that any education program is valuable only to the extent that it enhances overall grades and only if students choose to pursue that course of study in college. Such normative assumptions are dubious at best; common sense tells me that the chief value of music education, like that of art or physical education, lies in its contribution to the full development of a child, not in its influence on grades or choice of career. Without addressing this issue, the author's conclusion can be dismissed out of hand.

Another problem with the argument involves the implicit claim that only 20% of Solano students enroll in music courses because they are uninterested in music. This claim assumes that students have a choice in what courses they take in the first place; yet we are not informed that this is the case. It also unfairly assumes that no other factor influences students' decisions about whether to enroll in music courses. Perhaps Solano's current music teachers are unpopular; or perhaps the district lacks sufficient funds to meet current demand for music courses or to provide adequate facilities and instruments for more students. Since the author has not ruled out these other possible explanations for the low enrollment rate, the author's implicit claim that Solano students are not interested in music is doubtful at best.

Yet another problem with the argument involves the implicit claim that music education is not worthwhile because few Solano students pursue music as a college major. This claim assumes that all Solano students pursuing a career in music attend college in the first place; yet this is not necessarily the case. The claim also assumes that Solano students are properly advised about choosing their college major; yet it is entirely possible that Solano's high school advisers dissuade students from pursuing music. Since the author fails to rule out these possibilities, the fact that few Solano students pursue music in college lends little credible support for the author's conclusion.

A final problem with the argument involves Rutherford's increase in its students' grades the year after that district discontinued music programs. This increase might be attributable to numerous factors. Perhaps that year Rutherford received substantial funding to enhance its after-school tutoring program; or perhaps it hired more effective teachers that year. Or perhaps the outgoing graduating class one year was less bright overall than the incoming freshman class the next year. Any of these scenarios, if true, would discredit the author's assertion that music education contributes to lower academic grades. Besides, the author cites an increase during only one year—an insufficiently small range to draw any reliable general conclusion.

In sum, the author's argument for discontinuing music education is weak. To strengthen the argument the author must show that the cited statistics about Solano students reflect their lack of interest in music rather than some other phenomenon, and that the increase in Rutherford's grades was the result of its discontinuing music education.

Argument 237　Mira Vista College's job-placement record

This letter recommends that in order to improve its job-placement record Mira Vista College should offer more business and computer courses and should hire more job counselors. To support this recommendation the author points out that at Green Mountain College 90 percent of last year's graduates had job offers, but that only 70 percent of Mira Vista seniors who reported that they planned to seek employment had jobs within three months after graduation, and only half of these graduates were employed in their major fields of study. This argument is problematic in several critical respects.

First, the author assumes that Green Mountain's comparatively strong job-placement record is due to the fact that it provides more business courses and job counselors than Mira Vista, rather than some other factor. But this need not be the case. Perhaps Green Mountain students are exceptionally bright or resourceful to begin with. Or perhaps the quality of instruction and job counseling at Green Mountain is exceptionally high. Moreover, perhaps Green Mountain provides more business courses and job counselors than Mira Vista simply because Green Mountain is a larger school with more students; if so, then the comparative numbers are not likely to have any bearing on job-placement success. In short, without ruling out other possible explanations for the difference between job-placement rates, the author cannot reasonably conclude that additional business courses and job counselors would enhance Mira Vista's job-placement record.

Another problem with the argument is that the statistics comparing job-placement rates might be distorted in one or more respects. First, the author fails to indicate the percentage of Green Mountain graduates who find employment in their major fields of study. Without this information it is impossible to assess the comparative success of the two colleges in helping their recent graduates find such employment. Second, the author ignores the possibility that the time parameters defining the two schools' job-placement rates differ. Mira Vista's record was determined only three months after graduation. It is entirely possible that Green Mountain's record was based on a longer period of time, thereby distorting the comparative success of the schools in helping their recent graduates find jobs.

The cited statistics about Mira Vista's job-placement record might be unreliable in other respects as well. These statistics were based only on data from Mira Vista seniors who reported to the college's job-placement center. The author overlooks the possibility that only a small portion of Mira Vista seniors reported to begin with. The author also ignores the possibility that many of these reporting students later changed their minds about seeking employment or were offered jobs but turned them down. Without ruling out these possible scenarios, the author cannot reasonably rely on these statistics to support the claim that Mira Vista's job-placement record is comparatively poor and thus could be improved by Mira Vista's emulating Green Mountain.

In conclusion, the argument is unconvincing as it stands. To strengthen it the author must show that additional business courses and job counselors would in fact improve Mira Vista's job-placement rate, and that the comparison between the job-placement rates at the two schools is fair. Finally, the author provides no evidence whatsoever to support his recommendation for providing more computer courses; to justify this claim the author must provide supporting evidence.

Argument 238   Should the city of **Dalton** adopt a curfew for minors?

The author of this editorial argues that in order to reduce its rising crime rate the city of Dalton should establish a 10:00 p.m. curfew for minors under age 18. The author also claims that the curfew would control juvenile delinquency as well as prevent minors from becoming crime victims. To support these claims the author points out that Williamsville established a similar curfew four months ago, and that since then Williamsville's youth crime rate has dropped by 27% during curfew hours. The author also points out that in Williamsville's town square no crimes have been reported in the last four months, yet Williamsville residents had previously expressed particular outrage about the square's high crime rate. I find the editorial logically unconvincing in several respects.

To begin with, the author has failed to convince me that Williamsville's overall crime rate has declined, or that the curfew was responsible for any such decline. It is entirely possible that although that city's youth crime rate has declined, its adult crime rate has risen. If so, this fact would seriously call into question the author's claim that a similar curfew would reduce Dalton's overall crime rate. Even if Williamsville's overall crime rate has declined in the last four months, the decline is not necessarily attributable to the curfew. Perhaps Williamsville has also enhanced its police enforcement, or established social programs that help minors avoid delinquency. In short, without evidence that all other conditions that might affect Williamsville's crime rate have remained unchanged during the last four months, the author's claim that the curfew is responsible for the drop in that city's crime rate is dubious at best.

Moreover, the evidence involving the town square does not adequately show that Williamsville's curfew has been effective in reducing its crime rate. The number of crimes reported in the square does not necessarily reflect the number actually committed there. Also, it is entirely possible that Williamsville's residents had already abandoned the town square at night by the time Williamsville established the curfew. If so, then the mere fact that no crimes in the square have been committed or reported recently proves nothing about the effectiveness of the curfew.

Even if Williamsville's curfew was responsible for a decline in that city's overall crime rate, the editorial's claim that a similar curfew would be effective in Dalton is unwarranted. Dalton might differ from Williamsville in ways that would undermine the curfew's effectiveness in Dalton. Or perhaps the percentage of crimes that are committed by adults is far greater in Dalton that in Williamsville. In either case, a curfew that is effective in reducing Williamsville's overall crime rate might be far less effective in reducing Dalton's.

Even assuming the proposed curfew would reduce Dalton's overall crime rate, the author unfairly infers that the curfew would also curb juvenile delinquency. The author's definition of juvenile delinquency might embrace additional behaviors—ones that don't amount to crimes. Besides, a reduction in the overall crime rate does not necessarily indicate a reduction in the youth crime rate.

The author's further inference that the curfew would protect minors from becoming crime victims is also unwarranted. This inference depends on the assumption that all crimes against youths occur during curfew hours. Yet common sense informs me that many such crimes occur during other hours. The inference also rests on the assumption that it is adults who are committing all crimes against youths. Yet the author fails to account for the possibility that some crimes against youths are committed by other youths.

In sum, the editorial relies on a series of dubious assumptions, which render it wholly unpersuasive. To bolster the editorial's claims the author must provide clear evidence that the curfew, and not some other phenomenon, was in fact responsible for a decline in Williamsville's youth crime rate. The author must also show that the curfew would have a similar effect in Dalton, and that the curfew would result in a decline in not just the youth crime rate but also the overall crime rate. To better assess the author's final two claims I would need to know how the author defines "juvenile delinquency", and what percentage of crimes against Dalton's youth are committed by other youths.

Argument 239　A new dormitory for **Buckingham College**

In this memo, a dean at Buckingham College recommends that in order to meet expected enrollment increases the college should build an additional dormitory. To support this recommendation the dean points out that rental rates for off-campus apartments have been increasing, thus making it more difficult for students to afford this housing option. The dean also points out that a new dormitory would attract prospective students to the college. This argument is problematic in several respects.

A threshold problem with the argument involves the statistical reliability of the reports about off-campus rental rates. The dean indicates only that "student leaders" reported these statistics; the dean provides no information about how these students collected their data. It is entirely possible that the report was based on an insufficiently small sample, or a sample that was unrepresentative of the town's overall student rental market.

Secondly, the dean assumes that this current trend in rental rates will continue in the future; yet the dean offers no evidence to substantiate this assumption. These rates are a function of supply and demand, and it is entirely possible that construction of apartment houses will increase in the future, thereby reducing rental rates along with the need for an additional dormitory. Without considering this possible scenario, the dean cannot justifiably conclude that an additional dormitory is needed to meet future demand.

Thirdly, the dean assumes that as enrollment increases the demand for student housing will also increase. While this might be the case, the dean ignores the possibility that the increased enrollment will be the result of an increase in the number of students commuting to Buckingham from their parents' homes. This scenario, if true, would render the dean's argument for building a new dormitory untenable.

Yet another problem with the argument involves the dean's final claim that an attractive new dormitory would attract prospective students to Buckingham. Even assuming students in fact choose colleges on this basis, by relying on this evidence the dean essentially provides an argument against building the new dormitory. If an attractive new dormitory would increase demand for dormitory space, this fact would only serve to undermine the dean's conflicting claim that the new dormitory would help meet increasing demand for dormitory space.

In conclusion, the dean's recommendation is not well supported. To strengthen it the dean must provide clear evidence that average rental rates for off-campus student apartments have in fact been increasing, that this trend will continue in the future, and that this trend will in fact result in an increased demand for dormitory housing.

Argument 240   Finding new jobs for laid-off **XYZ company** employees

This XYZ company memo recommends that XYZ continue to use Delany instead of Walsh as its personnel service for helping laid-off XYZ employees find new jobs. To support this recommendation the memo points out that 8 years ago, when XYZ was using Walsh, only half of XYZ's laid-off workers found new jobs within a year. The memo also points out that last year XYZ employees using Delany's services found jobs much more quickly than those who did not, and that the average Delany client found a job in six months, compared to nine months for the average Walsh client. The memo also mentions that Delany has more branch offices and a larger staff than Walsh. I find the memo's argument unconvincing for several reasons.

To begin with, Walsh's prior rate of placing laid-off XYZ employees is not necessarily a reliable indicator of what that rate would be now. Perhaps the placement rate 8 years ago was due to a general economic downturn or some other factor beyond Walsh's control. For that matter, perhaps the rate was relatively high among all placement services during that time period. In short, without ruling out other possible reasons for Walsh's ostensibly low placement rate 8 years ago, and without convincing me that this rate was low to begin with, the memo's author cannot convince me on the basis of XYZ's past experience with Walsh that XYZ should favor Delany over Walsh.

The memo also makes two hasty assumptions about the benefits of Delany's services last year. One such assumption is that these services were in fact responsible for helping the laid-off XYZ employees who used those services find jobs more quickly. It is entirely possible that the comparative success of this group was due instead to their other aggressive job-seeking efforts, which might even have included using Walsh's services—in addition to Delany's. Also, the memo unfairly equates the speed with which one finds a job with job-seeking success. Common sense informs me that the effectiveness of a job search depends not only on how quickly one finds a job, but also on compensation, benefits, location, and type of work.

Furthermore, the difference in the two firms' overall placement time last year does not necessarily indicate that Delany would be the better choice to serve XYZ's laid-off employees. These employees might have particular skills or needs that are not representative of the two firms' clients in general. Besides, a single year's placement statistics hardly suffices to draw any firm conclusions. Last year might have been exceptional—perhaps due to some unusual event that is unlikely to reoccur, such as a major employer's move to an area that Delany serves, or out of an area that Walsh serves.

Finally, the fact that Delany has more branch offices and a larger staff than Walsh proves nothing in itself about which firm would be more effective in finding jobs for laid-off XYZ employees. Perhaps these employees generally look for jobs in geographic areas or industries outside of Delany's domain. Or perhaps the number of Delany staff members per office is actually lower than at Walsh. Either scenario, if true, would cast serious doubt on the memo's conclusion that XYZ should favor Delany over Walsh.

In sum, as it stands the recommendation is not well supported. To bolster it the memo's author must provide better evidence—perhaps from XYZ's records—that Delany's services have consistently helped laid-off XYZ employees find jobs. Instead of attempting to convince me that Walsh provided a disservice to XYZ 8 years ago, the author should provide better evidence that Walsh's services would be inferior to Delany's in the foreseeable future. Accordingly, to better assess the recommendation it would be helpful to compare the number of staff members per office at the two firms, and the level of experience of those staff members. It would also be useful to know what sorts of skills laid-off XYZ employees possess, and which firm, Delany or Walsh, serves industries and areas with more openings for people with those skills.

Argument 241　Cheating at **Groveton College**

In this editorial, the author concludes that colleges should adopt an honor code for detecting academic cheating. To support this conclusion the author points out that the first year after switching from a monitoring system to an honor system the annual number of reported cheating incidents at Groveton College decreased from 30 to 21, and that five years later the number was only 14. The author also cites a survey in which most students indicated they would be less likely to cheat under an honor system than if they are closely monitored. This argument is unconvincing for several reasons.

First and foremost, the argument relies on the assumptions that Groveton students are just as capable of detecting cheating as faculty monitors, and that these students are just as likely to report cheating whenever they observe it. However, without evidence to substantiate these assumptions one cannot reasonably conclude that the honor code has in fact resulted in a decline in the incidence of cheating at Groveton. Besides, common sense tells me that these assumptions are dubious at best; an impartial faculty observer is more likely to detect and report cheating than a preoccupied student under peer pressure not to report cheating among classmates.

The argument also assumes that during the five-year period all other conditions possibly affecting the reported incidence of cheating at Groveton remained unchanged. Such conditions include the number of Groveton students and the overall integrity of the student body. After five years it is entirely possible that these conditions have changed, and that the reported decrease in cheating is attributable to one or more such changes. Thus, without ruling out such alternative explanations for the reported decrease, the author cannot convince me that the honor code has in fact contributed to a decline in the incidence of cheating at Groveton.

The author's recommendation that other colleges follow Groveton's example depends on the additional assumption that Groveton is typical in ways relevant to the incidence of cheating. However, this is not necessarily the case. For instance, perhaps Groveton students are more or less likely to report cheating, or to cheat under an honor system, than typical college students. Lacking evidence that Groveton students are typical in these respects, the argument is indefensible.

Finally, the survey that the author cites might be unreliable in any of three respects. First, the author fails to assure us that the survey's respondents are representative of all college students. Second, the survey results depend on the honesty and integrity of the respondents. Third, hypothetical predictions about one's future behavior are inherently less reliable than reports of proven behavior. Lacking evidence that the survey is reliable, the author cannot reasonably rely on the survey in recommending that other colleges adopt an honor code.

In conclusion, to persuade me that other colleges should adopt an honor code in order to reduce cheating, the author must supply clear evidence that cheating at Groveton in fact decreased after the honor code was instituted there, and that it is this code that was responsible for the decrease. Finally, to better assess the usefulness of the survey I would need specific information about the survey's sampling methodology.